Radar and ARPA Manual

A. G. Bole, Extra Master Mariner, FRIN, FNI

W. O. Dineley, Extra Master Mariner, MPhil

Butterworth-Heinemann
Linacre House, Jordan Hill, Oxford OX2 8DP
A division of Reed Educational and Professional Publishing Ltd

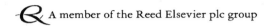 A member of the Reed Elsevier plc group

OXFORD   BOSTON   JOHANNESBURG
MELBOURNE   NEW DELHI   SINGAPORE

First published 1990
First published as a paperback edition 1992
Reprinted 1997

British Library Cataloguing in Publication Data
Bole, A. G.
  Radar and ARPA manual
  1. Ships. Automatic radar plotting aids. Use - manuals
  I. Title II. Dineley, W. O.
  623.89'33

ISBN 0 7506 0818 8

Printed and bound in Great Britain

Radar and ARPA Manual

⏷ be returned on or before
⏷ dated below.

CONTENTS

Preface   xiii

Acknowledgements   xiv

1   Basic radar principles
   1.1   Introduction   1

   1.2   Principles of range measurement   1
       1.2.1   The echo principle   1
       1.2.2   Range as a function of time   2
       1.2.3   The timebase   3
       1.2.4   Calibration of the timebase   4
       1.2.5   The synthetic display   6

   1.3   Principles of bearing measurement   8
       1.3.1   Directional transmission and
              reception   8
       1.3.2   Synchronization of scanner and
              trace   9
       1.3.3   The build-up of the picture   9
       1.3.4   The heading marker   10
       1.3.5   Bearing measurement   11

   1.4   Picture orientation   11
       1.4.1   Ship's-head-up orientation
              (unstabilized)   11
       1.4.2   True-north-up orientation
              (stabilized)   14
       1.4.3   Course-up orientation
              (stabilized)   14
       1.4.4   Choice of orientation   17

   1.5   Picture presentation   18
       1.5.1   The relative-motion
              presentation   18
       1.5.2   The true-motion presentation   21
       1.5.3   Choice of presentation   24

2   The radar system – operational principles
   2.1   Introduction   26

   2.2   Function of units   26
       2.2.1   The transmitter function   26
       2.2.2   The aerial function   28
       2.2.3   The receiver function   28
       2.2.4   The display function   29

   2.3   Transmitter principles   29
       2.3.1   The pulse repetition frequency   31
       2.3.2   The pulse length, power and
              shape   32
       2.3.3   The radio frequency of the
              transmitted pulse   37
       2.3.4   Selection of PRF and pulse
              length and their relationship
              with range scale   39

   2.4   Aerial principles   40
       2.4.1   Aerial concepts   40
       2.4.2   The horizontal beamwidth   40
       2.4.3   The vertical beamwidth   48
       2.4.4   Aerial rotation rate   50
       2.4.5   Aerial and display rotation link   52
       2.4.6   Heading marker data   54

   2.5   Receiver principles   55
       2.5.1   The radio frequency section   56
       2.5.2   The intermediate frequency
              amplifier   59
       2.5.3   The video section   66

   2.6   Display principles   69
       2.6.1   The cathode ray tube   69
       2.6.2   Real-time picture generation   75

2.6.3   Compass (or azimuth)
        stabilization   78
2.6.4   The provision of true-motion
        facilities   80
2.6.5   Echo paint   84
2.6.6   The radial-scan synthetic display 91
2.6.7   The raster-scan synthetic
        display   106

2.7   The siting of units on board ship 116
2.7.1   Aerial siting   116
2.7.2   The transceiver unit   117
2.7.3   The display unit   121
2.7.4   Compass safe distances   122
2.7.5   Exposed and protected
        equipment   123
2.7.6   Power supplies   123
2.7.7   High voltage hazards   123
2.7.8   Interswitching   123

3   Target detection

3.1   Introduction   126

3.2   Radar characteristics   127
3.2.1   Transmitter characteristics   127
3.2.2   Antenna characteristics   127
3.2.3   Receiver characteristics   127
3.2.4   Minimum detection range   128

3.3   Target characteristics   129
3.3.1   Aspect   129
3.3.2   Surface texture   129
3.3.3   Material   130
3.3.4   Shape   130
3.3.5   Size   131
3.3.6   Responses from specific targets 136

3.4   Target enhancement – passive   137
3.4.1   Corner reflectors   137
3.4.2   Arrays of reflectors   139
3.4.3   The Lunenburg lens   141
3.4.4   Buoy patterns   143

3.5   Target enhancement – active   143
3.5.1   The racon principle   143

3.5.2   The racon appearance on the
        display   144
3.5.3   Frequency and polarization   145
3.5.4   The ramark   150
3.5.5   Sources of radar beacon
        information   151
3.5.6   The Radaflare   151
3.5.7   Racons for survival craft   154

3.6   The detection of targets in sea clutter 154
3.6.1   The nature of the sea clutter
        response   155
3.6.2   The clutter problem
        summarized   159
3.6.3   The suppression of displayed sea
        clutter signals   159

3.7   The detection of targets in precipitation
      clutter   166
3.7.1   The nature of precipitation
        response   167
3.7.2   Attenuation in precipitation   168
3.7.3   The effect of precipitation type 168
3.7.4   The suppression of rain clutter 169
3.7.5   Combating the attenuation
        caused by precipitation   172
3.7.6   Exploiting the ability of
        radar to detect precipitation   173

3.8   The radar horizon   173
3.8.1   The effect of standard
        atmospheric conditions   173
3.8.2   Sub-refraction   177
3.8.3   Super-refraction   178
3.8.4   Extra super-refraction or
        ducting   179

3.9   False and unwanted radar responses 179
3.9.1   Introduction   179
3.9.2   Indirect echoes (reflected
        echoes)   180
3.9.3   Multiple echoes   184
3.9.4   Side echoes   184
3.9.5   Radar-to-radar interference   185
3.9.6   Second-trace echoes   187
3.9.7   False echoes from power cables 193

4 Automatic Radar Plotting Aids (ARPA), specified facilities

4.1   Introduction   194
      4.1.1   Stand–alone ARPAs   194
      4.1.2   Integral ARPAs   194
      4.1.3   The requirement to carry
              ARPA, and for operator
              training   195
      4.1.4   Compliance with the IMO
              Performance Standards   195

4.2   The acquisition of targets   196
      4.2.1   The acquisition specification   196
      4.2.2   Manual acquisition   196
      4.2.3   Fully automatic acquisition   197
      4.2.4   Automatic acquisition by area   197
      4.2.5   Guard zones   197
      4.2.6   Guard rings and area rejection
              boundaries (ARBs)   198

4.3   The tracking of targets   198
      4.3.1   The tracking specification   198
      4.3.2   Rate aiding   199
      4.3.3   The number of targets to be
              tracked   200
      4.3.4   Target loss   200
      4.3.5   Target swop   200
      4.3.6   The analysis of tracks and the
              display of data   201
      4.3.7   Tracking history   207

4.4   Vectors   209
      4.4.1   Relative vectors   210
      4.4.2   True vectors   210
      4.4.3   Trial manoeuvre   211

4.5   The ARPA display   212
      4.5.1   The continued availability of
              radar data in the event of an
              ARPA malfunction   212
      4.5.2   The size of the display   213
      4.5.3   The range scales on which ARPA
              facilities should be available   213
      4.5.4   The modes of display   213
      4.5.5   ARPA data should not obscure
              radar data   213

      4.5.6   The ARPA data brilliance
              control   213
      4.5.7   The ability to view the display 214
      4.5.8   The use of the marker for range
              and bearing measurement   214
      4.5.9   The effect of changing range
              scales   214

4.6   The display of alphanumeric data   214

4.7   Alarms and warnings   215
      4.7.1   Guard zone violation   215
      4.7.2   Predicted CPA/TCPA
              violation   215
      4.7.3   Lost target   216
      4.7.4   Performance tests and
              warnings   217

4.8   Connections with other equipment   217

5 ARPA – additional facilities

5.1   Introduction   218

5.2   Additional alarms and warnings   218
      5.2.1   Loss of sensor input   218
      5.2.2   Track change   218
      5.2.3   Anchor watch   219
      5.2.4   Tracks full   219
      5.2.5   Wrong or invalid request   219
      5.2.6   Time to manoeuvre   219
      5.2.7   Safe limit vector suppression   219
      5.2.8   Trial alarm   219

5.3   Automatic ground-stabilization   219

5.4   Navigational lines and maps   221

5.5   The potential point of collision (PPC) 222
      5.5.1   The concept of collision points 222
      5.5.2   The behaviour of collision
              points if the observing ship
              maintains speed   223
      5.5.3   The behaviour of the collision
              point when the target ship's
              speed changes   225
      5.5.4   The behaviour of the collision
              point when the target changes
              course   225

5.6   The predicted area of danger (PAD)   227
        5.6.1   The PAD in practice   228
        5.6.2   Changes in the shape of the
                PAD   228
        5.6.3   The movement of the PAD   229

6   The radar system – operational controls

6.1   Optimum performance   230

6.2   Setting-up procedure for an analogue
        display   230
        6.2.1   Preliminary procedure   231
        6.2.2   Switching on   231
        6.2.3   Preparing the display   232
        6.2.4   Obtaining the optimum
                picture   234

6.3   Setting-up procedure for a radial-scan
        synthetic display   236
        6.3.1   Preliminary procedure   236
        6.3.2   Switching on   236
        6.3.3   Preparing the display   237
        6.3.4   Obtaining the optimum
                picture   237

6.4   Setting-up procedure for a raster-scan
        synthetic display   240
        6.4.1   Preliminary procedure   240
        6.4.2   Switching on   240
        6.4.3   Preparing the display   241
        6.4.4   Obtaining the optimum
                picture   243

6.5   Performance monitoring   243
        6.5.1   The principle of the echo box 244
        6.5.2   Echo box siting   245
        6.5.3   Power monitors   247
        6.5.4   Transponder performance
                monitors   248
        6.5.5   Calibration levels   248
        6.5.6   Performance check procedure   248

6.6   Change of range scale and/or pulse
        length   249

6.7   The stand-by condition   250

6.8   Setting up the display for a true-motion
        picture presentation   250
        6.8.1   The controls   250
        6.8.2   Setting up a sea-stabilized
                presentation   255
        6.8.3   Setting up a ground-stabilized
                presentation   255

6.9   Controls for range and bearing
        measurement   256
        6.9.1   Fixed range rings   256
        6.9.2   Variable range marker (VRM)   258
        6.9.3   The Perspex cursor   258
        6.9.4   Parallel index   261
        6.9.5   The electronic bearing line
                (EBL)   261
        6.9.6   Free electronic range and
                bearing line   262
        6.9.7   Joystick and screen marker   263
        6.9.8   Range accuracy   263
        6.9.9   Bearing accuracy   264

6.10   Controls for the suppression of
        unwanted responses   264
        6.10.1 Sea clutter suppression   265
        6.10.2 Rain clutter suppression   267
        6.10.3 Interference suppression   267

6.11   Miscellaneous controls   268
        6.11.1 Echo stretch   268
        6.11.2 Second-trace echo
                elimination   268

6.12   Setting-up procedure for an ARPA
        display   268
        6.12.1 The input of radar data   268
        6.12.2 Switching on the computer   268
        6.12.3 Heading and speed input data   269
        6.12.4 Setting the ARPA brilliance   269
        6.12.5 Setting the vector time
                control   269
        6.12.6 Setting the vector mode   269
        6.12.7 Safe limits   269
        6.12.8 Preparation for tracking   269

6.13   Switching off   270

7   Radar plotting

7.1   Introduction   271

7.2   The relative plot   271
   7.2.1   The vector triangle   274
   7.2.2   The plotted triangle   274
   7.2.3   The construction of the plot   277
   7.2.4   The practicalities of plotting   277
   7.2.5   The need to extract numerical data   278
   7.2.6   The plot in special cases where no triangle 'appears'   278

7.3   The true plot   279

7.4   The plot when only the target manoeuvres   281
   7.4.1   The construction of the plot   283
   7.4.2   The danger in attempting to guess the action taken by a target   283

7.5   The plot when own ship manoeuvres   283
   7.5.1   The plot when own ship alters course only   283
   7.5.2   The construction of the plot   285
   7.5.3   The plot when own ship alters speed only   285
   7.5.4   The construction of the plot   287
   7.5.5   The use of 'stopping distance' tables, graphs and formulae   287
   7.5.6   The plot when own ship combines course and speed alterations   290
   7.5.7   The plot when own ship resumes course and/or speed   295
   7.5.8   The plot when both vessels manoeuvre simultaneously   295

7.6   The theory and construction of PPCs, PADs, SODs and SOPs   297
   7.6.1   The possible point of collision (PPC)   297
   7.6.2   The construction to find the PPC   297
   7.6.3   The predicted area of danger (PAD)   302

   7.6.4   The construction of the PAD   302
   7.6.5   The sector of danger (SOD)   302
   7.6.6   The construction of a sector of danger   305
   7.6.7   The sector of preference (SOP)   305
   7.6.8   The construction of a sector of preference   305

7.7   The plot in tide   305
   7.7.1   The construction of the plot   307
   7.7.2   The course to steer to counteract the tide   307
   7.7.3   The change of course needed to maintain track when changing speed in tide   307

7.8   The theory and practice of reflection plotters   309
   7.8.1   The construction of the reflection plotter   309
   7.8.2   Testing and adjustment   310
   7.8.3   Care and maintenance   310
   7.8.4   The practical use of reflection plotters   310
   7.8.5   Changing range scale   311
   7.8.6   The use of the 'free' EBL to draw parallel lines   311
   7.8.7   Fixed and rotatable surfaces – use with a ship's-head-up unstabilized display   311
   7.8.8   Flat and concave surfaces   311
   7.8.9   Use in conjunction with parallel indexing   312
   7.8.10   Reflection plotters and raster-scan displays   312

7.9   Manual plotting – accuracy and errors   313
   7.9.1   Accuracy of bearings as plotted   313
   7.9.2   Accuracy of ranges as plotted   314
   7.9.3   Accuracy of own ship's speed   314
   7.9.4   Accuracy of own ship's course   314
   7.9.5   Accuracy of the plotting interval   314
   7.9.6   The accuracy with which CPA can be determined   315

7.9.7   The consequences of random
        errors in own ship's course and
        speed   315
7.9.8   Summary   316

7.10   Errors associated with the true-motion
        presentation   317
        7.10.1 Incorrect setting of the true-motion
                controls   317
        7.10.2 Tracking course errors   318
        7.10.3 Tracking speed errors   318
        7.10.4 The effect of radial display non-
                linearity   319

7.11   Radar plotting aids   320
        7.11.1 The radar plotting board   320
        7.11.2 Threat assessment markers   321
        7.11.3 The 'E' plot   322
        7.11.4 Intelligent knowledge-based
                systems as applied to collision
                avoidance   322

7.12   The Regulations for Preventing
        Collisions at Sea as applied to radar and
        ARPA   323
        7.12.1 Introduction   323
        7.12.2 Lookout – rule 5   323
        7.12.3 Safe speed – rule 6   324
        7.12.4 Risk of collision – rule 7   324
        7.12.5 Conduct of vessels in restricted
                visibility – rule 19   324
        7.12.6 Action to avoid collision –
                rule 8   325
        7.12.7 The cumulative turn   326
        7.12.8 Conclusion   329

8   Navigation techniques using radar
    and ARPA

    8.1 Introduction   330

    8.2 Identification of targets and chart
         comparison   330
         8.2.1 Long range target
                identification   331
         8.2.2 The effect of discrimination   332
         8.2.3 Shadow areas   333

8.2.4   Rise and fall of tide   335
8.2.5   Radar-conspicuous targets   336
8.2.6   Pilotage situations   336

8.3   Position fixing   336
        8.3.1   Selection of targets   336
        8.3.2   Types of position line   337

8.4   Parallel indexing   338
        8.4.1   Introduction   338
        8.4.2   Preparations and precautions   339
        8.4.3   Parallel indexing, the
                technique   342
        8.4.4   Progress monitoring   353
        8.4.5   Parallel indexing on a true-motion
                display   356
        8.4.6   Modern radar navigation
                facilities   357
        8.4.7   Unplanned parallel indexing   361
        8.4.8   Anti-collision manoeuvring while
                parallel indexing   361

9   ARPA – accuracy and errors

    9.1 Introduction   362

    9.2 The test scenarios   362

    9.3 The accuracy of displayed data required
         by the Performance Standard   363

    9.4 The classification of ARPA error
         sources   368

    9.5 Errors that are generated in the radar
         installation   368
         9.5.1   Glint   368
         9.5.2   Errors in bearing measurement 370
         9.5.3   Errors in range measurement   370
         9.5.4   The effect of random gyro
                 compass errors   371
         9.5.5   The effect of random log
                 errors   372
         9.5.6   The magnitude of sensor errors
                 specified in the Performance
                 Standard   372

    9.6 Errors in displayed data   372
         9.6.1   Target swop   372

9.6.2 Track errors 373
9.6.3 The effect on vectors of incorrect
        course and speed input 375
9.6.4 The effect on the PPC of incorrect
        data input 379

9.7 Errors of interpretation 379
9.7.1 Errors with vector systems 379
9.7.2 Errors with PPC and PAD
        systems 372
9.7.3 The misleading effect of
        afterglow 373
9.7.4 Accuracy of the presented data 374
9.7.5 Missed targets 375

10 Extracts from official publications

10.1 Extract from Regulation 12, Chapter V of
     the IMO-SOLAS (1974) Convention as
     amended to 1983 384

10.2 Extracts from IMO Resolutions
     A222(VII), A278(VIII), A477(XII) 385
10.2.1 Performance Standards for
        Navigational Radar Equipment
        installed before 1 September
        1984 385

10.2.2 Performance Standards for
        Navigational Radar Equipment
        installed on or after 1 September
        1984 387

10.3 Extract from IMO Resolution A422(XI),
10.3.1 Performance Standards for
        Automatic Radar Plotting Aids
        (ARPA) 392

10.4 Extracts from IMO Resolutions A423
     (XI) and A277 (VIII), Radar Beacons,
     Transponders and Reflectors 397
10.4.1 Marine uses of radar
        beacons and transponders 397
10.4.2 Performance standards
        for radar reflectors 401

10.5 Extract from United Kingdom Merchant
     Shipping Notice M1158, The Use of
     Radar Including ARPA 401

10.6 Extracts from United Kingdom Statutory
     Instrument 1984, No.1203 405

Glossary of acronyms and abbreviations 409

Index 411

To Keith

Preface

This manual has been planned not only as a comprehensive practical reference for mariners on board ship and managers ashore, but also to provide all essential information for candidates following ENS, radar observer and professional certificate courses.

Over the past decade there have been considerable developments in ARPA design, but perhaps the more significant changes have been seen in the design of basic radar systems: ARPA features are now almost entirely integrated with the radar display – which means that neither can be treated in isolation. Thus this new manual supersedes our earlier *ARPA Manual*, representing a thorough revision and extension to cover the complete radar/ARPA installation.

The changes in radar displays that are likely to be of greatest significance to the observer are the developments in signal processing and the advent of raster-scan displays: these receive exhaustive treatment. The effects of changes in shipboard operations, such as false echoes from containers, are also dealt with.

Throughout the book the operational significance of the IMO Performance Standards is stressed, as is the role of radar and ARPA in navigation and collision avoidance.

With the completion of the SOLAS updating and fitting schedule in view, it has been possible to bring together a body of practical information on equipment and techniques which, it is hoped, will both serve the observer using traditional equipment and provide reliable guidance to the use of newer equipment for some years to come.

The companion volume, *The Navigation Control Manual*, covers the integration of radar and ARPA within the total navigation system. Together, the two books provide a comprehensive treatment of the theoretical and practical aspects of electronic navigation systems.

A.G.B.
W.O.D.

Acknowledgements

The authors wish to express their gratitude to:

The International Maritime Organization for permission to reproduce the various extracts from Resolutions Adopted by the Assembly;

The Controller of Her Majesty's Stationery Office for permission to reproduce the extracts from M 1158 and Statutory Instrument No. 1203 (1984);

Captain C. E. Nicholls of Liverpool Polytechnic for his major contribution to Chapter 8;

Mr B. Price of Sandown College, Liverpool for his helpful comments based on a reading of Chapter 2;

Mr Andrew O. Dineley for his assistance in producing the computer printout of the manuscript;

Families and friends without whose assistance, support and understanding this undertaking would never have been completed.

1 Basic radar principles

1.1 Introduction

The word RADAR is an acronym derived from the words *Radio Detection and Ranging*. In the United Kingdom it was initially referred to as *radio direction finding* (RDF) in order to preserve the secrecy of its ranging capability.

The scientist Heinrich Hertz, after whom the basic unit of frequency is named, demonstrated in 1886 that radio waves could be reflected from metallic objects. In 1903 a German engineer obtained a patent in several countries for a radio wave device capable of detecting ships, but it aroused little enthusiasm because of its very limited range. Marconi, delivering a lecture in 1922, drew attention to the work of Hertz and proposed in principle what we know today as marine radar. Although radar was used to determine the height of the ionosphere in the mid-1920s, it was not until 1935 that radar pulses were successfully used to detect and measure the range of an aircraft. In the 1930s there was much simultaneous but independent development of radar techniques in Britain, Germany, France and America. Radar first went to sea in a warship in 1937 and by 1939 considerable improvement in performance had been achieved. By 1944 naval radar had made an appearance on merchant ships and from about the end of the war the growth of civil marine radar began. Progressively it was refined to meet the needs of peacetime navigation and collision avoidance.

While the civil marine radars of today may, in size, appearance and versatility, differ markedly from their ancestors of the 1940s, the basic data that they offer, namely target range and bearing, are determined by exploiting the same fundamental principles unveiled so long ago. An understanding of such principles is an essential starting point in any study of marine radar.

1.2 Principles of range measurement

1.2.1 The echo principle

An object (normally referred to as a target) is detected by the transmission of a pulse of radio energy and the subsequent reception of a fraction of such energy (the echo) which is reflected by the target in the direction of the transmitter. The phenomenon is analogous to the reflection of sound waves from land formations. If a blast is sounded on a ship's whistle, the energy travels outward and some of it may strike, for example, a cliff. The energy which is intercepted will be reflected by the cliff. If the reflected energy returns in the direction of the ship, and is of sufficient strength, it will be heard as an audible echo which, in duration and tone, resembles the original blast. In considering the echo principle the following points can usefully assist in a preliminary understanding of radar detection:

(a) The echo is never as loud as the original blast.
(b) The chance of detecting an echo depends on the loudness and duration of the original blast.
(c) Short blasts are required if echoes from close targets are not to be *drowned* by the original blast.
(d) A sufficiently long interval between blasts is required to allow time for echoes from distant targets to return.

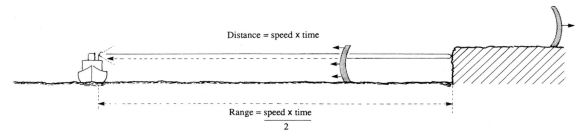

Figure 1.1 The echo principle

While the sound analogy is extremely useful, it must not be pursued too far as there are a number of ways in which the character and behaviour of radio waves differ from those of sound waves. In particular at this stage it is noteworthy that the speed of radio waves is very much higher than that of sound waves.

1.2.2 Range as a function of time

It is almost self-evident that the time which elapses between the transmission of a pulse and the reception of the corresponding echo depends on the speed of the pulse and the distance which it has travelled in making its two-way journey. Thus, if the speed of the pulse is known and the elapsed time can be measured, the range of the target producing the echo can be calculated.

While it is recognised that the velocity of radio waves is dependent on the nature of the medium through which they travel, for the practical purpose of marine radar ranging the speed may be assumed to have a constant value of 300 000 000 metres per second. Because this number is rather large, it is expedient in practical calculations to use the microsecond as the time unit. One μs represents one millionth part of a second (i.e. 10^{-6} seconds). The speed can thus be written as 300 metres per μs. Using this value it is possible to produce a simple general relationship between target range and the elapsed time which separates the transmission of the pulse and the reception of an echo in any particular case (see Figure 1.1).

Let D = the distance travelled by the pulse (metres)
     R = the range of the target (metres)

T = the elapsed time (μs)
S = the speed of radio waves (metres/μs)

Then $D = S \times T$
and $R = (S \times T)/2$
hence $R = (300 \times T)/2$
thus $R = 150T$

The application of this relationship can be illustrated by the following example.

Example 1.1   Calculate the elapsed time for a pulse to travel to and return from a radar target whose range is (a) 50 metres (b) 12 nautical miles.

(a) $R = 150T$
thus $50 = 150T$
hence $T = 50/150 = 0.33\mu$s

This value is of particular interest because 50 metres represents the minimum detection range that must be achieved to ensure compliance with the IMO Performance Standards for Navigational Radar Equipment (see Sections 10.2.1 and 10.2.2). While this topic will be fully explored in Section 3.2.4, it is useful at this stage to note the extremely short time interval within which transmission and reception must be accomplished.

(b) $R = 150T$
Since 1 nautical mile = 1852 metres,
             $12 \times 1852 = 150T$
hence $T = 12 \times 1852/150 = 148.16\mu$s

This result is noteworthy as it represents the elapsed time for a commonly used marine radar range scale. Further reference will be made to this value in the succeeding section.

1.2.3   The timebase

It is clear from the values established in the previous section that the elapsed times are of the order of millionths of a second and are thus so short as to be beyond the capability of any conventional time-measuring device. This difficulty is overcome by using an electronic device known as a cathode ray tube (CRT). The electronic principles of this important device are discussed in some detail in Section 2.6.1; it is sufficient at this stage to appreciate that its display feature is a glass screen across which travels a very small spot of light. The speed of this travel can be accurately controlled at values which allow the spot to transit the screen in as little as a few microseconds. At such speeds it moves literally 'faster than the eye can see' and hence appears as a line rather than a spot, but it is important that the concept of a moving light spot is appreciated as it is fundamental to an understanding of radar display principles.

The CRT can be used to perform an electronic stopwatch function by arranging that the time taken for the spot to cross the screen is the same as the time taken for a radar pulse to make the two-way journey to a target at a chosen range. (This can be compared with a mechanical stopwatch in which the second hand transits the circumference of a dial in the same time as the earth rotates through approximately 15 seconds of arc. It is useful to illustrate the principle with reference to the method originally employed in the early radars of the 1940s. While this type of display, known as A-scan, is no longer used in civil marine applications (other than in the form of an oscilloscope such as may be used for servicing) it demonstrates the principle clearly and is a suitable point from which to progress to a description of the ways in which the display has been subsequently refined.

1.2.3.1   The A-scan display

In the A-scan display, the spot is used to produce a horizontal line (the trace) which originates close to the left-hand side of the screen of the CRT. The following features are of particular importance:

(a)   The trace commences at the instant each radar pulse is transmitted and this event is indicated by an

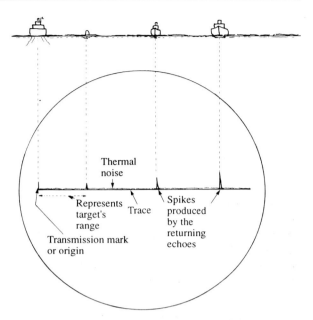

Figure 1.2   The A-scan display

instantaneous vertical deflection of the spot which produces a 'spike', known as the transmission mark.

(b)   The speed of the spot (the sweep rate) is adjusted so that it completes the trace in the same time as a radar pulse will take to travel to and from a target located at the maximum range which the scaled line is presently intended to represent. When the spot has completed the trace, the brilliance is automatically reduced to zero and the spot flies back to the origin to await the transmission of the next pulse. At this event it initiates a further trace along the same path as its predecessor.

(c)   A returning echo is used to generate an instantaneous vertical deflection of the spot, thus producing a further spike. The amplitude of this spike, within certain limits (see Section 2.5.2.5) is a function of the strength of the echo.

Consideration of these three features and Figure 1.2 will indicate that the horizontal distance between the transmission mark and the echo spike is a measure of the range of the target. Using the result from Example

1.1(b), it is evident that if the full extent of the trace is to represent a range of 12 miles (the selected range scale) the spot must complete the trace in approximately 148μs. This quantity is referred to as the *timebase* and it is on this value that the displayed range of all targets is based. If a target lay at a range of 6 miles, its echo would return in half the timebase and would be displayed at half the maximum range of the scale in use. Different range scales are obtained by operating the range scale selector which selects the correct timebase for the chosen range scale. For example, on the 3 mile range scale the spot must travel four times faster than on the 12 mile range scale and hence a timebase of approximately 37μs would be selected.

A limitation of the A-scan display is its inability to display information from any direction other than that in which the antenna (or aerial) is trained at that moment. This shortcoming led to the development of the plan position indicator (PPI).

In radar terminology the words *antenna*, *aerial*, and *scanner* are all used to describe the device which beams the transmitted energy into space. Throughout this text these words may be regarded as synonyms.

1.2.3.2   The radial-scan plan position indicator (PPI) display

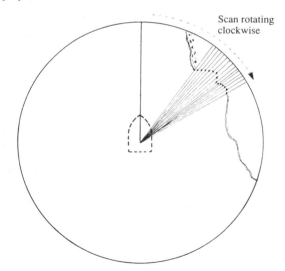

Figure 1.3   The radial-scan PPI display

In a radial-scan PPI display, the spot produces the trace in the form of a radial line whose origin is (normally) placed at the centre of the circular screen (Figure 1.3). An echo return from a target is used to produce an increase in the brilliance of the moving spot. To this end, a competent observer will, in setting up the display, adjust the brilliance of the trace so that it is barely visible (see Section 6.2.3.1), hence maximising the probability that small increases in brilliance will be detected. Within certain limits (see Section 2.5.2.5) the brightening of the trace by a target return is a function of the strength of the received echo. As with the A-scan display, the origin of the trace coincides with the instant of transmission of the pulse and the duration of the trace is the selected timebase. Thus a target which lies at the maximum range represented by the selected scale will appear at the edge of the screen.

When the spot has completed the trace, the brilliance is automatically reduced to zero and the spot flies back to the origin to await the incidence of the next transmission. At this event it initiates a further line which, in contrast with the A-scan case, is drawn along a path which is separated from the previous one by a small angle (about one tenth of a degree). In a PPI system the antenna rotates continuously and automatically in a clockwise direction, generating approximately some 3600 lines in one complete rotation. The resultant rotating trace makes it possible to display simultaneously targets in all directions in the correct angular relationship, one to another. Echoes painted by the trace as it passes will glow for a short period due to a property of the screen known as persistence or afterglow. Thus, in general the picture persists until refreshed on the next revolution of the trace (see Section 1.3.3). The PPI display is particularly suited to collision avoidance and navigational applications; the angular build-up of the picture will be described in Section 1.3.3.

1.2.4   Calibration of the timebase

It has been shown that by making the duration of one trace equal to the timebase of the selected range scale, the echo of a target will be displayed at a distance from the origin which is proportional to its range. Thus, when

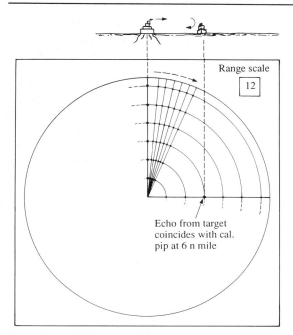

Range scale

12

Echo from target
coincides with cal.
pip at 6 n mile

Figure 1.4 Calibration marks

Table 1.1 Timebase and calibration interval values

Range scale (n miles)	Timebase duration (μs)	Calibration interval (n miles)	(μs)	Remarks
0.75	9.3	0.25	3.1	Normally only 3 rings
1.5	18.5	0.25	3.1	
3	37.0	0.5	6.2	
6	74.1	1.0	12.4	6 rings in each case
12	148.2	2.0	24.7	
24	296.3	4.0	49.4	
48	592.6	8.0	98.8	

observing the display, it may be possible to estimate the range of a target by mentally dividing the trace into equal sections. However, to measure a range with an acceptable degree of accuracy (see Section 6.9.8), the subdivision must be carried out by electronic methods.

A device known as an oscillator is used to generate a succession of signals which occur at *equal intervals of time*. It is arranged that the first signal of any group coincides with the instant of transmission and that the interval between successive pulses is a sub-multiple of the timebase of the selected range scale. Each signal is used to produce an instantaneous brightening of the spot, and as a result bright marks, sometimes called *calibration pips* or *calibration marks*, will subdivide the trace into equal intervals of time and therefore, by virtue of the timebase value, into equal intervals of range. Hence, on the 12 mile range scale, as illustrated by Figure 1.4, the echo from a target at a range of 6 miles will arrive after transmission by an elapsed time equal to half the timebase, and therefore will be displayed at the same time, and in the same place, as the 6 mile calibration pip. (Notice that

the 6 mile calibration pip is the third from the origin, the mark at the origin counting as zero.) It is evident that the range scale selector must control not only the timebase duration but also the interval between calibration marks. This is illustrated, for some range scales, by the values in Table 1.1.

The timing of the calibration marks can be achieved with an extremely high degree of accuracy which in turn becomes implicit in the accuracy with which the range of a target can be measured provided that its echo coincides with a mark. If the echo lies between two marks, some form of interpolation will be necessary. In some circumstances it may be that this can be done by eye, but in other cases an acceptable degree of accuracy (see Section 6.9.1) will demand electronic assistance.

Interpolation is facilitated by the generation of a single pip, known as a *variable range marker*, which occurs at a selected elapsed time after transmission. The time is selected by the operation of a manual control which is also connected to some form of numerical read-out. The latter will show the number of miles of timebase represented by the selected time. Thus, as illustrated by Figure 1.5, if the observer adjusts the variable range marker to read 3 miles, the single pip will be produced approximately 37μs after transmission, i.e. after one quarter of the 12 mile timebase.

In conclusion, it is clear that the precision with which the calibration marks are produced is fundamental to the accuracy of range measurement. For a detailed treat-

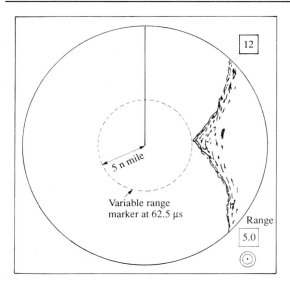

Figure 1.5   The variable range marker

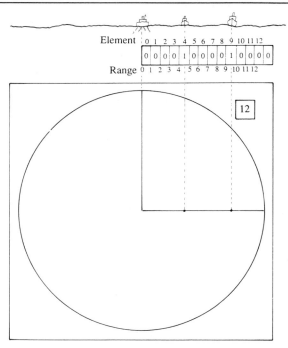

Figure 1.6   Storage of range data

ment of the correct procedure for their use and the accuracy which can be achieved, the reader is referred to Section 6.9.

1.2.5   The synthetic display

The displays produced in the ways so far described have become known as 'real-time' displays. The term describes the fact that the echoes are written on the trace concurrently with their reception, rather in the way in which one might write down a navigation warning, as it is received. It was recognised for many years that if the range data could be stored in such a way that it could be manipulated, considerable benefits might accrue, such as the ability to improve the picture quality and to carry out automatic tracking of targets. Pursuing the analogy of the navigation warning somewhat further, this may be compared with writing down the warning quickly as it is broadcast and subsequently re-writing it slowly and neatly. As with most analogies, care should be exercised in its indefinite pursuit. The term *real-time display* is used to differentiate between the traditional type of display and the modern, computer controlled 'Synthetic Display'.

The microprocessor, a computer device capable of storing and manipulating data at very high rates, became available from the early 1970s; as the cost of computer memory decreased through the 1980s, a revolution took place in the way in which range (and other) data was handled. As a result, in modern radar systems the range data is stored in a computer memory. The data, once processed, can be used to synthesize a picture for display on a radial-scan PPI. Such a picture is sometimes referred to as a *re-timed display*. Since the mid-eighties it has become progressively more common to produce the picture on a television screen. Such a display is referred to as a *raster-scan* PPI in order to distinguish it from the traditional *radial-scan* PPI. Detailed consideration of raster-scan displays is deferred to Chapter 2 (see Section 2.6.7), as an understanding of basic radar principles is more readily gained from a study of the radial-scan display. However, regardless of whether the synthetic picture is finally produced on a raster-scan or radial-scan PPI, the principle of range measurement is as described below.

For a general introduction to the principle of storage, the computer memory may be likened to a large number of 'two-position' switches each of which can be either on or off. Typically the computer will sample the received signal 1200 times in the duration of one complete radial trace. The sampling process commences at the instant of transmission and the result of each sampling is registered using, consecutively, each of 1200 memory elements. If a returning echo is present at the time of sampling, the appropriate switch is set to 'on', whereas if no echo is present the switch is left in the 'off' position. Thus the range of each echo will be implicit in the number of the memory element in which its presence is recorded.

In diagrams, it is usual to depict each element of memory as a box in which the number '1' appears if the switch is on and the number '0' appears if the switch is off. This form of representation is particularly suitable because the computer uses a counting system known as *binary* in which there are only two digits, namely '1' and '0' (see Section 2.6.6.1). Further, it is practical to show 12 elements, rather than 1200. Subject to these qualifications, Figure 1.6 illustrates the generation of one radial line of a synthetic picture when the 12 mile range scale has been selected. In writing the data into the memory, which will be carried out in the duration of the 12 mile timebase (i.e. approximately $148\,\mu s$), the sampling process stores a '1' for each received echo and thereby the range of each target producing a detectable echo is implicit in the place in which it is registered in the memory. For example, a target in element 7 lies within the range limits 7 to 8 nautical miles (using 1200 elements, a target in element 700 would lie within the range limits 7.00 to 7.01 nautical miles).

In reading the range data out of the memory, a standard rectangular pulse is produced for each '1' in the memory. If the data is read out in the duration of the 12 mile timebase (i.e. approximately $148\,\mu s$) and the sweep rate produces a trace whose radial duration is the same, each of these pulses will produce a brightening of the trace at a distance from the origin which is proportional to the range of the targets which produced the echoes.

In the example that has been chosen, the range data was written in and read out at the same rate. In a synthetic display this will only be true for one range scale.

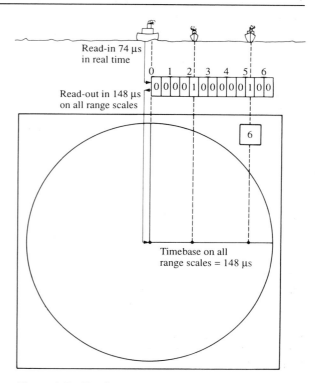

Figure 1.7 Fixed sweep rate display

This is best illustrated by considering what will happen if the 6 mile range scale is selected (Figure 1.7).

When the 6 mile range scale is selected, the data must be written into the memory over the duration of the 6 mile timebase (i.e. approximately $74\,\mu s$) because the writing time is determined by the speed of radio waves. The received signal will be sampled twice as often so that, if 12 elements are used to represent 6 miles, each element of memory will represent a range interval of 0.5 miles. (If 1200 elements were used, the range interval would be 0.005 miles.) If the stored range data for 6 miles is read out of memory at half the rate at which it was written in (i.e. at the same rate as it is read out on the 12 mile range scale) *and* the sweep rate is maintained at the value for the 12 mile scale (i.e. giving a timebase of approximately $148\,\mu s$), a radial trace representing 6 miles will be produced.

Table 1.2 Range data – typical write and read times

Range scale (n miles)	Write time (μs)	Read-out (μs)	Sweep time (μs)
0.75	9.2	148	148
1.5	18.5	148	148
3	37.0	148	148
6	74.1	148	148
12	148.2	148	148
24	296.3	148	148
48	592.6	148	148

Thus, in general, where computer storage is used to develop a radial PPI display, the range data for each radial line is written into memory during one timebase of the selected range scale but is read out in a fixed time, and displayed at a fixed sweep rate both of which are independent of the range scale selected. The duration of the fixed read-out time will be determined by the individual radar designer. Commonly, but not invariably, it is made equal to the 12 mile timebase. A representative set of values is shown in Table 1.2. Calibration marks and a variable range marker will be available on a synthetic display but it should be borne in mind that the interval between the calibration pips will depend on the fixed sweep rate chosen by the designer. Additionally it may be possible to have the computer read out the range of a target directly from the knowledge of the number of the memory element in which it lies.

The above process is sometimes called digital storage, because the presence or absence of an echo is registered by the binary digits '1' or '0'. It is considerably more complex than the above introduction might suggest and there is great variation in the way in which radar designers have exploited the basic principle. For example, the simple model described produces synthetic echoes all of which are identical in brightness. In some systems this is true but it is by no means invariably the case. Further, if (as in practice) some 1200 memory elements are used, many targets will register sequentially in more than one element. The topic is discussed in greater detail in Section 2.6.6.

1.3 Principles of bearing measurement

1.3.1 Directional transmission and reception

To examine the principles of bearing measurement it is useful to return to the sound analogy of Section 1.2.1. If the suggested blast was transmitted in low visibility it would not be easy to assess the precise direction from which the sound had returned. The difficulty arises from two principal features:

(a) The whistle   If it is well placed it will transmit sound in all directions and thus echoes will return from all directions.

(b) The ear   Evolution has designed the human ear to be highly receptive over more than 180 degrees on either side of the head.

These two properties are precisely the reverse of what is required. To determine the bearing of a target, transmission in the horizontal plane must be restricted to one direction at a time, and reception must be restricted to that same direction.

In a marine radar system a single antenna (known as the scanner or aerial) is used for both transmission and reception. It is designed in such a way (see Section 2.4.2) as to focus the transmitted energy in a beam which is very narrow in the horizontal plane. The angle within which the energy is constrained is called the *horizontal beamwidth* (Figure 1.8). It must have a value of not more

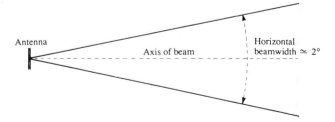

Figure 1.8 The horizontal beam

than 2.5° if it is to comply with IMO Performance Standards for Navigational Radar Equipment (see Section 10.2). However, horizontal beamwidths of less than 2° are commonplace and shipborne civil marine radars are available with values as low as 0.75°. The reception property of the antenna is such that it will only detect energy which has returned from within the angular limits of the horizontal beamwidth. It follows from the directional characteristic of the antenna that only those targets which lie in the direction of the beam will appear on the trace. Thus a single trace represents the ranges of targets lying along a specific line of bearing.

1.3.2 Synchronization of scanner and trace

An essential feature of the modern marine radar display is that it should provide continous coverage over 360° of azimuth. To achieve this both the scanner and the trace are rotated, at the same rate, clockwise, continuously and automatically. To comply with IMO Performance Standards (see Section 10.2) the duration of one revolution must not exceed 5 seconds; values of about 2 to 3 seconds are typical for shipborne radar.

The interval between successive transmitted pulses (and hence between the start of successive traces on the PPI) may fall within a range of values (see Section 2.3.1) but for the purposes of illustration an average value of 1/1250s (800 μs) will suffice. If a representative time for one revolution of the scanner is taken to be 3 seconds, one can deduce that some 3600 pulses are transmitted during one revolution and that the scanner rotates through 0.1° between pulses. Thus while the rotation is continuous, it may be found convenient to imagine that the antenna scans the area around the ship in about 3600 steps of 0.1° and that each step is represented by a separate trace on the screen. The picture is thus 'built up' of approximately 3600 radial lines.

1.3.3 The build–up of the picture

The echo of a detectable target will be 'painted' once per revolution of the scanner. The inside of the CRT screen is coated with a luminous material (see Section 2.6.1.2)

so that any area, once painted, will glow for at least 2 to 3 seconds. Thus the afterglow can be made sufficiently long to cause the echo paint to persist until it is painted again on the next revolution. (There are a few marine systems in which the persistence is less than one revolution but they are very much the exception.)

Because the scanner and trace rotate at the same rate, the radar beam and the trace describe equal arcs in equal intervals of time. Thus targets will be displayed in the correct angular relationship, one to another. If two ships subtend an angle of 50° at the observing vessel, the centres of their echoes will be separated on the PPI by a similar angle. As the beam sweeps across a geographical feature, such as a coastline, echoes on successive traces will add together, side by side, to produce a plan representation of that feature (see Figure 1.9).

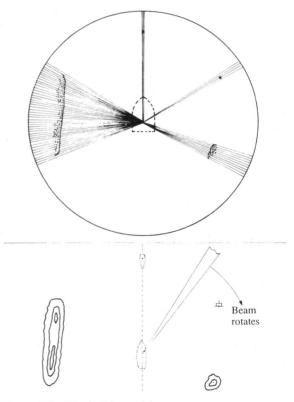

Figure 1.9 The build-up of the picture

The calibration marks, which may be switched on or off by the observer, will be painted on each trace and thus when switched on will appear as concentric circles. The variable range marker will similarly appear as a single circle of variable radius.

1.3.4 The heading marker

In general, a bearing is the angle between the direction of a chosen reference and that of an object of interest. On a PPI display the fundamental reference is the instantaneous direction of the observing vessel's head. As the axis of the horizontal beam crosses the ship's fore-and-aft line in the forward direction, a set of contacts is closed, producing a pulse of a few milliseconds duration. This pulse is used to increase the brilliance of the spot and hence produce the complete brightening up of several successive traces, resulting in the distinctive 'heading marker' or 'heading indicator' (see also Section 2.4.6). Thus all targets are displayed, not only in the correct angular relationship to one another but also in the correct angular relationship to the observing ship's heading (see Figure 1.9).

The angle between the observed vessel's heading and the direction of the horizontal beam is known as the *aerial angle*. In the case of a synthetic display (see Section 1.2.5) the instantaneous value of the aerial angle will be measured and stored in digital form alongside the corresponding set of range data (see Section 2.6.6).

The IMO Performance Standards (see Section 10.2) require that the line be displayed with an error of not greater than ±1° and that its thickness should not exceed half a degree. The procedure for checking this accuracy is discussed in Section 6.9.9. Clearly, because both targets and the heading marker are produced by a brightening of the spot, there is a danger that a target may be masked if it lies in the direction of the heading marker. The specification recognises this danger by requiring that there is a provision for switching the heading marker off. However, the provision must be such that the heading marker cannot be left in the *off* position. Normally this requirement is complied with by the use of a spring-loaded switch which is biased in the *on* position. The danger of the heading marker being left in the *off* position is that, in the absence of the correct reference, an erroneous reference (such as the bearing marker – see Section 6.9.5) might be used inadvertently.

The appearance of the heading marker confirms the orientation of the picture (see Section 1.4) and consequently whether the bearings are relative or true (see Figure 1.10).

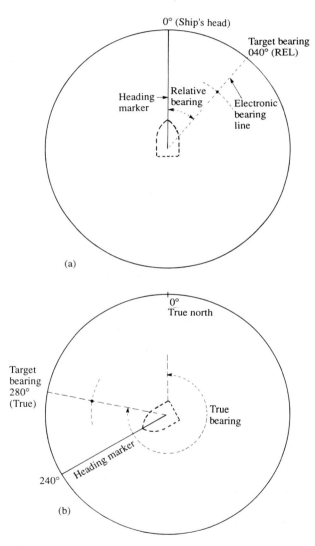

Figure 1.10 Measurement of bearing: (a) relative bearing, (b) true bearing

1.3.5 Bearing measurement

The picture described above offers a plan view representation of the area surrounding the ship in such a form as to make it possible to measure the range and bearing of any detected target. It is this characteristic that gave rise to the term 'plan position indicator' which distinguished the rotating trace display from the earlier A-scan display. It is also this characteristic which makes the display particularly suitable for use in collision avoidance and navigation.

The IMO Performance Standards (see Section 10.2) require that provision be made for quickly obtaining the bearing of any object whose echo appears on the display. In practice such provision may be fulfilled by a variety of mechanical and electro-mechanical devices which enable the observer to measure the angle between the heading marker and the object of interest. In general the target is intersected either by an engraved line along the diameter of the rotatable disk of transparent plastic located above the screen of the CRT, or by an electronic line emanating from the origin of the display (see Figure 1.10). The bearing is read off, in the former case from some form of fixed circular scale around the edge of the screen and in the latter case from an analogue or digital indicator coupled to the bearing marker control. In a synthetic display it may be possible to have the computer read out the bearing of a target directly from a knowledge of the radial line on which its echo appears. A variety of bearing measurement facilities and the correct procedure for their use are discussed in Section 6.9.

1.4 Picture orientation

In marine radar literature, there is frequently an understandable descriptive overlap between the concepts of picture 'orientation' and picture 'presentation'. In this text (as in *The Navigation Control Manual*), orientation is defined as the choice of directional reference to be represented by the 000° (12 o'clock) graduation on the fixed bearing scale around the CRT (see Figure 1.11). Although the heading marker should always appear at the instant the axis of the beam crosses the fore-and-aft line in the forward direction, it is in theory possible to rotate the whole picture so that the 000° graduation on the fixed bearing scale represents any direction. In practice one of three preferred directions will be chosen, namely:

1 The ship's instantaneous heading, in which case the orientation is said to be *ship's-head-up* (*unstabilized*).
2 True north, in which case the orientation is said to be *true-north-up* (*stabilized*).
3 The ship's true course, in which case the orientation is said to be *course-up* (*stabilized*).

Picture presentation (see Section 1.5) will be used to specify the reference with respect to which echo motion is displayed. In more general terms, the type of presentation indicates to the observer that the movement of the displayed echoes is shown with respect to his own ship, or with respect to the water, or with respect to the ground, i.e. *relative motion* or *true motion* (*sea-stabilized*) or *true motion* (*ground-stabilized*).

1.4.1 Ship's-head-up orientation (unstabilized)

This orientation is so called, because the observer views the picture with the heading marker (and thus the ship's head) at the 'top' of the screen (see Figure 1.11). When the original PPI displays were introduced, it was the only orientation available. At that time, no provision was made for 'azimuth stabilization', by which is meant the input of compass information to the display (see Section 2.6.3). In the absence of such an input it is not possible effectively to maintain either of the other two preferred orientations. In modern marine radar systems, almost invariably the ship's-head-up orientation is unstabilized, i.e. a compass signal is *not* used in the control of the orientation. Historically there have been two designs which did associate the ship's-head-up orientation with azimuth stabilization but they were special cases in that the stabilization was applied twice. With the advent of raster-scan displays, the concept may well be exploited again in the future.

The single attractive feature of the ship's-head-up orientation (unstabilized) is that it corresponds directly

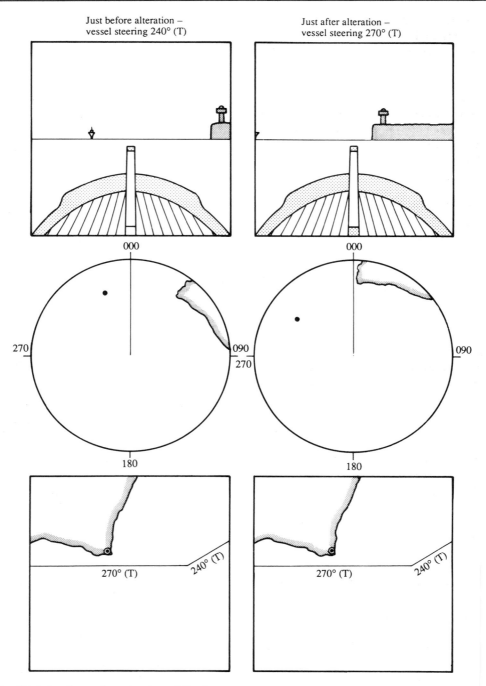

Figure 1.11   Ship's-head-up orientation (unstabilized)

with the scene as viewed through the wheelhouse window. A well placed display unit will be sited so that the officer viewing the screen faces forward. (United Kingdom vessels are required to have at least one display sited in this way – see Section 10.6.) Thus, irrespective of whether the officer is viewing the radar screen or looking forward through the wheelhouse window, objects on the starboard side of the ship will lie on the right and those on the port side will lie on the left.

A major shortcoming of the unstabilized orientation is that at every change in the direction of the observing vessel's heading, the entire picture (apart from the heading marker), will rotate by an equal but opposite angle (see Figure 1.11). This characteristic limits the usefulness of the orientation in three specific ways:

1 If a large alteration of course is made, any areas of land echoes are smeared across the screen, making it difficult to identify specific features. The afterglow created during the alteration may obscure isolated fixed or floating targets for some time after the vessel is steady on her new course (see Figure 1.11).

2 In ideal conditions the ship's heading would coincide at all times with the chosen course; in practice, due to the effect of wind and sea, the ship will 'yaw' about the correct heading. On a display using an unstabilized orientation, this superimposes an angular wander on the movement of all targets (see Figure 1.12) which limits the ease and speed with which bearings can be measured. It becomes necessary to choose an instant when the target can be intersected with the cursor or electronic bearing line *and* the vessel's instantaneous heading read off simultaneously, or, alternatively, to wait until the vessel is *right on* course. The latter is necessary because the bearings read off from this orientation are measured relative to the ship's head and must be converted to true bearings for use in collision avoidance and navigation. The practical procedure for obtaining bearings from an unstabilized orientation is described in Section 6.9.3.

3 The disruption of the echo movement due to yaw limits the ease and speed with which an observer can plot the movement of targets for collision avoidance purposes, even if a reflection plotter is used (see Section 7.8.7). Further, an unwary or untrained observer

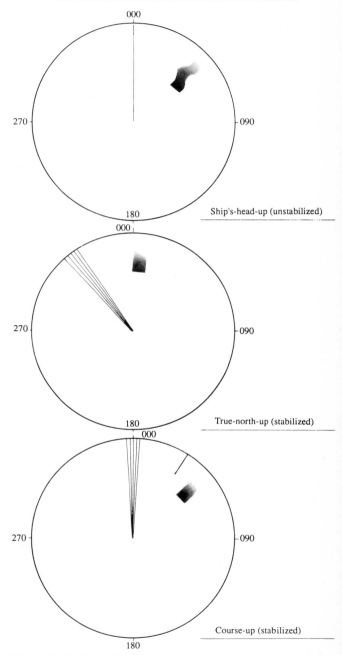

Figure 1.12 The effect of yaw
Observing vessel's course 330° (T), yaw ± 4°
Target vessel approaching on steady bearing of 015°(T)

may be dangerously misled by such angular move-ments. For example, a small change of course by the observing vessel may give the impression that the bearing of a target is changing, while in fact the true bearing is remaining constant. The extremely impor-tant topic of systematic observation of target move-ment is discussed at length in Chapter 7.

1.4.2   True-north-up orientation (stabilized)

In true-north-up orientation, the heading marker is aligned with that graduation on the fixed bearing scale which corresponds with the instantaneous value of the ship's heading. As a result, the 000° graduation repre-sents true north. Thus the observer views the picture with north at the 'top' of the screen and it is for this reason that the orientation is so named. Compass stabi-lization is essential so as to maintain the orientation true-north-up when the observing vessel alters course or yaws about her chosen course (see Figures 1.12 and 1.13). In the absence of stabilization, the picture would rotate by an amount equal and *opposite* to any change in the observing vessel's heading (see Section 1.4.1). The compass stabilization signal is used to produce simultan-eously a commensurate rotation of the picture in the *same* direction as the change of heading. As a result there is no *nett* rotation of the picture, the heading marker rotates to the new value of heading, and true north remains coincident with the 000° graduation on the fixed bearing scale. The stabilization signal can be derived from any transmitting compass but in practice the signal source is almost invariably a gyro compass. The process whereby the signal is used to effect stabi-lization is described in Section 2.6.3.

The addition of compass stabilization overcomes the serious, inherent limitation of the ship's-head-up (unsta-bilized) orientation by removing the angular smearing which is associated with any change in heading. Not only does this eliminate the masking of targets by the afterglow generated during an alteration of course, but it allows true bearings to be read off directly and quickly from the fixed bearing scale without the need to check the direction of the ship's head at the same instant. These features are of particular importance in both collision

avoidance and navigation applications. Further, there is no angular disruption of the tracks of targets as their echoes move across the screen. This greatly facilitates the systematic observation of targets for collision avoidance purposes and removes a characteristic which, probably more than any other, has demonstrated over many years its potential to mislead the untrained or unwary observer (see Section 7.12.7).

The orientation compares directly with the chart and very many observers find this agreeable or at least acceptable. However, despite the advantages of stabi-lization, some officers have a subjective preference for the ship's-head-up orientation. They find it awkward or uncomfortable to view a north-up orientation, particu-larly when the vessel is on southerly courses. This point of view is advanced by some river and estuary pilots who argue that in locks and narrow channels the angular smearing is secondary when compared with the impor-tance of port and starboard through the window corres-ponding with left and right on the radar screen. It is a view also held by some more senior officers whose initial radar experience was gained before the availability of azimuth stabilization and by some whose prime concern is visual conning of the vessel. Since then there has been a steady increase in the number of observers having a preference for a stabilized orientation.

1.4.3   Course-up orientation (stabilized)

In a course-up (stabilized) orientation the heading marker is aligned to the 000° graduation on the fixed bearing scale at an instant at which the vessel is right on the chosen course. By virtue of the azimuth stabilization, changes in the vessel's instantaneous heading are reflec-ted by sympathetic angular movement of the heading marker, thus maintaining the ship's course (referred to as the reference course) in alignment with the zero of the fixed bearing scale. For the same reason, the angular wander of echoes associated with an unstabilized display is eliminated. In some modern systems a north marker is displayed at the edge of the screen (see Figure 1.14).

Provided that the observing vessel does not stray very far from her chosen course, this orientation effectively combines the attractive features of both of the orienta-tions previously described. It eliminates the angular

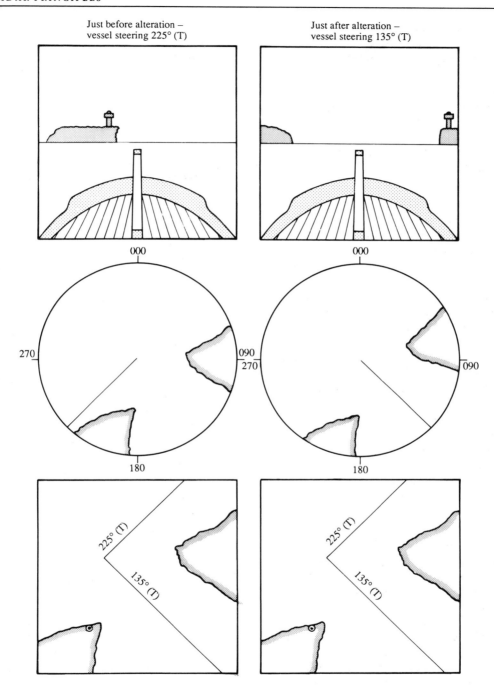

Figure 1.13   True–north–up orientation (stabilized)

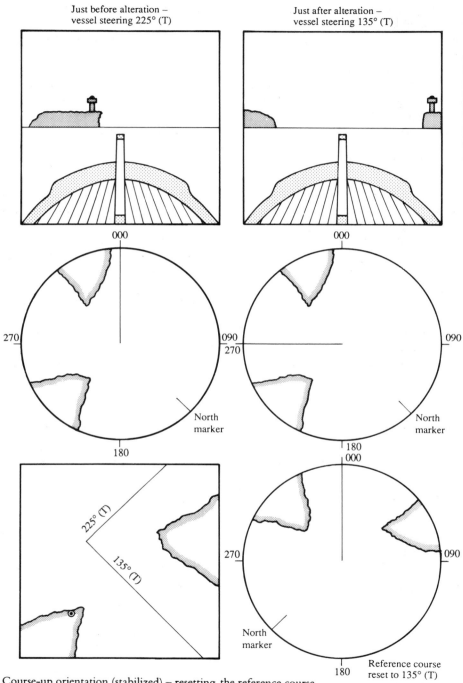

Figure 1.14   Course-up orientation (stabilized) – resetting the reference course

wander of the picture due to yaw, while maintaining the heading marker in a substantially (though not exactly) ship's-head-up position.

Inevitably a major alteration of course will become necessary either due to the requirements of collision avoidance or to those of general navigation. When the vessel is steadied on the new course the orientation, although not meaningless, will have lost its property of being substantially ship's-head-up. The problem is that the orientation is still *previous-course-up* and the picture must be reorientated to align the heading marker with the zero of the fixed bearing scale at an instant when the vessel is right on the new chosen course (see Figure 1.14). In older systems it was necessary to carry out the realignment by rotating a manual control, but in most modern displays it can be achieved simply by pressing a button.

1.4.4   Choice of orientation

The fundamental function of any civil marine radar is to afford a means of measuring the ranges and bearings of echoes and hence to make possible the tracking of target movements for collision avoidance and the determina-
tion of the observing vessel's position in order to ensure safe navigation. The ease with which these objectives can be attained is affected by the choice of orientation. Where the various techniques of collision avoidance and navigation are described in this text, appropriate attention will be given to the influence of orientation. The theory of the production of the orientations is described in Section 2.6.3 and the practical setting up procedures in Chapter 6. It is appropriate at this point to summarize the features of the three orientations so far described in the context of the foregoing fundamental requirements (see Table 1.3).

Except in specialized pilotage situations, the ship's-head-up unstabilized orientation has nothing to offer other than its subjective appeal, because by its very nature it regularly disrupts the steady-state condition conducive to measurement of bearing and tracking of echo movement (see Figure 1.12). True-north-up and course-up orientations do not exhibit this angular disruption and hence are equally superior in fulfilling the fundamental requirements. Fortunately they are complementary in that while one is north-up, the other is orientated in such a way as not to alienate the user who has a ship's-head-up preference (see Figure 1.12).

Table 1.3   Picture orientations compared

Feature	Orientation		
	Ship's-head-up, unstablized	True-north-up, stabilized	Course-up, stabilized
Blurring when observing vessel yaws or alters course	Yes: can produce very serious masking	None	None
Measurement of bearings	Awkward and slow	Straightforward	Straightforward
Compatibility with reflection plotter	Very limited	Straightforward	Straightforward
Angular disruption of target trails when observing vessel yaws or alters course	Yes: can be dangerously misleading	None	None
Correspondence with wheelhouse window view	Perfect	Not obvious	Virtually perfect except after large course change
Correspondence with chart	Not obvious	Perfect	Not obvious

1.5   Picture presentation

As suggested in Section 1.4, there is frequently some overlap between the concepts of picture orientation and picture presentation. In this text, as in *The Naviagation Control Manual*, the term 'picture presentation' will be used to indicate if the movement of displayed echoes is shown with respect to (a) the observing vessel, (b) the water, or (c) the ground. In all three presentations, the observing vessel is represented by the electronic origin of the display, i.e. by the centre of rotation of the trace.

1.5.1   The relative-motion presentation

In the relative-motion presentation the origin of the display is stationary and the movement of all targets is shown with respect to the observing vessel. Commonly the origin is located at the centre of the circular screen (or, in the case of a raster-scan display, at the centre of the display circle) but this need not be the case as off-centred relative-motion presentations are available in many dis-

play systems. The essential feature is that the origin is stationary and as a consequence targets exhibit their motion relative to the observing vessel. This is best illustrated by an example. (The scenario used to illustrate the three cases listed in Section 1.5 is subject to the assumption that the effect of leeway may be neglected.)

For the purpose of illustration it is convenient to consider the case of an observing vessel on a steady heading of 000° (T) at a speed of 10 knots through the water in a tide (which is uniform throughout the area) setting 270° (T) at a rate of 4 knots. The chart (see Figure 1.15 (a) also shows four targets:

(i)   Vessel *A* which is located 7 miles due north of the observing vessel and is stopped in the water heading 045° (T).

(ii)   Vessel *B* which is located 8 miles due east of vessel *A* and is on a steady heading of 270° (T) at a speed of 10 knots through the water.

(iii)   Vessel *C* which is located 5 miles due north of vessel *A* and is on a steady heading of 180° (T) at a speed of 5 knots through the water.

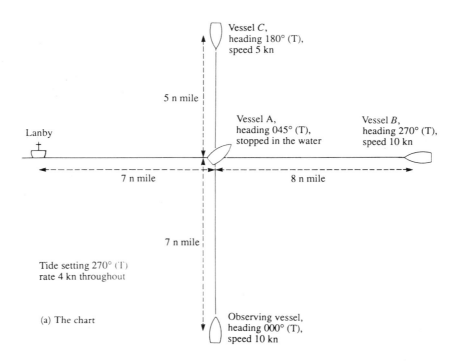

(a) The chart

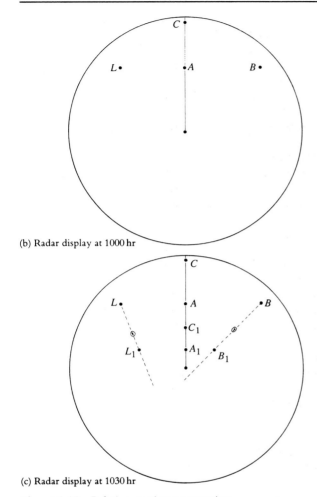

(b) Radar display at 1000 hr

(c) Radar display at 1030 hr

Figure 1.15   Relative-motion presentation

(iv) A large automatic navigational buoy (lanby) *L* which is anchored and therefore is stationary over the ground. Its position is 7 miles due west of vessel *A*.

To assist in the understanding of relative motion, Figure 1.15(b) represents the observing vessel's PPI as it would appear at 1000. For comparison, Figure 1.15(c) represents the same PPI showing the positions of the echoes as they would appear at 1030 together with a record of their 1000 positions. It will be noticed that the shape of the echoes gives no indication of the outline of

the targets. This fundamental limitation of marine radar will be discussed at length in Section 2.6.5. Consider now the movement of each of the four echoes in turn, commencing with that of the water-stationary target *A* which offers a simple basis on which an understanding of all relative motion can be built. It is important to remember that it is being assumed that the observing vessel maintains a steady heading. If the vessel were yawing, azimuth stabilization would be essential to achieve the continuity of movement described below.

In the period 1000 to 1030 the observing vessel will move north by a distance of 5 miles through the water. Because the origin remains stationary, and the range of target *A* decreases at 10 nautical miles per hour, it follows that the echo of *A* will move down the heading marker by a distance of 5 miles in the 30 minute interval. This reveals the basic property of the relative-motion presentation which is that the echo of a target which is stationary in the water will move across the screen in a direction reciprocal to that of the observing vessel's heading, at a rate equal to the observing vessel's speed through the water.

Consider now the movement of the echo of vessel *B* which at 1000 was 8 miles due east of the stationary vessel *A*. As *B* is heading directly toward *A* at 10 knots, it follows that its 1030 position will be 3 miles due east of *A*. Figure 1.15 (c) reveals that the afterglow trail left by the echo of vessel *B* offers an indication of how far off the target will pass if neither vessel manoeuvres. However, the echo has moved across the screen in a direction and at a rate which is quite different from the target's course and speed. An appreciation of this fact is absolutely essential if the presentation is to be interpreted correctly and used in assessing collision avoidance strategy. Further consideration of the figure will show that the relative motion of echo *B* is the resultant of that of a water-stationary target (which is determined by the observing vessel's course and speed through the water) and the true motion of the vessel *B* through the water. The proper use of radar for collision avoidance is based on systematic observation and analysis of both the relative motion and the true motion of the other targets in an encounter (see Chapter 7).

Consider now the movement on the screen of the echo of vessel *C*. At 1000 its position was 5 miles due north of the water-stationary vessel *A* and heading directly towards it at 5 knots. It follows that at 1030 its position will be 2.5 miles north of vessel *A*. As shown in Figure 1.15 (c), because the echo of vessel *A* has itself moved across the screen by 5 miles in a direction of south, the aggregate movement of echo *C* is 7.5 miles in the same direction. Thus, as in the case of vessel *B*, the echo has moved across the screen in a way that is different from the movement of the vessel through the water. However it should be noted that, by coincidence, the track across the screen of echo *C* is in the same direction as that of the water-stationary target *A*. This reveals a further feature of the relative-motion presentation, which is that the echoes of targets which are stopped in the water, targets which are on a reciprocal course to the observing vessel and targets which are on the same course as the observing vessel, but slower, will all move across the screen in the *same* direction (but at different speeds). This feature has the potential to mislead the untrained or unwary observer into confusing, for example, a target that is being overtaken with one that is on a

reciprocal course. This further emphasises the necessity of systematic analysis of the information presented, as opposed to inspired guesswork, when using the radar for collision avoidance (see Chapter 7).

Initially the east/west distance between the lanby and the stationary ship was 7 miles. As the tide is setting the stationary vessel down on to the buoy at 4 knots, it follows that this distance will have reduced to 5 miles by 1030. A study of Figure 1.15 (c) will show that the echo of the buoy has moved across the screen in a direction and at a rate which are the resultant of the motion of a water-stationary target and the reciprocal of the tide. Further consideration of this point will reveal that a property of the relative-motion presentation is that a land-stationary target will move across the screen in a direction which is the reciprocal of the observing vessel's ground track at a speed equal to the speed of the observing vessel over the ground. This property is exploited in the use of radar for navigation (as opposed to collision avoidance); the various procedures are set out in Chapter 8.

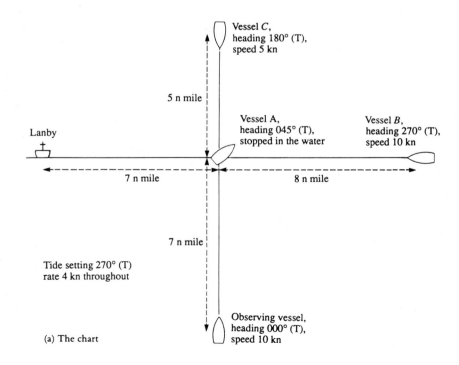

Vessel *C*, heading 180° (T), speed 5 kn

5 n mile

Lanby

Vessel A, heading 045° (T), stopped in the water

Vessel *B*, heading 270° (T), speed 10 kn

7 n mile   8 n mile

7 n mile

Tide setting 270° (T) rate 4 kn throughout

(a) The chart

Observing vessel, heading 000° (T), speed 10 kn

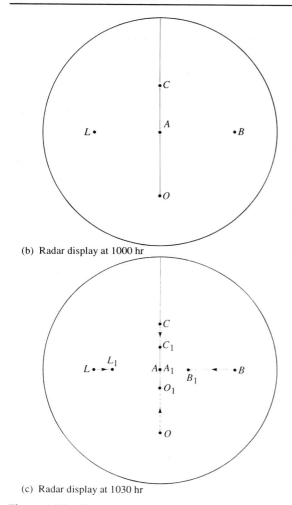

(b) Radar display at 1000 hr

(c) Radar display at 1030 hr

Figure 1.16 True-motion sea-stabilized presentation

1.5.2 The true-motion presentation

It has been shown that in a relative-motion presentation the movement of all echoes across the screen is affected by the course and speed of the observing vessel. In a correctly adjusted true-motion presentation, the echo movement of all targets is rendered independent of the motion of the observing vessel. This is achieved by causing the origin of the picture to track across the screen in a direction and at a rate which correspond with the motion of the observing vessel. Immediately one must ask the question, 'Should the observing vessel's course

and speed be measured with respect to the water or with respect to the ground?'. The answer will have a fundamental effect on the movement of the displayed echoes. At this juncture, it is important to recognise that either reference can be used: it is appropriate to consider both possibilities and subsequently debate the suitability of each.

If the course and speed through the water are selected, the true-motion presentation is said to be sea-stabilized. It was shown that with azimuth stabilization, the input of ship's heading data is used to maintain true north (or the ship's chosen course) in a fixed direction on the screen. By simultaneously feeding in speed data (measured with respect to the water) it is possible to stabilize the picture so that a water-stationary target is maintained in a fixed position on the screen. This is illustrated by the same scenario as was used in section 1.5.1.

1.5.2.1 True-motion sea-stabilized presentation

To produce a true-motion, sea-stabilized presentation, the origin of the picture must be made to track across the screen in a direction and at a rate that correspond with the observing vessel's course and speed through the water. In the example in the illustration (Figure 1.16) the course is 000° (T) and the speed is 10 knots.

Figure 1.16 (b) shows the PPI of the observing vessel as it would appear at 1000. The origin of the picture is offset in such a way as to make optimum use of the available screen area (see Section 6.8.2, paragraph 5). Figure 1.16 (c) shows the position of the four echoes as they would appear at 1030 together with an indication of their 1000 positions for the purpose of comparison. The movement of each of the four echoes will now be considered in turn, commencing with target *A* which is stopped in the water.

In the interval 1000 to 1030 the origin will move due north by a scale distance of 5 miles, while in the same time target *A* will remain on the heading marker but its range will decrease by 5 nautical miles. It follows that the nett motion of the echo of target *A* will be zero. Consideration of Figure 1.16 reveals the basic property of a correctly set up true-motion sea-stabilized presentation, which is that the echo of a target which is stationary in the water will maintain constant position on the screen.

At 1000 the moving target *B* was located 8 miles due east of vessel *A*. As it is heading directly toward *A* its bearing from *A* will remain steady but the range will have decreased to 3 miles by 1030. Figure 1.16(c) shows that the echo of target *B* will move across the screen in a direction and at a rate which corresponds with the target vessel's course and speed through the water. A similar argument will reveal that the echo of vessel *C* will move across the screen in a direction of 180° (T) at a scale speed of 5 knots. The presentation thus has the property that the afterglow trails offer an indication of the headings of all moving targets. This feature is complementary to the corresponding property of the relative-motion presentation (see Section 1.5.1). It must be stressed that collision avoidance strategy must be based on systematic analysis of the displayed target movements as detailed in Chapter 7.

As a result of the tide, the water-stationary vessel *A* will be set directly toward the lanby and by 1030 the east/west distance between the two will have reduced to 5 miles. It has been established that echo *A* will maintain its position on the screen and thus it follows that in the interval from 1000 to 1030 echo *L* will move east across the screen by a scale distance of 2 miles. Consideration of Figure 1.16 (c) will show that a third property of the true-motion sea-stabilized presentation is that land-stationary targets will move across the screen at a rate equal to the tide but in the opposite direction to the set.

In considering the properties of the true-motion, sea-stabilized presentation it is essential to appreciate that the accuracy with which the displayed target movements are presented is completely dependent on the accuracy with which the direction and rate of the movement of the picture origin represents the observing vessel's course and speed through the water. The true-motion presentation is only as good as the input data.

The mechanics whereby the tracking of the origin is achieved, the practical procedure for setting up the presentation and the effect of errors and inaccuracies are covered in Sections 2.6.4, 6.8 and 7.10 respectively.

Because the scenario used a heading of north for the observing vessel, the question of whether the orientation

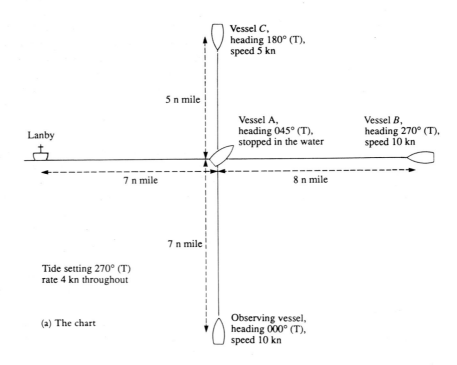

Vessel *C*,
heading 180° (T),
speed 5 kn

5 n mile

Lanby

Vessel *A*,
heading 045° (T),
stopped in the water

Vessel *B*,
heading 270° (T),
speed 10 kn

7 n mile   8 n mile

7 n mile

Tide setting 270° (T)
rate 4 kn throughout

(a) The chart

Observing vessel,
heading 000° (T),
speed 10 kn

was north-up or course-up did not arise. It should be noted that either orientation can be used with true motion, irrespective of heading.

1.5.2.2 *True-motion, ground-stabilized presentation*

To create ground stabilization of a true-motion presentation, the origin of the picture is made to move across the screen in a direction and at a rate which correspond with the observing vessel's track over the ground. To achieve this, the input data must have a component

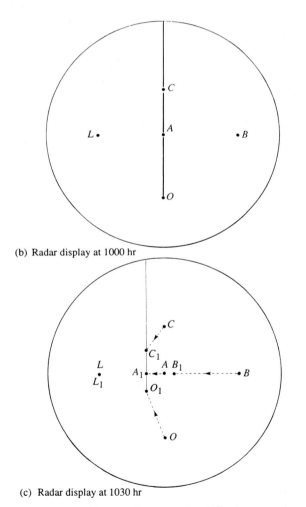

(b) Radar display at 1000 hr

(c) Radar display at 1030 hr

Figure 1.17 True-motion ground-stabilized presentation

which represents the observing vessel's course and speed through the water plus a further component which represents the set and rate of the tidal stream or current. There are several ways in which the resultant of these components may be deduced and applied as input data. A detailed description of the methods is set out in Section 2.6.4.4. At this stage it is important to appreciate that the accuracy of the presentation depends on the accuracy of both components. In particular it should be remembered that the values of set and drift may have to be based on past positions. For comparison purposes it is convenient to illustrate the presentation with reference to the same scenario as was used in the two preceding examples. Figure 1.17(b) shows the PPI of the observing vessel as it would appear at 1000, while Figure 1.17(c) shows the echoes as they would appear at 1030 together with recorded plots of the 1000 positions. It should be noted that the origin of the picture has moved in a direction which differs from that of the heading marker. The latter represents the direction in which the observing vessel is heading at any instant and is independent of any tidal influence.

In this case it is helpful to start by considering the ground-stationary target L. Reference to Figure 1.17(c) shows that in the period 1000 to 1030 the origin of the display will have moved to a position which is a scale distance of 5 miles due north (representing the vessel's movement through the water) and 2 miles due west (representing the set and drift experienced) of its 1000 screen location. In the same interval, the north/south distance between the observing vessel and the lanby will have decreased by 5 nautical miles (the d.lat.) while the east/west distance will have decreased by 2 miles (the departure). It follows from these two statements that the echo of the buoy L will exhibit neither north/south movement nor east/west movement across the screen. This reveals the key property of the correctly set up true-motion ground-stabilized presentation, which is that the echo of a land target will remain stationary on the screen.

Consider now vessel A which is stopped in the water heading 045° (T). As previously established, it will be set directly toward the buoy by a distance of 2 miles in the period 1000–1030. It follows from this, and the fact that echo L is stationary on the screen, that the echo of vessel

A will move in a direction of due west by a scale distance of 2 miles in the interval considered. This reveals a second property of the true-motion ground-stabilized presentation, which is that the echo of a target which is stopped in the water will move across the screen in a direction and at a rate that corresponds with the set and rate of the tidal stream.

Having regard to target *C*, it is clear that at 1030 its position will be 2.5 miles north of vessel *A*. A study of Figure 1.17 (c) will show that, because the movement of echo *A* represents the tide, the echo of vessel *C* will therefore move across the screen in a direction and at a rate which is the resultant of the set and drift of the tidal stream, and her course and speed through the water. This shows the general property of the correctly set up true-motion ground-stabilized presentation, which is that echoes of vessels that are underway will move across the screen in a direction and at a rate which represents their track over the ground. The example of the vessel *A* which is underway but stopped is a special case of this general rule. The movement of the echo of vessel *B* also illustrates this feature, but perhaps not so dramatically because it is heading in the same direction as the set of the tidal stream.

Consideration of the movements of echoes *A* and *C* in particular will emphasise how an untrained or unwary observer might be misled into *erroneously* concluding that vessel *A* was slow-moving and crossing showing a red sidelight (when in fact it is stopped in the path of the observing vessel) and that vessel *C* was a passing vessel showing a red sidelight (when in fact it is head on).

It is thus essential to appreciate that in this presentation the movement of the echoes of vessels that are underway does *not* represent their headings. Information on headings is essential for the proper use of radar in collision avoidance. It follows that, in principle, this presentation is not appropriate as a basis for planning collision avoidance strategy and can be dangerously misleading if used for this purpose. This extremely important topic is further discussed in Sections 2.6.4.4 and 6.8.3.

As noted in the previous section, it should be appreciated that either north-up or course-up orientation can be used with true motion.

1.5.3   Choice of presentation

The choice of presentation made in any given circumstances will be influenced by a number of factors. The available equipment may not offer the choice of all three presentations described in this chapter. Material to the decision will be the question of whether the radar is being used primarily for collision avoidance or for position fixing and progress monitoring. It may be that the requirements of both must be satisfied with a single presentation. Subjective preferences are likely to make themselves felt. It is appropriate to defer more detailed discussion of the factors affecting such a choice until after further consideration has been given to the operating principles of the radar system, the practical procedures for the setting up and maintaining of the presentations, and the general philosophy of the use of radar for collision avoidance and navigation (see Chapters 6, 7, and 8). However, at this stage it is useful, for comparison purposes, to summarize the major features of each presentation and comment briefly on its suitability for use in collision avoidance and navigation.

In the relative-motion presentation the echo movement of targets which are underway is that of the target relative to the observing vessel. Systematic observation of this movement readily offers a forecast of the distance off at which a target will pass (the closest point of approach or CPA) and the time at which the target will reach its closest point of approach (TCPA). This information is an effective measure of the risk of a close-quarters situation developing. The presentation gives no direct indication of the heading or speed of target vessels. Such information is essential to the choice of avoiding action in encounters with other vessels and has to be obtained by the resolution of a vector triangle. This may be done graphically or with the aid of some semi-automatic plotting device, or automatically by computer. Thus the relative-motion presentation gives direct indictation of some of the information required for collision avoidance but the remainder must be found by deduction (see Chapter 7).

The echoes of land targets on a relative-motion presentation trace out a trail which is the reciprocal of the observing vessel's track made good over the ground.

This feature is particularly useful in progress monitoring and position fixing when the radar is being used for navigation as opposed to collision avoidance (see Chapter 8).

The true-motion sea-stabilized presentation makes the headings and speeds of targets available directly but the observer is required to deduce the CPA and TCPA. In respect of the use of radar for collision avoidance it can be seen that the relative motion and the true-motion sea-stabilized presentations are complementary. The true-motion does have the added advantage that it makes it very much easier to identify target manoeuvres and, further, the continuity of target motion is not disrupted when the observing vessel manoeuvres.

The true-motion ground-stabilized presentation has little to offer other than its ability to maintain land targets in a fixed position on the screen. No apology is made for re-stating the fact that it gives no direct indication of any collision avoidance information.

Table 1.4 summarizes the features of the presentation described above.

Table 1.4   Presentations – summary of features

Feature	Presentation		
	Relative motion	True-motion sea-stablized	True-motion ground-stabilized
Ease of assessing target's CPA/TCPA	Directly available	Resolution required	Resolution required
Ease of assessing target's course, speed and aspect	Resolution required	Directly available	Resolution required – potentially misleading
Need for additional sensor inputs: course and speed	No	Yes	Yes
Need for data on tide set and rate	No	No	Yes
Displayed information relative to:	Observer	The water	The ground
Particular application for collision avoidance/navigation	Partial contribution to collision avoidance data Ideal for parallel indexing	Partial contribution to collision avoidance data	Difficult to achieve without ARPA but if achieved provides stationary map
Limitations for collision avoidance	Target heading not directly available	CPA not directly available	No collision avoidance data directly available
Limitations for navigation	Movement of land echoes may hinder target identification	Limited movement of land echoes	None if stabilization effective

2 The radar system – operational principles

2.1 Introduction

In Chapter 1 the fundamental principles of range and bearing measurement which underly the generation of a marine radar picture were discussed and the way in which the target information is displayed for use in navigation and collision avoidance was described in general terms. The operation of marine radar systems is now studied in greater detail in order to provide the reader with that thorough understanding of the relevant engineering and communication principles which is essential for safe and seamanlike application of the practical procedures described in Chapter 6.

An overall appreciation of system operation is readily achieved by reference to a simple block diagram (see Figure 2.1) in which the system is represented by a small number of main functional units. This makes it possible to identify the relationships between the units before proceeding to a more detailed anatomy of each functional block. It must be appreciated that while Figure 2.1 subdivides the system in such a way as to best illustrate operational principles, it may not coincide exactly with the physical subdivision of the units installed on board ship. For example, part of the receiver is commonly situated in the same cabinet as the transmitter, but the remainder may well be located in the display console. Such details of physical distribution may be neglected when considering general principles but are clearly relevant to a full understanding of a shipboard installation.

Accordingly the typical physical subdivision of a system will be discussed in Section 2.7.

2.2 Function of units

This section gives a brief description of the function of each block in the diagram and the interrelationship between the units, to provide a concise overall picture of radar operation. In subsequent sections a detailed exposition of the principles employed in each unit and of the characteristics required will be given. The treatment of these principles is substantially qualitative and should be readily followed by any reader having a rudimentary background of school physics.

2.2.1 The transmitter function (see also Section 2.3)

The function of the transmitter is to generate pulses of electromagnetic energy having the correct repetition frequency, length, shape, power and radio frequency. The pulses normally travel to the aerial by way of hollow copper tubing which has a precisely machined rectangular or circular cross-section and is known as *waveguide*.

It is sometimes considered convenient to visualize the radio energy as flowing, like water, along the inside of the tube and there is no doubt that this is a helpful and practical way of illustrating how the waveguide works.

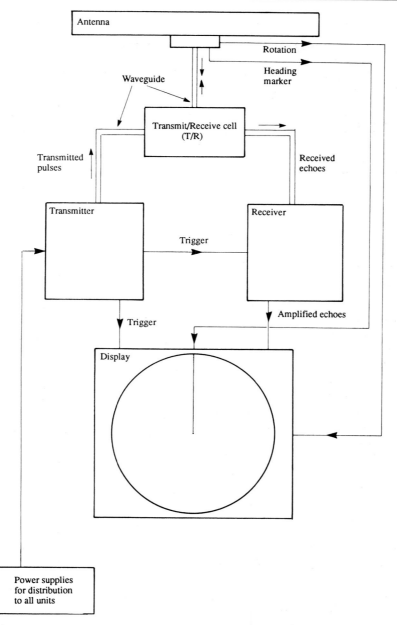

Figure 2.1   Simple block diagram of a radar system

Nonetheless, in the interests of veracity it must be stated that the energy actually travels, in the form of electric and magnetic fields, within the conducting walls of the waveguide. However there is no simple qualitative explanation for this mode of transmission. We are left with the choice between accepting the water analogy or pursuing a mathematical treatment which is beyond the scope of this book.

Historically, waveguide was used because of the considerable losses which were encountered in attempting to transmit the extremely short wavelengths associated with radar frequencies along conventional cables of any significant length. While some manufacturers have now developed co-axial cables which will pass radar frequencies, others still consider waveguide to be the more suitable method. (A co-axial cable is one having a central conductor surrounded by insulating material and a screening sheath.)

An essential feature of range measurement is that timing must commence at the instant of transmission (see Section 1.2.3.). This is achieved by using the same pulse to initiate transmission as is used to start the corresponding trace on the CRT display. This pulse is known as the 'synchronizing pulse' or 'trigger' and is shown in the block diagram as travelling along the line connecting the transmitter to the display.

In the block diagram a further line is shown connecting the transmitter to the receiver. This also carries the trigger pulse but in this case the pulse is used to initiate sea clutter suppression. Sea clutter is the name given to the echoes which are returned by the sea waves in the vicinity of the observing vessel (see Section 3.6). A variety of techniques exist for suppressing this unwanted effect. Most depend on the fact that the maximum response occurs at minimum range and hence suppression can conveniently be initiated by the trigger pulse.

2.2.2   The aerial function (see also Section 2.4)

Aerial, scanner and antenna are all names commonly used to describe the device which radiates the radio energy into space and intercepts the returning echoes. Its construction defines the power distribution of the radar beam in both the horizontal and the vertical planes. In order to achieve the required directional characteristic (see Section 1.3.1) the horizontal limits must be narrow. By contrast, the beam is wide in a vertical sense in order to maintain adequate performance when a vessel is rolling (or pitching) in a seaway. The IMO Performance Standards (see Section 10.2) set out certain range performance requirements and these must be achieved when the vessel is rolling or pitching up to ± 10°. While in theory one might contemplate using some form of gyro stabilization to maintain the beam in a horizontal plane, in practice the standard has the effect of defining a minimum vertical beam width of 20°.

To achieve the desired 360° of azimuth coverage (see Sections 1.3.2 and 2.4.4) the scanner is rotated continuously and automatically in a clockwise direction (when viewed from above). A signal representing this rotation, either in analogue or in digital code form, must be relayed to the PPI display in order to drive the trace in sympathetic rotation whith the scanner. (In a raster-scan display the signal will update the aerial angle against which the range data is being read in.) The transmission of this signal is represented in Figure 2.1 by one of the two lines connecting the aerial unit to the display. The second line carries the heading marker pulse (see Section 1.3.4) which fully brightens several successive traces as the axis of the main beam crosses the ship's fore-and-aft line in the forward direction.

Where the waveguide extends from the aerial to a *remote* transmitter/receiver, some form of rotating joint is required in the waveguide to allow the energy to pass from the fixed part of the aerial unit to the rotating part. This is achieved by using two short sections of circular waveguide (one fixed and one rotating) and a special co-axial joint.

2.2.3   The receiver function (see also Section 2.5)

The function of the receiver is to amplify the very weak echoes intercepted by the aerial so as to generate pulses whose form and power will produce a visible response on the screen of a cathode ray tube (or provide a suitable input for digital storage).

It will be noticed that because a single aerial is used for transmission and reception, the waveguide is common to both transmitter and receiver. It would thus appear that the powerful pulses generated by the transmitter might be able to pass directly into the receiver. The receiver is protected from this by a device known as a transmit/receive switch (or T/R cell) which is situated in the waveguide immediately before the input to the receiver. The T/R cell blocks the input to the receiver during transmission; it will be discussed further in Section 2.5.

In effect there are thus two inputs to the receiver, the received signals from the aerial and the trigger pulse to initiate sea clutter suppression. The output line from the receiver carries the amplified signals to the display.

2.2.4 The display function (see also Section 2.6)

The prime function of the display is to indicate the presence of detectable objects by generating, on the screen of the cathode ray tube, a visible response whose angular and radial position with respect to the heading line and the origin of the trace are representative of the bearing and range, respectively, at which the corresponding target lies. A less formal way of expressing this is to state that the display generates a radar picture. Four input signals are necessary to produce such a picture (see Figure 2.1). Each of these signals, namely trigger, echo signals, heading marker and aerial rotation, has already been mentioned in this chapter when its source was discussed. However, in consolidating an understanding of the mechanics of producing a radar picture it is helpful to summarize them as follows:

1 *The trigger.* This ensures that each trace commences at the instant of a transmission (see Section 1.2).
2 *The amplified echoes.* Each echo on any given trace produces a brightening of the spot on the cathode ray tube at an elapsed time after the transmission which initiated that trace. The length of the elapsed time is directly proportional to the range of the target which reflected the echo and hence the distance of the echo from the origin is a measure of its range (see Section 1.2).
3 *The rotation signal.* This signal causes the trace to rotate at the same angular rate as the aerial. Conse-

quently all targets on any given trace will appear in the correct angular relationship to all other targets on the PPI (see Section 1.3).
4 *The heading marker signal.* This generates the brightened radial indicator corresponding with the forward direction of the ship's fore-and-aft line, thus providing a reference from which bearings can be measured (see Section 1.3).

These four fundamental signals that generate the radar picture are shown as inputs to the display in Figure 2.1. It should be borne in mind that the time relationship between the signals is of particular importance. These are illustrated by Figure 2.2 which uses some representative values. Figure 2.2 is drawn in two parts because, although all four signals are repetitive in their nature, the former two recur several thousand times per second whereas the latter two have a period of a few seconds. It is thus not practical to show the time sequence of all four signals on the same time axis.

It will be noticed in Figure 2.2(a) that there is a comparatively long delay between the completion of one trace and the commencement of the next. This is a design feature of all marine radars and is incorporated in an attempt to ensure that echoes from distant targets do not arrive after the transmission of the next pulse. If this does occur, echoes from two different transmissions may appear on the same trace. The late responses, which will display at a range very much shorter than the correct value and may mislead the observer, are known as *second trace echoes*. They are discussed in detail in Section 3.9.6.

Before leaving the simple block diagram it must be mentioned that the four input signals described above would produce an unstabilised relative-motion picture. The addition of a compass input would be necessary if azimuth stabilization was required, while true motion would necessitate an input of the ship's speed. Such additional inputs are discussed in Sections 2.6.3 and 2.6.4.

2.3 Transmitter principles

In Section 2.2.1 it was noted that the function of the

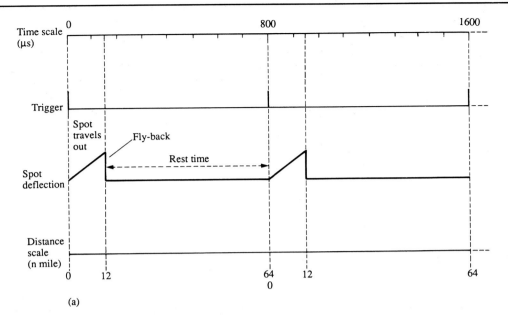

(a)

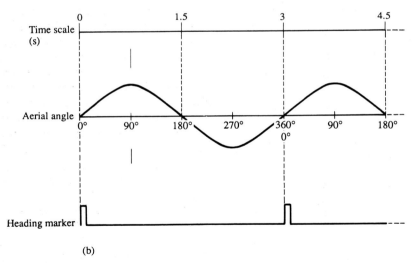

(b)

Figure 2.2   Typical time sequence of display input signals
(a)   High-frequency signals: PRF = 1250 pps, range scale 12 n mile
(b)   Low-frequency signals: Aerial rotation = 20 rpm

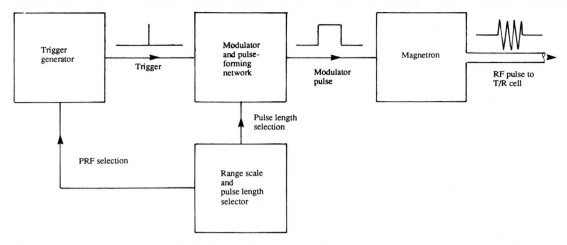

Figure 2.3 The transmitter – a block diagram

transmitter was to produce pulses of radar energy having the correct repetition frequency, length, shape, power and radio frequency. In this section a more detailed study of the transmitter shows how these important properties are determined and discusses their relevance to the operation of marine radar.

Figure 2.3 shows the three essential elements of the transmitter:

1 The trigger generator, which controls the repetition frequency of the transmitted pulses.
2 The modulator and associated pulse-forming network, which define the length, shape and power of the transmitted pulses.
3 The magnetron, which determines the radio frequency of the pulse which travels up the waveguide to the aerial.

When a pulse is transmitted, each element operates sequentially and it is thus appropriate to describe the characteristics of the pulses in the order set out above.

2.3.1 The pulse repetition frequency

The trigger generator is a free-running oscillator which generates a continuous succession of low voltage pulses known as *synchronizing pulses*, or *trigger* pulses. Com-

monly they are referred to simply as *triggers*. Each trigger causes the remainder of the transmission elements to generate a radio frequency pulse which is sent up the waveguide to the antenna. The trigger generator thus controls the number of radar pulses transmitted in one second. The latter quantity is referred to as the *pulse repetition frequency* (PRF) or sometimes the *pulse repetition rate* (PRR). Because the trigger generator controls the PRF, it is sometimes referred to as the PRF generator.

Most PRF generators make available two or three pulse repetition frequencies from which the observer may select the one most appropriate. In practice this may be achieved by designing the oscillator to 'free run' at the highest required frequency and using every second trigger to produce a medium PRF and every fourth trigger to produce a low PRF. Typical values might be 3400, 1700 and 850 pulses per second. In civil marine radars it is unusual to find PRFs outside the range 400 to 4000 pulses per second (pps). It is common practice to quote the PRF as a number, leaving the units of pulses per second to be understood.

In general there is a requirement for a low PRF when long range scales are selected and a high PRF in the case of short range scales. This is to some extent, but not completely, dependent on the duration of the transmitted pulse (the pulse length). Where more than one PRF is available it will be found that selection of the appropriate value is made automatically according to the range scale *and* pulse length selected by the observer. The relationship between selected range scale and PRF is discussed after the concept of pulse length has been introduced in the next section.

2.3.2 The pulse length, power and shape

The function of the modulator and its associated pulse-forming network is to produce a pulse of the correct length, power and shape on each occasion that it is activated by the trigger. Pulse length and power are of considerable importance in the effective detection of targets, as is pulse shape in the accurate measurement of their range.

2.3.2.1 The pulse length

Pulse length is defined as the duration of the transmitted radar pulse and is usually measured in microseconds (μs). In general, if a long pulse is used, the probability of detecting a target (other than one at extremely short range) will be higher than if a short pulse is used under the same circumstances. This important general theoretical principle is implicit in the fact that any given radar receiver can amplify long pulses more effectively than short pulses. This receiver characteristic is discussed in Section 2.5; however, the designer must take this principle into consideration when deciding which pulse lengths to make available to the observer, as must the observer in selecting a pulse length appropriate to the task in hand.

In stating the above general principle a proviso was made concerning the case of a target at extremely close range. This was necessary because in such circumstances the strength of the echo is likely to be so great that the effectiveness of amplification will be of minor importance. The critical factor in such a case is that where the radar uses the same waveguide and aerial for both transmission and reception (see Figure 2.1), it cannot perform both functions at the same time. The T/R cell (see Section 2.2.3) blocks the receiver for the duration of the transmitted pulse. It follows that the shorter the pulse length employed, the smaller the theoretical minimum

detection range will become, i.e. closer targets will be detectable (see Section 3.2.4).

In certain special circumstances, such as those where targets are difficult to detect against the background of sea or weather clutter, the use of a short pulse may improve the probability of detection of a wanted target. It is important to appreciate that this does not contradict the above principle but attempts to exploit it by reducing the response from both the clutter and the wanted target in the hope that the clutter can be removed from the screen while the target's echo is retained (see Section 3.6.3).

Two, three or even four pulse lengths may be available, according to the complexity of the system design. In civil marine radar it is unusual to find pulse lengths outside the range of 0.05 to 1.3 μs. It is likely that the pulse length produced by the system in any given circumstance will depend on both the pulse length requested by the observer and the range scale selected.

The philosophy of this semi-automatic selection is that if the radar is being used for general surveillance on the longer range scales, a long pulse is more appropriate because the receiver will have to handle weak signals returning from distant targets. On shorter range scales the returns are likely, in general, to be stronger and the observer is more likely to be concerned with the detail of the picture. The theoretical minimum radial length of any echo as it is eventually displayed on a conventional PPI is determined by the pulse length. Hence the shorter the pulse length the better the detail. The ability of the radar to display separately two targets which are on the same bearing and closely spaced in range is known as range discrimination and this is discussed fully in Section 2.6.5.5. Thus, in general usage, a short pulse is likely to be more appropriate on the shorter range scales. There are fewer occasions on which it may be helpful to use long pulses on the shorter range scales and short pulses on the longer range scales.

Where two pulse lengths are offered it is common for a long pulse to be automatically selected on range scales of 12 miles and upwards, and a short pulse on scales below that value. There is likely to be some facility for the observer to override the system selection and choose a long pulse on the shorter scales, though there may be a bar on selecting the long pulse on a very short range scale. In such systems it is less common to find an override facility allowing the short pulse to be used on the longer range scales.

Where more than two pulse lengths are offered, the selection becomes more complex and can take a variety of forms. An example is illustrated in Table 2.1. Notice that although there are three pulse lengths available, only two are available on any given range scale, with the

Table 2.1 PRF and pulse length — some representative values

| Range scale selected (n mile) | Pulse length selected | | | |
| | Short | | Long | |
	PRF (Hz)	PL (µs)	PRF (Hz)	PL (µs)
0.25	2000	0.05	2000	0.05
0.5	2000	0.05	1000	0.25
0.75	2000	0.05	1000	0.25
1.5	2000	0.05	1000	0.25
3.0	1000	0.25	500	1.0
6.0	1000	0.25	500	1.0
12	1000	0.25	500	1.0
24	500	1.0	500	1.0
48	500	1.0	500	1.0

exception of the shortest and two longest scales which will allow only the shortest and longest pulse lengths respectively.

The correct use of pulse length selection requires an understanding of a number of interacting factors which will be discussed at the appropriate points in this text. However at this stage it is useful to summarize the various factors as set out in Table 2.2.

2.3.2.2   The power of the transmitted pulse

It is almost self-evident that the range at which a target can be detected is dependent on the power of the transmitted pulse. While many other factors can affect the range at which detection may take place, in any given circumstances the *theoretical* maximum radar detection range is limited by the transmitter power. It can be shown (see Section 3.1) that the theoretical maximum detection range varies as the fourth root of the transmitter power.

The power of the radar pulse is a function of its amplitude (see Figure 2.4) which is determined by the pulse-forming network and its associated circuitry (see Section 2.3.2.4). For small craft radar systems a transmitter

Table 2.2 Short and long pulses — features compared

Feature	Short pulse	Long pulse
Long range target detection	Poor. Use when short range scales are selected	Good. Use when long range scales are selected and for poor response targets at short range
Minimum range	Good. Use when short range scales are selected	Poor. Use when long range scales are selected and minimum range is not a major consideration
Range discrimination	Good	Poor
Effect on echo paint	Short radial paint. Produces a well defined picture when short range scales are selected	Long radial paint when short range scales are selected but the effect is acceptable when long range scales are selected
Effect on sea clutter	Reduces the probability of the masking of targets due to saturation	Increases the probability of the masking of targets due to saturation
Effect in precipitation	Reduces the probability of the masking of targets due to saturation	Increases the probability of the' masking of targets due to saturation. However the use of long pulse helps to combat the attenuation caused by precipitation and will increase the probability of detecting targets which lie beyond rain.

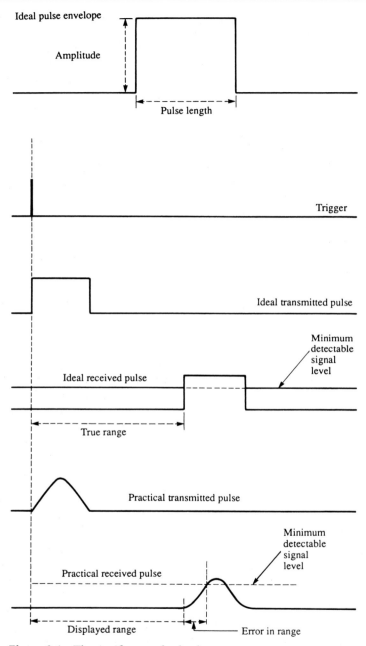

Figure 2.4   The significance of pulse shape

power of as low as 3 kW may be used, whereas for merchant ships powers in the range 10 to 60 kW may be encountered.

2.3.2.3   The pulse shape

The pulse shape is of particular significance in the accurate determination of range. Ideally the outline (or envelope) of the pulse should be rectangular and, particularly, the leading edge of the pulse should take the form of a vertical rise. The significance of this is illustrated by Figure 2.4 which shows the envelope of an ideal pulse and then compares the range measurement obtained using an ideal pulse shape with that obtained using a pulse shape which is less than ideal.

Because of the great disparity between the strength of the transmitted pulse and that of the returning signals, it is not practical to show their amplitudes to scale. Thus, when considering Figure 2.4, it must be appreciated that the transmitted pulse is of extremely high power whereas the received echo, even after amplification, is comparatively weak and will only be observed where its amplitude rises to the minimum level at which the receiver can detect signals. That level is called the 'minimum detectable signal' and is a receiver characteristic which is described in Section 3.2.3.

It follows that the *elapsed time* on which range measurement is based (see Section 1.2.2) commences at the instant of the trigger and ends when the received signal crosses the threshold of detection. Figure 2.4 shows that the range obtained will be in error by an amount which depends on the time taken by the received signal to reach minimum detection level. The time taken for the pulse amplitude to reach 90 per cent of its maximum value is known as the *rise time* of the pulse and ideally should be zero, as would be the case with a perfectly rectangular pulse. In practice, such an ideal cannot be realized, but the modulator and its associated pulse-forming network are designed in such a way as to produce a pulse having a rise time which is so short as to introduce a negligible ranging error. (Consideration must also be given to rise time in the design of the radar receiver, to ensure that it is capable of responding to the very fast rise times of the pulses produced by the transmitter and thus to avoid further degradation of

ranging accuracy. This topic is covered in Section 2.5.2.4.)

While not being such crucial characteristics as rise time, the forms of the upper limit of the envelope and of the trailing edge are also important. The former should be flat in order to produce an echo of uniform brightness, and the trailing edge should be steep in order to give a clean-cut termination of the displayed echo so as to minimize any overlap with a subsequent return (see also *range discrimination* in Section 2.6.5.5). Both of these properties are achieved by the careful design of the pulse-forming network and the characteristics of the receiver.

2.3.2.4   The modulator unit

Having considered the length and form which the envelope of the pulse must take, some attention will now be given to the way in which the envelope is generated. The pulse-forming network (PFN) may be considered to be a reservoir of electrical energy which is charged up comparatively slowly from the power supply in the period between pulses and is discharged very quickly in the duration of the pulse envelope. Consider an example in which typical values such as a PRF of 1000 and a pulse length of $1\,\mu s$ are used. The interval between pulses, which is referred to as the pulse repetition period (PRP), is $1000\,\mu s$ and hence the time during which the energy can be stored is $999\,\mu s$. As the energy is released in only $1\,\mu s$ (i.e. very nearly one thousandth of the time in which it was stored), it is apparent that a comparatively low power source can be used to produce a very high power radar pulse, albeit for a very short duration.

The modulator unit includes a very fast-operating switch which allows the discharge of the energy stored in the PFN. A solid state device known as a silicon controlled rectifier (SCR) is suited to this task. (In some literature it is referred to as controlled silicon rectifier (CSR).) The SCR, like a diode, will allow current to pass in one direction (the forward direction) but not in the other direction (the reverse direction). However, in the case of the SCR, forward current will only begin to flow when a trigger pulse is applied to a control electrode. When the trigger pulse is present the opposition to current offered by the device drops instantly to virtually

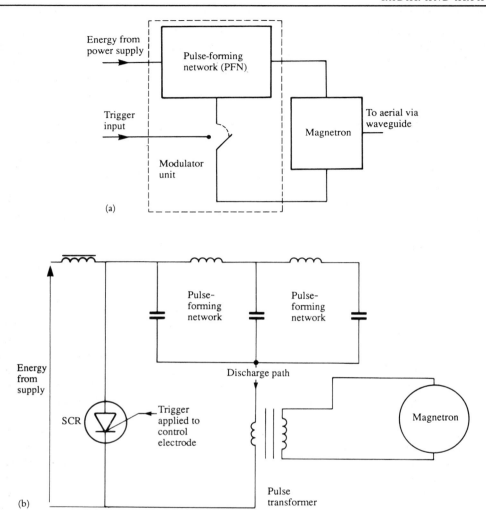

Figure 2.5 The modulator unit
(a)   block diagram
(b)   circuit diagram

zero, producing a pulse of current having an extremely fast rise time.

The storage property of the PFN is essentially that of electrical capacitance. When energy from a capacitor is discharged through a resistance, the rate of discharge is not constant but shows an exponential decay. This clearly would be unsatisfactory because to produce a

rectangular pulse the rate of energy discharge must be constant as long as energy remains in the storage network. Figure 2.5(b) shows that the PFN is a network made up of a number of sections of capacitive and inductive elements and it is the interaction of these elements which produces the constant rate of discharge required. No signal is needed to terminate the pulse, as that event will occur immediately all the energy has been discharged. The duration of the discharge is a function of the total amount of capacitance and inductance. Different pulse lengths (e.g. long, medium and short) are obtained by switching in the appropriate number of network sections. The network of elements giving the special property of constant discharge rate is commonly known as an 'artificial line' because its behaviour resembles that of an extremely long transmission cable. An explanation of the mechanics of the constant discharge would not be appropriate here; the reader who wishes to pursue the topic is referred to any good radar engineering text.

The pulse of current from the PFN is discharged through the primary winding of a step-up transformer whose secondary voltage is used to fire the magnetron which is the final unit in the transmitter.

2.3.3 The radio frequency of the transmitted pulse

A special type of radio valve called a 'magnetron' is used to produce a burst of radio frequency energy (which will radiate into space), the outline or *envelope* of which matches that generated by the modulator and its associated circuitry (see Figure 2.3). The radar transmission represents a special case of amplitude modulation in which the modulating waveform (the input to the magnetron) switches the carrier (the fixed-amplitude radio waves generated by the magnetron) on and off. Thus we have a signal capable of being radiated into space (because it is a radio frequency oscillation) but which has impressed on it, by virtue of its envelope, the pulse characteristics discussed at length in Section 2.3.2. Looking ahead to the consideration of receiver principles (see Section 2.5) it should be apparent that the receiver must be capable of demodulating the returned signals and hence extracting the envelope of the pulse.

2.3.3.1   Choice of frequency

By international agreement two groups of radio frequencies are allocated for use by civil marine radar systems. One group lies in the X-band and includes those frequencies which lie between 9300 and 9500 MHz.

These frequencies correspond with a wavelength of approximately 3 cm. The second group lies in the S-band, includes the frequencies lying between 2900 and 3100 MHz and corresponds with a wavelength of approximately 10 cm. Because a radar frequency is always a very large number, it is often found more convenient to speak in terms of wavelength.

While the precise frequency allocations made for civil marine radar were a matter of human agreement, the general area of the allocation was pre-ordained by the laws of physics which demand that the wavelength used be of the order of a few centimetres. A fundamental requirement of marine radar is that of directional transmission and reception, which is achieved by producing a narrow horizontal beam. It will be shown in Section 2.4.2 that, to focus the energy into a narrow beam, either a short wavelength or a large aerial must be used. When it is considered that there is a practical limit to the size of aerial which can be fitted and rotated on board a merchant ship, it is apparent that the general order of the wavelength is similarly limited. Wavelengths lower than about 3 cm are unsuitable because they experience unacceptable attenuation in the gases of the atmosphere and exacerbate the problems of sea and weather clutter (see Table 2.3 and Sections 3.6 and 3.7).

Historically, much civil marine X-band radar development work was done by manufacturers in Great Britain and Europe while in the USA S-band marine radars were more common. There are some circumstances in which X-band performance will be superior to S-band and others in which the reverse will be the case. In the 1950s and 1960s it was uncommon for ships to be fitted with more than one radar and thus the choice of wavelength had to be made at the procurement stage. Now that the fitting of two radars is quite commonplace, the need to make such a choice is avoided if S-band and X-band systems are fitted. In such a case the observer has the freedom to select the system whose wavelength is best suited to the prevailing circumstances (see also *Interswitching* in Section 2.7.8).

As suggested above, there are many ways in which the characteristics of X-band and S-band transmissions are complementary and a knowledge of these leads to more effective use of the equipment. The various cir-

Table 2.3   X-band and S-band compared

Feature	Comparison
Target response	For a target of a given size, the response at X-band is greater than at S-band
Bearing discrimination	For a given aerial width the horizontal beamwidth effect in an S-band system will be approximately 3.3 times that of an X-band system
Vertical beam structure	The vertical lobe pattern produced by an S-band aerial is about 3.3 times as coarse as that from an X-band aerial located at the same height.
Radar horizon	The radar horizon with S-band is slightly more distant than with X-band
Sea clutter response	The unwanted response from sea waves is less at S-band than at X-band, thus the probability of targets being masked due to saturation is less
Precipitation response	The probability of detection of targets which lie *within* an area of precipitation is higher with S-band transmission than with X-band transmission
Attenuation in precipitation	In any given set of precipitation conditions, S-band transmissions will suffer less attenuation than those at X-band

cumstances in which these complementary characteristics can be exploited will be discussed in detail at the appropriate points in this volume; for the moment, it is sufficient to compare their respective characteristics, as set out in Table 2.3.

2.3.3.2   The magnetron – outline of operation

The magnetron (or cavity magnetron as it is more correctly named) was invented in Great Britain in 1939 and to this day is considered by civil marine radar manufacturers to be the first choice as a generator of very short pulses of radar energy. (A modern alternative, the dupletron, is available but only for power output levels up to about 3 kW.) When first produced, the magnetron joined the large family of thermionic valves which populated the early radars; now, fifty years on, it is one of the two valves to survive the solid state revolution (the other is the cathode ray tube).

The magnetron is essentially a diode valve in which the anode is a copper cylinder into which are cut cavities (in the form of holes and slots) of very precise dimensions. The cathode is a pillar located along the central axis of the cylinder. A horseshoe magnet applies an extremely powerful magnetic field which acts along the axis of the cylinder. In the absence of the magnetic field one might expect electrons to flow, in an orderly fashion, radially from the cathode to the anode when a pulse is applied to the cathode. Because the magnetic field created by the permanent magnet is at right angles to the electric field created by the pulse, the electrons are

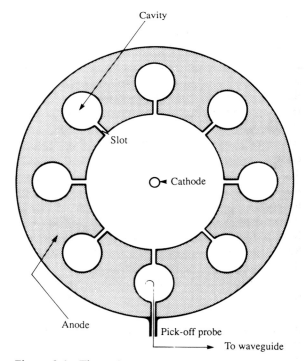

Figure 2.6   The cavity magnetron

deflected from the path which would take them directly to the anode (an application of the motor principle). Many electrons will eventually reach the anode only after a complex oscillatory journey in which their paths may alternately be directed toward and away from the anode and their speed increased and decreased. The movement of each electron will be further affected by the electromagnetic influence of the millions of other electrons moving in its vicinity. The effect is extremely complex but it can be summarized by saying that if the change of electron velocity is regular and repetitive then there will be associated with such change a sympathetic fluctuating electromagnetic field. If this is of sufficiently high frequency, it will be capable of radiation into space. There are certain limits of steady electric field (provided by the modulator pulse) and steady magnetic field (provided by the permanent magnet) outside which oscillation will not take place. However, if values are selected which lie within the appropriate limits, the frequency of the oscillations that develop is determined by the physical dimensions of the cavities.

Of the energy supplied to the magnetron, less than half contributes to the maintenance of the oscillations during transmission. Much of the remainder is dissipated as heat in sufficient quantity to require the fitting of cooling fins to the magnetron assembly. It follows that the temperature of the magnetron will increase quite rapidly during the warm-up period (usually considered to be about half an hour) which follows the initial switching on, with a consequent change in the size of the cavities because of expansion of the copper cylinder. The transmitted radio frequency is subject to progressive change during this period. This has important implications when consideration is given to maintaining the receiver in tune (see Sections 2.5.1.3 and 6.2.4.2). Systems which comply with the IMO Performance Standards will have a 'stand-by' condition (see Section 6.7) in which the magnetron is kept warm by means of a conventional valve heater while not being used for transmission. When the system is returned to the transmitting condition, the supplementary heating is reduced or removed as the natural heating returns. During this transition period a similar drift in frequency can be expected.

The output from the magnetron is picked up from one of the cavities by a small probe which couples the radar pulse to the waveguide by means of which it is conducted to the aerial.

2.3.4 Selection of PRF and pulse length and their relationship with range scale

In preceding sections of this chapter it has been suggested that there is a relationship between PRF, pulse length and range scale. A study of Table 2.1, which shows some representative values, will indicate that such an association does exist. Now that both PRF and pulse length have been described, it is appropriate to discuss why the three quantities should be interdependent.

For any given range scale the period between pulses (PRP) must be at least as long as the timebase for that range scale so that the spot has time to write the current radial line and return to the origin of the display before the next line is initiated (or, in the case of digital storage, to allow sufficient time for the range data to be read into the memory in real time). If the pulse repetition period was made equal to the timebase, ambiguity would arise because echoes from a range in excess of the chosen range scale might well arrive during the next timebase (see Section 2.2.4). A time delay, known as the receiver rest time, must thus be inserted between the completion of one timebase and the commencement of the next in an attempt to reduce to a minimum the probability of this happening. The combined length of the timebase and the receiver rest period must be sufficiently long to ensure that, other than in exceptional circumstances (see Section 3.9.6), all echoes that will be returned from any given pulse arrive before the next pulse is transmitted. This defines a minimum pulse repetition period and thus a maximum PRF for any given range scale.

However, to define the minimum acceptable pulse repetition period, an estimate must be made of the maximum range from which it is reasonable to expect echo returns. This range is dependent on, among other factors, the transmitted pulse length (see Sections 2.3.2.1, 2.5.2.4 and 3.2.1), which is one of the variables with which we are presently concerned. Clearly, in estimating the necessary rest period, consideration must be given to the pulse length which is to be employed on the chosen range scale. Longer pulse lengths will increase the maximum range from which returns can be reasonably expected (see Sections 2.5.2.4, 3.2.1 and 3.2.3) and thus necessitate a longer receiver rest period, a longer pulse repetition period and hence a lower PRF. This represents a major reason why each available pulse length is associated with a particular PRF (see Table 2.1).

The pattern which emerges from Table 2.1 is that the long pulses are used on the longer range scales and are associated with the low PRF, while the short pulses are used on the short range scales and are associated with the high PRF.

While the selection of short pulse will reduce the probability of detection of any one return (see Section 2.5.2.4), it should be noted that this will tend to be offset to a limited extent by the fact that the use of a higher PRF will result in more pulses being fired at any given target.

2.4   Aerial principles

The aerial unit is required to focus the transmitted energy into a beam, rotate the beam at an appropriate angular speed, relay rotation and heading marker data to the display and intercept returning signals within the same directional limits as those specified for the transmitted beam. Each of these functions will now be discussed in detail.

2.4.1   Aerial concepts

It has already been established in general terms that the beam should be narrow in the horizontal plane and wide in the vertical plane (see Section 2.2.2). Before these requirements are studied in detail it is helpful to consider some basic aerial concepts.

2.4.1.1   The point radiating source

This is an ideal concept which cannot be realized in practice but offers a useful basis on which to explain radiation from an aerial. The point source is a source of radiation

which is assumed to have no dimensions. Clearly any source must have some dimensions but the farther the target lies from the source of radiation the less significant the dimensions become and the more closely any observed effects will approach those which could be expected from a point source.

2.4.1.2   The isotropic source

This is an extension of the concept of the point source and assumes a point source which radiates uniformly in all directions. Again, this cannot be realized in practice because any practical aerial will radiate better in some directions than in others. In fact the essential characteristic of a radar aerial is that it does precisely that, radiating particularly well in one chosen direction. However, a convenient measure of its directional ability can be obtained by comparing the radiation from the practical aerial with that which would be obtained from an isotropic source.

2.4.1.3   Power density

As the power delivered from the transmitter to the aerial moves outward in space it becomes distributed over a continuously increasing area and thus the power available to be reflected by any intervening target decreases progressively. Power density is a measure (W/m^2) of the power per unit area available at any location in the area of influence of an aerial.

To illustrate the concept, consider a *lossless* isotropic radiator to be situated in space. If a pulse is transmitted, the power will travel outward, being uniformly distributed over the inside surface of a sphere of ever increasing radius. If the power delivered by the transmitter to the aerial is W watts then the power density at a distance r metres from the aerial will be given by the power W divided by the surface area of a spere of radius r. This can be written as

$$\text{power density} = P_r = \frac{W}{4\pi r^2}$$

This relationship forms part of the radar range equation set out in Chapter 3 which shows the theoretical relationship that exists between transmitter power and target detection range.

It can be seen from the above that in the case of an isotropic source the power density is the same in all directions, whereas for a practical aerial it will be greater in some directions than in others. The shape of a directional beam can be illustrated by plotting the power density values for different directions from the aerial and this gives rise to what is known as a *power pattern*. However, a power pattern is only valid for one particular range.

2.4.1.4   Radiation intensity

For many purposes this is a more convenient measure of the radiation from an aerial because it is independent of the range at which it is measured. Radiation intensity is defined as the power per unit solid angle, i.e. the power incident on that portion of the surface of a sphere which subtends an angle of one radian at the centre of the sphere in both the horizontal and the vertical planes. To illustrate the concept, consider again the case of an isotropic radiator located in space. If the power delivered to the aerial is W watts then as it travels outwards it will be uniformly distributed over the surface area of a sphere of ever expanding radius but which subtends a constant angle of 4π radians at the centre of the sphere. Thus the radiation intensity at any point in the field of an isotropic radiator is given by

$$\text{radiation intensity} = U = \frac{W}{4\pi}$$

In the same way as described for power density, radiation intensity can be plotted for different directions from the aerial and this gives rise to what is known as a *radiation pattern*. It is clearly a three-dimensional figure but in dealing with radar beams it will be unnecessary to attempt to show all three dimensions simultaneously; it is more convenient to use a two-dimensional figure to illustrate either the horizontal beam pattern or the vertical beam pattern as is appropriate to the topic under discussion. Figure 2.7 illustrates the concept, showing the horizontal radiation pattern for an isotropic source and, for comparison purposes, that of a directional aerial.

The radiation in any given direction is represented by the length of a line drawn from the origin, in the chosen

direction, which terminates at its intersection with the pattern. The line can be measured in watts per unit solid angle, but as we are principally concerned with representation of shape it is more convenient to use what is known as a 'normalized pattern', in which units are unnecessary. In the normalized pattern the maximum

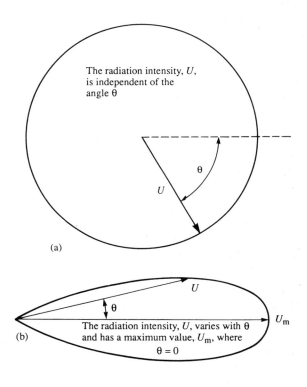

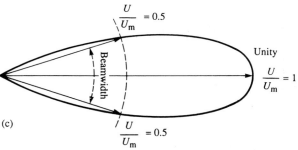

Figure 2.7 Examples of radiation patterns
(a)   A radiation pattern for an isotropic source
(b)   An absolute pattern for a directional source
(c)   A normalized pattern for a directional source

value is considered to be unity and the other values represent the ratio of the radiation intensity in the chosen direction to that of the maximum radiation intensity. It is of interest that if a power pattern is normalized it will give the same shape as the normalized radiation pattern. This might well have been stated at the outset, but it is important to appreciate that while the patterns have the same shape if normalized, the absolute patterns are not measured in the same units. When normalized, the shape produced by both patterns is commonly referred to as an *antenna (or aerial) radiation pattern*.

2.4.1.5   Beamwidth

In considering the shape of the beam we are particularly concerned with its angular width. The beamwidth is defined as the angular limits within which the power does not fall to less than half its maximum value at the same range. This is readily extracted from the normalized radiation pattern as illustrated by Figure 2.7(c).

2.4.1.6   Aerial gain

This is a measure of the effectiveness with which the aerial can radiate the power delivered to it by the transmitter, within specified angular limits of azimuth and elevation. Aerial gain is given the symbol G_0 and is defined as

$$G_0 = \frac{\text{maximum radiation intensity from the chosen aerial}}{\text{maximum radiation intensity from a reference aerial}}$$

The reference aerial is assumed to be a *lossless* isotropic radiator supplied with the same power level.

Clearly the aerial gain is a ratio having no units. Its maximum possible value would occur in the ideal situation in which none of the energy supplied by the transmitter was wasted and all of it was concentrated within the infinitely narrow limits of a straight line. In practice this ideal cannot be achieved because some of the transmitter power will be dissipated in overcoming electrical resistance in the aerial and the energy cannot be concentrated along a single line. However, good design techniques make it possible to reduce the electrical losses in

the aerial to very small values, and the special aerials used in marine radar can, where required, concentrate the power within very narrow limits of azimuth.

An alternative indicator of the measure of concentration achieved by the aerial is called *directive gain* or *directivity*. This is given the symbol D and is defined as

$$D = \frac{\text{maximum radiation intensity}}{\text{average radiation intensity}}$$

This quantity is independent of the aerial losses and is thus a perfect merit figure for describing the ability of the aerial to concentrate the power in a narrow beam.

Both aerial gain and directive gain are of interest to the radar designer, but their numerical values are so close to one another as to render the difference somewhat academic as far as the civil marine radar observer is concerned. However, it would be wrong in principle to use directive gain rather than aerial gain in stating the radar range equation (see Section 3.1) and hence both terms are defined here in the interests of rigour.

2.4.1.7.   Receiving characteristic

In the above introduction the antenna has been treated essentially as a transmitting element. It must be remembered that in marine radar the same aerial is used for transmission and reception. By the principle of reciprocity, whatever is said in relation to the directional nature of transmission will apply equally well to reception.

2.4.1.8   Polarization

The energy travelling outward from the aerial is in the form of an electromagnetic wave having electric and magnetic fields which are at right angles to one another and to the direction of propagation. The polarization is defined as the direction of the plane of the electric field. To comply with the IMO Performance Standards (see Section 10.2), all marine radars using the X-band must be capable of being operated with horizontal polarization. Historically, circular polarization (see Section 3.7.4.6) was offered for a time by one civil marine radar manufacturer but at the present time it is unusual to find any aerial which is not solely designed for horizontal polarization.

2.4.2   The horizontal beamwidth

To achieve the directional transmission necessary for the accurate measurement of bearings (see Section 1.3) the horizontal beamwidth must be narrow. This also has the effect of producing very high aerial gain by concentrating all the available power in one direction at a time. Further, such directional transmission is necessary in order to give the system the ability to display separately targets which are at the same range and closely spaced in bearing. This property is known as *bearing discrimination* and will be discussed under 'Display principles' in Section 2.6.5.6.

The wavelengths of the electromagnetic energy contained in radar pulses are much longer than those of visible light but in many ways the radiation exhibits characteristics which are reminiscent of the laws of optics. Until the late 1950s, designers exploited this resemblance by using a parabolic reflector to focus the radar beam, much in the same way as a polished mirror is used in a motorcar headlight or in an Aldis lamp to focus a beam of light. Although in civil marine radar this technique has now been superseded by direct emission from slots cut in one face of a length of waveguide (described as *slotted waveguide*), it is still used in many other surveillance applications. It is worthy of some study as it demonstrates in a relatively simple way how the radiation can be focussed into a narrow beam. Further, it provides a platform on which to base some understanding of the modern slotted waveguide aerial which produces a horizontal beam that has an almost identical pattern but which uses a direct emission technique, the mechanics of which are somewhat more difficult to visualize (see Section 2.4.2.2).

2.4.2.1   The parabolic reflector

The significant optical property of the parabolic reflector is that if a point source of light is placed at a particular point, known as the focus, which lies on the axis of symmetry, all the rays of light striking the mirror will be reflected parallel to the axis. Such an ideal situation would produce a perfectly parallel pencil beam of light (Figure 2.8(a)). If radar microwave energy is used instead of light, the results are remarkably similar. How-

ever, because in practice the energy cannot be emitted from a single point, it follows that most of the energy originates from points which are very close to, but not at, the focus. In physical form the source looked like a reversed nozzle (see Figure 2.10) and was produced by flaring out the end of the waveguide so that, while the

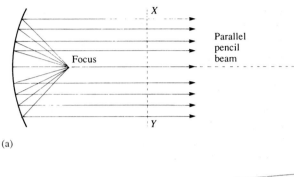

(a)

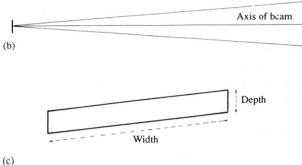

(b)

(c)

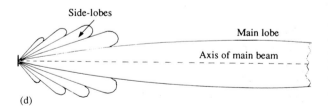

(d)

Figure 2.8   Focusing the horizontal beam with a parabolic reflector
(a)   Parabolic reflector
(b)   Fan-shaped beam
(c)   Aperture
(d)   Radiation pattern produced by a practical aerial

horizontal dimension was increased slightly, the vertical dimension was increased considerably. The flaring was necessary for reasons of impedance matching which are beyond the scope of this text. The device was known variously as a flare, a hog horn or simply a horn. The latter term is quite descriptive because, in its effect on microwaves, the behaviour of the device is somewhat analogous to that of an acoustic horn. The result of using a source whose dimensions are not negligible is the production of a horizontal beam which tends to diverge slightly in a fan shape and is illustrated in simple form by Figure 2.8(b).

A further departure from the ideal arises because the wavelengths used in marine radar are not negligible when compared with the size of the reflector, as would be the case with visible light.

The practical radar beam has a more complex form than the simple fan illustrated in Figure 2.8(b). An understanding of why this should be so is assisted by further consideration of Figure 2.8(a). A second geometrical property of the parabola is that if any line such as XY is drawn perpendicular to the axis of symmetry of the parabola, then the distance along any reflective path from the focus to that line will be the same irrespective of the reflective path which is followed. The implication

of this is that if all rays of energy were in phase when they left the source (which will be the case) they will be in phase as they cross this line.

The line XY has been drawn some little distance away from the parabola for the sake of clarity. If it were to be moved so that it just touched the ends of the parabola then it would bridge the 'mouth' of the reflector. Thus all the rays will leave the 'mouth' in phase with one another. The aerial thus behaves as if the radiation were emerging from a rectangular surface whose width is equal to that of the length of the line XY and whose depth is the vertical extent of the paraboloid (see Figure 2.8(c)). This area is known as the 'aperture' and its dimensions in relation to the wavelength determine the geometry of the beam. The horizontal beamwidth is determined by the width of the aperture and the vertical beamwidth by its depth. Source and reflector thus behave like a rectangular aperture from which emerges a plane wave with uniform phase-distribution across the aperture.

It can be shown that uniform phase-distribution across a plane aperture will produce a radiation pattern of the form shown in Figure 2.8(d). It will be noticed that most of the radiation is concentrated in a central main beam or lobe, but that some radiation manifests

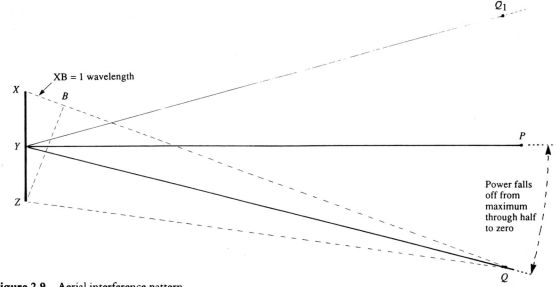

Figure 2.9 Aerial interference pattern

itself as a series of subsidiary beams, known as side lobes, the maximum radiation intensity of each of which is considerably less than that of the main lobe. The radiation intensity of individual side lobes decreases as their angle from the axis of the main beam increases.

The distribution of the radiation in the lobe pattern which is produced by uniform phase-distribution across a plane aperture can only be fully justified by a mathematical analysis which is beyond the scope of this text. However, by some more simple considerations it can be illustrated that such a pattern is not entirely unexpected.

If one considers a point P (Figure 2.9) which lies on the normal to the aperture, it is reasonable to accept that the distance from P to any point on the aperture is the same provided that P is a distant point. For the purposes of this simple explanation very short ranges will not be considered and hence the distance PY will be of the order of cables if not miles. The aperture width is likely to be 2–3 metres at the most, and hence the line XYZ can be considered to be a portion of the circumference of a very large circle. It can be concluded that all radiation arriving at P will be of uniform phase and will produce constructive interference, i.e. all the individual signal strengths added together will produce a strong resultant.

By contrast, consider a point Q which lies at an angle to the normal such that the distance XQ exceeds the distance ZQ by one complete wavelength. (At a frequency of 9400 MHz the difference need only be 3.19 cm). The distance XQ will thus exceed the distance YQ by half a wavelength and hence radiation emitted from X will arrive at Q antiphase to that emitted from Y. Each radiating element of the aperture between X and Y can be associated with a corresponding element between Y and Z which, together with it, will produce antiphase signals at point Q. It follows that at point Q, and anywhere along the line YQ produced, destructive interference will result in the nett radiation being zero. Hence the radiation intensity falls from maximum on the normal to the aperture (the axis of the main beam), to zero at some angle defined by point Q. Since the figure is symmetrical, a similar reduction in radiation will take place on the other side of the axis to the limit indicated by Q_1. It is self-evident that somewhere between these two angular limits must lie the half power points which by convention define the limits of the horizontal beamwidth. A similar consideration for angles greater than PYQ will reveal the presence of the side lobes.

It can be shown that the horizontal beamwidth is given by the expression

$$\text{HBW (in degrees)} = K \times \frac{\text{transmitted wavelength}}{\text{aperture width}}$$

where K is a constant which has a theoretical value of 51. Authorities differ on the value of this constant that can be achieved in practice. Clearly there are limits to the precision with which any aerial unit, be it parabola or waveguide, can be constructed. However, it is sufficient to say that for practical purposes a value for K of 70 adequately describes the horizontal beam produced by modern civil marine radars using a slotted waveguide aerial.

The important principle is that the horizontal beamwidth is directly proportional to transmitted wavelength and inversely proportional to the effective width of the aerial aperture, i.e. the horizontal beamwidth is a function of the ratio of wavelength to aerial width. The order of the quantities involved is best illustrated by two numerical examples in which a value of $K = 70$ will be assumed.

Example 2.1 Calculate the aerial width necessary to achieve a horizontal beam width of 2° with X-band transmission at 9400 MHz.

$$300 \times 10^6 = \text{frequency} \times \text{wavelength}$$

$$\text{thus wavelength} = \frac{300 \times 10^6}{9400 \times 10^6}$$

i.e. wavelength $= 0.032$ m (3.2 cm)

$$\text{HBW} = K \times \frac{\text{transmitted wavelength}}{\text{aperture width}}$$

$$\text{thus } 2 = \frac{70 \times 0.032}{\text{aperture width}}$$

$$\text{hence aperture width} = \frac{70 \times 0.032}{2}$$

i.e. aperture width $= 1.12$ m

Therefore to produce a horizontal beamwidth of 2° with X-band transmission at 9400 MHz, an aerial width of not less than 1.12 m is necessary.

Example 2.2 A marine radar aerial operating in the S-band with a wavelength of 9.87 cm has a width of 3.8 m. Calculate the horizontal beamwidth.

$$\text{HBW} = \frac{K \times \text{transmitted wavelength}}{\text{aperture width}}$$

thus

$$\text{HBW} = 70 \times \frac{9.87 \times 10^{-2}}{3.8}$$

i.e. $\text{HBW} = 1.82°$

Therefore a marine radar aerial of width 3.8 m, transmitting a wavelength of 9.87 cm, will produce a horizontal beamwidth of 1.82 degrees.

It is clear from the examples why the internationally agreed frequencies (see Section 2.3.3.1) allocated to civil marine radar were bound to be of an order which would give a wavelength of not more than about 10 cm. Longer wavelengths would require an aerial size so large as to preclude practical installation on a merchant ship.

It is evident that for the same horizontal beamwidth an S-band aerial must be three times the width of a corresponding X-band aerial. In general, available S-band aerials are not as large as this and hence X-band systems normally have narrower beamwidths. To comply with the IMO Performance Standards (see Section 10.2), a horizontal beamwidth of not more than 2.5° is required. Radars designed for use on large merchant ships normally offer horizontal beamwidths somewhere in the range 0.65° to 2° for X-band operation and 1.7° to 2° in the case of S-band.

Figure 2.10 shows two examples of parabolic reflectors. These are included partly for historical interest and partly because they illustrate much of what has been said in this section.

The single cheese aerial is representative of the early days of marine radar and its 'mouth' clearly illustrates the concept of 'aperture'. Two major problems associated with the cheese aerial were the accumulation of dirt within the cheese and the shadowing along the axis of the main beam caused by the hog horn. These shortcomings were removed by the development of the tilted parabolic cylinder. In this design the reflecting surface was tilted so that the horn could be located below the parabola and therefore out of the path of the reflected energy. The parabolic surface was made circular in a vertical sense in order to produce a wide vertical beam (see Section 2.4.3). It must be appreciated that the aperture in this case is the area of the parabola projected on to a plane surface perpendicular to the axis of the radiated beam and not the total surface area of the reflector.

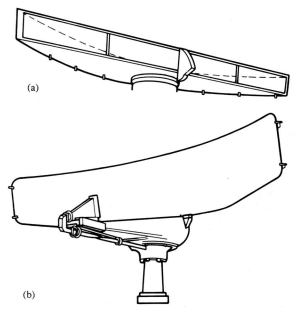

Figure 2.10 Early parabolic reflectors
(a)   The single cheese aerial
(b)   The tilted parabolic cylinder

2.4.2.2   *The slotted waveguide aerial*

It can be shown that if a narrow slot is cut in an infinite sheet of conducting material, and an alternating signal is applied across the slot at its midlength, it will act as an effective radiator of electromagnetic waves provided that the frequency of the applied signal corresponds with a wavelength which is approximately twice the length of the slot, i.e. if the slot length is approximately half a wavelength. It may be difficult to visualize how such an effect can take place and there is no simple explanation. Those readers who wish to study the effect in more detail are referred to a text dealing with antenna theory. For a practical understanding it will be found sufficient to consider that the slot behaves like a short radio aerial with the exception of the fact that the polarization of the emitted wave is perpendicular to the long side of the slot, i.e. a vertical slot will radiate a horizontally polarized wave.

In the slotted waveguide aerial, the principle of the slot radiator is exploited by cutting a number of slots in one side of a length of waveguide. The slots interrupt the pattern of alternating current flow along the wall of the guide and hence a signal is effectively applied across the centre of each slot. The intact remainder of the waveguide approximates to the infinite conducting sheet. Although the principle assumes an infinite sheet, quite effective results are obtained with comparatively small areas. As the slots measure approximately half a wavelength along their major axis, the conditions for radiation are fulfilled.

The slots are spaced along the length of the guide in such a way as to ensure that all slots are excited in equiphase. The slotted waveguide aerial thus constitutes a large number of radiators having a uniform phase distribution across a plane aperture. This will produce a radiation pattern having the same shape as that illustrated in Figure 2.8(d). Further, the horizontal beamwidth of the pattern can be described by the same relationship between transmitted wavelength and aperture width as was set out in Section 2.4.2.1. However, if the waveguide is fed from one end, as is normally the case in civil marine radars, the pattern will be rotated by a small amount away from the feed end of the guide so that the axis of the main lobe will make a horizontal angle of approximately 3° to 4° with the normal to the aperture. This angle is frequency-dependent and is known as the *angle of squint*. It should present no problem provided that the correct steps are taken to check regularly that the display heading marker occurs at the instant that the axis of the main lobe crosses the fore-and-

aft line in the forward direction (see Section 6.9.9). However, it is important to appreciate that the axis of the main beam will therefore not be fore-and-aft when the long axis of the aerial is athwartships.

Figure 2.11(a) shows a detail of the aerial waveguide with a typical pattern of slots. For a horizontally polarized wave one might expect all the slots to be vertical. In practice, the first few slots at the feed end and the last few at the remote end are indeed vertical but between these limits they are inclined to the vertical by a small angle which varies across the face of the guide. Alternate slots are inclined in opposite directions. The need for this refinement of the slot pattern arises from electrical impedance considerations which are beyond the scope of this book. However, it should be noted that despite the angling of the slots, the emitted radiation is horizon-

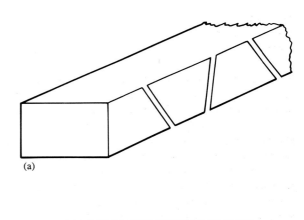

(a)

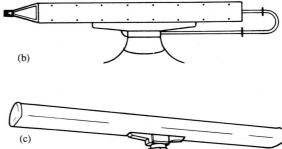

(b)

(c)

Figure 2.11   The slotted waveguide aerial
(a)   Detail of waveguide slots
(b)   Slotted waveguide aerial
(c)   Enclosed slotted waveguide aerial

tally polarized because the horizontally polarized components of radiation from all slots reinforce one another (they are all substantially vertical) while the vertically polarized components of radiation from alternate slots cancel (this is because they are angled in opposite directions).

Figure 2.11(b) shows a full slotted waveguide aerial assembly of a type which has the advantage that all of the parts can be clearly seen. The width of the aperture is determined by the length of the slotted unit. In the vertical plane the aperture is bounded by conducting sheets forming a horn which guides the waves from the narrow vertical dimension of the slotted unit to an aperture of a depth consistent with the correct vertical beamwidth (see Section 2.4.3). A sheet of glass reinforced plastic (GRP – which is often referred to by the proprietary name of Fibreglass) protects the aperture from the ingress of water and dirt. GRP is transparent to radar waves (see Section 3.3.3). (The GRP construction of the aerial window may include graphite to improve its transparency in addition to a polarizing filter to prevent the entry of stray unwanted vertically polarized waves.) Most paints are not transparent to radar energy and the cover commonly carries the legend 'do not paint'. As illustrated in Figure 2.11(c), a modern practice is to enclose the entire assembly in a GRP envelope.

The slotted waveguide aerial superseded the parabolic reflector for a variety of reasons, important among which was its ability to produce direct emission and to offer higher aerial gain by reducing the power radiated in the side-lobes. Such radiation not only represents a loss of power but can give rise to spurious echoes (see Section 3.9.4).

2.4.3   The vertical beamwidth

It was established in Section 2.2.2 that the minimum vertical beamwidth for compliance with the IMO Performance Standards was 20° because of the need to maintain the required performance when rolling and pitching. A further factor in favour of a wide vertical beam is that it reduces the possibility that a target at close range will escape detection by passing under the lower limit of the beam (see Section 3.2.4). The production of a wide beam presents no problems, but if it is allowed to

become too wide the radiation intensity will become unacceptably low. Commercially available aerials normally offer values which lie in the approximate range 20° to 25°, i.e. just a little more than is required to comply with the performance standard, although a value as high as 30° may be encountered.

The aperture is much smaller in the vertical plane than in the horizontal and thus one would expect the vertical radiation pattern to be characterized by a wide main lobe flanked by side-lobes. If the aerial were placed in space this expectation would be fulfilled and, neglecting the side-lobes, the radiation pattern would be of the form shown by Figure 2.12(a). However, as the aerial is placed a relatively short distance above the surface of the sea, the pattern is modified because much of the energy which would form the lower half of the lobe in free space (see Figure 2.12(b)) is reflected from the sea and forms an interference pattern with that energy which has not been reflected.

Figure 2.12(c), which is not to scale, illustrates how the interference pattern is created. Consider two rays of energy which arrive at point P, one having travelled directly and the other having been reflected from the surface of the sea at B. Let us suppose that the reflected path length is one half wavelength longer than the direct path length. It can be assumed that a 180° phase shift takes place on reflection at the sea surface and hence the signals arriving at point P will be in phase. (180° phase shift due to path difference and 180° phase shift due to reflection.) Thus, assuming that there is no loss of energy on reflection, the signal strength at point P will, due to the addition of the reflected signal, be twice what it would have been if the aerial were located in free space. If the reflected path is produced further it must in due course intersect with a further direct ray at a point at which the path difference is a full wavelength. At that point there will be 180° phase difference (360° due to path difference and 180° due to phase shift on reflection) between the direct and reflected signals and the resultant signal strength will be zero. Clearly this pattern of maxima and minima must repeat itself with height.

Understanding of the form of the pattern can be assisted by noting that the signal conditions at point P, while arising in the way described above, are exactly the same as would be the case if the aerial were located in free

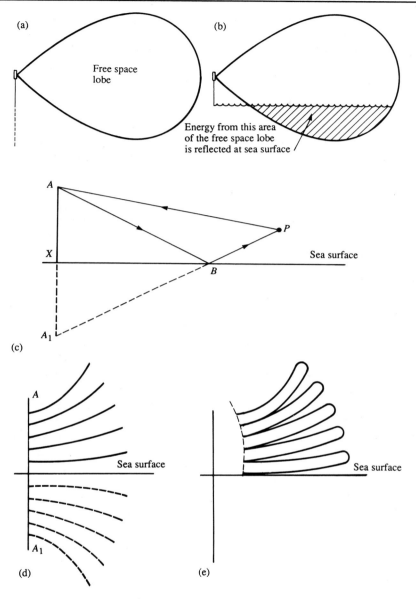

Figure 2.12 The vertical radiation pattern
(a)   Main vertical lobe in free space
(b)   Main vertical lobe close to sea surface
(c)   The interference pattern
(d)   Hyperbolic pattern

(e)   Vertical lobe pattern – only a few lobes are shown. In practice, the number of lobes per metre of scanner height is approximately:
      At X-band 33
      At S-band 10

Note   The horizontal extent represented in (e) is 2 × that represented in (b)

space and a second aerial, transmitting in antiphase, were located at A_1 such that $AX = A_1X$. This arrangement (with the exception of the 180° phase shift and the restricted vertical beamwidth) is analogous to the layout of the transmitting stations in hyperbolic position-fixing systems such as Decca and Loran, where A and A_1 correspond to the transmitting stations and the distance $A - A_1$ to the baseline. All points having the same path difference will lie along a hyperbola and the pattern of maxima and minima in the vertical plane will take the form of a family of such hyperbolae. This is illustrated by Figure 2.12(d), but it must be appreciated that the analogy should not be pursued very close to the baseline because of the restricted vertical beamwidth.

As a result of the existence of alternate maxima and minima the single main lobe in free space is broken up into a family of lobes of the form shown in Figure 2.12(e). The diagram shows only a few lobes in order to illustrate the pattern of maxima and zeros. In practice, for X-band transmission, there will be approximately 33 lobes per metre of scanner height. Thus the lobes are much more numerous and more closely spaced than could possibly be illustrated in a diagram of reasonable size. For S-band signals the figure is approximately 10 lobes per metre of scanner height. Thus the S-band vertical pattern has fewer, more widely spaced lobes. The radiation intensity along the axis of a lobe is twice what it would be in free space and an area of zero radiation lies between each pair of lobes. It can be shown that the elevation of the lowest maxima in degrees is approximately 14 times the ratio of wavelength to aerial height. For X-band transmission with an aerial height of 20 metres the lowest maxima will be approximately 8.5 metres above the sea at a range of 12 miles. This gives some idea of the coarseness of the pattern when considered in relationship to many practical targets.

2.4.4   Aerial rotation rate

To comply with the IMO Performance Standards (see Section 10.2) the scan (i.e. the rotation of the beam) must be clockwise (as seen from above), continuous, and automatic through 360° of azimuth at a rate of not less that 12 rpm. The equipment is required to operate satisfactorily in relative wind speeds of up to 100 knots.

This is achieved by rotating the directional aerial by means of an electric motor driving through a reduction gear train. The speed of rotation of the aerial is a significant factor in the overall performance of a marine radar system.

It will be noted that there is a lower limit to the permitted aerial rotation rate, but no maximum is specified. One can speculate that those who drew up the standards concluded that the cost of manufacturing and maintaining very high speed aerial rotation would create a natural upper limit.

If an aerial rotates at 12 rpm, the echo position is updated once every 5 seconds either as a repainting of the echo or as a rewriting of range and bearing data into memory. Clearly a digital memory will retain the echo data until overwritten, but the displayed echo on a PPI will only remain visible on the screen for a period determined by the strength of the echo and the persistence of the screen (see Sections 1.3.3 and 2.6.1.2). Hence if too low an aerial speed is employed, weak echoes, or possibly an entire sector of the picture may fade completely before being refreshed by a further paint on the next scan. While fading due to low scanner speed can be offset by using longer tube persistence, this may bring with it further problems associated with afterglow when range scale or picture presentation is changed. Excessive afterglow is a particular problem when an unstabilized orientation is used (see Section 1.4.1). The choice of aerial rotation rate and tube persistence is made at the design stage and in almost all civil marine radars is such that, except in the case of echoes very close to the threshold of detection, the picture persists for at least the period of one aerial rotation. However, worldwide this is not invariably the case.

An increase in aerial rotation rate will reduce the update period and allow shorter tube persistence. However such an increase cannot be pursued indefinitely because it reduces the time for which the beam actually dwells on any given target. Consider an aerial which is rotated at N rpm and has a horizontal beamwidth of HBW degrees. The time, in seconds, taken for the beam to rotate through HBW degrees is given by

$t = HBW/6N$

This also represents the time taken for the beam to sweep

across a point target (a target whose dimensions can be regarded as negligible: like a point radiation source (see Section 2.4.1.1), a point target is a theoretical concept which cannot be realized in practice but it is a useful aid to the analysis of some aspects of radar performance). In the time t seconds the radar will transmit a number of pulses given by

$$S = PRF \times t$$

where S represents the theoretical maximum number of pulses which could strike a point target. Thus we have

$$S = PRF \times \frac{HBW}{6N}$$

The greater the number of pulses which are fired at a target, the greater is the probability that one or more of these pulses will be reflected from the target and return a detectable echo. Thus the greater the value of S the higher the probability of detection. It can be seen from the above relationship that an increase in aerial rotation rate will tend to reduce the number of possible strikes per point target. Thus N and PRF are interrelated and a suitable combination must be chosen at the design stage. Clearly a low value of N can be offset by increasing the PRF but the possibility of second trace echoes (see Sections 2.2.4 and 3.9.6) places an upper limit on this option. Such a limit is a function of range scale and pulse length (see Section 2.3.4).

In recognition of the fact that not every strike will necessarily produce a detectable echo, because of the various other factors which can reduce the probability of target detection (see Chapter 3), it is generally believed that the radar design should have a capability of producing not less than 10 strikes per point target. Consider the following numerical example:

Example 2.3   A marine radar system has a PRF of 1000 and a horizontal beamwidth of 2°. Calculate the aerial rotation rate necessary to achieve at least 10 strikes per point target.

$$S = PRF \times \frac{HBW}{6N}$$

thus

$$10 = 1000 \times \frac{2}{6N}$$

hence

$$N = 1000 \times \frac{2}{60}$$

i.e.

$$N = 33.3 \, rpm$$

Thus an aerial rotation rate of 33.3 rpm or less is necessary to achieve at least 10 strikes per point target with a PRF of 1000 and a horizontal beamwidth of 2°.

In the late 1960s a radar system was produced with the exceptionally high aerial rotation rate of 80 rpm. This had the advantage of improving the overall picture brightness because, in the very short update period of three quarters of a second, the brightness of an echo had barely begun to decay before the echo was repainted. The very high rotation rate necessitated a similarly exceptionally high PRF of 6000 on the short range scales.

A further point of interest is that if the rotation speed is progressively increased, a speed will be reached at which the observer ceases to be conscious of the traditional rotating trace and sees merely a steady picture. In theory this will happen when the update period is so short that the decay in echo brightness between paints is not noticeable. What is noticeable is to some extent dependent on expectation. For example, with a very high aerial rotation rate an observer using the picture for navigation and collision avoidance might not be conscious of the rotating trace, whereas someone looking specifically to see if there was a rotating trace might well discern it. This is a fair description of the effect at about 80 rpm.

The above idea does not seem to have found general favour with radar designers and subsequently no civil marine system has offered aerial rotation rates even approaching the value quoted above. Most modern civil marine radar systems use aerial rotation rates in the range 22 to 33 rpm (although some small boat radars do use rates as high as 45 rpm). As the pursuit of the bright steady picture has now taken the road of the digital PPI and raster–scan displays, it seems unlikely that high aerial rates will be seen in the predictable future.

2.4.5   Aerial and display rotation link

A signal which represents the rotation of the aerial must be relayed to the display in order to maintain sympathetic rotation of the trace and/or update the aerial angle data in the digital memory. The signal can be analogue (e.g. a fluctuating voltage) or digital (e.g. a succession of binary numbers) in its form. However, even where a digital signal is required, it is common to find that an analogue signal is transmitted to the display and there converted to digital form. It is therefore appropriate to consider analogue transmission at this stage and subsequently to discuss the conversion to digital form in Section 2.6.6.4, which deals with display principles.

A variety of methods have been and still are used to transmit rotation from aerial to display. Modern methods fall into two broad categories; those which generate a fluctuating signal whose instantaneous value and polarity is a function of aerial angle, and those which generate a pulse train whose repetition rate is a function of instantaneous aerial speed.

2.4.5.1   Synchro system

A synchro system is suitably representative of the first category and will be described in block diagram form (see Figure 2.13).

The aerial element of the system is known as a synchro transmitter and consists of a rotor wound with many turns of wire and mounted so as to be able to rotate within a cylindrical chamber formed by a set of three fixed multi-turn windings having an angular separation of 120° and known as the stator. The rotor wind-

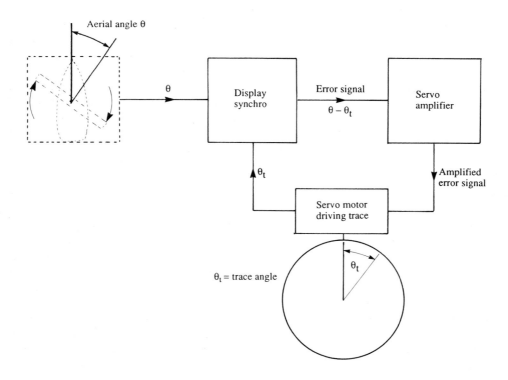

Figure 2.13   Transmission of aerial rotation using a synchro system

ing is energized with an alternating voltage of constant peak amplitude and thus by transformer action induces voltages in the three stator windings. The three values of induced voltage will form a unique combination for any given angular position of the rotor. If the rotor is driven on a 1:1 basis by the aerial, then the combination of voltages will constitute an analogue representation of aerial angle because it will vary in sympathy with aerial rotation.

The display element of the system is known as a synchro transformer or receiver and is constructed in a similar way to the synchro transmitter. Each stator winding of the display transformer is connected to its partner in the aerial unit and thus the voltages induced in the synchro transmitter are reproduced in the display unit. Hence we have in the display, at any instant, a unique combination of three stator voltages which is a measure of aerial angle. The resultant of these voltages will be induced, by transformer action, in the winding of the synchro transformer rotor. For any given combination of stator voltages the voltage so induced will, in both polarity and magnitude, depend on the relationship between the angle of the rotor in the aerial and that in the display. The voltage is known as the *error voltage* or *error signal* because it is a measure of the misalignment of the rotors. However, it is important to appreciate that when the misalignment is 90° the voltage induced in the display rotor will be zero. It may be helpful to consider this as being analogous to the radio direction finding null obtained when rotating the search coil under the influence of the voltages induced in the fixed coils of a goniometer. Clearly there are two zero positions. In the synchro case the ambiguity is resolved by the change of polarity which takes place at zero.

Until the late 1970s most (though not all) civil marine radar systems produced a rotating trace by means of a coil assembly which was rotated around the neck of the cathode ray tube (see Section 2.6.1.3) and many are still used at sea today. In such a system the rotor of the synchro transformer in the display is geared to the same motor as controls the rotation of the coil assembly which produces the rotating trace. This motor is driven by an amplified version of the error signal. This arrangement is known as a servo system (see Figure 2.13) and the factor by which the error signal is amplified is known as the gain of the servo amplifier.

To understand the operation of the servo system, consider initially that the synchro rotors are misaligned by 90° (not 270°!). The error signal will be zero. Let the aerial now be moved, in one step, through an angle of exactly 90° clockwise. The error signal will reach its maximum positive value and will cause the motor to drive the trace and the display synchro rotor rapidly clockwise. As the rotor rotates, the error signal will decrease and, neglecting the effects of angular momentum and friction, the rotor and trace will come to rest when the error voltage is zero and they have both rotated through 90°. Thus the system causes the trace to rotate through the same angle as the aerial.

If the aerial is now rotated at constant angular speed, the trace will similarly rotate but with a small angular lag. The lag arises because the misalignment between the aerial synchro rotor and the display synchro rotor must differ by slightly more than 90° to produce an error signal to drive the servo motor. The magnitude of error signal, and hence the angular lag required to achieve any given constant speed of rotation, is determined by the frictional resistance offered by the servo motor and the associated trace drive mechanism. The angular lag increases with speed of rotation. The presence of the angular lag will not introduce a bearing error as long as it remains constant, because it will generate a constant error signal and a constant servo motor speed. This will produce a steady state condition in which, because the lag is constant, the trace rotation speed will be the same as that of the aerial. This satisfies the basic condition required for bearing measurement as described in Section 1.3.3.

In practice, the aerial will not turn at a perfectly constant rate as it will be subject to angular acceleration and deceleration due to, for example, variations in air resistance as it rotates in the wind. Under these circumstances the angular lag will vary and the design of the system must ensure that this does not introduce unacceptable bearing errors. The IMO Performance Standards (see Section 10.2) require that any means provided for obtaining bearings should enable the bearing of a target whose echo appears at the edge of the display to be measured with an accuracy of ±1° or better. Clearly this ±1° must represent the aggregate of the accuracy with which the echo is displayed and the instrument accuracy of the measuring facility. The question of bearing accuracy is discussed in detail in Section 6.9 but it is important at this stage to recognise that any errors introduced by variations in angular lag must be sufficiently small that, when aggregated with other error contributions, they result in an error of not more than 1°.

If the aerial temporarily accelerates by a small amount it will tend to leave the trace behind. However, with the increase in angular lag, the error signal will increase and hence promote an acceleration of the trace rotation. Ideally, in the interests of bearing accuracy this will increase the speed of the trace rotation so that it matches that of the aerial with minimal time delay and negligible increase in angular lag. This can be achieved by using a very high gain servo amplifier and ensuring minimum frictional resistance in the mechanism to be driven. There are limits, however, to how far this ideal can be pursued.

If the servo amplifier gain is made too high, a small increase in angular lag will produce a very large increase in the amplified error signal. This may well impart sufficient angular acceleration to the trace assembly that it is travelling much faster than the aerial when the correct steady state angular lag is reached and it therefore may overtake the aerial direction. If this happens, a negative error signal will reduce the speed of the trace rotation and again, if this is done too violently, overshoot in the other sense will take place. Thus, after an aerial acceleration, if the gain is too high the trace speed will tend to oscillate about the new aerial speed, the amplitude of the oscillation gradually being reduced by the frictional effects in the system. (It has already been argued that for rapid response the latter should be minimized, in which case the tendency to oscillate will be increased.) Conversely, if the gain is too small, the trace speed will be slow to respond to the small changes in aerial speed which are inevitable in practical conditions at sea. Thus at the design stage a compromise value of servo amplifier gain must be selected which will produce the most rapid response possible without generating oscillations. This decision involves quantitative considerations of the mechanical inertia and frictional effects present in the system which are beyond the scope of this text. The reader who wishes to pursue this topic further is referred to any standard text on control engineering.

In many modern PPI systems the rotating trace is produced by a fixed coil assembly energized by voltages controlled by a digital computer. However, it is common to find that the rotation signal is generated in the aerial drive unit by a synchro transmitter (or similar analogue device) and the signals are used as input to a device in the display which converts the aerial angle into a binary code. It is more appropriate to discuss this under the heading of 'Display principles' in Section 2.6.6.4. In a raster-scan system the update of aerial angle may be achieved by analogue transmission to the display and subsequent analogue-to-digital conversion.

2.4.5.2 Aerial rotation pulse generator

Some modern digital systems relay the rotation data to the display by means of a device which transmits a train of pulses, the instantaneous repetition rate of which is dependent on the instantaneous speed of aerial rotation. A common value is 1 pulse per degree of aerial revolution. These pulses are used as input to a digital computer which updates the aerial angle in memory and controls the rotation of the trace. As with synchro-to-digital conversion, this will be discussed further in Section 2.6.6.4.

2.4.6 Heading marker data

The function of the heading marker is to indicate on the display the forward direction of the ship's fore-and-aft line. It forms the fundamental reference from which bearings are measured (see Sections 1.3.4 and 2.2.2). The signal is normally initiated by the mechanical closing of a switch located in the aerial drive unit. The closing of the switch activates circuitry in the display unit (see Section 2.6.2) which produces a pulse to fully brighten a number of successive traces. The IMO Performance Standards (see Section 10.2) require that the thickness of the displayed heading line be not more than 0.5°. It follows that the duration of the heading marker pulse must be not more than approximately 1/720th of the period of the aerial rotation. For an aerial rotation speed of 20 rpm the duration would be approximately 4 ms. The number of traces forming the heading marker will also depend on the PRF. With an aerial speed of 20 rpm and a PRF of 1000 the number will be approximately 4. The number of traces for any set of values can be obtained by using the relationship set out in Section 2.4.4 for calculating the number of strikes per point target and substituting the angular width of the heading marker for that of the horizontal beamwidth.

A number of methods have been used to operate the heading marker switch. One such method uses a small cam on a rotating part of the aerial unit to depress the switch as it goes past once during each revolution of the aerial. In all systems it is possible to adjust the point at which contact is made over a range of azimuth of about 5° to 10° so that the instant of heading marker display can be made to coincide with that of the axis of the main beam crossing the ship's fore-and-aft line in the forward direction. It is of critical importance that the setting is made correctly on installation and that the accuracy of the setting is checked by the observer regularly thereafter (see Section 6.9.9). The IMO Performance Standards require that the heading marker be displayed with an error not greater than ± 1° (see Section 10.2).

In some modern systems generation of the heading marker is achieved without mechanical contact by using an electronic sensing device known as a 'Hall effect switch'.

Some systems also offer the facility of a stern marker for the benefit of craft such as short sea ferries which regularly navigate stern-first.

2.5   Receiver principles

The function of the receiver is to amplify the weak returning echoes intercepted by the aerial and hence produce pulses of a strength and form which will generate a visible response on the screen of the display. In older systems the pulses will, in analogue form, produce a brightening of the rotating trace on a PPI. In more modern systems the pulses will be converted into digital form (see Section 2.6.6) and read into memory. After processing they will be read out of memory and used to produce either a radial-scan or a raster-scan PPI. The memory may also produce data for automatic target tracking (see Section 4.3.6.1).

The returning pulses are extremely weak and the receiver must be sufficiently sensitive to detect, at its input, signals having a strength of as little as one millionth of a volt. As explained in Section 2.2.3, the transmitter and receiver share a common section of waveguide. If the extremely powerful transmitter pulse (of the order of kilowatts) was allowed to enter the sensitive receiver, permanent damage would result. This is prevented by the T/R cell. For the purposes of this book the T/R cell may be considered to be an electronic switch which blocks the receiver branch of the waveguide during transmission.

The receiver must amplify the weakest signals by a factor of between 1 and 10 million in order to make them large enough to produce a picture. When the signals arrive at the antenna they are in the form of bursts of radio energy having a frequency lying in the X-band or S-band and an evelope resembling the shape originally imparted to them by the modulator and pulse-forming network (see Section 2.3.2.3). For engineering reasons which are beyond the scope of this treatment it is not practical to produce devices which will amplify signals at frequencies in the bands used for radar transmission and reception (approximately 9300–9500 MHz and 2900–3100 MHz). It is therefore necessary to reduce the frequency of the signal contained within the envelope of the pulse to a value at which such amplification is possible. The device which performs this function is known as the *mixer* and operates in association with another device known as the *local oscillator* (see Figure 2.14). The value of lower frequency adopted may vary with manufacturer but it is usually in the region of 60 MHz and is referred to as the intermediate frequency (IF).

The signals leaving the mixer are amplified progressively by a series of amplifier stages (probably about 6 to 8 in number) which together constitute the IF amplfier. From the output of the IF amplifier the signals are passed to a device known as a *detector* which extracts the envelope from each burst of IF energy and hence the signals are ideally once more in the form of *rectangular* pulses. They are then referred to as *video pulses* because they are capable, after some amplification in the video amplifier, of producing a picture on a cathode ray tube.

It is evident that the signal path through the receiver can be divided into three convenient sections:

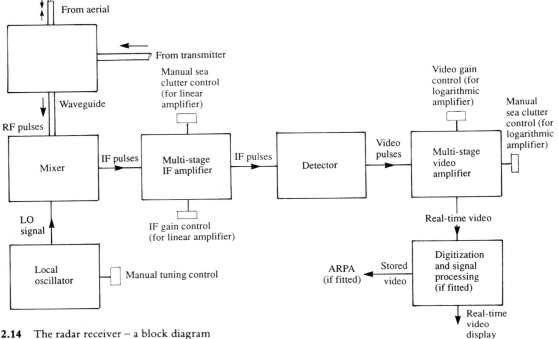

Figure 2.14 The radar receiver – a block diagram

1 The radio frequency section comprising the mixer and local oscillator.
2 The intermediate frequency section comprising the various stages of the IF amplifier.
3 The video section comprising the detector and video amplifier stages.

The sections are particularly convenient as they each represent a stage at which, in setting up and using the radar system, the observer may exercise control over the receiver. The tuning control invariably operates in the radio frequency section. Gain and clutter controls may operate in either the IF or the video section, depending on the receiver design.

2.5.1 The radio frequency section

2.5.1.1 The mixer principle

It can be shown that if two sinusoidal signals of differing frequencies are mixed, the resultant complex signal con-

sists of a number of sinusoidal components one of which has a frequency which is equal to the difference between the two frequencies which were mixed and which is known as the beat frequency. (Other components generated include the sum of the mixed frequencies, twice the higher frequency and twice the lower frequency, to name but a few.) The principle is more correctly known as the heterodyne principle and the radar receiver is said to be of the superheterodyne type.

The principle is applied in the radar receiver by mixing the incoming weak echoes, which are bursts of radio signals at magnetron frequency, with a continuous low power radio frequency signal generated by a device known as the local oscillator. The envelope of the pulse produced at the output of the mixer will contain, among others, a component whose frequency is equal to the difference between that of the magnetron and that of the local oscillator. This signal is used as input to the IF amplifier. The IF amplifier is carefully pre-tuned by the manufacturer (to the chosen IF) so that it will respond only to that component of the mixer output which lies at the chosen beat frequency. As a result, all the other frequency components generated by the mixing process are rejected. Thus the IF section deals with pulses whose envelope resembles the shape originally imparted by the transmitter and which encloses bursts of oscillations at a frequency which is sufficiently low to be amplified using conventional techniques.

2.5.1.2 Tuning principles

Since the IF amplifier is pre-tuned to the chosen IF frequency it follows that the local oscillator must be adjusted so that the frequency which it generates differs from that of the magnetron (and thus the incoming wanted signals) by an amount equal to the chosen intermediate frequency. It is this adjustment which the observer makes when tuning the receiver. The manual tuning control will be located on the display unit so that the observer can view the picture while making the necessary adjustments, but it is important to appreciate that it exercises its influence at the very earliest stage of the receiver.

It is evident from the simple description of the magnetron presented in Section 2.3.3.2 that the generation of microwave frequencies is a complex process. While from an engineering point of view the local oscillator presents fewer problems because there is no requirement

for extremely high power or very short pulses, the generation of the oscillations nevertheless depends on some form of resonant cavity. Here, it is sufficient to say that the oscillations are generated in a single cavity (as opposed to the multiple cavities of the magnetron). Coarse control of the generated frequency is obtained by variation of the physical size of the cavity (this is an installation or service adjustment), while fine control is exercised by small variations in the electronic conditions associated with the cavity (this is an operator/observer adjustment). Clearly stability of the local oscillator frequency is of great importance as any drift in its output value will de-tune the receiver and result in the loss of targets.

Because the IF amplifer is pre-tuned to a fixed frequency, the response of the receiver to incoming signals can be as illustrated in Figure 2.15. The response curve can be centred on any chosen frequency within the appropriate band and it will be observed that it has a bell-shaped characteristic which is symmetrical about that frequency. It is not possible to produce circuitry which will respond at a single frequency and exclude all others. The response will be maximum at the tuned frequency and will decay on either side of that value. The range of frequencies over which the response can be considered to be significant is referred to as the *bandwidth* of the receiver.

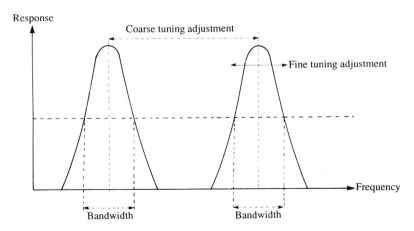

Figure 2.15 The response of the radar receiver

In most other applications of radio receivers great care is taken to ensure that the bandwidth is as narrow as physically possible. For example, in a broadcast receiver one wishes to obtain maximum response from the desired station and to avoid interference from stations operating on nearby frequencies. In radar systems designed to receive pulsed signals, the bandwidth is deliberately widened. It can be shown that the effect of a very narrow bandwidth is to distort the shape of the pulse to an extent which increases as the pulse length becomes shorter. The increase in bandwidth carries the penalty of loss of response and susceptibility to interference from other radar systems. The value adopted by the designer is thus of necessity a compromise and as it is essentially an IF amplifier characteristic it will be further discussed under that heading (see Section 2.5.2.4).

In most marine radar systems the bandwidth, when long pulse is selected, normally lies in the range 3 to 5 MHz and in the range 15 to 25 MHz in the case of short pulse selection.

2.5.1.3 Manual tuning control

Most modern marine radar systems have a manual tuning control, situated on the display unit, which enables the observer to carry out fine tuning of the receiver. Coarse tuning should have been carried out by shipboard or shore-based service personnel in such a way as to ensure that the optimum setting of the display control lies close to the centre of its travel. If the optimum setting is found to approach one end of the travel, the coarse tuning should be re-adjusted by a person qualified to service the equipment.

It is crucial to the safe and proper use of marine radar for collision avoidance and navigation that a procedure is adopted which ensures that the manual tuning control is correctly set when the equipment is switched on and that thereafter it is regularly checked and readjusted as may be necessary due to the warming up of the equipment and the passage of time (see Sections 2.3.3.2 and 2.5.1.2). The appropriate procedure is described in detail in Sections 6.2.4.2 and 6.3.4.3).

2.5.1.4 Automatic tuning

It is possible to design circuitry which will seek and find the correct local oscillator frequency when the radar equipment is first switched on and which will maintain the receiver in tune despite changes which may occur due to warm-up or with the passage of time. Such a facility is correctly termed automatic frequency control (AFC) and should not be confused with limited automatic tuning facilities such as *pull-in* or *lock* which are described in Section 2.5.1.5.

In the past, marine radar systems offering fully automatic tuning were not uncommon, but since the 1970s they have tended to become the exception rather than the rule. In systems with full AFC there is usually no facility for the observer to carry out manual tuning at the display position but it will normally be possible for service personnel to switch out the automatic control and adjust the tuning from within the receiver unit.

Even where fully automatic tuning is available, it is essential for the observer to check (with reference to displayed signals) after switching on, and at regular intervals thereafter, that the facility is achieving optimum tuning. This is best done by use of the performance monitor (see Section 6.5).

2.5.1.5 Limited automatic tuning

Such a facility is sometimes referred to as *pull-in* or *lock* and is supplementary to a manual tuning control. Provided that the observer has initially set the manual tuning control at or very close to the correct setting, the pull-in circuitry has the ability to maintain the receiver in tune despite small variations in local oscillator or transmitter frequency during warm-up or with the passage of time.

It is important to appreciate that if the observer does not adjust the manual control to bring the receiver frequency within the limits of pull-in or if for any reason the frequency to which the receiver is tuned subsequently drifts outside these limits, the automatic system will be unable to re-tune the receiver without manual intervention.

Frequently such a limited tuning facility is complemented by a visual indicator (such as a neon light or a magic eye) which is designed to register whether or not the receiver frequency lies within the limits of the automatic tuning. It is important not to confuse such tuning indicators with others which are merely some measure of received signal strength. Tuning indicators are not required under the IMO Performance Standards and it would be unwise to make use of such devices without a clear understanding of the significance, accuracy and limitations of their indication. It should not be necessary to make use of such devices as the criteria set out in Sections 6.2.4.2 and 6.3.4.3. (which are based on the observation of displayed signals) will always provide a more reliable check on the setting of the tuning control. Thus, as with fully automatic tuning, it is essential for the observer to check regularly, by reference to displayed signals, that optimum tuning is being maintained.

2.5.2 The intermediate frequency amplifier

The intermediate frequency (IF) amplifier accepts the echoes produced by the mixer (which are in the form of weak bursts of IF signal within an envelope resembling that produced by the modulator) and boosts them to the level at which it is possible to extract the pulse envelope. As there is a limit to the factor by which any single amplifier stage can increase the strength of a signal, the IF amplifier is assembled in the form of a series of individual stages which progressively amplify the received echoes. It is now necessary to consider some of the characteristics of an amplifier stage and examine how they behave when connected together.

2.5.2.1 Stage gain and saturation

A single amplifier stage may be considered to be a *black box* such that if a signal is applied at the input to the stage an amplified version of the signal will appear at the output. Up to a certain level of input signal (known as the limiting input) the ratio of the strength of the output signal to the strength of the input signal is constant. It is known as the stage gain and is a measure of the magnification of the signal. Thus, below the limiting input, all signals will be amplified by the same factor.

If progressively increasing signals are applied to the input of the amplifier (see Figure 2.16) a situation must eventually arise (at the limiting input) where the output reaches the maximum value which the amplifier can produce. The latter is known as the limiting output.

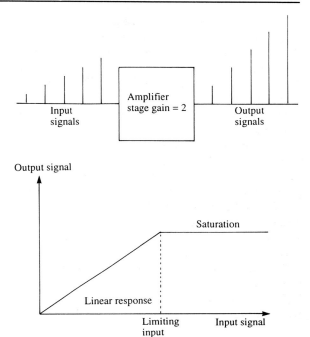

Figure 2.16 A simple amplifier stage

Further increase in the input signal will produce no further increase in the output. The amplifier is then said to be saturated. Thus all input signals which exceed the limiting input will produce the same output. This characteristic is of particular importance in the interpretation of a marine radar picture as it tends to create a substantially monotone picture in which all the strong echoes are displayed with equal brightness. It may allow echoes from the sea waves around the ship, or from areas of rain, to mask the presence of echoes very much stronger than themselves. The importance of this serious limitation of marine radar is dealt with in detail in Sections 3.6 and 3.7.

2.5.2.2 Overall gain

The gain offered by a single stage is a fraction of what is required to amplify the weakest signals received by the system. A large overall gain can be achieved by connecting a number of stages in series to form a multi-stage amplifier.

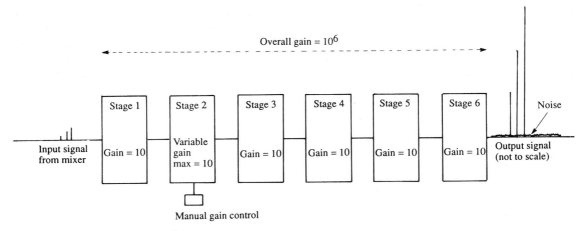

Figure 2.17 A multi-stage amplifier

The overall gain of the amplifier is given by the product of the gains of individual stages. Thus, in the example illustrated by Figure 2.17, if all stages have a gain of 10 the overall gain of the amplifier is 10^6, i.e. one million. Where such an amplifier is used in practice it would be normal for the observer to have control of the gain of one of the earlier stages while the gain of the remaining stages would be pre-set.

2.5.2.3 *Thermal noise*

In any electrical conductor or device at temperatures other than absolute zero there exists random movement of electrons due to thermal agitation and thus there will be random movement of electric charge. This produces an effect known as thermal noise, or sometimes as white noise, because like white light, it is equally distributed across the full frequency spectrum. The movement of the charge manifests itself as a minute random electrical signal which in the case of an amplifier stage will appear at the output of the stage. Although when initially generated the noise signal is of very low level, if it is amplified by a number of stages in a multi-stage amplifier its amplitude may be increased by a factor of as much as a million (see Figure 2.17), rendering it strong enough to produce a detectable signal on the radar display.

The term 'noise' was adopted because, when the phenomenon was first noticed in audio systems, it could be heard as background crackling in earphones and loudspeakers which made it difficult to hear weak signals. In a radar display it appears visually as a close-grained background speckling on the display. As the observer must attempt to discern the echoes of targets against this background, the level of noise generated in the first stage of the amplifier is of fundamental importance in determining the system's ability to display weak echoes. If the returning echo is weaker than the noise produced in this first stage it will not be capable of detection, as successive stages of amplification will merely increase the amount by which the noise exceeds the required signal. However, if initially the signal is stronger than the noise, successive stages of amplification will magnify this difference and improve the probability of detection. Echoes which are close to noise level will always be difficult to detect.

The level of noise displayed on the screen, and hence the probability of detecting weak targets, will depend on how the observer sets the gain control. If the gain is set too low, weak echoes will be lost because they will fail to display. If the gain is set too high, weak echoes will be lost, not because they will not displayed, but because they will be masked by the background. The correct practical procedure for setting the gain control is discussed in detail in Chapter 6.

2.5.2.4   Bandwidth

The IF amplifier is pre-tuned to a chosen frequency and will respond only to signals at, or within the bandwidth limits of, that frequency. The amplifier is required to handle a sinusoidal signal having a frequency of typically 60 MHz and which is modulated by a rectangular waveform. It can be shown that a rectangular waveform is built up from a large number of sinusoidal waveforms consisting of a fundamental frequency and components

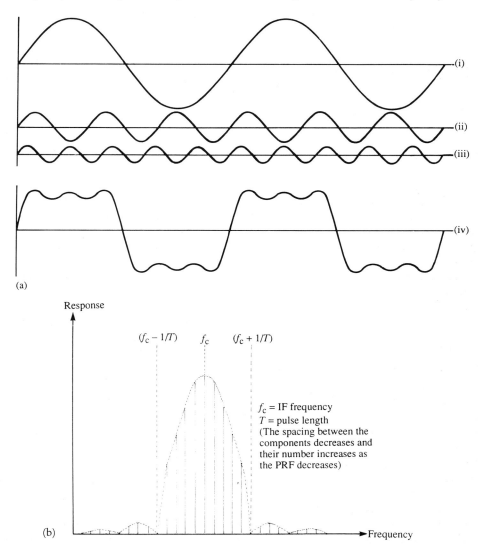

Figure 2.18   Rectangular pulses
(a)   Frequency spectrum of a rectangular pulse
    (i)   Sine wave at amplitude A units, frequency f
    (ii)   Sine wave at amplitude $A/3$ units, frequency $3f$
    (iii)   Sine wave at amplitude $A/5$ units, frequency $5f$
    (iv)   Sum of (i) + (ii) + (iii) → tends toward a square wave
(b)   The frequency components of an IF pulse

known as harmonics at multiples of that fundamental frequency. A proof of this requires a mathematical analysis well beyond the scope of this text. However, Figure 2.18(a) does show graphically that the assembly of a family of sine waves will tend towards a rectangular waveform.

The signal to be amplified is a complex waveform each element of which is a burst of sinusoidal signal (referred to as the IF carrier) contained within a rectangular envelope (referred to as the modulating waveform). It can be shown that the fundamental and harmonics of the modulating waveform will combine with the carrier frequency to produce a family of frequency components, known as side frequencies, which lie above and below the intermediate frequency and whose magnitude decreases with separation from the centre frequency (see Figure 2.18(b)). In order to preserve a reasonably rectangular pulse shape the IF amplifier must be able to respond to at least the stronger side frequencies. The shorter the duration of the received pulse, the more important this requirement becomes. It is for this reason that marine radars are designed with a bandwidth which is wider than would be the case in many other radio systems (see also Section 2.5.1.2). The bandwidth is normally considered to extend on either side of the centre frequency to the frequencies at which the response has fallen to half that at the centre frequency.

However, the bandwidth cannot be widened indefinitely (see Figure 2.19) and the value selected by the designer is of necessity a compromise. The curve in Figure 2.19(a) is representative of a sharply tuned amplifier which has high gain at the centre frequency and high selectivity because the bandwidth is very narrow. Clearly the high central response is desirable. However, the narrow bandwidth will reject the side frequencies and distort the shape of the pulse. This will reduce the accuracy of range measurement which is dependent on the echo having a sharp leading edge (see Section 2.3.2.3).

The curve in Figure 2.19(b) is representative of an amplifier having a wide bandwidth. The latter characteristic will ensure that the side frequencies necessary for good pulse shape will not be rejected but this has been bought at the expense of a decrease in central response.

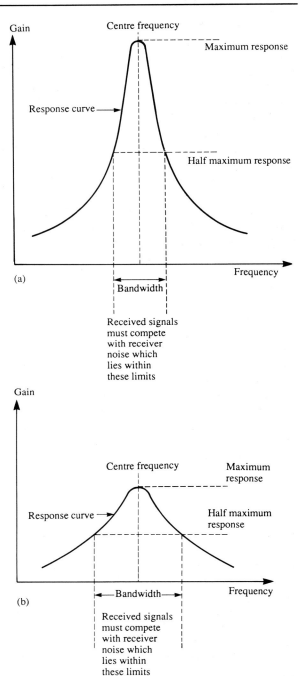

Figure 2.19   (a) Narrow bandwidth and (b) Wide bandwidth

Thus the designer must achieve a bandwidth which is sufficiently wide to achieve acceptable pulse shape yet not so wide as to inordinately reduce the amplification provided.

A further factor which the designer must consider is the presence of noise. White noise (see Section 2.5.2.3) is generated across the full spectrum of frequencies but only those components which fall within the bandwidth of the receiver will be accepted. Thus increasing the bandwidth allows more noise to be accepted and hence reduces the probability of detection of weak echoes. Again the designer must compromise.

Most civil marine radars designed for large merchant vessels achieve this compromise in part by arranging for the IF amplifier to have two bandwidths which are under the indirect control of the observer by means of the pulse length selector (see Section 2.3.2.1). The narrower bandwidth is switched in if the observer, directly or indirectly, selects long pulse. The logic employed is that if long pulse has been selected, the observer must be concerned with distant targets and detection can be awarded a higher priority than range accuracy. Thus selection of long pulse has the effect of improving the probability of detecting distant echoes.

If the short pulse is selected, the wider bandwidth is used on the basis that the observer will make such a selection when observing targets on the shorter range scales and that as a result some amplification can be traded for an improvement in pulse shape.

2.5.2.5 The linear IF amplifier

Traditionally this is the type of multi-stage amplifier which was employed in all marine radar systems. It is now being progressively superseded by the more modern logarithmic amplifier (see Section 2.5.2.6) in radar systems which are designed for use on large merchant ships. However, a large number of older systems using a linear amplifier are still used at sea and some systems designed for smaller vessels continue to use the older technique.

Figure 2.20 shows a representative arrangement of a linear amplifier having six stages connected together in series. For continuity, the first element of the video stage is also shown. This is known as the detector and its func-

tion is to extract the envelope from the amplified IF signal (see Section 2.5.3.1).

This type of amplifier is so called because, provided that saturation does not take place at any stage, there is a linear relationship between the output and input signals, i.e. the overall gain is constant. Thus, provided that the input signal is below that value (the limiting input) which will produce saturation of the last stage, all echoes will be amplified by the same *factor*.

The major shortcoming of the linear amplifier is that it has a limited dynamic range (see Figure 2.20) and a large proportion of received signals will saturate the amplifier under normal conditions. This will allow unwanted responses such as those from the sea and from precipitation to mask even very strong targets (see Sections 3.6 and 3.7). At the root of the problem is the fact that the radar receiver has to handle a very large range of input signal levels. The ratio between the strongest and weakest signals at the input may be of the order of $10\,000 : 1$ (for example, a supertanker to a wooden boat).

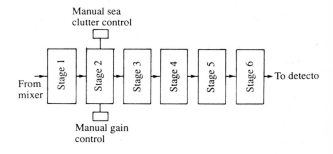

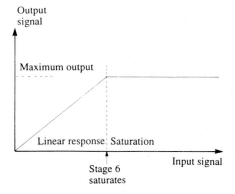

Figure 2.20 The linear IF amplifier

To achieve detection, the weakest signals have to be amplified by a factor of about 1 million which clearly will cause the stronger echoes to saturate the last, and probably a number of earlier stages of the amplifier. Normally all but one or two of the stages will have fixed gain while the observer will have the ability to modify the overall gain by means of the *IF gain control* (usually referred to simply as the gain) and the *sea clutter control*. The latter is a specialized form of gain control which will be discussed in detail in Section 3.6.3.1. These controls may operate in the same or separate stages.

The observer has to seek to offset the shortcomings which the limited dynamic range imposes by judicious adjustment of the overall gain. If the gain is adjusted so that the noise just appears on the display then there will be maximum probability of detecting weak targets, but strong echoes will all appear equally bright and masking will take place. If the gain is adjusted so that masking is eliminated then noise and weaker echoes will be insufficiently amplified to be displayed on the screen. The detailed practical procedures for dealing with this conflict are set out in Section 6.10.

2.5.2.6   *The logarithmic amplifier*

The logarithmic amplifier is designed to reduce the range of input signals that will saturate the receiver. Some marine radar systems offered logarithmic amplification from the mid-1960s, but it is since the early 1970s that the use of this technique has progressively become more commonplace.

The amplifier is so called because at the higher levels of signal input the output signal is proportional to the logarithm of the input. The logarithmic nature of the response is best demonstrated by mathematical analysis which is beyond the scope of this book, but a practical understanding of the operation can be obtained by consideration of Figure 2.21. To facilitate comparison the amplifier is assembled from the same number of stages as the linear amplifier in Figure 2.20.

The essential feature of the logarithmic amplifier is that the gain and limiting output of all stages must be the same, whereas in the case of the linear amplifier this need not necessarily be the case. Further, instead of a single output being taken from the last stage as in the case of

the linear type, an output is taken from each individual stage. These contributions are summed to form a composite output. For reasons which are beyond the scope of this work it is expedient to extract the envelope of each contribution before the addition is performed. For this reason the type illustrated is often referred to as a *successive* detection amplifier. Alternatively it is sometimes said that the stages are connected together in *cascade*.

As mentioned previously, it is essential that the gain of each individual stage is fixed and equal to that of all of the others. For this reason the observer has no control of the gain in this unit. Where a logarithmic amplifier is employed, both gain and sea clutter controls operate at a later stage in the video section.

Consider the situation where the input just saturates the last stage. Although the contribution from the last stage will have reached its maximum, further increase in the input signal will nonetheless produce an increase in the total output because of the contributions from the earlier unsaturated stages. It follows that the total output will not saturate until the input signal is sufficiently large to saturate the first stage. Thus, comparing linear and logarithmic amplifiers, it is evident that the former produces a saturated output when the *last* stage saturates whereas the latter will not do so until the input signal has risen to such a level as to saturate the *first* stage. Hence the logarithmic amplifier increases the range of signals which can be handled without saturating the receiver. This increase makes it possible to design a receiver which will not be saturated other than by exceptionally strong echoes. A wide range of echoes may still saturate the screen phosphor (see Section 2.6.1.2) but this is more easily dealt with by the observer than saturation which takes place early in the IF amplifier.

It can be shown that, provided that the last stage does not saturate, the amplifier has a linear characteristic with an overall gain slightly less than a linear amplifier configured from the same stages. At signal levels above this, but below that which will saturate the first stage, the characteristic is logarithmic. Some understanding of the nature of the response can be obtained from the relationships, set out below, between input and output for a six-stage logarithmic amplifier configured as in Figure 2.21.

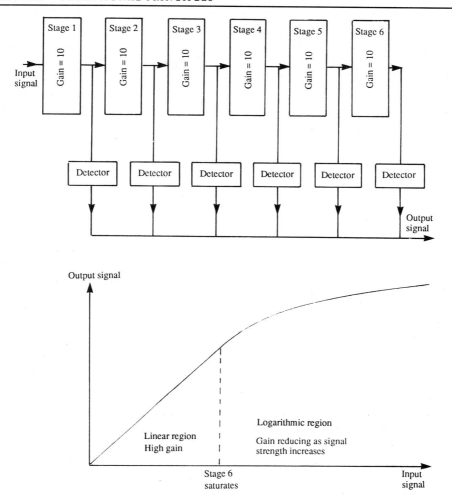

Figure 2.21   The logarithmic amplifier

Input	Output
v_s	$V+v$
AV_s	$2V+v$
A^2v_s	$3V+v$
A^3v_s	$4V+v$
A^4v_s	$5V+v$
A^5v_s	$6V$

where v_s is the input signal which will just saturate stage 6

A is the gain of each stage
V is the saturated output of each stage
v is the contribution of the unsaturated stages which has a maximum value of $v = V/A + V/A^2 + V/A^3 + V/A^4 + V/A^5$.

Before comparing the input and the output colums, it should be noted that v must always be very much smaller than V (its largest component cannot exceed V/A, where A is the stage gain). Comparing the input and output columns, and for the moment ignoring the effect of v, we can obtain an appreciation of the response. It should be noticed that at the lower values shown in the table, a tenfold increase in input signal produces a doubling of the output signal. As the input signal level increases, the proportional increase in output produced by a tenfold increase in input progressively decreases until, toward the top end of the values tabulated, a tenfold increase in input merely produces a 20% increase in output signal. Thus the overall gain falls off at high levels along a curve which can be seen to be approximately logarithmic.

A simpler illustration of the logarithmic relationship between input and output is obtained by (i) considering v_s to be unity, (ii) using a stage gain of 10 and (iii) neglecting v which is a small quantity. On this basis the values given above approximate to:

Input	Output
1	V
10	$2V$
100	$3V$
1 000	$4V$
10 000	$5V$
100 000	$6V$

The effect of this logarithmic response is to emphasise the difference between different input echo strengths at the lower end of the range while maintaining a small but finite difference between the ouput echo strengths at the top end of the range. This considerably reduces the problems created by the masking of targets by sea and precipitation echoes, renders the adjustment of manual clutter controls less critical and provides an IF output which will make possible the use of automatic clutter suppression techniques in the video section (see Sections 3.6, 3.7, and 6.10).

2.5.3   The video section

For the general public the word 'video' has tended to take on a new and popular meaning with the advent of mass produced television tape recorders for use in homes. However, it should be appreciated that for the purposes of this work 'video' means *that signal which, when applied to the CRT, produces the picture.*

The function of the video section is to extract the envelope (i.e. the rectangular outline) of each received pulse and to amplify and condition it so that it can be used as input to computer memory for storage and processing and/or used to produce a visible response on the screen of the cathode ray tube.

2.5.3.1   *The detector*

The function of the detector is to extract the rectangular envelope from the amplified IF signals (see Figure 2.22). In engineering texts it is sometimes referred to as the *second detector*, the mixer being considered to be the first detector. (This arises because the process involved is fundamentally the same.) Alternatively the term *demodulator* may be used. This arises from the general terminology of radio communication in which the term modulation is used to describe the process whereby a signal representing intelligence (e.g. speech, music or data) which cannot be transmitted directly into space, is superimposed on a radio frequency signal (known as a carrier). In the radar case the modulating signal is represented by the rectangular pulse envelope (see Figure 2.4) and the carrier by the radio frequency oscillations produced by the magnetron (see Section 2.3.3.2). Hence, considering the IF oscillations as representative of the original carrier, the function of the demodulator or detector is to recover the modulating signal, i.e. the rectangular envelope (see Figure 2.23).

When it is recalled that the waveform of the envelope is the sum of a fundamental frequency and its harmonics (see Section 2.5.2.4), it will be appreciated that the frequency characteristic of the detector must be such that it will respond to the *relatively* low frequencies of the envelope (usually of the order of a few megahertz) but reject the relatively high intermediate frequency which will normally be in the region of 60 MHz.

2.5.3.2   *The video amplifier*

This unit boosts the pulses which are produced at the output of the detector to a level at which they are suitable for storage in memory or capable of producing a visible response on the screen of the cathode ray tube (see Section 2.6.1). The amplifier may comprise several stages and, like the IF amplifier, each stage must have

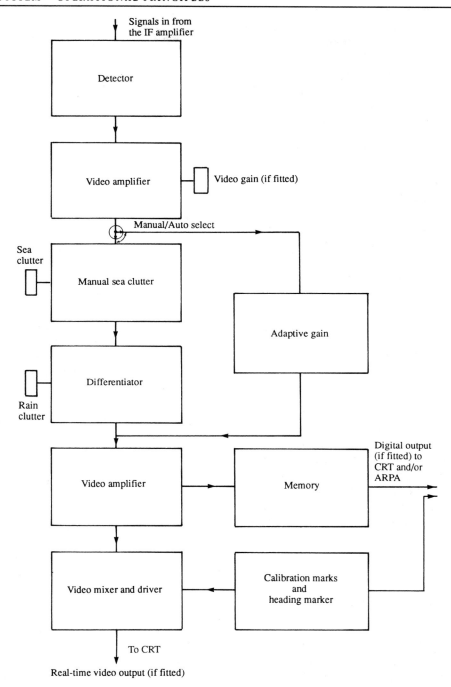

Figure 2.22 The video section

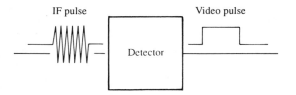

Figure 2.23   Recovering the pulse envelope

sufficient bandwidth to pass an adequate range of the harmonics which are present in a rectangular waveform. In most modern marine radar systems the video bandwidth is fixed but there are some systems in which the video bandwidth, rather than the IF bandwidth, is switched with pulse length. As the amplitude of the signal is increased through successive stages, its polarity may change from positive to negative with alternate stages. This arises because the operation of many single-stage amplifiers introduces a 180° phase shift between input and output signals. This point need not concern the radar observer but readers who wish to pursue the point are referred to any electrical engineering text dealing with voltage amplifiers.

In older systems, where the video amplifier was preceded by a linear IF amplifier, it was normal to find that the observer exercised control of the gain (by means of gain and sea clutter controls) in the IF stage and that the overall gain of the video section was fixed. However, a few systems did offer a separate video gain control with a view to offering a limited level of independence where the display unit was used as a slave in an interswitched configuration (see 'Interswitching' in Section 2.7.8). In modern systems employing a logarithmic IF amplifier, the gain and sea clutter control is invariably exercised in the video section because operator control of the IF gain would destroy the logarithmic law of the IF section (see Section 2.5.2.6).

Consideration of Figure 2.22 shows that, after the initial section of the video amplifier, the signal path has been split into what can be conveniently called the manual channel and the automatic channel. This configuration will only be found in modern systems in which the video section is preceded by a logarithmic amplifier. In older systems employing a linear amplifier, only the manual channel will be present and it will not normally

offer any control of sea clutter as this will have been performed at IF.

2.5.3.3   The manual channel

Where both channels are provided, the manual channel allows the observer to carry out manual suppression of sea clutter echoes by means of a special type of gain control, sometimes referred to as swept gain or sensitivity time control (STC). The safe and successful operation of this control requires a sound knowledge of the phenomenon known as sea clutter and a skill which can only be obtained with practice. This topic is dealt with in Sections 3.6 and 6.10.

The second facility offered by this channel is known as *differentiation*. By adjustment of a manual control the observer is able to change the shape of the displayed pulse from that of a rectangle toward that of a spike. This may improve the ability of the display to show separately echoes which are on the same bearing and closely spaced in range, i.e. it may improve range discrimination (see Section 2.6.5.5). This control is often labelled *rain clutter* because it may assist in detecting targets which are masked by echoes from precipitation. Again, the use of this control calls for skill and knowledge; the topic is dealt with in Sections 3.7.4.4 and 6.10.2.

2.5.3.4   The automatic channel

The automatic channel provides a facility whereby the signal level is continually sensed and the overall gain is varied automatically in an attempt to remove unwanted signals such as those from sea waves (sea clutter) and precipitation (rain clutter). This automatic technique is known as adaptive gain and can only operate successfully on signals which have been processed initially by a logarithmic amplifier. When the automatic channel is selected, the manual channel is bypassed and thus the manual sea and rain clutter controls are disabled. Adaptive gain is described in detail in Section 3.6.3.3.

2.5.3.5   Further video amplification

There may or may not be further video amplification before the signals are fed off to memory and/or mixed with calibration signals before being displayed. The latter operations are more conveniently described under the heading of display principles below.

2.6   Display principles

The function of the display is to present the radar picture in such a way that, where a detectable response is returned, the observer may reveal the presence of the echo, measure its range and bearing, and track the movement of the target which has produced it.

From the invention of radar to the present day the radar picture has been presented on the screen of a cathode ray tube and this is likely to continue to be the case for many years to come. The prospect of a civil marine radar picture on a flat electronic panel lies somewhere in the future but it would be a brave person who would forecast when it will be commercially available.

While the cathode ray tube has retained its central position in the radar display over the years, the way in which the picture is presented has undergone three major revolutions over the same period. The first of these was the change from A-scan to PPI (see Section 1.2.3) but as this is of purely historical interest it will

not be mentioned further. From the early 1970s the change from a real-time picture to a synthetic picture (see Sections 1.2.5 and 2.6.6) began, although the radial-scan PPI was retained. From the mid-1980s the first raster-scan displays appeared (see Sections 1.2.5 and 2.6.7) in which the radial scan PPI is replaced by a raster-scan PPI generated on a television-type display. This last revolution will not take place overnight and it will be a very long time before the last civil marine radial-scan PPI display is finally switched off.

In this section consideration will be given to the principles of real-time and synthetic pictures displayed on a radial-scan PPI display and to raster-scan displays. As the cathode ray tube is the fundamental element of all such displays it is appropriate to discuss its operation in some detail. As the vast majority of radar cathode ray tubes at sea today use a radial-scan tube, the general treatment will be based on that type. The tube used in raster-scan radars differs in some respects from the radial-scan tube, and these differences will be highlighted in Section 2.6.7. which deals with this new type of display.

2.6.1   The cathode ray tube

The CRT (Figure 2.24) is an evacuated narrow glass tube which funnels out at one end to produce a circular

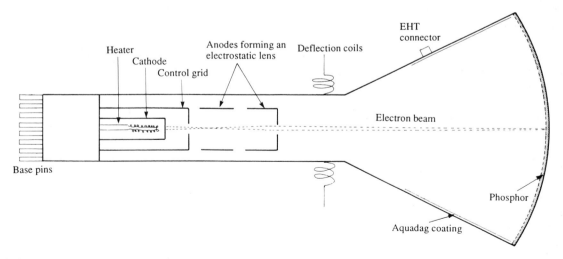

Figure 2.24   The cathode ray tube

screen. Electrons are emitted at the narrow end of the tube and formed into a very narrow beam which strikes the inside of the screen at the other end and there produces a spot of light whose brightness, size and position may be controlled (see also Section 1.2.3). The generation and control of the spot is best described by considering the CRT to comprise three major elements:

1 The electron gun which emits the electron stream.
2 The coated screen which reacts to produce light when struck by the electrons.
3 The deflection system which controls the location at which the beam strikes the screen.

Each of these elements will now be considered in turn.

2.6.1.1 *The electron gun*

An electron is the fundamental particle which carries unit negative electrical charge. The electron gun is an arrangement of cylindrical metal components which are known as electrodes.

The electrodes are located along the axis of the tube and their function is to liberate, accelerate and concentrate the electrons into a narrow beam which is fired toward the screen.

The electrode which emits the electrons is called the cathode and it is from this that the tube takes its name. The various electrodes which attract the electrons towards the screen are called anodes. These are maintained at very high positive potentials with respect to the cathode in order to accelerate the electrons to speeds of tens of thousands of kilometres per second. The strength of the electron stream is controlled by an electrode known as the control grid, normally referred to merely as the grid.

The cathode is a metal cylinder closed at the end nearer the screen and is coated on the outside with an oxide having an atomic structure such that electrons are emitted from the surface at a relatively low level of heat. The emission is promoted by heating the cathode indirectly as a result of passing electric current through a wire filament, known as the heater, which is located inside the cathode cylinder. The electrons emitted by the cathode form a cloud in its vicinity known as the space charge. As the cloud builds up, the loss of negative charge to the cloud renders the cathode positive with

respect to the cloud; hence some electrons tend to be recaptured. However, at any given temperature a state of dynamic equilibrium will be reached in which as many electrons are leaving the cloud as are joining it and thus a space charge of constant population will surround the end of the cathode. Electrons are drawn from this cloud and accelerated toward the screen to form the electron beam. Returning echoes, after being amplified by the receiver (see Section 2.5), are applied to the cathode as a pulse of negative polarity which will produce an increase in the strength of the beam and hence a brightening of the spot.

The grid is cylindrical in shape with one end closed except for a small hole which constrains electrons travelling along or close to the tube axis to pass through and emerge in the form of a convergent beam. It is located between the cathode and the first anode but closer to the cathode (see Figure 2.24). The grid potential can be adjusted by the observer, using the brilliance control, and will be a few tens of volts negative with respect to the cathode. The effect of the grid potential is to offset the attraction of the anode system to a greater or lesser extent, thus allowing the observer to control the strength of the electron beam and hence the brightness of the spot. Clearly the beam strength could, in theory, be varied by adjusting the anode potentials. However, it is much more practical to exercise control at the grid which is close to the cathode, as this allows small variations in a relatively small voltage to produce an effect which would require large variations in potentials having values of hundreds or thousands of volts at the anode. An automatic signal, known as the *bright-up pulse*, will also be applied to the grid. This ensures that the spot brightness selected by the observer is available when each radial line is being drawn but that it is suppressed when the spot is returning to the origin. Such automatic suppression may also take place when change of range scale or similar operations are performed. (In some systems the video signal has also been applied to the grid instead of the cathode.)

The brilliance control must be correctly set by the observer in the *no signal* condition, i.e. with the input of received signals to the cathode suppressed. This is of fundamental importance as the observer detects echoes by noticing the increase in the *no signal* spot brightness caused by the arrival of an echo (see Section 1.2.3.2). The practical procedure for carrying out this extremely important adjustment is set out in Section 6.2.3.1.

There will normally be two or three anodes in the electron gun and considerable variations in design detail are possible. For example, the cylinders may be of different diameters and lengths. Further, both ends of any one cylinder may be open, or one end may be partially closed to form a small hole, coincident with the axis of the tube. However, a satisfactory understanding of the principles involved can be obtained by considering the simple arrangement of two anodes shown in Figure 2.24. The two anodes are maintained, by a power supply, at a potential which is several hundreds of volts positive with respect to the cathode. Having regard to the interactive force which exists between charged particles (unlike charges attract one another while like charges repel), it is evident that the electrons which are free in the space charge around the cathode will experience a vigorous attraction and will be accelerated toward the positively charged surfaces of the anodes (which are fixed). The electrons will reach the vicinity of the anodes travelling at extremely high speed and those which are close to the axis of the tube will be fired through the small hole in the second anode, thus forming a narrow beam projected at the screen. The electrons then come under the influence of the final anode which takes the form of a conductive coating applied to the inside of the cone-shaped portion of the tube. This is maintained at a potential which is several tens of thousands of volts positive with respect to the cathode and accelerates the electrons towards the screen at an extremely high speed.

It might seem that the incidence of a continuous stream of negatively charged particles would result in an accumulation of free electrons on the screen. This does not occur as the surplus free electrons are drawn off by the final anode and returned through the power supply to the cathode. Thus the CRT forms a continuous electrical circuit in the external portion of which the current flows along wires while within the vacuum of the tube the current flow is manifest in the form of the electron beam.

Further consideration of Figure 2.24 shows that, although the beam emerging from the grid is initally convergent, the geometry is such that crossover takes place and the beam is divergent when it enters the anode assembly. The interaction between like-charged particles will further contribute to this divergence. Such a beam would produce a large and poorly defined spot on the screen. As the spot is effectively the pencil point with which the picture is drawn on the face of the tube, it is essential that it is small and well defined (see Sections 1.2.3 and 2.6.2). This requires that the electron beam should converge to a point which is coincident with the screen. In modern systems this is achieved by arranging for the second anode to have a potential which is a little more positive than that of the first anode. This has no transverse effect of electrons flowing along the axis of the tube but those whose paths are off the axis experience a force which acts toward the axis. The magnitude of the force experienced by any given electron increases with its distance from the axis. Thus in addition to its perhaps more obvious function of accelerating the electron stream toward the screen, the anodes of the electron gun fulfil a focusing role analogous to that of an optical lens. The anode arrangement forms an electrostatic lens whose focal length is controlled by the difference in potential between the first and second anodes (see Figure 2.25).

A rigorous treatment of the lens operation is beyond the scope of this work but the reader who wishes to study the topic further is referred to any electrical engineering text which deals with electron optics.

The difference in potential between the two anodes is adjusted by means of the focus control. The stability of most modern focusing systems is such that this control should seldom need adjustment and for this reason it is usually located inside the display unit, on the basis that it will be preset on installation and that any subsequent adjustment will be made by competent service personnel. It must be appreciated that although the control is preset, it is not automatic and if for any reason the focus voltage does deviate from the correct value it will not correct itself. In this condition the beam will converge to a point which lies either inside or outside the tube, producing a spot which is too large and hence a poorly defined picture. It is therefore important that the observer checks that the tube is correctly focused. The appropriate practical procedure for carrying this out is described in Section 6.2.3.2.

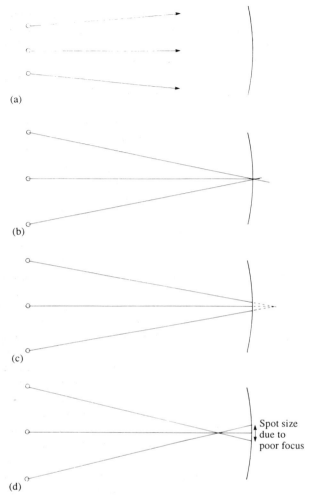

(a)

(b)

(c)

(d)

Spot size
due to
poor focus

Figure 2.25   Focusing the electron beam
(a)   Mutual repulsion produces divergent beam
(b)   Correct focus: beam converges to point on screen
(c)   Incorrect focus: beam converges to point beyond
      screen
(d)   Incorrect focus: beam converges to point inside screen

2.6.1.2   The screen

The function of the screen is to react with the electron beam to produce a small bright spot of light at the point at which the beam strikes it. This is made possible by coating the inside of the glass with a material known as a

phosphor which has the property that when bombarded by electrons it will emit light immediately and for some time thereafter. The instantaneous generation of light by electron bombardment is called fluorescence and for any given phosphor the brightness of the light emitted is a function of the strength of the electron beam. Hence, subject to the limits of saturation of the receiver (see Section 2.5.2.1) and of the phosphor (which will have a maximum light emission capability), stronger targets will produce brighter echoes. With a purely fluorescent coating, light emission will cease immediately the bombardment ceases (as in the case of strip lighting) whereas in the case of a phosphor the light level emitted will decay over a period giving the property known as persistence or afterglow. A wide variety of chemicals are employed in the production of phosphors and the compound selected will depend on the brightness, persistence and colour most suited to the particular application.

In the case of a radial-scan PPI display, the choice of persistence involves some compromise. Long afterglow ensures that strong targets persist for at least one aerial revolution and increases the likelihood of the observer spotting a weak echo. Further, it causes moving targets to leave more obvious afterglow trails. The trails may assist the observer in an early appraisal of encounters with other vessels, but great care must be taken in interpretation (see Section 2.6.7.5 and Chapter 7). However, excessive persistence may produce serious masking when the range scale is changed or where an unstabilized orientation is selected (see Section 1.4.1). Although some radial scan displays for special applications have used a green phosphor, the vast majority of radial-scan civil marine radars employ a phosphor which emits a pale orange glow.

The phosphor has a limited life because continued excitation of the material progressively destroys the sensitivity of the coating. This is described as CRT burn. Evidence of it can be seen on old CRTs, particularly in the area around the origin and where markers such as range rings are regularly displayed. The effect is inevitable but its serious onset can be delayed by intelligent use of the controls (see in particular Sections 6.9.8 paragraph 7 and 6.10.1.1 paragraph 5). The consequence of the loss of sensitivity is that echoes will not brighten the screen in the burned areas and so may go undetected for a period of time. This can be particularly dangerous when a true-motion presentation is selected if the origin is tracking toward the burn at the centre of the screen.

The dynamic range of signals which can be displayed by the phosphor is limted. As a result, if the receiver noise is just visible, the strongest signals will saturate the screen. This problem is analogous to the saturation which takes place in the receiver (see Section 2.5.2.5) but the adjustments required to cope with screen saturation are much less critical than is the case with saturation which takes place at an early stage in the receiver. Provided that the receiver does not saturate, and the signals are not digitized (see Section 2.6.6), the range of input signals to the tube will be continuous but the range of screen brightness levels which can be discerned by an observer is to some extent subjective and authorities differ on its value. It is unlikely to be less than 8 or more than 15. In general, where digital techniques are used this latter continuous range will be lost (see Section 2.6.6.7).

The surface of the phosphor remote from the glass is coated with a very fine metallic (normally aluminium) spray. The spray is sufficiently fine to be transparent to the electron bombardment and forms a conducting surface which assists in the return of free electrons to the final anode surface and hence to the power supply. A proportion of these electrons will have originated at the cathode while others will have been dislodged from the screen by the impact of the beam. The aluminized screen also serves to enhance the brightness of the picture by reflecting the light from the phosphor that would otherwise be lost by radiation to the inside of the tube.

The IMO Performance Standards (see Section 10.2) specify, according to the gross tonnage of the vessel, the minimum effective diameter of the display which must be available. Three diameters are listed, namely 180 mm, 250 mm and 340 mm. These dimensions correspond to cathode ray tubes having overall diameters of 9, 12, and 16 inches respectively (228 mm, 305 mm and 406 mm).

2.6.1.3 The deflection system

The function of the deflection system is to move the spot across the screen in the correct direction and at the correct rate to produce the rotating trace necessary for the build-up of the picture (see Section 1.3.3). Deflection can be carried out by electrostatic or electromagnetic methods, but the latter technique is invariably employed in civil marine radar applications.

Electromagnetic deflection exploits the motor principle whereby a conductor carrying an electric current in a magnetic field experiences a force which acts at right angles both to the direction of current flow and the direction of the magnetic field. A simplfied representative arrangement is illustrated in Figure 2.26.

An explanation of the mechanics of deflection is best commenced by assuming that initially the electron beam, as indicated by the spot, is at the centre of the screen and that the deflection system is not energized. Consider that a voltage is now applied to the scan coil and that accordingly a current flows. This will magnetize the core with the polarity indicated and create the conditions required for the application of the motor principle. In applying the principle it is important to appreciate that, because by convention current flows from positive to negative, the electron beam represents a conventional current flowing from screen to cathode (i.e. in the reverse direction to the electron flow). Thus in Figure 2.26 the current is flowing into the page, the magnetic field lies in the plane of the page and hence the deflection of the spot will be at right angles to both. Should the reader wish to check the validity of the direction of deflection, the application of Fleming's Left-hand Rule will offer the necessary confirmation (an explanation of Fleming's Left-hand Rule should be found in any text dealing with basic electromagnetism).

It is almost self-evident that the extent to which the spot is deflected will depend on the strength of the deflecting magnetic force. Clearly there will be some value, let it be called F_E, which will deflect the spot to the edge of the screen. It will be remembered that, in the case of a real-time display, a single trace is produced by moving the spot from the centre of the screen to the edge of the screen at constant speed in the duration of the timebase appropriate to the selected range scale (see Section 1.2.3). Thus, by the application of a suitable signal to the scan coil, the deflecting force can be made to increase at a uniform rate from zero to F_E in the duration

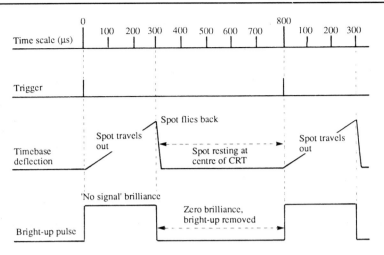

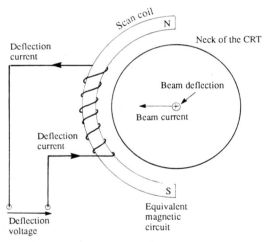

Figure 2.26 Rotating-scan coil deflection: time-sequence diagram for PRF = 1250, range scale 24 n mile

of one timebase. For example, the duration of the rise will be approximately 150 µs when the 12 mile range scale is selected. At the end of the timebase the deflecting force must fall rapidly to zero, allowing the spot to fly back to the centre of the screen. During flyback the spot brilliance will be automatically reduced to zero by the removal of the bright-up signal. The time relationship between the deflecting force, the trigger and the bright-

up signal for the 12 mile range scale, assuming a PRF of 1250, is illustrated by Figure 2.26. The deflection signal is sometimes referred to as a *sawtooth* waveform because of its distinctive shape. The circuitry which develops the waveform of the correct duration and slope for the range scale selected by the observer is called the *timebase generator*.

To build up the picture the trace must rotate in sympathy with the aerial (see Section 1.3.3). In the traditional analogue display this is most commonly achieved by physically rotating the scan coil assembly about the neck of the CRT. The motor which drives the assembly forms part of a proportional error servo system whose mode of operation is described under 'Aerial principles' in Section 2.4.5. Such an electromechanical system will still be found in a very large number of civil marine radars at sea today, although since the mid-1970s there has been a progressive shift toward the use of digital techniques and fixed-scan coils (see Section 2.6.6.4).

In order that the picture will be correctly orientated the scan coil assembly must be aligned such that at the instant the heading marker contacts make, the direction of deflection, and hence the displayed heading marker, accurately intersect the correct graduation on the fixed-bearing scale around the outside of the screen. In older systems a manual control was provided to allow the observer to rotate the picture to the correct orientation. In more modern systems, auto-alignment is offered directly by the orientation/presentation selector.

For convenience of explanation it was assumed that, in the absence of the deflection signal, the electron beam would settle along the axis of the tube and hence produce a spot coincident with the centre of the screen. For a variety of reasons it cannot be guaranteed that in practice there will be absolutely zero magnetic field influencing the neck of the tube and hence the spot may settle close to but not exactly at the centre of the screen. The IMO Performance Standards (see Section 10.2) require that, after installation and adjustment on board, the specified bearing accuracy must be maintained without further adjustment irrespective of the movement of the vessel in the Earth's magnetic field. Special screening is sometimes used to isolate the scan coils from ambient magnetic fields. In many circumstances it is of particular importance that the observer should be able to locate the origin of the picture exactly at the centre of the screen (see Section 6.2.3.3). To this end, two fixed coils, set at right angles to one another, are also fitted around the neck of the tube in such a way that one coil allows horizontal adjustment of origin location while the other allows vertical adjustment. The observer is able to locate the origin in the centre of the screen by adjusting two corresponding display controls which are referred to as

shift controls or centring controls. Normally the controls will only allow a small amount of movement but in some displays it may be possible to offset the origin by as much as 75% of the radius. Where this facility exists the controls are more correctly called off-centring controls and are normally, but not necessarily, associated with a true-motion presentation. This aspect of off-centring is discussed further in Section 2.6.4. The correct practical procedure for checking and adjusting the centring controls is set out in Section 6.2.3.3.

2.6.2 Real-time picture generation

The method of picture generation described in this section is representative of the technique used in the development of the earliest civil marine PPI radars and which, in principle, remained unchanged until the 1970s. The term real-time display is used to describe the fact that each radial line of the picture is written during the time taken by each radar pulse to travel the two-way journey to the maximum range of the scale in use. Modern displays employ digital computer techniques to store, process and then reproduce the radar data. The latter development was introduced in Section 1.2.5 and will be considered in detail in Sections 2.6.6 and 2.6.7. Despite the advent of digital techniques, there are vast numbers of real-time displays at sea today and they are likely to be with us for many years to come. The traditional display is sometimes also referred to as an analogue display, or alternatively it is said to produce analogue video by which is meant the strength of the displayed echoes is analogous to the strength of the echoes received. More fully, this means that the displayed echoes may lie anywhere in a continuous range between noise level and saturation and that, within these limits, linear amplification will produce display echoes whose brightness is proportional to the strength of the received signals that produced them.

The picture which appears on the screen of the CRT is generated by the combination of a number of signals in a carefully time-related sequence; an outline treatment of this was presented in Section 2.2.4. It is necessary at this stage to recapitulate and consider the relationship between these signals in more detail. Some of these signals originate in the transmitter, receiver and aerial units (see Sections 2.3, 2.4 and 2.5, respectively), while others are generated within the display. An understanding of the relationship between the signals which generate the picture in a real-time display will be assisted by a study of Figures 2.27 and 2.28. Figure 2.27 shows the distribution of the signals within the display. However, it is equally important to appreciate the time relationship which exists between the signals (Figure 2.28).

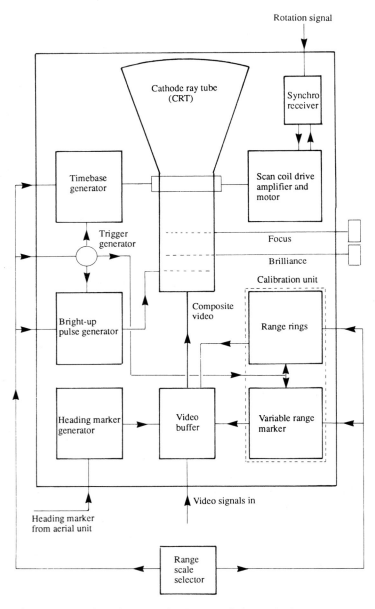

Figure 2.27   Block diagram of real-time radial-scan display

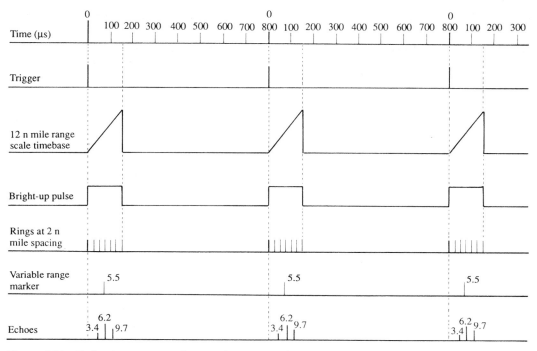

Figure 2.28 Radar time-sequence diagram for PRF = 1250, range scale 12 n mile, range ring interval 2 n mile, VRM set to 5.5 n mile

It should be remembered that there are four signal inputs to the display, namely rotation, trigger, heading marker and video, which are illustrated in Figure 2.27. The rotation system has been fully described in Sections 2.4.5 and 2.6.1.3.

The trigger originates in the transmitter (see Section 2.3). It may be considered to signify the *time zero* of the radar timing sequence and provides the synchronizing link between transmitter and display. It should be noticed that it initiates both the time base and bright-up signals. This ensures that the spot leaves the origin at the instant of transmission and is visible from that instant. Both timebase and bright-up units are capable of producing waveforms of a duration appropriate to each of the display range scales. At any given instant the value available will be determined by the position of the range scale selector. This ensures that the spot draws each trace in the correct time and that it is only visible on its outward journey.

The trigger is also applied to the calibration unit. From the explanation of the calibration of the timebase presented in Section 1.2.4 it is evident that the time period for both the fixed marks and the variable mark must be initiated at the instant of transmission. The interval between successive calibration marks is a function of the range scale selected and thus the calibration oscillator must be able to offer the correct frequency of oscillation for each range scale. In older systems this was achieved by employing a separate oscillator for each range scale. A more modern approach is to use a single oscillator whose frequency, usually known as the clock frequency, is that required for the shortest range scale. If the second shortest range scale is twice the range of the shortest, then the correct calibration interval is easily derived by using every second pulse of the clock frequency. Provided that successive range scales increase by the constant factor of two, which is normally the case, the correct calibration interval for each range scale can be obtained by using each alternate calibration mark from the next lower range scale. The precision with which the observer may measure range is dependent on the accuracy with which the calibration marks are generated (see Section 6.9).

The term 'video' has been used above to describe the echo signal which has been processed in the various stages of the receiver as described in Section 2.5. It is this signal which, when applied to the cathode of the tube, will produce an increase in spot brightness for each detected echo. However, it has to be combined with other signals which also produce an increase in spot brightness. These comprise the heading marker signal which is generated in the aerial unit (see Section 2.4.6) and the calibration signals which are generated within the display. The raw heading marker signal from the aerial will normally pass through some preliminary circuitry in the display before being mixed with the other signals. The combination takes place in a unit known as a video buffer (or mixer) and it can be thought of as a device which allows each of the signals access to the output path leading to the cathode but will prevent any one input signal entering the circuit of any of the others.

The combined signal will be referred to as the *composite video* and it takes the form of a sequence of negative-going pulses, each of which will produce a brightening of the spot. As the received echoes are boosted through the several stages of the video amplifier (see Section 2.5.3.2), the polarity of the pulses may change from positive to negative in alternate stages. A similar situation may arise during the development of other waveforms such as trigger, calibration marks and bright-up. For time-sequence considerations polarity is not important and thus for ease of illustration Figure 2.28 uses positive polarity, i.e. signal strength increases toward the top of the page. This convention will be preserved throughout this text in all illustrations related to echo strength, and hence amplitude is indicative of brightness.

2.6.3 Compass (or azimuth) stabilization

The IMO Performance Standards (see Section 10.2) require that means be provided to enable the display to

be stabilized in azimuth and states that the accuracy of alignment with the compass transmission should be within 0.5° with a compass rotation rate of 2 rpm.

The time-related combination of signals described by Section 2.6.2 will produce a picture which is inherently unstabilized. This will be adequate for use with the ship's-head-up orientation only (see Section 1.4.1). In Section 2.6.1.3 it was indicated that, on installation, the scan coils would normally be aligned in such a way that at the instant when the axis of the main beam crosses the fore-and-aft line, the spot will be deflected along that radial which lies over the 000° graduation on the fixed-bearing scale. Provided that the heading marker contacts have been correctly set (see Section 6.9.9), such an alignment will ensure that the heading marker appears in the ship's-head-up position.

If a true-north-up (stabilized) orientation (see Section 1.4.2) is required, an additional signal will be necessary to provide compass stabilization. When switched in, this signal will re-align the scan coils, and subsequently maintain them in the correct angular relationship with the aerial direction so that at the instant when the heading marker contacts make, the spot will be tracing out that radial which respresents, on the fixed-bearing scale, the vessel's instantaneous true heading. As a consequence, at the instant the axis of the main beam sweeps through true north, the spot will draw the trace which passes through the 000° graduation on the same scale. In some older systems, known as manually aligned systems, the observer was required to carry out the initial alignment and thereafter the stabilization signal maintained the correct angular relationship. Most modern systems offer auto-alignment.

To generate the course-up (stabilized) orientation (see Section 1.4.3), a compass stabilization signal is also necessary. However, in this case the initial alignment of the scan coils with respect to the aerial direction is such that at the instant when the axis of the main beam sweeps through the direction of the ship's true course, the spot is tracing out the radial which passes through the 000° graduation on the scale. If, but only if, the vessel is right on her course, the heading marker will also pass through that graduation.

In seeking an understanding of the methods by which compass stabilization is achieved it is helpful first to con-

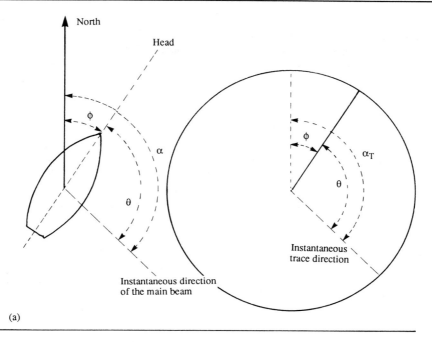

(a)

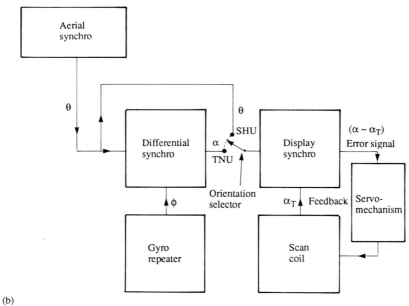

(b)

Figure 2.29 Compass stabilization
(a) Angular quantities
(b) Block diagram

sider the three angular quantities which are involved. These are illustrated in Figure 2.29(a) which is drawn with particular reference to the true-north-up orientation.

The *aerial bearing* (α), by which is meant the angle of the axis of the main beam, measured clockwise from true north, is indicated on the display by the angular position of the trace as read from the fixed bearing scale. In Figure 2.29(a) it can be seen that, at any instant, the angular position of the trace with respect to the 000° graduation is the sum of two constituent angles. One of these is the *aerial angle* θ through which the axis of the main beam has rotated since the last heading marker. This angle is continuously updated by the aerial/trace servo system (see Sections 2.4.5 and 2.6.1.3). The second angle is the instantaneous value of the ship's heading ϕ and it is this angle which must be supplied when a stabilized orientation is selected and which must be updated with every subsequent change in the vessel's heading.

The process of stabilization is illustrated in block diagram form by Figure 2.29(b). It should be noticed that the figure is similar to Figure 2.13 with the addition of the differential synchro and the compass input. The differential synchro may be considered to be a device which adds the ship's heading to the aerial angle and hence produces an input of aerial bearing (instead of aerial angle) to the scan coil servo mechanism. Applying the principles described in Section 2.4.5.1, the servo system will drive the trace in such a way that its radial direction on the fixed bearing scale maintains alignment with the instantaneous true direction of the axis of the main beam.

The differential synchro has a stator winding similar to that of a synchro receiver. In Section 2.4.5.1 it was explained that such a set of windings would produce a unique signal for any given aerial direction and it is in this form that the aerial angle forms the input to the differential unit. The output stage of the differential synchro is a similar set of windings which can be rotated through 360° with respect to the stator. The output angle differs from the input by an amount equal to the misalignment between the fixed and the free sets of windings. The reader who seeks a more technical description of a differential synchro is referred to any good control engineering text.

The stabilizing signal is almost invariably derived from a gyro compass by way of a repeater motor. The motor may be one of several different varieties, common among which is the step-by-step type which produces a step angular change of shaft position for a fixed fraction (usually $\frac{1}{6}$) of each degree of heading change detected by the master gyro. Through an appropriate ratio gear train the output shaft of the step motor drives the shaft on which is mounted the moving coil assembly of the differential synchro. For a full treatment of the operation of gyro repeater systems the reader is referred to any good text on the gyro compass.

In many older radar systems the two angles were added mechanically by means of a differential gearbox. The electromechanical system described in this section is representative of the method used in a very large number of radar systems at sea today though there is a growing tendency for part or all of the process to be carried out using microprocessor techniques. This is discussed further under the heading of synthetic displays in Sections 2.6.6 and 2.6.7.

The description of the stabilization process has been presented in terms of a true-north-up orientation but the example of course-up orientation could equally well have been chosen.

2.6.4 The provision of true-motion facilities

To generate a true-motion picture it is necessary to arrange for the origin of the display to move across the screen in a direction and at a rate that corresponds with the motion of the observing vessel through the water or over the ground (see Section 1.5.2). This is achieved by energizing two sets of off-centring coils wound on a yoke around the neck of the CRT. The operation of the coils is based on the same electromagnetic principle as that of the shift coils described in Section 2.6.1.3 and the true-motion off-centring may well be produced by the same coils. However, whereas the shift controls normally permit only a small amount of movement to allow the correct setting-up of a centred display, the true-motion off-centring controls (referred to as reset controls) allow the origin to be located anywhere within a playing area which typically extends to some 60–75%

of the radius from the centre of the screen. Initially the observer will use the reset controls to locate the origin so as to make the best possible use of the screen area (see Section 6.8.2). Thereafter a unit, usually referred to as the true-motion computer, takes over control of the off-centring coils and continuously updates the screen location of the origin in accordance with input values of direction and speed. As the origin tracks across the screen, sooner or later it will be necessary to reset the origin as the view ahead becomes limited. The observer may at any time temporarily override the computer by using the reset controls. On release of the latter the computer will resume control and the origin will commence tracking from the new location.

2.6.4.1 *The analogue true-motion computer*

The function of the true-motion computer is to resolve the direction and rate of the observing vessel's true motion into N/S and E/W components and to use these two components to energize the off-centring coils. In the original true-motion units developed in the late 1950s the resolution was carried out solely by mechanical methods using specialized gearboxes. These were in due course superseded by techniques which were electromechanical rather than purely mechanical. The arrangement illustrated by Figure 2.30 is suitably representative of the majority of analogue systems at sea today. It is important to appreciate that the electromechanical arrangements constitute an analogue computer and should not be confused with the microprocessor techniques which are becoming progressively more common and are associated with synthetic displays (see Sections 2.6.6 and 2.6.7).

The central unit of the true-motion computer is a device known as a resolver. This may be considered to be an electromechanical *traverse table* which converts direction and distance into d.lat. and departure. (Readers who are concerned to understand the technical details of resolvers are advised to consult a good control engineer-

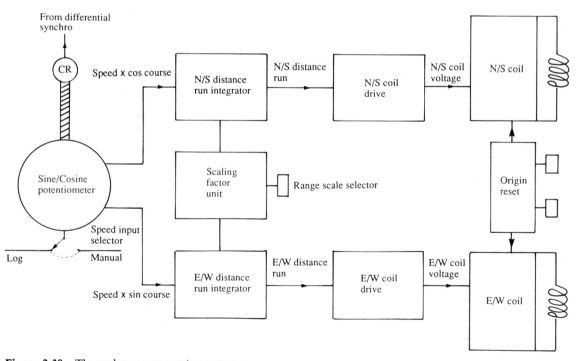

Figure 2.30 The analogue true-motion computer

ing text under the references of ball resolvers and sin/cos potentiometers). For sea-stabilization (see Section 1.5.2.1) the inputs to the resolver are the observing vessel's course and speed and the outputs are the signals which must control the N/S and E/W movements of the origin. Where ground-stabilization (see Section 1.5.2.2) is required, additional inputs relating to the tide will be required and these will be discussed separately in Section 2.6.4.4.

There are two outputs from the resolver, one of which is proportional to (ship's speed × cosine heading) while the other is proportional to (ship's speed × sine heading) and these are fed to two parallel channels. In each channel is connected a unit known as a *distance-run integrator* (see Figure 2.30). The integrator is a device which samples the instantaneous resolved speed at short regular intervals and hence develops an output signal which changes progressively with distance run. If the heading is in the first quadrant, the ouput from both integrators will increase with distance run. If it lies in any other quadrant at least one of the outputs will decrease. The signal from each integrator is processed by an amplifier and used to control the current in the shift coil to which it is connected and hence the electromagnetic deflecting force generated by that coil. Thus the location of the origin, which represents the rest position of the electron beam (see Section 2.6.1.3), is determined by the resultant of the mutually perpendicular forces exerted by the shift coils and its movement will be controlled by the progressive changes in these forces.

For any given input speed, the origin must track across the screen at a scale speed which is consistent with the range scale selected by the observer. It is for this reason that a scaling factor signal, controlled by the range selector, is fed to the integrator (see Figure 2.30). True-motion facilities are not normally available on the very long or the very short range scales, because in the former case target movements would be so slow as to be barely perceptible, while in the latter case the disruption of tracking caused by the need to reset would arise too frequently to be acceptable.

The IMO Performance Standards (see Section 10.2) do not require the fitting of true-motion. However, where it is fitted, they specify that the accuracy and discrimination should be at least equal to that which is otherwise required. A further requirement is that the motion of the origin of the trace should not, except under manual override conditions, continue to a point beyond 75% of the radius of the display. The standards allow the fitting of automatic resetting facilities. Within the limits of the standards, the exact nature of the manual and automatic resetting arrangements made available by different manufacturers vary considerably.

A consequence of the provision of any off-centred presentation is that it requires the display of some targets at ranges in excess of the nominal selected range scale. For example, on the 12-mile range scale with 70% off-centring, the view in one direction will be 1.7×12 miles, i.e. 20.4 miles. Thus where true-motion facilities are provided, it is necessary for the timebase to be greater than that which would be required on a centred display for the same range scale. The practical procedures for setting up and maintaining a true-motion presentation, including the use of various reset facilities, are described in Section 6.8.

The preceding description has been presented in terms of a true-north-up orientation. A course-up orientation is also possible but in that case the vessel's speed is resolved into components which are parallel and perpendicular to the reference course (see Section 1.4.3).

2.6.4.2   *The compass input*

The compass input is almost invariably derived from a gyro repeater motor which, through appropriate gearing, drives the input shaft of the resolver. The repeater will commonly be the same one as is used to provide compass stabilization (see Section 2.6.3).

2.6.4.3   *The speed input*

The speed input may be derived from a log or it may be fed in manually by the observer. Most true-motion computers are designed to operate with a log which generates a train of constant amplitude voltage pulses, the repetition rate of which is proportional to the indicated speed.

There are a variety of ways in which the pulse train can be used to produce an analogue of the speed. One method is to use a device known as a smoothing circuit.

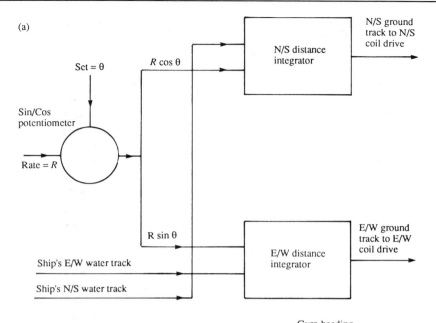

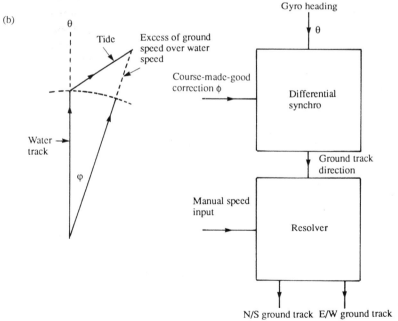

Figure 2.31 Tidal inputs for ground stabilization
(a)   Direct tidal input: set θ, rate R
(b)   Indirect tidal input: course-made-good correction ϕ,
      manual ground speed

This accepts a fluctuating input signal and from it produces an output signal whose amplitude is the average value of the input. Since all the log pulses have the same amplitude, the average amplitude will be directly proportional to the frequency at which the pulses are repeated. Thus for any given log speed, the output signal will be a steady voltage whose value is proportional to that speed. This signal can be conditioned if necessary and used as the speed input to the resolver.

An alternative approach is to use an electronic counting circuit which will produce a fixed step of scale distance run for each pulse received from the log. This will give distance travelled which may be used directly or may be differentiated with respect to time to give speed.

Where a manual speed input is used, the observer normally selects the required value by adjusting a control which operates a numerical scale and a unit known as the *artificial log*, both of which are driven by the same shaft. The circuitry of this unit either mimics a log by generating a pulse train at a repetition rate consistent with the speed selected by the observer or may generate an analogue speed voltage directly.

2.6.4.4   Tide inputs

To generate a ground-stabilized presentation, additional inputs representing the effect of the tide will be necessary. While the precise form which the input controls take varies with manufacturer, in principle they all fall into one of two categories according to whether the set and rate are fed in directly or indirectly.

In systems using direct input, the observer feeds the tidal information in terms of set and rate. The set control drives the shaft input of a second resolver, the tide resolver, while the rate control adjusts a manual rate input to the same resolver. The resolver produces two output components which represent the N/S and E/W components of the tide. The operation is exactly analogous to the resolution of the observing vessel's course and speed as described in Section 2.6.4.1. Hence the N/S motion of the ship through the water and the N/S motion of the water over the ground can be summed at the input to the N/S integrator so as to produce an output which is an analogue of the N/S component of the vessel's ground track. A similar addition will be performed in the E/W channel as illustrated by Figure 2.31(a).

The alternative approach adopted in other systems is to feed the tidal data in indirectly by means of a course-made-good correction and a speed-made-good correction. This is illustrated in Figure 2.31(b).

The course-made-good correction is defined as the angle between the course through the water and the direction of the ground track measured in degrees to port or starboard from the course through the water. The correction is made by a control which jointly operates an angular scale and, through appropriate gearing, a shaft which forms one of two inputs to a differential gearbox. The other input is the shaft driven by the compass repeater (see Section 2.6.4.2) while the output shaft of the gearbox drives the resolver of the true-motion computer. Variations in the position of the course-made-good correction control will slew the resolution angle to one side or the other of that indicated by the gyro repeater and hence cause the origin to track crabwise across the screen at an angle to the direction indicated by the heading marker.

The speed-made-good correction is the difference between the speed through the water and the speed over the ground. A separate control is not normally provided, and so the adjustment is made indirectly by selecting manual speed input and setting the manual speed control to the ground speed rather than the water speed.

From the observer's point of view, advantages and disadvantages can be claimed for both approaches and the practical implications of this will be discussed in Section 6.8.3 paragraph 5. In general it should be remembered that any type of ground stabilization generates a picture which is not suited to the normal use of radar for collision avoidance and may seriously mislead the untrained or unwary observer.

2.6.5   Echo paint

'Echo paint' is a term used to describe the size and shape of an echo as it appears on the screen. Except in the case of extremely large or very close targets, the echo paint is almost if not totally dependent on certain characteristics of the radar system and virtually independent of the size and shape of the target. This is an extremely important limitation of civil marine radar and is best explained by considering the echo of a point target. The latter is a theoretical concept which supposes a target that has the ability to reflect radar energy but which has no dimensions. Clearly this cannot be realized in practice, but in due course it will be seen that, because of the dominant effect of the radar characteristics, many practical targets behave in a manner closely resembling that of a point target. Figure 2.32 shows a situation in which a radar

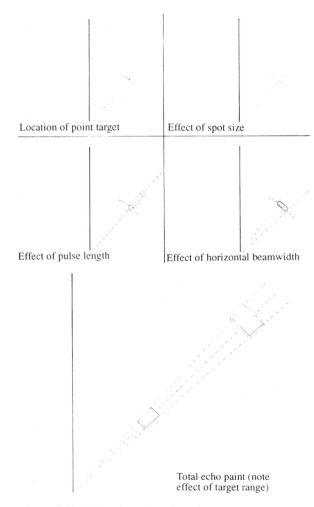

Location of point target

Effect of spot size

Effect of pulse length

Effect of horizontal beamwidth

Total echo paint (note effect of target range)

Figure 2.32   The echo paint of a point target

beam sweeps across two point targets and illustrates how the echo paint is built up.

The characteristics of the radar system which affect the size and shape of the displayed echo are spot size (CRT), pulse length (transmitter) and horizontal beamwidth (aerial unit). Each of these will be discussed in turn.

2.6.5.1   The effect of spot size

The spot produced on the screen of the CRT may be regarded as the *pencil point* with which the radar picture is drawn. While the spot can be focused to a fine point, the mutual repulsion of electrons within the beam (see Section 2.6.1) sets a lower limit to the spot diameter which can be achieved in practice. In civil marine radar applications this minimum is in the region of 0.5 mm (values between 0.3 and 0.6 mm are not uncommon) and represents the smallest mark that can be made on the screen. The distance represented by the spot diameter will vary inversely with screen diameter and will decrease when the shorter range scales are selected. This is illustrated by the following numerical example:

Example 2.4   A certain vessel has two radar displays, having screen diameters of 340 and 250 mm respectively. In both cases the spot diameter is 0.5 mm. Calculate the range represented by one spot diameter on the 12 mile and 1.5 mile range scales.

On the 340 mm screen
The number of spot diameters per screen radius is given by

$$N_{340} = \frac{170}{0.5} = \underline{340}$$

When the 12 mile range scale is selected, the range represented by one spot diameter is given by

$$R_S = \frac{\text{range scale in metres}}{\text{spot diameters per radius}}$$

$$= \frac{12 \times 1852}{340}$$

$$= \underline{65.36 \text{ metres}}$$

In the case of the 1.5 mile scale,

$$R_S = \frac{1.5 \times 1852}{340}$$

$$= 8.17 \text{ metres}$$

On the 250 mm screen
The number of spot diameters per screen radius is given by

$$n_{240} = \frac{125}{0.5} = 250$$

When the 12 mile range scale is selected, the range represented by one spot diameter is given by

$$R_s = \frac{12 \times 1852}{250}$$

$$= 88.9 \text{ metres}$$

In the case of the 1.5 mile scale,

$$R_S = \frac{1.5 \times 1852}{250}$$

$$= 11.11 \text{ metres}$$

It is important that the observer checks that the spot is correctly focused (see Section 6.2.3.2) otherwise the picture will suffer from loss of definition.

2.6.5.2   *The effect of pulse length*

A detected echo produces a brightening of the spot and the length of time for which this brightening occurs will depend on the duration of the received echo and hence on the pulse length. Thus each pulse which strikes a point target and is successfully detected will produce a paint on the screen which is one spot diameter wide and which has a radial extent related to pulse length. Consideration of the timebase principle (see Section 1.2.3) indicates that this radial extent is equivalent to half a pulse length. The appearance of the factor of one half may be puzzling at first sight but it can easily be justified

by a simple numerical example. Let a radar be switched to the 12 mile range scale. This means that in the time a radar pulse travels 24 miles (i.e. 12 miles out and 12 miles back), the spot traces out a screen distance which represents 12 miles. Let a pulse length of 1 μs be selected. In the interval during which a single pulse is being received, radar waves will travel 300 metres (see Section 1.2.2) but the spot will trace out a screen distance of 150 metres. Thus, in terms of distance, the radial extent of the echo paint of a point target is half the pulse length (see Figure 2.32).

2.6.5.3   *The effect of horizontal beamwidth*

The IMO Performance Standards (see Section 10.2) permit a maximum horizontal beamwidth of 2.5°. As the beam sweeps across the point target, it will be struck at regular intervals (the pulse repetition period) by a number of pulses. Thus the echo paint is built up of a number of the radial elements each of which is one spot diameter wide and of a radial length equivalent to half the pulse length. This is illustrated by Figure 2.32. The angular width of the paint of a point target will depend on the horizontal beamwidth, while the number of radial elements is additionally dependent on the PRF and the aerial rotation rate (see Section 2.4.4). The angular elongation of the echo paint is sometimes referred to as half-beamwidth distortion because it has the effect of extending the paint by half the beamwidth on either side of the nominal echo position. The angle contained between the limits of the main lobe of the horizontal beam is constant (see Section 2.4.2) but the length of the arc which subtends this angle at the aerial increases in proportion to the range at which the arc is measured. Thus the length which this angular distortion produces increases with the range of the target (see Figure 2.32).

2.6.5.4   *Practical considerations*

In the case of a point target, the aggregate of the effects described above is a paint whose size and shape depends on the spot size, pulse length, and horizontal beamwidth of the radar system and also on the range of the target. To appreciate the practical significance of these effects it is helpful to consider the following numerical example:

Example 2.5   A marine radar system has a screen of effective diameter 250 mm and spot size 0.5 mm. The horizontal beamwidth is 2°, the pulse length is 1 μs and the display is switched to the 12 n mile range scale. A point target X is detected at a range of 10 miles. Calculate the radial length and the angular width of the echo paint as it appears on the screen, and hence determine the distances, in nautical miles, which these dimensions represent.

Let D = spot diameter, P = radial effect of pulse length and A = angular elongation due to horizontal beamwidth. Let the total dimensions of the echo paint be given by T_R (radial length) and T_A (angular width).

P = screen distance moved by spot in the duration of one pulse

$$= \frac{\text{screen radius}}{\text{timebase duration}} \times \text{duration of pulse}$$

$$= \frac{125}{148.16} \times 1 \text{ mm}$$

Thus

$$\underline{P = 0.84 \text{ mm}}$$

A = radius of screen at which target lies × HBW in radians

$$= \frac{125 \times 10}{12} \times 2 \times \frac{\pi}{180} \text{ mm}$$

Thus

$$\underline{A = 3.64 \text{ mm}}$$

The radial length of echo paint is given by

$$T_R = \frac{D}{2} + P + \frac{D}{2} = D + P$$

$$= 0.5 + 0.84 \text{ mm} = \underline{1.34 \text{ mm}}$$

The angular length of the echo paint is given by

$$T_A = \frac{D}{2} + A + \frac{D}{2} = D + A$$

$$= 0.5 + 3.64 \text{ mm} = \underline{4.14 \text{ mm}}$$

Thus the echo paint has a radial length of 1.34 mm and an angular width of 4.14 mm

In the example chosen, the radius of the screen (125 mm) represents 12 miles, from which it can be deduced that the natural scale of the PPI is such that 1 mm represents 177.8 m. If this were to be applied to the dimensions of the echo paint this would suggest a target of approximate radial dimension 238 m and approximate angular dimension 736 m. This we know to be absurd. The area which is bounded by these dimensions is referred to as the *resolution cell*. Thus while it is possible to determine the range and bearing of a target with the necessary degree of accuracy by taking the measurement to the centre of the nearer edge of the echo paint (this represents the location of the echoing surface, see Figure 2.32), the size and shape of the paint of all but very large targets bear little or no relationship to the size and shape of the target which produced it. A radar reflector (see Section 3.4) has almost negligible dimensions, but if located at the position of the point target suggested in Example 2.5, would produce an echo paint which covers a screen area equivalent to that of several very large ships. Hence, only when a target has reflecting surfaces which extend beyond the resolution cell does it begin to contribute significantly to the size and shape of the echo.

It is evident that, except at extremely close ranges, a ship will in general produce an echo approaching that of a point target. If the calculation in Example 2.5 is performed for the same radar system, but with the point target located at a range of 2 miles, it will be found that the radial dimension remains unchanged at 1.34 mm (as it is not a function of range) while the angular dimension decreases to 1.23 mm. Thus, if a small target closes from a range of 10 miles to a range of 2 miles, its echo shape will change from one in which the angular width is the greater dimension to one in which the reverse is the case. It is noteworthy that radar characteristics selected in the above examples are representative and do not illustrate the worst possible case. Civil marine radar thus has a very limited ability to display picture detail.

In the use of radar for collision avoidance the principal significance of the above limitation is that the shape of the displayed echo of a ship gives no indication of how the vessel is heading. Heading inference drawn from the shape of the echo is likely to be dangerously misleading. For example, to the unwary or untrained observer, targets toward the edge of the screen may *appear* to be broadside-on (because of the dominance of the angular distortion) whereas targets towards the centre of the screen may *appear* to be head-on. The importance of understanding the specious nature of the impression created by the shape of the echo cannot be overstressed. The techniques for deducing a reliable indication of the heading of other vessels is set out in Chapter 7. The size of the resolution cell also presents limitations when the radar is used for navigation. These will be alluded to briefly in the following two sections and their significance to radar navigation will be discussed in detail in Section 8.2.2.

2.6.5.5 Range discrimination

Range discrimination, which may also be referred to as range resolution, describes the ability of the radar system to display separately the echoes of two targets which lie on the same bearing but which are closely spaced in range. The discrimination is normally expressed in terms of the number of metres by which the targets must be separated in order to prevent their echoes overlapping on the screen. In discussing discrimination it must be assumed that both targets are illuminated by the radar beam. If the more distant target is in a blind area caused by the nearer target, no echo will be displayed, irrespective of the ability of the radar to discriminate. The IMO Performance Standards (see Section 10.2) set out the requirement for range discrimination in terms of two small targets which lie on the same azimuth and which are separated by 50 metres in range. To comply with the standard, the equipment must, on a range scale of 2 miles or less, be capable of displaying the echoes of two such targets as separate indications when the pair lie at a range of between 50% and 100% of range scale in use.

A study of the factors which limit range discrimination is best commenced by considering two targets lying on the same bearing and investigating the conditions which must be satisfied for two separate echoes to arrive at the aerial. Figure 2.33 shows the limiting case and two other cases for comparison purposes.

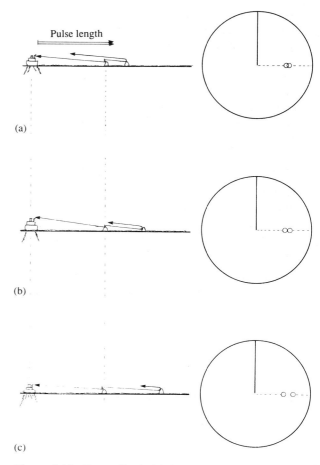

Figure 2.33 Range discrimination
(a) Targets separated by less than $\frac{1}{2}$ pulse length: echoes merge
(b) Targets separated by exactly $\frac{1}{2}$ pulse length: echoes just touch
(c) Targets separated by more than $\frac{1}{2}$ pulse length: echoes display separately

A study of the Figure 2.33 will show that if the targets lie on the same bearing, the leading edge of the second echo will just touch the trailing edge of the first echo when the range separation of the targets is half the length of the transmitted pulse. Thus, in theory, the range discrimination can be calculated by expressing half the pulse length in terms of metres. In practice, the radial paint is further elongated by the effect of spot size. For a given screen size and spot diameter, the influence of the spot size on the dimensions of the resolution cell becomes less significant on the shorter range scales. The influence of pulse length is independent of screen size. In theory it is also independent of range scale but in practice shorter range scales are normally associated with shorter pulse lengths (see Section 2.3.4). The range discrimination is equal to the radial dimension of the resolution cell and this is illustrated by the following numerical example which uses some representative values.

Example 2.6　A radar display has a screen diameter of 250 mm and a spot size of 0.5 mm. On the 12 mile and 1.5 mile range scales the pulse lengths are 1.0 and 0.05 μs respectively. Calculate the range discrimination on each of the given range scales.

On the 12 mile range scale
The range represented by one spot diameter is given by

$$R_S = \frac{\text{range scale in metres}}{\text{spot diameters per radius}}$$

$$= 12 \times \frac{1852}{250} \text{ m} = 88.9 \text{ metres}$$

The range represented by half pulse length is given by

$$R_P = \frac{\text{pulse length in microseconds}}{2} \times 300$$

$$= \frac{1.0}{2} \times 300 \text{ m} = 150 \text{ metres}$$

Range discrimination $= R_S + R_P$

$$= 88.9 + 150 \text{ m} = 238.9 \text{ metres}$$

On the 1.5 mile range scale

$$R_S = 1.5 \times \frac{1852}{250} \text{m}$$

$$= 11.11 \text{ metres}$$

$$R_P = \frac{0.05}{2} \times 300 \text{ m} = 7.5 \text{ metres}$$

Range discrimination $= 11.11 + 7.5 \text{ m} = 18.61 \text{ metres}$

It is interesting to note that on the longer range scale the pulse length effect is dominant, whereas on the shorter range scale the reverse is the case.

Best range discrimination can be obtained by selection of the shortest available pulse length and by ensuring optimum focusing. Care must be taken that the latter is not defeated by excessive brilliance, gain or contrast settings (see Sections 6.2.3.1, 6.2.4.1 and 6.3.4.1). In certain circumstances range discrimination may be improved by the use of the differentiator (rain clutter) control (see Section 3.7.4.4).

2.6.5.6 *Bearing discrimination*

Bearing discrimination, which may also be referred to as bearing resolution, describes the ability of the radar system to display separately the echoes of two targets which lie at the same range but are closely spaced in bearing. The discrimination is normally expressed by the number of metres by which two targets, if they lie at the same range, must be separated in azimuth in order that their echoes will appear separately on the screen. The IMO Performance Standards (see Section 10.2) set out the requirement for bearing discrimination in terms of two small similar targets both situated at the same range between 50% and 100% of the 1.5 or 2 mile range scales. To comply with the standard, the equipment must be capable of displaying the echoes separately when the targets are separated by not more than 2.5° in azimuth.

If two targets lie at the same range and are closely spaced in bearing, a minimum requirement for angular discrimination is that the trailing edge of the rotating beam must leave the first target before the leading edge illuminates the second target. This is illustrated by Figure 2.34.

Figure 2.34 shows the limiting case of discrimination and two other cases for comparison purposes. It follows from the illustration that, in theory, the radar can only discriminate between targets which are separated by at least one horizontal beamwidth. In practice, the angular elongation is further increased by the spot size. Thus bearing discrimination is limited by the angular width of the resolution cell.

It is important to appreciate that the distance repre-

Targets separated by

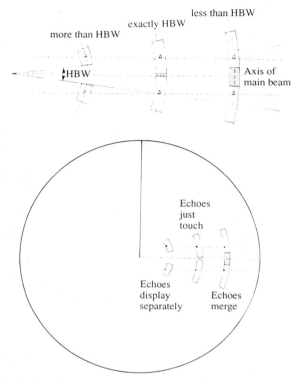

Figure 2.34   Bearing discrimination

sented by the horizontal beamwidth increases in direct proportion to the range at which the discrimination is being considered. The influence of spot size will be less on larger screens and on shorter range scales. Some representative values are illustrated by the following numerical example.

Example 2.7   A radar display has a screen of diameter 250 mm and spot size 0.5 mm. If the horizontal beamwidth is 1.5°, calculate the bearing discrimination at a range of 10 miles when the 12 mile range scale is selected and 1 mile when the 1.5 mile range scale is selected.

At 10 miles
The length of the arc of the horizontal beamwidth at 10 miles is given by

A_B = range × horizontal beamwidth in radians

$$= (10 \times 1852) \times 1.5 \times \frac{\pi}{180} \, \text{m}$$

$$= 10 \times 1852 \times 1.5 \times \frac{22}{7 \times 180} \, \text{m}$$

$$= 485.05 \, \text{metres}$$

The arc represented by one spot diameter is given by

$$A_S = \frac{\text{range scale in metres}}{\text{spot diameters per radius}}$$

$$= 12 \times \frac{1852}{250} \, \text{m} = 88.9 \, \text{metres}$$

Bearing discrimination $= A_B + A_S$

$$= 485.05 + 88.9 \, \text{metres}$$
$$= 573.95 \, \text{metres}$$

At 1 mile

$$A_B = 1 \times 1852 \times 1.5 \times \frac{22}{7 \times 180} \, \text{metres}$$

$$= 48.5 \, \text{metres}$$

$$A_S = 1.5 \times \frac{1852}{250} \, \text{m} = 11.11 \, \text{metres}$$

Bearing discrimination $= A_B + A_S$

$$= 48.5 + 11.11\text{m} = 59.61 \, \text{metres}$$

It is noteworthy that, in general, the major influence is that of the horizontal beamwidth. The latter depends on aerial and transmitter characteristics, which for any single installation lie beyond the direct control of the observer (see Section 2.4.2). The observer may, however, ensure the best available discrimination by checking that the spot is correctly focused (see Section 6.2.3.2). Care must be taken that this is not defeated by excessive brilliance, gain or contrast settings (see Sections 6.2.3.1, 6.2.4.1 and 6.3.4.1). If the use of an off-centred picture will allow the target to be displayed on a shorter range scale, the influence of spot size can be reduced.

A serious shortcoming of the use of civil marine radar for collision avoidance is its inability to offer direct indication of the heading of other vessels. Beamwidth distortion is a major contributor to this shortcoming. It also limits the usefulness of the radar for navigation by merging coastline details, such as bays and lock entrances which lie within one horizontal beamwidth. The significance of this is discussed in Section 8.2.2.

At least one manufacturer is now using digital signal processing techniques in an attempt to offset the effect of the signals received from the angular limits of the beam (see *beam processing* in section 3.9.5.1).

2.6.6   The radial-scan synthetic display

The progressive availability of low cost microprocessor technology, which began in the 1970s and accelerated through the 1980s, has made possible the application of computer techniques to civil marine radar systems. This led to the development of what is known as the synthetic display (see Section 1.2.5), at the heart of which is a digital computer. Real-time analogue signals (see Section 2.6.2) are stored in computer memory prior to being processed and used to generate the picture. Synthetic displays designed for large commercial vessels became available from the late 1970s but until about 1985 invariably used what was essentially a radial scan PPI. To the casual observer it might appear that nothing much had changed. However closer and informed inspection would show that there were major changes in the characteristics of the picture (see Section 2.6.6.7).

From the mid-1980s the development of civil marine radar entered a new phase when raster-scan displays that were capable of compliance with the IMO Performance Standards became available. These employ a CRT of a type similar to that of a television set. Its appearance and character differ so markedly from those of a traditional marine radar display that it is described separately in Section 2.6.7.

In terms of the use of radar for collision avoidance and navigation, the processing delays involved in picture generation are infinitely small and can be neglected. However, the effect of the processing which takes place in that short time cannot be neglected. The storage of

radar signal data in memory makes it possible to sample, manipulate and analyse the data. From this facility a number of benefits accrue. These include the ability to increase the overall brightness of the picture and to apply certain comparison techniques which assist in the suppression of unwanted responses (see Sections 3.6.3.3, 3.6.3.4 and 3.9.5.1). Storage is also the starting-point for the design of systems which offer automatic tracking of targets and the computation of data related to target motion (see Chapter 4). One can speculate that the pursuit of the latter ability more than of any other led to the birth and growth of the synthetic displays in civil marine radar systems. While benefits do accrue from storage, it is important to appreciate that the processing, in changing the character of the picture as compared with that of a real-time analogue display, also introduces limitations. These will be highlighted as the various types and aspects of processing are described. It is particularly important to note that the response of a synthetic picture to the adjustment of certain controls will differ from that of an analogue display (see Sections 6.3 and 6.4).

2.6.6.1   *Digital storage*

Radar signals may be stored digitally so that the information, now referred to as data, may be processed and recovered. The adjective *digital* derives from the fact that the data is stored as a pattern of binary digits. Binary is a system of counting in which there are only two digits, namely '0' and '1'. This contrasts with the decimal system which uses ten digits. In the binary system both (i.e. all) digits can be represented simply by a single electronic switch. In the *off* position it represents binary zero and in the *on* position binary one. It may be helpful to think of each element of memory as a mechanical on/off switch, but it must be appreciated that nothing moves and that the 'switch' is an electronic device which has two possible states. The change of state takes place in a time which for all practical purposes is instantaneous.

The comparison between decimal and binary number systems is illustrated by Figure 2.35. Underlying both systems is the concept of *place value*. This means that the significance of any digit is dependent on the column in which it is written. Thus in decimal, the digit 3 can represent 3, or 30 or 3 times any power of 10. In the

Decimal

The columns in which the four digits (ONE, FOUR, SIX AND ZERO) are written may be labelled in any of the three ways shown.

Thousands	Hundreds	Tens	Units
1000	100	10	1
10^3	10^2	10^1	10^0
ONE	FOUR	SIX	ZERO

The significance of the arrangement is

ONE	×	1000	=	1000
FOUR	×	100	=	400
SIX	×	10	=	60
ZERO	×	1	=	0
TOTAL				1460

Binary

This requires eleven columns which can be labelled in either of the two ways shown. The binary digits can be indicated in any of the three ways shown.

2^{10}	2^9	2^8	2^7	2^6	2^5	2^4	2^3	2^2	2^1	2^0
1024	512	256	128	64	32	16	8	4	2	1
ONE	ZERO	ONE	ONE	ZERO	ONE	ONE	ZERO	ONE	ZERO	ZERO
ON	OFF	ON	ON	OFF	ON	ON	OFF	ON	OFF	OFF
1	0	1	1	0	1	1	0	1	0	0

The significance of the arrangement is:

ONE	×	1024	=	1024
ZERO	×	512	=	0
ONE	×	256	=	256
ONE	×	128	=	128
ZERO	×	64	=	0
ONE	×	32	=	32
ONE	×	16	=	16
ZERO	×	8	=	0
ONE	×	4	=	4
ZERO	×	2	=	0
ZERO	×	1	=	0
TOTAL				1460

Figure 2.35 Decimal and binary representations of the number 1460

binary system the digit 1 can represent 1 or 1 times any power of 2.

To understand digital storage as described in this text, the reader will not require the ability to count in binary. However, it is essential to appreciate that any number can be represented by a bank of switches, some of which are on and some of which are off, and that this is the method employed in the memory units of digital computers. It follows that if radar signals are to be stored in commercially available computer memory they must be represented in this form. The pattern of ones and zeros may represent either a number or some other intelligence such as the prescence or absence of echoes on one particular bearing. In such applications the binary pattern is commonly referred to as a *digital word*.

Each element of memory is known as a *bit* which derives from the contraction of the words 'binary digit'. The elements are usually arranged in groups of eight (or binary multiples of eight) which form a *byte*. Total memory capacity used in a radial-scan display may amount to thousands of bits. This may be described in terms of kilobytes each of which represents 1024 bits (the power of 2 nearest to 1000). In raster-scan displays, memory capacity will involve millions of bits and the unit used is the megabyte which represents 1 048 576 bytes. (This is the power of two which is nearest to one million.) The physical entity which forms a block of memory is referred to as a register or switch register. Where the arrangement of ones and zeros represents a number, the digit on the extreme left is referred to as the most significant bit (MSB) while that at the other extreme is the least significant bit (LSB).

2.6.6.2 Threshold detection

The simple principle underlying the storage of echoes is that the presence of an echo is recorded as a binary 1 while the absence of an echo is represented as a zero. To facilitate this, the analogue signal from the video amplifier (see Sections 2.5.3.2 to 2.5.3.5) must be conditioned to produce a two-level signal representing presence and absence of echoes. This operation is carried out by a device known as a threshold detector and is illustrated by Figure 2.36.

A threshold detector may be considered to be a special

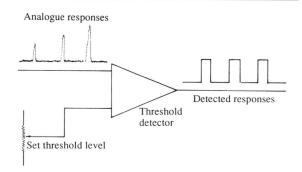

Figure 2.36 Threshold detection

type of amplifier which has two inputs, one of which is known as the signal input while the other is referred to as the threshold level. The output of the threshold detector can have only two values, one of which is high and the other of which is zero. As shown by Figure 2.36, the video signal is applied to the signal input and the threshold input is preset to a chosen value related to the expected level of received signals. The circuitry within the amplifier is configured in such a way that only if the input signal exceeds the threshold level will the high output be produced. Thus the output from the threshold detector represents the presence or absence of echoes and this data can be read into computer memory as described in the next section.

It should be noticed that in the process of threshold detection, the intelligence relating to echo strength has been lost. This is of particular significance to the radar observer. In some older systems this loss was accepted at the design stage but later systems have introduced multi-threshold storage to retain some of the intelligence relating to echo strength. It is appropriate to describe the general principles of echo storage in terms of single threshold detection and subsequently to discuss its limitations together with developments designed to offset them (see Sections 2.6.6.7 and 2.6.7.4).

In a variation of the arrangement shown in Figure 2.36, the gain of the receiver is preset by its logarithmic characteristic (see Section 2.5.2.6) and the observer exercises control by virtue of the fact that the display gain control operates the threshold level. In principle, both approaches are similar in that an increase in the setting of the gain control moves the baseline of the noise and the threshold level toward one another.

It appears that the threshold detector *decides* whether or not an echo is present. However it is important to appreciate that this *decision* is based on the value of the threshold level (which will normally have been preset on installation) and on the setting of the gain control selected by the observer. Ideally one would wish that, as illustrated by Figure 2.36, the combination of these settings would produce an output for all echoes and no output for thermal noise (see Section 2.5.2.3). Clearly this is not possible in practice because the noise amplitude is a rapidly fluctuating value. If no noise crosses the threshold, weak echoes close to noise level may not be detected, whereas if noise signals are allowed to cross the threshold they will produce the same output as an echo. The relationship between gain setting, noise amplitude and threshold level is of crucial importance in the detection of targets on a synthetic display. It is discussed in detail in section 2.6.6.7 and the practical procedure for setting the gain control on a synthetic display is set out in Section 6.3.4.2.

2.6.6.3   Storage of range

The concept of range storage was introduced in Section 1.2.5 but now must be examined in more detail. The method used is best understood by studying the storage of the echoes on a single trace and subsequently considering the whole family of radial lines which make up the picture. The video signal is stored by sampling the output from the threshold detector several million times per second and writing (i.e. storing) the result of each sample in individual elements of a type of switch register known as a random access memory (RAM). The device is so called because, under the control of the computer, data can be written into and read (i.e. recalled) from the memory. This distinguishes it from a read only memory (ROM) from which data can be recalled but into which data cannot be written. The latter type of memory is used for storing the programmes necessary for computer control.

The output from the threshold detector is sometimes referred to as a *logic* waveform. This is because it is in a form (i.e. two states only – high or low) which is com-

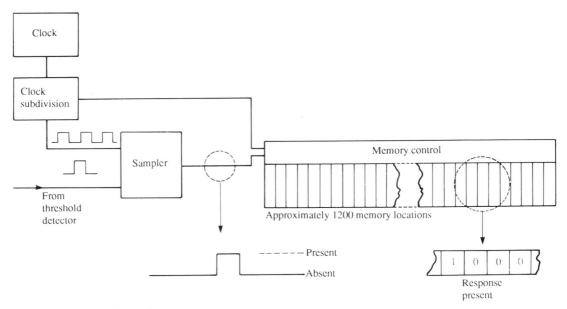

Figure 2.37   Video sampling and storage

patible with a very large family of two-state electronic devices, known as logic elements, which can automatically perform a wide range of logical functions of which sampling and comparison are but two examples. The principle of video sampling is illustrated in Figure 2.37.

The logic element in Figure 2.37 is an *AND* gate, which is a two-state device whose characteristic is such that its output will always be low (corresponding to binary zero) unless both of its two inputs are high. The logic waveform from the threshold detector forms one input while the other derives from an electronic clock. The latter provides a train of extremely short pulses at a very high and constant rate which commence at the instant of transmission. Reference to Figure 2.37 will show that the sampling gate will only produce a high output (corresponding to a binary one) if a radar echo is present at the same instant as a clock pulse. Hence the output of the sampling process indicates the presence or absence of an echo at extremely short, regular times intervals. The result of each sample is written into one of a very large number of separate memory locations or cells which are contained within the RAM. It is important to appreciate that the writing of the data must be done in real time, e.g. the data for one line of the 12 mile range scale must be written in $148.16\,\mu s$, the duration of the 12 mile timebase (see Example 1.1(b) in Section 1.2.2).

The writing process is supervised by the computer memory control which, through complex logic circuitry, ensures that the data is read in sequentially with range. A binary one is set if the sample indicates the presence of a target, otherwise a zero is written. Thus the range of any detected target is implicit in the number of the cell in which it is recorded. For example if 1200 cells represent the 12 mile time base, a target at 6 miles would register a binary one in cell number 600. The number of memory elements allocated to represent one radius depends on the sampling rate and will vary with manufacturer but is generally in the region of 1000 to 1200. It must be appreciated that larger targets may register in several consecutive range cells.

Commercially available RAMs are produced in blocks which are configured in such a way that the total number of memory locations is a power of two, for example 1024 (1 kilobit). Typically, two blocks of 1 kilobit might be used in series to represent one trace. To allow for the generation of a true motion picture, provision for about 70% off-centring will usually be made. Thus 2×1024, i.e. 2048 bits will represent 170% of the tube radius. The number of bits per radius is given by $2048 \times 100/170 = 1204$, i.e. approximately 1200.

If the interval between clock pulses is too large, echoes may escape detection or inadequate range accuracy and discrimination may result. The sampling rate, and hence the clock frequency must be sufficiently high to avoid any of these eventualities. This is best illustrated by a numerical example.

Example 2.8 A marine radar system uses its shortest pulse length of $0.05\,\mu s$ on the 1.5 mile range scale. Calculate a suitable sampling rate and quantify its effect on range accuracy and discrimination.

(a) *Pulse length consideration*
In order that no returning echo will be missed, sampling must occur at least once per pulse length.

Least sampling rate (LSR) = 1/pulse length

$$= 1/0.05 \times 10^{-6}$$

$$= \underline{20\,\text{MHz}}$$

Thus to sample once per pulse, LSR = 20 MHz. This is illustrated by Figure 2.38 in which consideration of pulse A will show that, regardless of its phase relationship with the clock pulses, it cannot escape sampling.

(b) *Range accuracy consideration*
If one memory location is allocated to each sample, then the number of locations N is given by

$$N = \frac{\text{timebase}}{\text{interval between samples}}$$

$$= \frac{1.5 \times 1852}{150} \times \text{LSR}$$

$$= 18.52 \times 10^{-6} \times 20 \times 10^{6} = 371$$

The range interval (I) represented by each memory location is given by

$$I = \frac{1.5 \times 1852}{371} = 7.5 \text{ metres}$$

It follows that the stored range of any given target will be an integer multiple of 7.5 m. Reference to echo B in

Figure 2.38 shows that a target at a range of almost 48.75 m will have a stored range of 45 m. This represents the maximum error which is half the sample range interval and is within the 70 m accuracy specified by the IMO Performance Standard (see Section 10.2) for this range scale. It follows that if the target is moving with respect to the observing vessel its range will appear to change in steps. This is called *range quantizing error* and is

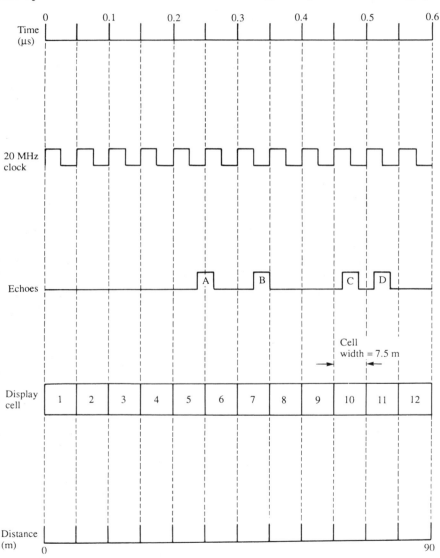

Figure 2.38 Sample rate considerations

of particular significance in automatic tracking (see Section 9.5.3.2).

(c) *Range discrimination consideration*

Reference to echoes C and D in Figure 2.38 will show that the targets producing them are 7.5 m apart (half pulse length) and thus are at the limit of range discrimination. Their stored echoes will just touch because they are in adjacent cells. It should, however, be noted that they will continue to be in adjacent cells until their separation is increased by a further half the sample range interval. The separation is well within the 50 m required by the IMO Performance Standard (see Section 2.6.5.5 and 10.2).

It is evident from the above calculations that a sampling rate of 20 MHz would be adequate to produce one sample per pulse and that the quantizing effect would be a fraction of the ranging error permitted by the IMO Performance Standards (it can be deduced that approximately 371 memory locations per radius would meet the standard.) However, in practice, to produce high resolution storage so that automatic tracking can be offered (see Section 9.5.3.2), many radar designers use clock frequencies which are effectively between two and three times higher (i.e. approximately 40–60 MHz) than that suggested in Example 2.8 and consequently allocate a correspondingly larger number of cells to each radius (of the order of 1000–1200). In practice the clock will run at a fixed frequency (the master or basic frequency) equal to that required for the shortest range scale/pulse length. When longer range scales/pulse lengths are selected, submultiples of the master frequency will be obtained by the use of successive *divide by two* devices. These are logic devices which produce an output pulse for every alternate input pulse received. Physical constraints normally limit the master clock frequency to the order of 32 MHz, though it is possible, by using two memory banks in parallel and a technique known as multiplexing, to produce an effective sampling rate of twice that frequency. It should be appreciated that if a higher sampling rate is used a point target will be written sequentially in more than one memory location.

Thus far, this section has described the real-time storage of the data on a single trace. The pattern of ones and zeros so obtained is referred to as a *range word*. Clearly, by repeating the procedure the entire picture can be stored by generating a range word for each of the radial lines which make up the picture. This is illustrated by the left-hand side of Figure 2.39. In generating a radial-scan synthetic picture on the screen (see Section 2.6.6.5), each range word is read out of memory almost immediately after it has been read in. Thus a single block of memory having a capacity of one range word can be used to store each line in turn, obviating the need to have a separate block for each individual line. However, where a raster-scan picture is to be produced (see Section 2.6.7), the entire picture must be held in store in the form of the matrix illustrated by Figure 2.39.

2.6.6.4   *Storage of bearing*

This is achieved by converting the analogue signal which represents aerial bearing (see Sections 2.4.5 and 2.6.3) into a digital signal which is called a *bearing word*. The mechanics of the conversion from analogue to digital vary with manufacturer but all systems use the principle that aerial bearing is an angle which increases progressively from 0° to 360° (relative) as the scanner rotates and can thus be represented by a binary number which increases from zero to some maximum at the same rate and in the same time. Most civil marine systems designed for large vessels use a 12-bit word. A pattern of 12 binary ones represents the decimal number 4095 ($2^{12} + 2^{11} + \ldots + 2^0$). If the zero condition is taken into account, there are 4096 binary increments between zero and maximum and hence the 12-bit word can be used to represent 4096 unique angles between 0° and 360°. This means that the angle can be stored in steps of 360°/4096, i.e. just under $\frac{1}{10}$ of a degree. Thus the appropriate incremental bearing word can be read into memory alongside the corresponding range word in the memory matrix as illustrated in Figure 2.39.

A study of the matrix reveals that the range and bearing of any target is defined by the column and row in which its digital sample appears. The range of any target is specified by the product of its consecutive range cell number and the range cell interval (see Section 2.6.6.3). Similarly, the bearing is specified by the number of incremental steps which have occurred since binary zero. If a ship's-head-up orientation is selected, the aerial

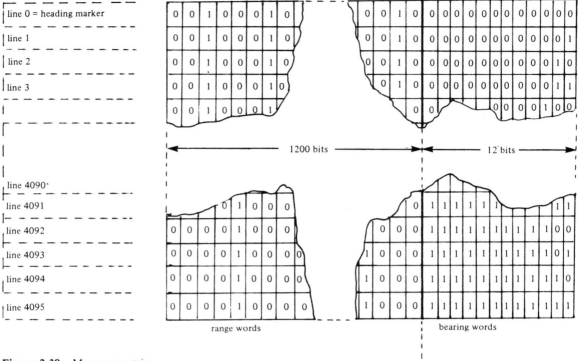

Figure 2.39 Memory matrix

count will be set to zero at the instant that the axis of the main beam is directly ahead and the heading marker contacts close, whereas in the case of true-north-up orientation, zero aerial count will be coincident with true north.

In many systems, the rotation signal is transmitted to the display in synchro or similar analogue form (see Section 2.4.5) and there converted into digital form. For each angular position of the aerial between 0° and 360° the resultant synchro signal available in the display has a value which is unique in magnitude and polarity. A purpose-built solid-state logic device known as a *synchro/digital converter* samples the synchro signal at very short regular intervals and hence calculates the aerial angle which will increment in binary steps from 0 to 4096 as the aerial rotates. An alternative approach is to employ an aerial-driven pulse generator which will typically produce one pulse per degree of rotation. The pulse train is used as input to a computer circuit which

generates 4096 pulses per 360 degrees of rotation. Effectively, the computer circuit fills in the missing pulses between the 360 received from the aerial by sensing the angular speed of the aerial from the interval between successive raw aerial pulses.

A third method employs an electromechanical device known as a *shaft encoder* which is driven 1 : 1 by the aerial. Although in civil marine applications this technique is much less common than the other two, it is worthy of some study as it provides graphic illustration of analogue-to-digital angle conversion.

Figure 2.40 shows that the moving element of a shaft encoder is a disk formed from a series of concentric rings of equal depth. Each ring is subdivided into an equal number of sectors. The number of sectors per ring increases outward from the centre in binary progression, i.e. the nth ring has 2^n sectors. In any given ring, sectors are connected to either a high level or a low level logic signal on an alternate basis, i.e. any sector will be at a

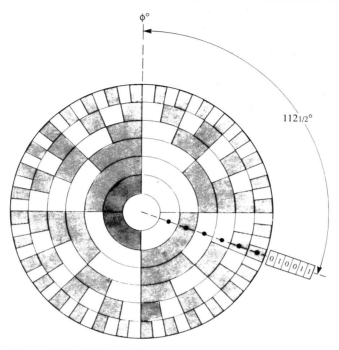

Figure 2.40   Shaft encoder

logic level different from either of its angular neighbours. A family of sliding contacts (or brushes) lies along a radius with one contact being allocated to each ring. As the disk rotates below the group of fixed contacts, the latter will pick off a pattern of binary ones and zeros which represents the aerial angle and which can be read into memory as a bearing word. It should be noticed that the number of unique words which can be produced by the encoder is equal to the number of segments in the outer ring, i.e. the ring which generates the LSB.

For clarity of illustration, Figure 2.40 shows an encoder having only five rings, i.e. a six-bit encoder. It has $64(2^6)$ segments in the outer ring and thus the digital angle will increase in steps of $360°/64$, i.e. $5.625°$ (one half compass point). Clearly, although this is suitable for purposes of illustration, its steps are much too coarse to be of practical use. In Section 1.3.2 it was established that a real-time picture is built up of approximately 3600 radial lines and that there is one radial line for each transmitted pulse. To emulate this, the aerial angle should be digitized in steps of about $\frac{001}{10}°$ which would require approximately 3600 segments in the outer ring of the shaft encoder. The nearest binary value higher than 3600 is 4096 and thus a 12-bit encoder is appropriate.

Brushes and slip rings provide a convenient illustration of the shaft encoder principle but they are noted for their poor operation, especially in the hostile marine environment. In modern systems, optical techniques are employed.

In general, whatever the type of the transmission device, if it is attached directly to the aerial driveshaft most of the errors resulting from gearing backlash can be eliminated.

The aerial bearing is obtained from the sum of the aerial angle and the vessel's instantaneous heading (see Section 2.6.3). This addition may be performed by adding the analogue signals (e.g. by means of a synchro transformer) or by digitizing both quantities individually and performing the addition thereafter. From the observer's point of view the distinction is academic.

2.6.6.5 *Synthetic picture generation*

The preceding sections have shown that the analogue video and rotation signals can be digitized and stored in memory in real-time. This section will consider how the range and bearing data are read out from memory and used to generate a radial-scan synthetic picture. The read function is illustrated in block diagram form by Figure 2.41, which also includes the units associated with the write function because the timings of both functions are inextricably linked, as shown by the time sequence diagram of Figure 2.42.

Immediately the last element of range data associated with any given radial line has been stored, the reading out of that line commences. The data which is read out may be processed as described in Section 2.6.6.6 or it may pass directly to circuitry which conditions it and mixes it with the heading line, the calibration marks and other internally generated signals to produce a composite video signal of sufficient power to drive the cathode of the CRT (see Section 2.6.1). In some texts this stage is

described as being *analogue*. This is intended to indicate that the circuitry is neither computer memory nor low-voltage logic but is of the conventional type normally used to handle analogue signals. It is, however, somewhat misleading because the signal is clearly digital in character and is no longer analogous to the echoes which produced it, since it is either a single-level signal (see Figure 2.43) or a small number of discrete values (see Figures 2.44 and 2.45). In most, though not all, systems a contrast control is provided. This allows the observer to adjust the brightness level of the synthetic echoes which represent the presence of targets. It is important to appreciate that all targets stored at the same level will have the same brightness. The correct procedure for the adjustment of the contrast control is discussed in Section 6.3.4.1. It should be noted that the function of the contrast control on a radial-scan radar display is somewhat different from the control of the same name found on a domestic television set and on some raster-scan displays (see Section 6.4.3.1).

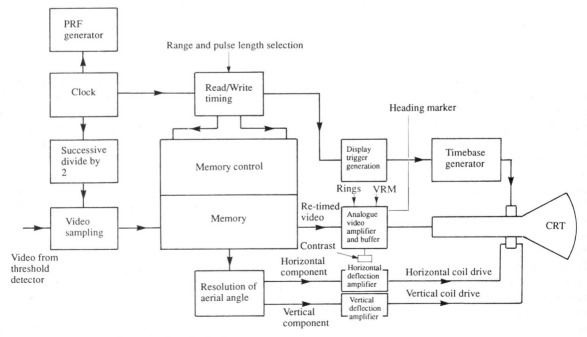

Figure 2.41 Block diagram of synthetic picture generation

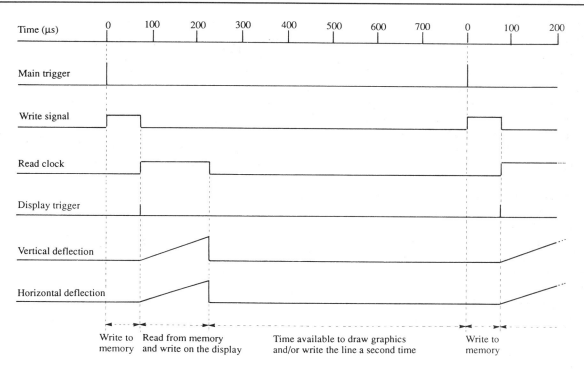

Figure 2.42   Time-sequence diagram for a radial-scan synthetic picture

Clearly, it is essential that the data for any radial line is written into memory in real time, i.e. in the duration of the timebase of the selected range scale, since that is the interval in which it is received. Thus the time taken to write the data into memory varies with selected range scale. However, the data can be read out of memory at a constant rate so long as this is done in the same time as it takes for the spot to travel from the centre to the edge of the screen. In a radial-scan synthetic display the read-out and sweep times are the same on all range scales and normally correspond with the timebase of either the 6 or the 12 mile range scale, depending on manufacturer. This means that, on the shorter range scales, the sweep time is slower than it would be in the case of a real-time display. Certain benefits accrue from a slow fixed read-out time. From an engineering and production point of view it is advantageous, since it dispenses with the need to provide separate timebase circuitry and associated switching for each range scale. It also avoids the need to produce the very fast sweep times demanded by a real-time picture on the very short range scales. If, for the purposes of discussion, we assume that the read-out time is $148.16\,\mu s$ (i.e. the timebase on the 12 mile range scale) then it is evident that, on all range scales less than 12 miles, the time taken for the spot to cross the screen will be a multiple of that which would be required for a real-time display. This slowing down of the spot increases the inherent brightness of the picture.

It has long been recognised that, other than in conditions of darkness, a real-time picture cannot be viewed successfully without the aid of a hood or visor. This is particularly the case on the shorter range scales because the spot travels so fast that it has very limited ability to excite the phosphor (see Section 2.6.1.2). In a radial-scan synthetic display, the effect of the relatively slow sweep rate is to extend the range of ambient light conditions in which it is unnecessary to use a hood. However, the improvement is not sufficient to allow full daylight viewing.

On range scales greater than 12 miles the spot speed will be greater than in the real-time case. This in itself will tend to reduce the inherent brightness of the picture, but the effect will be offset by the high synthetic brightness of the displayed echoes and possibly by writing each line more than once (the only theoretical limit to writing each line several times is the need to complete writing before the start of the next time sequence). With regard to echo brightness, the reader is reminded that in a real-time picture the echo brightness of weak targets is a function of signal strength (see Sections 2.5.2.5 and 2.6.1), whereas in a synthetic picture the equal brightness of all displayed echoes is a function of the setting of the contrast control which may be adjusted to suit the ambient light conditions. This is illustrated by Figure 2.43, while the correct practical procedure for the adjustment of the contrast is discussed in Section 6.3.4.1. To improve further the inherent picture brightness on the longer range scales, each line may be written twice (or possibly more often), since on these scales the lowest PRF will be used (see Section 2.3.4), thus offering a suitably long PRP. The faster timebase on the longer range scales will extend the radial paint of a small target and may assist detection by making it more obvious.

The radial-scan synthetic picture is sometimes referred to as *re-timed video* because it is not read out at the same rate as it was written into memory. There will of course be one range scale on which write and read times are the same. In some earlier synthetic displays a memory bypass was included which allowed the observer to select either a synthetic or a real-time pic-

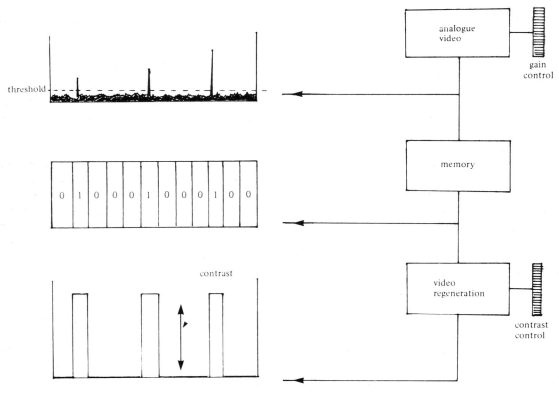

Figure 2.43   Single-level video

ture, albeit on that one range scale only. To the radar observer this was an extremely attractive feature as it allowed an assessment of the setting of the gain and tuning controls to be made against simple, traditional criteria (see Section 6.2.4), while also ensuring that one range scale would remain available in the event of memory failure. Unfortunately, more recent designs have ceased to offer this facility.

As each range word is read out of memory, so too is the corresponding bearing word (see Figure 2.39). The digital computor calculates the sine and the cosine of the instantaneous aerial angle and uses each of these to control the magnitude of two analogue deflection signals which drive two sets of fixed deflection coils that are wound mutually at right angles on a yoke assembly around the neck of the tube. These are named the X coils and the Y coils because they produce deflection parallel to the horizontal and vertical axes respectively (see Figure 2.41). The spot deflection is thus produced by two forces whose directions are at right angles to one another and whose magnitudes vary in sympathy with the sine and cosine of the aerial angle. Hence, although there is no physical rotation of the coils as was described in Section 2.6.1.3, the trace will rotate in sympathy with the aerial angle (see Figure 2.29).

From an engineering point of view there is considerable virtue in using fixed rather than rotating coils. It dispenses with the progressive wear and continual mechanical noise which are undesirable features of rotating coil assemblies and their associated motors and gearboxes. For technical reasons beyond the scope of this text, at very high sweep rates it is easier to achieve accurate and effective beam deflection by using rotating rather than fixed coils. By making possible a relatively long sweep time on the very short range scales (16 times longer on the $\frac{3}{4}$ mile range scale), the advent of digital storage made the use of fixed coils even more attractive to the radar designer.

True-motion facilities (see also Section 2.6.4) can be provided by digitizing and resolving the analogue course and speed inputs and hence energizing a fixed set (possibly the same set as described above) of off-centring coils.

This section has been concerned with setting out the principles on which the generation of a radial-scan syn-

thetic picture is based and has highlighted the ways in which the techniques differ from those already described for real-time pictures. It must be appreciated that the technical differences between the ways in which the two types of pictures are generated result in the synthetic echoes having characteristics which are radically different from those produced on the traditional real-time display. Failure to appreciate this may result in serious misinterpretation of the picture and maladjustment of the controls. The significance of these differences is discussed in Sections 2.6.6.7, 6.3 and 6.4.

2.6.6.6 Signal processing

While the received signal is stored in memory it can be processed in a variety of ways. In the case of civil marine synthetic radial-scan systems, this provision normally takes the form of interference suppression, noise reduction and echo stretching techniques. Normally these facilities can be selected at will by the observer. Their operation and use are described in Sections 3.9.5.1 and 6.11.1.

2.6.6.7 Multi-level synthetic video

In the description of single-level threshold detection (see Section 2.6.6.2), attention was drawn to the fact that intelligence relating to echo strength is lost by this process. This can be seen clearly from Figure 2.43 which shows that recieved echoes of differing strengths produce synthetic echoes all of which have the same brightness. Clearly there is merit in this approach as it has the effect of emphasizing the echoes of very weak targets. Such a target, which may be difficult to detect on an analogue display, will produce an obvious synthetic echo of full brightness even if it barely crosses the threshold. This benefit must be traded against the loss of indication of echo strength and the implications of this loss require serious consideration.

In an analogue receiver, echoes may have any amplitude over a continuous range from receiver noise to amplifier saturation level (see Sections 2.5.2.3 and 2.5.2.1). Although the range of received echoes is continuous, the excitation characteristic of the screen (see Section 2.6.1.2) is such that the stronger signals may saturate the phosphor. Further, there is a limit to the number of discrete brightness levels which the phosphor can display. This is probably not more than eight and is a measure of the intelligence which is lost by single-level storage. However, the usefulness of this intelligence is a matter of some debate. Some mariners do draw conclusions from the strength of the displayed echoes but the validity of these conclusions is very much open to question when it is recognised that a yacht with a radar reflector (see Section 3.4) may return an echo whose strength compares favourably with that from a medium-sized ship. Irrespective of the debate as to the intelligence that can (or cannot) be deduced from a knowledge of echo strength, it is beyond dispute that an understanding of this loss of a continuous range of echo strengths is essential when judging the correct setting of the gain and tuning controls of a synthetic display. The importance of this is discussed further under practical procedures in Sections 6.3.4.3 and 6.4.4.

A major practical problem associated with single-level storage is that any noise which does cross the threshold will be displayed with the same brightness as the echoes from even the strongest targets (see Section 2.6.6.2). This does not compare favourably with an analogue picture in which the brightness of noise echoes is a fraction of that of strong echoes. As radial-scan synthetic displays have developed, designers have attempted to offset this problem by introducing two or more thresholds in order to increase the number of brightness levels which can be allocated to displayed echoes. It is evident that one threshold is necessary for each proposed brightness level. The principle of two-level storage is illustrated by Figure 2.44, which for reasons of clarity shows only 12 range cells per screen radius.

Two thresholds, designated high and low, are used and a separate range word is allocated to each threshold. A target which crosses the high threshold must also cross

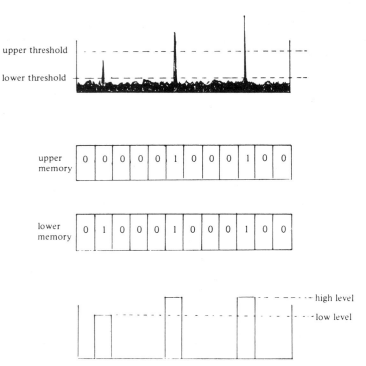

Figure 2.44 The principle of two-level threshold detection

the low threshold and will thus be stored as a binary one in both range words. A target which crosses the low-level threshold only will be stored in one range word only and of course a target which fails to cross the low threshold will be stored as a zero in both words. It follows that some intelligence as to signal strength has been preserved and that signals can be classified as *high-level* and *low-level* and thus used to produce one of two brightness levels on the display. (Many systems produce the effect by exciting the phosphor two (or more) times per strong target and thus use the integrating property of the phosphor to obtain the high level brightness.) The relative levels of the thresholds and the ratio of high-level to low-level brilliance are not under the control of the observer and will vary with manufacturer. Figure 2.44 shows a fairly small ratio of high to low level echo brightness which is typical of some earlier systems.

More recent designs have tended to choose a ratio in the region of 10 : 1 and to place the thresholds fairly close together. The problem of trying to set a single threshold to the correct level was mentioned in Section 2.6.6.2. The general philosophy of twin thresholds is probably best explained in terms of the single-threshold problem. If a single threshold is set too high, weak echoes will not be displayed; if it is set too low, excessive noise will cross

the threshold and will make it difficult to detect weak targets because their echoes will have to compete for the observer's attention with a large number of noise pulses, all of which will be of the same brightness as the echoes which are sought. Clearly the perfect setting which would show all echoes and no noise cannot be achieved and in practice, with a single threshold, a compromise must be accepted in which a certain amount of stored noise is tolerated. By employing two thresholds, with one set a little higher than the compromise level, i.e. just clear of the noise peaks, and one a little lower, i.e. just below the peaks of the noise, the problem can be greatly eased. All but the very weak targets will cross the high threshold and produce high-level synthetic echoes which will be obvious against the low-level echo background. The weak echoes which are close to the level of the noise peaks will be detected and, like these peaks, will be displayed as low-level synthetic echoes. The observer thus should have no problem in detecting all but the very weakest echoes as they are the only ones which have to compete with the stored noise. The lower level of video is sometimes referred to as *grey level* and this is illustrated by Figure 2.45.

The positions of the twin thresholds relative to one another are normally preset by the manufacturer but the

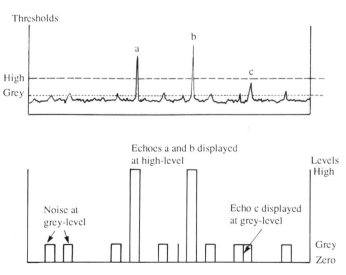

Figure 2.45 Two-level video with grey level

position of the lower threshold with respect to the noise is adjusted by the observer by means of the gain control. The correct procedure for judging the correct amount of noise, and hence the setting of this control, is described in Section 6.3.4.2.

Many modern radial-scan synthetic displays offer high-level and grey-level video, but there are some systems which offer three or four levels. Given the limited dynamic range of the phosphor, one can speculate as to exactly how many threshold levels are necessary fully to mimic an analogue display. One system produced in the mid-1980s pursued this goal by offering sixteen brightness levels. It has to be said that the latter approach is very much the exception rather than the rule.

Single-level video will exacerbate the masking effect of sea and rain clutter (see Sections 3.6 and 3.7).

The video produced by threshold detection is sometimes referred to as quantized video. The term *quantized* refers to the fact that the brightness of the displayed echoes can only take one of a number of discrete levels and does not have a continous range of possible values.

2.6.7   The raster-scan synthetic display

In this type of display the radar picture is produced on a television screen and is built up of a large number of horizontal lines which form a pattern known as a raster (see Section 2.6.7.1). It is a logical development of the radial-scan synthetic display but is much more complex and requires a very large amount of memory (Figure 2.39). For both user and designer a number of benefits accrue from the adoption of raster-scan in preference to the more traditional radial-scan techniques, but some deficiencies have also to be accepted. The design factors will be highlighted where appropriate in the following technical description, while Section 6.4 is devoted to the factors which affect the practical setting up and interpretation of the picture. From the observer's point of view, the most obvious advantage of raster-scan is the brightness of the picture which allows it to be viewed, at a distance, by several observers in almost all conditions of ambient light. Most, if not all mariners who have ever used a radial-scan display would agree that its most significant practical limitation is the difficulty of viewing it in daylight.

Probably the attractiveness of daylight viewing more than any other benefit has ensured the development of the raster-scan display, despite any disadvantages that may have to be accepted.

2.6.7.1   *The monochrome television CRT*

In the mid-1980s the introduction of this type of viewing device to civil marine applications represented a major departure from almost fifty years of radar tradition in which the conventional circular screen CRT (see Section 2.6.1) was taken for granted. In the early 1970s one manufacturer did present a marine radar picture on a monochrome television screen, but it was generated from a conventional rotating trace tube which produced a picture on an electronic image-retaining panel. The latter was viewed by a television camera which relayed the picture to the television screen by a closed-circuit television link. Such a system was analogue in its nature and fundamentally different from the modern raster-scan display in which the picture is written into computer memory and read out onto the television screen.

Some systems produce a monochrome picture, while others offer several colours. The following description relates to a monochrome display, i.e. one which can display one colour and black. Colour tubes are described separately in Section 2.6.7.7.

The significant difference between a conventional radar CRT and its television counterpart is that the latter has a rectangular screen. The screen size is specified by the length of the diagonal and the width and height of the screen are in the approximate ratio 4 : 3. Starting in the top left-hand corner of the screen, the spot writes the picture by tracing out a pattern of horizontal lines from top to bottom (see Figure 2.46), each individual line running from left to right. While each line is being written the spot brightness is determined by the no-signal setting of the brilliance control as modified by the video signal. Between lines, while the spot flies back from right to left, the brilliance is suppressed. The majority of television tubes are mass-produced for use in domestic television receivers and therefore the number of horizontal lines which form a complete picture (referred to as a frame or field) must conform to an agreed standard. In Europe the agreed line standard is 625 lines per frame, whereas in the USA the value is 525. A lesser number of

Spot writes horizontal line   Spot flies back after line

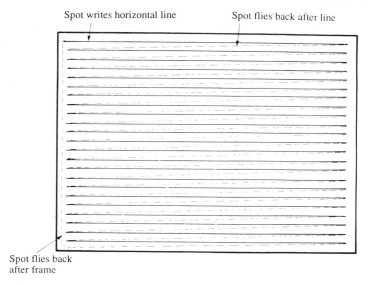

Spot flies back
after frame

Figure 2.46   Television raster

tubes are produced for special high-resolution applications and are available with a higher line standard such as 1024. Clearly it has been long established that line standards in the region 525–625 produce an acceptable domestic television picture. The question of its suitability for marine radar will be discussed in this section but at this stage it is worth noting that a major advantage of using established line standards is the ready availability of relatively cheap mass-produced components which have been tried and tested in the television industry.

The moving picture viewed on a domestic television is in fact a succession of still pictures (or frames) produced at an extremely high repetition rate in the same way as a movie film is produced from a succession of stills. Provided that the interval between stills is sufficiently small, i.e. the frame repetition rate is sufficiently high, the human eye will fail to notice any flicker between successive stills, and will perceive smooth movement. For a movie film this requires a frame rate of about 25 per second. Unfortunately this is not fast enough for television pictures because, whereas in screening a film each still is totally exposed immediately, on a television screen it is exposed progressively from

top to bottom. As a result, television requires a frame rate of about 50 per second. This was unattractive to television designers because there are technical difficulties in generating as many as 50×625 lines per second.

The necessary compromise was achieved by a technique known as *interlace*. By generating only the odd numbered lines (1,3,5,...,625) in one sequence and the even numbered lines (2,4,6,...,624) in the next sequence it is possible to renew half the picture 50 times per second but the entire picture only 25 times per second. Because the odd and even lines are interlaced, the human eye sees the picture as being renewed 50 times per second and does not perceive any flicker. This allows the designer to halve the rate at which the horizontal lines are generated. In domestic television receivers, for practical reasons, the frame rate is derived from the frequency of the national electricity supply, resulting in frame rates of 50 or 60 per second according to the country in which it is to be used. It is this extremely high refresh rate which gives the raster-scan radar display its daylight viewing potential. In practice, it is not possible to use all of the horizontal lines for picture presentation, a few being lost at the top and at the bottom. However from the radar observer's point of view this is of academic interest and will not be discussed further.

Unfortunately, interlace, the very technique which is used in domestic television to remove flicker, introduces a flicker effect when a marine radar picture is displayed on a television screen. This arises because a television picture is derived from a television camera which scans a rectangular matrix (i.e. one set out in terms of X and Y) and the picture is read onto the screen at a similar rate and in a similar format; a raster-scan radar display, however, is derived from a relatively slowly updating radial data pattern (i.e. in terms of range and bearing) but read onto the screen as a rectangular matrix (see Section 2.6.7.2) with a high refresh rate. This presents the radar designer with a dilemma. The choice is between selecting mass-produced television technology for its ready and economic availability or opting for more specialized tubes (and associated electronics) and dispensing with interlace to remove the flicker which some observers find tiring and obtrusive. Given the limited sea experience which observers have had with raster-scan displays, it is not surprising that some manufacturers elected to use interlace while others decided to refresh the full picture 50–60 times per second.

The television CRT has two sets of fixed deflection coils. One set produces horizontal deflection to generate the lines of the raster, while the other produces the vertical deflection necessary to ensure that successive lines are drawn progressively further down the screen from top to bottom. Both the deflection waveforms will have the distinctive *sawtooth* shape illustrated in Figure 2.26 which accompanied the description of rotating coil deflection presented in Section 2.6.1.3, but their repetition rates will differ from the conventional radar case and from one another. The line frequency will be a large multiple of the frame frequency. The precise values will depend on the standard adopted: if one considers the European standard, the frame rate will be 50 per second while, assuming interlace, the line rate will be $50 \times 625/2$ which is 15.625 kHz.

The general properties of phosphors were discussed in Section 2.6.1.2 and it was established that, by the correct choice of chemical constituents, a phosphor having an appropriate colour and persistence can be manufactured.

For general monochrome television use the colour is white. This is not ideal for the conditions under which a civil marine radar is viewed. The radar display tends to be viewed from a shorter distance than with television and the observer has to concentrate to a very much greater degree on picture detail for long periods of time. For monochrome raster-scan applications most designers elected to use a green phosphor, probably because this was the colour readily available from CRT types already produced in reasonable numbers for other applications. While there is very limited experience of how observers will react to raster-scan displays, it is believed that a green phosphor provides comfortable viewing and that it is not likely to produce excessive tiredness and stress. Orange is also a suitable colour but the phosphor is not as readily available in television CRTs and has a greater tendency to *burn* (see Section 2.6.1.2). In general, however, television tubes burn less easily and less quickly than traditional radar CRTs and this represents another benefit of the use of raster-scan. The television tubes are also cheaper, but the complexity of the necessary signal processing renders the raster-scan display unit more expensive than its predecessor.

It was mentioned in Section 2.6.7.1 that in the early 1970s one manufacturer presented a marine radar picture on a monochrome television screen using analogue conversion techniques. The system in question offered two modes of viewing. In the positive mode, light-coloured targets were displayed against a black background, whereas in the negative mode the colours were inverted. This option gave the observer the freedom to select the mode most suited to the ambient light conditions and it remains to be seen if monochrome digital raster-scan displays will in due course offer this option. Some colour raster displays provide day and night viewing modes (see Section 2.6.7.8).

In contrast with a rotating trace tube, the television screen uses a phosphor which has an extremely short persistence. Longer persistence is not only unnecessary, because of the high refresh rate, but would be a positive nuisance when any detail of the picture changed. However, the short persistence does mean that moving targets will not leave the characteristic afterglow trails associated with a conventional radar display. Raster-scan displays may use data storage techniques to generate artificial trails; these are described in Section 2.6.7.5.

As in any CRT, the spot diameter (see Section 2.6.5.1) determines the smallest area of light that can be produced on the screen. Thus, along each horizontal line there will be a finite number of picture elements, referred to as *pixels*, the total number of which will be determined by the number of spot diameters per screen width. Assuming a spot diameter of 0.5 mm (values as small as 0.3 mm are available) and the European line standard, a 584 mm (23 inch) tube, which is the minimum size on which it is possible to produce a 340 mm PPI, will have approximately 940 pixels per line. It follows that the whole screen will be represented by a rectangular matrix of pixels comprising 625 rows and 940 columns. Thus to produce a synthetic radar picture on a television screen the stored radar data must be read out to the screen in terms of X and Y co-ordinates and not in terms of range and bearing as was the case for a radial-scan display (see Section 2.6.6.5). In a raster-scan display the co-ordinate conversion is carried out by the digital computer within the display and the process is known as digital scan conversion (DSC).

2.6.7.2 Digital scan conversion

Each element of the radar picture may be stored in terms of its range from the origin and bearing from the heading marker, or true north (see Sections 2.6.6.3 and 2.6.6.4). Such storage is said to be in terms of *polar co-ordinates*. Alternatively, each element may be stored in terms of its northings and eastings from the origin, in which case the co-ordinates are said to be *cartesian*. By the very principle of its operation the radar generates the raw data in polar co-ordinates and the function of the digital scan conversion unit is to calculate the corresponding cartesian co-ordinates. The operation is similar to that carried out by the navigator who lays off a range and bearing on the chart to indicate the ship's position and then reads off the latitude and longitude from the scale borders of the chart to record it in lat./long. form in the log book. The technique is illustrated in block diagram and graphic form by Figure 2.47.

For clarity of illustration, Figure 2.47 shows the polar memory to have only twelve elements per radius rather than the representative practical value of 1200 suggested in Sections 2.6.6.3 and 2.6.6.4. To assist in comparison, the cartesian memory is also shown as having 12 elements either side of the origin along both the X and the Y axes. In practice, cartesian memories have less elements per unit radius; the significance of this important point will be discussed in Section 2.6.7.3.

Figure 2.47 shows that the input to the DSC unit is the retimed video and digital angle. For any given polar location specified by a range R and an angle θ, the cartesian co-ordinates will be given by

$$X = R \times \text{sine } \theta \qquad \text{and} \qquad Y = R \times \text{cosine } \theta$$

The arithmetic unit of the digital computer calculates the X and Y values of incoming raw radar data from the polar location R, θ which is then stored (either as a one or a zero) in the cartesian location X, Y.

After one rotation of the aerial, the cartesian memory will contain all the data for one complete radar picture. The digital computer can read out this data and repeatedly generate a picture on the television screen at a rate which is independent of the aerial rotation speed. Thus the raster-scan picture can be refreshed at a rate of about 50–60 times per second, which is about 150–180 times as often as is the case with a radial-scan display which can only be refreshed after each rotation of the aerial (approximately 3 seconds). It is vital to appreciate the significant difference that exists between the refreshing of the picture and the updating of the picture. A real-time radial-scan radar display is updated and refreshed at the same time once per revolution of the aerial. A raster-scan display is refreshed once per television frame but only updated once per aerial revolution, since updating can only take place when more recent data has been read into the cartesian memory.

In Figure 2.32 it was shown that the shape of the radar resolution cell was the area of a sector contained between two concentric arcs. The process of scan conversion will tend to degrade this resolution because, if the radar resolution cell even partially overlaps a cartesian memory location, the entire corresponding screen location will be brightened. This is illustrated in Figure 2.47. Any variation of the target return from aerial revolution to revolution will change the pattern of cartesian cells in a way which is more noticeable than is the same effect on a traditional rotating-trace display. This variation of picture content can prove to be distracting and tiring. It may also be found to stress the observer.

2.6.7.3 The raster-scan PPI

The IMO Performance Standards (see Section 10.2) require the equipment to produce a plan display with an effective diameter of not less than 180 mm, 250 mm or 340 mm, depending on the size of the vessel. The application of these standards effectively chooses the diameter of a conventional circular screen, whereas, given the shape of the television type screen, the designer has to decide where within the rectangle to have the display computer draw the appropriate size of circle. There is no general consensus on this point; three representative examples are shown by Figure 2.48 and it should be noted that the remaining screen space is used to give a read-out of numerical data or control status. A major advantage of the raster-scan display is the ease with which auxiliary data can be written around or within the picture area (no mechanical dials or scales are necessary).

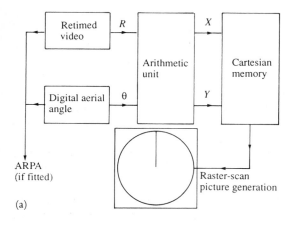

(a)

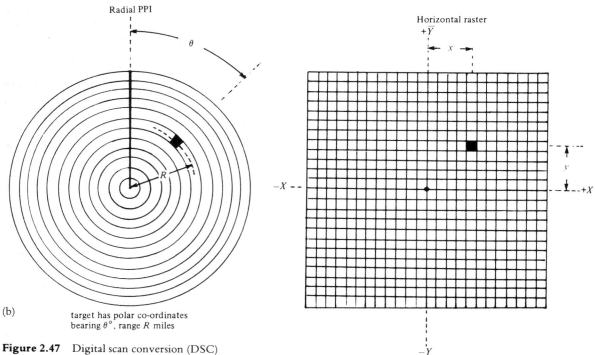

(b)

target has polar co-ordinates
bearing $\theta°$, range R miles

target has rectangular co-ordinates
$Y = +y, X = +x$

Figure 2.47 Digital scan conversion (DSC)
(a) Block diagram
(b) Memory arrangement

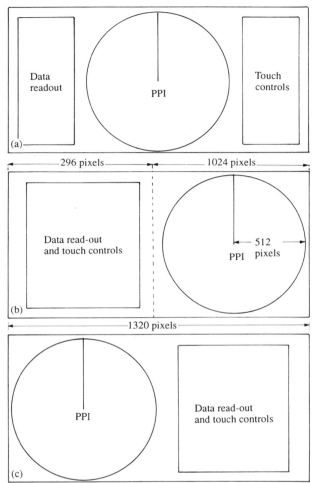

Figure 2.48 The raster-scan PPI: the pixel numbers shown represent high-resolution memory

In some modern systems the television screen has a touch-sensitive characteristic and the observer can operate certain controls simply by touching the appropriate screen location. This is achieved by means of a thin overlay consisting of two layers of plastic between which lies a matrix of a very large number of elemental areas whose conductivity is sensitive to finger pressure. Another modern approach is to exploit the principle of infra-red remote control which is used extensively in the domestic television market.

It is now appropriate to consider the allocation of memory locations, or cells, to represent the picture. To produce a simple illustration of a DSC in Figure 2.47, only twelve memory locations were allocated to represent the radius of the PPI. In Section 2.6.7.1 it was shown that the minimum size of television screen capable of showing a 340 mm PPI would have a matrix of approximately 940 by 625 pixels. Clearly there should be at least one memory cell for each pixel. In practice, designers may arrange that the ratio of memory cells to pixels is a little greater than unity, thus ensuring that the available screen resolution is fully exploited. The arrangement of memory locations is referred to as a *memory plane* and they are in general only produced in a limited number of preferred sizes. Commonly available formats have 512, 768, 1024 or 1360 cells per horizontal or vertical dimension. From these values rectangular matrices having an aspect ratio of approximately 4 : 3 can be produced. A representative allocation of pixels is shown in Figure 2.48(b).

The memory plane associated with Figure 2.48(b) is suited to a television screen having a frame rate of 1024, as in the vertical dimension the ratio of pixels to lines is unity. Having 1320 cells in the horizontal dimension, the aspect ratio of the memory plane closely approaches the 4 : 3 ratio of the screen. The diameter of PPI circle which can be drawn is limited by the vertical dimension of the screen; by using the values given in Figure 2.48(b), this results in an allocation of 512 cells per PPI radius.

In Section 2.6.6.3 storage of range was discussed in detail, including the relationship between sampling rate and allocation of memory. Reference to that section, and in particular to Example 2.8, will show that 512 cells per radius exceed the minimum consistent with the least sampling rate and that required to ensure adequate range discrimination and accuracy. However, it is less than the 1000–1200 which was quoted in the same section as being typical of what is used in practice for radial storage. This apparent inconsistency merits some explanation. Values of 1000–1200 cells per radius are normally employed so that the stored data can be used as an input to automatic tracking. Radar systems which provide automatic tracking are referred to as automatic radar plotting aids (ARPA) and are described in detail in Chapters 4, 5 and 9. The storage resolution required for automatic tracking is much higher than that required for synthetic picture generation for reasons which are set out under the heading of range quantization errors in Secion 9.5.3.2. Because the radial memory is overwritten line by line as the aerial rotates (see Section 2.6.6.3), the total capacity is a fraction of that required for a cartesian memory. In the case of raster-scan ARPAs it is thus expedient to use the radial memory to feed both the tracking unit *and* the cartesian memory, while the latter is used to refresh the picture.

The raster-scan display does use more memory than is strictly necessary for adequate sampling, accuracy and resolution. A major reason for this is that otherwise the steplike characteristic of the picture would be obtrusive. This is best understood by considering the generation of a circle, for example a range ring. On a radial-scan display this is achieved by illuminating a very large number of resolution cells each of which is a tiny arc. This is completely analogous to the use of a pair of drawing compasses and should result in a perfect circle. On a raster-scan display the circle is produced by illuminating the correct combination of pixels, which are not arcs but rectangles, resulting in steps between adjacent elements of the *circle*. For example, in a vertical sense adjacent pixels forming the circle must be on different lines, and unless these lines are very close together the steps will be obtrusive. A cosmetic technique known as anti-aliasing can be used to camouflage the effect but, in general, designers rely on initially selecting sufficiently high resolution. The steps will also affect the shape of displayed echoes and, if pronounced, could add to the difficulties of the identification of coastlines and other navigational features (see Section 8.2).

In Figure 2.48 the origin of the display (i.e. the own-ship position) is shown at the centre of the PPI circle. If the memory location corresponding to the origin remains fixed, a relative-motion presentation will result. It is, however, possible to arrange that the targets leave true-motion trails by generating synthetic afterglow (see Section 2.6.7.5). If the origin's co-ordinates in the memory plane are updated in sympathy with the observing vessel's course and speed, the origin will move across the PPI circle and a true-motion presentation will be produced. As with any true-motion presentation, whether produced by moving the origin or by

generating synthetic true afterglow, the accuracy of the displayed target motion is crucially dependent on the accuracy of the course and speed inputs (see Sections 1.5.2, 2.6.4 and 2.6.6.5).

2.6.7.4 Multi-plane memories

The memory plane associated with Figure 2.48(b) can register a binary 1 or 0 in any of its memory cells. This limits its ability to merely indicating the presence or absence of a target (or an item of data). Some of the implications of such a restriction were discussed in Section 2.6.6.7. Most raster-scan systems use multi-plane memories, normally having three or four layers. The principle is illustrated for three layers in Figure 2.49.

Figure 2.49 shows that with three memory layers it is possible to store three elements of binary information for each screen location, i.e. the number 1 or 0 may appear in each of the three cells which form a vertical column. This gives rise to eight possible permutations

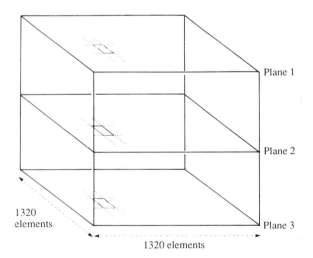

Figure 2.49 The principle of multi-plane memories. Use of the corresponding element from each plane allows the following combinations:
Plane 1. 0 0 0 0 1 1 1 1
Plane 2. 0 0 1 1 0 1 0 1
Plane 3. 0 1 0 1 0 0 1 1

and these can be exploited to produce multi-level video having eight different levels of target brightness. Multi-plane memories also make it possible to generate synthetic afterglow (see Section 2.6.7.5) and to perform a variety of signal processing techniques (see Section 2.6.7.6).

2.6.7.5 Artificial afterglow

Due to the long persistence of the phosphor of a radial-scan radar CRT (see Section 2.6.1.2), echoes which move across the screen leave distinctive afterglow trails. Such trails can be of assistance to the radar observer in making an early appraisal of a developing encounter but care must be taken in their interpretation (a full appraisal of an encounter requires radar plotting or equivalent systematic observation of detected objects, as set out in Chapter 7). Because the very short persistence of the phosphor of a raster-scan tube does not allow the trails to build up, most manufacturers make provision for the generation of synthetic afterglow.

Synthetic afterglow is generated by recording the presence of a target not only in the main echo memory plane(s) but also in a further history plane. When a target moves on to a new memory location in the echo plane, its previous location in that plane reverts to the zero condition and in the absence of the history plane that pixel would not be brightened. However, the data in the history plane continues to cause that pixel to be brightened to a progressively lesser extent for some time after the echo has vacated the corresponding cell in the echo plane. Thus the recent past positions of a moving target will form a trail which fades progressively with time. The mathematical law on which the fading is based is pre-programmed but in some systems the observer can select, from one of two values, the length of time over which the fading takes place. It is normally possible for the user to switch the afterglow facility on or off. Where a colour CRT is used (see Section 2.6.7.7) the trails can be generated in a colour which is different from that of the echoes.

Because the trails of all targets are generated over a fixed period of time, their lengths are directly related to the rate at which the target is moving across the screen. This is a significant improvement when compared with real-time afterglow trails. The latter are dependent not only on the rate at which the echo is moving but also on the strength of the echo and the sensitivity of the phosphor in a particular area of the screen. An observer who fails to appreciate this may be seriously misled.

Provided that a suitable course and speed input are available, it is in theory possible for the display computer to deduce either relative-motion trails or true-motion trails irrespective of the picture presentation selected by the observer. A particular application of this is the generation of a true-motion presentation by generating true trails while maintaining the origin in the centre of the PPI circle, or in a suitably off-centred position. Great care should be taken in ascertaining which trails are being generated and it is of paramount importance to remember that the accuracy of true trails, like that of true-motion, is dependent on the accuracy of the input course and speed.

Since they are visible in bright ambient light, the addition of synthetic afterglow may assist with the detection of targets in the background of clutter (see Section 2.6.7.8 and Section 3.6). However, because all displayed echoes are transferred to the history plane there can be a significant build-up in both thermal noise and all forms of clutter. Where the facility is being used, the afterglow should be cleared if the background builds up to a level at which it can impair the detection of genuine echoes.

2.6.7.6 Signal processing

As suggested in Section 2.6.6, a benefit which accrues from the storage of radar signal data is the ability to sample, manipulate and analyse that data. In radial-scan systems only a fractional sector of the picture is maintained in memory (see Section 2.6.6.3) and this in general limits the processing techniques to those of interference suppression, noise reduction (see Section 3.9.5.1) and echo stretching (see Section 6.11.1). Because in raster-scan systems the data for a complete picture is stored, the number of processing techniques which can be performed is increased. Such techniques are mainly devoted to improving the probability of detection of targets in clutter and it is appropriate to delay consideration of these until after a study of the phenomena of clutter and the corresponding manual techniques of clutter reduction (see Sections 3.6 and 3.7).

2.6.7.7 *The colour television CRT*

Red, green and blue are known as the three primary colours of light because by mixing them in suitable proportions it is possible to produce most of the colours that the eye can perceive. The phosphor used in a colour television tube has three individual components, one for each of the primary colours, and they are arranged in a rather special way which is illustrated by Figure 2.50.

The colour tube also differs from its monochrome counterpart in that it has three electron guns, designated red, green and blue, each of which activates its own component of the phosphor. As illustrated in Figure 2.50, the phosphor is a mosaic of minute strips of the primary colour phosphor materials arranged in elemental groups of three which are called *triads*. In every such group there is one strip of each primary colour. The shadow mask is a metal sheet in which slots are cut to allow each electron beam to excite the phosphor strips of its own colour and to prevent it falling on the strips of the other two primary colours. This is achieved by very

careful attention to the geometry of the positions of the guns, the positions of the phosphors on the tube and of the slots in the mask. The strength of the beam emitted by each gun is controlled individually by the input picture signals and thus the colour emitted by any given triad depends on the instantaneous balance between the individual beam strengths. The raster is generated by sweeping the three beams across the screen as a group, using the basic principles of beam deflection described in Section 2.6.7.1.

The description given above is a fairly simplified exposition of the principle. Modern colour tubes employ many refinements of the above principles to improve the brightness, focus and colour quality of the picture.

In a single-beam tube the smallest area of light that can be produced on the screen, sometimes referred to as the minimum resolvable picture element, is determined by the spot diameter (see Section 2.6.5.1); the implications of this for a raster-scan radar were discussed in Section 2.6.7.1. In a colour CRT the minimum resolvable element is determined by the spot diameter of each beam and the geometry of the triad. Thus the resolution of a colour tube is inherently poorer than that of a com-

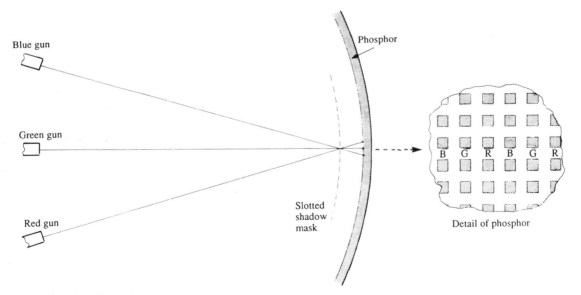

Figure 2.50   The colour television CRT

parable monochrome version. The materials used to produce the coloured phosphors are relatively costly and this, together with other design and manufacturing factors, renders the colour tube the more expensive of the two. The delay in the appearance of colour raster-scan radar displays has been due to the excessive costs of tubes with an acceptable screen resolution. The presence of the shadow mask reduces the potential light output of the tube and thus makes it difficult to achieve brightness levels comparable with that of monochrome.

2.6.7.8   *The use of colour in radar picture generation*

In the early to mid-1980s there was vigorous debate concerning the contribution that colour could make to enhancing the raster-scan picture. As mentioned in the previous section, the use of colour can result in the loss of resolution and brightness in addition to its tendency to be more expensive. However, it can be argued that it does improve the observer's ability to discern picture detail while viewing the display from some distance. There is the temptation to extrapolate the television-based argument that 'colour is better than black and white'. This argument is specious because, although the advent of colour undoubtedly added the dimension which ensured the future of sports like snooker as television spectacles, there is no direct parallel with the radar picture. In marine radar the use of colour is only productive if it is used to contribute useful and unambiguous information to the observer. If it does this, it makes a positive contribution to the presentation of information albeit one that brings the concomitant penalties of resolution, brightness and cost. Extra cost arises not only from the expense of a colour tube but also from the more complex signal processing which is required. Certain engineering problems relating to magnetic effects, vibration and temperature also have to be overcome.

Some of the earliest colour raster-scan radars used the additional dimension of colour to indicate signal strength. It will be remembered from Figures 2.44 and 2.45 that, by employing digital storage, it is possible to produce a *two-level* picture. It follows that with suitable computer assistance these two levels could be shown as different colours. In early systems three colours, red, amber and green, were used to show high, medium and

low signal levels. A wide range of factors affect the strength of signal returned by any given target (see Chapter 3) and there is considerable doubt as to how valuable this information is to the observer (see Section 2.6.6.7). An argument which was sometimes offered was that 'targets show as a different colour against the background of clutter'. A major limitation of marine radar is the ability to detect targets whose signal strength is close to clutter level (see Sections 3.6 and 3.7) and it is almost self-evident that a marginal target would change colour almost continually. This is likely to confuse and mislead the observer and in this regard the use of colour does not make a positive contribution to the information available to the observer.

More recent approaches to the application of colour have tended to support the view that the use of several colours to indicate relative signal strength is counter-productive and they have employed a single colour (for example, yellow or amber) for the present position of all targets, irrespective of signal strength. A second colour (possibly brown) can be used to indicate random responses (such as those from sea clutter) while persistent echoes retain the main echo colour. This facility can be selected at will by the observer but must be used with care and with an understanding of the principle involved. It has to be appreciated, for example, that buoys, boats and similar small floating targets may well return intermittent responses. The technique clearly involves analysis and correlation of signals, the principle and application of which are described in detail under 'Clutter suppression' in Section 3.6.3.4.

An important decision for the designer is the choice of background colour, i.e. that which represents the absence of signal (or data). There is some debate on this issue. One opinion is that for daylight viewing blue is an improvement on the traditional black background. However, its brightness tends to destroy night vision on the bridge and where blue is provided for daylight viewing it is normal for black to be available for selection at night. There is an opposing view that a black background is more suitable for both day and night use. It is probably true to say that many designers have an open mind on the choice of background (and other) colours and their views are likely to be reinforced or modified by the reaction of users as more and more observers gain experience of the use of both mono-chrome and colour raster-scan radars at sea.

Synthetic afterglow (see Section 2.6.7.5), sometimes referred to as *target tracks* or *trails*, is shown in a colour which contrasts with the background, for example black on blue or blue on black.

Assimilation of picture information is assisted by using a separate colour for the graphics associated with range and bearing measurement, for example range rings, variable range markers, electronic bearing lines, heading markers, bearing scales and data readouts.

The use of red as a warning colour for selected graphics or data suggests itself but set against this is the fact that red does not tend to show up as well as other colours.

2.6.7.9   *The future of raster-scan radar at sea*

The first marine raster-scan radars to appear on the market were designed for the small craft. This arose largely because, although designers recognised, among other benefits, the daylight viewing potential of using a television-style presentation, they were also very much aware of the cost and difficulties of producing the picture on a screen sufficiently large to allow compliance with the IMO Performance Standards (see Section 10.2.2). The latter requires a 340 mm diameter PPI circle for systems on large vessels. However, in due course many of the problems were accepted or overcome and by the mid-1980s a number of manufacturers were offering raster-scan radars which complied with the IMO Performance Standards even for vessels whose gross tonnage exceeded 10 000.

There is no doubt that raster-scan is the form of the radar picture of the future and, while it may take many years, it is certain to replace completely the traditional rotating trace display. The latter was never able to offer daylight viewing and the ability of the raster-scan display to do so has, probably more than any of its other benefits, and despite its limitations, ensured its success. However, it must be appreciated that the first generation of raster-scan systems represents the designer's perception of what is most likely to assist the observer in using and interpreting the radar system. Only a small proportion of observers have had any experience of raster-scan radar systems that comply with the IMO Performance Standards and thus there has been very little feedback from users. It will be important to establish how the majority of observers react to concentrating on the detail of a television-style radar picture for long periods of time, particularly in terms of the level of stress and tiredness that this may produce.

The question of whether all designers will eventually offer a full size colour display will also take time to answer. Some designers take the view that it is necessary to await the development of higher quality colour tubes because they believe that, of the large colour CRTs which are currently available, none offers the necessary brightness and resolution. This is reflected in their policy of offering a large monochrome display, supplemented by an optional smaller colour slave display. Other designers have indicated their faith in readily available large colour tubes by producing raster-scan systems with a 340 mm diameter colour PPI.

There is also some debate as to which colours should be used and how they can best be allocated to enhance the daylight viewing characteristic of the picture and to make a positive contribution to the ease with which the observer can extract and interpret the picture information. There are pleas for standardization of colours so that observers are not confused by the products of different manufacturers and there is merit in this suggestion. However, if regulations enforcing standardization are implemented at too early a stage in a new development such as colour radar, they can stifle potential improvements.

The first-generation raster-scan displays of the early to mid-1980s represented the most dramatic change that has taken place in the method of *painting* the radar picture since the A-scan was replaced by the radial-scan PPI (see Sections 1.2.3.1 and 1.2.3.2). It is to be hoped the second generation will reflect the professional mariner's reaction to the first generation which may well give the answers to some of the issues that are currently a matter of debate.

2.7   The siting of units on board ship

The preceding treatment of marine radar principles was based on a subdivision of the radar system into four units, namely, transmitter, aerial, receiver and display.

This approach is particularly helpful when discussing theoretical principles but the subdivision does not represent the physical units into which the shipboard system is divided. In practice the transmitter and some parts of the receiver are commonly located within the same unit, known as the *transceiver*. The ideal siting of the shipboard units is dictated by a number of navigational criteria but the extent to which such ideals can be realized is limited by certain engineering considerations. In general, the units should be sited so as to avoid failure or undue maintenance difficulties due to heat or fumes and they should be mounted sufficiently rigidly to prevent the performance and reliability of the system being adversely affected by vibration. Particular navigational and engineering aspects of the siting of each of the physical units will be discussed in the following sections and finally an exposition of the concept of interswitching duplicate units will be given.

2.7.1 Aerial siting

It is appropriate to consider the siting of this unit first since a poorly sited aerial can completely offset any benefits that can be gained elsewhere. In the theoretical treatment of aerial principles it was indicated that the aerial unit comprised the scanner, a device to transmit the rotation signal and a heading marker generator (see Sections 2.2.2 and 2.4). This also effectively represents the physical contents of one type of practical aerial unit. A second type of aerial unit also includes some or all of the transmitter and part of the receiver. The implication of the siting of these additional elements within the aerial unit will be discussed in Sections 2.7.2 and 2.7.3. In general, the scanner must be sited on a rigid structure which will not twist and give rise to bearing errors.

The scanner is the eyes and ears of the radar system and its siting is of crucial importance. However, the siting has to take into account a number of conflicting factors and is of necessity a compromise. In most cases radar observers will have had no say in the acceptance of this compromise but it is important that they appreciate the factors which may affect optimum results.

2.7.1.1 Blind and shadow sectors

Blind and shadow sectors occur when the radiation

from the aerial is intercepted by obstructions (for example, masts, funnel etc.) on board the vessel. The effect is illustrated by Figure 2.51 and it can be seen that it is analogous to that of optical shadows cast when a source of light is obstructed. In the interests of rigour it has to be said that because of the longer wavelength, radar waves

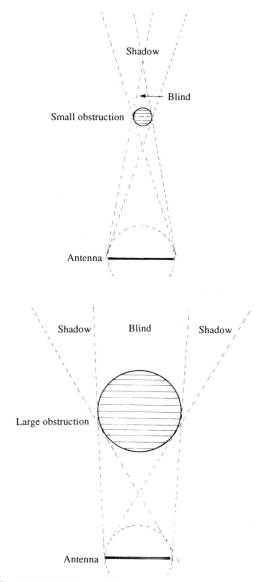

Figure 2.51 Blind and shadow sectors

experience greater diffraction than light waves. Diffraction is the term used to describe the effect when radiation passes close to a solid object which gives it a slight tendency to bend round the object. In this respect the use of S-band (see Section 2.3.3.1) will tend to reduce the shadow extent when compared with X-band transmissions.

No radiation is incident on the area of a blind sector, whereas a shadow sector represents an area of reduced sensitivity, i.e. an area on which less radiation is incident than would be the case in the absence of the obstruction. The size of the antenna, the size of the obstruction and its proximity to the aerial site will determine the angular width of the sector and whether it is 'blind' or 'shadow' in character.

The IMO Performance Standards (see Section 10.2) require that the aerial system be installed in such a manner that the efficiency of the display is not impaired by the close proximity of the aerial to other objects. It draws particular attention to the need to avoid blind sectors in the forward directions.

It might appear at first sight that the best approach is to locate the aerial unit sufficiently high as to be above all obstructions. This may be possible on some ships but in general the penalties which are paid for excessive aerial height (see Section 2.7.1.3) will disqualify this apparently *perfect* solution. Although it may not be possible to use the vertical location of the aerial to eliminate blind and shadow sectors, suitable attention to the horizontal siting may reduce the seriousness of their effects. This is illustrated by Figure 2.52.

Figure 2.52(a) shows a fairly traditional siting with sectors ahead and on both bows. Figures 2.52(b) and (c) show how these can be relocated astern or on one side. In considering these solutions it should be remembered that, although in clear weather the collision regulations allocate responsibilities to vessels which relate to the crossing and overtaking situations, when vessels are not in sight of one another the give way/stand on allocation of responsibilities does not apply. Both vessels have a responsibility to take action to avoid a close-quarters situation (see *The Navigation Control Manual*, Chapter 22).

There are practical limits to the physical separation between the aerial unit and the transceiver (see Sec-

tion 2.7.1.3) and hence if the aerial is sited forward so too must be the transceiver. In bad weather the latter may thus be exposed to vibration and access for maintenance may be a problem. Such siting may also involve very long cable runs to the display. This is a drawback both from the point of view of signal attenuation and because of susceptibility to damage, with the attendant difficulties of locating and repairing such damage should it be sustained.

If the aerial is sited off the vessel's fore-and-aft line it is important to remember that the origin of the picture represents the location of the aerial. This factor may be of particular significance in pilotage situations because, as illustrated by Figure 2.52(d), failure to appreciate it could result in the observer being seriously misled as to the position of the vessel with respect to mid channel.

All radar observers should be aware of the nature and extent of the shadow sectors on board their vessel. The prudent method of ensuring this is to measure the sectors and illustrate the results on a suitable plan-view diagram posted near the radar display (see Figure 2.53). In addition, the information should be recorded in the radar log. In some vessels the trim or draught may affect the shadow pattern and if this is believed to be the case it will be necessary to measure the sectors in more than one condition of loading.

The angular extent of the sectors can be measured by observing the response of a weak isolated target such as a buoy which is not fitted with a radar reflector (see Section 3.4) and is located at a range of about one mile. The ship should be swung through 360° and the limits of the sectors determined by measuring the bearings on which the echo disappears and subsequently reappears. It is important that a weak target is chosen to ensure that the areas of reduced sensitivity are effectively revealed. A good target, such as a buoy with a radar reflector, may return an echo which is so strong that a response is obtained despite the loss in energy caused by the offending obstruction. The measurement procedure should be carried out in calm conditions so that the echo is not masked by clutter (see Section 3.6) and to avoid an intermittent response due to the rolling motion of the buoy.

An alternative approach is to measure the sectors against the background of the sea clutter pattern (see

Section 3.6). For the same reasons given in the preceding paragraph for selecting a weak target, strong clutter conditions should be avoided. The measurements should not be taken when the vessel is in confined waters as the sectors may be obscured by indirect echoes (see Section 3.9.2) due to reflections from the obstructions which produce the shadow sectors.

Having measured the shadow pattern, it is important

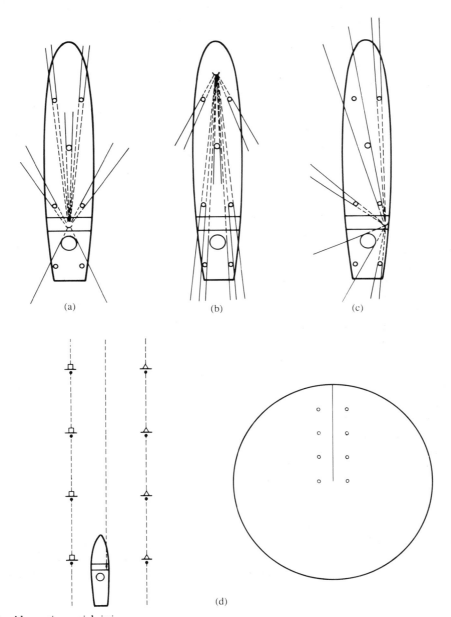

Figure 2.52   Alternative aerial sittings

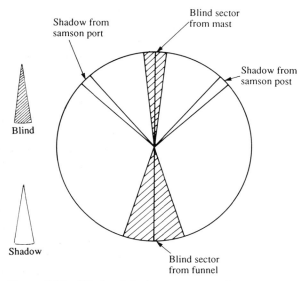

Figure 2.53   Blind and shadow sector record

to appreciate the danger of a target approaching on a steady bearing which lies within one of the sectors. Collisions have resulted from this cause. In poor visibility this danger must be addressed by ensuring that from time to time the vessel is *briefly* swung either side of the course by half the width of the largest sector in an attempt to reveal the presence of any targets within the blind and shadow sectors. In some situations the natural yawing motion of the vessel may adequately fulfil this function.

In ships which frequently navigate astern, for example short sea ferries, the aerial siting must be such as to avoid shadow sectors astern. In many cases such vessels are fitted with a dedicated docking aerial at the stern.

2.7.1.2   Indirect echoes

Obstructions close to the site of the aerial may reflect some of the radar energy on both its outward and return journeys. This gives rise to false echoes known as *indirect* (or *reflected*) echoes. These are discussed in detail in Section 3.9.2.

2.7.1.3   Aerial height

As suggested in Section 2.7.1.1, the location of the aerial

above all obstructions is not a simple matter. The height at which the aerial is sited is inevitably a compromise. There are benefits and drawbacks to siting the aerial as high as possible. In respect of shadow sectors, it is worth bearing in mind that if a vessel has crosstrees or similar reflecting areas on the masts, an aerial sited above the level of such an obstruction will cast a shadow on the water, whereas with a lower siting it may cast the shadow in space.

In favour of a high aerial siting is the fact that the distance to the radar horizon, and hence the theoretical maximum detection range of targets, increases with aerial height. This topic is discussed in detail in Section 3.8. The minimum range at which targets can be detected also depends on aerial height. Excessively high and low aerial sitings may increase or decrease this important limit and the implications of this, including the effect on the accuracy with which very short ranges can be measured, are discussed in Section 3.2.4. In general, very short range accuracy is improved with a low aerial. Some vessels have two interswitched aerials (see Section 2.7.8), one high and one low, to obtain the advantages of each.

A serious penalty incurred by the siting of the aerial at a great height is the effect on the amplitude and range of sea clutter response. The amplitude of sea clutter echoes and the maximum range at which they are detectable increases with aerial height. These responses produce a pattern of echoes around the origin which can mask even very strong targets. The danger of targets being lost in sea clutter returns represents one of the most serious limitations of marine radar and is discussed in detail in Section 3.6. Excessive aerial height will exacerbate this fundamental problem and serious consideration must be given to this factor when a shipboard radar installation is planned.

A further problem associated with a high aerial site is the loss of energy which occurs when the transmitted pulse and received signals travel along the necessary lengths of waveguide. These losses place a maximum limit of about 21 m on the separation between transceiver and aerial. In some systems the problem can be overcome by locating part or all of the transceiver within the aerial unit (see Section 2.7.2).

It is evident from this section that choosing an optimum aerial height involves reconciling a number of conflicting factors. The height selected in practice may be limited by the size and type of the vessel, but experience has shown that a height of between 13 and 20 m above the water level offers the best overall radar performance.

2.7.1.4 Susceptibility to damage

The site of the aerial unit should be well clear of halyards and similar rigging which might be liable to become entangled with the rotating scanner. Alternatively, the aerial can be located in a protective arrangement such as a *radome*. The latter is a spherical moulding made of glass reinforced plastic (GRP) within which the scanner is free to rotate. The surface of the radome must be kept clean because while GRP (more commonly referred to as Fibreglass) is transparent to radar energy (see Section 3.3.3), salt, dirt and similar deposits which may accumulate on the surface of the radome are not. In civil marine applications, the use of radomes is in general limited to small craft where the aerial length is less than about one metre.

2.7.1.5 Radiation hazard (see also Section 2.7.2)

It is believed that there is no radiation hazard to shipboard personnel provided that the aerial is rotating. This is based on the premise that the level of radiation outside the turning circle of the aerial is safe. However, *harmful* effects, particularly to the eyes, can be experienced at very short distances from a stationary aerial if energy is being radiated. The distance will depend on the transmitted power, but in civil marine radars designed for merchant ships it is usually in the region of 0.3 to 0.6 m. Many administrations require, and good practice dictates, that manufacturers should make radiation level measurements from which it is possible to determine the safe distance. This distance should form part of a warning contained in the operator's manual and should also be printed on the aerial unit. In the case of slotted waveguide aerials, the safe distance warning is normally written on the GRP envelope or protection panel (see Section 2.4.2.2). If it is necessary for personnel to approach within the safe distance of a stationary aerial, it is important to ensure that the equipment is not trans-

mitting and to take steps to prevent the equipment being switched to the transmit condition. A good practice is to have the person qualified to service the equipment remove the fuses from the transceiver and aerial-turning equipment when this work is being carried out and to place a prominent warning notice on the display.

Service personnel may have to carry out adjustments which require transmission from a stationary aerial, to undertake work on a waveguide while the transmitter is operating and to disconnect the waveguide from the transmitter. All such operations incur a risk of exposure to dangerous levels of radiation. It is essential that such work is only undertaken by fully trained and experienced service personnel. *Permanent damage to the eyes* is likely to result from looking down a waveguide from which radar energy is being radiated. Some appreciation of the possible harmful effects of radiation can be obtained by recognizing that a domestic microwave oven uses radar waves to cook meals in a very short space of time.

It is important to note that some cardiac pacemakers can be affected by radar-frequency radiation.

2.7.1.6 Effect on radio direction finder (RDF)

Metal elements close to the direction-finding loop aerial may introduce errors into RDF bearings and this factor may influence the choice of radar aerial site.

2.7.2 The transceiver unit

The transceiver unit is so called because it houses the transmitter (see Section 2.3) and part of the receiver (see Section 2.5). In addition to the mixer, the latter may comprise either the entire IF amplifier (see Section 2.5.2) or a portion of it sometimes referred to as the *pre-IF amplifier*.

Ideally, the transmitter and at least the early stages of the receiver should be located as close to the aerial unit as possible. This reduces the attenuation of the powerful transmitted pulse on its journey up the waveguide to the aerial and, of even greater importance, the attenuation of the weak returning signals as they travel down the waveguide to the receiver. By siting the transceiver close to the aerial unit, it is inevitable that in most cases it will therefore be remote from the display unit. However, by ensuring sufficient receiver gain within the transceiver (see Section 2.5.2.2) the signal can be amplified to an adequate level to make the journey along co-axial cable from the transceiver to the display.

Waveguide is expensive and thus siting the transceiver in close proximity to the aerial also reduces the overall cost of the installation. The cross-section of the waveguide is of critical importance to correct propagation and it must be *plumbed in* with great care, particular attention being given to ensure that bends and twists are formed in such a way as to prevent distortion of the waveguide dimensions. It is usual to have specially preformed sections for bends and twists. In an ideal situation the aerial unit would be mounted vertically above the transceiver so as to allow the use of a straight waveguide run. This is seldom possible in practice. Long waveguide runs are always at risk of accidental damage. The ingress of water or dirt will seriously affect the performance of the guide. Some modern waveguide systems are filled with a suitable gas in an attempt to maintain the guide cavity in a dry condition and, by pressure indication, to serve as an indicator of any accidental puncture in the wall of the guide.

In some systems the transceiver is fitted within the aerial unit. This may dispense with the need for a rotating waveguide joint (see Section 2.2.2), eliminates the waveguide run and reduces signal attenuation to a minimum. This approach suffers from the major disadvantage that there may be serious difficulties in servicing the unit in situ, especially in bad weather. The availability of replacement boards or units has reduced the seriousness of this problem.

In general, civil marine radar equipment should not produce undue interference in other radio equipment. However, good practice dictates that radar units in general, and the transmitter in particular, should not be sited close to radio communications equipment.

While modern transceivers are quiet by comparison with older types, the possibility of acoustic noise being a nuisance to personnel on or off watch is a factor which might influence siting of the unit.

The magnetron (see Section 2.3.3.2) is sited within the transceiver and clearly this, together with the associated waveguide, represents a radiation hazard. However,

only service personnel should be exposed to such risk and they should have appropriate training to deal with this danger. In some cases there may be risk from X-radiation and if this is the case many administrations require that the transceiver, or other unit should carry a warning notice.

2.7.3 The display unit

The display unit will contain the units necessary to perform the display functions described in Section 2.6. It will also house the video amplifier stages and perhaps some stages of the IF amplifier, the number of which will depend on what proportion of the receiver is located in the transceiver. Provided that there is adequate gain in the transceiver, the display can be located at quite a distance from it. Because the receiver is split between transceiver and display, some service procedures may require transceiver adjustments whose effect is best judged by viewing the display. If the two units are separated by a great distance, a communication link may greatly facilitate such servicing. This need may well be fulfilled by the use of portable VHF or UHF radios.

Where a single display unit is provided it will most likely be located in the wheelhouse because this allows the observer to view the radar and maintain a visual lookout. In the case of dual displays both may be sited in the wheelhouse or, alternatively, the second display may be placed in the chartroom. The advent of raster-scan displays (see Section 2.6.7) makes the provision of multiple displays a simple matter and allows considerable scope for remote control by means of a separate control panel associated with a long cable or by employing a cordless infra-red transmitter.

With the traditional analogue display (see Section 2.6.2), daylight viewing has always been a problem and one practical alternative to the use of a viewing hood or visor is to site the display within an area which can be screened by curtains or tinted glass. The advent of the radial-scan synthetic display (see Section 2.6.6) eased this problem to some extent while raster-scan displays should ensure daylight viewing in almost any ambient light condition. A fairly low level of light emanates from the traditional display and this caused few problems at night, though in certain circumstances reflection of the PPI glow and dial lights in the wheelhouse windows could impair night vision. The light level produced by a raster-scan display is considerably higher and this factor has to be considered in choosing a suitable site for the display.

At night it is practical for several observers simultaneously to view the traditional real-time analogue display, but in daytime the viewing hood makes this impossible. A major benefit of the modern raster-scan display is the elimination of this limitation.

It has been established that in general navigators prefer to have the display sited so that it is viewed when facing forward.

2.7.4 Compass safe distances

Many administrations require that all radar units, because of their potential magnetic influence, be tested to establish the safe distance by which they should be separated from the standard magnetic and from the steering magnetic compass. In the United Kingdom the compass safe distance must be indicated on a tally plate attached to the unit concerned. Some radar spares, in particular magnetrons (see Section 2.3.3.2), have very strong magnetic effects. They may be marked with a magnetic safe distance but if not should be stowed at least 7 m from magnetic compasses.

2.7.5 Exposed and protected equipment

Some radar equipment, such as the aerial, must be designed to withstand the elements while others are intended to be protected from the weather. Certain administrations require the class of equipment to be indicated on each unit.

2.7.6 Power supplies

In general, civil marine radar systems are not designed to operate directly from the mains supply. Normally a power supply unit is provided which can be configured to accept a range of power supply inputs and to convert any one of these to the voltage and frequency required.

In older systems it was common for such units to be rotary converters which were noisy by virtue of the mechanical nature of their operation. More modern systems use static inverters, but despite the absence of moving parts these too can emit obtrusive acoustic noise. The siting of this unit should be chosen to avoid disturbance to either those involved in watchkeeping or those who are off watch.

2.7.7 High voltage hazards

Lethal voltages may exist at various points within shipboard radar equipment. The charge held by high voltage capacitors may take some minutes to discharge after the equipment has been switched off. Maintenance adjustments which require the removal of the outside cover of units should only be attempted by fully qualified personnel.

2.7.8 Interswitching

The IMO Performance Standards (see Section 10.2) require vessels greater than 10 000 tons gross to be fitted with two radar installations. Many vessels below this tonnage limit also carry two radars because the benefits of such a dual installation are recognised. In order to maintain a high degree of reliability and flexibility where a dual installation is fitted, some or all of the units may be made interswitchable and capable of serving either or both displays. This allows unserviceable units to be isolated and also permits the servicing of units requiring maintenance, without affecting the availability of the overall system. The IMO Performance Standards (see Section 10.2) require that, where interswitching is fitted, the failure of either radar must not cause the supply of electrical energy to the other radar to be interrupted or adversely affected. A specific limitation of interswitching is that aerial units are only compatible with transceivers designed for the same wavelength, e.g. an X-band aerial cannot be used with an S-band transceiver. A typical fully interswitched system is illustrated in Figure 2.54.

Suitable selection of the characteristics of individual units will extend the capability of the system as a whole

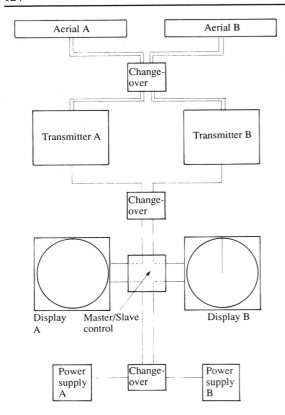

Figure 2.54 Interswitched systems

(see hereafter) to deal with a variety of conditions and circumstances.

2.7.8.1 *Choice of frequency*

The characteristics of S-band and X-band systems are to some extent complementary (see Section 2.3.3.1) and an interswitched system which offers both options has much to recommend it. It allows the observer to select the frequency which is most appropriate to the particular task in hand. For example, the masking response from sea and rain clutter (see Sections 3.6 and 3.7) is less with S-band whereas, with comparable aerial size (see Section 2.4.2.1, X-band in general offers better bearing discrimination (see Section 2.6.5.6).

2.7.8.2 *Choice of picture orientation and presentation*

An interswitched system makes possible the simultaneous availability of two different orientations or presentations. In particular, the relative-motion and true-motion presentations are complementary (see Section 1.5.3) and a dual system allows the observer to exploit this.

2.7.8.3 *Choice of aerial location*

In Section 2.7.1 the question of aerial siting was discussed and it is apparent that in the case of a single aerial the result is a compromise. With an interswitched dual installation, by careful choice of aerial siting it is possible to ensure that each siting gives particular benefits and that these can be exploited by the observer according to the prevailing circumstances. For example, the installation might have one high and one low aerial, one centred and one offset aerial or one forward and one midships aerial. The particular trade in which a vessel is involved might influence the choice of aerial sites.

2.7.8.4 *Partial interswitching*

A smaller degree of flexibility with lower cost may be achieved by partial interswitching. For example, one aerial and one power unit might serve two transceivers and two displays. Alternatively, a single aerial, transceiver and power supply might be provided with two displays, one as master and one as a slave.

2.7.8.5 *Switching protection*

Normally the equipment is protected during switching by the *stand-by* condition (see Section 6.7). In some systems this has to be done manually while in others access to the interswitching control is protected by an interlock.

2.7.8.6 *Master and slave controls*

Where two displays are driven from the same transceiver, one display must be designated as master and the other as slave. This has significance in that it affects the use of the operational controls. The master display will control the receiver tuning (see Sections 2.5.1.2, 6.2.4.2

and 6.3.4.3). If the receiver is of the linear type (see Section 2.5.2.5), the gain and sea clutter functions will be controlled from the master display, whereas with a logarithmic receiver (see Section 2.5.2.6) control can be exercised from each display. Normally the master display will control PRF and pulse length (see Sections 2.3.1 and 2.3.2.1) whereas the selected range scale is controlled by each display. As a result the pulse length and PRF could be inappropriate to the range scale selected at the slave display. To overcome this problem, at least one system has presented, at the slave display, an indication of the range scales that may be selected there.

The display will be protected by suitable circuitry from any technical incompatibility but the observer must be aware of any operational limitations, such as minimum range, discrimination and saturation, which may result (see Sections 3.2.4, 2.6.5 and 2.5.2.1). Pure display functions such as brilliance, range rings, range markers, EBL, centring and rain clutter are available at each display (see Chapter 6).

To overcome problems of mutual interference (see Section 3.9.5), a transmission synchronization circuit may be incorporated in the interswitching unit.

3 Target detection

3.1 Introduction

The ability of the radar system to detect and display a given target depends on a large number of factors some of which are constant and others which may vary in quite a complex manner. The significance of some of these factors may be almost self-evident while that of others may be much less obvious. The *rada range equation* is an expression which attempts to formalize the relationship between the maximum range at which a target can be detected and the parameters on which that range depends. In the form in which the equation is used by radar engineers to predict detection ranges of targets by taking into account all conceivable factors, it is indeed lengthy and complex, containing statistical and empirical components. However, in its simplest form as set out below, it provides at a glance an indication of the significance of many of the factors which are of concern to the radar observer :

$$R_{\max} = \sqrt[4]{\left(\frac{P \times G_0 \times A \times \sigma}{4 \times \pi^2 \times S_{\min}} \right)}$$

where $R_{\max}$ = maximum detection range
  P = transmitter power
  G_0 = antenna gain
  A = antenna aperture area (m^2)
  σ = target radar cross-section (m^2)
  $S_{\min}$ = minimum detectable signal

All but one of the variables appearing in the equation relate to the characteristics of the radar system and each of these is discussed in turn in Section 3.2. The sole representative of the target is its radar cross-section which is a measure of the size of the target as 'seen' by the radar. Except in the case of certain simple shapes, this is a complex quantity, often having a statistical nature; the implications of this are discussed in Section 3.3. This simple form of the radar equation assumes that the radar and the target are in free space. In practice they are both located on a curved earth having a surface of varying character and surrounded by an atmosphere in which various weather effects may be manifest. The simple equation takes no account of the surface over which, or the medium through which, the radar pulse travels, because many of the effects are extremely difficult to quantify. However, a suitable qualitative treatment of these factors is presented in Sections 3.6, 3.7 and 3.8.

While each of the various factors will be discussed in turn, it is essential to appreciate that in assessing the ability of the radar to detect a target *all* factors will have to be considered and it must be recognised that the relative significance of individual factors will vary with circumstances.

A further result which follows from the equation is that, in general, the signal strength received varies inversely as the *fourth* power of the range of the reflecting surface. (This can be shown by replacing $S_{\min}$ with the more general term S_r representing received signal strength and then making S_r the subject of the equation.) It is thus important to appreciate that, for distant targets, a small increase in range may produce a comparatively large decrease in response. The response from almost all wanted targets follows this law, but some unwanted responses such as those from the sea and from precipitation do not, these will be discussed in Sections 3.6 and 3.7 respectively.

3.2 Radar characteristics

The radar characteristics which appear in the radar range equation as set out above relate directly to the system units described in Sections 2.3, 2.4 and 2.5. One (the power) relates to the transmitter, two (antenna gain and aperture) relate to the aerial and one (S_{min}) relates to the receiver. It is thus appropriate to consider the characteristics under these headings.

3.2.1 Transmitter characteristics

As might be expected, the ability to detect distant targets can be improved by using a more powerful transmitter (see Section 2.3.2.2). In a single radar installation the transmitter power will be a factor which is beyond the control of the observer. However, in dual or interswitched systems (see Section 2.7.8) it may be possible to make a choice between two transmitters of differing powers. The important factor which the radar equation reveals is that the maximum detection range varies as the fourth root of transmitter power. The power of transmitters designed for fitting to large vessels varies with manufacturer, but 10 kW and 50 kW are representative of low and high values. However, it must be noted that a five-fold increase in power only yields an improvement in predicted detection range of approximately 50%. This relationship must also be considered when contemplating the use of a lower power transmitter to reduce unwanted responses (see Sections 6.10.1.1 and 6.10.2.2).

It may seem strange that the pulse length (see Section 2.3.2.1), which is clearly a transmitter characteristic, does not appear in the expression for detection range. Simple observation will show that long range detection is improved by the use of longer pulse lengths. The effect of pulse length is in fact implicit in the quantity S_{min}, the minimum detectable signal, which is a function of pulse length and is discussed in Section 3.2.3.

3.2.2 Antenna characteristics

The radar equation shows that maximum detection range is a function of antenna gain and aperture area.

Clearly these two quantities are related, as a study of Sections 2.4.1.6, 2.4.2.1 and 2.4.3 will reveal. For a given rectangular aperture area, an increase in one dimension at the expense of the other will increase the aerial gain in the plane of the larger dimension. It can be shown that G_0 is directly proportional to A and can thus be replaced in the equation by G_0^2. Hence the predicted maximum detection range varies as the square root of antenna gain. Thus aerial gain has a greater influence than transmitter power on long range performance.

As in the case of transmitter power, where a single radar installation is fitted the observer will have no choice in the matter of aerial gain. In a dual system or interswitched system (see Section 2.7.8.3) the observer may benefit from the ability to select the more suitable aerial. It should be remembered that bearing discrimination will also be improved by selection of the higher gain aerial.

It may seem strange that wavelength does not appear in the equation. It is in fact implicit in the aerial gain and the target radar cross-section, both of which are functions of wavelength (see Sections 2.4.2 and 3.3.5.4).

3.2.3 Receiver characteristics

In the absence of unwanted echoes the criterion for the detection of an echo is that the target response must exceed that of the thermal noise generated at the first stage in the receiver (see Section 2.5.2.3). Thus S_{min}, the minimum detectable signal, is a function of receiver sensitivity. While the theoretical maximum sensitivity is of course limited by the extent to which the radar design can minimize the amplitude of the noise generated in the first receiver stage, it cannot be stressed too strongly that the observer will degrade this sensitivity if the tuning and gain controls are set incorrectly (see Sections 6.2.4, 6.3.4 and 6.4.4).

Whatever the level of noise generated by the first stage of the receiver, the amount of noise which reaches the display depends on the bandwidth of the receiver (see Section 2.5.2.4). This bandwidth must be wider when shorter pulses are selected and hence the receiver sensitivity is inherently poorer in that condition. The receiver sensitivity, and hence the maximum range at which targets can be detected, is thus a function of the pulse length selected by the observer.

Further study of the radar range equation shows that the transmitter power appears as a large quantity on the numerator of the expression while the receiver sensitivity is represented by a small number in the denominator. Radar designers recognise that small improvements in the noise performance are as effective as massive increases in transmitter power; as a result, in recent years efforts have been concentrated on trying to improve receiver performance. This principle is at least as important to the radar observer because it must be borne in mind that minor maladjustments of the tuning or gain controls can have the same effect as a large loss in transmitter power.

Where wanted echoes are present among unwanted signals such as clutter and spurious echoes, it may not be possible to exploit fully the sensitivity of the receiver because the minimum detectable signal level will be determined not by the amplitude of the noise but by the amplitude of unwanted signals. The difficulties posed by such circumstances are discussed in Sections 3.6, 3.7 and 3.9.

It must be appreciated that the available receiver sensitivity can only be fully exploited if the radar display is set up correctly and the controls maintained in correct adjustment to suit changing conditions and requirements. Some adjustments are routine while others, such as searching for targets in clutter (see Sections 6.10.1 and 6.10.2), require considerable skill and practice. In this connection particular attention is drawn to the various practical procedures set out in Chapter 6. There is little doubt that, but for the difficulty of quantifying it, the skill of the radar observer is a factor which would appear in the radar range equation.

3.2.4   Minimum detection range

The radar range equation is specifically concerned with the prediction of maximum detection ranges and in many circumstances the radar observer is concerned with this aspect of target detection. However, there are certain circumstances, for example pilotage situations, in which the minimum detection range is of particular importance. The importance of a small minimum

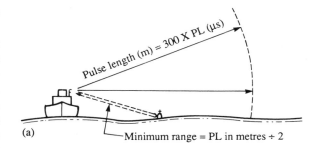

(a)

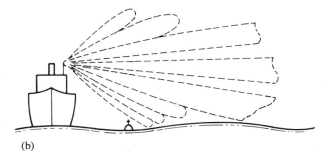

(b)

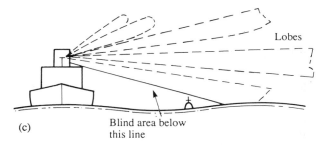

Figure 3.1   Factors affecting minimum detection range
(a)   Pulse length
(b)   Vertical beam structure
(c)   Ship structure shadowing

detection range is recognised by the IMO Performance Standards (see Section 10.2) which require that specific target types be clearly displayed down to a minimum range of 50 m. The various factors affecting minimum detection range are illustrated by Figure 3.1.

Clearly the radar cannot receive echoes while the pulse is being transmitted and this limitation determines the *theoretical minimum detection range*. The trailing edge of the transmitted pulse will clear the aerial after the start of the timebase by an elapsed time equal to the duration of one pulse length. This instant will coincide with the arrival of an echo from any reflecting surface which lies at a distance of one-half pulse length from the aerial (see Figure 3.1(a)). The theoretical minimum detection range can thus be determined by calculating the distance travelled by radar energy in one-half the duration of the transmitted pulse.

Example 3.1   Calculate the theoretical minimum detection range for a radar which has three pulse lengths, the durations of which are 1.0, 0.5 and 0.1 μs.

To achieve the minimum detection range the observer should select the shortest available pulse length. Half the duration of the shortest pulse length (PL) is given by

$$\frac{\text{PL}}{2} = \frac{0.1}{2}\,\mu s$$

The distance travelled by radar energy in this time is given by

$$D_{min} = \frac{0.1}{2} \times 300\ \text{m (see Section 1.2.2)} = 15\ \text{m}$$

The theoretical minimum detection range $= 15$ m

It is evident that the theoretical minimum range illustrated by this example (which uses a typical short pulse length) is considerably less than that required by the IMO Performance Standards. In practice, the theoretical minimum range cannot be achieved for three principal reasons, namely:

1 At close range the target may be below the lower extent of the vertical beam (see Section 3.2.4), though of course it may be illuminated by the vertical side-lobes. Assuming that the beam is not intercepted by the ship's structure (see below), the range at which the lower edge intersects the sea increases with aerial height (see Figure 3.1(b)).
2 At close range the target may be shadowed in the athwartships direction by the ship's side or in the fore-and-aft direction by the ship's bow or stern. The likelihood of this shadowing decreases with aerial height.

The question of whether the minimum range is limited by this factor, or by the lower limit of the beam described in item 1, depends on the height at which the aerial is sited, its location with respect to the ship's fore-and-aft line and the dimensions of the vessel (see Figure 3.1(c)).
3 The T/R cell takes a finite time to de-energize.

3.3 Target characteristics

Energy in the pulse which is intercepted by the target is then available for return towards the antenna and hence to the receiver which is now in a receptive state. The amount of energy which is returned toward the antenna, as opposed to that energy which is absorbed and scattered by the target, is dependent upon the following five prime characteristics of the target.

3.3.1 Aspect

The simplest approach to target response is to consider that the energy suffers 'specular' reflection, i.e. the sort of reflection that occurs when light strikes a plain mirror. Aspect is the angle which the radar rays make with the plane of the mirror and, as can be seen in Figure 3.2, the response will be good when the aspect is 90° and poor at virtually all other angles.

3.3.2 Surface texture

The extent to which reflection is specular is dependent upon the surface texture of the target, i.e. whether the surface is 'rough' or 'smooth'. Whether a surface is rough or smooth has to be related to the wavelength of the waves which are striking it. A surface which reflects light poorly because the indentations or facets in the surface are of the same order as the wavelength of the light (approximately 0.001 mm) will appear smooth to radar waves whose wavelength (some 3 to 10 cm) is very much longer, and specular reflection will result. It should be noted that objects which appear rough to radar waves, and therefore scatter a large proportion of the waves, can occasionally improve the response from a

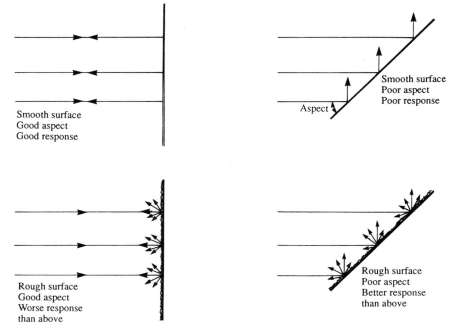

Figure 3.2   The effects on target response of aspect and surface texture

target which has an intrinsically poor aspect (see Figure 3.2).

3.3.3   Material

In general, materials which are good conductors of electricity also return good radar responses. This occurs as a result of absorption and re-radiation of the waves at the same wavelength as those received, rather than from simple specular-type reflection.

Some bodies absorb radiation but, when they re-radiate, the wavelength is different from that at which it was received; still other bodies absorb radiation and re-radiate very little of the energy (this results in the temperature of the body rising, i.e. the received radiation is coverted to heat). Some materials are simply transparent to radar energy. GRP behaves to a large extent in this way, steel will return good responses, while wooden boats generally produce poor responses.

3.3.4   Shape

It is frequently suggested that shape might be considered as the variable aspect of an object. This is true, but when attempting to assess the degree of response which one might expect from a particular target it is often convenient to consider the target as of fixed shape but able to change its aspect (e.g. a conical buoy rolling in a seaway).

Figure 3.3   Some effects of material on target response

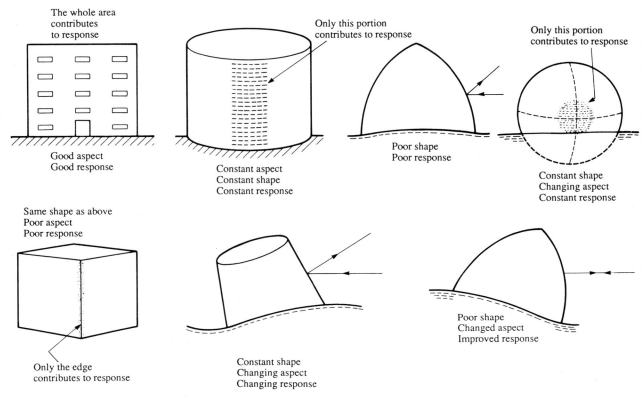

Figure 3.4   The effect of target shape on target response

3.3.5   Size

In general, the more energy intercepted by the target, the better the response is likely to be, i.e. the response is related to the area of the target irradiated by the beam (at any instant). This is not necessarily the same as the intrinsic size of the target. Since the radar beam is angularly wider in the vertical plane than in the horizontal, tall targets will in general produce stronger responses (all other factors being equal).

Consider two targets presenting the same area to the radar; if the linear width of the horizontal beam at the range of the targets is equal to the linear width of target A then, in the case of B, only the small irradiated portion of the target will contribute to echo strength, while, in the case of A, virtually the total area will be irradiated.

It is essential to understand clearly that what is being considered here is target response as opposed to actual target size (and therefore its potential *brightness* on the screen) and not its displayed size (i.e. the *area* of the screen which it occupies).

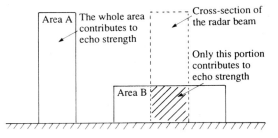

Figure 3.5   The effect of irradiated area on echo strength
Area A = Area B = cross-section of the radar beam

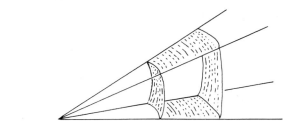

Figure 3.6   The resolution cell

Figure 3.7   The portion of the vessel irradiated

It is also necessary here to consider the 'resolution cell' in relation to the three-dimensional size of the target. The cell is defined by the transmitted pulse length, the horizontal beamwidth and the vertical beamwidth.

Only that portion of the target which falls within the resolution cell at any instant can contribute to the response. In general, as the beam sweeps over small targets, they will fall completely within the resolution cell. With larger targets, all the energy may be intercepted when the target is at short range, whereas at longer ranges, as the cell 'expands', the target may still exceed the horizontal beamwidth but is unlikely to fill the vertical beam.

Where, within the cell, the target is sloping, e.g. a coastline, two consequences of the slope need to be considered.

3.3.5.1   Sloping surfaces – the effect of coherence on response amplitude

Consider the face of the slope to be made up of small steps. The radial length of the step will determine the phase relationship of the elements of the returning composite wave. If the elements are out of phase on their return to the antenna then the echo strength will be poor, while if they are in phase the response will be good.

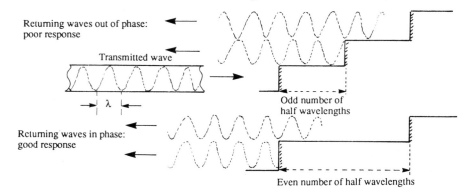

Figure 3.8   The effect of coherence on echo strength

Note The radial length of the steps being considered here is of the order of a fraction of a wavelength (and will take the form of an odd number of quarter wavelengths).

3.3.5.2 *Sloping surfaces – the effect of signal integration on echo strength*

In this case, the steps which are to be considered are of the order of one-half pulse length, i.e. half of 0.1 to 1 μs, which equates to a radial distance of some 15 to 150 m.

Consider a stepped sloping surface (Figure 3.9) where each step is 10 m in length and the radar pulse length is 0.2 μs, i.e. the spatial length of the pulse is $0.2 \times 300 = 60$ m.

It can be seen from Figure 3.9 that the responses from the individual steps on the target can integrate (i.e. add up) to a maximum from that portion of the target which lies within any one-half pulse length, but cannot increase indefinitely as the target increases in height. In the above example the one-half pulse length is 30 m.

If, with the same overall size of target, the step height and length are varied so that each step height is halved and the step length is halved, the same aggregate

response will be obtained, which is the integration of a larger number of smaller responses. It is evident that the land still rises to the same height over half the pulse length. This suggests an alternative approach, which is to consider only the vertical height over the one-half pulse length i.e. *projected height* (or, in three dimensions, the *projected area* – Figure 3.10).

Note (a) If the step lengths are not precisely the same and if the difference is of the order of one-half the wavelength, then the effects of coherence will also have to be considered when deciding on whether or not the elements of the response will integrate.

(b) If the facets are not true steps, random scattering will also have to be considered.

(c) As a result of the most favourable integration of the elements of the response, the maximum echo *strength* would be the same as if a flat plate were placed in the path of the pulse. The plate would have a vertical height equivalent to the projected vertical height of the target which lies within half the radial length of the transmitted pulse.

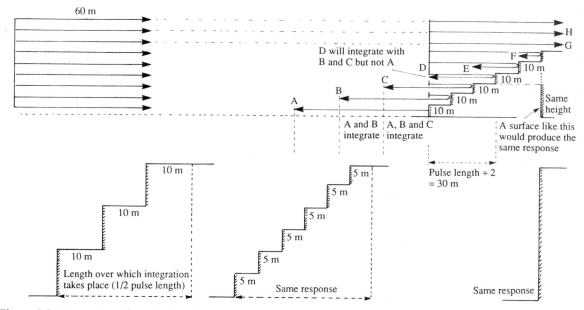

Figure 3.9 Integration of signals from sloping surfaces

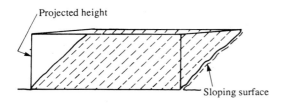

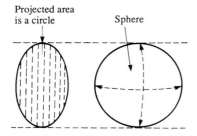

Figure 3.10   Projected area

Where a target is small in relation to the resolution cell, it is convenient to consider the projected area of the target (see also Section 3.3.5.4), but its surface texture, material, aspect and shape must not be ignored.

3.3.5.3   *The equivalent flat plate area (A$_t$) of a target*

This is the area of a flat plate orientated at right angles to the incident radiation which would return the same energy as the object. The equivalent flat plate areas for some common shapes are given in Figure 3.11.

Note   (a)   The values given in Figure 3.11 are maximum values, having been simplified by the removal of terms relating to aspect. If the aspect in either or both planes is changed, the response may decrease. For example, if the flat plate were tilted there would be a marked drop in response, whereas, with the cylinder, a change about a vertical axis would result in no change in response while a change about a horizontal axis would result in a marked drop in response.

(b)   In deriving the formulae, there is an assumption that the size of the object is very large in comparison with the wavelength. (The formulae should not be applied, for instance, to spherical rain drops.)

3.3.5.4   *The radar cross-section of a target (σ)*

The radar cross-section (or equivalent echoing area) of an object is the area intercepting that amount of power which, *when scattered isotropically*, produces an echo equal to that received from the object.

Since a sphere is generally accepted as a typical isotropic radiator (i.e. it radiates in all directions), this definition is indicating the cross-section of a sphere which, if it replaced the target, would produce the same response.

It can be seen that if there is some directivity in the target's response, its radar cross-section will be much greater than its actual physical cross-section or projected area.

Example 3.2   Compare the radar cross-section of a flat plate with that of a sphere if the plate is at right angles to the radiation; both plate and sphere have projected areas of 1m² and the wavelength in use is 3.2 cm.

$$\frac{\text{Radar cross-section of a flat plate}}{\text{Radar cross-section of a sphere}} = \frac{4\pi a^2 b^2 / \lambda^2}{\pi c^2}$$

$$\text{but} \quad a \times b = 1 = \pi c^2$$

$$= \frac{4\pi ab}{\lambda^2}$$

$$= \frac{4\pi A}{\lambda^2}$$

$$= \frac{4 \times 3.142 \times 10^4}{3.2^2}$$

$$= \quad 12\,273 \text{ times}$$

This means that the flat plate would produce a response some 12 000 times greater than the sphere or, alternatively, a sphere having some 12 000 times the projected area of the plate would have to be placed at the same range as the plate to produce the same response. It is interesting to note that any slight change in the aspect of the plate will result in a massive drop in the response, whereas no change will occur if the sphere is re-orientated.

One of the surface objects referred to in the IMO Performance Standards, in specifying range performance (see Section 10.2), is a navigational buoy having an effective echoing area of approximately 10 m². This

Target	Dimensions	Max. equivalent flat plate area A_t	Max. radar cross-section σ
Sphere	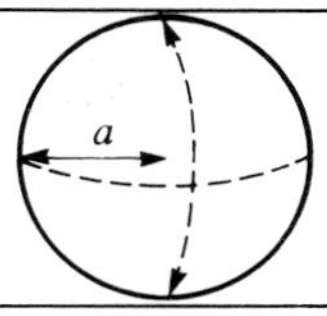	$\dfrac{a\lambda}{2}$	πa^2
Cylinder	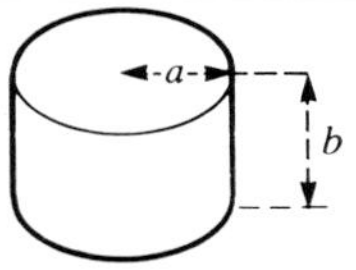	$b\sqrt{\dfrac{a\lambda}{2}}$	$\dfrac{2\pi ab^2}{\lambda}$
Flat plate	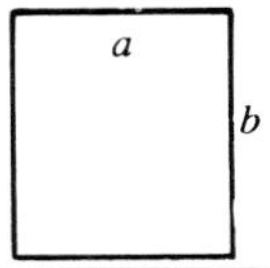	ab	$\dfrac{4\pi a^2 b^2}{\lambda^2}$
Dihedral corner	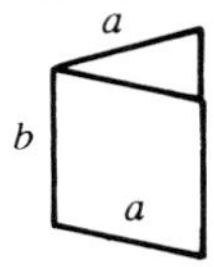	$ab\sqrt{2}$	$\dfrac{8\pi a^2 b^2}{\lambda^2}$
Triangular trihedral	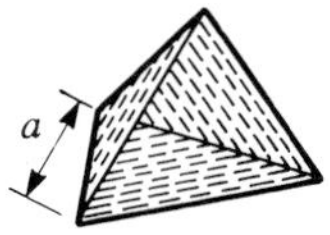	$\dfrac{a^2}{\sqrt{3}}$	$\dfrac{4\pi a^4}{3\lambda^2}$
Rectangular trihedral	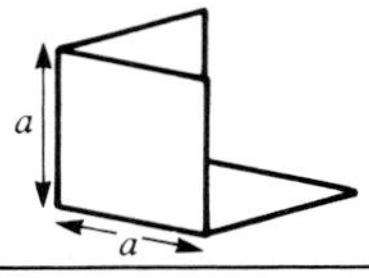	$a^2\sqrt{3}$	$\dfrac{12\pi a^4}{\lambda^2}$
Cone	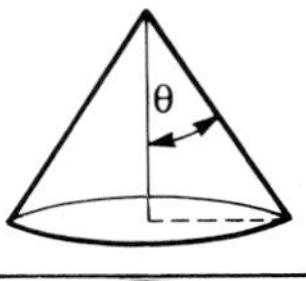	$\dfrac{\lambda^2 \tan^2\theta}{8\pi}$	$\dfrac{\lambda^2 \tan^4\theta}{16\pi}$
Lunenburg lens	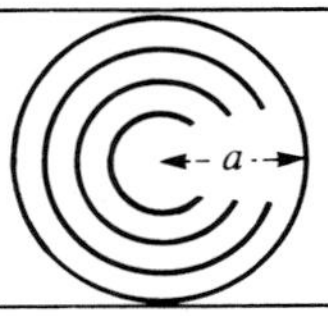	πa^2	$\dfrac{4\pi^3 a^4}{\lambda^2}$

Figure 3.11   Radar cross-sections and equivalent flat plate areas for some common targets

means one that produces the same strength of echo as a sphere having a projected area of 10 m², i.e. a spherical buoy having a diameter of some 12 ft.

The relationship between radar cross-section and equivalent flat plate area is given by the formula

$$\sigma = \frac{4\pi A_t^2}{\lambda^2}$$

3.3.5.5 The Rayleigh roughness criterion

It can be shown that the roughness of a surface depends on the size of the discontinuities in relation to the incident wavelength and the angle at which the radiation strikes the surface (the grazing angle). Application of the Rayleigh criterion indicates that the surfaces for all practical purposes are smooth if $(8 \times \delta h \times \sin \theta) < \lambda$, where λ is the wavelength and θ is the grazing angle (Figure 3.12).

Example 3.3 If the antenna is at a height of 15 m, at what distance, d, from the ship, will the sea surface appear smooth if wave height is 1 m (the radar is working in the X-band)? (At the limit of clutter, $8 \times \delta h \times \sin \theta = \lambda$.)

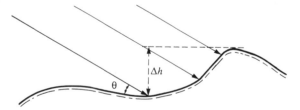

Figure 3.12 Grazing angle and roughness

$$\frac{8 \times 1 \times 15}{\sqrt{(225 + d^2)}} = 0.03$$
$$d^2 = 4000^2 - 225$$

The sea surface will appear smooth at a distance.
$$d \geqslant 4\,km\ (2.16\,n\ mile)$$

3.3.6 Responses from specific targets

3.3.6.1 Ice

Large icebergs, such as those which are formed on the east coast of Greenland and drift down toward the North Atlantic shipping routes, have been found to give greatly varying radar responses. Detection ranges as great as 11 nautical miles have been experienced while, on the other hand, quite large icebergs have approached to within 2 n mile without being detected. Even the same iceberg may give greatly differing responses when viewed from different directions.

Particular concern has been expressed because of radar's apparent difficulty in 'detecting ice'. The point should be made that the ice which causes most concern is that form which comprises what are known as growlers. Many theories have been put forward and there have been many practical experiments carried out to determine the best way to use the radar in areas where growlers are expected: two major points emerge.

1 Growlers are intrinsically poor targets because, as melting ice, the surface tends to be smooth and this does nothing to improve their essentially poor shape and aspect. They present a small projected area above the water and the signal returned is frequently of

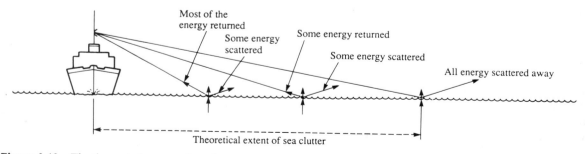

Figure 3.13 The theoretical extent of sea clutter

strength comparable to or weaker than that returned from the sea waves which are prevalent in the area in which the growlers are commonly found.

Theories relating to the effects of high temperature gradients in the immediate vicinity of the growler and also to the re-radiation characteristic of the ice have not proved conclusive.

2 In areas where growlers are to be expected, radar should not be relied upon to give adequate or even any warning of their presence, especially at night or in poor visibility. Speed and the visual lookout should be set with this in mind.

The best use of radar under these circumstances is:

(a) a dedicated radar watch by one observer;
(b) regular searching with the anti-clutter control on the short ranges (see Section 6.10.1), remembering to check at frequent intervals on the longer ranges for larger targets;
(c) use of the long pulse in weak clutter;
(d) use of the longer wavelength of the S-band radar.

3.3.6.2   *Radar-conspicuous targets*

Targets which are designated *radar-conspicuous* should be those which are known to provide good radar responses and are readily identifiable (see Section 8.2.5). In the past, particular land features which satisfied those criteria were highlighted on charts by the addition of the legend 'Radar Conspic'. This practice has been discontinued but there is no reason why observers should not mark their own charts in this way and also make notes in the radar log for the benefit of their successors.

3.3.6.3   *Ships*

The structure of ships is such that there are many natural 'corner reflectors' (see Section 3.4.1) and hence, when a target vessel is rolling and pitching in a seaway, its echo strength does not vary quite as much as might be expected. Some rather peculiar effects can be observed, although they are usually quite easily explained by reverting to first principles. For example, long vessels may appear as two or three individual echoes (each of which when tracked by ARPA might appear to be going in a slightly different direction). They may also be confused for a tug-and-tow or vice versa. Supertankers, because of their low freeboard, may not be detected at inordinately great ranges.

3.4   Target enhancement – passive

It is essential that some targets which would normally provide poor radar responses, e.g. buoys, glass fibre and wooden boats etc, are detected at an adequate range by radar. It was recognised at a very early stage in the development of radar that some form of echo enhancement was needed.

3.4.1   Corner reflectors

A corner reflector was seen as a simple device which would return virtually all of the energy which entered

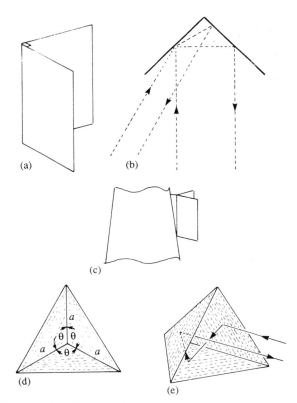

Figure 3.14   Corner reflectors

it, i.e., the energy would be returned in the direction from which it had come almost irrespective of the angle at which it had entered the corner (see Figure 3.14). In its simplest form, such a corner consists of two metal plates placed at an angle of 90° to each other, attached to a navigation mark which then returns an improved radar response and consequently is detectable at a greater range.

An essential principle of all echo enhancement is that it provides *reserve gain*, which means that, in adverse conditions of sea or weather clutter, the target's improved response can be expected to be greater than the clutter responses and therefore be detectable (see Sections 6.10.1 and 6.10.2), despite the reduced gain necessary for the suppression of the clutter.

While a simple corner is adequate on non-floating objects, if the attitude of the target is likely to change as it moves in a seaway it is necessary to use the now familiar *closed corner* or triangular trihedral (see Figure 3.14(d)) rather than the dihedral corner. The closed corner will ensure that the energy is returned even though the corner is moving through quite a large angle in both the horizontal and vertical planes.

3.4.1.1   *The accuracy of construction*

The angle between each pair of planes must be 90° and

very little error can be tolerated without affecting the efficient operation of the corner. Where, as a result of damage or careless construction, the angle is other than 90°, even by a very small amount, the response from the corner can be seriously impaired.

Figure 3.15 shows that, with a wavelength of 3 cm and a side length of 1.05 m (i.e. side length to wavelength ratio of 35); if the angle between the planes is 88° the gain is only 10 dB instead of the 30 dB that might be expected – this difference of 20 dB represents a reduction in response by a factor of 100. Note that with smaller sides but still working at the same wavelength, the loss would not be so severe.

Over the years, many designs for the 'home' construction of the corner reflectors and in particular 'collapsible' octahedral arrays (see Section 3.4.2.2) have been published, but it is never made clear how important is the precision required in the construction and assembly of the corners, in order for the full potential of the reflector to be achieved.

The suggestion that 'crumpled' aluminium foil (in a plastic container!) will provide adequate radar responses is a serious over-simplification. The physical principles of adequate enhancement require precise corners and that the size of each facet is at least greater than and preferably a function of wavelength.

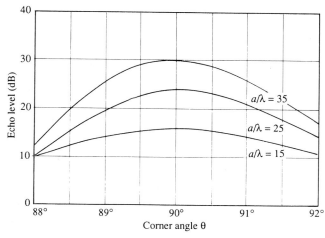

Figure 3.15   The effect of an error in all three corner angles of a corner reflector

3.4.1.2 *The response from a corner reflector*

The three forms of the corner reflector may be compared by referring to Figure 3.11. The following points should be noted.

1 Values shown are maximum values. Where aspect in either plane is changed, additional terms will need to be included in the equations.

2 A_t indicates the area of a flat plate, orientated so as to be perpendicular to the direction of the incident radiation. For example, a triangular trihedral reflector which has a side length a of 50 cm reflects as if it were a flat plate having an area of 1443.4 cm² and a 90° aspect.

This would appear to indicate that a corner reflector is not as good at returning a response as a flat plate. While this is true, the very important proviso is that a flat plate will only respond at optimum level when it is perpendicular to the incident radiation. If there is only a very slight change in aspect of the flat plate, the response will drop theoretically to zero; with the corner, the level will suffer very little reduction over some ± 50° of change in attitude.

A second point which is worthy of note is that the dihedral and rectangular trihedral corners both have better response figures than the triangular trihedral but the former's response is markedly susceptible to change of attitude while the latter does not have such a wide coverage angle since the square plates tend to intercept the incident radiation at an earlier stage as aspect is varied.

3.4.2 Arrays of reflectors

A single triangular trihedral corner does not provide 360° of azimuth coverage. By use of a group or array, irrespective of the direction from which it is viewed and of its attitude in the vertical plane, the response will remain virtually unchanged. The array may be incorporated in the basic structure of the navigation mark (Figure 3.16).

The following points should be noted with regard to arrays:

1 Reflectors which have surfaces of wire mesh, especially if a is greater than 20 times the wavelength, tend to warp and so produce poor results.

2 Deterioration of response is likely to result from (a) imprecise construction or damage (b) poor intrinsic orientation and (c) changes in coherence.

3.4.2.1 *Types of array*

The *didhedral array* has been found to be most appropriate for shore-based navigation marks because the rapid fall off in response associated with change of attitude in the vertical plane was not a factor.

The *octahedral array* (Figure 3.17) was until recently regarded as the standard for most situations.

In the *pentagonal array* (Figure 3.18), the polar diagram in the horizontal plane shows quite serious arcs of reduced response where the beam passes between the elements.

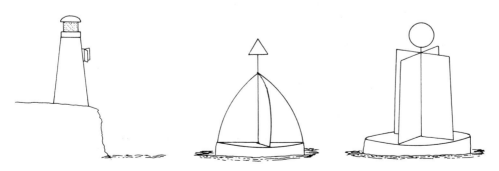

Figure 3.16 Arrays of reflectors incorporated into the structures of navigation marks

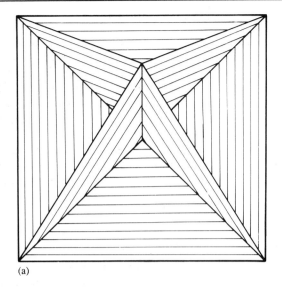

(a)

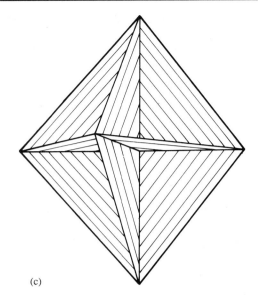

(c)

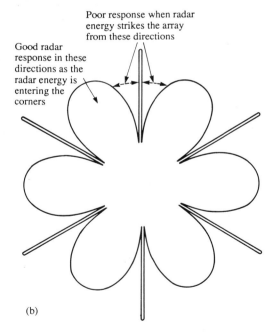

Poor response when radar
energy strikes the array
from these directions

Good radar
response in these
directions as the
radar energy is
entering the
corners

(b)

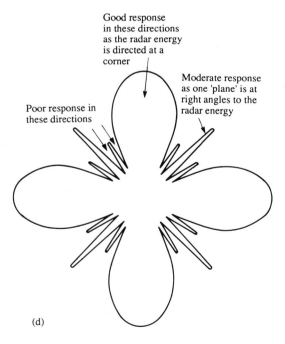

Good response
in these directions
as the radar energy
is directed at a
corner

Moderate response
as one 'plane' is at
right angles to the
radar energy

Poor response in
these directions

(d)

Figure 3.17   The octahedral array

(a)   Correct orientation

(b)   Polar diagram corresponding to (a)

(c)   Incorrect orientation

(d)   Polar diagram corresponding to (c) – the 'point-up'
orientation gives reduced response

In the vertical plane, as the navigation mark heels, the response falls off rapidly with angle of heel.

In the *double pentagonal array*, as can be seen from Figures 3.18(b) and 3.19 the interspaced corners fill out the polar diagram in the horizontal plane, thus improving the 360° coverage pattern.

3.4.2.2   Stacked arrays (Figure 3.20)

In order to overcome the effect of the gaps in the polar diagrams for the arrays described above, the individual triangular trihedral corners can be arranged in such a way that, as the response from one corner decreases, the response from the next corner starts to increase and so compensates for that drop. In this way, uniformity of response is maintained over 360° of azimuth.

An advantage of the many commercial forms of stacked arrays is that they are enclosed in a glass fibre housing which protects the metallic element from damage.

3.4.3   The Lunenburg lens

The Lunenburg lens has been in use for quite a number of years, both on navigation marks and on small craft, but frequently goes unrecognised. It comprises a series of concentric shells of differing refractive index.

(a)

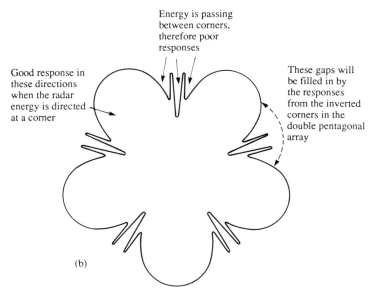

Energy is passing between corners, therefore poor responses

Good response in these directions when the radar energy is directed at a corner

These gaps will be filled in by the responses from the inverted corners in the double pentagonal array

(b)

Figure 3.18   The pentagonal array
(a)   The array   (b)   Polar diagram

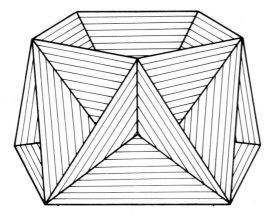

Figure 3.19   The double pentagonal array

3.4.3.1   *Principle of operation (Figure 3.21)*

Paraxial rays, impinging on the outer spherical surface, are refracted by different amounts at each shell interface so that they are focused at a point on the opposite surface of the sphere. Here the energy is reflected by a metal band in such a way that the exit path of the returning energy is in a direction reciprocal to that of the incident energy.

3.4.3.2   *The polar diagram*

Figure 3.22 gives the theoretical polar diagram, and Figure 3.23 shows its practical effect when applied to a buoy. It should be noted that in the horizontal plane there are no significant 'dropout' sectors. In the vertical plane the coverage is also good, allowing the buoy an angle of heel of some 35° or, conversely, the response will be enhanced even when the buoy is close to a vessel with quite a large antenna height.

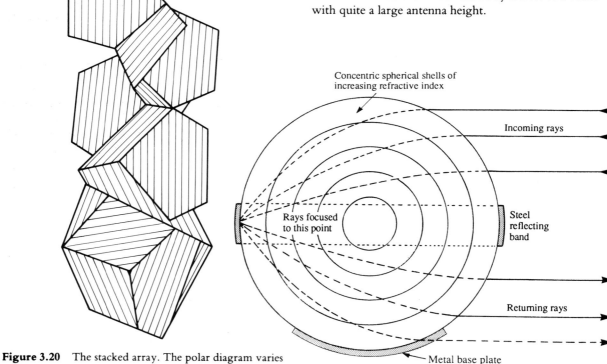

Figure 3.20   The stacked array. The polar diagram varies according to how the stack is constructed: in general, there are few blind spots even with 20° − 30° of heeling.

Figure 3.21   The Lunenburg lens - the principle

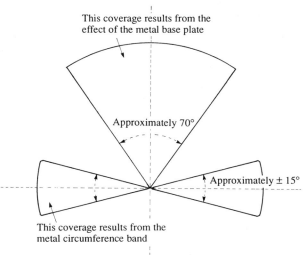

Figure 3.22 Theoretical vertical polar diagram of the Lunenburg lens. The horizontal polar diagram is virtually a circle, i.e. there are no 'preferential' directions.

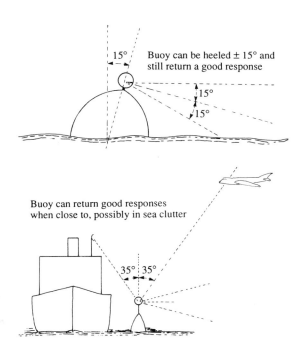

Figure 3.23 The vertical plane polar diagram applied to a buoy

3.4.4 Buoy patterns

Although the addition of a radar reflector array improves the overall radar response of a target, it does not assist in the identification of the target. Some experiments were carried out where targets (such as spar bouys) were fitted with arrays and placed in patterns. Although these patterns were readily recognisable on the radar display, the use of patterns as an aid to recognition has not received widespread acceptance. Patterns which exist naturally can prove most helpful.

3.5 Target enhancement – active

In about 1958 it became possible to apply what had been primarily military identification techniques to civil marine targets. These result in improved responses and facilitate identification. There were two major thrusts in the development of a solution – the *racon* and the *ramark*.

3.5.1 The racon principle (Figure 3.24)

A simple explanation of the operation is that the ship's radar pulse triggers the racon transmitter on the navigation mark, which then responds by transmitting a pulse (virtually instantaneously). This pulse is both longer and more powerful than the ship's transmitted pulse.

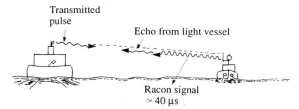

Figure 3.24 The racon principle

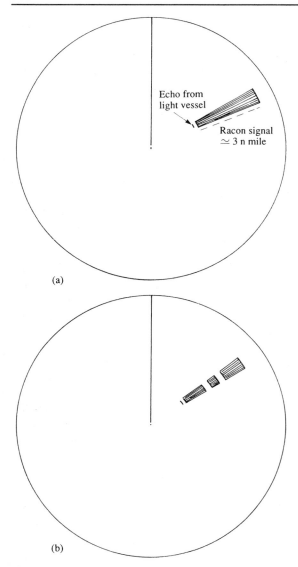

Figure 3.25 The racon appearance on the display
(a) Standard response
(b) Coded response

3.5.2 The racon appearance on the display

The racon signal appears on the radar screen as depicted in Figure 3.25 i.e. as a radial 'flash' some 1° to 2° in

angular width. Its radial length depends on the duration of the racon pulse, which is individual to the various manufacturers. Values are likely to lie in the range 20 μs to 40 μs, which represents a length on the radar screen of some 1.5 to 3 n mile.

3.5.2.1 Coding

The racon transmitter may be interrupted by on/off keying in such a way as to give a displayed racon signal of a specific appearance. This normally takes the form of an appropriate morse coding; for instance, a harbour authority might mark a shoal called 'King's Bank' by the morse letter K, as in Figure 3.25(b). This is of particular importance in aiding identification where there are several racons in the same area.

3.5.2.2 Racons at close range

When radar is being used in close proximity to a racon-equipped light vessel, it frequently occurs that energy transmitted in the sidelobes triggers the racon at times other than when the radar's main beam is scanning the light-vessel. In such cases, the 'racon clutter' (Figure 3.26) can cover a large arc of the radar screen close to the observing vessel (see also 'side echoes', Section 3.9.4).

Some racons are equipped with means to reduce the possibility of sidelobes triggering the racon. This is achieved by frequency-agile racons (see Section 3.5.3.3) storing the received signal strength at particular frequencies and then only responding when the signal strength at a particular frequency is close to the stored value.

Cheaper versions of the racon may use adaptive regulation of the racon receiver's sensitivity but this can result in weaker signals from more distant vessels being denied a racon response.

3.5.2.3 Racons at long range

Since one of the reasons for fitting a racon is to improve the detection range of what might otherwise be a poor response target, at longer ranges the response from the actual target may not be detected/displayed although the racon flash appears quite clearly. In this case, measuring the range to the nearest edge or the racon flash is

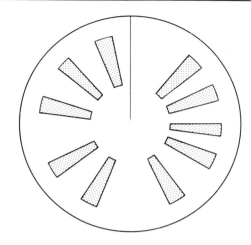

Figure 3.26   Racon clutter

acceptable as it will result in an error of only a few hundred yards (the racon receive/transmit delay time) and at long range such an error should not be significant. However, additional care must be exercised when navigating in close proximity to off-lying hazards while using a distant racon to fix position.

3.5.2.4   *The danger in using racons to assess correct tuning of the radar receiver*

It is advocated (see Sections 6.2.4.2, 6.3.4.3 and 6.4.4) that the radar receiver be accurately tuned by observing the change in display brightness of certain received signals while adjusting the tuning control. Racon signals *must not* be used in this way since:

(a)   The racon signal is frequently above saturation level and will not therefore show any marked change as the tuning control is varied.

(b)   The racon response will be displayed irrespective of the frequency to which the receiver is tuned (see Section 3.5.1), i.e. the racon will be displayed even when the receiver is off tune.

3.5.3   Frequency and polarization

It is evident that if the racon signal is to appear on the ship's radar, then the beacon response must be transmit-

ted at the transmission frequency of the ship's radar. During periods of restricted visibility in areas of high-density traffic, the demand on the racon can be extremely heavy, both in the number of interrogations and also the range of frequencies at which a response is required.

For example, at X-band the marine radar transmissions will fall within the approximate band 9300 to 9500 MHz. The radar receiver bandwidth, i.e. the band of frequencies within which an individual receiver can detect signals, is in the approximate range 2 to 20 MHz (see Section 2.5.2.4) and so it can be seen that some form of tunable oscillator is required within the racon transmitter if its responses to all interrogations are to be detectable.

One concession in the demand for a response is that it is not essential that the racon be 'observed' on every radar scan, i.e. every 3 seconds or so. This can also be beneficial in that there will be less likelihood of an observer failing to detect a real target which might be obscured by the racon flash.

Today only a few racons operate in the S-band but the number is increasing. Some combined S/X-band racons convert a received S-band signal to X-band for analysis and then convert back prior to transmission.

It is usual for the racon signals to be horizontally polarized, which means that radar systems using vertically polarized transmissions will not be able to receive racon signals.

3.5.3.1   Slow sweep racons

Rather than attempt to respond to each ship's radar pulse every time it is received, the racon oscillator is swept comparatively slowly across the marine radar band. Racon sweep periods of some 60 to 120 seconds are typical (Figure 3.27).

By careful consideration of radar receiver bandwidths, scanner rotation rates, and also the racon sweep time, some estimate can be made of duration and interval between racon appearances on an individual observer's radar display. This will in general be for sufficient time to allow the identification of the racon-fitted navigation mark (or to obtain a range and bearing of the racon itself). Typically, the racon flash will appear on

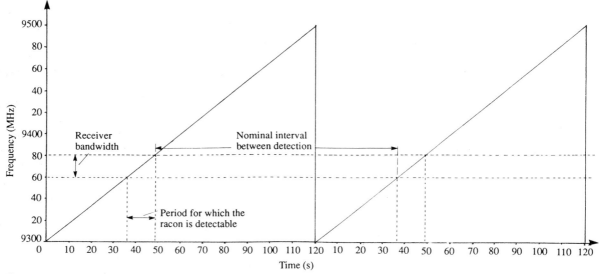

Figure 3.27   Slow time/frequency racon sweep

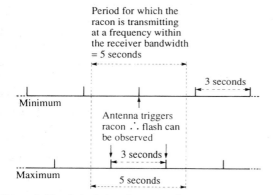

Figure 3.28   Calculation for Example 3.4
200 MHz in 100 s
therefore 10 MHz in 5 s
Time for 1 antenna rotation = 3 s
maximum 2 flashes
minimum 1 flash
Nominal interval between pulses = 100 s

some two to four consecutive scans of the ship's radar in each sweep period of the racon.

Although the frequency is shown as being continuously swept, an alternative technique which had similar results was to increase the frequency in discrete steps

which were held for a short period of time, with the overall 'sweep' period being as before.

Example 3.4   A racon with a sweep period of 100 s is triggered by a ship's radar which has an antenna rotation rate of 20 rpm and a receiver bandwidth of 10 MHz. Determine the theoretical maximum and minimum number of responses which can be expected during a single racon frequency sweep if the sweep band is 9300 to 9500 MHz. Find also the nominal interval between responses from consecutive racon sweeps.

3.5.3.2   *Fast-sweep racons (Figure 3.29)*

In this type, when triggered, the racon transmitter will rapidly (1 μs to 10 μs) sweep the particular radar frequency band, producing a series of brief flashes beyond the target. Each transmitted pulse will trigger the racon so that if it is triggered say, 10 times as it is swept by the radar beam on each scan, the paints will integrate on the radar screen to give a typical but distinctive displayed flash. The racon will display on virtually every scan but, because of low power, can be masked by noise, rain or sea clutter. There is no easy way of encoding the response.

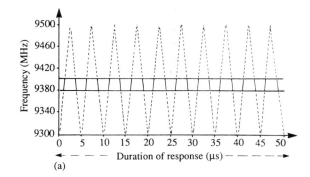

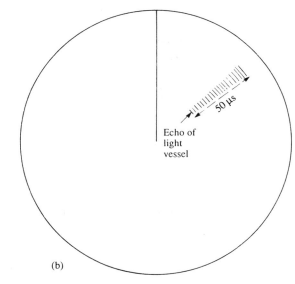

Figure 3.29 The fast-sweep racon
(a) Racon response
(b) Displayed response

Only a few fast-sweep racons are still in operation today.

3.5.3.3 Frequency-agile racons

In such a system, the frequency of the interrogating radar is measured, the racon transmitter is then tuned to that frequency and a (coded) response is transmitted. The time taken for this operation is some 0.4 μs, which corresponds to a ranging error of some 60 metres.

The block diagram of a frequency-agile racon is shown in Figure 3.30.

The following points should be noted:

(a) Racons which appear on each scan could mask other targets and so the racon is made to be 'silent' for a short period in each minute.
(b) The application of FTC (see Section 3.7.4) and some video processing techniques including 'interference suppression' (de-fruiting, see Section 3.9.5.1) can mutilate racon signals and should be switched off.
(c) The claimed 'mean time between failures' (MTBF) is some 10 years.
(d) With frequency-agile racons it is essential that the receiver is on tune, especially if the receiver bandwidth is narrow.

3.5.3.4 Racon 'clutter'

It has always been feared that with the proliferation of radar beacons, racon clutter could become a problem and mask targets. Alternatively, beacon responses can be masked by strong land and rain/sea clutter echoes.

Two solutions have been investigated:

1 *Beacon band operation*. This requires all radar beacons to transmit at a particular fixed frequency within a band at the edge of the marine radar frequency band, e.g. 9300 to 9320 MHz. A switch on the radar console sets the radar receiver to this 'fixed' frequency and only the radar beacons, but no targets, are displayed. The extra circuitry for all potential users could be expensive.
2 *Interrogated time-offset frequency-agile racons* (ITOFAR). When the frequency-agile racon is triggered at a very precise PRF (1343.1 pulses per second), it recognises it as an ITOFAR interrogation and delays its response by a very precise amount (374 μs). If the trigger to the display is delayed by the same amount, the racon signal will be displayed in what was previously the 'clear' outer portion of the radar screen on long range but is now at the correct range on the displayed range scale (see Figure 3.31). The circuitry required for this solution is less costly than for beacon band operation.

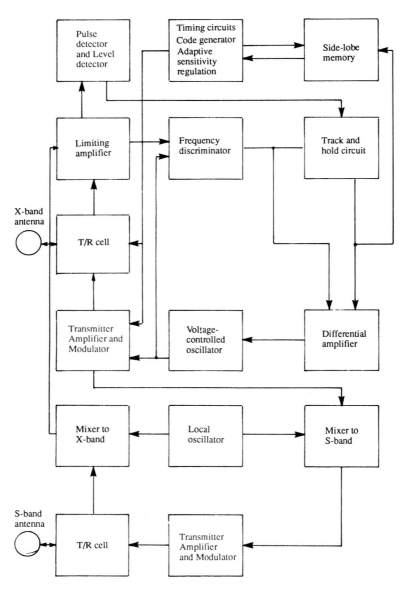

Figure 3.30   Block diagram of a frequency-agile racon
(based on a diagram of AGA-Ericsson Radio Systems of
Sweden)

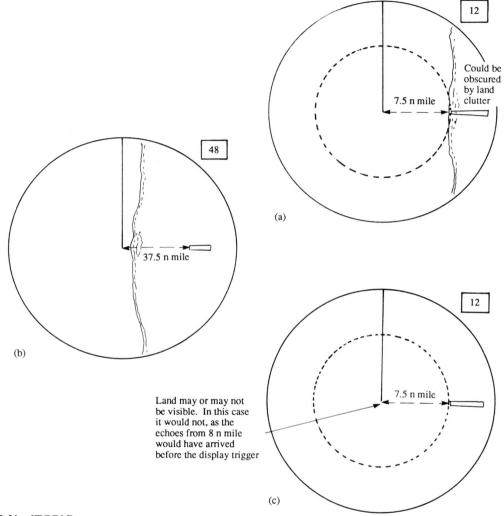

Figure 3.31   ITOFAR response
(a)   ITOFAR beacon response on all radars
(b)   Appearance of the ITOFAR beacon response when display trigger has not been delayed but beacon response has

(c)   Display of ITOFAR beacon response if ITOFAR operation is selected at the radar display

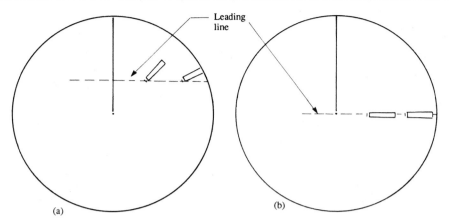

Figure 3.32 Leading line using two racons
(a) Approaching the line
(b) On the leading line

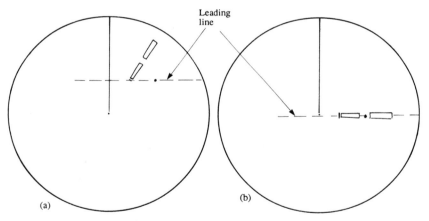

Figure 3.33 Leading line using a coded racon and buoy
fitted with a reflector
(a) Approaching the line
(b) On the leading line

3.5.3.5 Leading lines using racons

Figure 3.32 shows a leading line using two racons. Figure 3.33 shows a leading line using one racon and a buoy with a radar reflector.

3.5.4 The ramark

This is a radar beacon in which the frequency is swept continuously at such high speed that the transmission at each frequency is in effect continuous (not triggered).

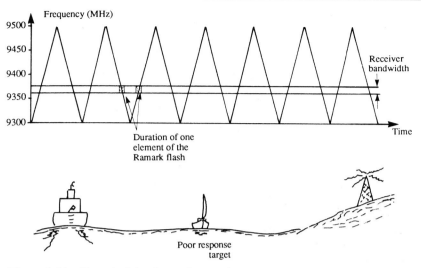

Figure 3.34   The principle of ramark operation

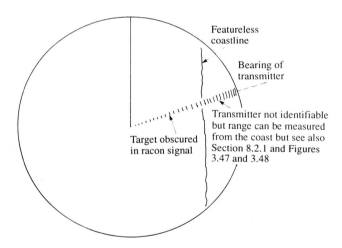

Figure 3.35   The appearance of a ramark on the radar display

Figure 3.34 illustrates the principle of ramark operation and Figure 3.35 shows the appearance of the ramark on the radar display.

3.5.5   Sources of radar beacon information

The *Admiralty List of Radio Signals* volume 2 contains information relating to racons working in both the S-band and the X-band as well as ramarks. Figure 3.36(a) gives typical extracts. Figure 3.36(b) shows chart symbols used on UK and US charts.

3.5.6   The Radaflare

This is a rocket which is fired from a pistol. At some 400 metres altitude, the rocket ejects a quantity of dipoles which respond strongly to 3 cm radar waves and at the

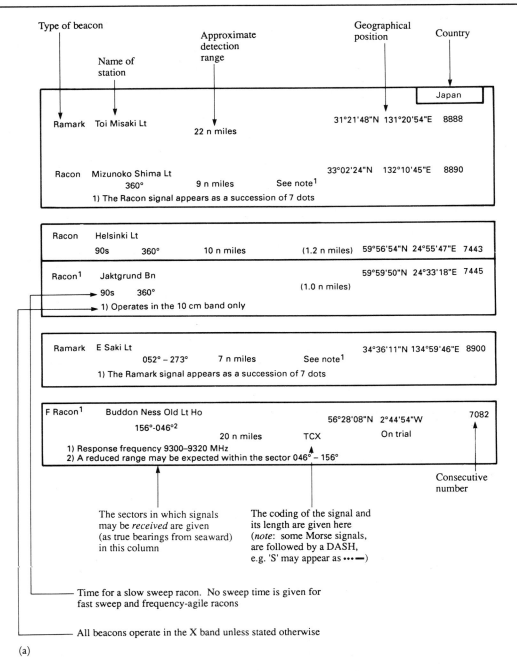

Figure 3.36

(a)   Examples of radar beacon information in *Admiralty List of Radio Signals* vol. 2

UK		
(o) Ra	Coast radio station providing range and bearing from station on request	
(o) Racon (K)	Radar transponder beacon with Morse identification responding within the 3 cm (X) band	
(o) Racon (K) (10 cm)	Radar transponder beacon with Morse identification responding within the 10 cm (S) band	
(o) Racon (3 & 10 cm)	Radar transponder beacons responding within the 3 cm and 10 cm bands	
Racon (o)------- Racon (o)------ - ----- Racons in line; Racons 270°		
⌒ Ra. Refl.	Radar reflector (not generally charted on IALA system marks)	
≌ Ra. Conspic	Radar conspicuous object	
(o) Ramark	Radar beacon transmitting independently of ship's radar emissions	
USA		
(o) Ra	Radar station	
(o) Racon	Radar responder beacon	
⌒	Radar reflector	
Ra (conspic)	Radar conspicuous object	
Ramark	Ramark	

(b)   UK and USA chart symbols

same time the rocket gives out a very bright white light. The radar response has a maximum detection range of 12 n mile and will last for some 15 minutes, depending upon weather conditions. It is intended for use as a distress signal for small craft.

3.5.7   Racons for survival craft

To assist in the detection and identification of survival craft and other small craft in distress, the IMO have specified a Search and Rescue Transponder (SART) which is a coded racon and which will appear on the radar screen as a series of twenty dots. Since the racon flash will always appear as a radial signal *beyond* the target, it will immediately indicate the course to steer to the target.

Two types of equipment are envisaged, one of which will be permanently attached to the craft or carried by an individual while the second is intended to eject and activate automatically on the sea surface in the event of collision or capsize.

It is intended that the beacons should respond to radar equipment working in the standard marine X-band. No modifications would be required for detection by normal shipborne equipment. It would also be detectable by the radar installed aboard some search and rescue aircraft.

A feature of the beacon is an audible or visible signal that lets the survivors know there is a craft in the area with operational radar. The increasing strength of the signal would indicate that the vessel using the radar is approaching and this is seen to provide a valuable psychological stimulus for survival.

Voluntary fitting of the beacons is recommended at the present time but it will become mandatory for certain classes of craft with the implementation of the Global Maritime Distress and Safety Service (GMDSS).

3.6   The detection of targets in sea clutter

In general, the term 'clutter' is used to describe the accu-mulation on the screen of unwanted echoes. Sea clutter describes the particular case of echoes which arise as a result of the radar energy being scattered back from the surface of the sea. The presence of sea clutter echoes may make it difficult or even impossible to detect wanted targets and this represents an important limitation of even the most modern civil marine radar systems. It is essential that the radar observer understands not only the nature of this phenomenon but also the principle of the various arrangements available to assist in combating the effect. Since the mid-1970s, with the advent of digital storage (see Section 2.6.6.1), the complexity of anti-clutter arrangements has increased progressively and the limitations of these must be appreciated.

The ever-changing surface of the sea represents an immensely complex population of varying radar targets. The radar cross-section (see Section 3.3.5.4) of any element of the sea surface fluctuates in a largely random fashion and can thus only be evaluated in terms of averages or probabilities. In an effort to identify the radar and sea surface characteristics which determine the magnitude of the sea clutter response, eminent radar engineers have spent much time and effort in using statistical techniques to obtain a mathematical model of the sea clutter mechanism. Because of the complexity of the problem, and in particular the difficulty of carrying out controlled experiments with the sea, it is not possible to reconcile completely the detailed mathematical predictions with the observed phenomena and to this extent it is true to say that the mechanism is not yet fully understood. However, a discussion of such quantitative considerations is beyond the scope of this manual and the reader who wishes to pursue the mathematical approach is referred to any good radar enginering text. To the extent of understanding required for effective radar observation, the mechanism can be explained in the fairly simple qualitative terms used in the following section.

From the point of view of the radar observer, the essence of the clutter problem is that targets weaker than the clutter returns cannot be detected and even targets which return responses which are very much stronger than the clutter may be masked if the clutter returns saturate the receiver or the display (see section 2.5.2.1).

3.6.1 The nature of sea clutter response

In absolutely flat calm sea conditions, the sea surface will behave like a mirror and specular reflection will take place (see Section 3.3.1). All radar energy which strikes the surface of the sea will be reflected away and none will be scattered back toward the antenna (some of the energy which strikes targets will travel via the sea surface, as described in Section 2.4.3).

If there is any wind at all it will tend to ruffle the surface of the sea producing small wavelets and as the wind strength increases so too will the height of the waves which are generated. In deep water the height and period of the waves depends on the wind speed, the fetch and the length of time for which the wind has been blowing. In shallow water the waves tend to steepen and the distance between successive wave crests decreases. When the wind is blowing against the tide, wave height and steepness will be greater than the observed wind would perhaps suggest. Where two wave patterns are present, as for example may occur in an area where a large wind shift has taken place with the passage of a frontal system, constructive interference between the patterns will produce, from time to time, wave heights larger than the individual component heights. As wave height increases for whatever reason, a point will be reached at which the waves break, producing confused tumbling water and wind-blown spray. A more complex and less predictable target is difficult to conceive.

Despite the complexity of the problem, one can consider there to be three elements which contribute to the aggregate response:

1 *Specular reflection from those sloping parts of the wavefront which present a good aspect to the incident radar energy.* This would be the sole contribution if the wind could produce a completely smooth sloping wavefront. It is well represented by the situation which arises when swell is present in calm conditions. (*Swell* is the term used to describe waves which have been generated by wind in some distant area and have travelled across the ocean.) Swell may be present in isolation or it may have locally generated *sea* waves superimposed upon it.

2 *Scattering of energy from the surface of the wavefront.*

Except when swell is present in flat calm conditions the sloping surface of the wavefront will be disturbed by the wind and will thus produce a surface texture which is *rough* in terms of the wavelengths used in civil marine radar (see Section 3.3.5.5). The face of the wave can be thought of as being composed of a large number of facets whose aspects change at random with the ruffling and tumbling of the surface water. The resulting backscatter of radar energy will yield responses whenever a favourably placed facet lies within the resolution cell (see Section 3.3.5). It is essential to appreciate that although these facets may be quite small, possibly a few square centimetres, they will produce echoes whose displayed size is determined by the resolution cell. Thus if a facet remains favourable for the time taken by the radar beam to sweep across it (say 10 to 20 milliseconds) it will produce an echo which is one half-pulse long, one beamwidth wide and subject to spot size effect.

3 *Reflection from water droplets close to the surface of the wave.* In higher wind conditions water from the crests tends to be blown off the wave and the droplets so formed will reflect radar energy if sufficiently large (see also Raindrops in Section 3.7.3.1).

Opinions differ as to the relative significance of each contribution, but it is nonetheless evident that a large number of independent targets capable of producing backscatter exist on and around the sloping surfaces of sea waves. The observed response from this backscatter depends on characteristics of both the waves and the radar installation and these will be considered in turn.

3.6.1.1 The effect of wave height

Although, as indicated in the previous section, various factors can affect wave height, in general as the wind force rises so too does the wave height. In attempting to translate the growth in wave height into an increase in clutter response one must consider not only the increase in the strength of signals received from nearby waves but also the increases in the range from which detectable signals are received.

The response from an individual wave increases with wave height up to a certain level and then tends to flatten

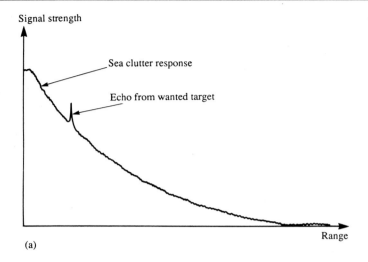

(a)

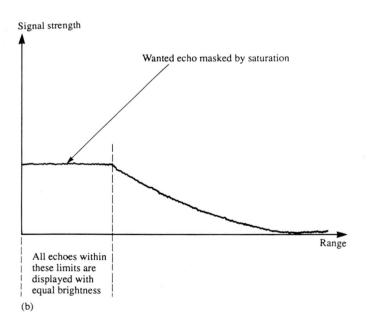

(b)

Figure 3.37   The variation of clutter response with range
(a)   Unsaturated response
(b)   Saturated response

off. The precise nature of the law is a matter for the scientist rather than the radar observer who is more concerned with the effects which can be observed on the display. As wave height increases, the clutter returns close to the observing vessel will in due course saturate the receiver or display; a further increase in wave height will be observed to extend the radius to which this saturation is manifest. Beyond the radius of saturation the amplitude of the displayed clutter signals will decay progressively with range (see Section 3.6.1.2) toward the maximum radial extent of visible clutter, at which the grazing angle has reduced to that at which the radar sees the surface as smooth (see Section 3.3.5.5). In conclusion, the range within which the observer must combat the masking effects of saturation will increase with wave height, as will the range within which targets are undetectable if their response is less than that of the ambient clutter.

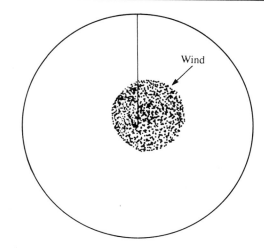

Figure 3.38   Sea clutter pattern in the open sea

3.6.1.2   *The variation of sea clutter response with range*

In the introduction to this chapter it was shown that, in general, received echo strength varies inversely as the fourth power of range. Sea clutter response does not obey this law and it can be shown that it varies inversely as (range)^3 except that at very short ranges this becomes (range)^2. This arises because the radar cross-section of sea clutter (which is a statistical quantity) is a function of range. A proof of this is beyond the scope of this work but if desired will be found in any good radar engineering text having a mathematical treatment of the sea clutter mechanism. The relationship between the two decay rates favours the detection of clutter except at very short ranges.

In the absence of saturation, the variation of sea clutter with range will be as illustrated in Figure 3.37(a). For the reasons set out in Section 2.5.2.5, saturation usually takes place in the case of the linear amplifier, resulting in the waveform being modified as illustrated in Figure 3.37(b). Comparison of sections of the figure shows the masking effect of the presence of sea clutter. The difficulties which arise from the masking and the benefit of employing a logarithmic receiver (see Section 2.5.2.6) will be discussed further in Sections 3.6.3.2.

3.6.1.3   *The effect of wind direction*

Even casual observation of the waves generated on the sea surface will reveal that the upwind wavefronts are steeper than their more gently sloping downwind counterparts. The steeper wavefronts present a more effective echoing surface and thus the radial extent of sea clutter echoes will be found to be greater to windward than it is to leeward, as illustrated by Figure 3.38.

The outer limit of the pattern represents the minimum detectable signal (see Section 3.2.3) and hence the radial extent of the pattern offers a suitable criterion by which to judge the setting of the tuning control (see Sections 6.2.4.2 and 6.3.4.3).

In coastal and estuarial areas the pattern may be modified by seas breaking on banks or in areas of shallow water and the waves may be steepened where the wind blows against the tide.

3.6.1.4   *The effect of antenna height*

Increased antenna height extends the radial limit of the overall sea clutter pattern which appears on the screen and also the range within which the clutter echoes saturate the receiver or the display (see Sections 2.5.2.1 and 2.5.2.5). This is illustrated by Figure 3.39.

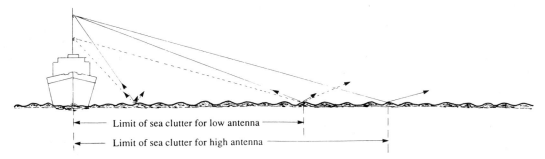

Figure 3.39 The effect of antenna height on sea clutter response

Sloping wavefronts close to the observing vessel present a more favourable aspect for the reflection of the radar energy than those at a distance. This arises because at large angles of depression the beam *looks down* at nearby wavefronts and there is as a consequence a high probability that some energy will be normal to the general surface of the wavefront. If the surface is smooth, specular reflection will take place but in most cases the surface will be sufficiently rough to ensure scattering and thus a response from surfaces which are not exactly normal to the beam (see Section 3.3.1). In theory, with the ship upright, one might expect the maximum depression angle to be 10°, i.e. half the vertical beamwidth (see Section 2.4.3), but in practice the energy in the lower vertical side-lobes will increase this effective angle considerably. As range from the observing vessel increases, the aspect of the wavefront will become progressively less favourable for reflection as the direction of the incident energy approaches that which is tangential to the top of the wave. At about this distance, most of the energy will just graze the crest of the wave and clutter echoes will not be detected beyond this limit.

3.6.1.5 The effect of radar wavelength

Like most aspects of the sea clutter phenomenon, experimental determination of the exact relationship between the wavelength being transmitted by the radar and the clutter response is difficult to achieve, as is an explanation of the results in terms of the necessarily complex theoretical mathematical model of the mechanism. There is general agreement that the response decreases with increase in wavelength, though there is some debate as to the significant power – (wavelength)^2 or (wavelength)^3. At best, the civil marine radar observer will have the choice between the selection of 3 cm or 10 cm wavelength (see Section 2.3.3.1) and for practical purposes can consider the clutter response to be directly proportional to wavelength. This is consistent with the concept of surface texture as set out in Section 3.3.5.5 which suggests that the *roughness* of the surface of the sloping wavefront will be greater for 3 cm than it will be for 10 cm radiation. It is similarly consistent with the theory that reflection from water droplets forms one component of the aggregate response (see Section 3.6.1).

Thus, in general, the sea clutter response will be less troublesome at S-band than it will be X-band and where dual antenna/transceiver units are fitted the observer may well be able to exploit the potential of S-band transmissions in adverse sea clutter conditions. It is also a factor which should be considered when planning the radar installation for a new vessel or updating an existing installation.

3.6.1.6 The effect of pulse length

In general, subject to any saturation, selection of long pulse rather than short pulse will improve the displayed response of any given target (see Section 2.5.2.4) and sea clutter is no exception to this rule. Thus if wanted targets are masked as a result of saturation (see Sections 2.5.2.1 and 2.5.2.5) it may be possible to combat the effect by judicious choice of pulse length. Selection of short pulse will reduce the response of both clutter and wanted targets and may bring the clutter response below saturation level or at least to a level which will allow the observer to apply smaller amounts of clutter suppression (see Section 3.6.3).

Selection of short pulse will also reduce the radial extent of the resolution cell (see Section 2.6.5.2). This effect can only begin to show if the distance between the farthest scattering element of a wavefront and the nearest scattering element (including any associated spray) of the next wave beyond exceeds half the transmitted pulse length. In certain sea conditions it is possible to recognise the line of approaching wavefronts, especially in ocean conditions where a long swell is present.

3.6.1.7   The effect of polarization (see Section 2.4.1.8)

In clutter conditions there is little if any difference between the response from horizontally polarized radiation and that which is vertically polarized. In almost all cases any difference is in any event academic since to comply with the IMO Performance Standards (see Section 10.2) relating to the ability to detect radar beacons (see Section 3.5), all systems operating in the 3 cm band must be capable of operating in a horizontally polarized mode. There is thus no stimulus for designers to produce an X-band system with vertical polarization. Although vertical polarization offers some improvement in target response in calm conditions, particularly at S-band, vertically polarized S-band systems are very much the exception rather than the rule. Thus, in general, polarization is not a system characteristic which is under the control of the observer.

In the past, a system offering circular polarization was offered in an attempt to reduce the response from droplets of precipitation. This is discussed under that heading in Section 3.7.4.6; at this stage it is relevant to observe that any reduction so gained would have an effect on that element of sea clutter response originating in reflection from spray. It must, however, be borne in mind that there is some debate as to the significance of the contribution of the droplet component to the aggregate sea clutter response.

3.6.2   The clutter problem summarized

Sea clutter echoes may make it impossible to detect

some targets, while the presence of others may only be revealed by skilful adjustment of the controls or with the assistance of some form of signal processing. Before discussing the techniques available for the suppression of sea clutter it is appropriate to summarize the clutter problem in terms of three distinct cases of target amplitude which are set out below and illustrated by Figure 3.40.

1 *Targets weaker than the ambient clutter.* A target which returns a signal that is weaker than the clutter surrounding it cannot be detected, because any technique used to suppress the clutter will also suppress the echo of the wanted target. Marginal targets may be recognised by the regularity of their paint.

2 *Targets stronger than ambient clutter that does not saturate the receiver or display.* Such a target is capable of detection but it may not be obvious because of the poor contrast when viewed against the background of the clutter echoes. This is likely to be a particular problem if the targets are only marginally stronger than the ambient clutter. The target may be made more obvious by suppression of the clutter returns.

3 *Targets stronger than ambient clutter that saturates the receiver or display.* Such a target will be masked because its echo will have exactly the same brightness on the display as all the sea clutter echoes surrounding it. It is capable of detection subject to suppression of the clutter signal. Skill is required to reveal targets which are only marginally stronger than the ambient clutter.

3.6.3   The suppression of displayed sea clutter signals

In Sections 3.6.1.4, 3.6.1.5 and 3.6.1.6 it was indicated that a judicious choice of antenna height, wavelength and pulse length would reduce sea clutter responses. Except in very light sea conditions it is unlikely that such reduction will alone be sufficient to combat the sea clutter problem and it will normally have to be supplemented by some form of active suppression applied in the receiver or the display.

3.6.3.1   The sea clutter control

The probability of detecting targets in clutter will be

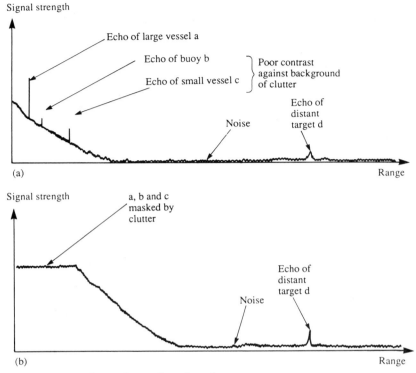

Figure 3.40   The masking effect of sea clutter returns
(a)   Clutter does not saturate receiver or display
(b)   Clutter saturates receiver or display

maximized by adjusting the controls so that the echoes of the targets paint against a background of light residual clutter speckle similar to the noise speckle used as the criterion for setting the gain control. This can be achieved for a target at any given range by reducing the setting of the gain control. However, it can be seen from Figure 3.41 that this may only be achieved at the expense of losing more distant targets and without achieving the desired degree of suppression for nearer targets.

Essentially, the problem is that the gain reduces the amplification uniformly across the radius of the timebase, whereas the clutter signals are strongest near the origin and decay with range (see Section 3.6.1.2).

The sea clutter control is a specialized type of gain control which reduces the gain at the origin of each radial line and restores it with time as each radial line is

written. The control thus allows a varying amount of suppression to be applied. The amount of initial suppression is variable and can be adjusted by the observer by the setting of the front panel control, whereas the rate at which the suppression decays is preset by the manufacturer (see Figure 3.42). The joint effect determines the radius to which suppression is effected.

The control is sometimes referred to as *swept gain* or *sensitivity time control* (STC) because of the time-related variation of the gain. Ideally the decay of the suppression curve should obey the same law as that governing the decay of the sea clutter response with range (see Section 3.6.1.2). Normally, it will be found that the suppression decays exponentially with time. This law was adopted in the very early days of marine radar for the very practical reason that it is the waveform generated by discharging a capacitor through a resistor and hence has the merit of simplicity, reliability and cheapness. It has stood the test of time because although the exponential decay ($e^{-\text{range}}$) is not exactly the same as that of $(\text{range})^{-2}$, it is a reasonable fit except at very short range. In any event, in practice the sea conditions may not exactly follow the theoretical predictions and hence the complications of producing a $(\text{range})^{-2}$ law would not be justified.

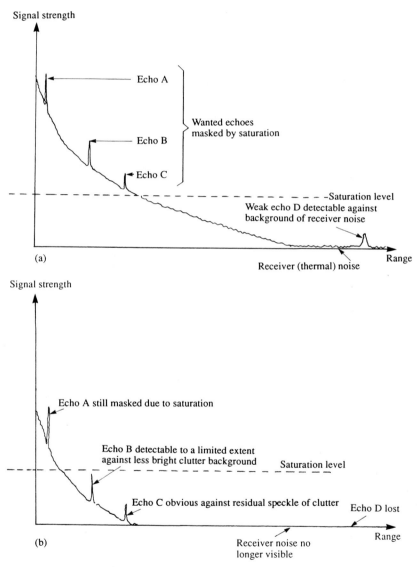

Figure 3.41 Suppression of clutter by use of the gain control
(a) Normal gain setting
(b) Gain suppressed

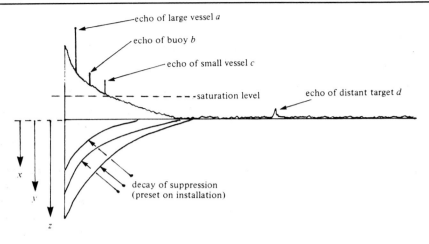

x, y, z represent varying degrees of initial suppression set by sea clutter control

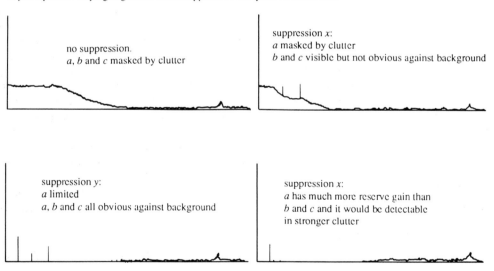

Ideally, the observer wishes to optimize the suppression to match the clutter response, thus leaving wanted targets painting against a light residual clutter speckle. This is illustrated in Figure 3.42 which shows three (excluding the zero setting) particular levels of suppression which have been chosen in such a way that while one level is optimum, the other two levels are representative of the cases of insufficient and excessive suppression *for that particular line* of responses on the display. However, the clutter response varies from line to line (see Section 3.6.1.3) and thus it follows that if the control is set correctly for one radial line, it is likely to be set incorrectly for most, if not all, other radial lines. Thus there is no single *correct* manual setting for the sea clutter control; to maximize the probability of detecting targets in clutter, the observer must, at regular intervals, systematically adjust the control in small steps through the extent of its travel from full clutter suppression to zero effect. This operation is known as *searching* and considerable skill and practice are required to perform it successfully. It is one of the most important skills associated with marine radar operation; the appropriate practical procedure is described in detail in Section 6.10.1.1.

3.6.3.2 The effect of receiver characteristic

In older systems which employ a linear IF amplifier (see Section 2.5.2.5), saturation is likely to take effect early in the amplifier chain. In such cases the sea clutter control will normally be designed to effect the suppression prior to such a point in the receiver. In heavy clutter conditions, extensive suppression may be required at an early stage in the receiver and particular care and skill will be required in carrying out the searching operation with the sea clutter control.

In more modern systems the use of a logarithmic amplifier (see Section 2.5.2.6) will ensure that in almost all cases an unsaturated output is available for input to the video section of the receiver (see Section 2.5.3). Thus saturation due to sea clutter returns will not normally take effect until some stage in the video amplifier (see Section 2.5.3) or possibly not even until the CRT, in which case, the sea clutter control will operate in the video section of the receiver. With a logarithmic amplifier, the masking effect of sea responses is likely to be less troublesome and the operation of the sea clutter control will in most situations be found to be less critical than in the case of a linear receiver.

From the treatment presented in Section 2.5.2.6 it is fairly evident that the use of a logarithmic amplifier reduces the risk of targets being masked by sea clutter because it extends the range of signals that will not saturate the IF amplifier. It can also be shown that the logarithmic relationship between receiver output and input also produces a swept gain effect on the clutter signals, thus further improving the potential performance of the system in heavy clutter conditions. Proof of this requires a mathematical treatment beyond the scope of this text. The reader who wishes to pursue this further is referred to a good radar enginerring text or to the various technical papers published on the subject of logarithmic receivers.

3.6.3.3 Adaptive gain

This is a more recent approach to automatic clutter suppression. In discussing the manual sea clutter control, the point was made that ideally the clutter suppression should be set correctly for each radial line. Clearly no human operator possesses the speed or dexterity to perform such a task but it can be achieved with a considerable degree of success by electronic means. The general name for the technique is *adaptive gain* and it is so called because the associated circuitry is designed to adjust continually the receiver gain so as to *adapt it* to the level of clutter present at any point on each radial line. For practical engineering reasons it is necessary to perform the adaptive gain process in the video stage of the receiver and, because it is necessary to deduce an analogue of the clutter response (see below), it must operate on an unsaturated signal. It follows that the technique cannot be used successfully in systems which have a linear receiver (see Section 2.5.2.5). As a result, the advent of adaptive gain in civil marine radar systems dates from the mid-1970s when solid-state logarithmic receivers became available for civil applications at sea. Since then it has become progressively more common because of the need for effective automatic clutter suppression in systems that use digital storage for picture generation and automatic tracking (see Section 2.6.6). If the clutter responses are not suppressed before digitization the masking problem is likely to be exacerbated, particularly if the clutter echoes are stored at high level (see Section 2.6.6.7). The principle of adaptive gain is illustrated by Figure 3.43.

The theory of adaptive gain is that if an analogue of the clutter signal is used to produce the suppression signal, only signals stronger than the clutter will be displayed. Examination of the combined target and clutter signal shown in Figure 3.43 reveals that its characteristic has two main components, one being the relatively slow general decay with range (see Section 3.6.1.2) from maximum at the origin to zero at the radial limit of the sea clutter response. Superimposed on this is the second component which has the form of relatively rapid spikes which represent the presence of targets and clutter peaks. The total signal can be thought of as a slowly changing average signal about which rapid excursions occur. The

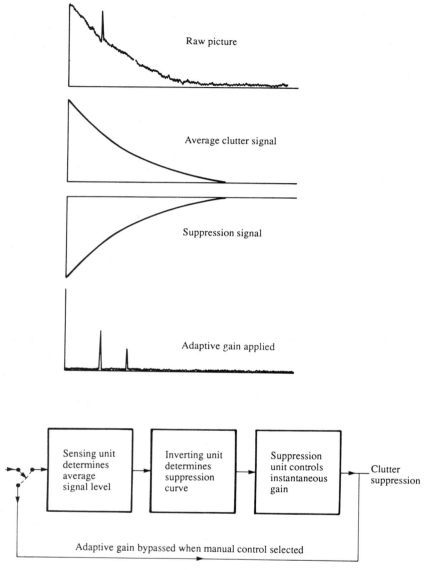

Figure 3.43   The principle of adaptive gain

reaction time of the sensing section (sometimes referred to as the integrator) of the adaptive gain circuitry (see Figure 3.43) is designed to be too slow to respond to the rapid excursions but sufficiently fast to react to the slowly changing average signal level. The sensing sec-

tion thus effectively filters out the high frequency fluctuations and generates a slowly changing average signal level which is inverted and used as a suppression signal to modify, continuously and instantaneously, the overall gain level set by the observer.

Clearly the slow reaction time of the sensing section will not allow it to respond immediately to a change from zero clutter at the end of one line to maximum clutter at the commencement of the next. This difficulty is overcome by using the initial clutter signal from the previous line to produce the suppression for the first part of the current line. The adaptive gain effect is normally enhanced by the limited use of a further technique known as *differentiation* which tends to emphasise the leading edge of echoes. This is described in detail in section 3.7.4.4.

If the suppression signal is a faithful analogue of the average signal level, the resultant video signal made available for display (see Figure 3.43) should comprise those signals which are rapid excursions from that level and which represent the presence of targets that are stronger than the clutter and also the clutter peaks. Targets which are much stronger than the clutter should be easy to detect as they will be displayed (on an analogue display) against the background of the light residual speckle of clutter peaks. Targets very close to clutter level will be difficult to detect and the observer may have to rely on an ability to recognise their regular paint against the background of random clutter echoes.

The setting up of the adaptive gain circuitry must be carried out by qualified service personnel but it should be done in consultation with experienced radar observers who, on the basis of systematic use, are in a postion to comment on the performance of the system in a wide variety of sea conditions. It has to be recognised that it is virtually impossible to adjust the adaptive gain circuitry so that it will give optimum response over the full range of wind and sea conditions between calm and gale force winds. For this reason, exclusive reliance *should not* be placed on the ability of such circuitry to remove clutter and to display only targets. The practical procedure for the use of the facility is set out in Sections 6.10.1.2 and 6.10.2.3.

Because of the averaging effect and the differentiation (see Section 3.7.4.4), adaptive gain circuitry will suppress radar beacon signals (see Section 3.5) and it is for this reason, among others, that the IMO Performance Standards (see Section 10.2) require that it should be possible to switch off those signal processing facilities which might prevent a radar beacon from being shown on the radar display. Adaptive gain will have a similar effect on radial performance monitor signals (see Section 6.5.5) and clearly must be switched off when a performance check is carried out. The effect of adaptive gain on land echoes will vary depending on whether the beam is parallel with or normal to the coastline; in general, it will tend to display the leading edge and suppress what lies behind. For this reason, identification of coastal features (see Section 8.2) is best performed with the adaptive gain facility switched off.

The adaptive gain facility may be effective in suppressing rain clutter responses (see Section 3.7.4.5). In some systems a single adaptive gain facility is offered, whereas in others separate sea and rain adaptive gain facilities may be provided. The adaptive gain principle described above is valid in both cases, the essential difference being that the sea clutter facility applies the adaptive gain to a limited preset range whereas the rain clutter facility is effective for the full timebase. The principal reason for separating the functions is that a sea clutter adaptive gain facility will allow suppression of proximate clutter while permitting the detection of more distant radar beacons. 'Adaptive gain' is a general engineering term: the display control which effects this function may be labelled in a variety of ways by different radar manufacturers (see Section 6.10.1.2). Normally, when the adaptive gain facility is selected the manual sea and rain clutter controls (see Sections 6.10.1.1 and 6.10.2.2) are disabled.

3.6.3.4   Rotation-to-rotation correlation

This is a further approach to automatic clutter suppression and is only available in systems which can store the range and bearing data for a full aerial rotation (see Section 2.6.6.4). The other methods of clutter suppression so far described use difference of amplitude (i.e. signal strength) in their attempt to distinguish between clutter and targets, though it has been mentioned that an observer may identify a weak target in clutter by virtue of the regularity of its paint when compared with random sea clutter responses. Rotation-to-rotation correlation sets out to perform this latter operation automatically.

The principle is similar to line-to-line correlation which is described in Section 3.9.5.1, but differs in that, instead of comparing the contents of two *different* range cells at the same range on successive lines, the comparison is made between the content of the *same* range cell on two (or more) successive aerial rotations. The theory of operation can be understood by asking the question: 'If a wave with a favourable aspect is present in a given range cell, what is the probability that a favourable wave will be present in the same range cell after one aerial rotation, i.e. after approximately 3 seconds?' Evaluation of this probability is clearly an exercise in statistics but it is fairly obvious that the probability of a wave being present in the same cell for two successive rotations is considerably less than that of a target. The difference between the probabilities will increase if the comparison is made for three or more rotations, provided of course that the target does not move out of the cell in question. Thus it is possible, to an extent which depends on the number of rotations over which the comparison is made, to distinguish between regular target returns and random clutter returns.

The way in which the probability theory is exploited and the name given to the facility (see Section 6.10.1.3) vary considerably with manufacturer. In a simple application of the principle, echoes which are present on successive rotations may be displayed at a higher level or in a different colour to those which appear at random from rotation to rotation. In a more complex approach, the comparison may be made over several successive rotations, and multi-levels of synthetic video (see Section 2.6.6.7) may be used to indicate the consistency of echo return by promoting them to higher levels of echo brightness as the number of successive rotations on which they appear increases. Demotion to a lower brightness level will occur if a target ceases to be consistent, though probably on the basis of a more tolerant law. The general effect of the correlation will be to favour consistent targets at the expense of clutter but it must be borne in mind that targets which return an intermittent response, such as a buoy or a small boat in a seaway, will be penalized.

It is essential for radar observers using such a facility on any particular system to be aware of the logical rules on which that version operates. It is also important to appreciate that echo brightness modified in this way is in no way a measure of echo strength.

Normally in radial-scan synthetic displays only one, or possibly two, radial lines are stored and it is for this reason that rotation-to-rotation correlation first became available only with the development of raster-scan displays suitable for use on large merchant vessels.

Rotation-to-rotation correlation tends to eliminate some receiver noise and it is thus important to switch the facility off when setting the gain control (see Section 6.4.4).

3.7   The detection of targets in precipitation clutter

Precipitation is the general term used to describe collectively various states in which water can manifest itself in the atmosphere, of which rain, snow and hail are examples. Reflections from precipitation can produce unwanted echoes on the screen and these are in practice (perhaps somewhat loosely) referred to as *rain clutter* though it is recognized that they may originate from other forms of precipitation. The effect of rain clutter in some ways resembles that of sea clutter but it has other characteristics which are quite different. Like the responses from the sea, those from rain can mask even strong target echoes by causing saturation within the receiver. They can also make it difficult to detect unsaturated responses against the background of clutter due to poor contrast, and impossible to detect targets whose response is weaker than that of the rain. However, precipitation echoes can occur anywhere on the screen and may well change their position quite rapidly. Additionally the transmitted pulse and the returning echo suffer scattering and attenuation (see Section 3.7.2) on their journey through the precipitation, thus reducing the received echo strength below what it would be in the absence of the precipitation. This has the effect of exacerbating the masking effect of the clutter and reducing the probability of detecting targets located beyond the area of precipitation. It is important to recognise that the solutions to the problems of detecting targets in and beyond rain are distinctly different (see Sections 3.7.5.1 and 3.7.5.2).

3.7.1 The nature of precipitation response

The area of precipitation can be considered to be an aggregation of a large number of randomly distributed individual particles which may take the form of water droplets, snowflakes or ice. Energy from the radar beam may strike these particles and will as a consequence be scattered in a multitude of directions. The aspect of some of the particles will favour backscatter, i.e. reflection in the direction of the antenna, and energy so reflected may produce detectable responses on the screen of the observing vessel. Like the backscatter from the multiple facets of sea waves (see Section 3.6.1), the mechanism is extremely complicated and quantitative analysis of the response involves complex statistical theory beyond the scope of this text. However, it is not altogether surprising that it can be shown that the amplitude of the response depends on the size and material of the particles, the number present per unit volume of space illuminated by the radar beam at any time and the range of the precipitation (also the energy in the pulse and the transmission frequency, although, for a particular radar at a particular time, these may be considered fixed: see Sections on pulse length, transmitted power/PRF and wavelength for the effects of deliberately varying each one).

3.7.1.1   The effect of particle size

As is evident from the treatment presented in Section 3.3, particle size is only significant when considered in relation to transmitted wavelength. Theoretical calculations show that, provided the particle diameter is small when compared to wavelength, for a given wavelength the scattering response increases in direct proportion to the square of particle diameter. Thus a doubling of particle size will produce a fourfold increase in response.

Conversely, for a given particle size, the response is inversely proportional to the square of transmitted wavelength. Thus in given precipitation conditions selection of an S-band (see Section 2.3.3.1) system as an alternative to X-band will reduce the rain clutter responses by a factor of approximately 0.1.

3.7.1.2   The effect of particle density

It is important to stress that the term 'density' is not used here to indicate the mass per unit volume of the particle material but in the sense of the number of particles present per unit volume of space illuminated by the radar beam at any time. Clearly, for any given particle size the response will increase with the particle density.

3.7.1.3   Precipitation rate

It is evident from the two preceding sections that the response from precipitation increases with both the density of the particle population and the size of the individual members. Both of these factors determine the precipitation rate which is a measurement meteorologists use to quantify precipitation in units of the volume falling per unit time. The term *precipitation* or *rainfall rate* is quite commonly used in discussing precipitation response. In general, the rain clutter response increases in proportion to the rainfall rate.

3.7.1.4   The effect of range

It was shown in the introduction to this chapter that in general, target response decays in proportion to the fourth power of range. By contrast, the response from precipitation falls off in proportion to the square of range. This arises because the radar cross-section of precipitation, a complex statistical quantity, is range dependent. A proof of this is beyond the scope of this manual but will be found in any good mathematical text on radar engineering. The relationship between the two decay rates favours the detection of clutter except at very short ranges.

The remote limits of the rain clutter pattern represent the minimum detectable signal (see Section 3.2.3) and hence the extent of the pattern offers a suitable criterion by which to judge the setting of the tuning control (see Sections 6.2.4.2 and 6.3.4.3).

3.7.2 Attenuation in precipitation

Even when the radar waves travel through clear atmosphere, some attenuation takes place. It occurs because some of the energy is absorbed by the gaseous constituents of the atmosphere, in particular oxygen and water vapour. The effect starts to become of practical significance only at wavelengths shorter than that of X-band. However, the presence of precipitation considerably increases the amount of attenuation that takes place. The extent to which the energy is absorbed depends on particle size, particle form (e.g. water or ice) and rainfall rate. It also increases exponentially with the distance travelled by the energy through the attenuating medium. In any given set of precipitation conditions, S-band transmissions will suffer less attenuation than those at X-band.

3.7.3 The effect of precipitation type

In the preceding sections, the strength of the response, the extent of scattering and the amount of attenuation to be expected from precipitation in general have been considered in terms of the physical characteristics that affect them. Such characteristics will vary with precipitation type and it is therefore appropriate to discuss the effects in terms of various forms in which the precipitation may be manifest.

3.7.3.1 Rain

In the case of rain the particles which effect the scattering and attenuation take the form of water droplets. The droplet size cannot exceed a diameter of about 5.5 mm because at this limit the surface tension which holds the water in droplet form is overcome and the droplet subdivides.

Large droplets tend to be found in tropical rainstorms and in general in the rain associated with vigorous convection such as occurs for example at and after the passage of a cold front. In such cases the droplet size is an appreciable proportion of the X-band wavelength, very strong clutter echoes will be produced and there will be serious loss of energy due to scattering and attenuation. The detection ranges of strongly responding targets within the rain area will be reduced and their echoes may be severely masked by saturation within the receiver. Weaker target responses, for example those from small vessels and buoys, will be rendered undetectable if their echoes are not stronger than that of the rain. While targets in clear areas beyond the rain will not be subject to masking, scattering and attenuation will significantly reduce their detection ranges. As the droplet size is a much smaller proportion of the 10 cm wavelength, and bearing in mind the square law relationship (see Section 3.7.1.1), it is evident that the effects will be significantly reduced by the selection of S-band under such circumstances.

The droplet size of rain associated with stratiform clouds, such as those which might be expected at a warm front, tends to be smaller than those so far described. However, it must be remembered that the response and attenuation depend not only on the size of the droplets but also on the number falling, i.e. on the rainfall rate.

Drizzle is a form of light rain characterized by low rainfall rate and small droplet size of less than about 0.25 mm and as a consequence is unlikely to cause serious problems other than in the case of very weak targets.

3.7.3.2 Clouds

The water droplets which form clouds are too small (less than 0.1 mm) to produce detectable responses even at X-band. However, if there is rain or other precipitation within the cloud it may well be detected.

3.7.3.3 Fog

Because of the very small particle size and density it is most unlikely that fog and mist will return detectable echoes. In most circumstances attenuation results in only a slight reduction in maximum radar detection range. However, in the special case of the intense fogs which arise in polar regions a significant reduction in detection range may occur.

Smog is an acronym of smoke and fog and describes the effect of the condensation of water droplets on the dirt particles in areas of industrial smoke. It is likely to produce a somewhat higher degree of attentuation than a clean sea fog.

3.7.3.4   Snow

Where no melting is taking place, snowflakes are single ice crystals or a conglomeration of such crystals. When precipitation rates are compared, snowfall rates are in general less than rainfall rates. If this is considered in parallel with the lesser response of ice, it is evident that the echoes from snow are likely to be less troublesome than those from rain. *Sleet* describes the condition in which the snow is partially melted and the response will tend toward that of water. The attenuation produced by snow is similarly less than in the case of rain.

The fact that snow reflects radar energy less effectively than rain may be considered to be fortunate but it must be borne in mind that where snow lies on the surface of wanted targets its relatively poorer reflecting property and its albeit limited absorption characteristic may reduce the detection range of good targets such as land and also render indetectable poor targets such as growlers (see Section 3.3.6.1).

3.7.3.5   Hail

Hail is essentially composed of frozen raindrops. Ice reflects radar energy less effectively than water and hence, size for size, hailstones will produce a lesser response than raindrops. Melting on the surface of the stone will improve its response toward that of water. In general, the precipitation rates associated with hail are lower than those experienced with rain and so clutter and attenuation from hail are likely to prove less troublesome than those from rain.

3.7.3.6   Dry sand and dust haze

Clearly such phenomena cannot be described as precipitation but, as the effects are similar, it is appropriate to consider them under this general heading. On the basis of particle size and distribution, theory suggests that the effects should be similar to those of fog; practical experience substantiates this. Detectable responses, though not impossible, are extremely unlikely, and a fairly low level of attenuation is to be expected. These characteristics may prove very useful in conditions where visual sighting is severely hampered.

3.7.4   The suppression of rain clutter

As suggested in Section 3.6, in some ways the rain clutter problem resembles that of sea clutter and it is thus not surprising that some suppression techniques may be effective in both cases.

3.7.4.1   The choice of pulse length

As in the case of sea clutter, selection of a shorter pulse length will reduce the amplitude of all received echoes and hence may well assist in the detection of targets within an area of rain by bringing rain clutter echoes below saturation and in general improving the contrast between clutter echoes and those of wanted targets. It will of course not assist in combating the attenuation caused by the presence of the precipitation (see Section 3.7.5).

3.7.4.2   The choice of wavelength

Selection of S-band as opposed to X-band transmission will increase the probability of detection of targets within an area of precipitation clutter by reducing the response from the precipitation and the associated attenuation.

3.7.4.3   Searching techniques

The probability of detection of targets within areas of precipitation may be improved by using the gain control or the sea clutter control to systematically suppress and restore the clutter signals in a searching fashion similar to that described in Section 3.6.3.1. Where the clutter surrounds the observing vessel, the sea clutter control is likely to prove helpful but it will not be effective for more distant precipitation. The practical procedures for carrying out such searches are described in Section 6.10.1.

3.7.4.4   The rain clutter circuit

This is an alternative approach to the problem of saturation and employs a technique known as differentiation which is performed in the video section. The signal is conditioned by circuitry which responds only to

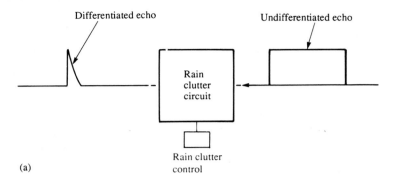

(a)

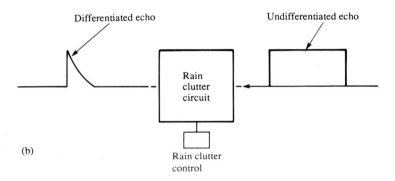

(b)

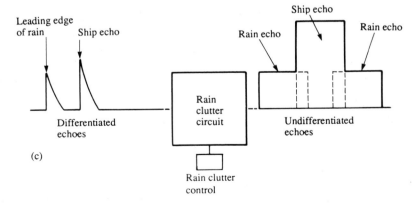

(c)

Figure 3.44   The principle of differentiation
(a)   High degree of differentiation
(b)   Low degree of differentiation
(c)   Separation of echoes by differentiation

increases in signal strength. The term 'differentiation' is mathematical in origin and essentially means to measure the rate of change of some quantity. The theoretical principle of operation is illustrated by Figure 3.44. Figure 3.44 (a) and (b) show the effect of varying degrees of differentiation on a single idealized rectangular pulse, while Figure 3.44 (c) shows three idealized rectangular echoes which overlap one another, saturate the receiver and hence are representative of the masking effect of rain clutter. The first pulse represents the rain echo which returns immediately ahead of the target response and the third pulse represents the rain return immediately following that of the target.

Because the circuitry responds only to those sections of the waveform where the signal strength is increasing, its effect is to remove the trailing edges of the echoes, thus making it possible to display the leading edge of the rain and that of the target as separate returns. Clearly the displayed echoes must not be made so short that they become difficult to discern. The finite radial length of the differentiated echo depends on the *time constant* of the circuit which is a measure of the time taken by the circuitry to respond to a levelling off or decrease in signal strength (see Figure 3.44 (a) and (b)). For this reason the rain clutter control may sometimes be referred to as the *fast time constant* (FTC). In some systems this is present by the manufacturer in which case the rain clutter control is an on/off ftc switch; in other systems it can be set by the observer over a continuous range of values. The effect of the rain clutter control on a practical set of echoes is illustrated by Figure 3.45.

Reference to Figure 3.45 shows that the two principal features of the differentiated output are the leading edges of the rain and the target which is stronger than the rain. It should also be noted that the raw rain signal shows a slow decrease with range, on which is superimposed a small high frequency fluctuation of the instantaneous signal level. Depending on the setting of the rain clutter control, the differentiated output will also tend to show to a greater or lesser extent the rising edges of the fluctuating peaks: targets close to rain level will have to compete with these for attention. Targets weaker than the rain response cannot be detected. It is emphasised that differentiation will be carried out before any digitization (see Section 2.6.6.1) and the output illustrated in Figure 3.45 is analogue.

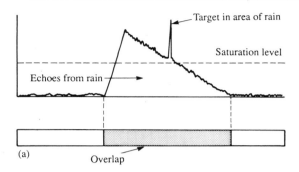

(a)   Overlap

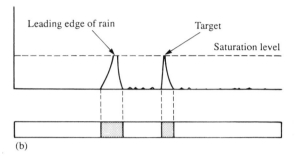

(b)

Figure 3.45   The effect of the rain clutter control
(a)   No rain clutter control applied: displayed echoes of rain and target overlap radially
(b)   Rain clutter control applied: there is radial (not necessarily amplitude) discrimination between leading edges of rain and target

It is important to appreciate that although the rain clutter control is so called, it is not necessarily the most effective way of dealing with rain echoes. Many users find the use of the gain control in a searching action much more effective. This is discussed further in Section 6.10.2, which sets out the practical procedures for detecting targets in rain. It is worth mentioning that the differentiating effect may be found particularly useful for improving discrimination on short range pictures.

3.7.4.5   Adaptive gain

This technique was described in detail in Section 3.6.3.3 and represents an automatic approach which may be found effective in the suppression of rain clutter echoes. In most systems, when adaptive gain is selected, a fixed amount of differentiation is also applied.

3.7.4.6 Circular polarization

For the reasons set out in Section 3.6.1.7 there is no stimulus for designers to produce X-band equipment other than with horizontal polarization. Hence, in civil marine applications, vertical polarization is very much the exception rather than the rule. In Section 2.4.1.8 it was explained that the terms 'vertical' and 'horizontal' refer to the plane of the fluctuating electric field associated with the electromagnetic wave.

The visualization of a circularly polarized wave may require some mental effort. Its effect is best explained by considering it to be produced by generating a horizontally polarized wave, and adding to it a vertically polarized wave which has the same amplitude and frequency but is a quarter-cycle out of phase with it. The polarization of the resultant wave thus rotates and hence the use of the term 'circular polarization'. On the return of echoes, the two components of the wave are separated and a further quarter cycle phaseshift is applied to the vertically polarized wave. If the two components of the wave have suffered identical reflection, they will be equal in amplitude, out of phase by one half-cycle and thus will cancel one another. Such symmetrical reflection will be experienced if the target is a small smooth sphere (radar cross-section is a function of polarization). In many circumstances a raindrop comes close to this ideal. Thus the response from raindrops will tend to be cancelled or at least considerably reduced. If the reflection of both components is not symmetrical then the degree of the cancelling will be reduced to a greater or lesser extent, depending on the lack of symmetry. The cancelling achieved in the case of other types of precipitation will not be as effective if the particle is not spherical, as in wet snowflakes. When compared with linear polarization, the response of wanted targets will also be reduced by the use of circular polarization. In general, cancellation can be expected, where the energy has suffered an odd number of reflections, but not with an even number. A ship target is a complex arrangement of many reflecting surfaces. It thus behaves as a large scatterer and the energy returned to the observing vessel will contain components which have suffered an even number of reflections.

The effectiveness of circular polarization for the suppression of precipitation thus depends on the reduction in response of wanted targets being less than that suffered by the precipitation. This hope may well not be realized in the case of small targets and this limitation must be firmly borne in mind should such a facility be available. In the past some civil marine radar systems offering this facility were produced but few, if any, are still at sea and there is no sign at present that they will be produced again. One might speculate that the additional cost and complication was not justified by the benefit gained.

3.7.5 Combating the attenuation caused by precipitation

The nature of the problem differs depending on whether the target lies within or beyond the area of the precipitation.

3.7.5.1 The attenuation of the signal from a target beyond precipitation

The response from a target beyond an area of precipitation will be reduced as a result of scattering and attenuation of the radar signal on its two-way journey through the precipitation (see Section 3.7.2). This attenuation can be combated by the selection of the S-band and the use of a longer pulse length. While searching for specific targets it may be useful temporarily to turn the gain above the normal setting or to use an echo-stretching facility (see Section 6.11.1) if the latter is available.

3.7.5.2 The attenuation of the signal from a target within precipitation

This is a more difficult problem: the only way in which this attenuation can be effectively reduced is by the use of S-band in preference to X-band transmission (see section 3.6.1.5). The other techniques suggested in Section 3.7.5.1 will certainly increase the target response but they will also increase the response from the precipitation, thus exacerbating the already serious problem of saturation.

3.7.6 Exploiting the ability of radar to detect precipitation

The ability of radar to detect precipitation at long range has been found useful in a number of meteorological applications. Shore-based radars having a range of several hundred miles have been used to track the movement of the large areas of precipitation present in hurricanes and other similar storms in order to provide warning of possible danger and damage from the associated weather conditions. The detection range offered by shipboard radar cannot provide sufficient warning to permit avoiding action. The presence of precipitation in other less dramatic weather systems has led to the use of long range surveillance radars in day-to-day general weather forecasting. Again, shipboard equipment does not offer the range necessary for weather forecasting but the ability to track the movement of precipitation in the short term can prove useful.

Early warning of the approach of precipitation should make it possible to ensure that the vessel is adequately prepared to deal with the additional problems this may pose in the use of radar for collision avoidance. The Master can be called in adequate time, the engine room staff can be prepared for manoeuvres and arrangements can be made for such additional bridge and lookout personnel as may be required. It may be possible to commence the plotting of targets before they enter areas of precipitation. This may well assist in the detection of targets even in the presence of masking as it is always easier to find an echo if its approximate location is known. The data extracted should also prove useful in planning collision avoidance strategy, although the observer must always be alert to the possibility of a target manoeuvring while masked.

In port, the ability to track approaching rain showers may make it possible to close cargo hatches in sufficient time to prevent cargo damage. At sea, the ability to avoid isolated showers might benefit a freshly painted deck or perhaps an outdoor event on a passenger vessel.

3.8 The radar horizon

At marine radar transmission frequencies (nominally 10 000 and 3 000 MHz), the paths followed by the signals may be considered as 'line of sight'. This means that even though the radar is delivering a powerful pulse and the target is capable, if irradiated, of returning a detectable response, the target will not be detected if it is below the *radar horizon*. This is analogous to the visual observation of objects in the vicinity of the horizon.

The effect of the atmosphere on the horizon is a further factor which must be taken into account when assessing the likelihood of detecting a particular target and especially when considering the expected appearance of coastlines.

3.8.1 The effect of standard atmospheric conditions

Under standard atmospheric conditions, the radar beam tends to bend slightly downward, the distance to the radar horizon being given by the formula

$$d_{\text{n mile}} = 1.22\sqrt{h_{\text{ft}}} \quad \text{or} \quad d_{\text{n mile}} = 2.21\sqrt{h_{\text{m}}}$$

where h is the height of the antenna in feet or metres.

It can seen from Figure 3.46 that the possibility of

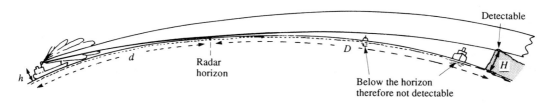

Figure 3.46 The radar horizon under standard atmospheric conditions

detecting targets beyond the radar horizon will, in addition to all the other factors discussed in this chapter, depend upon the height of the target (i.e. whether or not a responsive part of it extends above the horizon). Thus the theoretical detection range based purely on the antenna and target heights is given by the formula

$$R_d = d + D$$
$$R_d = 1.22\sqrt{h_{ft}} + 1.22\sqrt{H_{ft}} \quad \text{or}$$
$$R_d = 2.21\sqrt{h_m} + 2.21\sqrt{H_m}$$

where h and H are heights of the antenna and the target respectively in feet or metres. In both cases, R_d is the theoretical detection range in nautical miles.

This relationship is of course theoretical since it assumes that:

(a) Standard atmospheric conditions prevail.
(b) The radar pulses are sufficiently powerful.
(c) The target response characteristics are such as to return detectable responses.
(d) The weather conditions, such as precipitation etc., through which the pulses have to travel, will not unduly attenuate the signals.

3.8.1.1 The increase in detection range with increased antenna height

While in theory it is correct to say that detection ranges can be increased by increasing the antenna height, in practice there is a limit to the extent to which it is worth pursuing this increase. Above moderate height, the increase in detection range is minimal and not worth the effort (or the consequent additional expense of waveguide etc.). The reason for this can be appreciated by considering the theoretical relationship set out above: to double the distance to the radar horizon, the antenna will have to be four times as high. If the antenna is at a

height of 16 m, the distance to the radar horizon is 8.84 n mile. To double this to some 17.7 n mile would require an antenna height of some $(17.68/2.21)^2$ n mile = 64 m. This point should be borne in mind when considering the extent to which radars offering 96 n mile range scales can be effective.

It can be seen from Figure 3.46 that if targets are observed beyond the horizon, it must *not* be assumed that nearer targets will necessarily also be detected. Note that, although the cliff may be detected, there is no chance of receiving an echo from the buoy at this stage.

Consider a vessel having its radar antenna at a height of 16 m above the water. The distance to the radar horizon will be $2.21 \times 4 = 8.84$ n mile. This means that when assessing the possibility of detecting a target at a range greater than some 8.5 n mile, one must first consider whether or not the target has sufficient height.

The theoretical range at which a sheer cliff face rising to a height of 64 m should be detected on a vessel whose antenna is at a height of 16 m is

$$2.21\sqrt{(64)} + 2.21\sqrt{(16)}$$
$$= 2.21 \times 8 + 2.21 \times 4$$
$$= 26.5 \text{ n mile}$$

Note Although sheer cliffs immediately suggest a good response target, aspect must be borne in mind, i.e. whether the cliffs are 'square on' or at an angle to the radar rays.

Consider the case where a vessel has its antenna at a height of 16 m above the water and first detects land at a range of 23 n mile:

$$23 = 2.21\sqrt{(16)} \times 2.21\sqrt{H}$$
$$\text{therefore } H = \left(\frac{23 - (2.21 \times 4)}{2.21}\right)^2$$
$$= 41.05 \text{ metres}$$

Figure 3.47   The effects of target and antenna height

The indication here is that, if standard atmospheric conditions prevail, the land which is being detected must be at least 41 m high. When attempting to relate what is being observed on the radar to the chart, only land having a height of at least 41 m should be being considered. As can be seen in Figure 3.47, it would be completely incorrect to assume that the vessel is 23 n mile from the coastline.

Great care must be exercised when attempting to identify targets which are beyond the radar horizon. Using the example above (and Figure 3.47) it is evident that the land detected is unlikely to be the coastline but is probably higher ground lying inland. It is important to appreciate this principle as failure to do so gives the impression that the vessel is farther offshore than is in fact the case.

It should be noted that, when making in toward a sloping coastline such as that in Figure 3.48, the coastline as displayed on the radar screen can have a disconcerting effect of 'appearing' to come toward the vessel as more of the low-lying land comes above the horizon. This is especially so if it has been assumed that it was the coastline that was being observed in the first instance and positions have been laid off as if this were the case.

Considering a vessel with an antenna at a height of 16 m and assuming standard atmospheric conditions, if echoes from land are observed at a range of 26 n mile then whatever is being observed must be at least some 60 m high (see Table 3.1).

Table 3.1 gives the least theoretical height (in metres) of a target detected beyond the radar horizon for various antenna heights. Since the distance to the radar horizon in the above example is some 8.8 n mile, any target observed at a greater range than 8.8 n mile should be checked against the table to ensure that it has adequate height for detection.

3.8.1.2 Standard atmospheric conditions

'Standard' conditions are precisely defined as:

Pressure = 1013 mb decreasing at 36 mb/1000 ft of height

Temperature = 15°C decreasing at 2°C/1000 ft of height

Relative humidity = 60% and constant with height.

These conditions give a refractive index of 1.003 25 which decreases at 0.000 13 units/1000 ft of height.

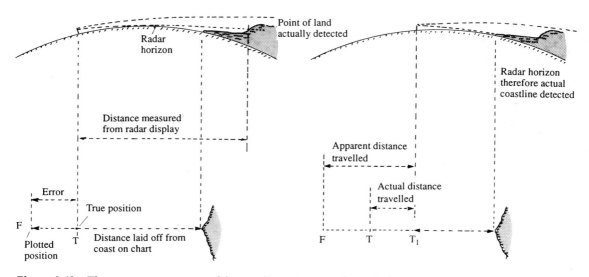

Figure 3.48   The apparent movement of the coastline as it comes above the horizon

The term 'standard' should not be confused with the term 'normal', which is extremely subjective and imprecise. Standard conditions are rarely likely to equate to what might be considered normal at any particular location on the earth.

It can be seen that the definition of 'standard' condi-

tions relates to the vertical composition of the atmosphere. The mariner is unlikely to be able to obtain a precise knowledge of this and so must rely on a more general appreciation of the weather conditions, the area of the world, and the time of the year, as well as on past experience for guidance as to the likelihood of the exist-

Table 3.1   Least height of a target detected beyond the radar horizon

Antenna height (m)

Detection range of target (n mile)	8	10	12	14	16	18	20	22	24	26	28	30
12	6.8	5.1	3.9	2.9	2.0	1.4	0.9	0.5	0.3	0.1	0.0	
14	12.3	10.1	8.2	6.7	5.5	4.4	3.5	2.7	2.1	1.5	1.1	0.7
16	19.5	16.6	14.3	12.2	10.5	9.0	7.7	6.5	5.5	4.6	3.8	3.1
18	28.3	24.8	21.9	19.4	17.2	15.2	13.5	11.9	10.5	9.3	8.1	7.1
20	38.7	34.7	31.2	28.2	25.5	23.1	21.0	19.0	17.2	15.6	14.1	12.8
22	50.8	46.1	42.1	38.6	35.5	32.6	30.1	27.7	25.6	23.6	21.7	20.0
24	64.5	59.3	54.7	50.7	47.1	43.8	40.8	38.1	35.5	33.2	31.0	29.0
26	79.9	74.0	68.9	64.4	**60.3**	56.6	53.2	50.0	47.1	44.4	41.9	39.5
28	96.9	90.4	84.7	79.7	75.2	71.0	67.2	63.7	60.4	57.3	54.4	51.7
30	115.5	108.4	102.2	96.7	91.7	87.1	82.9	78.9	75.3	71.8	68.6	65.6
32	135.8	128.1	121.3	115.3	109.8	104.8	100.2	95.8	91.8	88.0	84.4	81.0
34	157.7	149.4	142.1	135.6	129.6	124.1	119.1	114.4	109.9	105.8	101.9	98.2
36	181.2	172.3	164.5	157.5	151.0	145.1	139.7	134.5	129.7	125.2	121.0	116.9
38	206.4	196.9	188.5	181.0	174.1	167.8	161.9	156.4	151.2	146.3	141.7	137.3
40	233.2	223.1	214.2	206.1	198.8	192.0	185.7	179.8	174.3	169.0	164.0	159.3

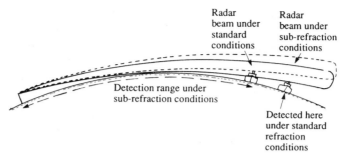

Figure 3.49 The effect of sub-refraction on detection ranges

ence of standard or non-standard atmospheric conditions and of the effects that they can have on the detection ranges of targets in the area.

In general, 'normal' conditions in the more highly frequented sea areas of the world tend to be super-refractive.

Note The attenuating and clutter effects of the atmosphere are considered in Section 3.7.2.

3.8.2 Sub-refraction

3.8.2.1 The effects of sub-refraction on detection ranges (Figure 3.49)

Sub-refraction occurs when the refractive index of the atmosphere decreases less rapidly with height than under standard conditions. As a result, the radar beam is bent downward slightly less than under standard conditions. This means that, with all other factors constant, the same target will be detected at a slightly reduced range. In practice, this is likely to mean something of the order of 80% of the detection range under standard conditions but will obviously depend on the severity of the conditions prevailing at the time.

3.8.2.2 Atmospheric conditions that give rise to sub-refraction (Figure 3.50)

These can be specified precisely but since the mariner is unlikely to have access to data relating to the vertical composition of the atmosphere it is perhaps more

appropriate to consider the conditions which, from experience, are likely to accompany this phenomenon. These are:

(a) An increase in relative humidity with height.
(b) A rapid fall in temperature with height.

Both of these conditions do not have to be satisfied at any one time but, obviously, the greater the changes in temperature and relative humidity with height, the greater will be the effect that they will have on the radar beam. This does not mean that, under extreme conditions, the whole beam will rise above the sea surface or that no targets will be detected at all.

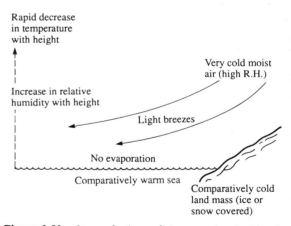

Figure 3.50 Atmospheric conditions associated with sub-refraction. The critical factor is land/sea (or sea/sea) temperature difference. When the sea is cold, sub-refraction can occur provided that the air is even colder

These conditions, to a greater or lesser extent, may be encountered virtually anywhere but are most likely in the polar regions, the Grand Banks (especially in the Gulf Stream with northerly winds), east of Japan in winter, and in the Mediterranean in winter.

Sub-refraction is generally associated with bad weather conditions, i.e. with low pressure systems, which is typically the time when radar is most likely to be needed.

3.8.3   Super-refraction

3.8.3.1   The effects of super-refraction on detection ranges (Figure 3.51)

Super-refraction occurs when the rate of decrease in refractive index with height is greater than under stan-

dard conditions. When super-refraction occurs, the radar beam tends to be bent down slightly more and so targets may be detected at ranges which are slightly greater than standard. Increases of some 40% are not uncommon.

Again, the mariner has no means of knowing exactly what sort of atmospheric conditions are being experienced and so has to rely on some form of subjective assessment; it is always best to err on the cautious side.

3.8.3.2   Atmospheric conditions associated with super-refraction (Figure 3.52)

These are:

(a) A decrease in relative humidity with height.
(b) Temperature falling more slowly than standard, or even increasing with height.

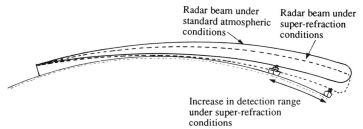

Figure 3.51   The effects of super-refraction on detection ranges

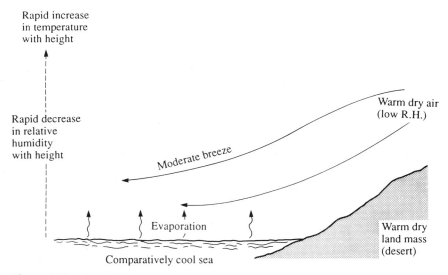

Figure 3.52   Atmospheric conditions associated with super-refraction

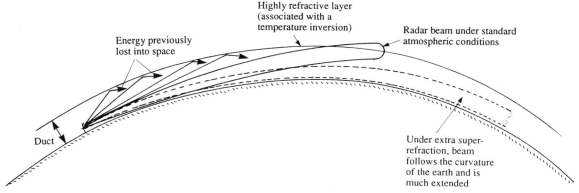

Figure 3.53   The effect of extra super-refraction

These conditions tend to be more frequently encountered in the maritime trading areas of the world, in particular, the tropics; other areas include the Red Sea, the Arabian Gulf, and the Mediterranean in summer.

Super-refraction is generally associated with fine settled weather, i.e. with high pressure weather systems.

3.8.4   Extra super-refraction or ducting

3.8.4.1   The effects of extra super-refraction (Figure 3.53)

Under these conditions, the radar energy is, in effect, trapped in a 'duct' formed by the Earth's surface and a highly refractive layer which may be as little as a 100 ft (30 m) above the ground. The effect is to concentrate energy which would otherwise have been lost into space together with the energy which would normally travel in the direction of the targets. This increased energy now follows the Earth's surface, thus reducing the constraint of the radar horizon and considerably extending the detection ranges of targets. This can result in the unwanted detection of 'second-trace echoes' (see Section 3.9.6).

3.8.4.2   Atmospheric conditions which give rise to extra super-refraction

If the rate of change of refractive index is of the order of 4 times the 'standard' rate, initially horizontal rays will follow the curvature of the Earth. It is more effective,

though, for the energy to be trapped between the Earth and a highly refractive layer (such as a temperature inversion), thus forming a duct in which the energy will travel in a similar manner to propagation within a waveguide with a 'leaky' upper wall.

Note   (a)   A temperature inversion by itself must be very pronounced to produce a duct.

(b)   Relative humidity gradients are more effective than temperature gradients alone.

The areas which are normally associated with extra super-refraction are the Red Sea, the Arabian Gulf, the Mediterranean in the summer with the wind from the south, and the area off the west coast of Africa in the vicinity of the Canary Islands. However, extra super-refraction can occur anywhere if the conditions are right. The usual indication that these conditions exist is the appearance of second trace echoes (see Section 3.9.6).

3.9   False and unwanted radar responses

3.9.1   Introduction

These responses may also be referred to as spurious echoes and are the result of a number of specific causes. In all cases, echoes are displayed on the screen in pos-

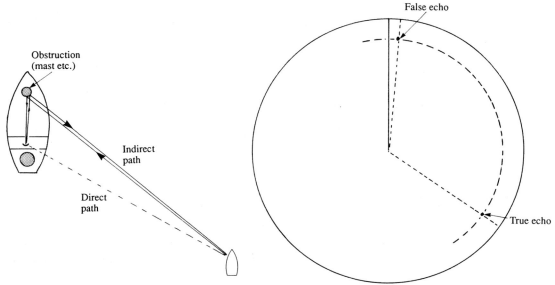

Figure 3.54   Indirect echoes

itions where no genuine targets exist. In general, these are likely when genuine targets are close but this is not always the case (see Section 3.9.6).

3.9.2   Indirect echoes (reflected echoes)

These can occur when radar energy is deflected in the direction of an object by some obstruction in the path of the radiated energy, either on board the ship or ashore.

The returning energy follows a reciprocal path and so causes an echo to be displayed in the direction of the obstruction. This form of false echo can be particularly misleading when the obstruction is on board the ship.

3.9.2.1   The effect of on-board obstructions

Consider the situation, depicted in Figure 3.54, where energy strikes the foremast and some of it is deflected in the direction of the target on the starboard quarter. Energy reflected by the target follows a reciprocal path and so returns to the antenna from a direction fine on the starboard bow (i.e. the reflection point on the foremast). As a result, a false echo will be displayed at a range which is similar to that of the genuine target (this assumes that the distance to the on–board obstruction is small by

comparison with the range of the target), but on the bearing of the obstruction (i.e. the foremast).

Typical of on-board obstructions which can give rise to this form of false echo are a mast, a funnel and cross-trees. In fact, any structure which intercepts energy in the beam can produce the effect. There is a tendency to associate indirect echoes with blind arcs and shadow sectors (see Section 2.7.1.1); while this is frequently the case, in recent times other less obvious causes have been identified. Most notable have been the indirect echoes resulting from reflections from the aft-facing surface of containers (Figure 3.55). Here, three points should be noted:

(a)   The traditional blind/shadow sector theory need not apply.
(b)   There is a likelihood of other true echoes appearing on the radar display on the same bearing as the false echoes.
(c)   The cause of the problem may change each time the stowage of the containers on deck is changed.

It is advisable, when containers are stowed in isolated stacks, that a warning of the possibility of indirect echoes is displayed alongside the radar.

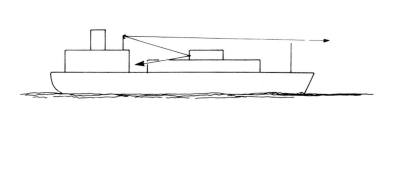 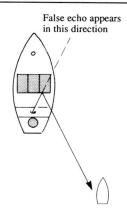

False echo appears
in this direction

Figure 3.55   Reflections from aft-facing surfaces of containers

3.9.2.2   The recognition of indirect echoes

The more obvious causes (blind and shadow sectors) should be studied in clear weather when there are a number of other vessels in the vicinity of the observing ship. Blind and shadow sectors should have been logged (see Section 2.7.1.1) and any echo which appears in these sectors should be regarded as suspect. Visual comparison with the radar should confirm whether the echo is genuine or indirect. Where it is decided that the displayed echo is indirect, it is reasonable to expect to find a genuine target at about the same range, although even this search may be inconclusive.

Many unusual causes of indirect echoes have been reported but, without a careful study of the conditions obtaining at the time, it is very difficult to come to reliable conclusions and to take steps to prevent their recurrence. Deck cargo, deck cranes, breakwaters, ventilators and a host of other on-board structures have aroused suspicion at one time or another.

Indirect echoes can give rise to serious concern when they appear ahead of the vessel, particularly at night or in restricted visibility. At night, it may be suspected that the 'vessel' ahead is not showing the necessary navigation lights or that the onset of restricted visibility is imminent.

If this phenomenon occurs in restricted visibility and it is considered necessary to manoeuvre to avoid what one must assume is a real target, the resulting apparent behaviour of the echo (if false) is quite unpredictable.

For example, the 'target' may appear to make a simultaneous countermanoeuvre or may even disappear (Figure 3.56).

The following safety precautions should be observed:

1   Where echoes are suspected of being false, they should be assumed to be real until proved false beyond all reasonable doubt.
2   Potential causes of indirect echoes such as blind and shadow sectors should be constantly borne in mind and any suspect arc investigated, preferably before arrival in areas of known restricted visibility.
3   Unexplained 'target' behaviour should be logged.
4   Where the cause of indirect echoes has been identified, steps to prevent their recurrence should be taken immediately.

3.9.2.3   The prevention of indirect echoes

Where shipboard structures have been identified as the cause of indirect errors, steps should be taken to prevent their future recurrence. In principle, this means that the energy striking the deflecting obstruction must be dissipated by re-direction, scattering or absorption.

Each cause has to be treated individually; typical solutions in the past have included attaching plates angled upwards to the crosstrees, welding angle iron to the after surfaces of the crosstrees and surfacing the obstruction with radar absorbent material (RAM).

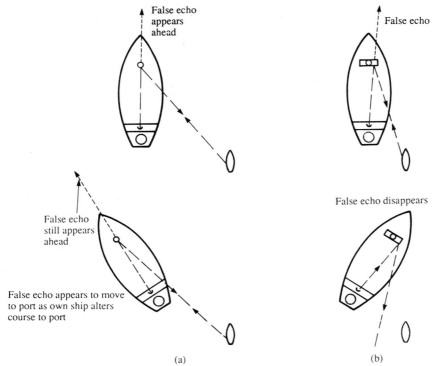

Figure 3.56   The effect of a manoeuvre by own ship on an indirect echo

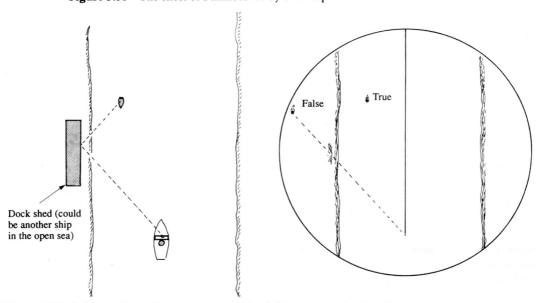

Figure 3.57   Indirect echoes which occur as a result of objects external to the ship

Note Where attempts are made to scatter the energy by 'roughening' the surface, it must be remembered that facets must be of the order of wavelength (see Section 3.3.2).

3.9.2.4 *Indirect echoes from objects external to the ship (Figure 3.57)*

These can frequently be seen when vessels are in built-up areas and other vessels are moving in the vicinity. Because of the conditions under which they occur, they are frequently not recognised.

In general, the obstructions which cause the deflection of energy tend to be large and the false echoes will display on the farther side of them. In many cases they will appear to move over the land, making it easy to recognise them and dismiss them as false. In the open sea, this recognition might not be quite so positive but there is always the consolation that the nearer of the targets on the same bearing is invariably genuine.

One special form of false echo arising from this cause can be extremely misleading. This is where the indirect echoes occur as a result of a bridge structure spanning the waterway. Consider a vessel approaching a bridge as in Figure 3.58. Energy reflected back and forth between the bridge and the vessel (in a similar manner to that described in 3.9.3) will result in a false echo appearing about as far beyond the bridge as the observer's vessel is from it. As the vessel approaches the bridge, so the false echo will appear to approach the bridge from the opposite direction. In most cases, the bridge will cross the waterway at right angles which will mean that, however the vessel manoeuvres in an attempt to avoid the '*other ship*', the observed echo will appear to have undertaken a complementary countermanoeuvre, i.e. the false echo's position will be on the perpendicular from the observing vessel to the bridge and its distance from the bridge will be about the same as that of the observing vessel.

Indirect echoes from objects ashore which result from reflections at the bridge can result in a considerable amount of 'clutter' appearing in the water area beyond the bridge. It should be noted that this clutter will be moving as the observing vessel moves and so changes its position in relation to the objects ashore. This clutter can also mask the real responses from other vessels using the waterway.

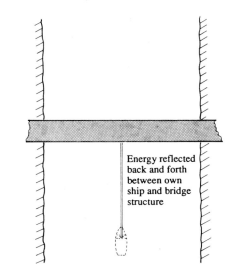

Figure 3.58 False echoes from bridges

3.9.3 Multiple echoes

Multiple echoes are likely when a target is close and energy bounces back and forth between the hulls of the target and the observing ship, with some of the energy entering the antenna at each return (Figure 3.59). The features of this form of response are that the echoes:

(a) Lie along a single direction.
(b) Are consistently spaced.
(c) Tend to move in accord.
(d) Tend to diminish in strength with the increase of range.

It should be noted that, while it would seem logical from Figure 3.59 for this form of response to occur when vessels are abeam, it has been observed to occur on virtually all relative bearings.

Since it is most unlikely to occur when vessels are close (maybe as much as 4 n mile but usually less), if the vessels are constrained within channels or rivers etc, the false echoes will be seen to be navigating outside the channel or even on the shore.

Note Because the outer echoes must keep on the same bearing line as the nearer ones, if plotted, their movement can be found to be higher than or contrary to that which might be anticipated.

The chances of multiple echoes can be reduced by ensuring that shorter pulse lengths are selected when using the lower range scales. It may be possible to produce this phenomenon deliberately in order to observe it, by selecting the longer pulse when on a lower range scale and with a close target.

In general, this form of false echo should not give real cause for concern since the genuine target producing the effect is always the nearest. Nonetheless, it is worth while to watch out for it in clear weather, when the absence of real targets beyond the nearest one can be confirmed.

Multiple echoes can also be produced by targets ashore, but the multiples will generally be lost amidst the confusion of other land echoes.

3.9.4 Side echoes

Side echoes are again associated with targets that are at close range, and result from the radar beam being surrounded by smaller beams or lobes (see Section 2.4.2).

In the case of the farther target in Figure 3.60, the radar beam sweeping over it will result in the display of an echo of angular width which is approximately equal to the horizontal beamwidth (see Section 2.6.5.3).

In the case of the nearer target, if energy is returned as

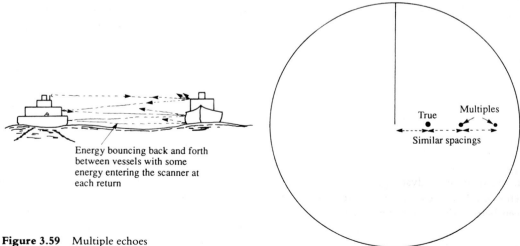

Energy bouncing back and forth
between vessels with some
energy entering the scanner at
each return

Figure 3.59 Multiple echoes

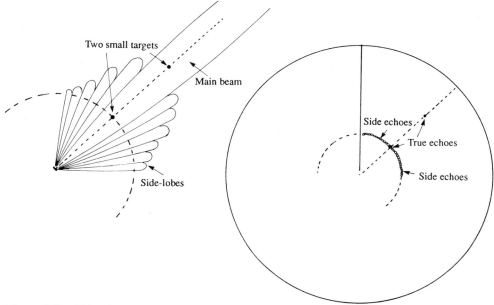

Figure 3.60   Side echoes

each lobe sweeps over it, the angular width of the displayed echo will be of the order of 100°. Some of the echoes will appear to be separate but all will be at the same range, i.e. as if all were lying on the same range circle.

This phenomenon is generally associated with smaller antennae and those which are dirty or damaged. While it is normal for the side echoes to be symmetrical about the genuine response, this may not be so in all cases; it is reasonable to expect the true response to be the strongest (see Section 2.4.2.1). If it is essential to identify the genuine echo, this can be achieved by the use of the gain or anti-clutter controls to suppress the weaker side echoes, as when dealing with sea clutter (see Section 6.10.1.1).

The effect of side echoes on sea clutter is to intensify the displayed clutter by integration of the echoes and this can be a definite disadvantage.

When side echoes are observed where they have not been seen before, their cause should be determined (a damaged or dirty antenna should be the first suspect) and rectified at the first possible opportunity.

3.9.5   Radar-to-radar interference

All civil marine radar systems are required to operate within a fairly narrow slot of approximately 200 MHz allocated in the X-band or S-band (see Section 2.3.3.1). When it is considered that the receiver bandwidth (see Section 2.5.2.4) of a marine radar system may be as much as 20 MHz, and given the high power and antenna height of a shipboard system, it is obvious that, except in mid-ocean, there is a very high probability of receiving interfering radiation from other vessels in the vicinity which are operating radar equipment.

If the radiation received is within the limits of the receiver bandwidth the signals will be amplified in the same way as those reflected from targets and will produce a visible response on the display. In the case of returned echoes there is a strict time sequence relationship between transmission and timebase cycles and both have the same repetition rate (see Section 2.3.1). By contrast, there is no synchronism in the relationship between the transmission sequence of the interfering radar and the timebase of the receiving system, nor are

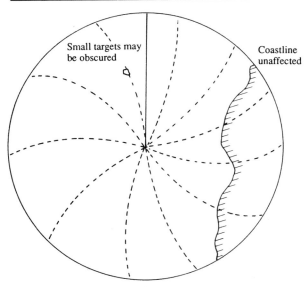

Figure 3.61   Radar-to-radar interference – appearance on the display

their repetition rates necessarily similar. As a result, the interfering signals produce a pattern on the screen which is totally random. It can take any form but frequently has a spiral character, as illustrated by Figure 3.61.

At best, the presence of interference may be a source of slight irritation which the practised observer may be able to cope with by mental filtering. In severe cases it may seriously impair the ability of the observer to detect targets.

If observers make prudent use of the stand-by condition (see Section 6.7), the general level of radar-to-radar interference present in the atmosphere can be reduced at source. Despite this, there is still a need to provide the observer with a means of suppressing displayed interference.

3.9.5.1   Interference rejection

Where picture data is stored, interference can be filtered out by comparing the signals present in successive range words (see Section 2.6.6.3) and rejecting those which do not appear on successive lines. The principle of operation is known as *line-to-line correlation* and is illustrated by Figure 3.62.

The underlying logic is that, because of the random nature of interference, the probability of two signals appearing in the same range cell on successive range words is negligible. By contrast, as a point target is swept by the radar beam, it will be struck by a number of successive pulses (see Section 2.4.4) all of which will register in the same range cell in successive lines. Thus interference will be removed by the correlation process, whereas the echoes of targets will be unaffected other than the rejection of the first strike. This loss is acceptable since even a point target should experience some 10 to 20 strikes. The output from the interference rejection circuit is known as *correlated video*.

Such a facility will also reduce the amount of displayed receiver noise and should therefore be switched off when setting the gain control (see Sections 6.2.4.1, 6.3.4.2 and 6.4.4). Correlation may also result in the rejection of the signals from some radar beacons (see Section 3.5). The IMO Performance Standards (see Section 10.2) state that it should be possible to switch off *any* signal processing facility that might prevent a radar beacon from being shown on the display (see also Adaptive gain in Section 3.6.3.3).

Some modern radar systems offer a more sophisticated facility described as *beam processing* by which all hits within the antenna beamwidth are compared with criteria for probability of detection. The information so derived is used to eliminate interference and reduce noise and, additionally, to reduce the angular width of the echo in an attempt to reduce the distorting effect of the horizontal beamwidth (see Section 2.6.5.3).

Mutual interference may be particularly troublesome where two X-band or two S-band systems are fitted on the same vessel. Where the two systems are interswitched (see Section 2.7.8), a pulse synchronization unit may be incorporated. This unit will synchronize the PRFs of both units and time-shift the transmissions in an attempt to ensure that neither system will transmit during the timebase of the other. This will not necessarily eliminate all interference from the adjacent system. However, the strongest interfering signals are likely to be those reflected from the ship's structure and nearby targets and these will be not be displayed. A pulse synchronization circuit will make no contribution to the reduction of interference generated by other vessels.

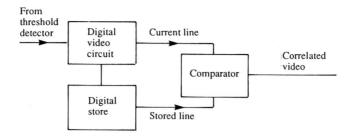

		Input line								Displayed line							
	S	0	0	1	0	1	0	0	0								
S	C	1	0	1	0	1	0	0	1	0	0	1	0	1	0	0	0
C	S	0	0	1	0	1	0	0	0	0	0	1	0	1	0	0	0
S	C	0	1	1	0	0	0	0	0	0	0	1	0	0	0	0	0
C	S	0	0	1	0	0	0	1	0	0	0	1	0	0	0	0	0
S	C	0	0	1	0	0	0	1	0	0	0	1	0	0	0	1	0
C	S	0	0	1	1	0	0	1	0	0	0	1	0	0	0	1	0
S	C	0	0	1	0	0	0	1	0	0	0	1	0	0	0	1	0
C	S	0	0	1	0	0	0	1	1	0	0	1	0	0	0	1	0
S	C	0	0	1	0	0	0	1	0	0	0	1	0	0	0	1	0
C	S	0	1	0	0	0	0	1	0	0	0	0	0	0	0	1	0
S	C	0	0	0	0	0	0	1	0	0	0	0	0	0	0	1	0
C	S	1	0	0	1	0	0	1	0	0	0	0	0	0	0	1	0
S	C	0	0	1	0	0	0	1	0	0	0	0	0	0	0	1	0

Figure 3.62 Line-to-line correlation

3.9.6 Second-trace echoes

The conditions which must exist before this form of false echo will appear are fairly exceptional:

(a) Extra super-refractive atmospheric conditions must exist.
(b) Targets must be in the vicinity of the ship and in areas which are precisely defined by the PRF selected by the observer at the time.

Nonetheless, false echoes of this type are regularly reported in the meteorological journals, while on many more occasions observations go unreported as they are not recognised for what they are.

Under conditions of extra super-refraction (see Section 3.8.4), the radar energy follows closely the surface of the Earth and travels to greater distances than under standard conditions. This means that echoes from distant targets can arrive back at the receiver one trace late (i.e.

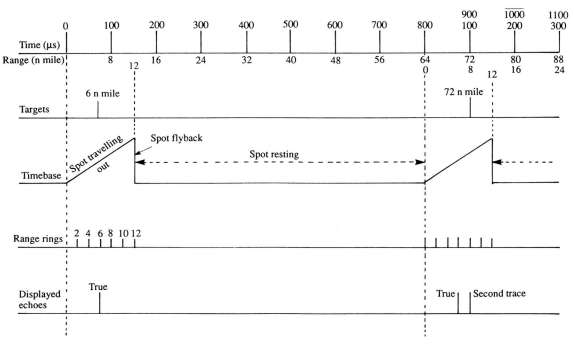

Figure 3.63   Time sequence graph

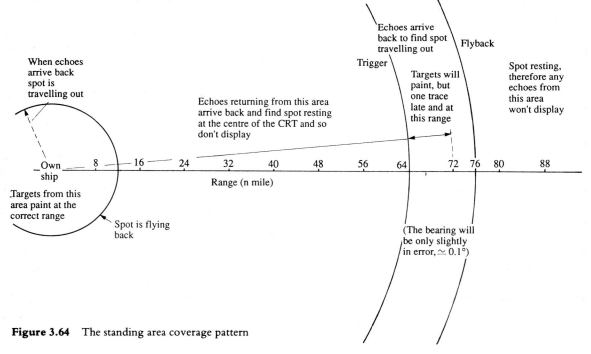

Figure 3.64   The standing area coverage pattern

on the 'second trace') or even later, be accepted by the receiver and so be displayed but obviously at an incorrect range.

Consider a radar system operating with the following parameters:

PRF = 1250 pulses/second (pps) and therefore the PRP = 800 μs (an echo which returns after an interval of 800 μs from transmission will be from a target which is at a range of 64 n mile).

Long pulse is being used on the 12 n mile range scale (timebase = 150 μs) and there are objects at 6 n miles and 72 n miles which will respond well to radar pulses if struck.

Note Under standard atmospheric conditions, the object at 72 n mile would be well below the radar horizon; also, the energy in the transmitted pulse would be insufficient to travel to and from targets at that range.

Figure 3.63 shows the time sequence graph for the above data. Consider how this can be translated to the area around the vessel. Figure 3.64 gives the standing area coverage pattern.

By allowing a fairly long resting period for the spot, radar designers are generally able to ensure that the energy in the pulse is sufficient to detect most targets out to the range of the scale in use (12 n mile in this case) but insufficient to return echoes from targets in the 64 to 76 n mile band, which would otherwise arrive while the receiver was again receptive and the spot on its way from the centre of screen to the edge. If this were not the case, an echo arriving back during this period would display together with those coming from within the range of the scale in use at the time.

Under extra super-refraction conditions, the situation changes in that the energy trapped in the duct is capable of returning echoes from much greater ranges and so second (or even third and fourth) trace echoes become a real possibility.

As can be seen from Figures 3.63 and 3.64, the positioning of the bands from which reception is possible is fixed by the PRF in use at the time, while the width of the band is equal to the range of the scale in use.

3.9.6.1   The recognition of second-trace echoes

It should be remembered that second-trace echoes are generally associated with fine weather conditions and so in most cases it will be possible to compare the radar picture with the visual scene. In some areas, notably the Red Sea and Arabian Gulf, some parts of the Mediterranean and off the west coast of Africa, extra super-refraction conditions are accompanied by a dry sand haze which can severely restrict visibility, thus rendering visual comparison with the radar picture impossible.

Where conditions are unfavourable for visual comparison, some indications as to the second-trace nature of the echoes may be recognisable. The radar picure should be compared with echoes from the coastline which might be expected from the vessel's present position. Where the DR position is sufficiently far in doubt, other effects should be sought.

Consider a long straight coastline which is returned as a second-trace echo. The coastline would be as depicted in Figure 3.65, with the distortion toward the origin of the display. Also, as the vessel steamed parallel to the coast, the 'point' of land would appear to remain abeam to starboard.

Alternatively, the relative track which the island would follow when plotted should be parallel to the heading marker but, as a second-trace echo, would produce a plotted apparent-motion line akin to the curve of the straight coastline. It might also move out of the band, either at long range or short range, and so disappear. The latter experience can be somewhat disconcerting, especially as the 'target' would appear to be on a collision course for much of the time.

To assess (assuming atmospheric conditions are appropriate) whether it is possible for echoes to be second-trace or multi-trace, it is necessary to study the charted coastline and the accuracy with which the vessel's position is known. This must then be related to the radar's PRF and range scale in use at the time.

Example 3.5   An echo is observed at a range of 4 n miles but visual observation shows nothing in the vicinity of the vessel. If the PRF is 1000 pps and the 12 n mile range scale is in use at the time, what could be the range of the true target? (atmospheric conditions suggest extra super-refraction).

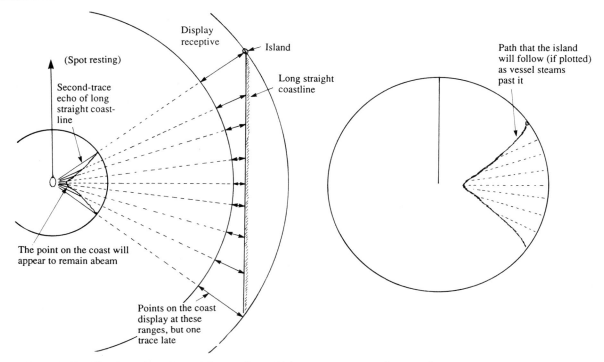

Figure 3.65   The distortion of a straight coastline which returns as a second-trace echo

PRF = 1000 pps therefore PRP = 1000 μs, which relates to 80 n miles.

The bands from which echoes could return are

80 − 92 n miles   160 − 172 n miles
240 − 252 n miles ...

therefore the target's range could be

84 n miles   164 n miles   244 n miles ...

In general terms, it can be shown that

$$R_{nt} = \text{PRP in n miles} + \text{target's displayed range}$$
$$= \frac{8 \times 10^4 \times (n-1)}{\text{PRF}} + R_d$$

where R_{nt} is the range (n miles) of an nth-trace echo
R_d is the displayed range of the target
n is the number of the trace on which the echo appears (the trace associated with transmission is counted as 1).

In the example above, if the false echo were third-trace then its range would be

$$R_{nt} = \left(\frac{80\,000 \times 2}{1000}\right) + 4 \text{ n miles}$$
$$= 164 \text{ n miles (as above)}.$$

3.9.6.2   The elimination of second-trace echoes

By using a knowledge of the PRFs selected by the observer on the various range scales, it is possible to vary the areas from which second-trace echoes are possible.

If, in the example above, it had been possible to change from a PRF of 1000 to one of 500 pps then the bands at 80 and 240 n miles would have been eliminated. By observing what happened to the echo when this change was made, some deduction as to the true range of the target could have been made. If, after the change of PRF, the echo still remained, the true target must have been at a range of 164 n miles; if it had disappeared, then

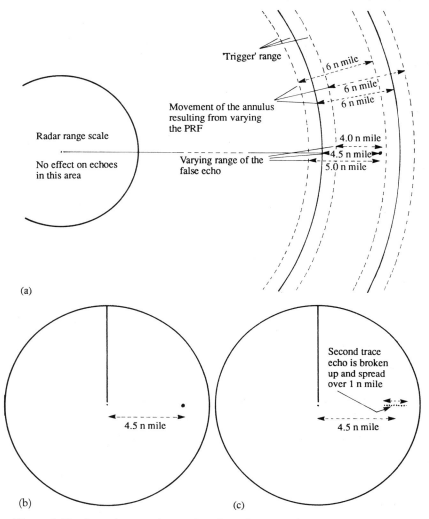

Figure 3.66 Second-trace echoes – the effect of varying the PRF
(a)   Effect on the standing pattern
(b)   The target as a second-trace echo with a fixed PRF
(c)   The effect of varying the PRF

its true range could have been either 84 or 244 n miles with the former being more likely. The principle here is to change to a lower PRF by selecting a longer range scale. If this is to be done, a knowledge of the parameters of the particular radar is essential.

Some designers have appreciated this principle. By means of the false target elimination (FTE) control, one radar system allows the observer to deliberately change the PRF to one which is not a submultiple of the PRF in use at the time, and so move the bands to totally differ-

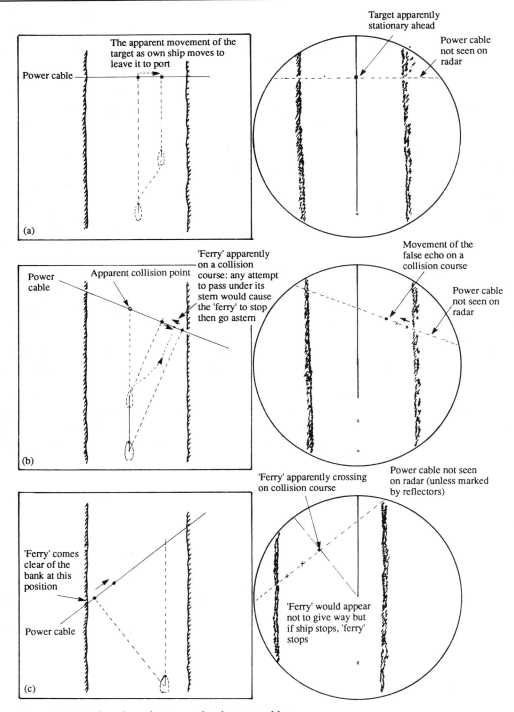

Figure 3.67 False echoes due to overhead power cables

ent areas which eliminate second-trace echoes arising from the original areas.

For a time, some radar systems incorporated an automatic elimination circuit which continually varied the PRF at a frequency of 50 Hz on the nominal value. This had the effect of moving the second-trace echo areas 50 times per second, which in turn had the effect of making the individual strikes of any second-trace echoes move in and out. Thus successive strikes would paint at different ranges and so would not line up side by side on the display and therefore no recognisable paint would result (see Figure 3.66). These circuits have been fitted in some radars; because they require no action on the part of the observer and appear to have no side effects which give cause for concern, their presence has gone largely unnoticed.

3.9.7   False echoes from power cables

It has for some time been recognised that electromagnetic waves can react with the electromagnetic field surrounding a cable carrying a current in such a way that a false echo appears on the radar display. The false echo so produced will appear in the direction of the perpendicular from the vessel to the power cable and at the range of the cable (Figure 3.67).

Unfortunately, the actual power cable itself does not produce a response and so it can be very difficult to associate the observed echo with the cable and thereby have some indication that the echo may be false. Where the cable is at right angles to the channel, the false echo will appear in the channel so that, however the vessel manoeuvres in the channel to avoid it, the false echo will always move into the vessel's path.

Where the cable is angled across the waterway, the false echo may initially appear among the shore echoes and so go unnoticed, but as the vessel approaches the cable, the false echo will appear on the water as if from a vessel on a converging course.

Consider the situations illustrated in Figures 3.67(b) and 3.67(c). As the vessel approaches the cable, a 'vessel' would appear to put out from the starboard bank and proceed on a collision course. Any attempt by the observing vessel to pass under the 'stern' of the false echo would cause the false echo to return toward the bank, i.e. again into the vessel's path. If the observing vessel stopped, the 'target' would also appear to stop.

In Figure 3.67(c), the false echo would put out from the port bank, again on a collision course. Here the logical manoeuvre would be for the observing vessel to move farther over to the starboard side of the channel. The false echo would continue to crowd the observing vessel into the starboard bank. The result of stopping or a port manoeuvre would be as described above.

On some waterways, power cables have had radar reflectors fitted to them in order that their line will appear on the radar display. The unusual behaviour of echoes in the vicinity of the cable may thus be associated with the cable and should be treated with due caution.

4 Automatic Radar Plotting Aids (ARPA), specified facilities

4.1 Introduction

With computers developing at an ever increasing pace, it was only a matter of time before their capabilities were harnessed to assist the mariner in resolving the continuing problem of tracking targets and analysing their movements when faced with heavy traffic.

In the past, many semi-automatic devices were developed to assist in this task but only those systems which conform to the IMO Performance Standards for Automatic Radar Plotting Aids (ARPA) are rightfully entitled to be classified as ARPAs (see Section 10.3).

The IMO Performance Standard for an ARPA requires that it should '... *reduce the workload of observers by enabling them to automatically obtain information so that they can perform as well with multiple targets as they can by manually plotting a single target*'.

It also states:

'The display may be a separate or integral part of the ship's radar. However, the ARPA display should include all the data required to be provided by a radar display in accordance with the performance standards for navigational radar equipment'.

In the early days, ARPAs of both broad categories existed and were generally referred to as 'stand-alone' and 'integral' (Figure 4.1).

4.1.1 Stand-alone ARPAs

These were primarily intended as additions to conventional radars. They provided all of the ARPA facilities but derived their data from a 'host' radar. This was an attractive means of upgrading the ship's radar system without incurring the expense of removing the existing radar and installing a new ARPA system. Stand-alone equipment had to be interfaced to a variety of existing equipment and while it was the less expensive and more expedient of the two alternatives, it was never the ideal solution and so, today, most of the ARPAs being fitted fall into the 'integral' category.

4.1.2 Integral ARPAs

In the modern integral ARPA a computer, usually referred to as the processor, is incorporated in the radar/ARPA system so that the ARPA data etc. can be displayed on the same screen as the conventional radar data. The main operational advantage is that the radar and ARPA data are readily comparable. In practical terms, it is much better that the same manufacturer is responsible for the design, testing, installation and functioning of the system. Gradually the trend has been for all ARPA development to follow this form, although there is still a small group who continue to develop stand-alone modules.

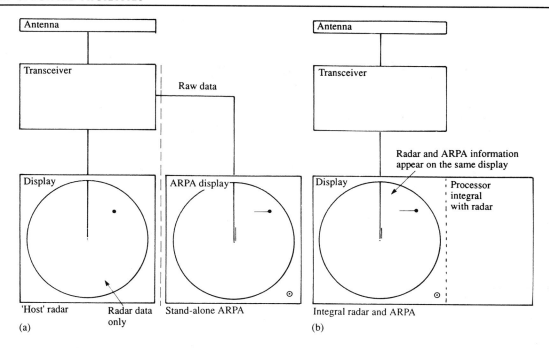

Figure 4.1
(a)   Stand–alone ARPA and   (b)   integral radar and ARPA

4.1.3   The requirement to carry ARPA, and for operator training

The IMO–SOLAS (1974) Convention as amended up to 1983 (see Section 10.1) sets out a schedule whereby various sizes and types of vessels are required to be fitted with an approved ARPA (i.e. one complying with the IMO Performance Standards) over a period of four years which ended on 1 September 1988. As a result, all tankers of 10 000 gross tons and upwards and all ships other than tankers of 15 000 gross tons and upwards should be fitted with an approved ARPA. In the particular case of vessels constructed on or after the 1 September 1984, all vessels of 10 000 gross tons and upwards should be fitted with an approved ARPA.

Note   Some exceptions are allowed where ships were fitted with ARPAs which pre-date the IMO Performance Standards. It should also be borne in mind that vessels registered in countries which are not signatories to the IMO convention will not necessarily comply with the carriage requirement. Such vessels are, however, likely to run into problems with Port State Control if they attempt to visit countries which are signatories.

When a ship required to be fitted with an ARPA is at sea and a radar watch is being kept on the ARPA, the installation shall be under the control of a person qualified in the operational use of ARPA, who may be assisted by unqualified personnel. UK Statutory Instrument 1984 No. 1203 para. 41 (see Section 10.6)

4.1.4   Compliance with the IMO Performance Standards

Irrespective of which type of equipment is installed, it is still necessary for it to comply with the IMO Performance Standards as well as with the various requirements of national legislation. Only the facilities which are specified by the IMO Performance Standards will be considered in this chapter. Where appropriate, at the beginning of each relevant section, extracts from the IMO Performance Standards for ARPAs will be quoted (in the form of indented paragraphs) to the extent necessary to support the section. For the full text of the Standard, the reader is referred to Section 10.3.

All ARPAs are required to have certain facilities but, unfortunately, there has been no standardization among manufacturers either in the form of the provision or in the labelling of controls. At present the only consolation for the operator is that the required facilities will have been provided and type tested to ensure that they comply with the Performance Standards. However, there is good indication that international agreement on standard names and symbols for at least 12 ARPA controls is possible in the not too distant future.

4.2   The acquisition of targets

Acquisition is the term used to describe the process whereby target tracking is initiated. This may be 'manual', in which case the operator, using the screen marker (see below) indicates to the computer which targets are to be tracked, or may be 'automatic', when the computer is programmed to acquire targets which enter specified boundaries. When a target is 'acquired', the computer starts collecting data relating to that target.

A graphic symbol known as the *screen marker*, controlled by a joystick or tracker ball, is positioned over the target. When the 'acquire' button is pressed, an area centred on the screen marker is defined within the computer memory. This area is termed the 'tracking gate' or 'tracking window'. The gate is made to appear automatically on some ARPA displays; on others, the operator may display it if desired. Within the gate, the computer will expect to find evidence of a target, i.e. a binary 1 in the appropriate memory location (see Sections 2.6.6.1 and 4.3.6).

4.2.1   The acquisition specification

Target acquisition may be manual or automatic. However, there should always be a facility to provide for manual acquisition and cancellation. ARPAs with automatic acquisition should have a facility to suppress acquisition in certain areas. On any range scale where acquisition is suppressed over a certain area, the area of acquisition should be indicated on the display.

Automatic or manual acquisition should have a performance not inferior to that which could be obtained by the user of the radar display.

If automatic acquisition is provided, a description of the criteria of selection of targets for tracking should be provided to the user.

Although it would seem that anything is possible in today's technological climate, some practical problems still exist and fully automatic acquisition systems do not give quite the results which one might have been led to expect. The main problem with automatic acquisition is that the 'sensitivity' of the detection circuitry, if set too high, will acquire thermal noise and clutter, leading to false alarms, while if its sensitivity is reduced, poor-response targets can evade detection.

4.2.2   Manual acquisition (Figure 4.2)

In this case, the operator specifies the target to be acquired and subsequently tracked. To do this, a joystick

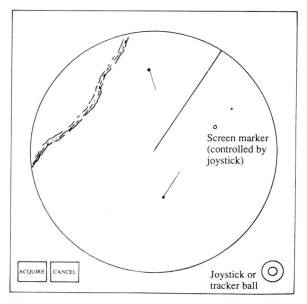

Figure 4.2   Manual acquisition

and screen marker or tracker ball and screen marker are used. The target is entered into (acquired) or removed from (cancelled) the computer memory when the *acquire* or *cancel* button is pressed.

In the latest ARPAs, tracking can be initiated by touching the position of the target on a special touch-sensitive screen (see Section 2.6.7.3).

4.2.3   Fully automatic acquisition

Every echo (up to some 200 maximum) which is detected in the receiver is tested against a set of published criteria. Large (land-sized) targets are rejected and the remainder prioritized according to the set criteria. (*Note* This may only be on the basis of range, e.g. the nearest 20, or, at the other extreme, it may involve tests of CPA, TCPA, range, bearing and other criteria). Tracking is then initiated on the first 20 in the priority order. Targets at the bottom of the list are deleted or acquired as their ranking changes, e.g. a target moving away may be dropped when there are 20 nearer than it. Some ARPAs have more complicated priority criteria where parameters can be varied by the operator.

4.2.4   Automatic acquisition by area (Figure 4.3)

In this type, an area around the ship is specified by the operator and any target that is detected within this area is acquired. Some prioritizing system must operate when the number of targets exceeds the number of tracking channels.

4.2.5   Guard zones (Figure 4.4)

In this system, zones (usually up to two) may be specified by arc and depth. Targets entering the zone will be acquired and an alarm activated. A 'tracks full' warning will be given when all tracking channels are in use and it will then be up to the operator to decide which of the acquired targets can be cancelled.

Note   Target 'A' may only be acquired at a late stage in the encounter and target 'B', which appears for the first time inside the inner zone, may not be acquired at all. Careful thought must be given when setting up guard zones and the display must be regularly observed.

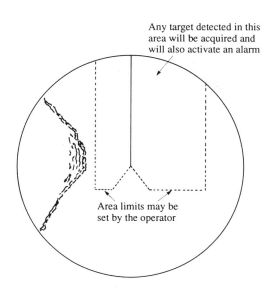

Figure 4.3   Automatic acquisition by area

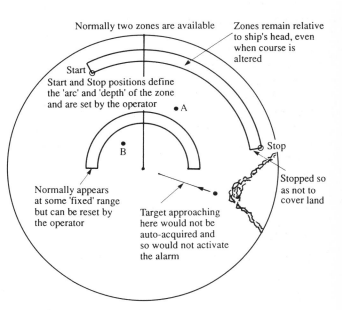

Figure 4.4   Guard zones

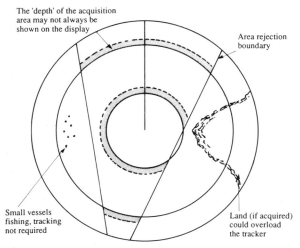

The 'depth' of the acquisition area may not always be shown on the display

Area rejection boundary

Small vessels fishing, tracking not required

Land (if acquired) could overload the tracker

Figure 4.5   Guard rings and ARBs

4.2.6   Guard rings and area rejection boundaries (ARBs)

With this method of acquisition, the usual provision is for up to two 'rings' (of predetermined depth) plus up to two area rejection boundaries (ARBs). The rings and ARBs may be positioned by the operator (Figure 4.5).

When a target is automatically acquired in a guard zone/guard area, it is usual for an alarm to be activated to attract the operator's attention (see Section 4.7.1). The target activating the alarm will be indicated on the screen by, for example, a flashing symbol.

In general, automatic acquisition has not been as successful as was at first predicted. There is a tendency to acquire sea clutter, rain clutter, noise and interference, while disassociated elements of land echoes will very quickly fill up the available tracking channels. Land echoes can be excluded by careful setting of the zones/areas and ARBs, but spurious targets (e.g. clutter), after having been acquired, are quickly lost and the 'lost target' alarm can sound continually.

While it is argued that automatic aquisition will reduce the operator's workload, in practice there is a tendency for it to acquire spurious targets, also to 'over-acquire' and so clutter the screen with unnecessary and unwanted vectors. This has led to auto-acquisition falling out of favour. Enquiries have indicated that it is

rarely used in areas of high-density traffic, but can be useful on long ocean passages where the number of targets is small and there is the danger of loss of concentration by the officer of the watch due to boredom.

Manual acquisition can be very quick and also selective and hence the perceived need for automatic acquisition has not really materialized.

Guard zones/areas should be regarded as an additional, rather than an alternative means of keeping a proper lookout.

4.3   The tracking of targets

4.3.1   The tracking specification

If the ARPA does not track all targets visible on the display, targets which are being tracked should be clearly indicated on the display. The reliability of tracking should not be less than that obtainable using manual recordings of successive target positions obtained from the radar display.

In many cases it may be obvious that a target is being tracked by virtue of the fact that its predicted movement will be indicated by a graphic line known as a vector (see Section 4.4). The line originates on the target and its remote end indicates the predicted position of the target after an elapsed time selected by the observer. However, the need for tracked targets to be clearly indicated on the display is important because in the early stages (up to about one minute) of tracking a fresh target, in most systems the vector is suppressed because the available data is unlikely to be sufficiently accurate or stable. Furthermore, in certain cases, even when the vector is present it may have zero length (e.g. the true vector of a stationary target or the relative vector of a target on the same course and speed as the observing vessel).

Once tracking is initiated, by whatever method, the tracker will continue to follow the target until tracking is cancelled (manually, or automatically because some other criterion has been met, e.g. 'more than 16 miles away and range increasing') or the target is 'lost'.

The precise nature of the algorithms used to ensure that the tracking window will faithfully follow the target varies with manufacturer. The fine detail of such methods are beyond the scope of this text but the general principle can be illustrated by the following description of the technique known as *rate aiding*.

4.3.2 Rate aiding

When the target is first acquired, a large gate is necessary since there is uncertainty as to the direction in which the target will move. Figure 4.6 shows how successive positions can be used to improve the forecast of the next position in which the target is expected to appear. The radius of the gate is really a measure of confidence in the tracking and the smaller this value becomes, the more precise the prediction will be. In this way it is possible to establish a feedback loop in the computer which will progressively reduce the size of the tracking gate.

The advantages of a reduced tracking gate are:

(a) A lower likelihood of target swop (see Section 4.3.5).
(b) An improved ability to track targets through rain and sea clutter.
(c) An ability to continue tracking, even when target response is intermittent.

One problem which can arise with reduced gate size is that if a target manoeuvres and, as a result, is not found by the computer in the predicted position, the computer may continue to track and look in the predicted direction and end up by losing the target altogether. To avoid this possibility, as soon as the target is missed, i.e. not found in the predicted position, the gate size is increased (and the tracking duration reduced – see Section 4.3.6). If the target is still detectable and subsequently found, the tracking will resume and a new track will gradually stabilize.

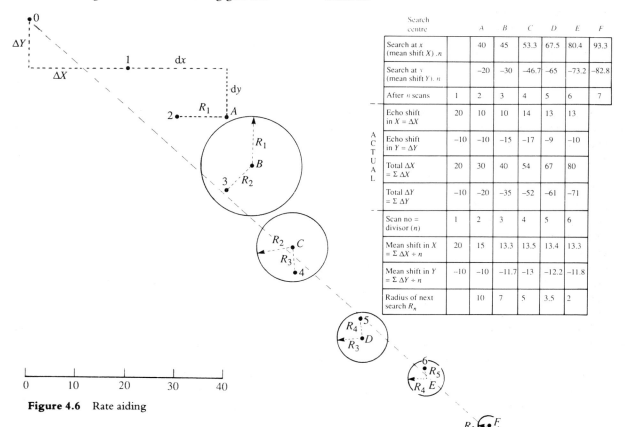

Search centre		A	B	C	D	E	F
Search at x (mean shift X) .n		40	45	53.3	67.5	80.4	93.3
Search at y (mean shift Y). n		−20	−30	−46.7	−65	−73.2	−82.8
After n scans	1	2	3	4	5	6	7
Echo shift in $X = \Delta X$	20	10	10	14	13	13	
Echo shift in $Y = \Delta Y$	−10	−10	−15	−17	−9	−10	
Total $\Delta X = \Sigma \Delta X$	20	30	40	54	67	80	
Total $\Delta Y = \Sigma \Delta Y$	−10	−20	−35	−52	−61	−71	
Scan no = divisor (n)	1	2	3	4	5	6	
Mean shift in $X = \Sigma \Delta X \div n$	20	15	13.3	13.5	13.4	13.3	
Mean shift in $Y = \Sigma \Delta Y \div n$	−10	−10	−11.7	−13	−12.2	−11.8	
Radius of next search R_n		10	7	5	3.5	2	

(ACTUAL)

Figure 4.6 Rate aiding

If, after six fruitless scans, the target is still not found then an alarm is activated and a flashing marker is displayed at the target's last observed position (see Section 4.7.3).

4.3.3 The number of targets to be tracked

The ARPA should be able to automatically track, process, simultaneously display and continuously update the information on at least:

  1 Twenty targets, if automatic acquisition is provided, whether automatically or manually acquired.
  2 Ten targets, if only manual acquisition is provided.

It has been suggested that 10 to 20 tracking channels might be insufficient in heavy traffic but from practical experience it has been found that ship's officers can quickly identify the targets which need to be tracked and acquire them. (Although at times there will be some 40 plus targets on the screen, not all of them will need to be tracked.) In fact, it has been found that an excess of vectors can produce 'ARPA clutter' and be counter-productive.

It should be noted that a higher tracking capability is required by the Performance Standard where the manufacturer has elected to provide automatic acquisition. This recognises the tendency of the latter facility to over-acquire (see Section 4.2.6) and compensates for it to some extent.

4.3.4 Target loss

Provided the target is not subject to target swop (see Section 4.3.5), the ARPA should continue to track an acquired target which is clearly distinguishable on the display for 5 out of 10 consecutive scans (see Section 4.7.3, lost target alarm).

(The term *scan* tends to be used rather loosely in radar terminology. Sometimes it is used to describe one line, as in the term 'interscan period', while on other occasions it refers to one aerial rotation. In the above context it refers to the latter.)

It should be noted here that if, for some reason, a response from a tracked target is not received on a particular scan, the ARPA must not immediately declare the target lost. Also it is implied that some form of 'search' for it must take place, e.g. by opening the tracking gate rather than merely looking in the limited area in which it was expected but failed to be detected.

4.3.5 Target swop (Figure 4.7)

The possibility of tracking errors, including target swop, should be minimized by ARPA design. A

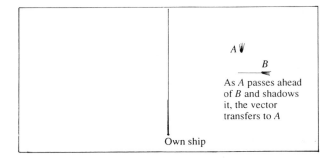

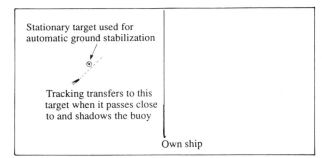

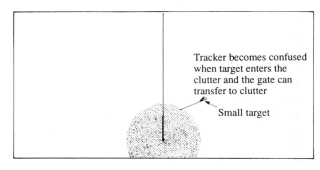

Figure 4.7   Target swop

qualitative description of the effects of error sources on the automatic tracking and corresponding errors should be provided to the user, including the effects of low signal–to–noise and low signal–to–clutter ratios caused by sea returns, rain, snow, low clouds and non–synchronous emissions.

Target swop is likely when two targets respond within the tracking gate at the same time. When this happens, the tracker can become confused and the vector(s) may transfer to the wrong target. To minimize this problem, the gate should be made as small as possible, the movement of the target should be predicted and the gate moved on at each scan as described under 'rate aiding' (see Section 4.3.2).

The two requirements that target swop be minimized by the ARPA design and that tracking be continued even if no response is received for a period of time are thus to some extent achieved by the common solution of rate aiding.

4.3.6 The analysis of tracks and the display of data

When a target appears on the radar and, in the case of automatic acquisition, enters within the acquisition area chosen by the observer or, in the case of manual acquisition, has been acquired by the observer, the ARPA should present, in a period of not more than one minute, an indication of the target's motion trend and display, within 3 minutes, the target's predicted motion in accordance with the Performance Standard described in Sections 9.2 and 9.3 of this text.

The paragraphs to which this section of the Performance Standards refer specify the format in which the data must be displayed and also set out accuracy levels which must be achieved. It would have been preferable for the contents of these paragraphs to be reproduced within the above extract. This is not practical since they are necessarily detailed because a number of formats such as vector, alphanumeric and graphic areas can be used and moreover the potential accuracy is a function of the geometry of the OAW triangle and must be stated in terms of specified scenarios (see Figures 9.1 to 9.4). In each case two levels of accuracy are specified:

1 A lower level relating to the target's motion trend, which is an early indication of the target's relative motion.
2 A higher level relating to the target's predicted motion; this means the best possible estimate of the target's relative and true motion data.

The contents of the various paragraphs are examined in detail in Sections 9.1 to 9.4. However, for the general discussion of tracking philosophy which follows, it is adequate to appreciate that essentially the Performance Standard requires the computer to deduce and display relative motion data to a specified level of accuracy after one minute of steady state tracking, and both relative and true motion data to a higher specified accuracy after 3 minutes of steady state tracking. Steady state tracking means that neither the target nor the observing vessel has manoeuvred and no significant change has taken place in the errors of the input sensors.

4.3.6.1 General tracker philosophy

In order to calculate the data required by the Performance Standard, the computer must store sequential positions of each tracked target and then analyse the movement represented by such successive positions so as to evaluate the relative motion and the true motion of each target. The computer is thus required to automate the operation which has traditionally been carried out manually by the recording of successive target positions (either by the plotting of ranges and bearings on a paper sheet or by the use of a reflection plotter) and the subsequent resolution of the OAW triangle (see Chapter 7). Automation of any process normally carried out by an intelligent being is always complex. The injection of pseudo–intelligence and the difficulty of satisfying conflicting requirements gives considerable scope to the inventiveness of the designer and it is not surprising that various solutions to the problem exist, all of which differ in mathematical detail to a greater or lesser extent. A detailed consideration of the options open to the designer in carrying out the data processing is beyond the scope of this text, but it is important for the observer to have some general knowledge of how the operation relates to the way in which the same task would be tackled by manual plotting. This understanding is relevant not only to the above extract from the Performance Standard but to that of Section 4.3.1, which requires the results to be at least as good as would be obtained by using manual recordings, and to the introduction to the Performance Standards (see Section 4.1), which requires that the ARPA should enable observers to perform as well with multiple targets as they can by manually plotting a single target. It should thus be appreciated that the ARPA is carrying out a task which could be undertaken manually by an observer, given the time and the inclination, and that there is no reason to believe that the results obtained by an ARPA are any better, or any worse, than those that can be achieved by such an observer.

For acceptance by the ARPA, data must be in digital form, since the necessary calculations must be performed by a digital computer. Thus, in the first instance, the analogue radar data must be stored, radial line by radial line, in a digital memory. The presence of a response will be registered as a binary 1 in the appropriate range cell(s) and will be associated with the appropriate bearing word, as was described for the general radar memory in Section 2.6.6.3. Filtering techniques are used to establish the likelihood of any particular response being a target and hence whether or not it should be stored for tracking purposes. During each timebase the detected responses are read into what is known as the *prime register*, which is a group of memory elements of the form shown by one line of the memory matrix illustrated in Figure 2.39. During the rest (or interscan) period, the contents of the prime register are transferred into the number one register which is the first of a group of N identical registers. At the same time the contents of number one are transferred into number two, and so on down the group. The contents of the Nth register (i.e. the oldest data) are discarded. During the transfer period a comparison is made of the contents of the N cells in each column and if more than M out of N cells in the column contain a binary 1, a hit is registered in the correct location in a further section of the tracker memory which holds only filtered responses. The filtering technique helps to reduce the probability of false echoes reaching the tracker and also improves the chances of a real but weak or intermittent response being tracked.

Targets within the filtered area of the memory are selected for tracking when, either manually or automatically, a gate is placed over their responses. As the aerial sweeps past a ship-target, it will register a number of strikes (see Section 2.4.4) on successive timebases and it may be that such a target activates more than one successive radial range cell. In the case of picture storage (see Section 2.6.6.5) these digitized responses will aggregate in the memory to generate on the display an echo having the outline of the distinctive echo paint (see Section 2.6.5). Clearly it is neither necessary nor desirable for the computer to track each individual element present in the resolution cell. For this reason the input responses to the tracker are processed to produce a single registration which represents the location of the target to be tracked and about which the gate will in due course attempt to centre itself. The area of memory which is used to store the assembly of such registrations is known as the *hit matrix*.

If the target has been acquired, and is being successfully tracked, a tracking window will be centred on that particular memory location within the hit matrix which corresponds with the target's range and bearing. The co-ordinates of the window can be extracted and stored in a further area of the tracker memory. This area is sometimes referred to as the *track file* and there will have to be a separate track file for each tracked target. Thus, rotation by rotation, as the gate moves in steps following the target's position through the hit matrix, sequential positions of each tracked target can be stored in the appropriate track file.

The processor (which is that part of the computer which manipulates the data and carries out the mathematical operations) must operate on the recorded positions to calculate the most probable track of the target. It is difficult to carry out calculations based on positions which are expressed in terms of range and bearing because the rates at which the bearing and range change are not constant for a target on a straight track. Further, the spatial resolution varies with range (i.e. it is geometrical). For these reasons it is usual to convert the target positions into cartesian co-ordinates of northings and eastings, the mathematical operation being the same as that described for scan conversion in Section 2.6.7.2.

When laying off observed ranges and bearings on a

plotting sheet (see Section 7.8) the effect of inherent errors is that, even for a target on a steady track, the plotted positions do not form a perfectly straight line but are scattered about the correct track; the observer has to attempt to draw the line that is the best fit. Exactly the same effect occurs with automatic plotting and it is further exacerbated by quantizing errors introduced by the digital storage (see Sections 2.6.6.1 and 9.5). Since the data must eventually be displayed as a stable straight line vector, the processor must calculate a length and direction which represents the best fit to the scattered observations. This operation is known as smoothing and involves the application of quite complex mathematical techniques such as Kalman filtering, the mechanics of which are beyond the scope of this text. However it is important for the observer to appreciate that such smoothing does take place and to understand the implications.

If the smoothing is carried out over too long a period, the tracker will be insensitive to changes in tracks as a result of which small manoeuvres may go undetected and there will be a long delay before large manoeuvres become apparent. On the other hand, if smoothing is carried out over a short period, the output data will fluctuate, rendering decision-making difficult. Clearly the amount and duration of smoothing is a compromise and the difficulty of reconciling the twin requirements of sensitivity to target manoeuvres and data stability provides the designer with a considerable challenge. As a result, the particular algorithms used for smoothing vary in detail with manufacturer.

When a target is first acquired, the computer will commence storing positions, obtaining updated co-ordinates each time the aerial sweeps across the target (i.e. about once every 3–5 seconds). These positions will have an inherent scatter and initially the mean line will be very sensitive to plots which fall some distance from it. However, as the plotting duration increases and more plots are obtained, the mean line will stabilize and accuracy will improve. During the first minute of tracking the target will normally display only a symbol to indicate that it is being tracked. In most systems the vector (or other graphical indication of target movement) will be suppressed until sufficient observations have been obtained to produce the indication of the tar-

get's motion trend to the level of accuracy required by the Performance Standard. Some systems were designed to display vectors within a few seconds of acquisition. This should not be seen as a sign of instant accuracy. Accuracy demands a number of successive observations and until the one minute interval has elapsed there is no requirement to meet the Performance Standard accuracy. Any data derived directly or indirectly from these very early indications could be highly misleading. In general, where such early display takes place, a study of the instability of the vector (or other indication of movement) should convince the user that it is based on insufficient observations. After one minute the tracker will have smoothed about 12–20 observations and must then produce data to the lower of the two accuracy levels set out in the Performance Standard. In some systems a graphic symbol on the target is used to indicate that the data is based on more than one but less than three minutes of observation. As long as the target continues to be detected at the location predicted by the rate aiding (see Section 4.3.2), the tracking period is allowed to build up to three minutes, at which stage the processor will be able to smooth some 36–60 observations and must then reach the higher accuracy level. Thereafter as each new plot is added the *oldest* is discarded.

If a target response is not detected in the location forecast by the rate aiding, one possible explanation is that the target has manoeuvred. The tracking gate will be opened out and if the target is detected, tracking will continue. If the departure from the three-minute track is not significant, the processor will conclude that the departure was due to scatter and will continue to smooth the track over a period of three minutes. On the other hand, if the departure is significant, the processor will treat the situation as a target manoeuvre and will reduce the smoothing period to one minute. This reduction in smoothing period is analogous to the situation in which an observer decides that a target has manoeuvred and therefore discards a previous *OAW* triangle and starts a new plot. If steady state conditions resume, low level accuracy must be obtained within one minute and then the tracking period can again be allowed to build up to 3 minutes, allowing high level accuracy to be regained.

Most systems have two smoothing periods, a short period of about one minute and a long period of about three minutes. For compliance with the Performance Standard the periods must not be more than one minute or three minutes respectively but in practice manufacturers quite often use slightly shorter periods and hence reach the required accuracy a little more quickly than the standard requires.

While the mathematical detail of the smoothing is beyond the scope of this work, what is of importance to the observer is the question of whether the smoothing is performed on the relative tracks or on the true tracks. This is a fundamental decision which must be taken by the designer and there are merits in both choices.

In general trackers will *either*

(a) smooth and store the relative track of a target to produce directly the output relative-motion data and hence calculate the true-motion data from the smoothed relative-track data and the instantaneous input course and speed data, which is normally unsmoothed to avoid any loss of sensitivity to manoeuvres by the observing vessel; *or*

(b) smooth and store the true track of a target to produce directly the smoothed true-motion data and reconstitute the relative-motion data from the smoothed true-track data and the (normally unsmoothed) input course and speed data.

Note   In order to smooth and store true tracks, the normally unsmoothed course and speed data are applied to the raw relative-motion data (see Section 4.3.6.3).

In the steady state situation, i.e. where neither tracked target nor the observing vessel manoeuvres and no changes take place in any errors in the input data, both approaches will produce the same result. If a change takes place, the two different approaches will produce differing results over the succeeding smoothing period. To understand the differences it is necessary to consider in general terms how the calculations are performed.

4.3.6.2   *The storage of relative data*

In this approach the ranges and bearings of the tracked target are scan-converted, smoothed and stored to produce the direction and rate of the target's relative motion. The displayed relative vector (see Section 4.4.1)

and the CPA/TCPA (see Section 4.6) data are derived directly from this, as illustrated by Figure 4.8. The merit of this approach is that, just as when an observer constructs a relative plot, the CPA data is totally independent of the course and speed inputs to the system. This is a feature which many users believe to be of paramount importance because they take the view that the miss distance ranks in importance above all other data.

If the true-motion data relating to the target is requested, the computer will calculate that information by vector addition of the instantaneous course and speed data to the smoothed relative track. Thus, as might be expected, the accuracy of the true-motion data depends on the accuracy of the input course and speed data (see Section 9.6.3). Where trial manoeuvre data (see Section 4.4.3) is requested, the vector addition will involve the smoothed relative track and the proposed course and speed.

An inherent difficulty which besets relative track storage is that if the observing vessel manoeuvres, the direction and rate of the relative track of all targets will change. There will thus be a tendency for the relative vectors to become unstable, because the tracker is vainly attempting to smooth a curve to produce a straight line. It follows that, during the time of the manoeuvre and for a short period thereafter, relative and true track data will be suspect. The effect is likely to be particularly dramatic on board vessels such as ferries which can change their heading and speed by a large amount in a fairly short time; the tracking data may give the mistaken impression that all tracked targets are manoeuvring. This is not intended as a criticism of the systems which elect to store relative data but merely a recognition of the basic laws of relative motion which demand steady state conditions for a stable and reliable assessment of relative motion, however it is deduced. In general, the system will attempt to recover stability by smoothing the relative motion over the shorter period (approximately one minute) once the computer has decided that a significant track change has taken place.

4.3.6.3   *The storage of true data*

In this approach the ranges and bearings are scan-converted to produce cartesian co-ordinates. Before

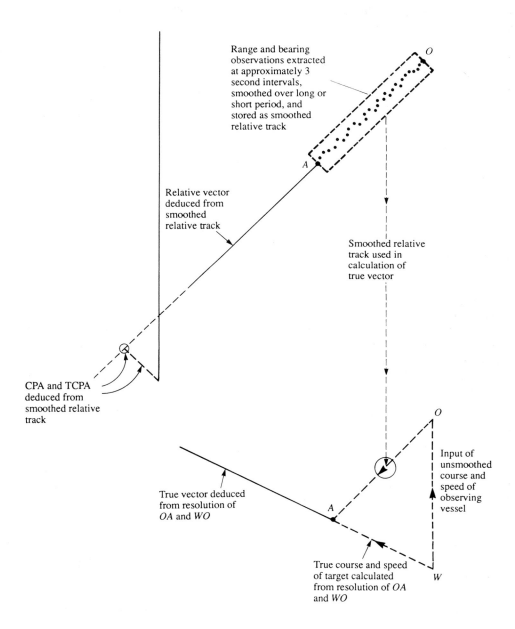

Range and bearing observations extracted at approximately 3 second intervals, smoothed over long or short period, and stored as smoothed relative track

Relative vector deduced from smoothed relative track

Smoothed relative track used in calculation of true vector

CPA and TCPA deduced from smoothed relative track

Input of unsmoothed course and speed of observing vessel

True vector deduced from resolution of *OA* and *WO*

True course and speed of target calculated from resolution of *OA* and *WO*

Figure 4.8   The storage of relative data

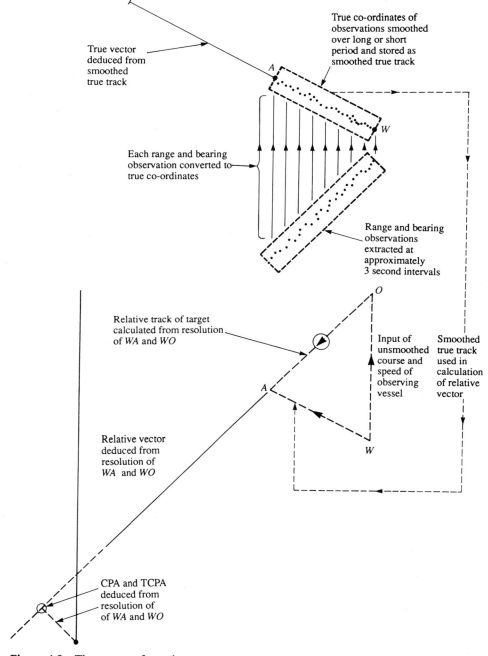

True vector
deduced from
smoothed
true track

True co-ordinates of
observations smoothed
over long or short
period and stored as
smoothed true track

A

W

Each range and bearing
observation converted to
true co-ordinates

Range and bearing
observations
extracted at
approximately
3 second intervals

O

Relative track of target
calculated from resolution
of *WA* and *WO*

Input of
unsmoothed
course and
speed of
observing
vessel

Smoothed
true track
used in
calculation
of relative
vector

A

W

Relative vector
deduced from
resolution of
WA and *WO*

CPA and TCPA
deduced from
resolution of
of *WA* and *WO*

Figure 4.9   The storage of true data

each position is stored, its co-ordinates are modified by the direction and distance moved by the observing vessel since the first observation (see Figure 4.9). The effect of this is to produce within the track file a succession of positions whose co-ordinates represent the unsmoothed true track of the selected target. These positions are smoothed to produce the best estimate of the target's true course and speed. The operation is analogous to the construction of a true plot, as described in Section 7.3.

If the relative-motion data relating to the target is requested, the computer will calculate that information by vector addition of the instantaneous input course and speed data to the smoothed true track of the target. Where trial manoeuvre data (see Section 4.4.3) is requested, the vector addition will involve the smoothed true track and the proposed course and speed.

The merit of this approach is that if the observing vessel manoeuvres, the relative vector will remain stable (though changing) because it is updated, rotation by rotation, being calculated from the smoothed true course of the target and the instantaneous course and speed of the observing vessel. On the debit side it would appear at first sight that the calculated relative motion of the target is dependent on the accuracy of the input course and speed data. This is not the case provided that the input course and speed data are consistent over a full smoothing period. If the input data error is constant for the full smoothing period, the smoothed true track will of course similarly be in error. The computer will then use the wrong input data and the consistently wrong true track and as a result will arrive at the correct relative motion (see Figures 4.9 and 9.11(b)).

It is thus evident that, provided any error in the input course and speed data is consistent for the full smoothing period, it will not affect the accuracy of the CPA/TCPA data. However, if there is a fluctuating error, for example due to an erratic log input, the relative vector will be inaccurate and unstable. While recognising the advantage of this approach in ensuring relative data stability during manoeuvres by the observing vessel, many users are concerned about the ability of random input errors to influence the CPA. Most users are prepared to tolerate some degree of instability or inaccuracy of true vectors when the observing vessel is performing a manoeuvre, but most, if not all, believe that the CPA is inviolate.

4.3.6.4   Storage philosophies compared

The two forms of storage which in general terms are described above represent two different approaches to dealing with the difficulty of maintaining stable tracking data when the observing vessel manoeuvres. This is an inherent difficulty which is experienced whether the plotting is carried out manually or automatically and arises from the fact that the basic information, i.e. range and bearing, is being measured from a moving vessel. The implications for tracking accuracy are discussed further in Section 9.6.3. However, at this stage it has to be emphasized that the observer must be alert to the likelihood of the data being inaccurate during non-steady state conditions and to the way in which the method of track storage will influence the nature of these inaccuracies.

4.3.7   Tracking history

The ARPA should be able to display, on request, at least four equally time-spaced past positions of any targets being tracked over a period of at least eight minutes.

This enables an observer to check whether a particular target has manoeuvred in the recent past, possibly while the observer was temporarily away from the display on other bridge duties.

Not only is this knowledge useful in showing the observer what has happened but it may well help him to form an opinion of what the target is likely to do in the furture. Manoeuvres by targets may be for navigational purposes and it may be possible to gain an indication from the general overview that this is the case. Alternatively, there may be an indication from the nature of the manoeuvre, when considered in relation to the general traffic pattern, that it has been undertaken for collision avoidance and hence the observer can be alert for a resumption of previous conditions.

'True history' is without doubt the only meaningful way in which this data can be displayed since the nature

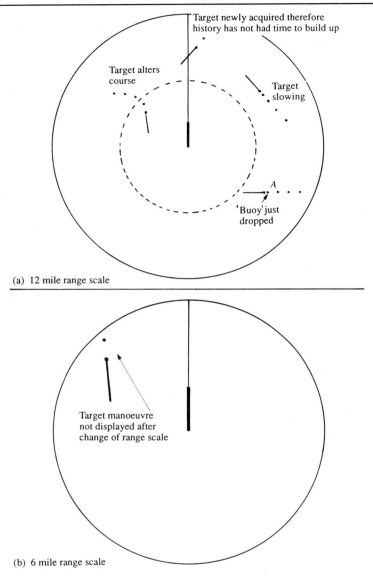

Figure 4.10 Tracking history

of the manoeuvre is readily apparent. A curve in the trail indicates an alteration of course by the target, whereas a change in the spacing of the dots will occur when there has been a change in speed. Since changes in speed are much slower to take effect, they are consequently more difficult to detect.

'Relative history' is not always provided but where it

is, it is important to remember that any change in the direction or spacing of the dots can result from a change of course, a change of speed, or a combination of the two. It is therefore essential that the true manoeuvre is identified. Relative history should be used with great caution (see Section 7.4.2). Relative history will not be considered further.

The history dots can be likened to a vessel dropping buoys (with radar reflectors) at *equal intervals of time*, thus a change in the spacing is indicative of a change in the target's speed but it is important to appreciate the significance of the distance between the echo and the last dot. For example, in Figure 4.10, target *A* has not just executed a crash stop but has just dropped a buoy and is now steaming away from it

When history is requested, only that of tracked targets can be displayed and even then the number of dots which are displayed will depend upon the period for which a particular target has been tracked. A target which has been tracked for two minutes can only display a maximum of two minutes' worth of history and so probably only one dot will be displayed, others being added as the tracking period increases.

Some manufacturers cause the plots to flash sequentially, e.g. 2 minutes ago, 4 minutes ago etc., while others cause the dots to decrease in brightness with time. The fourth plot is always removed as the latest plot is added to the display.

Although 'four equally time-spaced past positions over (at least) eight minutes' would suggest two–minute intervals, this is not necessarily the case. For a variety of philosophical as well as practical reasons, manufacturers have used intervals other than two minutes and so it is essential to establish just which intervals are being used on the display. On some equipment there is also an automatic change in time interval when range scale is changed. The argument for this option is that on the shorter range scales, the range spacing of two-minute dots could be so large as to place some or all of the dots 'off the screen' and hence not observable. As a result, an important target manoeuvre could be missed. On some equipment, 'fixed' or 'variable with range scale' spacings can be selected by an 'internal' switch, while another manufacturer has the switch as a front panel operator control.

Uneven tracks of targets or apparent instability of motion may be taken to indicate that tracking of that target is less precise than it might be and the displayed data should be treated with caution.

Because of the variations in the way this facility can operate, great care should be taken when observing history to ensure that one is certain of exactly what is being displayed. In particular, one must establish whether true or relative history is being displayed and also which time spacings are in use.

4.4 Vectors

The course and speed information generated by the ARPA for acquired targets should be displayed in a vector or graphic form (e.g. predicted areas of danger, see Section 5.6) which clearly indicates the target's predicted motion. In this regard:

1 ARPA presenting predicted (extrapolated) information in vector form only should have the option of true and relative vectors.
2 An ARPA which is capable of presenting target course and speed information in graphic form should also, on request, provide the target's true and/or relative vector.

(*Note* This means that vectors of some kind must be provided, irrespective of the availability of any other method such as PADs, used to display collision-avoidance information.)

3 Vectors displayed should either be time adjustable or have a fixed time-scale.
4 A positive indication of the time-scale of the vector in use should be given.

Vectors must be capable of indicating the rate and direction of the target's relative motion (relative vectors), or indicating the rate and direction of the target's proper motion (true vectors). The direction and rate forecast by a true vector will only be fulfilled if the tracked target maintains its course and speed. In the case of a relative vector, the fulfilment depends additionally on the observing vessel similarly maintaining course and speed.

In all cases, the displayed vector length is time related and normally can be adjusted by using a 'vector length' control. In addition, provision is made on some equipment for fixed time-scale vectors. In some systems, the latter are set for a fairly short period – say 6 minutes – which can prove useful when frequently changing range scale. If vectors are too 'long' then, when changing to a short range scale, they can extend beyond the edge of the screen. An alternative approach is to have a fixed physical length which remains the same irrespective of the range scale, e.g. 3 minutes on the 6 n mile range scale, 6 minutes on the 12 n mile range scale, etc.

Note Vectors of either of the two types can be displayed on a true or relative motion radar picture presentation, i.e. *true vectors* can be selected to appear on a *relative motion* presentation and vice versa. It was originally considered in some quarters that this might result in confusion and at least one manufacturer provides a default condition where relative vectors are displayed when relative motion is selected and, likewise, true vectors on the true motion presentation, with the alternative vector mode being temporarily selectable in each case by spring-loaded switch (see also Section 9.7,1, incorrect interpretation).

4.4.1   Relative vectors

As described in Section 4.3.6, the ARPA must track the target(s) for a period of time, after which a vector can be displayed as in Figure 4.11(a). Using the vector length control, the vectors can be extended to determine the CPA by observation against the background of the range rings and the TCPA can be read off from the vector length control.

4.4.2   True vectors

As an alternative, the observer may request that the true vector(s) be displayed (Figure 4.11(b)). In this case, own ship will also have a vector which will increase in length as the time control is increased. The likelihood of a close-quarters situation developing can be ascertained by running out the true vectors progressively to show the predicted development of the encounter. The dynamic nature of this technique appeals to many users but it must be borne in mind that any evaluation of CPA/ TCPA is a matter of trial and error and thus better avoided. It is essential to appreciate that the CPA is *not* represented by the point at which the target's true vector intersects own ship's true vector, except in the case of zero CPA.

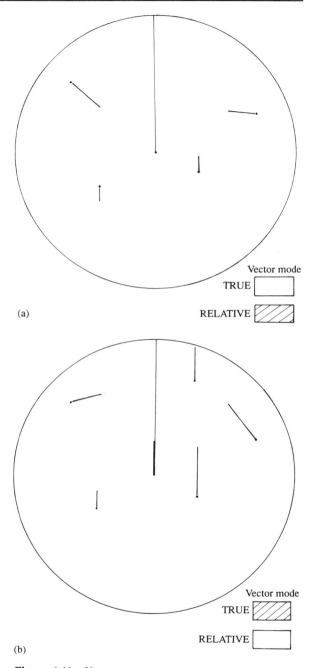

(a)

(b)

Figure 4.11   Vectors
(a)   Relative vectors
(b)   True vectors for the situation displayed in (a)

4.4.3   Trial manoeuvre

The ARPA should be capable of simulating the effect on all tracked targets of an own ship manoeuvre without interrupting the updating of target information. The simulation should be initiated by the depression either of a spring-loaded switch or of a function key with a positive identification on the display.

With the availability of computer assistance, the problem of predicting the effect of a manoeuvre prior to its implementation by own ship is much simplified. While it is relatively easy to visualize mentally the outcome of a manoeuvre where two ships are involved, in dense traffic this becomes very difficult. In particular, with large ships and limited sea room, it is necessary to plan and update the whole collision avoidance strategy as quickly as possible in light of the continually changing radar scene.

While planning, it is important to bear in mind the following points.

(a)   Own ship may temporarily need to be on a 'collision course' with more distant vessels, i.e. collisions may require sequential avoidance since it is unlikely that a single manoeuvre will resolve all the problems.

(b)   Extrapolation of the present situation using the trial manoeuvre facility with current course and speed as inputs can provide valuable information on which of the 'other' vessels in the vicinity may have to manoeuvre in order to avoid collisions between each other. Obvious avoiding manoeuvres may present themselves and should be watched for.

(c)   Constraints imposed by navigation may dictate the manoeuvre of 'other' vessels. This should be taken into account when planning strategy and watched for when carrying out the plan and assessing its effectiveness.

(d)   The ease with which this facility allows the navigator to establish the course to steer for a given passing distance may encourage the choice of a small alteration. This temptation must be avoided at all costs as it loses sight of the need to make a substantial alteration. The rules require the latter in recognition of the fact that other vessels may be using much more rudimentary methods of data extraction and may not be able to detect a small manoeuvre.

Unfortunately, although there is a single requirement for all approved ARPAs to possess a facility for simulating a trial manoeuvre, different methods of providing this have been devised by the various manufacturers.

When information relating to the proposed manoeuvre is fed in, the true or relative vectors which would result from such a manoeuvre are displayed on request. This, combined with the ability to adjust the vector length, can give a clear presentation of potential close-quarters situations between other vessels as well as with the observer's vessel.

It is important to select *relative vectors* when assessing the effect of a manoeuvre as this will give an indication of how far the target will pass clear (Figure 4.12). It is also possible to vary the inputs while observing this display and note the effect on the CPA.

The ARPA has to produce a plot similar to that discussed in Section 7.5.6. Unfortunately, manufacturers are given very little guidance by the Performance Standard with regard to the form of the simulation. There is a range of facilities available, with an increasing number of factors taken into account when presenting the trial data. In the simplest form, it is possible to feed in only the intended course and speed and observe their effect on the display.

There is a provision in some equipment for the manoeuvre to be instantaneous, but at some later time, e.g. after a delay of some 6 minutes. In some ARPAs it is possible for the vessel's handling characteristics to be included in the evaluation, but this will of necessity be restricted to one (or possibly two) conditions of loading.

On some equipment, provision is made for two successive manoeuvres to be displayed. This can be extremely helpful when endeavouring to assess the time for which an alteration must be held.

In order that there should be no confusion between the 'trial' data and the current situation, when trial is in operation the screen will display some distinctive indication such as the word SIM or TRIAL. The use of a 'T' to indicate trial is frequently mistaken for an indication that true vectors are being displayed. The letter 'T' as it

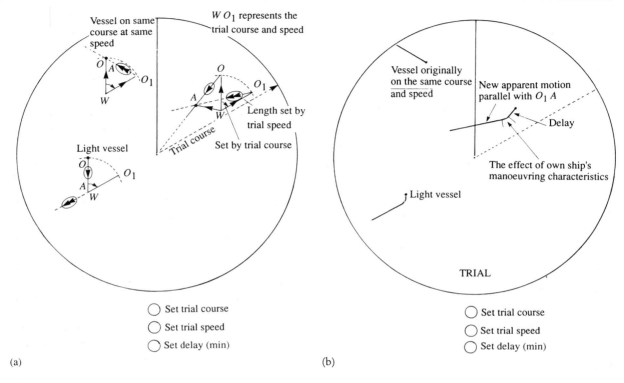

Figure 4.12 Trial manoeuvre display in the relative vector mode
(a)   Construction of relative vectors
(b)   The trial manoeuvre display

stands is meaningless and has not been particularly help-ful. There is the danger that one officer sets up the display and another officer (or the master) observes it without realizing the special nature of the display.

The provision of the spring-loaded switch, recommended in the specification, means that the observer has to make a positive decision to operate the switch and hold it over while he observes the display. Few systems offer such a failsafe control.

Note   (i) While trial manoeuvres are being presented on the display, the computer continues its normal task of tracking all acquired targets.
(ii) Where 'predicted areas of danger' (see Section 5.6) are provided, the possible alterations of course should be simultaneouly apparent, but a 'trial speed' facility is also provided since any given family of PADs is drawn for a specific speed of the observing vessel.

4.5   The ARPA display

4.5.1   The continued availability of radar data in the event of an ARPA malfunction

The design should be such that any malfunction of ARPA parts producing data additional to information to be produced by the radar, should not affect the integrity of the basic radar presentation.

In general, this means that when an ARPA malfunction is detected (see Section 4.7.4) an alarm is activated and those ARPA facilities affected are disabled, the radar presentation continuing 'normally'. For example, a fault in the own ship tracking circuitry may cause the ARPA as well as the true-motion facilities to be discontinued, but the relative-motion radar display will still be available.

4.5.2   The size of the display

The size of the display on which ARPA information is presented should have an effective display diameter of at least 340 mm.

This is equivalent to the normal 16 inch radius radial CRT whereas a raster-scan display requires a 27 inch (690 mm) tube (measured on the diagonal).

4.5.3   The range scales on which ARPA facilities should be available

The ARPA facilities should be available on at least the following range scales:

1 12 or 16 miles
2   3 or 4 miles

There should be a positive indication of the range scale in use.

In actual practice, the provision is normally far in excess of this requirement: ARPA facilities are provided on all range scales from 1.5 n miles to 24 n miles inclusive.

4.5.4   The modes of display

The ARPA should be capable of operating with a relative-motion display with 'north up' and either 'head up' or 'course up' azimuth stabilization. In addition, the ARPA may also provide for a true-motion display. If true motion is provided, the operator should be able to select for his display either true or relative motion. There should be a positive indication of the display mode and orientation in use.

The term 'mode' is used here to describe the 'radar' features of picture orientation and picture presentation which are discussed in detail in Sections 1.4 and 1.5.

4.5.5   ARPA data should not obscure radar data

The ARPA information should not obscure radar information in such a manner as to degrade the pro-

cess of detecting targets. The display of ARPA data should be under the control of the radar observer. It should be possible to cancel the display of unwanted ARPA data.

There was a tendency in the past for alphanumeric data relating to the current operation, and also warnings, to appear on the radar screen temporarily (see Section 4.6). This practice has been discontinued in current ARPAs.

4.5.6   The ARPA data brilliance control

Means should be provided to adjust independently the brilliance of the ARPA data, including complete elimination of the ARPA data.

This control allows the observer to remove all ARPA data from the screen in order to see just which is radar and which is ARPA data. It can be particularly useful when searching for a poor-response target (e.g. in clutter) while still wishing to continue tracking the other vessels in the vicinity.

Unfortunately, many a mariner has been caught out by this control and has spent some frustrating minutes trying to find the screen marker, only to realize that the ARPA data brilliance control was turned down.

4.5.7   The ability to view the display

The method of presentation should ensure that the ARPA data is clearly visible in general to more than one observer in the conditions of light normally experienced on the bridge of a ship by day and by night. Screening may be provided to shade the display from sunlight but not to the extent that it will impair the observer's ability to keep a proper lookout. Facilities to adjust the brightness should be provided.

The reasons for this requirement are fairly evident but the way in which it has been complied with in practice has been somewhat uncertain. The provision of a tinted 'glass' cubicle has been the most effective as it has still allowed the watchkeeper to maintain a lookout while not requiring the traditional radar hood.

The introduction of radial-scan synthetic displays helped to a limited extent and, more recently, raster-scan radar displays have gone a long way to comply with this requirement without the need to resort to special radar cubicles.

4.5.8 The use of the marker for range and bearing measurement

Provisions should be made to obtain quickly the range and bearing of any object which appears on the ARPA display.

To comply with this requirement, most manufacturers have enabled the range and bearing of the screen-controlled marker to be displayed. In this way, the range and bearing of an object can be obtained by placing the marker over it. Like all range and bearing measuring devices, they should be regularly checked against the range rings and heading marker respectively (see also Sections 6.9.8 and 6.9.9).

4.5.9 The effect of changing range scales

After changing range scales on which the ARPA facilities are available or re-setting the display, full plotting information should be displayed within a period of time not exceeding four scans.

It should be appreciated that, in order to fulfil this requirement, the ARPA needs to track and plot the acquired targets continually out to some 16 miles, irrespective of the range scale selected by the operator. Because of this, if the shorter range scales are selected and accompanied by a short pulse, targets at a longer range returning a poor response may be lost.

4.6 The display of alphanumeric data

At the request of the observer the following information should be immediately available from the ARPA in alphanumeric form in regard to any tracked target.

1 Present range to the target.
2 Present bearing of the target.
3 Predicted target range at the closest point of approach (CPA).
4 Predicted time to CPA (TCPA).
5 Calculated true course of target.
6 Calculated true speed of target.

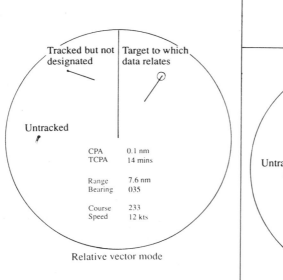

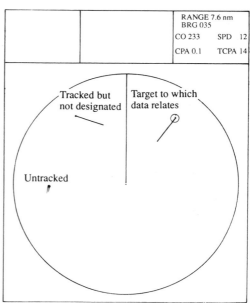

Figure 4.13 The display of alphanumeric data

When a target is 'marked' or 'designated', i.e. the joystick and gate are used to indicate to the computer the target about which data are required, data relating to that target can then be read out in alphanumeric form, i.e. range, bearing, CPA, TCPA, course and speed (Figure 4.13). In some systems the data available also includes the distance at which it is predicted that the target will cross ahead (BCR) and the interval which will elapse until this event occurs (BCT). The readout may be on a separate tote displaying all quantities, or, in some cases, displaying the data in sequential groups of two items or on the radar screen itself.

Although vectors are suppressed during the first minute of tracking (for the reasons described in Section 4.3.6), the observer can normally select a target during that period and read out the alphanumeric data. This is acceptable as a means of quickly obtaining the range and bearing of the target, but it must be appreciated that other alphanumeric values will at that stage be based on only a few observations and hence can be dangerously misleading.

When *trial manoeuvre* is selected, some systems continue to provide the real alphanumeric data while others produce the trial values. In the case of any given ARPA, it is essential to establish exactly which data are being made available.

4.7   Alarms and warnings

It should be possible to activate or de-activate the operational warnings.

4.7.1   Guard zone violation

The ARPA should have the capability to warn the observer with a visual and/or audible signal of any distinguishable target which closes to a range or transits a zone chosen by the observer. The target causing the warning should be clearly indicated on the display.

It is possible to specify an area in the vicinity of own ship, e.g. at 10 miles, a zone 5 cables in depth (see Figure 4.14) which, if entered by a target, would activate an alarm. It

is usual to have two zones, one which may be at some pre-set range and the other at a range which may be varied according to circumstances.

The target which has activated the alarm may be made to 'flash' or alternatively be marked in some other way, such as having a short bearing marker through it. In some equipments, the range and bearing of the target entering the zone is displayed in numerical form. It is important to remember that a target which is detected for the first time *at a lesser range than* the guard ring will not activate the alarm: this warning system should not be regarded as an alternative to keeping a proper lookout, but rather as an additional means of ensuring the safety of the vessel. Each guard zone may be set for 360° coverage or for a specific sector of threat. See also Figures 4.3 to 4.5.

Note   This provision is normally coupled with the 'automatic acquisition' facilities, in which case, in addition to activating the alarm, the target will also be acquired if there is an available tracking channel. Even where automatic acquisition is not provided, the guard zone facility is still required.

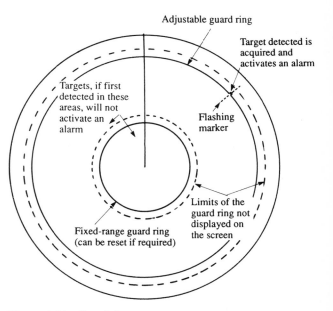

Figure 4.14   Guard rings

4.7.2 Predicted CPA/TCPA violation

The ARPA should have the capability to warn the observer with a visual and/or audible signal of any tracked target which is predicted to close to within a minimum range and time chosen by the observer. The target causing the warning should be clearly indicated on the display.

It is possible to specify a CPA and TCPA (sometimes referred to as *safe limits*) which will activate an alarm if *both* are violated. For example, if the CPA and TCPA controls are set to 0.5 n mile and 30 min respectively and a target which is being tracked will come to a CPA of less than 0.5 n mile in less than 30 min, then the alarm will be activated (see Figure 4.15). This will occur, even if the 'relative vector' has not been extended into the specified area. The displayed echo and vector of the target activating the alarm may be made to flash or, alternatively, marked in some other way.

Where own ship's heading marker intersects a predicted area of danger (PAD) (see Section 5.6), a warning will be activated and will continue until such time as own ship's course is altered to clear the PAD.

4.7.3 Lost target

The ARPA should clearly indicate if a tracked target is lost other than out of range and the target's last tracked position should be clearly indicated on the display.

Consider a target which is being tracked but, for one of a number of reasons does not return a detectable response on one scan: the tracker will open up the gate and, if it finds a response, will continue to track as described in Section 4.3.6.1. If it fails to find a response, it is required that the tracker should continue to search for the echo in an area where it might be expected for up to five successive scans. If, after this searching, the target is still not

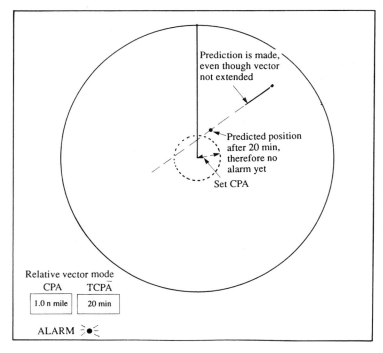

Figure 4.15 CPA/TCPA alarm settings

detected, the 'target lost' warning is activated and the last observed position of the echo is marked on the screen. It is also normal to activate an audible alarm.

4.7.4 Performance tests and warnings

The ARPA should provide suitable warnings of ARPA malfunction to enable the observer to monitor the proper operation of the system. Additionally, test programmes should be available so that the overall performance of the ARPA can be assessed periodically against a known solution.

In the case of conventional radar, there was always a basic requirement to ensure that the radar controls were properly adjusted and that correct operation of the radar had been established by means of a performance check (see Section 6.5).

All ARPA equipments incorporate some form of self-diagnostic routine which monitors the correct operation of the various circuits. This check is repeated at regular intervals (which may range from once per hour to many times per second) or on request from the operator. In the event of a fault, a warning is given to the operator and, in some cases, an indication of the cause or location (e.g. printed circuit board No. 6) of the fault is also given.

However, it must be appreciated that some faults cannot be detected internally, e.g. a failure of certain elements in a numeric read-out can cause an 8 to appear as a 6 or a 9 to appear as a 3 etc. In such cases, a typical test may provide for the operator to switch all of the elements on so that each indicator should display an 8.

To ensure that the processor which deals with data has sufficient overall accuracy, four test scenarios are specified (see Sections 9.1 and 9.2) together with the tolerances within which the output must fall. All ARPAs should be able to conform to this level of accuracy.

Where the effect of a fault is confined to certain facilities, those facilities may be 'shut down' (e.g. true motion not available), while allowing the remainder of the system to continue to be used.

4.8 Connections with other equipment

The ARPA should not degrade the performance of any equipment providing sensor inputs. The connection of the ARPA to any other equipment should not degrade the performance of that equipment.

5 ARPA – additional facilities

5.1 Introduction

With increased processing capability, manufacturers have been able to provide facilities additional to those specified in the IMO Performance Standards, some of which, in particular alerts, mariners had indicated would be of value.

Further design potential was realized by providing a facility whereby the ARPA would automatically deduce reliable values for the vessel's course and speed over the gound by tracking a designated stationary target. Such a facility, known as *automatic ground-stabilization*, can provide a reliable input to the ARPA but it is not the correct input for collision avoidance. The implications of this are discussed in Section 5.3.

With memory becoming less expensive, the means for the storage and display of navigation lines and simple 'maps' became a possibility, and the availability of automatic ground-stabilization made it possible to maintain such maps in a fixed position on the screen.

Also, some designers saw the potential for development in other areas, primarily in the provision of assistance in determining a collision avoidance strategy – notably potential points of collision (PPCs) and predicted areas of danger (PADs).

5.2 Additional alarms and warnings

In addition to the alarms and warnings specified, manufacturers have seen fit to provide alarms and warnings which they consider to be of benefit to the mariner.

5.2.1 Loss of sensor input

One occurrence which will activate a warning is the loss of a sensor input such as arises if log or gyro compass data is missing. It is important here to note that the ARPA has no way of knowing what values to expect and so can only warn of their absence. (The warning 'log error' means that the ARPA is receiving no input from the log, *not* that the value it is receiving is in error.)

5.2.2 Track change

This alarm is associated with an algorithm which quantifies departures from the predicted tracks of targets. The target(s) activating the alarm will be indicated by some graphic symbol. Its operation is likely to be associated with the change from a long to a short smoothing period (see Section 4.3.6.1).

It can be useful, but it does depend on the application of some arbitrary decision as to when the change in track is 'significant'. There is the possibility on some equipment to reduce the sensitivity of this alarm where it is found that the incidence of false alarms is too high. In some systems, the track change alarm will be activated by large or rapid manoeuvres performed by the observing vessel. This is likely to arise where relative track storage is used (see Section 4.3.6.2). In general, this condition can be recognised as all targets will exhibit the track change symbol.

5.2.3   Anchor watch

This facility attempts to offer automatic warning of the observing vessel or other vessels dragging in an anchorage. If a known stationary target (for example, a small isolated navigation mark) is acquired and designated as such then an alarm will be activated if the designated target moves more than a preset distance from the marked position. If the stationary target appears to move, then it must be due to the observing vessel dragging her anchor. Alternatively, it will give a warning if another 'tracked' vessel in the anchorage drags her anchor; it will, of course, be activated if such a vessel heaves up her anchor and gets under way.

5.2.4   Tracks full

Since there is a limit to the number of targets which an ARPA is capable of tracking, in areas of high traffic density, there may well come a time when all the tracking channels are in use. This is particularly likely when automatic acquisition (see Sections 4.2.4, 4.2.5 and 4.2.6) is in operation. An alarm will warn the operator to inspect the untracked targets for potential dangers and to transfer tracking from less important targets which are being tracked.

5.2.5   Wrong or invalid request

Where an operator feeds in incorrect data or data in an unacceptable form, e.g. course 370°, an alarm and indicator will be activated and will continue until the invalid data is deleted or overwritten.

5.2.6   Time to manoeuvre

Where a 'delay' facility is provided with trial manoeuvre (see Section 4.4.3), an alarm may be provided to warn the officer of the watch that it is, say, one minute until 'time to manoeuvre'. Depending on the size of ship and its manoeuvrability, this warning can be used as an indication to apply helm and/or ring the telegraph.

5.2.7   Safe limit vector suppression

This facility, if selected, suppresses the vectors of targets whose predicted motion does not violate the safe limits (see Section 4.7.2) and is an attempt to reduce ARPA 'clutter'. The computer continues to track the targets whose vectors are suppressed. If any of them should manoeuvre in such a way as to violate the set safe limits, the vector of that target will reappear and the safe limit alarm will be activated. If a decision is taken to use this facility, considerable thought must be given to the implications of the selected values of safe limits. In general, it is advisable to switch the facility off before contemplating a manoeuvre.

5.2.8   Trial alarm

This facility is analogous to the safe limit alarm but operates only when the trial manoeuvre is selected. It is not available on all systems.

5.3   Automatic ground-stabilization

The difficulties of achieving ground-stabilization on a raw radar display are outlined in Section 6.8.3. With computer assistance, ground-stabilization can be achieved easily and automatically. In general this stabilization is also applied to all true target vectors. It is particularly important to appreciate the implications of this, which are discussed later.

An isolated land target with good response is selected as reference. It is acquired and tracked by one of the ARPA tracking channels and then designated as a fixed target. This makes it possible for the tracker to calculate the ground track of the observing vessel and hence to maintain the movement of the electronic origin of the display in sympathy with it. When using this facility the observer should be particularly watchful for other targets which approach the reference target and, in particular, for those which pass between the observing vessel and the reference target. If the intervening target shadows the reference target the chances of target swop (see Section 4.3.5) may be greatly increased. If target swop does involve the reference target, it may have quite dramatic effects on the presentation of all vectors, particularly if the reference attaches to a fast moving target. If such an eventuality seems likely, it may be

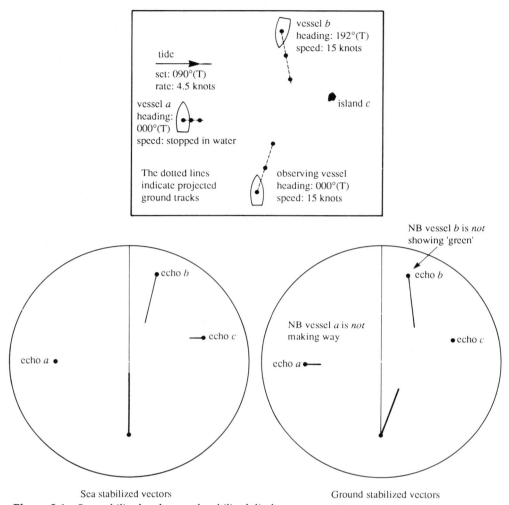

Figure 5.1 Sea-stabilized and ground-stabilized displays

expedient to move the reference to another fixed target.

In most designs the facility has been developed in such a way that the same stabilization is applied to the radar picture presentation and to the true vectors, i.e. either both are sea-stabilized or both are ground-stabilized. (There is currently one exception to this rule.) Thus in general, where automatic ground-stabilization is selected, true vectors will indicate the ground tracks of targets and *not* their headings. Failure to appreciate this can render the presentation dangerously misleading if it is

mistakenly used in the planning of collision avoidance strategy. This is illustrated in the right-hand display of Figure 5.1. One might expect the danger of observers being misled in this respect to be less than in the case of a raw radar display (see Section 1.5.2.2) because, except in case of an along-track tide, there will be angular displacement of the observing vessel's vector from the heading marker. Experience has indicated that this optimism cannot be justified in all cases.

The useful feature is that it makes true-motion parallel indexing a practical proposition, which is scarcely if at all the case with manual ground-stabilization (see Section 8.4.5). It also makes it possible to maintain electronic navigation lines and maps (see Sections 5.4, 8.4.6.2 and 8.4.6.3) in a fixed position on the screen. Some users find the availability of a fixed map particularly attractive in coastal navigation. However, it must be stressed that the penalty paid is that the presentation may not afford traffic heading information and may therefore in principle be unsuitable for collision avoidance.

Automatic ground-stabilization can also be achieved by using the output from a twin axis doppler log which is locked to the ground (see Section 6.8.1.3).

5.4   Navigational lines and maps (see also Section 8.4.6.3)

Most ARPAs offer a graphics facility whereby electronic lines can be drawn on the screen. The position, length and orientation of the lines can be adjusted, thus making it possible to produce parallel indexing lines (see Sec-

tion 8.4) and to delineate navigational limits in channels, traffic separation schemes, poor-response coastlines etc. It may also be possible to indicate points of interest such as isolated rocks and floating marks with a specific symbol.

The range of facilities available under the general heading of a navigation lines package is considerable. In simple facilities only some ten to fifteen lines may be available, thus merely allowing the construction of fairly crude patterns or maps (see Figure 5.2). The pattern may be lost if the equipment is switched off and it may or may not be possible to edit or move the pattern around the screen, once drawn. More advanced packages will allow the observer to prepare and store the pattern at a convenient time when passage planning and subsequently to recall it when required. It will then be possible to move the pattern around the screen in order to align or realign it with displayed radar echoes and there will be provision for easy editing. A non-volatile memory may allow the storage of several maps even when the equipment is switched off. The most comprehensive mapping facilities will provide for the permanent storage of maps containing as many as a

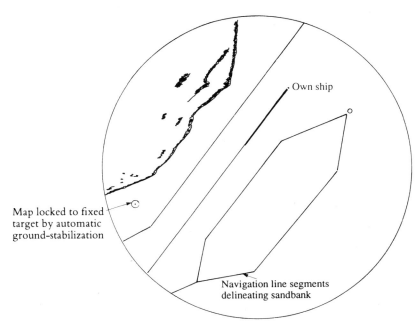

Figure 5.2   Map presentation

thousand or more elements. While there is no rigid distinction in names between the two extremes, the simpler packages tend to be referred to as navigation lines while the more comprehensive are usually described as mapping facilities. The facility will frequently be used in association with automatic ground-stabilization (see Section 5.3).

5.5 The potential point of collision (PPC)

The potential point of collision (PPC) is that point toward which the observing ship should steer at her present speed (assuming that the target does not manoeuvre) in order for a collision to occur.

Some designers have recognized that the positions of these points can be quickly calculated and displayed for all tracked targets. The argument made for displaying the PPCs is that they assist in developing a collision avoidance strategy by showing the navigator, at a glance, the courses which are completely unacceptable because they intersect a collision point. This is the only contribution which can be claimed for PPCs. They do not give any indication of *miss distance* (other than in the zero case) and any attempt to extrapolate the clearing distance either side of the point will be fraught with danger. A safe course is one which, among other things, results in passing at a safe distance, which implies a knowledge of clearing distance. Safe and effective use of PPCs depend upon a thorough understanding of the factors which affect their location and movement. As is evident from the following treatment this is, in many cases, not a simple matter. Some systems make it possible to display these points as small circles when, but only when, true vectors are selected.

5.5.1 The concept of collision points

When two ships are in the same area of sea, it is always possible for them to collide. The point(s) at which collision can occur may be defined and depends upon:

(a) the speed ratio of the two ships,
(b) the position of the two ships.

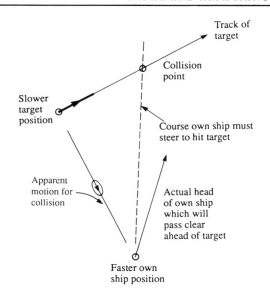

Figure 5.3 Single point of collision

Considering any two ships, usually one is moving faster than the other; the possibility that one is at exactly the same speed as the other and will maintain that ratio for any period of time is remote enough to be disregarded for the moment.

The ship which is the faster of the two will always see displayed one and only one collision point, since it can pursue the target if necessary. This collision point is always on the track of the target as shown in Figure 5.3.

The ship which is the slower of the two may see displayed two collision points, both of which must be on the target track. One exists where the slow ship heads toward the target and intercepts it, while another exists where the slow ship heads away from the target but is struck by it. The two cases appear in Figure 5.4. Alternatively there may be no way for the slower ship to collide with the faster (even though the faster may collide with the slower) because it is just not fast enough to reach the target (see Figure 5.5).

Note A critical in-between case of one collision point exists where the slow ship can just reach the track of the fast ship.

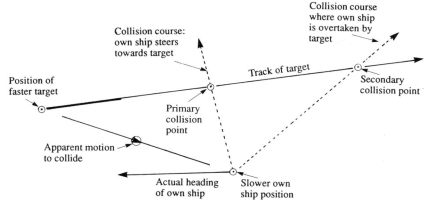

Figure 5.4 Dual points of collision

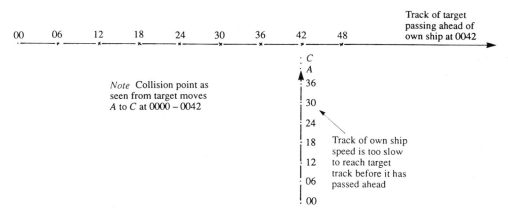

Figure 5.5 No points of collision

5.5.2 The behaviour of collision points if the observing ship maintains speed

5.5.2.1 The initial collision case

It is important to realize that collision points exist, whether an actual collision threat exists or not. The only significance is that in the event of an actual collision threat, the collision points are the same for both ships. Figure 5.6 shows how the collision points move in a collision situation and how they will appear to the two ships involved. On the faster ship, the single collision point appears on the heading marker and moves down, decreasing in range as the collision approaches. On the slower ship, one of the two collision points will move down the heading marker, while the other moves down a steady bearing.

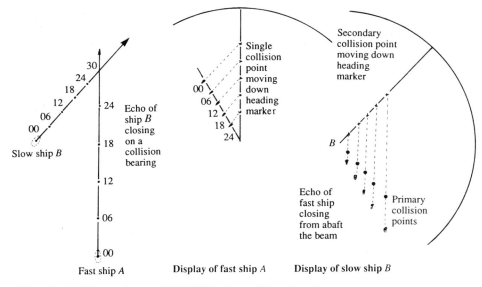

Figure 5.6   The movement of the PPC in the collision situation

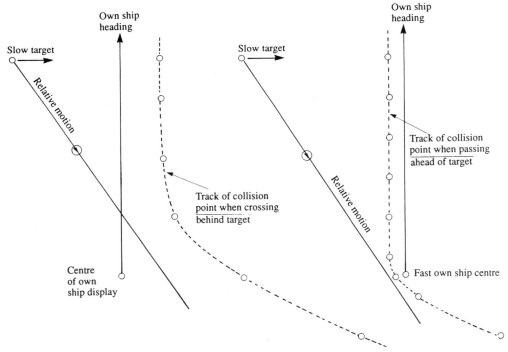

Figure 5.7   The track of the collision point

5.5.2.2 The non-collision case

In a non-collision case, the collision point moves according to well defined rules but it will never cross the heading marker. In the case of the faster ship, the movement depends on whether the fast ship will cross ahead of, or behind the target ship. Figure 5.7 shows the two possible cases and typical track lines.

The case of the slower ship is more complicated because of the two collision points and the possibility of no collision point existing. If the observing ship's course is to pass between the two collision points, they will pass down either side of the observing ship, generally shortening in range, and then draw together under the stern of the observing ship. As they meet they become one collision point before they finally disappear, as in Figure 5.8.

If the observing ship is steering to pass astern of the fast ship, the collision points will draw together, form one point and then disappear. It is noticeable that the collision point more distant from the target ship, usually termed the secondary point, moves much faster than the point nearer to the target, which is termed the primary collision point.

5.5.3 The behaviour of the collision point when the target ship's speed changes

If the speed ratio is infinitely large, e.g. when the target is stationary, then obviously the collision point is at the position of the target. If the observing ship maintains speed while the target begins to increase speed, the collision point will begin to move along the target track. When the target speed has increased to that of the observing ship, the secondary collision point will appear at infinity. Further increase of the target speed will move the primary and secondary collision points toward each other (not necessarily by equal amounts); eventually, own speed in comparison to target speed may be so slow that the two points will merge and then disappear. This behaviour is shown in Figure 5.9.

5.5.4 The behaviour of the collision point when the target changes course

If the two ships have the same speed, the collision point moves on a locus which is the perpendicular bisector of

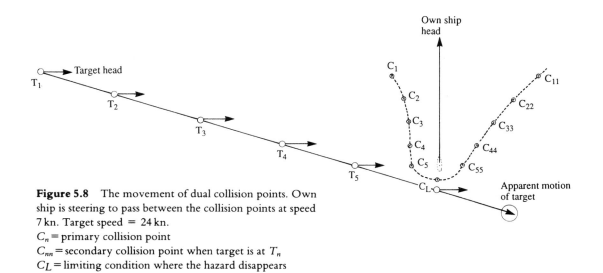

Figure 5.8 The movement of dual collision points. Own ship is steering to pass between the collision points at speed 7 kn. Target speed = 24 kn.
C_n = primary collision point
C_{nn} = secondary collision point when target is at T_n
C_L = limiting condition where the hazard disappears

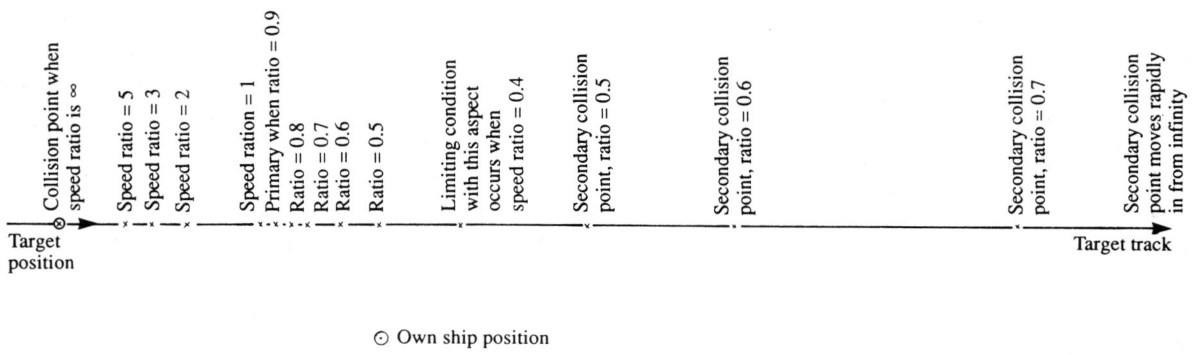

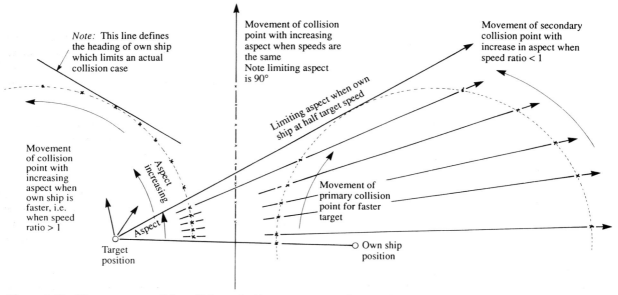

Figure 5.9   The behaviour of the collision point with the change of speed ratio (i.e. own speed : target speed)

Figure 5.10   The movement of the collision point(s) as target aspect changes, drawn for speed ratios of 2:1 and 1:2

the line joining the two ships. The greater the aspect, the farther away the collision point will be (Figure 5.10). Theoretically, the limiting aspect in this case is 90°, but then the collision point would be at infinity and hence an aspect of some 85° plus is considered the practical limit.

5.5.4.1   *For a slower observing ship*

When the observing ship is slower than the target, two collision points exist and they are seen to be on the circumference of a circle whose centre and radius are dependent of the speed ratio; the circle is always on the 'observing ship' side of the unity speed ratio locus. A limiting aspect can be defined which is also dependent on the speed ratio. A slower observing ship will mean that a target will have a smaller limiting aspect angle.

Aspects greater than the limit pose no hazard since the observing ship can never catch up with the target.

5.5.4.2   For a faster observing ship

When the observing ship is the faster, the circle of collision points lies on the target side of the equal-speed locus. As the aspect increases, the collision point moves farther away from the observing ship. There is no limiting aspect and collision is always possible.

An interesting point to note in Figure 5.10 is that the inverse of the idea of a limiting aspect to the slow observing ship appears when the observing ship is faster; this is effectively a limiting course for the observing ship. If the actual heading is to the remote side of this line, all collision points appear on the one bow. If own heading is inside this limiting direction, the collision point will move across the heading marker as the target changes aspect.

5.6   The predicted area of danger (PAD)

The shortcomings of collision points can be listed as follows:

(a)   Inaccuracies in data acquisition are likely to displace the points.
(b)   No account is taken of the dimensions of the ships involved.
(c)   They offer no quantitative indication of miss distance which is the essential data required for collision avoidance.

The logical development is to construct, around the PPC, a plane figure which is associated with a chosen passing distance and in the calculation of which due margin of safety can be allowed for the effects of data inaccuracies and the physical dimensions of the vessels involved. The area within the figure is to be avoided to achieve at least the chosen passing distance and is referred to as a predicted area of danger or PAD. The technique was patented by Sperry Marine Systems and is exclusive to the ARPAs produced by that company. The PAD approach is an extremely elegant solution to the problem of how best to present collision avoidance data. It is essential that the user has a thorough understanding of the principles underlying the presentation with particular reference to the location, movement, shape and change of shape of the PAD. As will be seen from the following explanation, this is not a simple subject.

In the case of the collision point there is a course which intercepts the target's track at the given speed ratio, whereas in the predicted area of danger there are generally two intersection points. One of these is where the observing ship will pass ahead of the target and the other where the observing ship will pass astern of the target. The angle subtended by these two limiting courses will depend upon:

(a)   The speed ratio.
(b)   The position of the target.
(c)   The aspect of the target.

As shown in the case of the collision point, a faster observing ship must always generate a single cross-ahead and cross-astern position. A slower observing ship produces much more complex possibilities and, depending on the three variables noted above, these may include:

(a)   Two cross-ahead and two cross-astern points.
(b)   One cross-ahead and two cross-astern points.
(c)   Two cross-astern points.
(d)   No hazard.

In the case of the single or primary collision point, the position at which the observing ship will cross ahead of the target is always farther from the target than the collision point, while the cross-astern point is always nearer to the target.

In the case of a slower observing ship, where there is a secondary collision point, the second cross-ahead position is nearer to the target and the associated cross-astern position more remote from it (see Figure 5.11).

To indicate limits within the 'cross-ahead/cross-astern' arc, it is necessary to draw a bar parallel to the target's track and at the intended miss-distance closer to the observing ship's position.

The limits defined by the arc and the bar are such that, if the observing ship were to cross those limits, then it would be at a less distance than the desired miss-distance from the target. Figure 5.12 shows the generation of the two boundaries in the case of a slower observing ship.

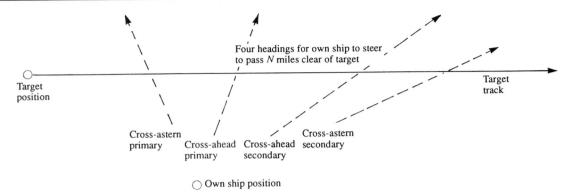

Figure 5.11   The sequence of cross-ahead/cross-astern points

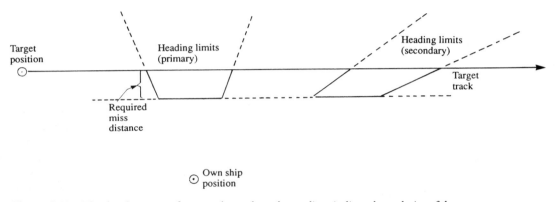

Figure 5.12   The development of areas to keep clear: heavy lines indicate boundaries of danger areas

5.6.1   The PAD in practice

In order to produce an acceptable system for practical operation, these limits are normally encapsulated by a symmetrical figure such as an ellipse or a hexagon.

In the case of the ellipse, the major axis is equal to the difference between the cross-ahead and cross-astern distances as measured from the target, while the minor axis is equal to twice the intended miss–distance. In the case of the hexagon, it is drawn from a rectangle and two isosceles triangles. The base of the triangle is always twice the miss–distance and the vertical height is one quarter of the distance E_1E_2 as shown in Figure 5.13. It should be noted that the collision point is not necessarily at the centre of either of the traditional figures.

In many cases the stylized figures do not follow the limits exactly, but any bias is on the safe side.

5.6.2   Changes in the shape of the PAD

Due to the lack of symmetry in the geometry which generates the area, the cross-ahead and cross-astern positions do not move symmetrically about the collision point when the miss-distance is changed. The cross-ahead position usually moves more markedly than the cross-astern position (see Figure 5.9, showing the movement of the two collision points, where the primary movement is much slower than the secondary). The overall result is an asymmetrical growth of the area with the cross-ahead position moving rapidly away from the collision point.

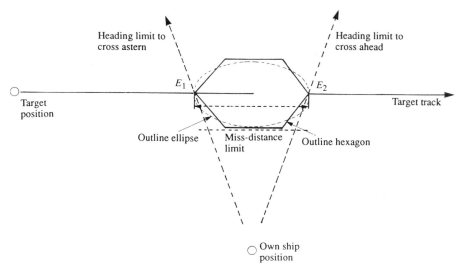

Figure 5.13   Acceptable symmetrical figures

5.6.3   The movement of the PAD

5.6.3.1   The collision case

As in the case of the collision point, when a danger area is violated by the heading marker the danger area will continue to move down the heading marker with the cross-ahead and cross-astern points on opposite bows. The shape of the danger area may change but it will never move off the heading marker. In the case of a slower ship, where either of the two predicted areas is violated, the other will move in toward the target and eventually merge with the one on the heading marker.

In the limiting case where the observing ship's heading marker just touches the limit of either of the predicted areas of danger, the limit will remain in contact with the heading marker, although the shape of the area may change considerably.

5.6.3.2   The 'passing clear' case

In the non-collision case where the heading marker does not violate one of the danger areas, the areas themselves will move across the screen, changing in shape and position. The movement will be very similar to that described for the collision point in Figure 5.7, depending on whether the observing ship is heading farther ahead than the cross-ahead position or farther astern than the cross-astern position. In the case of the dual areas of danger, although the movement will generally be the same as that shown for the dual collision points, a special case can arise when two danger areas may merge. This special case indicates the possibility of two cross-astern positions existing but no cross-ahead position. It is also possible that cross-astern positions may exist and an area of danger be drawn, which does not embrace an actual collision point.

5.6.3.3   Special cases

In some cases, for example, an end-on encounter, a cross-ahead and cross-astern position is not valid. In this context it is necessary to consider a pass-to-port and pass-to-starboard as defining the limits of the miss-distance. In the practical case, this results in the generation of a circle about the target's position.

6 The radar system — operational controls

6.1 Optimum performance

A major aim of the radar observer should be to ensure that all the targets which can be detected *are detected*. This is sometimes described as achieving the maximum probability of detection of targets. For any given radar system, the performance is limited in all circumstances by certain design parameters such as transmitter power, aerial gain and receiver sensitivity (see Section 3.2). On any particular occasion the performance of the system may be further limited by weather and atmospheric conditions (see Sections 3.6, 3.7 and 3.8). Although design features and environmental conditions place limits on the potential performance of the system, the ability of the observer to set and maintain the operational controls in correct adjustment determines whether or not such potential performance is realized. Maladjustment of the controls may result in a failure to detect targets at a sufficiently early stage or may allow them to escape detection completely. It is therefore of crucial importance that the radar observer knows, understands and implements the correct practical procedures for the setting up of the operational controls and for maintaining them in optimum adjustment according to changing requirements and circumstances.

Further, when basic data is extracted by making measurements from the display, the observer must ensure that the full potential accuracy is realized. Maladjustment of certain controls may impair the accuracy of such measurements and this must be avoided by the use of the proper procedures.

This chapter presents detailed practical procedures which, if followed, will ensure the correct initial setting of the controls at switch-on and the appropriate subsequent adjustments necessary to maintain optimum performance. The procedures also deal with the use of the controls in routine tasks, including the combating of the adverse effects of weather conditions and the extraction of basic radar and ARPA data from the display.

There exist long established criteria by which the setting of the radar controls can be judged. These criteria derive historically from the characteristics of the traditional analogue picture (see Section 2.6.2) and cannot necessarily be applied directly to a synthetic display. Some controls found on modern synthetic displays (see Sections 2.6.6 and 2.6.7) have no counterpart on their analogue ancestors. For these reasons this chapter, in dealing with setting-up procedure, will treat real and synthetic displays separately (see Sections 6.2, 6.3 and 6.4). The setting up of an ARPA display requires the optimization of the radar controls and the correct adjustment of the ARPA controls to achieve effective and accurate tracking and this is also treated separately (see Section 6.12). Where the procedure deals with routine tasks such as clutter suppression, the differences between traditional and digital techniques will be highlighted.

6.2 Setting-up procedure for an analogue display

The operational controls are all located on the display

unit and for this reason the procedure is commonly referred to as *setting up the display*. However, it should be borne in mind that some of the controls do not perform display functions. The tuning control operates within the radio frequency section of the transceiver (see Sections 2.5.1 and 2.7.2). The gain and sea clutter controls also perform receiver functions (see Sections 2.5.2 and 2.5.3), although the section of the receiver in which they operate may well be located within the display unit. The pulse length selector (which may also be affected by the range selector) operates in the transmitter (to control the pulse length and PRF – see Section 2.3.4) and in the receiver (to control the bandwidth – see Section 2.5.2.4).

6.2.1 Preliminary procedure

Before switching the equipment on the following preliminary checks should be carried out:

1 Ensure that the antenna is clear. In particular it is important to check that no personnel are working on or close to the antenna and that there are no loose halyards or other such rigging which may foul it.
2 Check that the power switch that makes the ship's mains available to the installation is on. This switch may not necessarily be located in the wheelhouse.
3 Set the following front panel controls to zero effect:
 (a) Brilliance: This precludes the possibility of the screeen being flooded with light when the set becomes operational and hence the danger of the phosphor being damaged (see Section 2.6.1.2). In any event this is the first control to be adjusted when setting up and it is convenient to start from zero effect.
 (b) Gain, range rings brilliance, variable range marker brilliance, sea clutter and rain clutter (any automatic clutter controls should be switched off): All of the controls mentioned here have some effect on the overall brightness of the picture and, if they are not set to zero effect, they make it very difficult to judge correctly the setting of the brilliance control.

6.2.2 Switching on

It is convenient to consider that this operation carries out three distinct functions:

1 The supply of power to the antenna.
2 The supply of power to the transceiver and display.
3 The switching of the system from the *stand-by* condition to the *operational* condition (see below).

In some systems an individual switch may be associated with each function. It is perhaps more common to find that a single switch combines functions 1 and 2. In a further variation, a single multi-position switch may service all three functions.

The application of power to the system initiates a warming-up period. Very high voltages (EHT) and working temperatures are associated with certain elements of the system, in particular the transmitter (see Section 2.3) and the CRT (see Section 2.6.1). Good engineering practice dictates that such elements should be raised gradually to working temperature before the high voltages are applied. Some form of thermal or other delay timer will normally be used to isolate the EHT during the warming-up period, which is likely to exceed one and a half minutes. The maximum duration is set by the IMO Performance Standards (see Section 10.2) which require that, after switching on from cold, the equipment should become fully operational within 4 minutes. For situations other than that of a cold start the same section of the standard requires the provision of a stand-by condition from which the equipment can be brought to an operational condition within 15 seconds.

The precise status of the equipment in the stand-by condition may vary with manufacturer but in all cases the transmitter will be in the quiescent state, i.e. it will be maintained at or close to working temperature but no pulses will be transmitted. The use of the stand-by condition is discussed in detail in Section 6.7. If the operational condition is selected at initial switch-on (see function 3 above), the system will automatically switch from the stand-by condition to the operational condition when the warming-up period has elapsed. While the system is warming up the observer may make the following selections:

Orientation and presentation. This selection is a matter of personal choice and navigational circumstances. Features which might influence such a selection are considered in Sections 1.4.4, 1.5.3, Chapter 7 and Chapter 8.

Range scale. It is usually best to set up on a medium range scale such as 12 miles. The likelihood of echoes and sea clutter which have not been affected by saturation (see Section 2.5.2.1) make such a scale best suited for judging the quality of the picture when it is subsequently obtained.

Pulse length. This should be appropriate to the range scale selected, e.g. medium range scale would suggest medium pulse length (see Section 2.3.4).

6.2.3   Preparing the display

This involves the setting of the controls directly associated with the CRT (see Section 2.6.1) so as to prepare the tube to display a marine radar picture; they should be adjusted in the sequential order set out below. In modern systems some of these controls may be preset. Nevertheless it is important to check that the preset control is having the desired effect, since they have no automatic correcting action. If they go wrong, they will stay wrong.

6.2.3.1   Setting the brilliance

The brilliance control sets the *no signal* level of the spot brightness (see Section 2.6.1.1). Since the presence of an echo is indicated by a temporary increase in that brightness, the setting of this control is fundamental to successful echo detection.

The brilliance control should be set so that the rotating trace is barely visible. If the brilliance is set lower than this, weak echoes may be missed because a small increase in electron beam strength may be insufficient to make the spot visible. Conversely, if the setting is too high, echoes may be missed, not because they are not displayed, but because a small increase in spot brightness may be difficult to see against an already bright background. The latter effect is sometimes described as lack of contrast (this use of the word contrast should not be confused with its use to name one of the controls associated with synthetic displays — see Sections 2.6.6.5, 6.3.4.1 and 6.4.3.1).

Excessive brilliance will tend to de-focus the spot, resulting in a reduction in discrimination and the accuracy with which ranges and bearings can be measured (see Sections 2.6.1.1, 6.2.3.2, 6.3.3 and 6.4.3.2).

6.2.3.2   Setting the focus

This control, by adjusting the position to which the electron beam is converged (see Section 2.6.1.1), determines the spot size. As the latter is one of the factors which affects the area of echo paint (see Section 2.6.5.1) the control must be set to produce the smallest possible spot diameter.

To set the focus control, switch on the range rings and adjust the control until the range rings appear as sharp as possible. Choose a ring half-way between the centre and the edge of the screen, as it is difficult to achieve perfect focus over the whole screen. Poor focus is evidenced by the ring appearing thick and *woolly*. In modern marine equipment the focus is invariably preset and no user control is provided. When the check has been completed the rings should be switched off.

Where focus adjustment is necessary, it is important that it is carried out after the brilliance has been correctly set because an excessive brilliance setting will tend to defocus the spot.

6.2.3.3   Centring the origin

A pair of centring or shift controls (see Section 2.6.1.3) allow the observer to make small adjustments to the position of the origin of the rotating trace. As its name suggests, the *horizontal shift* (or centring) control produces horizontal movement of the origin, i.e. movement parallel to the 090/270° axis of the graduated circular bearing scale which surrounds the tube (see Section 1.3.5), while the *vertical shift* produces movement at right angles to this direction.

Although the picture may subsequently be used in an offset position, when first setting up the display, the position of the origin should be adjusted to coincide with the centre of the bearing scale and the centre of the Perspex cursor (see Sections 1.3.5 and 6.9.3). This is necessary to facilitate the subsequent alignment of the displayed heading marker with the bearing scale (see Section 6.2.3.4). Further, it should be noted that failure to centre the origin of the trace will result in errors in bearings which are obtained by the use of the Perspex cursor (see Section 6.9.3).

The centre of the Perspex cursor disk is normally marked by a cross formed by the intersection of the main cursor line, which is engraved along a diameter, and a short line which bisects it at right angles. To centre the origin, the cursor should be aligned to the 000°/180° direction on the bearing scale and the horizontal shift control should be adjusted to place the origin below the engraved diameter. The vertical shift control should then be adjusted to place the origin below the cross at the centre of the Perspex cursor disk and thus (assuming that there has been no mechanical damage to the mounting of the disk), at the geometrical centre of the bearing scale.

Because the cursor disk is located some distance above the tube face, care must be taken to avoid parallax by ensuring that the eye is directly above the centre of the screen when judging the position of the origin. In many display units the cursor markings are engraved on the top and bottom surfaces of the Perspex disk. By adjusting the eye position so that the top and bottom sets of lines are in transit, i.e. such that only a single cross can be seen, the observer can ensure that the effect of parallax has been eliminated. Alternatively, use may be made of the visor or viewing hood. Most displays have some such arrangement which can be removed at night but which, when fitted, allows the display to be viewed in daylight. This will be designed to ensure that the eye is placed in such a position as to avoid parallax.

6.2.3.4 Orientating the picture

The picture must be correctly orientated by rotating it so that the heading marker intersects the correct graduation on the circular bearing scale surrounding the tube. In many older systems it was necessary to rotate the picture manually, whereas in more modern systems auto-alignment takes place provided that the compass repeater has been correctly set to the vessel's heading. The procedure will thus depend on the preferred orientation and can be set out as follows:

Ship's-head-up (unstabilized) – see also Section 1.4.1. The ship's-head-up orientation should be selected. Where a manual alignment control is provided, the heading marker should be rotated to align it with the 000° graduation on the bearing scale. In the case of an auto-aligned system, the display should be observed to ensure that the heading marker has aligned correctly.

True-north-up (stabilized) – see also Section 1.4.2. It is expedient to start by selecting the ship's-head-up (unsta-

bilized) orientation as this ensures that the heading marker will not yaw in sympathy with the azimuth stabilizing signal until the observer is ready to switch in the latter (see Section 2.6.3).

The display compass repeater should be correctly aligned to the vessel's instantaneous true heading. The alignment control which adjusts the repeater normally operates in association with a clutch mechanism. When the control is pressed in against a spring, the gyro repeater card is disconnected from the gyro follow-up system and it can be freely rotated to the desired reading by turning the alignment control. On release of the control, the clutch re-engages the repeater card to the gyro follow-up system and the alignment control can be rotated freely. The repeater should be aligned to the true course and, at an instant when the vessel is right on course, the alignment control should be released. A check should then be made to ensure that the repeater does follow variations in the ship's heading.

Where a manual alignment control is provided, the heading marker should be rotated to align it with that graduation on the bearing scale which corresponds with the vessel's true course. At an instant when the vessel is *right on course*, the true-north-up orientation should be selected (see also Section 1.4.2).

In the case of an auto-aligned system, true-north-up should be selected and the display should then be observed to ensure that the heading marker has aligned correctly.

In both cases, after the heading marker has been aligned, the display should be observed for a short period to ensure that the heading marker is following variations in the ship's heading.

Course-up (stabilized) – see also Section 1.4.3. It is expedient to start by selecting the ship's-head-up (unstabilized) orientation as this ensures that the heading marker will not yaw in sympathy with the azimuth stabilizing signal until the observer is ready to switch in the latter (see Section 2.6.3).

The display compass repeater should be correctly aligned to the vessel's instantaneous true heading in the same way as described for the north-up orientation.

Where a manual alignment control is provided, the heading marker should be rotated to align it with the 000° graduation on the bearing scale. At an instant when the vessel is *right on course*, the course-up orientation should be selected.

In the case of an auto-aligned system, course-up should be selected and the display should then be observed to ensure that the heading marker has aligned correctly.

In both cases, after the heading marker has been aligned, the display should be observed for a short period to ensure that the heading marker is following variations in the ship's heading.

In the particular case of course-up orientation, it will be necessary to reset the reference course each time the vessel makes a sustained alteration of course. In older systems this will have to be done manually, while in more modern systems it is merely necessary to press some form of reset control when the vessel is steady on the new course.

It is essential to appreciate that, irrespective of the orientation which is selected, all bearings are measured from the reference of the heading marker (see Section 6.9); if the picture is not correctly orientated, all bearings read from the graduated scale around the CRT will be in error. The operation of aligning the heading marker on the bearing scale should not be confused with that of the alignment of the heading marker with the ship's fore-and-aft line. The latter operation is concerned with ensuring that the heading marker contacts (see Section 2.4.6) close and produce the heading marker signal at the instant the radar beam crosses the ship's fore-and-aft line in the forward direction. This alignment cannot be checked with reference to both visual and radar observations (see Section 6.9.9).

6.2.4 Obtaining the optimum picture

Optimum picture is obtained by setting the receiver controls to maximize the detection of weak echoes. This involves the adjustment of, firstly, the gain control and, secondly, the tuning control.

6.2.4.1 *Setting the gain control*

The gain control, which is sometimes referred to as the sensitivity control, adjusts the amounts by which all received echoes and receiver noise are amplified (see

Section 2.5.2). It should be advanced until a low level, close-grained speckling can be seen all over the screen. The speckling is the visual indication of the phenomenon known as thermal or receiver noise. This important feature is described in detail in Section 2.5.2.3 which explains that signals weaker than the noise cannot be detected and that those signals close to noise level will only be detected with difficulty. The problem is analogous to attempting to listen for the fog signal of another vessel against the background of audible noise from the engine and other sources on board the observing vessel.

Because it determines the minimum level of detectable signal, the amplitude of displayed noise, and thus the setting of the gain, is of critical importance. Noise is a fluctuating signal and if the gain is set too low the peaks will not be displayed and genuine echoes close to noise level may well escape detection (see Figure 6.1.) If the gain is set too high, again weak echoes may be lost, not because they are not displayed but because, as a result of

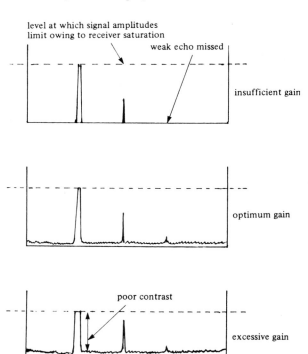

Figure 6.1 Setting the gain control

poor contrast, they may not be obvious against the background of the noise (see Figure 6.1). Further, excessive noise may also make it difficult to detect even strong echoes. If strong signals saturate the receiver (see Sections 2.5.2.1 and 2.5.2.5) additional gain will not increase their brightness but will increase the amplitude of the noise echoes and hence reduce the contrast which is related to the signal-to-noise ratio.

Excessive gain may cause defocusing of the spot, resulting in loss of discrimination and measurement accuracy (see Sections 2.6.5, 6.3.4 and 6.4.4).

In the presence of extensive and strong echoes, e.g. in harbour, it may be difficult to assess reliably the level of speckles present. In such circumstances it may be found helpful temporarily to set the tuning control well away from the optimum position while the gain is adjusted.

6.2.4.2 Setting the tuning control

The function of the tuning control is to adjust the frequency of the receiver (see Section 2.5.1) so that it coincides with that of the transmitter, rather in the same way as one might tune a broadcast receiver to listen for a distant station.

If the receiver is only slightly mistuned, the extent of the bandwidth (see Section 2.5.2.4) may still allow stronger echoes to be displayed even to the level of saturation. It is important not to be misled by this because

weak echoes will most certainly be lost. It is thus important to establish criteria against which it is possible to make a sensitive assessment of the setting of the tuning control.

One of the most sensitive criteria is the response of a weak echo from land (see Figure 6.2). The tuning control should be adjusted while carefully watching such a response. As the correct frequency is approached, the brightness of the displayed echo response will increase. It will peak at the correct setting and decay after that setting has been passed. By adjusting the control to achieve the maximum displayed brightness of such a target, the correct setting may be easily and reliably found. As the correct setting is approached it will be necessary to adjust the control in progressively smaller steps. It is important to appreciate that after each small adjustment is made, it is necessary to wait until the echo is re-painted in order to judge what effect and adjustment has had. If the coarse tuning has been set correctly by service personnel (see Section 2.5.1.2), the correct setting for the display tuning control should lie close to the centre of its range of travel. If the correct position is found to approach either end of the range of travel, the coarse tuning control (which will be located inside the transceiver) should be readjusted by qualified service personnel.

Strong echoes should not be used because they may saturate the receiver even when it is mistuned and if this is the case their displayed response will not be sensitive to

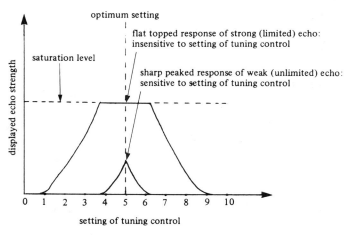

Figure 6.2 Setting the tuning control

the position of the fine tuning control. A land echo is chosen because it will give a constant response against which to judge the setting. If, for example, the echo of a buoy were chosen, the observer would be unable to tell the difference between fluctuations due to movement of the buoy in a seaway and those due to adjustment of the control.

Alternative acceptable criteria involve adjusting the control to achieve:

1 The maximum radial extent of sea clutter echoes. These are described in Section 3.6.
2 The maximum area of precipitation echoes. These are described in Section 3.7.
3 The maximum extent of the receiver monitor signal. This is discussed in Section 6.5.

Some displays offer features such as *magic eyes*, tuning meters and tuning indicators. They should not be used in preference to the above criteria. Such devices are not required by the IMO Performance Standards and the danger of the observer being misled by such indicators is discussed in Section 2.5.1.5.

The tuning may drift as the equipment warms up and to a lesser extent with the passage of time (see Section 2.3.3.2). The setting of the control should therefore be checked frequently during the first 30 minutes after switching on and periodically thereafter.

Where full automatic tuning is provided (see Section 2.5.1.4), a performance check should be carried out to ensure that optimum tuning is being achieved. The procedure for carrying this out is described in Section 6.5.6.

6.3 Setting-up procedure for a radial-scan synthetic display

In many respects the setting-up procedure for a radial-scan synthetic display is identical to that for an analogue display. Differences do however exist and these will be highlighted in Sections 6.3 to 6.3.4.3. The differences arise largely because, as a result of the digitization of the radar signals (see Section 2.6.6), it is not always possible to judge the settings of the gain and tuning controls by the criteria traditionally used in the case of analogue displays. Further, the contrast control which is almost invariably a feature of the synthetic display has no counterpart on the traditional analogue display. While it is true to say that some analogue displays did offer interference suppression, in general signal processing (see Section 2.6.6.6) is only available with synthetic displays.

6.3.1 Preliminary procedure

The procedure is the same as described for an analogue display in Section 6.2.1, with the exception that the contrast control should be set to zero effect and any signal processing facilities (such as interference suppression or echo stretching) should be switched off. In some systems it will be found that the contrast is preset.

6.3.2 Switching on

The procedure is essentially the same as described for an analogue display in Section 6.2.2. However, in the more modern systems it may well be found that orientation, presentation, range scale and pulse length are selected automatically on switch-on. The conditions automatically selected are known as the *default conditions*.

The use of default conditions has been made possible by the availability of modern controls designed particularly for computer applications. Traditionally, marine radar controls have been analogue in their action, normally taking the form of rotary knobs and multi-position mechanical switches, but there is a tendency for more and more of these controls to be replaced by electronic switches which send a digital signal to the display computer when operated by touch or pressure. They may take the form of push buttons or touch-sensitive switches. The touch-sensitive screen described in Section 2.6.7.3 is an extension of this technique.

On receipt of the signal, the display computer will carry out some programmed change in the status of the equipment. The controls can be configured and programmed to operate in a variety of ways. They may operate on the *alternative action* or *toggle* principle, i.e. one push or touch selects a function and a further push deselects that function. Alternatively they may be used to control more than one function, e.g. the first push selects function 1, the second push selects function 2 and the third push de-selects both functions. They can be used in pairs to perform an incremental action. For example, each push of one control may select the next higher range scale while its partner will reduce, in steps, the range scale selected. The list of variations is almost endless but the common feature of all actions is that, other than the actual push or touch, the action is not mechanical.

The display computer can be programmed to select the default conditions when the power is first applied at switch-on. For example, it might default to true-north-up orientation, relative-motion presentation, 12 mile range scale and long pulse. If the observer wishes conditions other than those to which the system defaults, the necessary selection can be made by pushing the appropriate switches immediately after switch-on.

In older systems all of the controls are likely to be of the mechanical type. Default conditions are not possible because these controls will remain in their last selected positions and the observer will need to make positive selection of the initial conditions required. Some systems may have a mix of analogue and computer controls.

6.3.3 Preparing the display

The procedure is identical to that described for an analogue display in Section 6.2.3.

6.3.4 Obtaining the optimum picture

It is in this area that the setting up procedure for a synthetic display diverges from that of the traditional analogue display.

6.3.4.1 Setting the contrast control

Traditionally the term contrast has been used to describe, in general, the difference between two levels of brightness and, in particular, the difference in brightness between the echoes and the background noise on an analogue display. In a synthetic display, contrast is the name given to the control which adjusts the brightness of all synthetic echoes (see Section 2.6.6.5). If the control is set to zero no synthetic echoes will be displayed. Con-

versely if the control is set to high, individual echoes will *bloom*, i.e. become large and defocussed. Between these two extremes is a wide range of settings intended to allow the observer to adapt the overall brightness of the display to suit the ambient light conditions. (Compare this with the analogue case, in which the brightness of the weaker echoes is limited by the extent to which the noise restricts the amount of gain that can be applied.) In some systems the contrast is preset by the manufacturer.

There is a 'chicken and egg' relationship between the contrast and gain/tuning. Some measure of contrast must be applied initially or there will be no visible signal on which to judge the setting of the gain and tuning. Conversely, it may not be possible to make a final decision as to the setting of the contrast until after the gain and tuning have been adjusted, because the overall picture brightness is to some extent dependent on picture content. The correct strategy is to find an initial contrast setting which gives sufficient brightness to allow the subsequent setting of the gain and tuning controls. The operator's manual will normally give guidance but, if not, the setting can be found easily by experiment. If there is not enough time to experiment, set the contrast control to the middle of its travel. The setting is not crucial at this stage as the control may well be readjusted after the setting of the gain and tuning controls. Furthermore it is important to appreciate that the control affects only the brightness of the picture; it does *not* affect the content, which depends upon the setting of the gain and the tuning.

The procedure is thus iterative and can be summarized as follows:

1 Select the initial setting of contrast.
2 Set the gain correctly (see Section 6.3.4.2).
3 Readjust the contrast if necessary to suit the ambient light conditions.
4 Set the tuning correctly (see Section 6.3.4.3).
5 Readjust the contrast if necessary.

6.3.4.2 Setting the gain control

The gain must be set to achieve the optimum relationship between the threshold level and the noise amplitude (see Section 2.6.6.2). In some systems, by operating the gain, the observer controls the threshold level while in

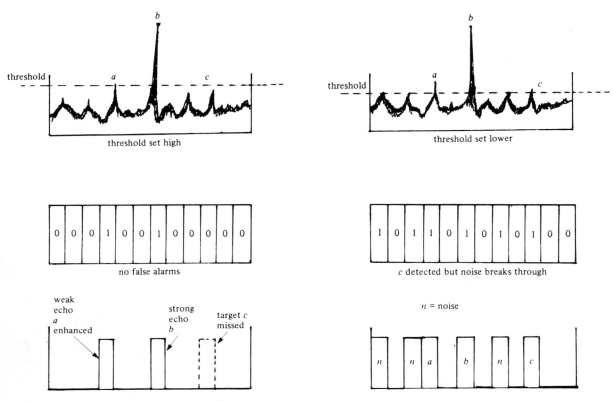

Figure 6.3   Target detection and threshold setting

others the receiver gain is affected. The difference is academic as, in both cases, advancing the setting of the gain control brings the threshold closer to the noise.

Ideally one would wish the gain to be set so that the threshold level is sufficiently low to display all detectable echoes yet sufficiently high to miss the noise. Because noise is a very rapidly fluctuating signal, such an ideal cannot be achieved. If the setting of the gain is sufficiently high for all detectable targets to cross the threshold, many noise peaks will also cross the threshold. Conversely, if the gain is set so that no noise peaks cross the threshold, detectable targets may well be missed. For the case of a single-level digitized picture, the dilemma is illustrated by Figure 6.3. Clearly a compromise setting must be found. The ease with which this setting can be made depends on the number of discrete video levels offered by the system (see Section 2.6.6.7).

In the single-level video case any noise which crosses the threshold will be displayed with the same amplitude as a detectable echo. This makes it much more difficult to assess the background noise than in the analogue case, where there is a very obvious amplitude difference between most echoes and the noise background. In some older synthetic displays it is possible to revert to an analogue picture, albeit in some cases on only one range scale (see Section 2.6.6.5); the difficulty can then be avoided by setting the gain while viewing the analogue picture. Later synthetic displays do not offer the analogue option and in such cases it is necessary to live with the difficulty of single-level noise and targets. With practice the observer should be able to identify the noise by its random nature and the radial length of individual noise pulses. The peaks of real noise are sharply spiked and thus the number of successive elements of a range word (see Section 2.6.6.3) occupied by a single noise pulse is likely to be noticeably less than that occupied by most genuine targets. This does not mean that every very short digital response is necessarily noise. A weak received echo which barely crosses the threshold may well activate only one range cell.

The difficulty of achieving a suitable noise setting is reduced where more than one video level is offered. The extent to which the additional levels are beneficial in this regard depends not just on how many levels are provided but also on how they are disposed (see Figures 2.44 and 2.45 in Section 2.6.6.7). The arrangement shown in Figure 2.44 is clearly an improvement on the single-level case, but only those systems which provide a *grey level*, as illustrated by Figure 2.45, assist the observer in identifying the noise as easily as with real signals. The grey-level approach makes it comparatively easy to judge the setting of the gain control because it can be set so that the noise produces an even speckled background at *low threshold*. Although a fair number of noise pulses will cross the grey-level threshold, because they are displayed at a fraction of high-level amplitude, the practised observer will not confuse them with strong echoes. Further, although low-level echoes will have the same amplitude as the noise, their coherence, persistence and radial length will favour detection when compared with the random noise pattern.

6.3.4.3 *Setting the tuning control*

The use of a weak land echo as the sensitive criterion by which to judge the setting of the tuning control (see Section 6.2.4.2) cannot be applied in the case of a synthetic display due to the quantizing effect of digital storage (see Section 2.6.6.7). This is illustrated for a single video level system by Figure 6.4.

Reference to Figure 6.4 shows that there may be little or no relation between the amplitude of the synthetic echo and the analogue response which produced it. The setting of the tuning control must not be judged with respect to the amplitude of the synthetic echoes because their brightness is not sufficiently sensitive to the position of the control. Even if several video levels are offered, the displayed echo strength will change only when the real echo moves into a new inter-threshold

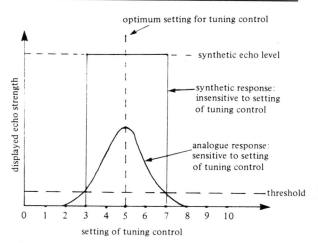

Figure 6.4 Setting the tuning control – the effect of quantizing

band, and even then in steps which may be quite large. Only if the synthetic display provided as many digital levels as there are phosphor brightness levels (see Section 2.6.1.2) would this limitation be removed. The vast majority of systems do not attempt to attain this goal.

In some older synthetic displays it is possible to revert to an analogue picture, albeit in some cases on only one range scale (see Section 2.6.6.5). The difficulty can then be avoided by adjusting the tuning control while observing the analogue picture. With later synthetic displays that do not offer the analogue option it is necessary to adjust the control to achieve one of the following results:

1 The maximum radial extent of sea clutter echoes: these are described in Section 3.6.
2 The maximum area of precipitation echoes: these are described in Section 3.7.
3 The maximum radial extent of the receiver monitor signal: this is discussed in Section 6.5.

It should be noted that all the above criteria are suitable because they are based on the area of response rather than on its brightness.

In the case of systems which have a grey level it may be possible with practice to choose an isolated land target and tune for the maximum area displayed at grey level.

The tuning may drift as the system warms up and to a lesser extent with the passage of time. The setting of the control should therefore be checked frequently during the first thirty minutes after switching on and periodically thereafter.

Where fully automatic tuning is provided (see Section 2.5.1.4), a performance check should be carried out to ensure that optimum tuning is being achieved. The procedure for carrying this out is described in Section 6.5.6.

The warning on the limitations of tuning indicators set out in Section 6.2.4.2 is equally valid for synthetic displays.

6.4 Setting-up procedure for a raster-scan synthetic display

The raster-scan display is based on digital storage and as a result the setting-up procedure relates in many ways to that described for the radial-scan synthetic display. However, significant differences do exist due to the 'television' nature of the display and the availability of signal processing made possible by the greater inherent memory capacity of the raster-scan system. Such differences are highlighted in the succeeding Sections 6.4.1 to 6.4.4.

6.4.1 Preliminary procedure

The procedure is essentially the same as that described for a radial synthetic display in Section 6.3.1. However, although the antenna safety checks are of vital importance regardless of the type of display, it may not be necessary to set certain of the raster-scan system controls to zero before switching on.

In general, the low burn characteristic of the phosphor used in television CRTs (see Section 2.6.7.1) renders it unnecessary to turn the screen brilliance to zero before switching on. By comparison, the radial-scan display is more susceptible to burn damage, not only because of the phosphor characteristic, but because of the slowly rotating trace. The light from a 20 ms burst of excessive brilliance would be dissipated over an entire

television frame, whereas it would be concentrated within a sector of about 2° on a radial-scan display.

In Section 6.4.3.1 it will be seen that the adjustment of raster-scan screen brilliance is more subjective and much less critical than in the radial-scan case. For this reason the presence of range rings or a variable range marker (VRM) is not likely to cause the observer to set the control incorrectly: it is not necessary to switch these two functions off before the power is applied to the display. In some systems it will be found that the range rings and VRM actually default to the *on* condition. The contrast between the background and the range rings/VRM is determined by the setting of the screen contrast and as a result separate range ring/VRM brilliance controls are not normally provided.

In the radial-scan case the contrast must be set initially to zero (see Section 6.3.1) to ensure that there is no possibility of the observer's assessment of the *no signal* brilliance setting being influenced by the presence of any very strong echoes which might display even with the gain set to minimum. The subjective nature of the screen brilliance setting mentioned in the previous paragraph (and described in Section 6.4.3.1) renders it unnecessary to set the contrast to zero.

The gain, sea clutter and rain clutter controls should be set to zero. In addition, particular attention should be paid to ensuring that signal-processing facilities, such as interference suppression, echo stretch, adaptive gain and rotation-to-rotation correlation, are inoperative (see Sections 3.9.5.1, 6.11.1, 3.6.3.3 and 3.6.3.4 respectively). In some raster-scan systems these facilities default to the *off* condition at switch-on. The setting of the gain is fundamental to achieving the correct relationship between threshold and noise levels (see Sections 2.6.6.2 and 2.6.6.7). All of the other foregoing controls and facilities also affect the echo content of the picture and may result in the gain being set incorrectly if not switched to zero effect when the gain level is assessed.

6.4.2 Switching on

The procedure is similar to that for the radial-scan synthetic display described in Section 6.3.2, but in the case of a raster-scan display it may be found that the system defaults to the stand-by condition at switch-on. Generally the range of functions which have default conditions is likely to be more extensive than with a radial-scan display. In addition to orientation, presentation, range scale, pulse length and signal processing, this may include the status of the range rings, the variable range marker and the electronic bearing line. If the observer does not wish any given default setting, appropriate selection can be made after switch-on.

If the raster-scan display uses a colour CRT the steel shadow mask (see Section 2.6.7.7) may become magnetized with the passage of time. The effect of such magnetism is to degrade the purity of the colours displayed on the face of the tube. When the system is switched on, a degaussing circuit automatically demagnetizes the shadow mask. In a domestic television display, if the colour purity is degraded during normal use the mask can be demagnetized by switching the set off and switching it on again. Clearly it may not be convenient or practical to do this in the case of a marine radar, which may have to run continuously for a long period. Some form of spring-loaded switch or similar arrangement will be provided to operate the degaussing circuit when required.

Most modern raster-scan displays warm up very quickly and the synthetic PPI circle, bearing scale, range rings and other graphics may well be visible within as

little as 30 seconds (assuming that the brilliance and contrast have not been set to zero). It may be possible to select the operational condition at switch-on, but the system will remain in the stand-by condition until the transmitter delay expires. The latter is a transmitter function. As in all systems, it must not exceed 4 minutes (see Section 6.2.2) but is unlikely to be less than 1.5 minutes.

6.4.3   Preparing the display

The procedure involves preparing a television screen to display a marine radar picture; here there are major differences when compared with that appropriate to a radial-scan display.

6.4.3.1   *Setting the screen brilliance*

The setting of the brilliance is judged by a criterion which differs fundamentally from that traditionally used in radial-scan displays, where the control adjusts the brilliance of the slowly rotating trace and the criterion for optimum setting can be rigidly specified in terms of the principle on which echoes are displayed (see Section 6.2.3.1). In a high-refresh-rate television display, the screen brilliance controls the brightness of the entire picture frame. The perceived brightness of the picture is

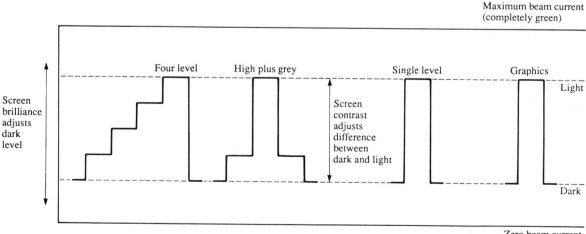

Figure 6.5   The relationship between raster-scan screen brilliance and contrast settings

largely a function of the ambient light conditions. It is also affected by the screen contrast control which defines the difference between dark and light for both graphics and echoes. In some systems the contrast is preset. The relationship between the brilliance and contrast settings for a green monochrome display is illustrated by Figure 6.5.

Reference to Figure 6.5 shows that the screen contrast adjusts the difference in brilliance level between the darker/darkest areas of the screen and the brighter/brightest areas. In general, the graphics will be single-level, i.e. bright on dark, and this will also be the case for target echoes in a simple single-threshold system. Where multi-level video is offered, the number of levels of echo brightness is the same as the number of thresholds used for the storage of range (see Section 2.6.6.7). (If rotation-to-rotation correlation is not switched off, the number of levels may be related to the number of rotations used – see Section 3.6.3.4.) The perceived effect of the screen contrast will depend to some extent on the screen brilliance setting. At higher brilliance settings, a greater absolute difference between light and dark will be necessary for an observer to perceive a difference between the two levels. Similarly, at very low levels of brilliance both light and dark levels may be so dark as to be indistinguishable.

Clearly there is an interrelationship between screen brilliance and screen contrast. Both contribute to the overall brightness of the picture as perceived by the observer and must be adjusted alternately until the best joint setting is found. The assessment of 'best' is a matter of subjective judgement for which a simple specific criterion, such as that prescribed for the radial case, cannot be given. However, consideration of the following factors will assist in making the judgement.

Excessive brilliance. If the overall brightness is too high the picture will be uncomfortable to view in the same way as any source of bright light. Tiredness, stress and headaches may result. At night the high level of illumination associated with the display may impair night vision and distract the watchkeeper by producing reflections on the inside of the wheelhouse windows and other such surfaces. Even at maximum screen contrast setting it will be difficult to achieve an adequate difference between background and picture content, because both will already be very bright.

Insufficient brilliance. If the overall brightness is too low it will be difficult to view the display and distinguish picture detail in full daylight, particularly at a distance. Even at maximum screen contrast setting, it will be difficult to achieve an adequate difference between background and picture content, because both will be very dark.

Excessive contrast. If the screen brilliance is set at a level which is comfortable to the eye, excessive screen contrast will make the picture stark and harsh.

Inadequate contrast. Insufficient contrast will result in a picture which is flat and featureless.

In most cases it will be found that if at switch-on the screen brilliance and contrast controls are left in the position in which they were last used, the settings will be sufficiently close to the optimum as to require only a small amount of adjustment to suit the new ambient light conditions. If the controls have been set to zero or have been badly maladjusted, the following procedure should be used:

1 If the system offers alternative daytime and nightime monochrome or colour combinations, select the option appropriate to the ambient light conditions.
2 Set the screen brilliance and screen contrast controls to the middle of their travel. The PPI circle, synthetic bearing scale and other graphics should be visible. (If they are not, advance each control in turn by small amounts until the graphics are visible.)
3 Adjust the screen brilliance to a level consistent with comfortable viewing in the ambient light conditions and such that the light issuing from the display does not interfere with the keeping of a proper lookout.
4 Adjust the screen contrast to achieve an obvious but comfortable difference in tone between the graphics and the background.
5 It may be necessary to make further repeated small alternate adjustments to the screen brilliance and screen contrast controls to obtain optimum overall level of brightness.

6.4.3.2 Checking the focus

It would be most unusual to find a raster-scan display in which the focus was not preset. Nevertheless, when preparing the display the focus should be checked. The graphics, in particular alphanumeric characters, are a good indicator of focus. If they are blurred and indistinct, focus adjustment is necessary and this should be carried out by qualified service personnel.

6.4.3.3 Centring the origin

The use of shift controls to centre the origin is not applicable to raster-scan displays because, in a centred display, the limit of the PPI is a graphics circle drawn about the origin as centre and the bearing scale is written in graphics and is concentric with it. Despite a visual impression which might suggest the contrary, there is no rotating trace corresponding to the radial-scan display. The appearance of rotation arises because, in the approximately 20 ms period required to refresh one frame of the cartesian raster, the radial memory is updated in an angular sector of about 2°. Thus the observer may see the moving pattern of updated data which gives the impression of a trace rotating in sympathy with the aerial.

All facilities for measuring bearings are generated graphically and in the default condition emanate from the electronic origin. In some systems the origin can be off-centred within the PPI circle.

6.4.3.4 Orientating the picture

In principle the procedure is the same as that described for a traditional radial-scan display in Section 6.2.3.4. In general, raster-scan displays default to one of the preferred orientations when the system is switched on. Although the heading marker normally automatically aligns itself to the input provided by the display compass repeater, the latter must be aligned to the master compass by the observer.

6.4.4 Obtaining the optimum picture

In a raster-scan display the synthetic echoes are generated by threshold detection followed by digital storage

(see Sections 2.6.6.1 and 2.6.6.2) and it is not always possible to judge the settings of the gain and tuning controls by the criteria traditionally used in setting up analogue displays. As a result, the procedure for setting the gain and tuning controls on a raster-scan display is the same as that described for a radial-scan synthetic display in Sections 6.3.4.2 and 6.3.4.3 respectively. Additionally, it should be borne in mind that rotation-to-rotation correlation (see Section 3.6.3.4) tends to eliminate some receiver noise: this facility should be switched off when setting up. It should be remembered that in the raster-scan case the screen contrast (which has a different function from that of the contrast control in a radial-scan display − see Section 2.6.6.5) will have been set at the same time as the screen brilliance. The presence of the digital noise background and a large number of digital echoes may have some slight effect on the overall brightness of the display and may necessitate minor readjustment of screen brilliance and/or screen contrast.

The warning on the limitations of tuning indicators set out in Section 6.2.4.2 is equally valid for raster-scan systems.

6.5 Performance monitoring

As soon as practical after the initial setting-up of the display, the system performance should be monitored. In the case of a shore-based radar system it may be possible to assess the level of performance from a knowledge of the identity of those targets which were at the limit of detection when the system was installed and the performance was tested and optimized by the manufacturer. However, at sea it is usually not possible to discern whether or not the system is giving optimum performance merely by viewing the displayed picture, because the observer does not have exact knowledge of which targets should be seen. Although the picture may look good, the observer cannot be sure that the equipment is operating at the level of performance that was intended by the manufacturer. In the open sea in calm, foggy weather, the absence of echoes, despite the presence of receiver noise, may be due to a loss in performance rather than an empty ocean. Failure to appreciate this fundamental principle could lead to a very dangerous situation. The absence of echoes deprives the observer of the normal criteria by which to judge the setting of the tuning control.

The IMO Performance Standard (see Section 10.2) requires that means be available, while the equipment is in use operationally, to determine readily a significant drop in performance relative to a calibration standard established at the time of installation, and that the equipment is correctly tuned in the absence of targets. This facility is commonly referred to as a *performance monitor*. The sensitive element which makes monitoring possible is usually a unit known as an echo box and is described in the next section. Some modern systems use a device known as a transponder (see Section 6.5.4).

6.5.1   The principle of the echo box

Any normal target which was mounted on the ship to reflect signals for test purposes would be unsatisfactory because, apart from the fact that it would probably be inside minimum detection range (see Section 3.2.4), the strength of the echo would probably be so great as to saturate the receiver even if the performance was well below optimum. The problem is commonly overcome by using what is known as an echo box.

The echo box is essentially a hollow metal container of precisely machined dimensions. In theory a variety of shapes can be used but, in practice, modern systems normally use a cylinder about the size of a small food can. The theory of the operation of the echo box is quite complex but its behaviour can be described in fairly simple terms. When a pulse of radar energy is transmitted into the box, the energy reverberates within the cavity and if, but only if, the cavity is the correct size in relationship to the wavelength of the radar signal, intense oscillations build up over the duration of the pulse length. At the end of the transmitted pulse the oscillations continue but their amplitude gradually decays over a period which is much longer than the duration of the transmitted pulse. As long as the oscillations persist, radar energy is re-radiated from the box. The energy re-radiated from the echo box can be treated in the same way as other returning radar signals and thus

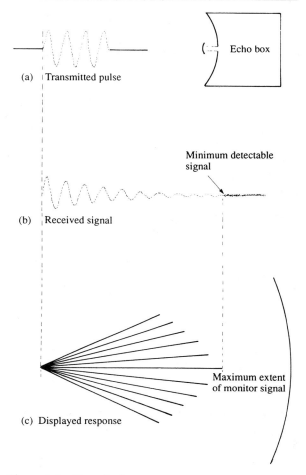

Figure 6.6   The echo box response

produces a visible, radial response on the display which is known as the *performance monitor signal*. This general principle is illustrated by Figure 6.6 but it should be noted that the angular extent of the monitor signal depends on other factors which are discussed in Section 6.5.2. The echo box and its associated circuitry is referred to as a performance monitor.

It may be found helpful to liken the action of the echo box to that of a bell which rings for a long time after being struck by a comparatively swift blow. In fact, engineers often refer to the re-radiation from the box as 'ringing'. (A full explanation of the action of the echo box is beyond the scope of this work, requiring an understanding of the theory of the resonant cavity: the reader who wishes to pursue this is referred to any good radar engineering text.)

Pursuing the analogy of the bell further, the length of time for which a nearby listener hears the bell ringing depends on the vigour with which it has been struck, and the sensitivity of the listener's ear at the frequency emitted by the bell. Applying this reasoning to the echo box, it should be evident that the radial extent of the monitor signal on the display is a measure of the performance of the radar system since it depends on:

1 *The transmitter performance.* The energy entering the echo box is a function of transmitted power and pulse length (see Sections 2.3.2.1 and 2.3.2.2). Thus the greater the amount of transmitted energy, the longer the echo box will ring.
2 *The receiver sensitivity.* The re-radiated signal is capable of detection until its amplitude has decayed to less than that of the receiver noise (see Section 2.5.2.3). Thus the more sensitive the receiver, the greater is the visible extent of the monitor signal (see Figure 6.6).
3 *The receiver tuning.* The frequency re-radiated by the echo box is the same as that of the transmitter and maximum monitor signal depends on the receiver being tuned to the same frequency (see Section 2.5.1.2).
4 *The display control settings.* Maladjustment of the display controls may prevent the observer detecting the full potential extent of the signal emitted by the echo box.

It is evident that if the system is adjusted by the manufacturer to optimum performance on installation (or after a service visit), and the radial extent of the monitor signal is measured at that time, the observer can be supplied with an objective calibration, in terms of miles and cables, against which to judge the performance of the system in the future. In particular this facilitates an assessment of the setting of the tuning control in the absence of echoes. It should be noted that if the echo box is sited external to the radar system, e.g. on some part of the ship's structure, it additionally monitors the aerial and waveguide performance. However, if the echo box is

located within the radar system, as is quite common, it only monitors the transmitter and receiver functions. The implications of echo box siting are discussed further in the next section.

6.5.2 Echo box siting

In older systems it was common for the echo box to be mounted in a blind sector on a mast, Samson post or other part of the ship's structure. Such boxes were large and rectangular in shape with a parabolic reflector to focus the received energy at the entrance to the cavity. They are now really only of historical interest. One of a number of subsequent variations which developed from this was the incorporation of the echo box within the aerial drive unit and the fitting of a horn (see Section 2.4.2.1) with a short length of connecting waveguide below the level of the scanner, as illustrated by Figure 6.7(b).

As the beam sweeps the horn once per revolution, some 10–20 pulses (see Section 2.4.4) will energize the horn and be conveyed down the waveguide to the echo box. This approach, like all external sitings, has the virtue that the length of the monitor signal is a measure of aerial and waveguide performance in addition to that of the transmitter and receiver. Such an echo box and its associated circuitry can justifiably be referred to as an *overall performance monitor* because it monitors the performance of all units of the system. The principal drawback of an external echo box is the general expense of producing such a unit (in particular the cost of making it suitable for above-deck fitting) and the problems which result if water does penetrate the system. The monitor can be switched on and off by means of an attenuator which effectively blocks the short length of waveguide when the signal is not required. Because external echo boxes are only energized as the radar beam sweeps across them, they produce a monitor signal which has a limited angular width the form of which is illustrated in Figure 6.7(c). This form is commonly described as a *plume.*

Many systems site the echo box on the waveguide just on the aerial side of the T/R cell (see Section 2.2.3) as illustrated in Figure 6.7(a). This dispenses with the need

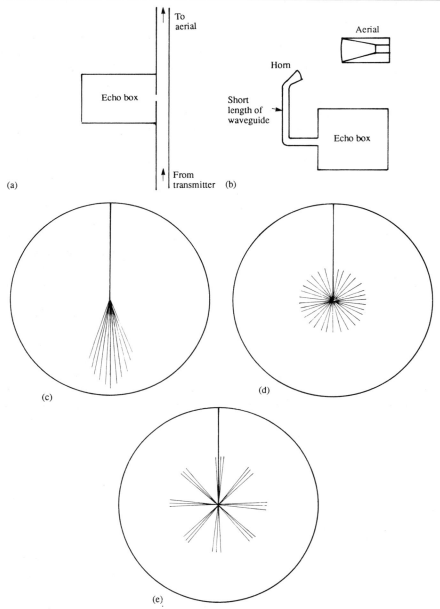

Figure 6.7   Echo box siting and the performance monitor signals
(a)   Echo box located on waveguide between transmitter and aerial
(b)   Echo box located below aerial
(c)   'Plume' from external echo box
(d)   'Sun pattern' from internal fixed-tune echo box
(e)   'Multi-plume' from internal echo box with oscillating plunger

to make the unit suitable for above-deck mounting and allows the unit to be more compact and less expensive. However, it does have the serious shortcoming that it does not monitor aerial or waveguide performance. If the echo box is sited in this position it forms, with the associated circuitry, a *transceiver monitor* and to comply with the IMO Performance Standards this must be supplemented by some arrangement which monitors the radiation from the antenna. Such an arrangement is normally referred to as a *power* or *output monitor* (see Section 6.5.3).

In the transceiver monitor the cavity is cylindrical and its size can be varied by adjusting a plunger. This allows service personnel to tune the cavity (i.e. make the cavity the correct size) so that it will ring at the magnetron frequency. The monitor can be switched on or off from the display position by means of some form of electromechanical control which de-tunes the cavity when the monitor signal is not required. Because the echo box is located on the waveguide, the response is not sensitive to aerial direction and hence the monitor signal extends for the full 360° of azimuth. The resulting pattern is sometimes referred to as a *sun* and is illustrated in Figure 6.7(d). Some observers might have a natural reluctance to switch on a monitor which produced such an extensive pattern. It is also sometimes argued that it is more difficult to discern the extent of a sun pattern than that of a plume, in which the contrast on either side assists in identifying the pattern. Some manufacturers break up the sun pattern as shown in Figure 6.7(e) by driving the tuning plunger in and out of the cavity. The echo box rings each time the plunger passes the tuned position, producing a 'family' of plumes which rotate at a speed governed by the relationship between the periods of the plunger oscillation and that of the aerial rotation. A plunger which makes a single sweep of the cavity and is triggered once per scan by the antenna as it rotates will produce a plume.

6.5.3   Power monitors

Where a transceiver monitor is fitted, the performance of the system is only monitored as far as the location of the echo box. Thus the presence on the display of a monitor signal of the specified length is no guarantee of optimum radiation from the aerial, which may be reduced by a variety of causes such as puncture or distortion damage to the waveguide, the presence of moisture or dirt in the waveguide space, damage to the antenna or the accretion of dirt or ice on the GRP envelope which protects the antenna.

The sensitive element commonly used in power monitors is a neon tube – a glass envelope which is filled with the inert gas neon and contains two separate metal electrodes. Neon gas has the particular property that it normally behaves as an insulator but, if it is subjected to an adequate level of radio frequency radiation, the gas is ionized and behaves as a conductor. Thus, within the tube, in the quiescent condition the electrodes are insulated from one another, whereas, when the gas ionizes in the irradiated state, the electrodes are effectively connected by a conducting medium. The neon tube is mounted close to the scanner so that radiated energy from the beam falls on it at each revolution. The tube is connected in series with some circuitry which produces a visual indication at the display position. In the absence of adequate radiation the de-ionized neon will interrupt the circuitry and give a visual indication of an absence of power. If the output power from the aerial is adequate, the ionized neon will complete the circuitry with a low-resistance path, giving a visual indication of the presence of radiation at the aerial output. (The particular feature of the neon tube is that the ionization level can be fixed very precisely.

The form of visual indication employed can vary considerably with manufacturer. It may take the form of a simple light which is illuminated when adequate power is present, or the signal from the neon may be used to indicate the output power by the deflection of a meter. The meter scale may well have a red arc or some other feature to give an indication of an unacceptably low output power level. In both cases it is likely that the indication will be smoothed over a period of one aerial revolution, otherwise the light or meter reading would fluctuate as the beam swept across the neon sensor. Some systems have used the signal detected by the neon to produce on the display a plume whose radial length represents the level of output power.

6.5.4 Transponder performance monitors

The sensitive unit of this modern type of performance monitor is an active (as opposed to passive) element known as a transponder, which is located on the aerial drive unit in such a way that it is irradiated by the beam as it sweeps past. The transponder reacts to reception of the radio frequency pulses by transmitting, after a short delay, a low-level coded response at the same frequency. A threshold set within the active element ensures that the response will only be given if the received signal is above a power level determined by the manufacturer.

The power level within the limits of the horizontal beam of the radar system falls off on either side of the axis. Thus, as the beam sweeps past the transponder, the latter responds over an arc bounded by the limits at which the radiated power is above the preset level. The transponder is thus a monitor of transmitted power.

The response returned to the aerial is treated as any other received signal and thus the ability to receive the

response is a measure of receiver response. The response is displayed in the form of a series of arcs (see Figure 6.8), the angular limits of which are a measure of performance.

The angular limits are measured by the manufacturer when the performance is known to be optimum and supplied as a calibration level against which performance can be judged.

6.5.5 Calibration levels

Given the wide variety of purely arbitrary ways in which the monitor information may be displayed, and considering, in particular that, for example, one manufacturer may use a plume as an indicator of output power whereas another may use it as a transceiver monitor signal, it should be evident that it is essential to study the operator's manual to establish which signal or indicator to observe and to appreciate precisely what it measures.

The calibration levels should be measured by the manufacturer when the performance of the system is known to be optimum. In the case of a sun or plume pattern, such measurement will be made in miles and cables. The following information should be shown on a tally close to the display:

1 The length of the signal (or status of indicator) consistent with optimum performance.
2 The length of the signal (or status of indicator) corresponding to a significant drop in performance.

If the overall performance is not monitored by a single signal or indicator, the values for both transceiver and power monitors should be shown separately and unambiguously.

6.5.6 Performance check procedure

It must be remembered that the length of the monitor signals (or the status of other indicators) is influenced by the position in which the operational controls have been set. When carrying out a performance check it is vital that controls are set as instructed in the maker's manual – otherwise comparison with the calibration level is meaningless.

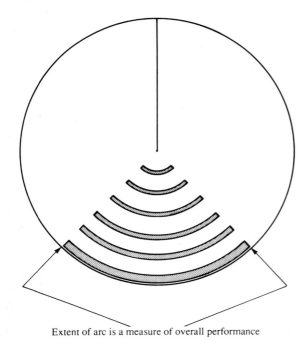

Extent of arc is a measure of overall performance

Figure 6.8 Transponder monitor signal

It cannot be stressed too strongly that the way in which the performance signals are displayed, and the extent to which they monitor the performance, vary considerably from manufacturer to manufacturer and even with different types made by the same company. Thus the important basic rule for carrying out a performance check is: *Consult the maker's manual and follow exactly the instructions given therein.*

A performance check should be carried out as soon as practicable after setting up and thereafter at regular intervals. In the United Kingdom the Department of Transport in Notice M1158 (see Section 10.5) recommends that a check should be carried out before sailing and at least every four hours when a radar watch is kept. This should be regarded as a minimum.

6.6   Change of range scale and/or pulse length

During normal operation of the radar system it will be necessary for a variety of reasons to change range scale from time to time. For example, having considered factors such as traffic density, speed of the observing vessel and the frequency of observation, a suitable range scale may have been selected on which to carry out radar plotting (see Section 7.2.4) but it may be necessary to change to a longer range scale at intervals in order to fix the vessel's position or to obtain early warning of approaching vessels. When using the radar for position-fixing or progress-monitoring it may be necessary to change scale in order to maximize the available accuracy of range and bearing measurement (see Sections 6.9.8 and 6.9.9). From time to time during general observation it may be necessary to select a suitable scale on which to search for targets among sea clutter returns. Many other circumstances will arise in which the range scale selected for some aspects of watchkeeping is not suitable for others. Intelligent use must thus be made of the range scale selector.

A change of range scale may be associated with a change in pulse length and some pulse lengths may not be available on all range scales (see Section 2.3.4).

Change of pulse length may be necessary for a variety of reasons such as the need to improve range discrimination, minimum range, detection in sea clutter, long-range detection and detection in and beyond areas of rain (see Sections 2.6.5.5, 3.2.4, 3.6, 2.5.2.4, and 3.7 respectively).

In analogue displays, particularly in older systems, it may be found that the *no signal* brilliance level alters with change of range scale and also with change of pulse length. In the case of change of range scale this occurs because in a real-time display the spot speed alters (see Section 2.6.1.3). For example, when changing to a shorter range scale, the spot will travel faster, the time for which it dwells on each element of the phosphor will become shorter and the perceived brightness of the trace will decrease. Because the setting of the gain also contributes to the overall *brightness* of the picture, it is difficult to detect and compensate for this change. The correct procedure for ensuring that optimum picture is maintained is as follows:

1 Turn down the gain. This reduces the problems of the afterglow generated by the previous picture but, more importantly, allows the brilliance level to be observed.
2 Change the range scale and/or pulse length.
3 Reset the brilliance control if necessary.
4 Restore the gain.

In a modern radial-scan display with a fixed timebase (see Sections 1.2.5 and 2.6.6.5) the problem should not arise in theory, but it is prudent to check that this is in fact the case.

In a raster-scan display the screen brilliance is independent of range scale selection. It may however be found that, if a change of range scale produces a large change in the distribution of the picture content, slight adjustment of the screen brilliance may make viewing more comfortable. For example, if a change is made from a very long range scale, where the clutter pattern (see Section 3.6.1.2) is a tiny bright area around the origin, to a very short range scale, where the bright clutter pattern covers most of the screen area, the overall brightness of the picture may appear to increase and comfort may dictate a slight decrease in the screen brilliance setting accompanied possibly by a small contrast adjustment.

6.7   The stand-by condition

As indicated in Section 6.2.2, the IMO Performance Standards require that such a condition be available.

The detailed nature of the stand-by condition will vary with manufacturer, but in all cases transmission is inhibited. Thus, although the radar is virtually ready for immediate use, limited-life components in the transmitter are not operational. A further, more general benefit is that the amount of radar-to-radar interference (see Section 3.9.5) experienced by other vessels (which may need to operate their radar systems) will be reduced over a potentially large geographical area. The life of components and hence the reliability of the radar system will be far less affected by continuous running than by frequent switching on and off, so that in periods of uncertain visibility it is better to leave the radar in full operation or in the stand-by condition.

Rule 7(b) of the Collision Regulations requires that 'proper use shall be made of radar equipment if fitted and operational'. There are many occasions on which *proper use* means continuous running. However, there are other occasions, for example in the open sea on a clear day with fog forecast, when the stand-by condition constitutes proper use. Thus, compliance with the letter and spirit of the rule is ensured as there is no excessive delay should the equipment be required quickly yet there is no unnecessary transmission in the meantime.

If the equipment is to be left on stand-by, the controls may be left in the optimum position, but the settings, particularly that of the tuning control, should be checked immediately on returning to the operational condition.

If the equipment is likely to be on stand-by for a long period, it is probably better in the case of a radial-scan display to set the controls listed in the setting-up procedure (see Section 6.2.1 and 6.3.1) to minimum effect and set up immediately on returning to the operational condition. Under the same circumstances in the case of a raster-scan display the gain, sea clutter and rain clutter controls should be set to minimum effect and all signal-processing facilities should be switched off, all being subsequently reset on returning to the operational condition.

6.8   Setting up the display for a true-motion picture presentation

The basic quantities measured by a marine radar system are range and bearing and, as a consequence, the system inherently produces a relative-motion presentation (see Section 1.5.1). To generate a true-motion presentation additional circuitry and controls must be fitted to the display (see Section 2.6.4). In many systems the additional circuitry and controls form a discrete module which can be added directly to an existing relative-motion display. A fundamental principle of the true-motion presentation is that the displayed information is only as true as the input data from which it is generated. It is of critical importance that the correct procedure should be followed both for the setting-up of the true-motion presentation and for the monitoring of its accuracy.

6.8.1   The controls

The format of the true-motion control panel and the precise nature of the individual controls vary somewhat with manufacturer but the underlying principles are the same for all systems. In the following sections the controls are described in general terms, with some indication of the variations in detail that may be encountered in practice. Subsequent sections set out the practical procedures for setting up sea-stabilized and ground-stabilized true-motion presentations.

6.8.1.1   *The presentation selector*

This may take the simple form of a two-position switch offering the choice between relative-motion and true-motion. In most systems it will be found that it is not possible to select true-motion on very long or very short range scales. On very long range scales echo movement is so slow as to be barely perceptible, whereas on very short scales the movement of the origin will be so rapid as to require resetting (see Section 6.8.1.4) at unacceptably short intervals.

In some systems the presentation selector may be combined with the orientation selector and might, for example, offer the observer the choice of some or all of the following options:

- Ship's-head-up relative-motion.
- True-north-up relative-motion.
- Course-up relative-motion.
- True-north-up true-motion.
- Course-up true-motion.

6.8.1.2   The compass repeater

The compass repeater determines the direction in which the origin will track (see Section 2.6.4.2). With very few exceptions the repeater merely reproduces *changes* in the heading detected by the master gyro and has no inherent sense of absolute direction. It is vital that the repeater is correctly aligned to the vessel's true course because, if it is not, the origin will track in the wrong direction, causing all the displayed tracks to be in error, and may dangerously mislead the observer (see Section 7.10.2).

The compass repeater normally takes the form of a conventional circular compass card or a three-digit readout, though in some older systems no card was provided and the repeater was aligned by rotating the heading marker to the appropriate graduation on the circular bearing scale around the PPI.

6.8.1.3   The speed input

Normally two controls are provided. One control, the input speed selector, enables the observer to choose the input either of a signal from the ship's log or of an artificial log signal generated within the radar display (see Section 2.6.4.3). The artificial log position is sometimes referred to as *manual speed*. The second control is used to set the speed generated by the artificial log.

The input speed selector is commonly a two-position switch, though in some cases it has a third position labelled *zero speed*. The use of this third position is described in Section 6.8.1.5. Alternatively, all three

functions can be combined in a single rotary control similar to that used to combine the on/off and volume functions on a domestic radio. In the *off* position ship's log is selected, the *on* position at zero gives the zero speed function, and advancing the control gives a continuously variable manual speed setting.

As in the case of the course input, it is vital that the correct value of speed is fed in, otherwise all the displayed tracks will be in error and may dangerously mislead the observer (see Section 7.10.3).

Most shipboard logs measure speed through the water and will thus, if selected, produce a sea-stabilized presentation. The doppler log is an exception to this rule. Where a doppler log is used to provide the speed input, particular care must be taken to establish the answers to the following questions:

1 Is the log measuring speed through the water or speed over the ground?
2 Is the log a single-axis or a dual-axis type?

Most doppler logs can be set to operate either on signals returned from the water mass or on signals returned from the ground. These two options are commonly referred to as *water lock* and *ground lock*, respectively. In very shallow water it will only be possible to obtain ground lock, while in very deep water only water lock will be possible.

A single-axis doppler log uses one transducer which measures fore-and-aft movement only. If the log is ground locked and the vessel is experiencing a tide having an athwartships component, the reading will be neither the speed through the water nor the speed over the ground (see paragraph 3 below).

A dual-axis doppler log has a second transducer which additionally measures athwartships movement. The output from the dual-axis doppler log can be in the form of the individual velocity components or their resultant. Some radar displays are designed to accept both a fore-and-aft input and an athwartships input and to cause the origin to track in sympathy with the resultant of both, whereas others will only accept a single input. The possible effects on the true-motion tracking of these various options are illustrated by Figure 6.9 (see also Section 7.9.3) and can be analysed by considering the following three possible cases:

1 If the doppler log is correctly water locked the input speed to the true-motion computer will represent the speed through the water whether it is a single-axis or a dual-axis log and irrespective of whether the radar display is designed to accept single-axis or dual-axis inputs (assuming that leeway can be neglected). The effect of this input will be to produce a sea-stabilized presentation.

2 If the doppler log is correctly ground locked, and the radar display is designed to accept a dual-axis input, the resultant input to the true-motion unit will represent the vessel's speed over the ground. The effect of this will be to produce a ground-stabilized presentation. Attention is drawn to the danger of using this presentation when planning collision avoidance strategy (see Section 1.5.2.2).

3 If the doppler log is ground locked, and it is of the single-axis type and/or the radar display is designed to accept a single-axis input only, the speed fed to the true-motion computer will be neither the vessel's speed over the ground nor the vessel's speed through the water: it will be the vessel's speed through the water plus that component of the tide which lies in the direction of the vessel's course (see Figure 6.9). The effect will be to produce an erroneous presentation which is neither sea-stabilized nor ground-stabilized. Such a presentation will be highly misleading and could lead to the development of a dangerous situation. The effect of errors on the true-motion presentation is discussed in Section 7.10.

It is evident that, where a doppler log is used, great care must be taken to establish the nature of the input to the true-motion computer. Failure to do so may result in inadvertent use of the ground-stabilized presentation or the use of a presentation with an inherent error in the speed input.

In some older systems a provision was made for using the propeller revolutions as a speed input. Errors can arise when using this source, as particularly in large vessels, there will be a finite time delay between a change in revolutions and the consequent change in the ship's speed through the water. Additionally, an allowance must be made for propeller slip, of which the value may vary significantly with weather and condition of loading. Particular problems will arise where variable-pitch propellers and/or twin screws are fitted.

6.8.1.4   The reset controls

As the origin tracks across the screen, the view ahead decreases and from time to time it will be necessary to reset the position of the origin.

In some systems the reset controls function in the same manner as shift controls (see Sections 2.6.1.3 and 2.6.4), producing N/S and E/W movement of the origin. Analogue reset controls normally operate in association with a clutch mechanism similar to that used when aligning a gyro repeater (see Section 6.2.3.4). When the origin is tracking they have no effect and turn freely, but when the control is pushed in against the action of a spring, a clutch disengages the drive from the true-motion computer and allows the observer to move the origin anywhere within a fairly large circular limit which must not exceed 75 per cent of the radius from the centre of the screen (see IMO Performance Standard in Section 10.2). In more modern synthetic displays, where the display functions are computer controlled under the

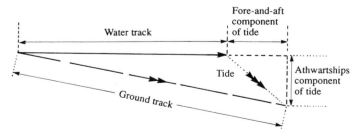

Figure 6.9   The use of a doppler log as speed input for true motion

direction of the observer, the equivalent action is achieved by holding in a push-button type control and *steering* the origin to the desired reset position by means of a joystick or tracker ball (see Figure 6.15).

An alternative approach is to offer the resetting facility in terms of direction and radius from the centre of the PPI. Where analogue controls are provided they will normally take the form of a rotary control with which to choose the direction and a second similar control for the radius. A third control of a push-button type will, when pressed, reset the origin in the chosen direction and at the chosen radius from the centre of the PPI. In modern synthetic displays a joystick or roller ball is used to place a graphics marker at the position within the circular resetting area to which it is desired to reset the origin. On pressing a reset button, the origin is reset to the screen co-ordinates of the joystick (or tracker ball) marker. A variation on this approach is to have two push-button controls, one of which performs the function already described. The second button, when pressed, resets the origin on the reciprocal of the observing vessel's course at the maximum permitted radius, thus seeking to make the best possible use of the screen area ahead (see Section 6.8.2).

If the observer fails to reset the origin and allows it to approach the outer extent of the tracking limit, the display will produce some form of automatic response. One approach is to illuminate a *reset warning* indicator supplemented by an audible warning. If this warning is ignored the origin will be stopped at the outer limit and the reset warning replaced by a *relative-motion warning*. There may be some provision to allow the observer to override this action manually in order to maintain observation of a developing situation but it has to be said that good practice dictates that an early and suitable occasion should be found to reset the origin to avoid being trapped in this dilemma. An alternative approach is that the display resets the origin automatically if the tracking limit is exceeded. This facility is usually associated with resetting that is based on direction and radius and in a computer-based system the reset position is likely to lie on the reciprocal of the vessel's course at the tracking limit. In similar displays with analogue controls it is more likely to be determined by the direction and radius to which the reset controls were last set.

In some systems automatic resetting takes place when a new range scale is selected. This function is not necessarily beneficial: it will disrupt manual tracking of echoes on a reflection plotter and may inhibit the observer from reducing range scale at the proper time (see Section 6.6).

6.8.1.5 The zero-speed control

Most systems have some provision for setting the origin speed to zero while true-motion is selected. Commonly it takes the form of a two-position switch. In one position (the ship's-speed position) it has no effect but in the other (the zero-speed position) it isolates the speed input to the true-motion computer. Alternatively it may be combined with the manual/log speed selector in the form of a three-position switch. This may seem a rather odd provision, since the whole point of the traditional true-motion display is to produce a moving origin. However, the reason for making this facility available can be understood by considering the complementary nature of the true-motion and relative-motion presentations (see Sections 1.5.1 and 1.5.2).

The sea-stabilized true-motion presentation gives direct indication of target heading but does not give a similar indication of CPA, whereas the relative-motion presentation gives that quantity directly. The operation of the zero speed control allows the observer to stop the origin temporarily and hence produce relative-motion tracks for a period of sufficient length to make it possible to assess the CPA of chosen targets. Having established this information, the observer can then restore the speed input on the basis that the assessed CPAs will be fulfilled provided that the targets do not manoeuvre. The true-motion presentation will give immediate indication should such manoeuvres occur and thus warn the observer of the need to re-assess the situation.

The zero-speed control must be used with extreme caution as there is always an inherent danger of mistakes being made when true and relative tracks are displayed on the same screen. For example, members of the bridge team, other than the observer who has operated the control, might mistake the consequent change in tracks for manoeuvres by target vessels. Conversely, the change in tracks may mask a change produced by the real manoeuvre of a target. If the facility is to be used, bridge organization must ensure that all team members understand an agreed procedure for the use of the control and that an appropriate convention is adopted in marking the reflection plot (e.g. by using a different colour or symbol) in order to ensure obvious differentiation between relative tracks and true tracks. The symbols used to indicate true-motion (plane arrow) and relative-motion (arrow in a circle) in the description of radar plotting in Section 7.2.3 would serve this purpose.

Ideally, the complementary nature of the true-motion and relative-motion presentations is best exploited by the use of two separate displays. The zero-speed function undoubtedly makes it possible to obtain true-motion and relative-motion from a *single* radar display but it has to be said that appraisal aids which use threat assessment markers (see Section 7.11.2) perform this function more effectively and with less possibility of confusion between relative and true tracks.

The zero-speed control may be labelled as such but other names used include *hold* and *check*. Even if a specific control is not fitted the technique can always be used by selecting manual speed and setting the speed to zero. A convenient method of achieving this involves using the true-motion presentation with a log speed input while leaving the manual speed setting permanently at zero. When the zero-speed facility is required it is merely necessary to select manual speed.

An alternative use of the zero-speed control is to achieve an *off-centred* relative-motion display. In many systems, when relative-motion is selected the origin can only be off-centred by the small scope allowed by the shift controls (see Section 2.6.1.3). However, by selecting the true-motion presentation it is possible to use the resetting arrangements to off-centre the display by a large amount and hence to extend the view ahead, albeit at the expense of the view astern. A possible extension of the off-centre presentation is to use the zero-speed technique for collision avoidance in the reverse sense to that already described in this section. In this way a relative-motion display is maintained but, from time to time, the zero-speed switch is set to the ship's-speed position, allowing the observer temporarily to view the true tracks of the targets.

In some systems such an off-centre presentation is actually available directly as one of the options offered

by the orientation/presentation selector (see Section 6.8.1.1.) without the need to achieve it by selecting true motion.

6.8.1.6   Tidal controls

Where the option to ground-stabilize the true-motion presentation is offered (see Section 1.5.2.2), additional controls are necessary to allow input of the observer's estimate of the set and rate of the tide (see also Section 2.6.4.4).

In many systems the tidal inputs simply take the form of two rotary controls. One control is adjusted on a 0°/360° scale to feed in the observer's estimate of the tidal set being experienced, while the other is set on a scale of knots, facilitating input of the estimated rate of the tidal stream. The origin of the display tracks along the resultant of the vector which represents the observing vessel's course and speed through the water and the vector which respresents the set and rate of the tidal stream. On some systems an additional three-position switch is provided to allow the observer to choose to have the selected rate of tide applied in the direction of the set control (as described above) or always ahead (contrary tide) or always astern (following tide). The two additional positions might be found useful in successive straight reaches of a winding river or channel where the true direction of the tide will vary from reach to reach but will always be in the direction of the reach. It must be appreciated that this assumes that the vessel maintains its heading parallel to the stream and takes no account of the inevitable cross component of tide on the bends.

In an alternative approach, the tidal set and drift are applied indirectly in terms of the difference between the observing vessel's course and speed through the water and that over the ground. The underlying principle is described in Section 2.6.4.4. The relevant controls are the *course-made-good* correction and the *manual speed* (see Section 6.8.1.3). The course-made-good correction control adjusts the angle by which the direction in which the origin tracks differs (to port or starboard) from the observing vessel's heading. The manual speed control is set to the ground speed rather than water speed. As a result, the origin tracks in a direction and at a rate which corresponds with the vessel's track over the ground.

In certain systems ground-stabilization can also be provided by the input of course and speed data from a dual-axis doppler log (see Section 6.8.1.3). Where the radar display forms an integral part of an Automatic Radar Plotting Aid, the tracking computer can be used to produce automatic ground-stabilization of the picture (see Section 5.3).

Irrespective of the source of the method used to obtain ground-stabilization, it must be remembered that ground-stabilized tracks do not indicate the headings of other moving vessels (see Section 1.5.2.2). Failure to appreciate this may result in the observer being dangerously misled in the planning of collision avoidance strategy.

6.8.2   Setting up a sea-stabilized presentation

1 Ensure that the optimum picture has been obtained as described in Section 6.2, 6.3 or 6.4 as appropriate to the type of display.
2 Check that the display is correctly orientated and azimuth-stabilized (see Section 6.2.3.4).
3 Select true-motion presentation.
4 Select log or manual speed input. Check that the log is reading the correct water speed (see Section 6.8.1.3) or that the manual speed control has been set to that value.
5 Adjust the reset controls so that the origin is placed to avoid the necesssity of frequent resetting by making the best possible use of the screen area, bearing in mind possible forthcoming manoeuvres.
6 Commence systematic plotting of the origin on the reflection plotter (see Section 7.10) to ensure that it tracks in the correct direction and at the correct rate. Such plotting will not be possible where the display is of the raster-scan type. In such cases the synthetic afterglow trails (see Section 2.6.7.5) should be selected. Check that the trail left by the observing vessel is consistent with the vessel's course and that the length of the trail, which is generated for a fixed time, is consistent with the vessel's water speed. The length of the trail can be measured with the variable range marker (see Section 6.9.2).
Remember that the true-motion presentation is only as true

as the course and speed information being supplied to it – in this case the course and speed through the water.

7 Be vigilant for loss of *view ahead* as the origin moves across the screen. Anticipate a suitable opportunity to reset the origin.
8 Reset the origin at an appropriate time and resume monitoring the tracking of the origin by reference to the reflection plot or synthetic afterglow.
9 It should be borne in mind that an underlying assumption of the true-motion presentation is that the target vessel is heading in the same direction as she is moving through the water. A vessel making leeway would not fulfil this condition. In many cases this does not present a serious problem since frequently the poor visibility associated with fog arises in calm conditions or with light winds. However, this is not always the case. Further, visibility may be severely restricted by precipitation accompanied by strong winds. In such circumstances due account must be taken of the possible disparity which may exist between the heading and water track of the target vessel.

It is important to appreciate that the problem is not peculiar to the true-motion presentation. Headings, whether calculated by manual resolution from the traditional relative plot (see Section 7.2) or derived by the most modern automatic tracking techniques (see Section 4.3.6), may be subject to the same disparity.

6.8.3   Setting up a ground-stabilized presentation

1 Correctly sea-stabilize the display.
2 Plot an isolated ground-stationary target on the reflection plotter (see Section 7.8.4) and deduce the set and rate of the tide. The ground-stationary target will move at a rate equal to that of the tide but in the reciprocal direction (see Section 1.5.2.2). In the case of a raster-scan display, the length and direction of the synthetic afterglow of the ground-stationary target should be measured using the *free* electronic bearing line and variable range marker (see Section 6.9.6).
3 Where set and drift controls are provided (see Section 6.8.1.6), adjust them to the values deduced in step 2.

4 Where direct tidal inputs are not supplied (see Sections 2.6.4.4 and 6.8.1.6), use the known values of the observing vessel's course and speed together with the set and drift established in step 2 to construct a vector triangle, the third side of which is the observing vessel's track over the ground. Figure 6.9 includes an example of such a triangle. The construction can be carried out on the reflection plotter by transferring the plot of the set and drift through the end of the plot used to monitor the tracking of the origin, assuming that the latter is correct. Alternatively, the construction may be carried out on a chart, plain paper or squared paper as convenient.

From the vector triangle establish the course-made-good correction and the ground speed. Set the course-made-good correction to the appropriate value, remembering the convention that *a starboard correction is applied if the ground track lies to starboard of the water track*. Select manual speed input and set the manual speed to the ground speed value.

5 Continue systematic monitoring of the ground-stationary target to ensure that it maintains its position as plotted on the reflection plotter. Re-adjust the tidal inputs if necessary to remove any residual movement.

In the case of direct tidal inputs the residual movement represents the reciprocal of the difference between the input and actual tide values and the observer must visualize this when deciding how to modify the tidal controls. In the case of a course-made-good input it is somewhat easier to decide how to modify the setting, as any athwartships movement of the echo of the ground-stationary target can be substantially removed with the course-made-good correction and any fore-and-aft movement substantially removed by adjustment of the manual speed control. The use of indirect inputs suffers from the disadvantage that the values change when the observing vessel alters course. In all cases it must be borne in mind that the tide, and thus the appropriate settings for the controls, will vary with the passage of time and with the position of the vessel. In estuarial conditions it is possible that the vessels observed may be experiencing a set and drift which are different from those experienced by the observing vessel.

6 Continue systematic plotting of the origin or observation of the artificial afterglow of the origin, as this is the only really obvious indication that the display is ground-stabilized. In observing any true-motion display, be wary of the case in which the tide is fore-and-aft as there will be no indication from the direction of the trail of the observing vessel.

7 As an alternative to the use of tidal input controls, the presentation can be ground-stabilized by the inputs from a dual-axis ground locked doppler log as described in Section 6.8.1.3.

6.9 Controls for range and bearing measurement

A wide range of facilities are provided to enable the observer to measure the range and bearing of targets. Some arrangements measure range and bearing while others measure one quantity or the other. In older systems the facilities are associated with rotary controls and mechanical scales, whereas more modern equipments employ a joystick/tracker ball and graphic read-out. There is considerable variation in the precise detail of facilities provided by different manufacturers but the principle is essentially the same in each case.

6.9.1 Fixed range rings

The IMO Performance Standard requires that fixed rings should be provided. The number of rings required depends on the range scale selected; a detailed schedule is set out in the standard (see Sections 10.2.1 paragraph 2(d) and Section 10.2.2 paragraph 3.4). There is also a requirement that the range scale displayed and the interval between the range rings should be clearly indicated at all times.

The fixed range rings take the form of a pattern of equally spaced circles concentric with the electronic origin of the picture. The pattern is generated by subdividing the timebase into equal intervals of time and rotating the trace through 360° as described in Sections 1.2.4 and 1.3.3. In a radial-scan display the rings should appear as perfect circles because all elements of a ring will be displayed at the same distance from the origin.

In a raster-scan display, a slight 'staircase' effect may be noticed due to the quantizing effect of scan conversion (see Sections 2.6.7.2 and 2.6.7.3). The effect will be most noticeable close to bearings of 0° and 180°, because in that area the circumference of the circle runs parallel or nearly parallel to the raster lines and will be exacerbated at lower line standards. The effect may offend the eye of the observer who is accustomed to the perfect circles of a radial-scan display, but it should be appreciated that it does not in itself represent a ranging error. This can be understood from consideration of the fact that a circular stretch of coastline at the range represented by the ring would have the same steps due to quantizing.

In a radial-scan display a facility will be provided to switch the rings on/off and to adjust their brilliance. This may take the form of a single control or two separate controls. The brilliance of the rings should be adjusted to obtain the finest possible line. Excessive brilliance will make the rings thick and fuzzy, thus making accurate range measurement more difficult. There also exists the risk that a weak target will be obscured.

The IMO Performance Standards require that the fixed range rings should enable the range of an object to be measured with an error not exceeding 1.5 per cent of the maximum range of the scale in use or 70 metres, whichever is greater. Thus, when using the range rings to measure the range of a target, the most open range scale appropriate should be selected so as to maximize the inherent accuracy of the measurement.

The measurement of range should be taken to the nearer edge of the echo, as this represents the leading edge of the returned echo. Time measurement commences at the leading edge of the transmitted pulse and thus elapsed time must be measured to the same reference on the received pulse (see Figure 2.4). It must be appreciated that the leading edge of the echo represents the range of the nearest *detectable* facet of the target and not necessarily the nearest part of the target (for example, possibly the bridge rather than the bow of a ship approaching head-on).

The circuitry which produces the range rings is simple, reliable and can be set up by service personnel with suitable test equipment to a high degree of accuracy.

The only situation in which an observer can fix the vessel's position with a sufficient degree of precision to be able to check the accuracy of the rings is when the vessel is alongside a berth (developments in the satellite position-fixing accuracy available for civil marine applications may one day invalidate this statement). It is possible for an observer to check the accuracy of the rings by observing the echo of an known small, isolated and steep-sided target when secure in a known charted position.

The range rings are highly suited to the measurement of the range of a target which lies on a ring and there may well be situations in which it is convenient to measure the range of a target as it crosses a ring. In general it will be necessary to interpolate between the rings and this is best done with the aid of the variable range marker (see Section 6.9.2).

If the decision is taken to interpolate by eye, a visual check should be made to ensure that the rings are equally spaced. A fault condition known as a *non-linear timebase* can develop in radial-scan displays, particularly in older systems. In this condition the spot does not travel at constant speed and as a result the ring spacing is cramped toward the origin (if the spot is accelerating) or toward the edge of the display (if the spot is slowing down). The ranges of targets whose echoes fall on a ring will not be affected (because both ring and displayed echo are affected by the same amount). However, a target which lies midway between two rings will have a range which does *not* lie midway between the ranges represented by the two rings. Thus linear interpolation between the rings is not possible. This is illustrated by Figure 6.10 for the case of the spot accelerating.

If this fault is noticed there is no need to switch off the set, as use of the variable range marker will give the necessary non-linear interpolation between the rings (see Figure 6.10). However, steps should be taken to have the fault corrected by qualified service personnel as soon as possible because the picture and the movement of echoes will be distorted (see Section 7.10.4).

There is inevitably a small amount of non-linearity at the beginning of each trace as the spot accelerates from the rest position (see Section 1.2.3), though in some systems arrangements have been made to start the spot a little early and a little before the origin to avoid this.

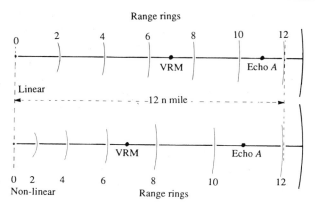

Figure 6.10 Timebase non-linearity
VRM set to 7 miles: on non-linear timebase it appears closer to the 6 mile ring than the 8 mile ring
Echo *A* has a correct range 11 miles: on a non-linear time base it appears closer to the 10 mile ring than the 12 mile ring

Non-linearity should seldom, if ever occur, on a good quality, well set up raster-scan display. If it does, the direction of the distortion will depend on whether it occurs in the horizontal or vertical timebase. In either case visual interpolation should be avoided and the fault attended to as soon as possible.

The factors affecting the inherent accuracy of range measurement and the procedure for ensuring that this accuracy is realized are summarized in Section 6.9.8.

6.9.2 Variable range marker (VRM)

The IMO Performance Standards (see Section 10.2) require that an electronic range marker with a numerical read-out of range be provided. It also requires that arrangements are made so that it is possible to vary the brilliance of the marker and to remove it completely from the screen and such arrangements will in general be similar to those described for the fixed rings in Section 6.9.1. The accuracy requirement, i.e. 1.5 per cent of the maximum range of the scale in use or 70 metres (whichever is greater) is also the same as that required for the fixed range rings.

The VRM is a variable-radius ring generated at a selected elapsed time after the instant of trigger as

described in Section 1.2.4. The elapsed time, and hence the radius of the ring, can be varied by the observer over a continuous set of values from zero to the limit of the maximum range scale. The radius of the VRM may be set by a rotary control which also drives a mechanical three or four digit scale. In more modern systems *increase* and *decrease* push-button controls (see Section 6.3.2) or a joy stick/tracker ball may be employed (see Section 6.9.7) and the read-out may form part of the graphics on a raster-scan display.

In the raster-scan case, the VRM will be similarly liable to exhibit the staircase effect described for the fixed range rings in Section 6.9.1.

Although the electronic circuitry which generates the VRM is simple and reliable, errors can frequently arise due to its association with controls, scales and read-outs which are of a mechanical nature. For this reason it is essential to check the accuracy of the VRM regularly by placing it over a ring and comparing the read-out value with that of the ring. To maximize the inherent accuracy of any range measurement made with the VRM, the most open range scale appropriate should be selected. The VRM brilliance should be adjusted to obtain the finest possible line and the range should be taken to the nearer edge of the echo (see also Section 6.9.1).

The factors affecting the inherent accuracy of range measurement and the practical procedure for ensuring that this accuracy is realized are summarized in Section 6.9.8.

6.9.3 The Perspex cursor

The IMO Performance Standards (see Section 10.2) require that provision be made to obtain quickly the bearing of any object whose echo appears on the display. On radial-scan displays, the Perspex cursor offers a simple mechanical means of satisfying this requirement.

It consists essentially of a Perspex disk mounted so as to be free to rotate about the centre of the circular bearing scale which surrounds the CRT. The disk is rotated either by hand through direct access to a part of the circumference or by a rotary control acting through gearing or some other form of drive. A line is inscribed across the diameter, usually on the upper and lower sides of the disk so that it is possible to tell when the eye is directly above the line and thus avoid parallax (see Section 6.2.3.3). Additional lines, known as parallel index lines, may also be engraved on the disk. These are described separately in Section 6.9.4.

A bearing is taken by rotating the cursor until the diametric line intersects the target (see Figure 6.11), avoiding parallax by use of the double engraved markings. The value is read off on the circular scale around the edge of the CRT. Bearings are quickly and easily obtained by this method.

Before using the cursor it is essential to check that the origin of the trace has been correctly centred (see Section 6.2.3.3). Failure to centre the origin will result in errors in the measured bearing. The magnitude of such errors will depend not only on the direction and distance by which the origin is off-centre but also on the range and bearing of the target, as illustrated in Figure 6.11.

The orientation selected will determine the type of bearing which is obtained as follows:

Ship's-head-up orientation. A bearing relative to the instantaneous direction of the ship's head will be obtained. To obtain a true bearing it is necessary to

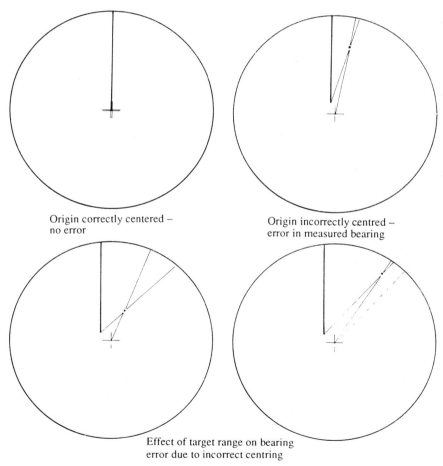

Origin correctly centered –
no error

Origin incorrectly centred –
error in measured bearing

Effect of target range on bearing
error due to incorrect centring

Figure 6.11   The use of the Perspex cursor and the importance of centring the origin

observe the ship's heading at the instant of taking the bearing and to add this to the relative bearing obtained, subtracting 360° from the total if necessary.

True-north-up orientation. A true bearing will be obtained directly.

Course-up orientation. A bearing relative to the reference course (see Section 1.4.3) will be obtained. To obtain a true bearing it is necessary to add the reference course to the relative bearing obtained, subtracting 360° from the total if necessary.

Some systems do provide arrangements to make it possible to read off true bearings when the ship's-head-up orientation is selected. One approach is to fit a gyro-stabilized bearing scale outside the fixed bearing scale which surrounds the tube. When the ship is right on course the scale is aligned so that the graduation representing the course coincides with the 000° graduation of the fixed bearing scale and, subsequent to alignment, the

gyro repeater signal rotates the outer scale in sympathy with the vessel's instantaneous heading. True bearings can thus be read off directly from the outer scale.

In general, the bearing should be taken through the centre of the echo because of the effect of horizontal beamwidth on echo paint (see Section 2.6.5.3). This is fairly straightforward where the echo is comparatively small and isolated as, for example, when measuring the bearing of a ship echo when carrying out radar plotting or the bearing of a small island when using the radar for navigation. Where bearings have to be taken of more complex coastal features it may be more difficult to decide on the location of the centre of the echo. This will be discussed under the use of radar for navigation in Section 8.3.

When taking a bearing, the most open range scale appropriate should be selected so as to place the echo as near to the edge of the screen as possible and hence to maximize the inherent accuracy of the measurement. This follows from the IMO Performance Standards (see

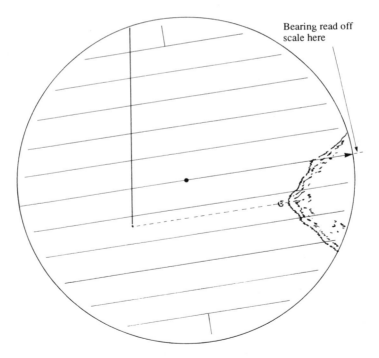

Figure 6.12   Taking a bearing using the parallel index cursor when off-centre

Section 10.2) which require that the means provided for obtaining bearing should enable the bearing of a target whose echo appears *at the edge* of the display to be measured with an accuracy of ±1° or better. It is essential to appreciate that the permitted error of ±1° refers only to the measurement of the angle and does not take into account other sources of bearing errors. The inherent accuracy of radar bearings is discussed, and the procedures for ensuring that the potential accuracy is realized are summarized, in Section 6.9.9.

6.9.4 Parallel index

This comprises a pattern of equally spaced lines (probably double engraved) inscribed parallel to and on one or both sides of the diametric cursor line. In some displays the pattern is inscribed in such a way as to be coincident with the fixed range rings when the display is centred. As illustrated by Figure 6.12, the facility offers a quick method of taking bearings when the picture is off-centred as, for example, when the true-motion presentation is in use.

To obtain a reasonable degree of accuracy, skill and practice are required. Care must be taken to avoid parallax, by using the double engraved lines or the visor where appropriate (see Section 6.2.3.3). In radar navigation this facility is of considerable use in association with a progress monitoring technique generally referred to as *parallel indexing*. This technique is described in detail in Section 8.4.

6.9.5 The electronic bearing line (EBL)

This may also be referred to as the electronic bearing indicator (EBI) or electronic bearing marker (EBM). It takes the form of a continuous or dashed line which is generated electronically (see Figure 6.13(a)). Because it emanates from the electronic origin it can be used even if the origin is not centred. In radial-scan displays the brilliance of the line will normally be continuously variable, from 'off' to 'maximum', under the control of the observer. In raster-scan displays the levels may be restricted to on/off or possibly to off/low/high, though the EBL brilliance will be indirectly affected by the setting of the screen brilliance control.

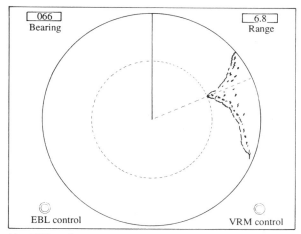

(a) EBL and VRM

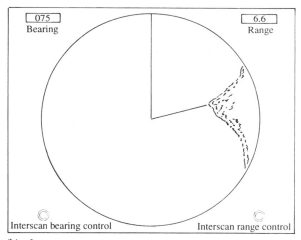

(b) Interscan cursor

Figure 6.13 Electronic bearing line, VRM and interscan cursor

In older radial-scan systems it is produced by the closing of a mechanical contact once per rotation of the scan coils (see Section 2.6.1.3). The angular position of the contact with respect to the scan coils is adjusted by a rotary control which also drives some form of circular or three-digit remote mechanical read-out. When adjusting the position of this type of EBL, the observer may have to wait for a period up to one aerial revolution to see whether or not the desired target has been intersected and hence it is somewhat slower than other methods of bearing measurement.

In modern systems the EBL can be made visible continuously by brightening it once per trace rather than once per revolution. This is achieved by using the spot to write the EBL in the rest period between timebases (see Section 2.6.2). For this reason, such an EBL is sometimes referred to as an *interscan cursor*. The cursor position is adjusted by a rotary mechanical control which also drives a mechanical or electronic read-out. The bearing measurement function may be combined with that of range measurement by making it possible to vary the length of the interscan cursor, in which case it may be referred to as an electronic range and bearing line (ERBL) (see Figure 6.13(b)). Alternatively, the continuous line may be retained and a variable range indication given by generating a mark of some sort at an adjustable point somewhere along the line.

In the synthetic radial and raster-scan displays the EBL or ERBL may be controlled by incremental touch controls (see Section 6.3.2), a joystick, or a tracker ball (see Section 6.9.7).

While the electronic circuitry which generates the EBL and ERBL has a high degree of inherent accuracy it must be remembered that the associated mechanical drives, scales and controls are a potential source of errors. For example, if the drive from the rotary control to the scale slips, the read-out can be seriously in error. For this reason it is prudent to check the EBL by superimposing it on the heading marker and checking that the bearing read-out is in agreement. Similarly, the ERBL should be checked for range measurement against the rings.

In general, the type of bearing (i.e. relative or true) which is read off using the EBL will depend on the orientation selected as described in Section 6.9.3. In some systems arrangements are made for the EBL to read off true bearings even when a ship's-head-up orientation is selected. This is only possible where there is a gyro repeater input, as the ship's instantaneous heading must be added automatically to the relative bearing to produce a true read-out. For any given system, care must be taken to establish the type of bearings available with each orientation.

As indicated in Section 6.9.3, when taking a bearing the most open range scale appropriate should be selected

and the bearing should be taken through the centre of the echo. The inherent accuracy of radar bearings and the procedures for ensuring that the potential accuracy is realized are discussed in detail in Section 6.9.9.

6.9.6 Free electronic range and bearing line

This facility takes the form of an ERBL the origin of which can be positioned at any point on the screen. It allows the observer to measure the range and bearing between two displayed targets, as illustrated by Figure 6.14.

The following three examples serve to indicate that there is a range of circumstances in which this facility might be found useful.

1 Approaching port it may be useful to ascertain the distance of other approaching vessels from the pilot station.
2 Having heard another vessel broadcast its position in terms of bearing from a well defined charted object, it may be possible to identify positively the radar echo of that vessel. (The incorrect use of VHF in collision avoidance can contribute to the development of a dangerous situation: the reader wishing to pursue this topic is referred to *The Navigation Control Manual*, Chapter 19.)

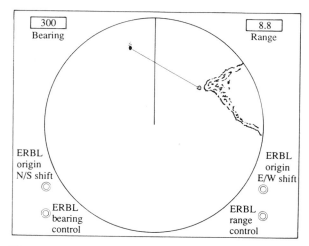

Figure 6.14 Free electronic range and bearing line

3 Having positively identified one land echo, it may be possible to identify positively others by measuring their range and bearing from the known echo.

Other applications which are particularly appropriate to a given trade will no doubt suggest themselves to readers. The facility is often used to draw *navigational lines* in systems which offer automatic tracking (see Section 8.4.6.3).

6.9.7   Joystick and screen marker

This facility makes use of the fact that in modern synthetic displays range and bearing data are stored in digital form (see also Section 2.6.6 and Section 4.5.8).

A joystick is a short spindle which is mounted on the display adjacent and normally to the right of the screen (see Figure 6.15). In its neutral position it lies perpendicular to the plane of the screen. A small sphere or other suitable hand-grip is fitted on the outer end of the spindle, while the inner end is pivoted in such a way that it can be moved fore-and-aft, athwartships or in any direction which lies between these two. The movement of the joystick controls two independent voltages which are analogues of the displacement of the joystick from its neutral position. If these analogue signals are converted into digital numbers they can be used to control the X and Y screen co-ordinates of a graphics marker and to

generate the corresponding digital angle and range in the form of a read-out of bearing and range. The engineering details of the technique by which the displacement of the joystick is translated into marker position/bearing and range may vary in detail with manufacturer.

The graphics marker is commonly a small circle or cross which is located at the origin of the picture when the joystick is in its neutral position. By steering the marker with the joystick, it is placed over the chosen target and the bearing and range are read out on a computer-controlled digital scale. This facility offers a simple and rapid method of range and bearing measurement. As with any form of range and bearing measurement, it should be monitored for errors by checking it against the rings and heading marker.

In some systems a tracker ball is used as an alternative to a joystick. This comprises a sphere, half of which projects above the top panel of the display. It is pivoted in such a way that it can be rotated in any direction, thus allowing control of the graphics marker in a similar fashion to that of the joystick.

6.9.8   Range accuracy

The IMO Performance Standards (see Section 10.2) require that the fixed range rings and the variable range marker enable the range of a target to be measured with an error not exceeding 1.5 per cent of the maximum range of the scale in use or 70 metres, whichever is greater. Where appropriate in the preceding descriptions of the various facilities available for range measurement, mention was made of procedures for ensuring that the potential accuracy is realized. For ease of reference it is appropriate to summarize these procedures in this section.

1 Adjust the brilliance of the VRM, or ERBL to obtain the finest possible line.
2 Measure the range to the nearer edge of the displayed echo.
3 Use the rings when the target is on or close to a ring.
4 Use the VRM, ERBL or joystick marker to interpolate between the rings.
5 Regularly check the VRM, ERBL or joystick marker against the rings.

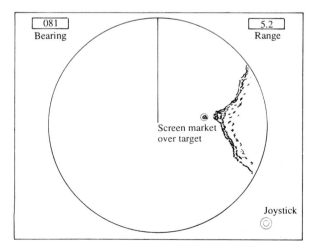

Figure 6.15   Joystick and screen marker

6 Use the most open scale appropriate.

7 When it is not necessary to display the rings, good practice dictates that they should be switched off in order to prolong the life of the phosphor area on which they paint (see Section 2.6.1.2).

6.9.9 Bearing accuracy

As stated in Section 6.9.3, the IMO Performance Standards require that the means provided for measuring bearings should enable the bearing of a target whose echo appears at the edge of the display to be measured with an accuracy of ± 1° or better.

It is essential to appreciate that the permitted error of ± 1° refers only to the measurement of the angle (whose accuracy will depend on the correctness of the alignment of scanner and trace/digital bearing word and the graduation accuracy of the measuring device). It does not take into account the accuracy of the heading marker (see Section 2.4.6) from which the angle is measured or of the accuracy of the gyro signal (see Section 2.6.3) used where azimuth stabilization is provided. The Performance Standards specify an accuracy of ± 1° for the heading marker and ± 0.5° for the gyro input. If these error sources are aggregated, a bearing measured from the display could be in error by 2.5° without the provisions of the Standards being contravened. However, it must be said that each error will have a component which is substantially constant throughout the period of taking a series of bearings. For example, only in the case of mechanical fault would one expect the error from the heading marker source to change from + 1° to − 1° during the taking of a series of bearings. The significance of the aggregate error will depend on whether the bearings are being used for radar plotting or for position-fixing. The implications of bearing errors are discussed separately in terms of their significance in the accuracy of radar plotting in Section 7.9 and of the accuracy of position-fixing in Section 8.3.

Where appropriate in the preceding descriptions of the various facilities available for bearing measurement, mention was made of procedures for ensuring that the potential accuracy is realized. For ease of reference it is appropriate to summarize these procedures in this section.

1 It is important to check regularly that the heading marker accurately represents the ship's fore-and-aft line. The procedure for carrying out this check is set out in paragraph 3.25 of Notice M 1158 issued by the United Kingdom Department of Transport and is reproduced in Section 10.5.

2 Ensure that centring has been carried out before using the Perspex cursor.

3 Ensure that the picture is correctly orientated.

4 Use an appropriate range scale with the target as near to the edge of the screen as possible.

5 Take care to avoid parallax when using the Perspex cursor or parallel index lines.

6 If using a ship's-head-up unstabilized orientation, the ship's head must be read at the instant of taking the bearing.

7 Check the EBL, ERBL or joystick marker by superimposing them on the heading marker, at which time the bearing and heading should agree. Any error should be noted, applied to bearings and the cause investigated.

8 For a small isolated target align the cursor, EBL, ERBL or marker with the centre of the target.

9 Temporarily reduce the gain if it will give a more clearly defined echo.

In general it should be borne in mind that radar range position circles have a much high inherent accuracy than is obtainable from position lines derived from radar bearings. Further, radar bearings are not as accurate as visual bearings.

6.10 Controls for the suppression of unwanted responses

Controls for the suppression of unwanted responses naturally group themselves under the headings of sea clutter, rain clutter and interference. Each of these controls will be dealt with in turn but it should be borne in mind that the usefulness of their effects is not necessarily limited to the heading under which they are considered. For example, the sea clutter control may assist in the detection of a target masked by proximate rain clutter or strong side-lobe response (see Sections 3.7.4 and 3.9.4) and the rain clutter control may be efficacious in improving range discrimination (see Section 3.7.4.4).

6.10.1 Sea clutter suppression

The theory of the sea clutter response and of the various techniques available for its suppression is treated in detail in Section 3.6 and it is intended in this chapter merely to deal with the appropriate practical procedures.

It should be appreciated that many targets will be visible *before* they enter the clutter area and the probability of detecting them within the clutter will be improved if their position is regularly monitored as they approach. As the range of any target decreases its response will improve (see Section 3.1), but once within the clutter it must compete for attention with clutter signals which will be weak at the point of entry but the response of which improves with decreasing range. If the clutter response overtakes that of the target the latter will be undetectable. Thus, where weak targets are approaching, it is important to attempt to detect them before this occurs. Very weak targets may of course be within the clutter area before they return a detectable response.

The above principle is well illustrated by the situation in which a vessel engaged in a Search and Rescue mission is attempting to locate the echoes of survival craft close to her in clutter conditions. Under such circumstances it may be that the rescue vessel cannot detect the echoes of the survival craft because of the clutter. Another vessel stationed sufficiently far away that the first vessel and the survival craft responses are clear of the clutter response may well be able to locate all the craft involved, because it does not have to view them against a clutter background.

6.10.1.1 *The manual sea clutter control*

It is evident from the theory that there is no single correct setting for the sea clutter control and that the correct use of the control is to perform regular *searching* operations. The practical procedure for carrying out searches can be set out as follows:

1 Turn the manual sea clutter control to maximum effect. This will immediately suppress the responses within the receiver but the afterglow of previously displayed echoes will persist on the screen for a short period. To maximize the possibility of detecting targets it is necessary to pause and allow the afterglow to fade.

2 Reduce the suppression by a small step and study the screen for the appearance of echoes.

3 Continue to reduce the suppression in small steps, pausing at each step to examine the screen for the appearance of echoes. In due course the clutter peaks will begin to appear and, as the suppression continues to be removed, it will become progressively difficult to detect targets against the clutter background. In this connection it should be remembered that sea clutter paints will tend to be random while those of targets will tend to be steady.

4 Repeat the search procedure at frequent intervals. The frequency with which this is done must be matched to the prevailing conditions. In particular, consideration should be given to the speed of the observing vessel, the visibility and the type of floating object which is likely to be encountered.

5 Between searches it is prudent to set the control so that just a few echoes are painting, thus extending the life of that important area of the phosphor (see Section 2.6.1.2).

6 The effectiveness of the searching operation may be assisted by the overall reduction in response which can be achieved by the use of a short pulse length, a logarithmic receiver and the selection of S-band transmission. In very heavy clutter, it may be found that even the full suppression offered by the sea clutter control is inadequate, in which case its effect will have to be supplemented by that of the gain control.

Where two transmitters of different powers are available, it may be helpful to select the one having the lower power.

Effective sea clutter searching requires considerable skill which can only be developed by practice. It is recommended that, wherever possible in clear weather, the observer should make use of opportunities to carry out such practice. It must always be remembered that targets weaker than the clutter cannot be detected.

6.10.1.2   Adaptive gain

When adaptive gain is selected, the manual sea clutter and rain clutter controls are rendered inoperative, a fixed amount of differentiation is applied, and the gain is varied instantaneously and automatically according to the dictates of a suppression waveform derived from the signals present on the current or previous radial timebase (see Section 3.6.3.3).

The name 'adaptive gain' is a general engineering term but the control which selects the facility may be variously named by different manufacturers. Examples include video processor, automatic clutter, auto sea clutter and CFAR (*constant false alarm rate* – a statistical term used in the theory of threshold detection). In this, unwanted targets, such as noise and clutter, which cross the threshold are referred to as *false alarms*. In the case of noise, which is a random phenomenon as described in Section 2.5.2.3, the false alarm rate, i.e. the number of false alarms per unit time, should be the same whatever the screen location. This makes it comparatively easy to make a judgement on threshold setting. In the case of sea clutter, the false alarm rate is likely to have a high value at the centre of the screen falling to a lower value where only noise is present, making the choice of threshold setting a problem. Adaptive gain seeks to simplify the problem of threshold setting by producing a *constant false alarm rate*, i.e. reducing the clutter to a noiselike response (see Section 3.6.3.3).

The particular virtue of adaptive gain is that, if correctly set up, it will provide near optimum instantaneous clutter suppression, line by radial line, hour after hour, without tiring, losing concentration or becoming distracted. In general, it is not possible to set up the circuitry so as to guarantee optimum performance over the entire range of sea conditions that may be experienced and exclusive reliance must not be placed on its ability to remove *all* clutter responses and display *all* targets. In some conditions, particularly heavy clutter, it may well be found that skilled use of the manual sea clutter control will provide a higher probability of detection. The adaptive gain facility should be regarded as having the ability to display *most* of the targets masked by clutter for *most* of the time. However, the observer must from time to time switch off the adaptive gain and

use the manual clutter control to check for targets close to clutter level. Commonly, the control for the selection of adaptive gain is integral with the manual clutter control.

The manual gain control remains operative and thus the observer maintains control of the gain level which obtains in the absence of automatic suppression. At initial setting up (see Sections 6.2.1, 6.3.1 and 6.4.1) the manual gain control should be set with the manual and adaptive clutter controls at zero effect. If the adaptive gain circuitry is functioning correctly, further adjustment of the gain should not be necessary. However, at any time that the observer suspects that excessive suppression is being applied, the gain may be adjusted to produce a higher level of residual speckle in order to ensure maximum probability of detection of targets.

For the reasons set out in Section 3.6.3.3, it may be necessary to switch off the adaptive gain facility in the following circumstances:

1 When attempting to detect radar beacons. In some systems separate automatic sea and rain adaptive gain controls are provided and it may be possible to detect a distant radar beacon while maintaining the ability to use the limited range of the automatic sea clutter adaptive gain facility.
2 When carrying out a performance check.
3 When attempting to identify coastlines.
4 In rivers, narrow channels and enclosed dock areas.

6.10.1.3   Rotation-to-rotation correlation

This facility is only available on raster-scan displays and seeks to remove clutter responses by identifying their random character (see Section 3.6.3.4). The signal produced as a result of the processing is sometimes referred to as *integrated video* and the control may be similarly labelled.

Only two states, *on* and *off*, are associated with the facility. In some systems the facility defaults to *off* at switch-on and the observer is required to make a positive selection if the correlation is required. In other systems the facility defaults to the *on* condition and the observer must switch it off if not desired. In some cases the switch is spring-loaded. In cases where the facility does default to the *on* state, it is important to switch it off when setting the gain control because it will produce some reduction in the displayed noise.

The use of the facility in combination with adaptive gain will greatly reduce the displayed clutter response. It will also make manual searching a simpler operation. However, it must be borne in mind that echoes close to clutter level, such as those from small boats, buoys and small icebergs, may also be random in their character. Small fast-moving targets may also be displayed at low level if the facility is selected.

6.10.2   Rain clutter suppression

The theory of the rain clutter response and of the various techniques available for its suppression is treated in detail in Section 3.7 and it is intended in this chapter merely to deal with the appropriate practical procedures.

As in the case of sea clutter, targets may well be visible before they enter areas of precipitation and it is self-evident that the task of detecting any target is made easier by knowing roughly where to look. Thus every effort should be made to track such targets so as to improve the probability of detecting them once they are within the clutter area. One must of course always be alert to the danger of a target manoeuvring within the clutter region. Rain clutter differs from sea clutter in that the echoes may appear in any part of the screen and may move quite rapidly. The probability of problems arising with targets being lost in precipitation can be anticipated if efforts are made to track the direction in which particular areas of precipitation are moving.

6.10.2.1   The rain clutter control

As described in Section 3.7.4.4, this controls seeks to deal with the saturation problem by displaying only the leading edges of echoes. Because it is so called, there is a tendency for observers to assume that it is the most effective way of dealing with rain echoes. On the basis of practical experience many users hold the view that the use of the gain control in a searching fashion is much more effective. It can of course be argued that this view is to some extent subjective. The important point to appreciate is that suppression and differentiation are two

quite different attempts to solve the same problem. Given the subjective element that exists, an observer should take every opportunity to establish which particular technique he or she finds most helpful, and whether the preference applies to particular circumstances.

6.10.2.2   Manual searching for targets within rain

The masking effect of rain can be dealt with as follows:

1 If the rain is close to the ship, searching with the sea clutter control may be effective.
2 In general the most effective technique is to use the gain control in a searching fashion.
3 If preferred, the rain clutter control may be used in a searching fashion, either alone or in combination with some suppression of the gain.
4 The effectiveness of the searching operation may be assisted by the overall reduction in response which can be achieved by the use of a short pulse length, a logarithmic receiver, the selection of S-band transmission, the selection of a low power transmitter or the selection of circular polarization.

6.10.2.3   Adaptive gain

This is an effective way of providing automatic rain clutter suppression. Attention however is drawn to the practical limitations of the technique set out in Section 6.10.1.2.

6.10.2.4   Searching for targets beyond precipitation

Because of the attenuating effect of precipitation (see Section 3.7.2), it may be difficult to detect weak targets which lie beyond areas of precipitation. It may be possible to overcome this difficulty by using S-band transmission, a higher power transmitter (if fitted) or selecting a longer pulse length. While searching for specific targets it may be useful temporarily to turn the gain above the normal setting, or use an echo-stretching facility if available (see Section 6.11.1).

6.10.3   Interference suppression

This is normally a two-position control which allows a

line-to-line correlation facility to be switched off or on. Such a facility will tend to reduce the noise content of the picture and should be switched off when initially setting the gain control. Certain types of step sweep racons can also be removed by this facility (see Section 3.5.3).

6.11 Miscellaneous controls

This section deals with some specialized controls which will not be found on all civil marine radars.

6.11.1 Echo stretch

In a synthetic display, the radial length of the displayed echo is normally fixed by the number of elements of memory activated by the detected response (see Section 2.6.6.3). Some systems offer an additional facility whereby the number of radial elements representing the target can be increased, as a result of which the observer can cause the displayed echoes to be stretched radially away from the origin in order to make them more obvious, while preserving the leading edge at the correct range. The rules which govern the stretching vary somewhat with manufacturer, but in general the availability of the facility is limited to:

1 The longer range scales.
2 Targets beyond a preset minimum range.
3 Targets whose received echoes exceed a preset duration.

Such a facility may be particularly useful when trying to detect distant land echoes. Once detection has been achieved and identification becomes a priority, the stretching effect will become counter-productive (see Section 8.2.1).

6.11.2 Second-trace echo elimination

Some systems provide a facility whereby second-trace echoes can be eliminated. The facility can normally be switched on or off. The theory of the techniques used to eliminate the second-trace echoes is described in Section 3.9.6.

6.12 Setting-up procedure for an ARPA display

Most automatic radar plotting aids offer a host of facilities, some of which are required by the IMO Performance Standards and others which are not (see Chapters 4 and 5). The precise way in which even the specified facilities are controlled varies considerably with manufacturer. This general treatment seeks to deal with the setting up of the display for basic tracking in terms of the important guiding principles which are common to all systems.

6.12.1 The input of radar data

Irrespective of whether the ARPA is of the integral or stand-alone type (see Sections 4.1.1 and 4.1.2), it is essential to ensure that the radar system supplying the raw data to the ARPA tracker is correctly set up (see Sections 6.2, 6.3, and 6.4). Particular attention must be paid to pulse length selection, tuning and *any* control that affects receiver gain (for example, the sea clutter control – see Sections 3.6.3.1 and 6.10.1). Failure to use the correct pulse length or to tune the receiver will reduce the probability of targets being detected and tracked by ARPA. The effect of the setting of the receiver gain controls on the video fed to the tracker varies from one manufacturer to another. In some systems the signal level fed to the tracker (see Section 4.3.6) is independent of the operator's gain controls, being continuously set by some form of adaptive gain or other form of automatic signal processing. In other systems, the manual gain control determines the signal level fed to both the tracker and the CRT. When first using an ARPA with which the observer is not familiar it is prudent to establish which gain control settings affect the input to the tracker. This can be done quite simply by acquiring a target, adjusting each relevant control in turn, and observing any consequent loss of tracking (see Section 4.7.3).

6.12.2 Switching on the computer

In some systems the ARPA computer is switched on

when the radar is switched to the 'operate' condition while in others a separate switch is provided. After the computer is switched on, it may be necessary to wait for a short time, not normally more than a minute, for the computer to carry out a self-checking programme.

When the computer becomes active, many ARPAs have default conditions by which all but the basic facilities are switched off. This ensures that the user obtains the additional facilities only if they are positively requested and is thus not confused by uncertainty as to the status of the controls nor plagued by the need to find the control necessary to switch off unwanted facilities. Care must be exercised where analogue controls are used as they are likely to remain as set by the last user.

6.12.3 Heading and speed input data

The observer should check that the correct heading and *water speed* information is being fed to the computer; if not, the necessary adjustments should be made. The procedure is essentially similar to that carried out when setting up a true-motion sea-stabilized presentation (see Section 6.8.2). It is vital that this check is made, otherwise no reliance can be placed on the tracking. The importance of heading and speed inputs cannot be over-stressed and the navigator must always be watchful for errors in these fundamental data sources.

6.12.4 Setting the ARPA brilliance

This control adjusts the brilliance level of the vectors and other graphics used to display the ARPA data (see Section 4.5.6). It is not usually possible to adjust this control correctly until after some targets have been acquired, since it is only at that stage that one can judge what level of brightness allows comfortable viewing of the vectors and other graphics in the ambient light conditions. When setting up it is usually best to set the control about mid-travel and to optimize it later when tracking has commenced.

6.12.5 Setting the vector time control

In many systems the vector time control will default to some non-zero setting, probably in the range of 6–12

minutes. This ensures that, when vectors are initially displayed after acquisition has commenced, they will in general have a length which is sufficient to be obvious but not excessive. In due course the length can be set to suit the traffic conditions and will of course have to be adjusted from time to time as the vectors are used to extract data from the display. Where there is no default condition the observer should, when setting up, adjust the vector time control to a suitable non-zero value, preferably in the range 6–12 minutes.

6.12.6 Setting the vector mode

Most systems will have a default condition which will select a particular vector mode (see Section 4.4) at switch-on. Some systems default to relative vector mode, some to true vector mode, while in others the default condition depends on the radar picture presentation that has been selected. A further variation is for the system to default to neither mode, requiring the observer to make positive selection of one mode or the other. The observer clearly must be able to select the alternate mode to the default condition but in some systems the vector mode is *ballasted* in the default condition, i.e., to select the other mode the observer must operate a spring-loaded control which returns to the default condition on release. Such are the variations found in practice that it is essential to consult the operating manual and discover what options are available.

6.12.7 Safe limits

The observer should set in suitable safe limits in terms of CPA and TCPA (see Section 4.7.2). The judgement of what is suitable is to some extent subjective. Excessive alerts can be distracting and counter-productive whereas, by contrast, if very small limits are used the dangerous target alarm will not be activated by a vessel which is standing into a close-quarters situation.

6.12.8 Preparation for tracking

If the observer is unfamiliar with the system some time should be spent in locating the joystick (or tracker ball), the *acquire* button and the *cancel* button and practising their use. This can be done using live targets if available or, failing that, use can be made of the synthetic targets provided by the training programme supplied with many ARPAs.

6.13   Switching off

When finally switching the radar off, if the system has analogue controls it is prudent to set the controls as you would wish to find them when initally switching on, i.e. as set out in Section 6.2.1. In many modern systems having computer controls and default conditions, this will not be necessary.

7 Radar plotting

7.1 Introduction

It may be argued that the prime function of the radar system is avoidance of collision, either with other vessels or with navigation marks in restricted visibility. After the initial euphoria of being able to detect other vessels in fog, the plethora of accidents involving vessels equipped with radar left no doubt as to the need for systematic observation of the radar display and for proper techniques for the extraction of data relating to other vessels. The method by which this information has been displayed to the navigator has seen a steady progression from paper plotting sheets via true-motion displays to the present day ARPAs. All have sought to provide the mariner with the most meaningful portrayal of the situation in the proximity of his ship with the least amount of distraction to the other bridge routines. In order to understand the more complex operations performed by ARPAs and for the benefit of those who are not so fortunate as to have that aid or where it has broken down, it is still necessary to have a fair degree of skill and dexterity in practical plotting. In order to maintain this dexterity, it is essential to engage in regular practice, preferably in clear weather where visual confirmation of results will build confidence in the information obtained when using the radar in restricted visibility.

7.2 The relative plot

Since the radar is carried along by the vessel as it proceeds, the direct measurements obtainable are always *relative to the observing vessel* (see Section 1.5.1). Thus, in order to determine the true courses and speeds of other vessels, it is necessary to resolve this observed relative or apparent motion into its components by using a knowledge of own ship's true course and speed. The means by which this may be achieved ranges from pencil-on-paper plotting sheets via reflection plotters and true-motion displays to computer-based collision avoidance systems. Irrespective of the mechanism used, if a complete appreciation of the dynamic situation in the vicinity of own ship is to be obtained, the relative motion of targets must be systematically recorded and the true motion derived by means of a plot. The techniques employed to extract the relevant data and the use to which it is put will form the major part of this chapter. Failure to carry out such systematic observation has resulted in many dangerous misconceptions (see Figure 7.1).

If systematic observations are made of the bearing and range of a displayed echo and the positions are plotted on a traditional plotting sheet or reflection plotter (see Section 7.8), the line joining the plotted positions will depict the target's apparent motion OA (Figure 7.2), which if extended will enable a measure of the target's closest point of approach, CPA, to be obtained. The time to closest point of approach, TCPA, can be obtained by stepping off the rate from O to A along OA extended to CPA. This does of course assume that both vessels maintain their present courses and speeds. If this condition is not met, the apparent motion will not be uniform, i.e. the echo will not move across the screen in a constant direction at a constant rate.

It is important to realize that the measurements obtained thus far are only subject to those errors inherent in the radar system itself (see Sections 7.9.1 and

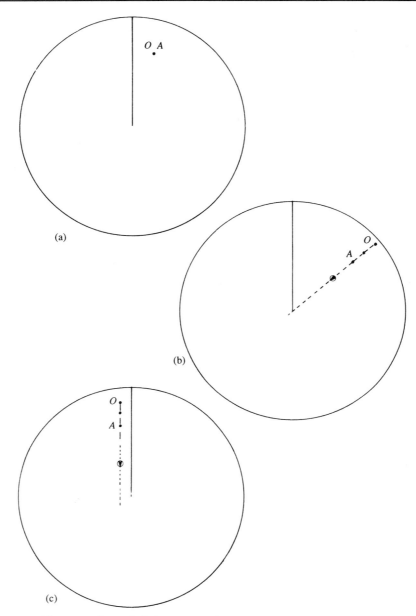

Figure 7.1   Common misinterpretations of relative-motion displays
(a)   The target, believed to be stopped, is in fact on the same course and at the same speed as own ship
(b)   A vessel which might be expected, if observed visually at night, to be showing both sidelights, i.e. to be head-on and to present no threat, is in fact crossing broad starboard-to-port and on a collision course
(c)   The target appears to be proceeding slowly on a reciprocal course, showing a red light: it is actually being overtaken and showing a stern light

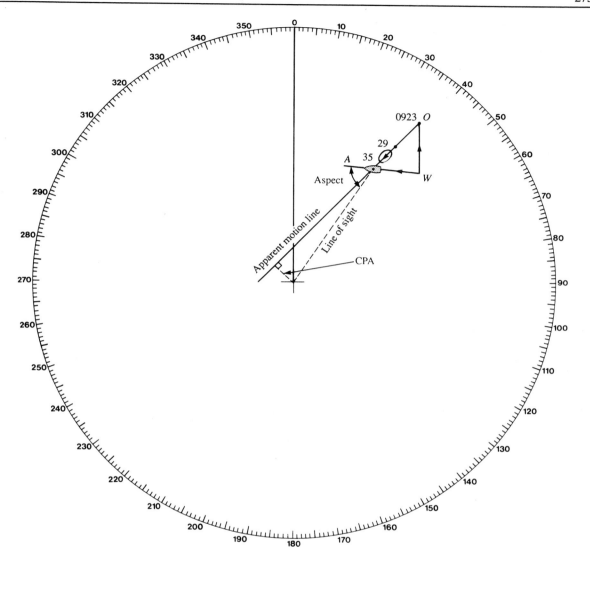

Distance (n mile)

Figure 7.2 The relative-motion plot

7.9.2) and in the observations and are therefore uncontaminated by errors (or blunders) to which other inputs – notably own ship's course and speed – might be subjected. For this reason, relative motion (or the relative plot) is probably the most reliable, although not the only data on which to base decisions.

While CPA and TCPA are two important pieces of information, it is essential that, prior to manoeuvring own ship, the true course and speed of the target(s) are derived and this can only be done by resolving the vector triangle.

7.2.1   The vector triangle

By plotting the apparent motion of a target and with a knowledge of own ship's true course and speed, it is possible to determine the true course and speed of the target (see Figure 7.3).

7.2.2   The plotting triangle

Example 7.1   While steering 090°(T) at 12 knots, the echo of a vessel is observed as follows:

> 0923 echo bearing 127°(T) at 9.5 n mile
> 0929 echo bearing 126°(T) at 8.0 n mile
> 0935 echo bearing 124°(T) at 6.5 n mile

At 0935, determine the target's true course and speed; CPA and TCPA; and aspect.

The data relating to the target in Figure 7.4 as extracted from the plot at 0935 is as follows:

Course: 008°(T)   CPA: 1.0 n mile   Aspect: Red 65°
Speed: 11 kn   TCPA: in 26 min

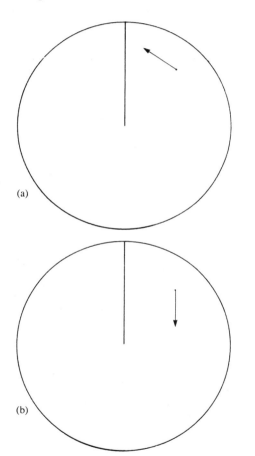

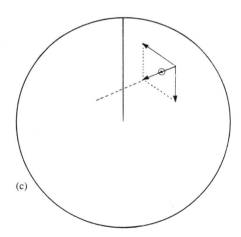

Figure 7.3   The vector triangle
(a)   With own ship stopped, target moves with true course and speed
(b)   With target stopped, own ship movement causes the target to appear to move
(c)   The resultant motion of the echo when both vessels are moving

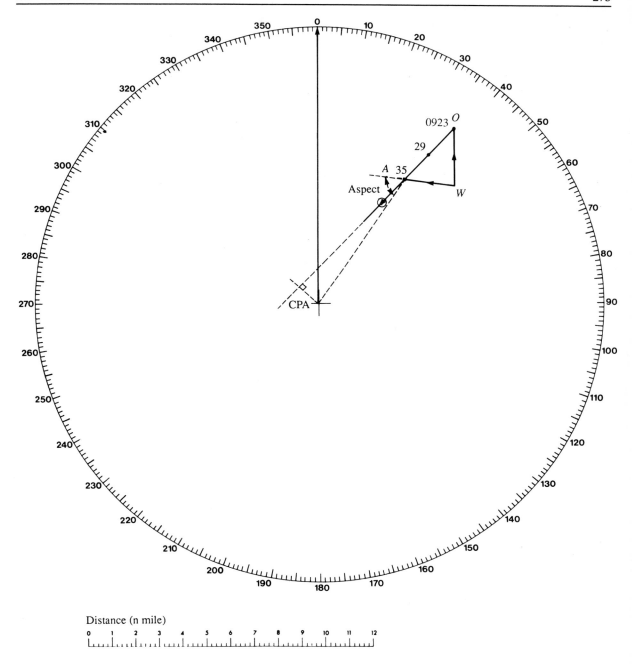

Figure 7.4 The relative plot for Example 7.1
(a) Ship's head up

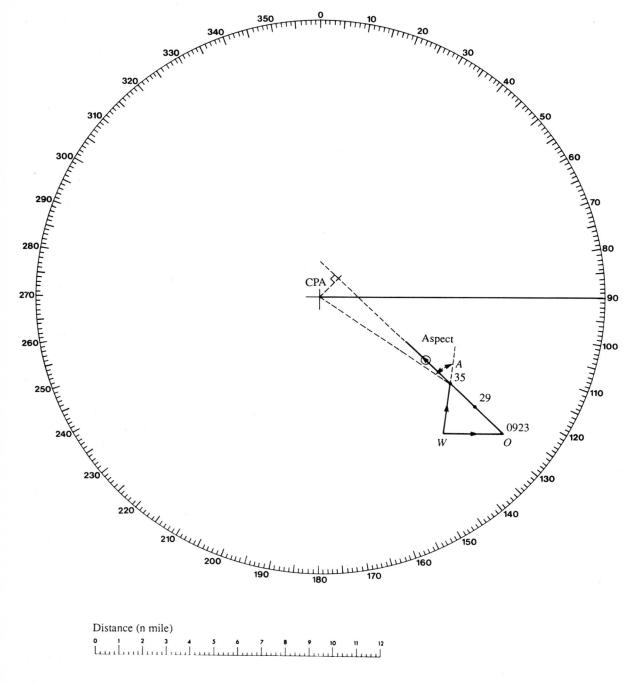

(b) True north up

7.2.3 The construction of the plot

(a) Draw in own ship's heading line on the plotting sheet.

(b) Plot the first position of the target. Label it O. Insert the time.

(c) Lay off a line to represent the apparent motion of a stationary target, from O, opposite to the direction of the heading line.

(d) Plot at least one intermediate position of the target to ascertain that its apparent motion is not changing. Insert the time.

(e) Plot the final position, with the time, and label it A. Ensure that the apparent motion is consistent in direction and rate. Join OA and label it thus: ⟶

(f) Produce the apparent motion line OA to find the closest point of approach (CPA) and the time to closest point of approach (TCPA).

(g) The 'plotting interval' is the time between the readings of range and bearing for O and A. Calculate the distance that own ship has steamed in this time and plot the position in which you would expect to find the stationary target W at the end of the plotting interval. (OW is derived from own ship's speed and course reversed.)

(h) If A and W coincide, the target is stationary. If they do not, the line W to A represents the proper motion of the target in the plotting interval.

(i) 'Aspect' is measured between the 'line of sight' and the WA direction as in Figure 7.4.

It can be seen that, whichever orientation is used for the plot, the answers obtained will be the same, but some consideration must be given to the actual practicalities of plotting and the way in which the results are to be used. Where it is not possible to compass-stabilize the radar display (see Section 2.6.3), the ships-head-up display will be the obvious choice. Where the radar display is capable of being compass-stabilized, it makes good sense to orientate the plot in the same way as the radar display, i.e. true-north-up when the radar display is true-north-up etc, especially when the vessel is on a southerly heading. There can be considerable confusion and even potential danger in trying to relate a ships-head-up plot to a displayed radar picture which is 'upside down' e.g.

when heading south. On the other hand, when conning the vessel and therefore relating the plot to the visual scene ahead of the vessel, it is sensible to orientate the display and to plot ships-head-up or course-up accordingly.

7.2.4 The practicalities of plotting

The way in which the plot is constructed in practice is very different from the way in which one theoretically tackles a plot, such as the example in Section 7.2.2 above. In the first place, ranges and bearings are obtained only at intervals of some 3 to 6 minutes (not all at the same time), and it is unlikely that the plotter will be able to enjoy the luxury of radar plotting as a dedicated task, having rather to dovetail this activity into the many other bridge duties. If plotting is not to become all-consuming or if it results in peaks and troughs of activity, some wrinkles will have to be adopted to assist in spreading the load:

(a) Always draw in the heading line before starting to plot.

(b) When a target is first plotted, draw in OW and graduate it in 3-minute steps up to about 12 minutes. This is not to suggest that one should plot slavishly at 3-minute intervals but, rather, that one should plot when the opportunity arises and interpolate visually between the 3-minute graduations on the OW line.

The frequency with which the target should be plotted is dependent on a number of factors, namely, the range, the approach rate and the CPA. A target which is closing fast will require more frequent plots than, say, one which the observing vessel is slowly overhauling.

(c) Make a quick, early plot after, say, 3 minutes. Although the triangle will be small and not particularly accurate, it will give early warning of the potential of the encounter which is arising and allow time for some pre-planning. *Do not wait 12 minutes* before drawing the first triangle.

(d) Obtain at least three consistently spaced positions in a reasonably straight line before being prepared to make a decision based on the plot.

(e) Plotted positions should be in a reasonably straight line and spaced at distance intervals which are related to the time intervals between the plots. Where a plotted position appears significantly different from what is anticipated, it should be investigated immediately for an error either in reading the range and bearing from the radar or in plotting the position. Where a change in apparent motion is found to have ocurred, a new triangle should be started (see Section 7.4).

(f) Only essential lines should be put on the plot and then kept to a minimum in length. Extending WA beyond A should be avoided as it can be dangerously misleading and mistaken for an indication of CPA. On the other hand, OA should *not* be stopped short but extended at least beyond CPA.

(g) It can be extremely helpful, especially when other officers are likely to observe the plot, to adopt some standard form of labelling (the labelling used in all figures in this text conforms with the United Kingdom Department of Transport's recommendations).

(h) Times should be placed alongside each plotted position. This is essential when the plotting interval varies as it can justify the unequal spacing of the positions. 'Minutes' are quite sufficient, with the occasional indication of the hour.

(i) TCPA should be given as the 'time to elapse', i.e. 'CPA in 16 minutes' rather than 'CPA at 1743' which is far less meaningful to someone who has then to check the time and subtract mentally. Also, time to elapse will in itself convey the degree of urgency in the situation.

(j) After some 12 minutes there should be no real need to continue plotting bigger and bigger triangles, but it is essential to continue to plot positions and ensure that the target's apparent motion is being maintained. As soon as the apparent motion is observed to change, a new plot should be commenced (see Section 7.4).

(k) Neatness is essential at all times. An untidy plot – lines everywhere, no labels, with times not related closely to plots, crossings out etc. – is likely to be more of a hindrance than a help. There is no merit in a plot which even the plotter has difficulty in understanding.

(l) The range scale on which to plot requires some consideration. As a general rule, plots should be initiated on the 12 mile range scale, but two differing requirements can arise. Where targets are likely to be closing fast, the earlier the plot is commenced the better, in which case the 12 mile range scale should be adequate; when targets are close, a shorter (3 or 6 mile) scale should be in use, possibly off-centred. The advantages of the shorter range scale are that there is better intrinsic accuracy and that changes in the target's movement are quickly and easily identifiable. As a target closes, a shorter range scale should be selected, but the plotter should, at intervals, temporarily return to the longer range scale(s) to search for newly arrived targets which could be a potential threat.

7.2.5 The need to extract numerical data

Plotting theory provides for the extraction of data in numerical form but this takes time and is needed only rarely. Also, the precision with which it is displayed often belies its accuracy and therefore the reliance which can be placed upon it.

Of the information normally available on a clearly constructed plot, CPA and the target's aspect/course should be directly observable with sufficient accuracy and without precise measurement. The target's speed should be mentally assessable by visual comparison with own ship's speed vector, i.e. by comparing WA with WO, which is known. By this means, the target's aspect/course, speed and CPA should be obtainable with sufficient accuracy for the practical assessment of the situation and only TCPA will require some form of measurement.

7.2.6 The plot in special cases where no triangle 'appears'

As can be seen in the cases shown in Figure 7.5, all of the vector values are represented but in some of the cases their value is zero while, in others, the vectors are superimposed, all of which requires a little more care in the drawing of the plot and its subsequent analysis.

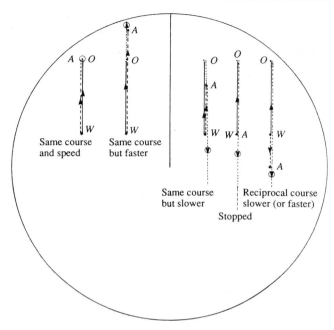

Figure 7.5 Plots where no triangle appears

7.3 The true plot

The data given in Example 7.1 in Section 7.2.2 can be plotted on graph paper or on the chart as a 'true plot' (Figure 7.6).

In this case, own ship's course line is laid off on the plotting sheet and own position marked. From this position the bearing and range of the target are laid off. Own ship's position at, say, 3 minute intervals is then marked off along the course line. What will be obtained directly is the target's course and the distance travelled in the plotting interval but, as already stated, perhaps the most important single piece of information available from a plot is the target's CPA, which is not immediately available and must be determined by the following geometrical construction:

(a) Lay off a line WO, parallel with the course line and of a length equal to the distance that own ship has travelled in the plotting interval.

(b) Join O to the current position of the target A and extend OA to pass O_2, i.e. own ship's current position, thus giving CPA. The static situation is identical with that depicted in Figure 7.4 and the required information is extracted in the same way. To this extent, relative and true plots are equally valid, but some practical points are worth noting:

(i) The convenience of a bearing scale and range circles on a relative plotting sheet are not possible with a true plot where own position is continually moving. In plotting the target's position, protractor (or equivalent) and dividers will have to be used and the operation will be somewhat slower.

(ii) Each target position will have to be laid off from own ship's current position, which can be very time-consuming if a number of targets are being plotted.

(iii) Any error in plotting own ship's position (i.e. an error in the course and/or speed input) will

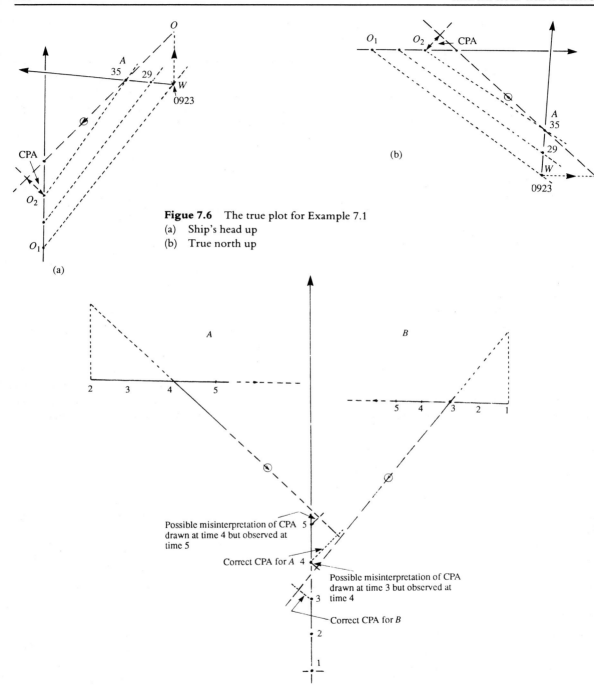

Figue 7.6   The true plot for Example 7.1
(a)   Ship's head up
(b)   True north up

Figure 7.7   The temporary nature of the apparent–motion line on a true plot

result in an error in the directly obtained answer, i.e. the course and speed of the target. *Note.* If this error is repeated when laying off *WO* the CPA of the target will in fact be correct.

(iv) Perhaps the most disconcerting product of this plotting technique is the temporary nature of the apparent-motion line. (Figure 7.7). It is essential to appreciate that the 'displayed' CPA relates to *only one* own ship position, after which the apparent motion line can be at worst misleading. Where a number of targets are being plotted on the same sheet, apparent-motion lines can relate to *different* own ship positions.

In general, where manual plotting has to be carried out, time is of the essence and in this respect the relative plot is better. For this reason the subsequent treatment will assume the use of the relative plot except in the case of reflection plotting on a true-motion display. In the latter case, a true plot can be easily and quickly produced.

(b) Say what action each target has taken. (Your vessel maintains course and speed throughout.)

The apparent-motion line *OA* which is produced when determining CPA and TCPA, depends upon four factors: Own ship's course and speed and the target's course and speed. If any of these factors changes then the apparent-motion line will also change. Changes in own ship's proper motion are known (but in this example remain unchanged) and the resulting apparent motion can be predicted (see Section 7.5), but where a change in the apparent motion of the target is observed, the procedure set out in Section 7.4.1 should be followed to determine the change in the target's proper motion.

Answer

		Target A	Target B
(a)	CPA :	collision	1.0 n mile
	TCPA :	24 min	25 min
	Course :	040°(T)	226°(T)
	Speed :	10 kn	10.5 kn
(b)		Target has altered course only: 50° to starboard	Target has stopped.

Note that target *B* is similar to that used in the previous example and although, in this case, the bearings are re-orientated, the plots CPA and TCPA are identical.

7.4 The plot when only the target manoeuvres

Example 7.2 Your own ship is steering 310°(T) at a speed of 12 knots. Echoes are observed as follows:

Time	Echo A	Echo B
0923	brg 270°(T) at 9.0 n mile	brg 347°(T) at 9.5 n mile
0929	brg 270°(T) at 7.5 n mile	brg 346°(T) at 8.0 n mile
0935	brg 270°(T) at 6.0 n mile	brg 344°(T) at 6.5 n mile

(a) Determine the CPA, TCPA, course and speed of each target.

Plotting is continued as follows:

0941	brg 270°(T) at 4.5 n mile	brg 341°(T) at 5.0 n mile
0947	brg 253°(T) at 2.8 n mile	brg 350°(T) at 4.0 n mile
0953	brg 206°(T) at 1.7 n mile	brg 004°(T) at 3.1 n mile

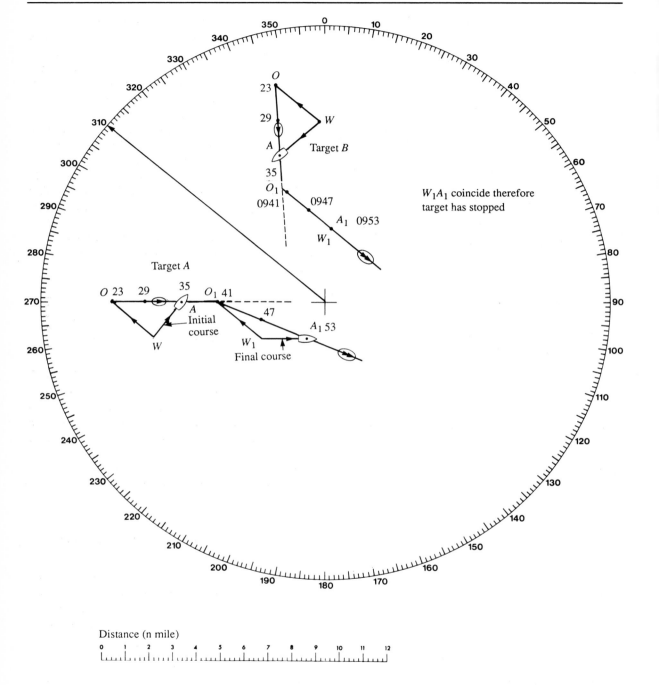

Figure 7.8 The plot when only the target manoeuvres (Example 7.2)

7.4.1 The construction of the plot (Figure 7.8)

(a) Own ship's heading line should have been drawn in.
(b) The *OAW* triangle should have been constructed and the basic information extracted.
(c) Continue to plot the apparent motion of the target, making sure the direction and rate are as predicted in the initial plot.
(d) *As soon as a change in the target's apparent motion is noticed*, plot more frequently and, when a new steady apparent motion is established, choose a position, label it O_1 and insert the time.
(e) Plot the new apparent motion as if it were a new target. Predict the new CPA and TCPA, also course and speed, from which any changes from the previous proper motion may be noted.

7.4.2 The danger in attempting to guess the action taken by a target

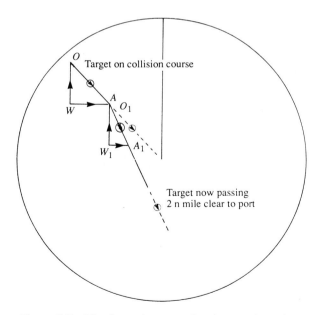

Figure 7.9 The danger in attempting to guess the action taken by a target

Since the change in the target's apparent motion can result from virtually any combination of changes in its course and speed, one should always construct a new plotting triangle and never attempt to assume a particular manoeuvre has taken place even though it fits in with what is both logical and desirable under the collision avoidance rules. In the typical crossing situation shown in Figure 7.9, one might expect the target to give way by altering her course to starboard. While the change in apparent motion would seem to indicate that this is what has happened, when the plot is completed, it is clearly indicated that the target has in fact reduced her speed. If the observing vessel is subsequently presented with the development of a close-quarters situation with another vessel, the assessment of the appropriate manoeuvre will be dangerously flawed if it assumes the wrong heading for the pre-existing target.

7.5 The plot when own ship manoeuvres

When it is decided (after assessment of the initial plot) that it is necessary for own ship to manoeuvre, it is essential to determine the effect of that manoeuvre *prior to* its execution and to ensure that it will result in a safe passing distance. After the manoeuvre has been completed, plotting must be continued to ensure that the manoeuvre is having the desired effect.

7.5.1 The plot when own ship alters course only

Because of the time taken for a change in speed to have any effect on the apparent motion line, the mariner will frequently select a change in course if it will achieve a satisfactory passing distance. This has some distinct advantages:

(a) It is quick to take effect.
(b) The vessel retains steerage way.
(c) The encounter may be more quickly cleared.

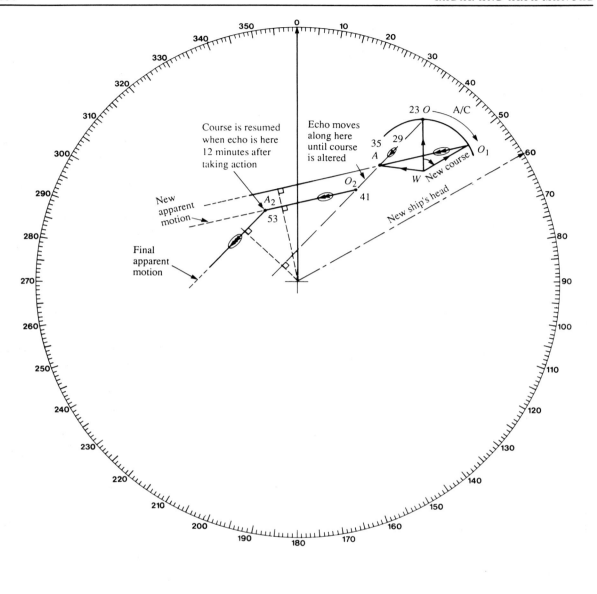

Distance (n mile)

Figure 7.10   The plot when own ship alters course only (Example 7.3)

(d) It is more likely to be detected if the other vessel is plotting.

(e) It complies with the spirit of rule 8c (see Section 7.12.6).

Example 7.3   With own ship steering 000°(T) at a speed of 12 knots, an echo is observed as follows:

0923	echo bears	037°(T)	at	9.5 n mile
0929	echo bears	036°(T)	at	8.0 n mile
0935	echo bears	034°(T)	at	6.5 n mile

At 0935 it is intended to alter course 60° to starboard (assume this to be instantaneous).

(a) Predict the new CPA and TCPA.

(b) Predict the new CPA and TCPA if the manoeuvre is delayed until 0941.

(c) Predict the range and bearing of the echo at 0953, if the (instantaneous) manoeuvre is made at 0941.

Answer

(a) CPA is 4.4 n mile, 13 min after the alteration, i.e. at 0948.

(b) CPA is 3.6 n mile, 10 min after the alteration, i.e. at 0951.

(c) Predicted range is 3.8 n mile on a bearing of 334°(T).

7.5.2   The construction of the plot (Figure 7.10)

(a) The original *OAW* triangle should have been drawn.

(b) With compasses at *W* and radius *WO*, draw an arc.

(c) Draw from *W* a line at an angle to port or starboard of *WO*, equal to the proposed alteration of course.

(d) Label as O_1 the point at which this line cuts the arc.

(e) Join O_1 to *A* – this now represents the new apparent motion in direction and rate.

(f) Draw in the ship's *new heading line* and expunge the old heading line.

(g) Until the manoeuvre takes place, the target will continue to move down the original apparent-motion line. Predict the position of the target at the time at which it is proposed to alter own ship's course and label it O_2.

(h) Draw O_2A_2 parallel with and equal to O_1A and produce if necessary to find the new CPA.

Note (a)   The prediction is based on the assumption that the target will maintain its course and speed. If the target also manoeuvres then the target will not follow the predicted apparent motion in both direction and rate and a new plot will have to be started.

(b)   It is assumed that the alteration of course is instantaneous. For a more practical prediction:

(c)   When manoeuvring at sea, to obtain a more realistic indication of the new CPA, one could predict the effect of the manoeuvre and check that it is acceptable. If so, bring the ship round to the new course and, when steadied on the new course, plot the position of the target and transfer the new apparent motion, O_2A_2, through this position.

7.5.3   The plot when own ship alters speed only

Example 7.4   With own ship steering 000°(T) at a speed of 12 knots, an echo is observed as follows:

0923	echo bears	037°(T)	at	9.5 n mile
0929	echo bears	036°(T)	at	8.0 n mile
0935	echo bears	034°(T)	at	6.5 n mile

At 0935 it is intended to reduce speed to 3 knots (assume this to be instantaneous).

(a) Predict the new CPA and TCPA.

(b) Predict the new CPA and TCPA if the manoeuvre is delayed until 0941 (assume an instantaneous reduction of speed).

(c) Predict the bearing and range of the echo at 0953, if the manoeuvre is made at 0941.

Answer

(a) New CPA is 4.8 n mile, 24.5 min after the alteration of speed, i.e. at 0959.5.

(b) New CPA is 3.9 n mile, 19 min after the alteration of speed, i.e. at 1000.

(c) At 0953 the bearing should be 007°(T), range 4.0 n mile.

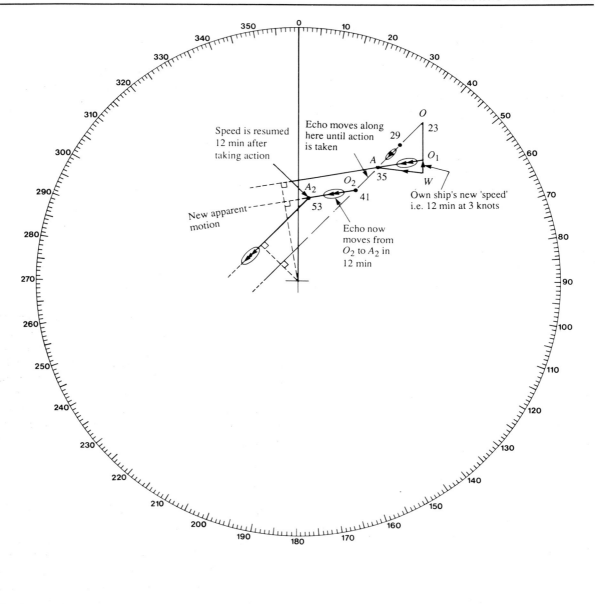

Speech labels within figure:

Speed is resumed
12 min after
taking action

Echo moves along
here until action
is taken

Own ship's new 'speed'
i.e. 12 min at 3 knots

New apparent
motion

Echo now
moves from
O_2 to A_2 in
12 min

O 23
29
A O_1
35   W
O_2
A_2 41
53

Distance (n mile)

0 1 2 3 4 5 6 7 8 9 10 11 12

Figure 7.11 The plot when own ship alters speed only (Example 7.4)

7.5.4 The construction of the plot (see Figure 7.11)

(a) The original OAW triangle should have been drawn.

(b) From W, measure off in the direction WO, the distance at the new speed that own ship will steam in the plotting interval and label the point O_1. Join O_1 to A. This represents, in direction and rate, the new apparent motion.

(c) Until the proposed alteration takes place, the target should continue to move along the old apparent-motion line. Predict the position of the target at the time it is proposed to alter own ship's speed and label it O_2.

(d) Lay off O_2A_2 parallel with and equal to O_1A and produce it if necessary to find the new CPA.

Note (a) This prediction is based on the assumption that the target will maintain its course and speed and that own change in speed is instantaneous.

(b) It should be appreciated that when changing speed, especially in large vessels, it can take a considerable time to achieve the required new speed. Because of this, the new apparent motion line, O_2A_2, will be much nearer own ship than predicted in the example above.

7.5.5 The use of 'stopping distance' tables, graphs and formulae

7.5.5.1 *Stopping distance tables produced by The Honourable Company of Master Mariners*

It is not indended here to provide a full explanation of these tables, but merely to indicate their existence and show briefly, some of the ways in which they can be used. They are based on the formulae:

$$S = V \times e^{-t/k}$$
$$D = \frac{V \times k(1 - e^{-t/k})}{60}$$

where S is the speed change in knots, t minutes after the speed demand is made

V is the speed through the water when the speed demand is made

e is 2.718 281 8

t is the time in minutes since the speed demand was made

k is a constant related to the ship type

D is the distance travelled while changing speed.

Note
$$S = dx/dt = V \int e^{-t/k} \, dt$$
Therefore
$$x = V(-e^{-t/k} \times k) + c$$
(when $t = 0$, $D = 0$ therefore $c = Vk$)
Therefore
$$D = -Vk(e^{-t/k}) + Vk$$

$$= \frac{Vk(1 - e^{-t/k})}{60}$$

(the 60 in the formula is to allow t in minutes)
The above represents speed and distance *changes* and will therefore only give the speed and distance to be expected when the speed demanded is *stop*, i.e. when the demanded speed change is the speed of the vessel. Where the speed change is a proportion of the actual speed at the time of the demand, the formulae below will need to be used. These will give the actual speeds t minutes after a speed change is ordered. It is these formulae that are used as a minimum basis for speed alterations in some marine navigation simulators.

Acceleration $\quad S = (V - v)(1 - e^{-t/k}) + v$

Deceleration $\quad S = ((V - v).e^{-t/k}) + v$

where V is the higher speed, v is the lower speed and the other values are as above.

The formula for speed reduction quoted in this section is a particular application of a general relationship which is used in science to describe many examples of physical decay. In this particular application the value of the constant k is the time, in minutes, for the vessel's speed differential to fall to 0.37 of its original value. The Honourable Company of Master Mariners recognized the potential benefit to mariners of a set of tables giving the solution of both the speed and the distance formula for various values of the constant k. However, rather than use k, it was decided to express the results in terms of a constant C, which is referred to as the *speed change constant* and is defined as the time in minutes taken for a vessel to reach a speed midway between her original speed and the new speed ordered. It was believed that the time taken for the speed differential to reach half its original value would be much more meaningful to the mariner than the factor of 0.37 (C is in fact 0.7k).

Stopping distances are tabulated for increasing values of speed-change constant or 'C' value. Table 7.1(a) gives the speeds which can be expected after a given number of minutes from a requested manoeuvre. For example, a vessel with a speed-change constant C of 6 is steaming at a speed of 16 knots when the engines are set to stop. The figures in the shaded column (16) indicate the speeds to be expected as the vessel slows, i.e. 13 minutes after 'stop' the vessel should be down to a speed of 3.5 knots.

Table 7.1(b) shows how far the vessel will have travelled in the intervening minutes since ringing 'stop' on the engines, i.e. in the 13 minutes, the vessel will only have travelled 1.8 n mile instead of the 3.5 n mile the ship would have travelled at 16 knots.

Note that the tables are headed 'speed difference.' In

Table 7.1   Stopping distances for a vessel having a Speed Change Constant (C value) of 6

(a) SPEED DIFFERENCE IN KNOTS   C6

Minutes	Speed difference (knots)										
	10	11	12	13	14	15	16	17	18	19	20
1	8.9	9.8	10.7	11.6	12.5	13.3	14.2	15.1	16.0	16.9	17.8
3	7.0	7.8	8.5	9.2	9.9	10.6	11.3	12.0	12.7	13.4	14.1
5	5.6	6.1	6.7	7.3	7.8	8.4	8.9	9.5	10.0	10.6	11.2
7	4.4	4.9	5.3	5.7	6.2	6.6	7.1	7.5	8.0	8.4	8.8
9	3.5	3.8	4.2	4.5	4.9	5.2	5.6	5.9	6.3	6.6	7.0
11	2.8	3.0	3.3	3.6	3.9	4.2	4.4	4.7	5.0	5.3	5.5
13	2.2	2.4	2.6	2.9	3.1	3.3	3.5	3.7	3.9	4.2	4.4
15	1.7	1.9	2.1	2.3	2.4	2.6	2.8	3.0	3.1	3.3	3.5
17	1.4	1.5	1.7	1.8	1.9	2.1	2.2	2.3	2.5	2.6	2.8
19	1.1	1.2	1.3	1.4	1.5	1.6	1.7	1.9	2.0	2.1	2.2
21	0.9	0.9	1.0	1.1	1.2	1.3	1.4	1.5	1.6	1.6	1.7
23	0.7	0.8	0.8	0.9	1.0	1.0	1.1	1.2	1.2	1.3	1.4
25	0.5	0.6	0.6	0.7	0.8	0.8	0.9	0.9	1.0	1.0	1.1
27	0.4	0.5	0.5	0.6	0.6	0.6	0.7	0.7	0.8	0.8	0.9
29	0.3	0.4	0.4	0.4	0.5	0.5	0.5	0.6	0.6	0.6	0.7

(b) DISTANCE DIFFERENCE IN MILES

Minutes	Speed difference (knots)										
	10	**11**	**12**	**13**	**14**	**15**	**16**	**17**	**18**	**19**	**20**
1	0.2	0.2	0.2	0.2	0.2	0.2	**0.3**	0.3	0.3	0.3	0.3
3	0.4	0.5	0.5	0.5	0.6	0.6	**0.7**	0.7	0.8	0.8	0.8
5	0.6	0.7	0.8	0.8	0.9	0.9	**1.0**	1.1	1.1	1.2	1.3
7	0.8	0.9	1.0	1.0	1.1	1.2	**1.3**	1.4	1.4	1.5	1.6
9	0.9	1.0	1.1	1.2	1.3	1.4	**1.5**	1.6	1.7	1.8	1.9
11	1.0	1.1	1.2	1.3	1.4	1.5	**1.7**	1.8	1.9	2.0	2.1
13	1.1	1.2	1.3	1.4	1.6	1.7	**1.8**	1.9	2.0	2.1	2.2
15	1.2	1.3	1.4	1.5	1.7	1.8	**1.9**	2.0	2.1	2.2	2.4
17	1.2	1.4	1.5	1.6	1.7	1.8	**2.0**	2.1	2.2	2.3	2.5
19	1.3	1.4	1.5	1.7	1.8	1.9	**2.0**	2.2	2.3	2.4	2.5
21	1.3	1.4	1.6	1.7	1.8	2.0	**2.1**	2.2	2.3	2.5	2.6
23	1.3	1.5	1.6	1.7	1.9	2.0	**2.1**	2.3	2.4	2.5	2.7
25	1.4	1.5	1.6	1.8	1.9	2.0	**2.2**	2.3	2.4	2.6	2.7
27	1.4	1.5	1.6	1.8	1.9	2.1	**2.2**	2.3	2.5	2.6	2.7
29	1.4	1.5	1.7	1.8	1.9	2.1	**2.2**	2.3	2.5	2.6	2.8
HR★	1.4	1.6	1.7	1.9	2.0	2.1	**2.3**	2.4	2.6	2.7	2.9

★HR is for all practical purposes the 'head reach', i.e. the distance the vessel will travel while running the way off (Figure 7.12).

the special case of stopping, the speed difference and the initial speed are the same. In the general case, the speed difference is that between the initial speed and the demanded speed. The values in the body of Table 7.1(a) give the excess of the expected speed over the demanded speed for 2 minute intervals from the time of the manoeuvre request. The distances in the body of Table 7.1(b) represent the excess of the actual distance run over that

which would have been the case if the speed reduction had been instantaneous.

7.5.5.2 'C' factors and their verification.

The speed-change constant (or 'C' factor) is specific to a particular ship and the tables produced by the Honourable Company of Master Mariners provide guidance on the ways in which it may be determined and also some of the conditions which may give rise to changes. Variations in 'C' factor may be expected when accelerating and decelerating, with changes in draft and also in differing wind conditions.

Note The tables give some indication of the 'C' values which vessels of particular displacements are likely to have but these are intended only for initial guidance and should not be used without experimental verification.

Example 7.5 With own ship steering 000°(T) at a speed of 16 knots, an echo is observed as follows:

  0900   echo bears 045°(T) at 11.0 n mile
  0906   echo bears 045°(T) at 9.0 n mile
  0912   echo bears 045°(T) at 7.0 n mile

At 0915, the engines are stopped. If the vessel has a speed change constant of 6, draw in the limit line which the target would not be expected to cross. (See Figure 7.12.)

7.5.5.3 Manoeuvring data which should be available on board

The International Maritime Organization (IMO) recommends in Resolution A160 (ES IV) that booklets containing manoeuvring information should be on board and available to the masters of large ships and also on board smaller ships, especially those carrying dangerous chemicals.

Part 1 of the booklet should contain manoeuvring data and/or diagrams (preferably the latter), typical of which are the turning circle and stopping curve diagrams (see Figures 7.13 and 7.14).

The form of the booklet should be such that additional information can be added from 'trials' and during the normal course of the voyage. Shipmasters are encouraged to add to this basic information as they gain experience in the handling of the vessel in conditions not covered by the original data.

Copies of the appropriate diagrams should be posted on the bridge.

7.5.5.4 The use of stopping curves drawn up from data recorded during trials

Consider a vessel proceeding at 16 knots. If the engines are put to *stop*, it will take some 3.2 n mile to run off the

way, i.e. the readings associated with *A*, Figure 7.14.

If the engines are put to *half astern*, the vessel will be stopped in the water in some 17 minutes having covered some 1.7 n mile in running the way off, i.e. the readings associated with *B*.

If proceeding at 10 knots and full astern is demanded, the vessel will be stopped in the water in 10 minutes having covered some 7 cables while running the way off, i.e. the readings associated with *C*.

The stopping curves are intended primarily for use when the engines are to be put astern in order to stop the vessel in the water, e.g. when picking up a pilot, anchoring or in an emergency.

Note The curves assume that the environmental and loaded conditions etc. are the same as when the trials data was obtained. They should only be used as a rough guide as to what might be expected. It should also be borne in mind that as speed reduces, a critical speed will be reached when the vessel will no longer answer to the helm. When it is necessary to reduce speed even more quickly, other techniques such as rudder cycling may have to be employed. The prediction of how the speed may change or the vessel may turn under any conditions of loading, weather etc. can be very difficult. While the tables give some indication as to what may be expected, one should always work with a margin of safety and not leave manoeuvres until the last possible moment which theory suggests.

7.5.6 The plot when own ship combines course and speed alterations

Example 7.6 With own ship steering 000°(T) at a speed of 12 knots, an echo is observed as follows:

  0923   echo bears 037°(T) at 9.5 n mile
  0929   echo bears 036°(T) at 8.0 n mile
  0935   echo bears 034°(T) at 6.5 n mile

At 0935 it is intended to alter course 40° to starboard and reduce speed to 6 knots (assume this to be instantaneous).

(a)   Predict the new CPA and TCPA.

(b)   Predict the new CPA and TCPA if the manoeuvre is delayed until 0941.

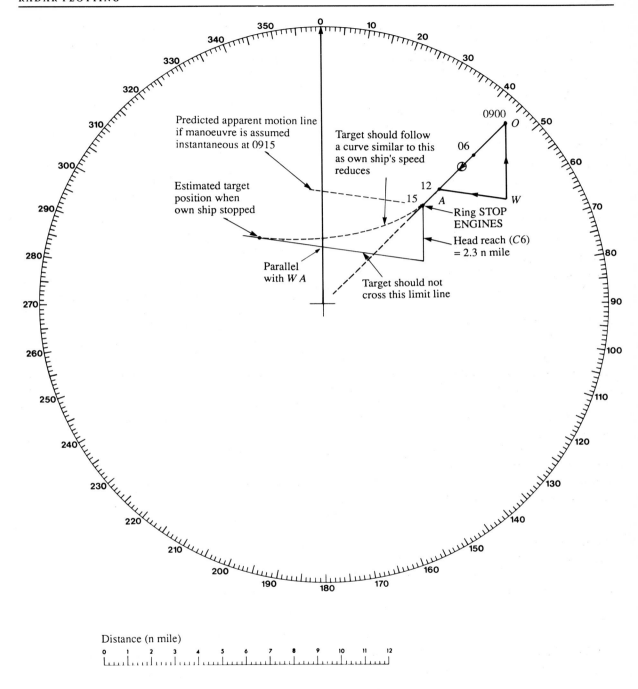

Figure 7.12   The plot when own ship stops: the effect of head reach (Example 7.5)

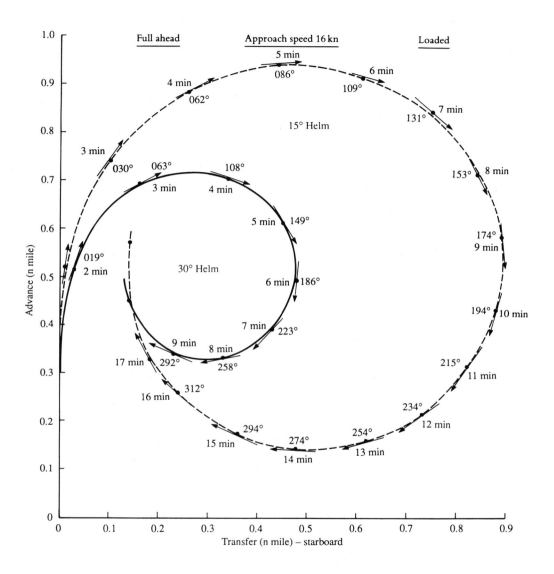

Figure 7.13 Turning circles

The response actually experienced may differ from that shown if any of the following conditions is not met:

Calm weather

No current or tidal stream

Water depth at least 2 × vessel's draught

Clean hull

Displacement 97 440 tonnes

Draught forward 9.14 m

Draught aft 9.14 m

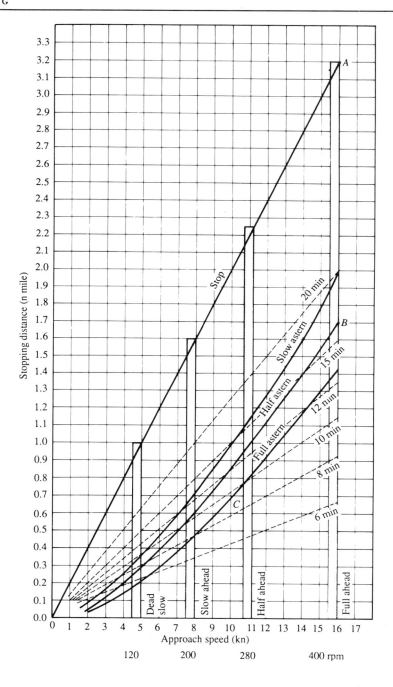

Figure 7.14 Stopping curves

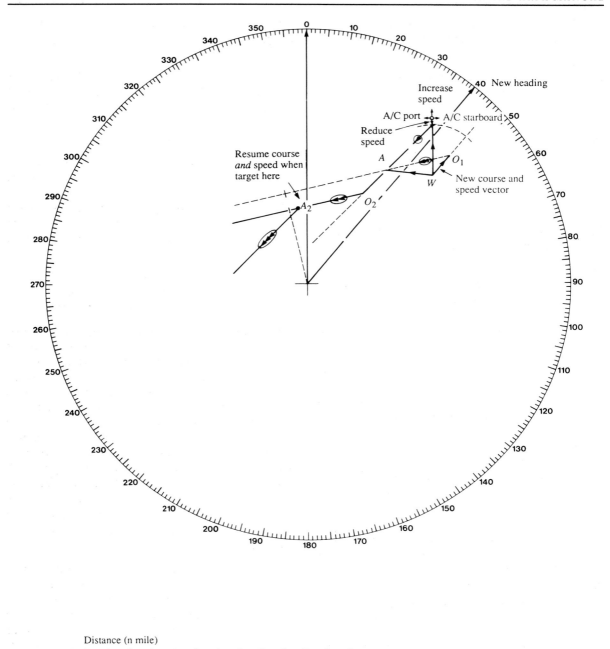

Figure 7.15   The plot when own ship combines course and speed alterations (Example 7.6)

(c) Predict the range and bearing of the echo at 0953 if the manoeuvre was made at 0941.

Answer (Figure 7.15)

(a) CPA is 4.4 n mile, 20 min after the manoeuvre. *Note* The new apparent motion direction is the same as that when course only was altered (see Figure 7.10) but the new rate, O_1A, is much slower.

(b) CPA is 3.6 n mile, 14.5 min after the manoeuvre at 0941, i.e. at 0955.5.

(c) Predicted range is 3.6 n mile on a bearing of 355°(T).

7.5.7 The plot when own ship resumes course and/or speed

When taking action to avoid a close-quarters situation, the action should be *substantial enough* and *held for long enough* to show up in the plotting of radar observers on other vessels.

In order to determine the effect of resuming own ship's course and/or speed:

(a) The original *OAW* triangle should have been drawn.

(b) The apparent motion after manoeuvring should have been predicted and, provided that the target has maintained its course and speed, the target will follow the new apparent motion line, O_2A_2.

(c) If the target still maintains its course and speed and own ship resumes her original course and/or speed, the direction and rate of the final apparent motion will be the same as in the original *OAW* triangle. Thus, from the target's predicted position at the time of resumption, draw O_3A_3 parallel and equal to OA and produce if necessary to find the new CPA after resumption.

(d) If it is required to find the time to resume so that the CPA will not be less than, for example, 4 miles, lay off a line parallel to OA and tangential to the 4 mile range circle. The point at which this final apparent-motion line crosses the second apparent-motion line should be labelled O_3. Predict the time at which the target will reach O_3. This will be the time to resume.

Note When predicting the movement of a target along an apparent-motion line, be sure to use the appropriate rate of apparent motion.

Example 7.7 Using Examples 7.3 and 7.4, predict in each case the CPA if the original course and speed respectively are resumed at 0953 (see Figures 7.10 and 7.11).

Answer

(a) If course is resumed at 0953, CPA = 3.5 n mile.

(b) If speed is resumed instantaneously at 0953, CPA = 2.4 n mile.

Note If the order for an increase in speed is given at 0953, then by the time the vessel has worked up to the required speed the target will have passed in excess of the 2.4 n mile CPA.

7.5.8 The plot when both vessels manoeuvre simultaneously

It has been assumed until now that only one of the two vessels in the encounter manoeuvres. In such cases, the resulting apparent motion can be predicted when own ship manoeuvres, or resolved when only the target manoeuvres. When ships of about the same size meet, it is not uncommon for them to commence plotting at about the same time and subsequently manoeuvre simultaneously or nearly so. If each vessel has plotted initially and completed the construction showing the effect of an own ship manoeuvre, then the target in each case will not follow the predicted apparent motion. In some cases this will result in each 'target' clearing by a greater distance than predicted but this will not always be the case. Thus it is essential when own ship manoeuvres:

(a) To predict the target's new apparent motion, assuming that it maintains course and speed.

(b) To ensure that the manoeuvre is having the (desired) predicted effect. It is not sufficient merely to assume that, because the target 'appears' to be going clear, it is moving in the direction *and rate* predicted. Where the predicted direction and rate are not as expected, a new plot must be started and the action taken by the target must be determined.

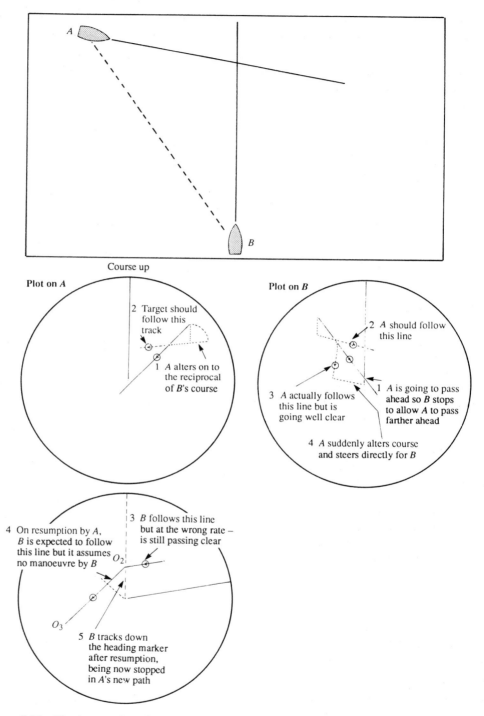

Figure 7.16 The danger of not determining the target's actual manoeuvre when apparently passing clear

The latter can have important consequences in deciding when it is safe to resume. No longer can it be assumed that the 'final' apparent motion will be parallel and equal to the original apparent motion, as was assumed in Section 7.5.7.

Consider the situation in fog, as set out in Figure 7.16.

If both vessels manoeuvre simultaneously or at nearly the same time, B as observed from A will move along the new apparent-motion line (but at the wrong rate, which is now much slower) and so appear to be going clear. No longer will B move along O_2O_3 when A resumes: it will move down parallel to the heading marker, since B is now stopped in the water.

If the apparent motion of B had not been predicted, monitored and re-appraised after the manoeuvre was detected, A might well have resumed course when B was at O_2, only to find a vessel stopped directly in its path. This would have manifested itself by B coming down A's heading marker and thus requiring sudden emergency action, possibly by both vessels at a very late stage in the encounter.

If systematic observation and interpretation is not carried out on B, as the way is run off, the relative motion plot would start to relate to the true situation, in which case B would have observed a vessel steering to pass clear down the port side but then appearing to turn to port and steer directly toward it. Having very little way on at this stage, there is very little that B can do to avoid the close-quarters situation.

The encounter considered above is frequently carried out with the best of intentions but it is clear that, where manoeuvres are executed without proper prediction, monitoring and re-appraisal, the consequences can be dire.

7.6   The theory and construction of PPCs, PADs, SODs and SOPs

The harnessing of computers and ARPAs to assist in the resolution of the plotting triangle led to the question of whether some assistance could be given which would be of a higher order than that provided by the *trial man-oeuvre* facility on the ARPA (see Section 4.4.3). Without going to the extreme of an *expert system* (see Section 7.11.4), some attempts were made to give a graphical representation of the encounter geometry which would assist the mariner in selecting an acceptable manoeuvre. The major problem was to devise a way in which this 'advice' should be presented to the mariner so that it was most meaningful. What follows is the theory and construction of the graphic representations that were devised; the philosophy and shortcomings are discussed in Chapter 5. It is stressed that it is not envisaged that an observer would construct these points or areas manually. Where available, they will be generated by computer graphics. However, it is essential that any observer who elects to use such facilities understands the principles upon which their construction is based.

7.6.1   The possible point of collision (PPC)

This is the point or points toward which own ship should steer at her present speed (assuming that the target does not manoeuvre) in order for a collision to occur (Figure 7.17 (a)). The logic of this is that if one knows the course(s) which will result in collision then, by not steering those courses, collisions will be avoided. Also, by picking one's way between the PPCs, a more far-reaching collision avoidance strategy can be evolved.

Example 7.8   With own ship steering 000°(T) at a speed of 10 knots, an echo is observed as follows:

    0923   echo bears 037°(T) at 10.3 n mile
    0929   echo bears 036°(T) at 8.5 n mile
    0935   echo bears 034°(T) at 6.7 n mile

Determine the bearing and range of the PPC(s).

Answer (Figure 7.17 (b))
(a) P_1 bearing 337° at a range of 4.4 n mile.
(b) P_2 bearing 270° at a range of 18.0 n mile.

7.6.2   The construction to find the PPC

(a)   Plot the target and produce the basic triangle.

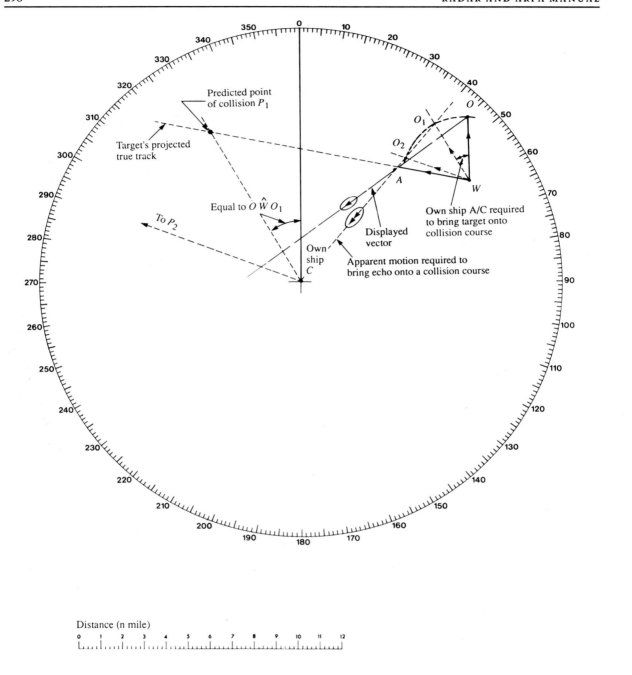

Figure 7.17

(a)   The possible point of collision (PPC)

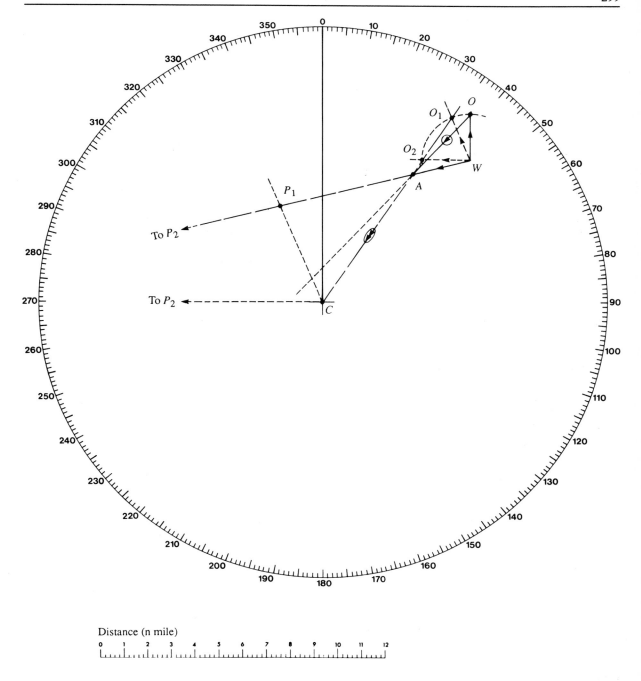

(b) Answer to Example 7.8

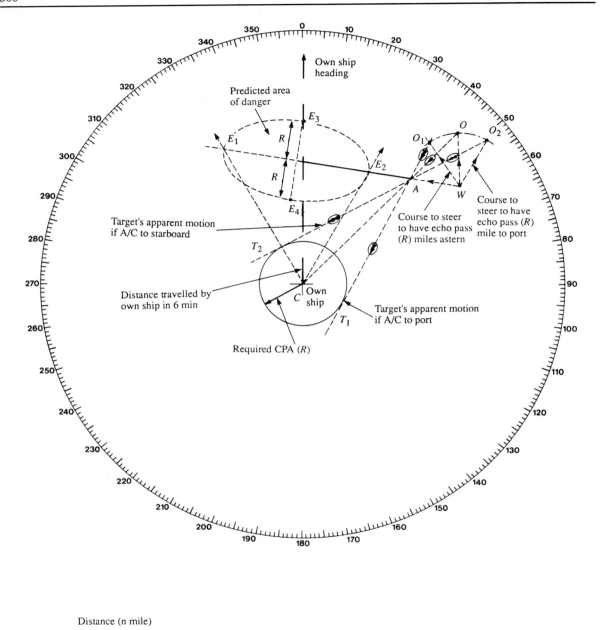

Figure 7.18
(a)   The predicted area of danger (PAD)

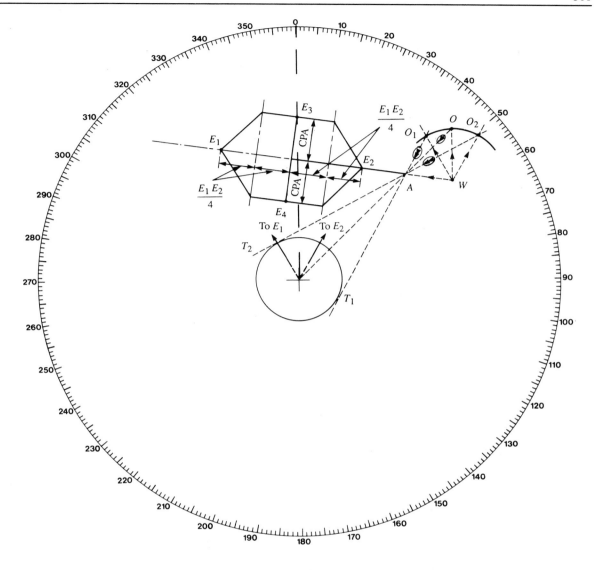

Distance (n mile)

(b)   Answer to Example 7.9

(b) Join the own ship position 'C' to the target's position 'A' and produce beyond 'A'.

(c) With compasses at W and radius WO, scribe an arc to cut CA produced at O_1 or, if own ship is the slower (i.e. $WO < WA$), at O_1 and O_2

(d) Join WO_1 (and WO_2).

(e) Draw CP_1 parallel to WO_1 to cut WA produced at P_1 (and CP_2 parallel to WO_2 to cut WA produced at P_2).

(f) P_1 (and P_2) is the PPC.

For a clearer appreciation of the determination of the PPC, Example 7.8 should be drawn out full size and to scale on a plotting sheet.

7.6.3   The predicted area of danger (PAD)

The PPC gives no indication of the course which needs to be steered to clear the PPC by some specific distance: to this end, the PAD was devised (Figure 7.18 (a)). A further improvement is that the target is connected to its PAD on the display, which was not the case with the PPC.

Example 7.9   With own ship steering 000°(T) at a speed of 12 knots, an echo is observed as follows:

1000   echo bears 045°(T) at 10.0 n mile
1006   echo bears 045°(T) at 8.5 n mile
1012   echo bears 045°(T) at 7.0 n mile

Plot the target and draw in the PAD for a 2.0 n mile clearing.

Answer See Figure 7.18(b).

7.6.4   The construction of the PAD

(a) Plot the target and produce the basic triangle.

(b) Draw lines AT_1 and AT_2 from the target's position A, tangential to a circle of radius equal to the required CPA. Produce beyond A.

(c) With compasses at W and radius WO, scribe an arc to cut T_1A produced and T_2A produced at O_1 and O_2 respectively.

(d) Join WO_1 and WO_2. These represent the limiting courses to steer to clear the target by the required CPA.

(e) Draw CE_1 and CE_2 parallel to WO_1 and WO_2 respectively, to cut WA produced at E_1 and E_2 respectively.

(f) At the mid-point of E_1E_2, draw the perpendicular to E_1E_2 and extend it in both directions. In each direction, mark off the 'required CPA' and label the points E_3 and E_4.

(g) Draw in the ellipse passing through the points E_1, E_2, E_3, and E_4 (or the hexagon as indicated in Figure 7.18 (b)).

For a clearer appreciation of the PAD, Example 7.9 should be drawn out full size and to scale on a plotting sheet.

7.6.5   The sector of danger (SOD)

In this approach, a line CH, equal in length and direction to OW is drawn from the centre of the plotting sheet. This line is referred to as the *own ship vector*. The sector of danger is an area constructed to provide a chosen passing distance. If the remote end of the own ship vector lies outside the SOD, a passing distance greater than the chosen value will be achieved, provided that the target does not manoeuvre.

Example 7.10   With own ship steering 000°(T) at a speed of 12 knots, an echo is observed as follows:

1000   echo bears 045°(T) at 11.0 n mile
1010   echo bears 045°(T) at 9.0 n mile
1020   echo bears 045°(T) at 7.0 n mile

Plot the SOD and suggest the minimum alteration of course to starboard at 1020 (instantaneous) which will achieve a 2 n mile CPA if own ship's speed is maintained throughout.

Answer. If own ship alters course to 027°(T) at 1020 then the target's new apparent motion will be along AT_1.

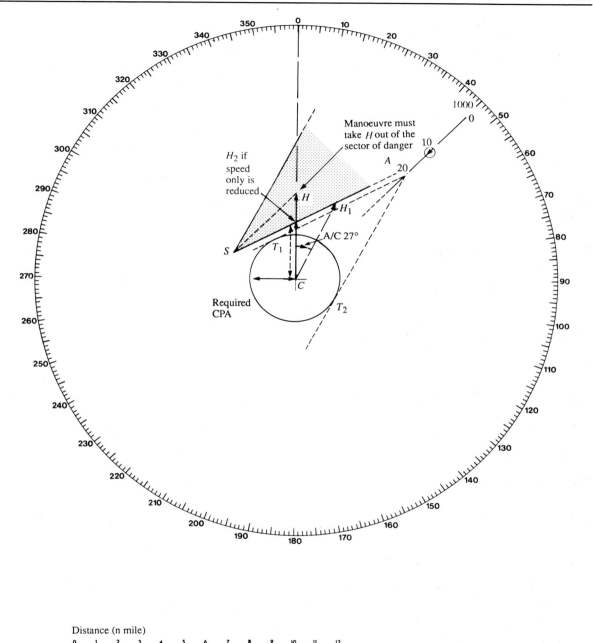

Figure 7.19 The sector of danger (SOD) – Example 7.10

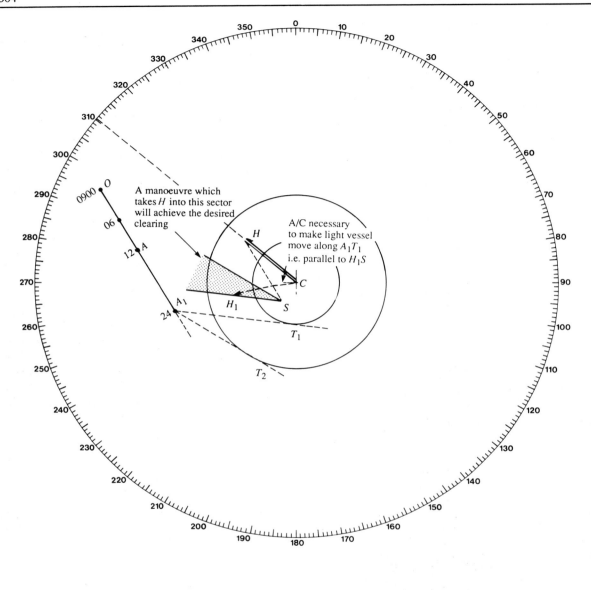

Figure 7.20   The sector of preference (SOP) – Example 7.11

7.6.6 The construction of a sector of danger

(a) Plot the target for a set period.

(b) Draw own ship's vector for the same period – *CH*, equal to the distance that own ship will travel in the plotting interval, i.e. equal to *OW*.

(c) Draw *HS* parallel and equal to *OA*.

(d) Draw AT_1 and AT_2 tangential to the 'required CPA' range circle. (*Note*. If it were intended to delay the manoeuvre, then the tangents would be drawn from the predicted position of the target at the manoeuvre time.)

(e) Parallel T_1A and T_2A through *S*.

(f) Any manoeuvre which takes *H* outside the shaded sector will achieve a CPA in excess of the required CPA.

(g) Swing *CH* until it just touches the sector boundary at H_1. This is the minimum alteration of course to starboard which own ship can make at the present speed to keep the target to a 2 n mile CPA.

Alternatively, 'speed' could have been reduced to CH_2 which would also have taken own ship's vector just outside the sector.

While this will take care of the geometry, it is essential to ensure that the manoeuvre selected is still in accordance with the collision avoidance rules and the practice of good seamanship (see Section 7.12).

7.6.7 The sector of preference (SOP)

This relates to a stationary target or navigation mark and is a sector into which one must steer to achieve a passing distance within prescribed limits (Figure 7.20).

Example 7.11 With own ship steering 310°(T) at a speed of 15 knots, a light vessel, identified by its racon, is observed as follows:

0900	echo bears 296°(T) at	10.0 n mile
0906	echo bears 290°(T) at	8.6 n mile
0912	echo bears 282°(T) at	7.4 n mile

It is intended to manoeuvre at 0924.

(a) Construct the SOP if the light vessel is required to pass at not less than 2 n mile nor more than 4 n mile to port.

(b) Determine the course alteration which would be needed to achieve a CPA of 2 n mile to port (assume the alteration to be instantaneous).

Answer. (b) Alter course to 258°(T), i.e. 52° to port.

7.6.8 The construction of a sector of preference

(a) Plot the stationary target for a set period of time.

(b) Draw own ship's vector for the same period, *CH*, equal to the distance that own ship will travel in the plotting interval, i.e. equal to *OW*.

(c) Draw *HS* parallel and equal to *OA*.

(d) Plot the position of the target at the time at which it is intended to manoeuvre, A_1.

(e) From A_1, draw tangents to range limits for clearing the target, A_1T_1 and A_1T_2.

(f) Parallel T_1A_1 and T_2A_1 through *S*.

(g) Any manoeuvre which takes *H* into the shaded sector will result in the target clearing within the limits for which the sector was drawn (provided that any tidal effect remains constant). This could be achieved by an alteration of course or speed or both. If *CH* is swung until it intersects either of the limits of the shaded sector then that will be the course required to achieve the specific CPA.

7.7 The plot in tide

Example 7.12 With own ship steering 310°(T) at a speed of 15 knots, the echo from a light vessel fitted with a racon is observed as follows:

0900	echo bears 346°(rel) at	10.0 n mile
0906	echo bears 340°(rel) at	8.6 n mile
0912	echo bears 332°(rel) at	7.4 n mile

(a) Find the set and rate of the tide.

(b) It is required that your ship should pass 2 n mile off, leaving the light vessel to port.

  (i) If action is taken instantaneously at 0912, find the alteration of course which would be necessary.

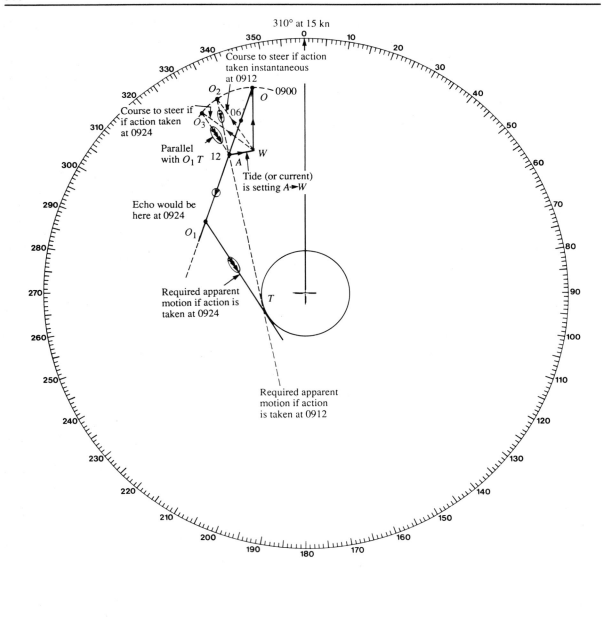

Figure 7.21   The plot in tide – Example 7.12

(ii) If instead, the action is to be taken at 0924 instead of 0912, find the alteration of course which would then be necessary.

Answer. See Figure 7.21

(a) Set = 032°(T) at 5 knots
(b) (i) course to steer at 0912 is 278°(T)
    (ii) course to steer at 0924 is 260°(T)

7.7.1 The construction of the plot

(a) Establish the identity of the target beyond all doubt (see Section 8.2). Plot the target and construct the basic triangle.
(b) W and A should coincide if there is no tide. If they do not, then A to W is the direction in which the tide is setting. Note that this is the reverse of what is normally deduced from a plot but since the target cannot be moving, it is the ship which must be experiencing set. The distance WA is the drift of the tide in the plotting interval and it is from this that the tidal rate can be calculated.

Note When plotting other (moving) targets while experiencing tide, it is their movement through the water which is evaluated. It is precisely this which needs to be known when applying the collision avoidance rules and so it is essential that *no* attempt should be made to apply the effect of tide or current to their courses as determined from the plot.

7.7.2 The course to steer to counteract the tide

(a) Plot the target and determine the tide or current.
(b) Predict the position of the target at the time at which it is intended to manoeuvre.
(c) Draw in the apparent motion which is required, e.g. $A_1 T$.
(d) Draw in a line in the reverse direction through A, i.e. AO_2 (and AO_3 for the manoeuvre at 0924).
(e) Swing WO to cut the line through A at AO_2 (and AO_3).

(f) WO_2 is the new course to steer (and WO_3 if the manoeuvre is delayed).

Note All of the above assume instantaneous manoeuvres. When handling large ships in tide, due allowance will need to be made for their handling characteristics, especially when a speed change is demanded.

7.7.3 The change of course needed to maintain track when changing speed in tide

When proceeding while experiencing tide, any change in own ship's course and/or speed and/or tidal set and/or rate will affect the vessel's ground track.

Example 7.13 While steering 090°(T) at a speed of 16 knots, a beacon marking the anchorage is observed as follows:

0900 echo bears 076°(T) at 10.0 n mile
0906 echo bears 070°(T) at 8.6 n mile
0912 echo bears 062°(T) at 7.4 n mile

It is intended to anchor 2 n mile due South of the beacon.

(a) Determine the set and rate of the tide.
(b) Determine the course to steer at 0912 to counteract the tide.
(c) If the speeds which are represented by the engine room telegraph settings of Half Ahead, Slow Ahead and Dead Slow Ahead are 9, 6 and 3 knots respectively, determine the courses to be steered as the speed is progressively reduced when approaching the anchorage.

Answer. See Figure 7.22

(a) The tide is setting 184°(T) at 5 knots.
(b) At 0912, alter course to 060°(T).
(c) Half Ahead – steer 052°(T)
    Slow Ahead – steer 035°(T)
    Dead Slow Ahead: it is necessary to steer 004°(T) and stem the tide but note that the tide is 1 knot greater than the ahead speed.

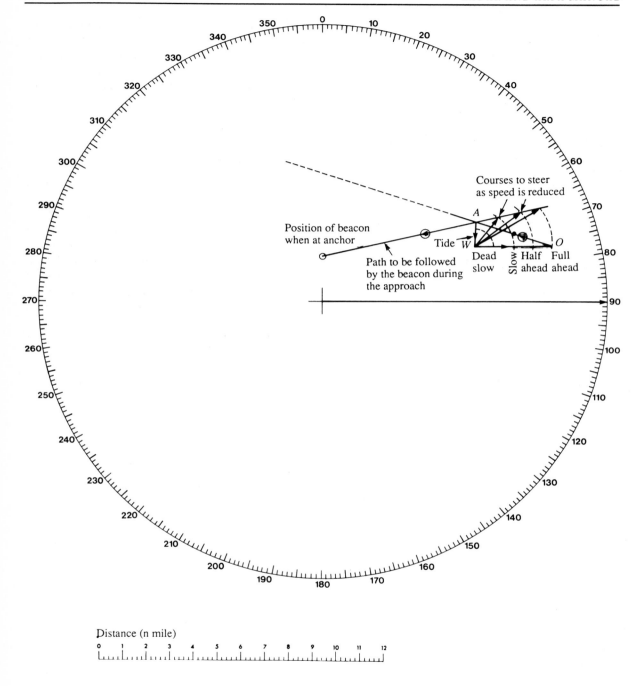

Figure 7.22   The course to steer in tide as speed is reduced – Example 7.13

7.8   The theory and practice of reflection plotters

The work involved in the transferring of data from the radar display to a plotting sheet is both time-consuming and a potential source of errors and so is a discouragement to practical plotting. The advantage of being able to plot directly on the screen surface was recognised at a very early stage in the development of radar. As a result, the anti-parallax reflection plotter was developed.

7.8.1   The construction of the reflection plotter

As can be seen from Figure 7.23, the plotting surface has the same curvature as the cathode ray tube (see Section 2.6.1). By inverting it and placing a flat partial reflecting surface midway between the two curved surfaces, it is possible to put a mark on the concave plotting surface such that its *reflection* will be aligned with the target's response on the CRT surface irrespective of where the observer's eye is positioned. This overcomes the problems of parallax which would arise if one were to try to plot on the plastic cursor placed some inches above the CRT surface.

7.8.2   Testing and adjustment

The relative positioning of all three surfaces is critical if paralactic errors are to be avoided. In many plotters, means are provided for adjusting the position of the partial reflecting surface as well as its 'tilt'. This is usually done by means of four adjusting screws. In order to test and adjust for freedom from parallax it is necessary to have four targets, one in each quadrant. These are marked on the plotting surface and then viewed from various directions and positions. If the plotted positions

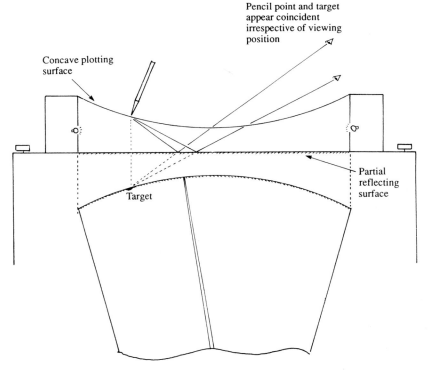

Figure 7.23   The reflection plotter

do not remain co-incident with all four targets, adjustment is necessary. This may take more than one 'round', as the adjustment of one screw can mean that all the others will require further trimming.

In order to overcome this need for adjustment, most modern plotters are now sealed units, but the plotter should still be regularly checked for misalignment.

7.8.3 Care and maintenance

The exposed surfaces and, in particular, the plotting surface should be wiped regularly with a dry cloth, taking care not to disturb the positioning of the surfaces.

On occasions, the plotting surface may require additional cleaning, when Perspex polish, supplied by the manufacturer, can be used. This should *never* be used on the partial reflecting surface.

It should be possible for the reflection plotter to remain in place but when it becomes necessary to remove it temporarily and store it, care should be taken to avoid it being bumped or scratched.

7.8.4 The practical use of reflection plotters, including the use of the Perspex cursor and parallel index

Plotting should be carried out on the plotting surface as if working on a plotting sheet but it is the 'reflections' which must be continually observed. Two techniques are peculiar to reflection plotting:

(a) It will be necessary to make a 'scale' rule for measuring distance on the plotting surface. This is done by brightening the range rings, placing a mark on each ring and then, using stiff card, marking the position of each ring on the card. Sub-divisions may be put in by eye or more precisely, using the variable range marker. See Figure 7.24.

(b) It will be necessary to draw parallel lines on the plotter surface, e.g. *OW* parallel to the heading marker. This is done by lining up the Perspex cursor (see Section 6.9.3) with the heading marker – the parallel index lines on the cursor will now be parallel with the heading marker. Align the edge of

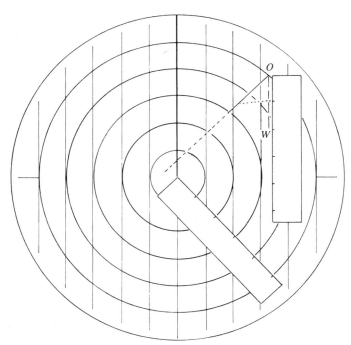

Figure 7.24 Constructing and using a scale rule

the scale rule with the nearest parallel index line below it – this may mean that one has to move the position of one's head slightly, or slide the card a short distance.

Note   When drawing a line from a point, tangential to a range ring, e.g. when determining the time to resume, it is best first to mark the position of the range ring on the plotter surface.

7.8.5   Changing range scale

The reflection plotter has two distinct advantages: namely, it eliminates the need for reading and transfer of ranges and bearings to a plotting sheet and it maintains the immediate contact between display and plot. However, there is a certain reluctance on the part of the observer to change range scale because of the perceived potential loss of the plot. Nonetheless, it is important that when targets are close, the most appropriate range scale is used. This will mean adapting the plot to the new range scale. As can be seen in Figure 7.25, once the target is within the inner portion of the screen, the range scale should be changed and the predicted apparent motion

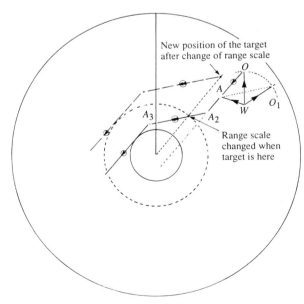

Figure 7.25   Changing range scale on a reflection plotter

line A_2A_3 drawn parallel through the new position of the target.

It can often prove useful to retain the original plot and, provided that the lines do not become confusing, they can be left on.

7.8.6   The use of the 'free' EBL to draw parallel lines (see Section 6.9.6)

The 'free' EBL can prove extremely useful for transferring parallel lines in conjunction with a reflection plotter in preference to the use of the parallel lines on the Perrspex cursor.

The EBL origin is positioned on the reflection of the line to be transferred and is rotated so that it is aligned with the line to be transferred. The EBL will maintain its orientation as it is moved about the screen using the joystick (see Figure 7.26).

7.8.7   Fixed and rotatable surfaces – use with a ship's-head-up unstabilized display

While using a plotter on a ship's-head-up unstabilized display, if it becomes necessary to alter own ship's course, the target and plot will come out of alignment as own ship changes course. For example, in Figure 7.27, after an initial plot, own ship alters course 55° to starboard; at the completion of the manoeuvre, the plot and target will be as depicted. To re-align the plot to the target, rotate the plotter surface anti-clockwise (i.e. in the opposite direction to the alteration of course) by the amount which own ship has altered course.

When a rotatable surface has not been provided, there are means by which the plot can be continued. However, they can be complicated and consequently confusing, and are best avoided.

When a fixed-surface plotter is provided, it is virtually essential that the true-north-up stabilized presentation is selected (see Section 1.4.2).

7.8.8   Flat and concave surfaces

The plotter described in Section 7.8.1 and in Figure 7.23 is typical of many plotters which are carried aboard ships

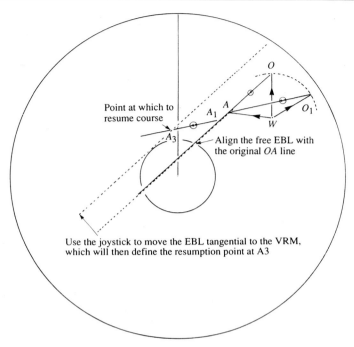

Point at which to
resume course

Align the free EBL with
the original *OA* line

Use the joystick to move the EBL tangential to the VRM,
which will then define the resumption point at A3

Figure 7.26   The use of the 'free' EBL to draw parallel lines.
Note Transfer the line to the plotting surface if the EBL is
required for another use; if not, leave it in place

today. The concave surface can be rather awkward to work on and so in recent years more complex plotters have been provided with flat plotting surfaces. This has been made possible by using a curved partial reflecting surface. However, apart from that, its use is exactly the same as for a plotter with a concave plotting surface.

7.8.9   Use in conjunction with parallel indexing

The provision of a reflection plotter made it possible for a prepared navigation plan to be marked out on the plotter and the movement of particular navigation marks to be observed in relation to their predicted movement. Any deviation from the pre-planned track

will be readily apparent and compensation can be made (see Section 8.4).

7.8.10   Reflection plotters and raster-scan displays

As yet it would appear that no manufacturer has produced an optical reflection plotter which can be used with a television-type CRT. Where the requirement to carry radar equipment includes a reflection plotter or equivalent means of plotting and especially where only one radar display is to be fitted, a raster-scan display is in effect precluded unless it has some form of electronic plotting facility such as the Kelvin Hughes 'E' Plot (see Section 7.11.3).

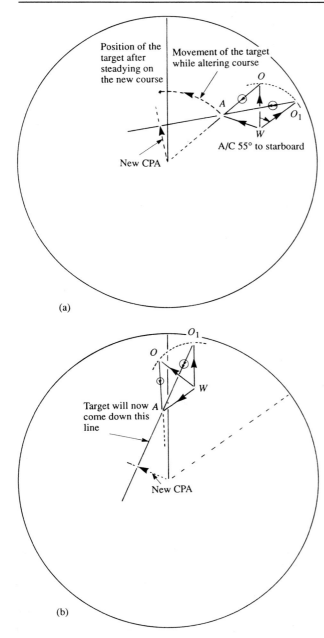

Figure 7.27 The use of a rotatable plotting surface
(a) Before or during alteration of course
(b) After rotation of the plotter

7.9 Manual plotting – accuracy and errors

The error in the result from any computation depends upon the accuracy of the data used. The intrinsic sources of error in the radar system relate to the measurement of ranges and bearings. Other data needed to complete the radar plot and subject to error are own ship's course and speed, and the plotting interval. Also, there are of course personal errors and blunders. While a *constant* (or systematic) error in input will result in a constant error in the answer obtained, it is the errors which are of a random nature which govern the size of the 'circle of uncertainty' around the plotted position which, if not actually drawn, should be borne in mind when plotting a position.

Note *Precision of measurement* and *accuracy of measurement* should not be confused. For example, it is no good being able to measure bearings to 0.1° if the 'free play' in the gearing is ±2°.

7.9.1 Accuracy of bearings as plotted

Errors in bearings may arise from any of the following causes:

1 The existence of inherent errors which fall within the limits allowed by the IMO Performance Standard (see Section 10.2). The individual error sources are discussed in detail in Section 6.9 where it is shown that they may aggregate to as much as ±2.5°. It is also indicated that some components of the total error can be expected to remain constant over a series of bearings and these will have the effect of slewing all plotted positions by a fixed amount. There will, of course, be a random component which is most likely to arise from an instantaneous misalignment of the antenna and trace and should not exceed ±1°. This error will have the effect of scattering the observed positions about the correct apparent motion.

2 Parallax when bearings are taken with the Perspex cursor (see Section 6.9.3).

3 Failure to centre the origin correctly when use is to be made of the Perspex cursor. The magnitude of this error will depend upon several factors which are described in Section 6.2.3.3.

4 Errors of alignment of the electronic bearing line. This error is likely to be constant over a series of bearings (see Section 6.9.5).

5 Failure to check the heading at the time a bearing is taken when a ship's-head-up unstabilized orientation is selected. This error is likely to be random.

6 Personal errors and blunders.

7.9.2   Accuracy of ranges as plotted

Sources of error in the measurement of range may include any or all of the following:

1 Range errors inherent in radar systems which comply with the IMO Performance Standards. These are described in Section 6.9. They should not exceed 1.5% of the maximum range of the scale in use or 70 metres, whichever is the greater. On the 12 n mile range scale this gives 1.8 cables or 333 metres. These errors should be constant over a series of ranges.

2 Inaccurate interpolation. This will give rise to random errors.

3 Mechanical errors in the variable range marker. Such errors should normally be constant over a series of ranges unless a serious mechanical fault exists.

4 Personal errors or blunders.

7.9.3   Accuracy of own ship's speed

In general, the means of obtaining the ship's speed can be flawed in the extreme and is the quantity most susceptible to error. Speed (or rather, distance travelled in the plotting interval) can be derived from a variety of sources, for example:

1 *Distance (towed) log.* In this case, it is not possible to know one's speed quickly, particularly when altering speed (e.g. in poor visibility). Also, it is common practice to hand the log when the engines are put on stand-by, so as to avoid fouling the propeller when the engines are put astern (some towed logs do have an additional unit which provide a read-out of speed).

2 *Speed (pitot, impeller, electromagnetic) log.* Although the speed may be read at any instant, the sensor is frequently withdrawn when the vessel is in shallow water, e.g. in port approaches.

3 *Engine revolutions.* This is only accurate in so far as 'slip' is accurately known and this is rarely the case when changing speed such as when manoeuvring in fog.

4 *Doppler log.* It should be borne in mind that if ground locked, this indicates speed over the ground which in tide can lead to misinterpretation of the aspects of other ships (see Ground-stabilization, Section 6.8.1.3). Also, there is some uncertainty as to just what 'speed' is being measured if using a single-axis sensor which is 'ground locked'.

5 *Speed derived from positions plotted on the chart.* There is a common misconception that this is the ship's 'correct' speed and on this basis it is used for plotting and as the manual input to the true-motion unit and ARPA (see Sections 6.8.1.3 and 6.12.3). It must be remembered that the speed derived is measured over the ground, whereas it is the speed through the water which is required for plotting. Thus, if there is any tide involved, its effect *must* be allowed for in order to deduce the water speed.

Note   The slower own ship's speed, the greater will be the proportionate effects of errors in the knowledge of own ship's speed. Unfortunately, the plot can be at its most inaccurate when both vessels are moving slowly as they might be when proceeding in fog.

7.9.4   Accuracy of own ship's course

Compass error should be small and relatively constant so, although it will produce errors in target course and speed, they too should be small and constant. Where the ship is off course for minutes at a time and this is not taken into account in the plot, errors in the target's course and speed will result (see Figure 7.29).

7.9.5   Accuracy of the plotting interval

The times of each plot are normally recorded to the nearest minute and so an error of up to half a minute can be quite common when plotting a position. This can

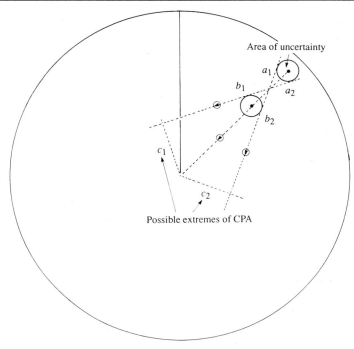

Figure 7.28   The accuracy with which CPA can be determined

mean an error of up to 1 minute in a plotting interval of, say, 5 minutes, i.e. 20%. As the plotting interval is used to calculate the distance run (OW), an error here will have the same effect as an error in speed.

7.9.6   The accuracy with which CPA can be determined

Random errors in obtaining the range and bearing of a target will mean that when a position is plotted, it should be surrounded by an *area of uncertainty* based on the errors referred to in Sections 7.9.1 and 7.9.2. In Figure 7.28, the apparent-motion line through the plotted positions indicates a vessel on a collision course. However, if 'worst accuracy' is considered, i.e. that the target's position is at a_1 and some time later at b_2 or, alternatively, is at a_2 and later at b_1, then the CPA of the target will lie in the range between c_1 to port and c_2 to starboard.

The means by which accuracy can be improved are:

(a)   Improve the inherent accuracy of the system, i.e. decrease the size of the circles of uncertainty.

(b)   Plot frequently. This has the advantage of being a quick check for blunders while also allowing for a better 'mean' line to be drawn through the plotted positions. It has been suggested that the time period for which plotting should be continued before accepting that the result is of sufficient accuracy should be calculated by allowing the target to traverse some $0.2 \times$ radius of screen, e.g. OA should be some 2.4 n mile when using the 12 n mile range scale.

7.9.7   The consequences of random errors in own ship's course and speed

We assume in the following that positions O and A are without error.

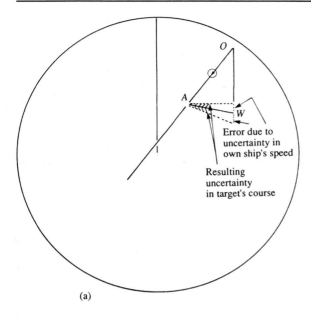

(a)

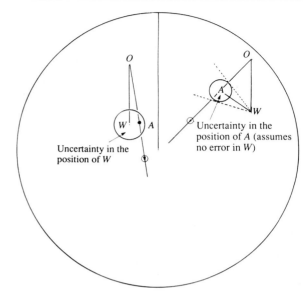

Figure 7.30   Slow-moving targets

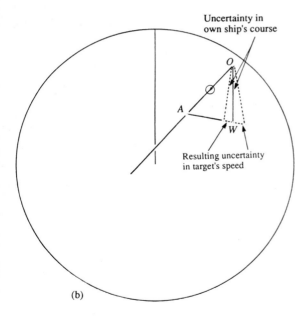

(b)

Figure 7.29   Errors resulting from inaccuracy
(a)   in own ship's speed
(b)   in own ship's course
   Note Assume no error in *O* or *A*

In the *OAW* triangle (Figure 7.29), the position of *W* is determined from a knowledge of own ship's course and speed. It is important to note here, that, when dealing with a slow-moving target, if *A* falls within the error circle around *W* then it is impossible to determine the course and/or speed of the target (see Figure 7.30).

7.9.8   Summary

1 It has been estimated that the full maximum error occurs only in some 1 per cent of encounters.
2 In deciding what is an acceptable CPA, the consequences of inaccuracies should be borne in mind and one should err on the safe side.
3 Small alterations of course and speed by plotted targets can be completely swamped by errors, especially when speeds are low.

In an attempt to evaluate the errors, the following have been suggested:

$$\text{Error in CPA} = \frac{\pm 0.03 \times \text{mean range}}{\text{range change}}$$

$$\text{Error in vessel's estimated course (degrees)} = \frac{103 \times \text{mean range}}{\left(\substack{\text{estimated speed} \\ \text{of target}}\right) \times \left(\substack{\text{plot interval} \\ \text{in minutes}}\right)}$$

$$\text{Error in target's speed (\%)} = \frac{180 \times \text{mean range}}{\left(\substack{\text{estimated speed} \\ \text{of target}}\right) \times \left(\substack{\text{plot interval} \\ \text{in minutes}}\right)}$$

7.10 Errors associated with the true-motion presentation

The true-motion display (see Section 2.6.4) is, in fact, a contrived mode of display in that the 'received data' is processed by applying the ship's course and speed in order to achieve the desired method of presentation. Because of this, the accuracy of this form of presentation is subject, in addition to the errors discussed in Sections 7.9.7 and 7.9.8, to errors which may arise in the accuracy with which the origin tracks across the screen.

7.10.1 Incorrect setting of the true-motion controls

When setting up the true-motion presentation, the method of course and speed input will have to be selected by the operator. The course input will invariably be from a repeating compass and will be automatic, but the repeater in the radar will have to be aligned with the master compass. Provided that this has been done correctly, errors from this source should be minimal (see Section 6.8.2).

The source of speed input can be provided by log, by manual input or with ARPA, by means of automatic ground-stabilization (see Section 5.3). The points discussed in Section 7.9.7 apply here and will affect the displayed movement of the target(s) (see Figures 7.32 and 7.33), but it is the setting of the 'manual' input of speed that warrants special attention.

While steaming at a steady speed it is possible to set the manual speed input and virtually forget about it, but

in fog, heavy traffic and in port approaches it may be necessary to change speed frequently. Amid all the other bridge activity, it must be remembered that the manual speed control on the radar will also need to be re-set each time there is a change in the demanded speed. It is logical at times like these to use the 'log' input to the true-motion unit but these are also the times when the log is least likely to be deployed.

It is very easy to order a change in speed and forget to change the manual speed input to the radar and so have it portray a most misleading presentation of the situation. Such forgetfulness will be less likely if the observer maintains a plot of the origin, as recommended in Section 6.8.2.

Consider own ship steaming at 16 knots, using manual speed input to the radar which is correct during the initial plotting period. Having passed ahead of vessel *A*, own ship now reduces speed (the other vessel maintains course and speed throughout) but forgets to alter the manual speed input to the radar. The target A would *appear* to alter course to starboard as indicated in Figure 7.31, but on 'visual' observation would still be showing

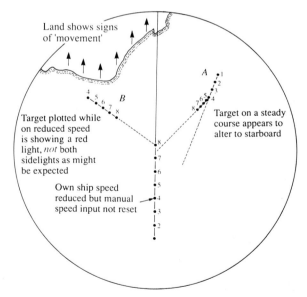

Figure 7.31 The misleading effect caused by failing to reset the manual speed input to the true-motion unit after a manoeuvre

a green light (her starboard side) instead of the expected red light. Careful observation of the land would show that it too is now 'moving' – but at times like this, one rarely has time to analyse the more subtle discrepancies on the display.

One must also be conscious of the fact that an error in the log input will produce a similar effect.

Other inputs which can inadvertently cause problems are the tide input controls (see Sections 2.6.4.4 and 6.8.1.6). When setting up the true-motion display, it is essential to check that these controls are set as required (see Section 6.8.3) or are completely inoperative. If allowed to remain as when previously in use, they can cause the origin to track in completely the incorrect direction and thus give a totally wrong impression of the direction in which the targets are tracking. Again, the

importance of plotting the origin (see Section 6.8.2) must be stressed.

7.10.2   Tracking course errors

In achieving true motion, the origin must track in the direction in which the vessel is travelling. If it does not, then the target's courses and/or speeds will be in error. The magnitude and direction of these errors will vary from target to target and will be dependent upon the encounter geometry and the magnitude and direction of the tracking error.

Causes of tracking course error can include a fault in the true-motion unit, incorrect alignment of the compass repeater (heading marker), and incorrect setting of the tidal correctors (see Sections 6.8.2 and 6.8.3).

7.10.3   Tracking speed errors

As with tracking course errors, these will result from errors in the movement of the origin across the display (see Figure 7.33). Causes may include a fault in the true-motion unit, an error in the transmitting log, an error in

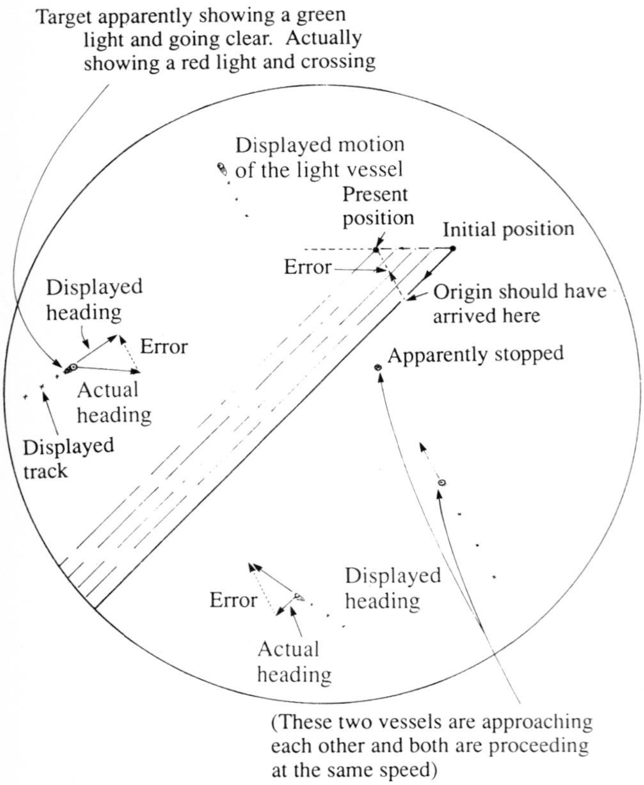

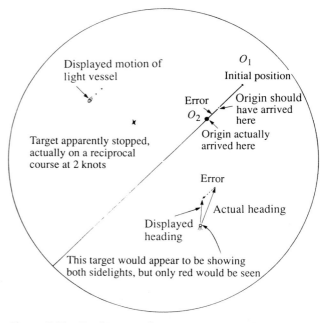

Figure 7.32   Tracking course errors on a true-motion presentation
True course 225° Speed 10 kn
Origin tracking 270° Speed 10 kn

Figure 7.33   Tracking speed errors on a true-motion presentation
True course 225° Speed 5 kn
Origin tracking 225° Speed 7 kn

the estimated speed, failure to re-set the manual speed control after ordering a change in speed and failure to re-set the tidal correctors.

It is essential not only to plot the origin of the display when using the true-motion presentation but also to ensure that the movement is correct in both direction and scale speed. This may mean that a future position of the origin must be predicted and marked on the reflection plotter. If the prediction is not achieved then the cause should be investigated.

7.10.4 The effect of radial display non-linearity

Where a radial display shows signs of non-linearity (see Section 6.9.1), care should be taken when the true-motion presentation is selected as the plot of a crossing vessel can be misleading. The extent to which the target movement can be in error is dependent upon the degree of non-linearity, the form of the non-linearity and the geometry of the encounter.

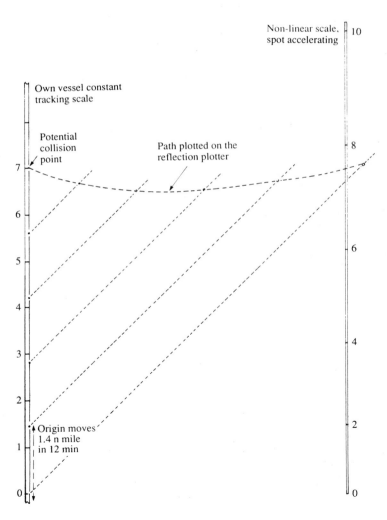

Figure 7.34   The effect of a non-linear timebase on the plotted true-motion track

Consider the situation as shown in Figure 7.34. The true situation is as follows:

Own ship course: 000°(T) speed: 7 knots
Target ship course: 270°(T) speed: 7 knots
Target range is 10 n mile on a bearing of 045°.
The origin is tracking correctly at a constant rate.

Note (a) On a relative-motion display, the target will remain on a steady bearing and will be on a range ring every 12 minutes (own vessel will travel 1.4 n mile in 12 min).

(b) Tracking is controlled by the true-motion unit, whereas linearity depends upon the timebase generator.

Figure 7.35 shows the effects manifest when the spot
(a) accelerates and
(b) decelerates.

7.11 Radar plotting aids

Many pieces of equipment have been developed over the years which were intended to assist the mariner in plotting and thereby interpreting the display. Apart from the reflection plotter, most are now only of historical interest, having been superseded by ARPAs (see Chapter 4) but one or two are worthy of individual mention.

7.11.1 The radar plotting board

This took a number of forms as various manufacturers attempted to provide something more permanent and durable than the paper plotting sheet. Effectively, this was little more than a plotting sheet, overlaid with Perspex or heavy transparent film, which was free to rotate and so assist in predicting the effect of an alteration of course by own ship.

It is not intended here to discuss its construction and use since it has been almost entirely superseded by the reflection plotter, but this was a fruitful area for personal innovation and some boards are still appearing for use in the pleasure boat market.

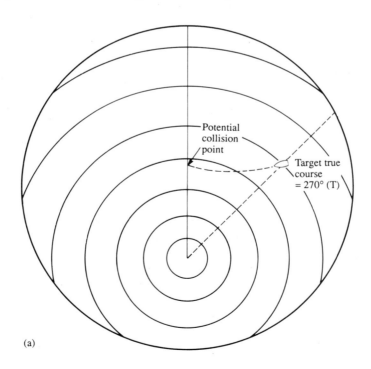

(a)

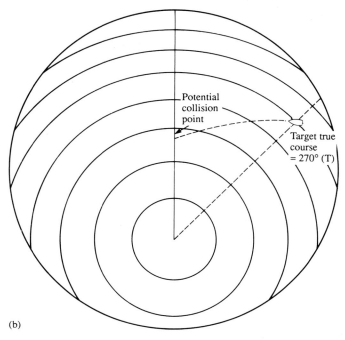

Potential collision point

Target true course = 270° (T)

(b)

Figure 7.35 The effects manifest when the spot (a) accelerates and (b) decelerates

7.11.2 Threat assessment markers ('matchsticks' or 'pins')

It has long been the practice of mariners to observe the compass bearing of an approaching vessel and, where there is no appreciable change, to assume that risk of collision exists. Unwary mariners have been seriously misled when using an unstabilized display as the source of bearing measurement.

With the increased use of compass-stabilized displays, the principle of observing the compass bearing of a target again manifested itself by mariners adopting the practice of placing the cursor on the target and observing how its bearing changed in relation to this datum.

Where it is necessary to monitor more than one target, the technique is difficult to implement. Recognising this problem, Decca Radar in 1966 made provision for the observer to use up to five 'threat assessment markers'. These are, in effect, sections of electronic cursor which can be positioned in range and azimuth so that, when placed on a target as shown in Figure 7.36, they will quickly show whether the bearing of the target is changing. The remote end of the marker, which represents a constant range and bearing from the observing vessel, is brightened and thus the marker resembles a match or pin.

Correct use of the markers provides much more information than merely an indication of change of bearing. It enables the observer to deduce the relative and true motion data for each marked target. To exploit this facility, the true-motion sea-stabilized presentation must be selected. Used in this way, the true plot of the target will indicate its true motion, but the position of the target in relation to the bright end of the marker will indicate its potential threat. By joining the 'head' of the marker to the current position of the target and extending the line, the CPA of the target can be assessed.

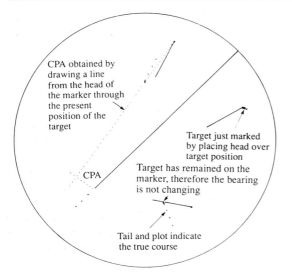

Figure 7.36   Threat assessment markers on a true-motion presentation

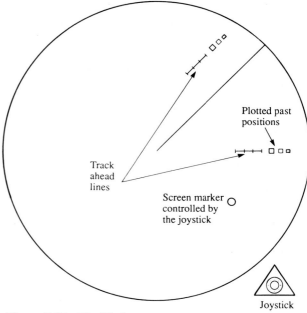

Figure 7.37   The 'E' plot

Note When used with a true-motion display, the markers track across the screen in the same manner as the origin but with their orientation and position in relation to the origin remaining unchanged.

Other manufacturers have produced variations on this basic idea. In one system, the markers are bright spots (i.e. only the head of the 'match' is shown) and a free electronic bearing line, having time divisions on it, is used to lay off the relative motion of the chosen target. In this particular system, if relative motion is selected, the marker traces out the track of a water-stationary target and there is a provision temporarily to move the marker to the O_1 plotting position (see Section 7.5) in order to assess the effect of a proposed manoeuvre by the observing vessel.

7.11.3   The 'E' plot

This system uses a joystick and marker to record 'electronically' the position of a target (Figure 7.37). The operator records the positions of targets at regular intervals, after which the data can be processed and extrapolated to provide the information available from a normal plot, i.e. course, speed, CPA and TCPA. Up to 10 targets can be manually tracked.

Manual recording as practised here should not be confused with manual acquisition followed by automatic tracking which takes place in the simplest of ARPAs.

The system is unique to Kelvin Hughes. However, other types of plotting aids using graphics are becoming common. Development of such facilities is a natural result of the need to provide plotting facilities on a raster-scan display which are at least equivalent to a reflection plotter (see Section 7.8.10), and has been assisted by the ease with which lines and points can be drawn electronically on such a display.

7.11.4   Intelligent knowledge-based systems as applied to collision avoidance

Under investigation at the present time is the potential use of computers to supply the mariner with advice as to the manoeuvre which will be most effective in the current circumstances.

The International Regulations for Preventing Collisions at Sea form a framework within which all manoeuvres must conform. Unfortunately, the regulations only work well for two-ship encounters, beyond which conflicts may arise. Further, terms such as 'early', 'substantial' and 'close-quarters' are quantitatively imprecise and so encoding of the rules is far from simple.

Computational techniques can now facilitate the encoding of 'experience': if experienced mariners are presented with complex encounters which are known to cause difficulty, their solutions can be analysed and the principles learned by the computer which can then apply them to a future similar (but not necessarily identical) encounter.

The systems at present under development are of necessity individual to the researchers and the international safety agencies would need to validate the rule base before they could be accepted for use at sea. There is also the intention to provide the mariner with a brief explanation of the reasons for the suggestion of a particular strategy.

The recommendation of a particular set of manoeuvres is not intended to take over the navigational function of the mariner but rather to support, in quantitative terms, the overall strategy which he himself would follow.

The limitations on manoeuvres imposed by terrestrial constraints will also be included as and when collision avoidance systems (ARPAs) become integrated with the electronic chart. In the meantime, the operator will have to indicate to the system, manoeuvres or areas which are unacceptable.

7.12 The Regulations for Preventing Collisions at Sea as applied to radar and ARPA

7.12.1 Introduction

The specific function of radar plotting (whether carried out on a paper plotting sheet, with the aid of an ARPA or with any of the intermediate facilities or techniques) is to provide the data on which a collision-avoidance strategy can be based. It is not intended that this section should represent a treatise on collision-avoidance strategy in restricted visibility. For that, the reader is referred to *The Navigation Control Manual*. This section aims to provide the radar observer with an appreciation of the need to carry out radar plotting (or equivalent systematic observation) in order to comply with the rules for preventing collisions at sea and with an understanding of the relationship between the data extracted and the provision of the Regulations to the extent necessary to provide informed support for the master or other officer responsible for the collision-avoidance strategy.

A notable feature of the 1972 Collision Regulations is that many specific references to the use of radar are made in the body of the rules. While some of these originated in the annex to the previous Regulations, some of the references are new and appear for the first time.

When considering the application of radar and ARPA to collision avoidance, it is particularly pertinent that the term *radar plotting or equivalent systematic observation of detected objects* (rule 7b) appears for the first time. Although the rules do not define this term, consideration of the various instructions and cautions given in the specific references to radar make it possible to deduce a procedure which would enable competent personnel to comply with both the letter and spirit of the rules. In this respect, ARPA should merely be seen as readily providing data which would otherwise have to be obtained from the radar by lengthy and tedious manual extraction.

7.12.2 Lookout – rule 5

Every vessel shall at all times maintain a *proper lookout* by sight and hearing as well as by *all available means appropriate* in the prevailing circumstances and conditions so as to make a full appraisal of the situation and of the risk of collision.

Although this rule does not specifically mention radar, there seems little doubt that radar is embraced by the term 'all available means'; for its ability to detect targets and in its role as a source of information allow an observer to make a more complete appraisal of the situation. It would also appear that there is an implied requirement to use the equipment in clear weather where it can augment or clarify the visual scene, e.g. in dense traffic, especially at night.

7.12.3   Safe speed – rule 6

Every vessel shall at all times proceed at a safe speed so that she can take proper and effective action to avoid collision and be stopped within a distance appropriate to the prevailing circumstances and conditions.

In determining a *safe speed* the following factors shall be among those taken into account:

(a) By all vessels;
  (i)   the state of visibility;
  (ii)   the traffic density including concentrations of fishing vessels or any other vessels;
  (iii) the manoeuvrability of the vessel with special reference to stopping distance and turning ability in the prevailing conditions;
  (iv)   at night the presence of background light such as from shore lights or from backscatter of her own lights;
  (v)   the state of wind, sea and current, and the proximity of navigational hazards;
  (vi)   the draught in relation to the available depth of water.

(b) Additionally, by vessels *with operational radar*:
  (i)   the characteristics, efficiency and limitations of the radar equipment;
  (ii)   any constraints imposed by the radar range scale in use;
  (iii) the effect on radar detection of the sea state, weather and other sources of interference;
  (iv)   the possibility that small vessels, ice and other floating objects may not be detected by radar at an adequate range;
  (v)   the number, location and movement of vessels detected by radar;
  (vi)   the more *exact assessment of the visibility* that may be possible when radar is used to determine the range of vessels or other objects in the vicinity.

In listing the factors to be considered when determining a safe speed, this rule devotes a complete section to those factors which can be determined by the use of radar. It is important to realize that the factors listed extend beyond the context of basic radar into that of collision-avoidance systems such as ARPA.

7.12.4   Risk of collision – rule 7

(a) Every vessel shall *use all available means* appropriate to the prevailing circumstances and conditions to determine if risk of collision exists. If there is any doubt, such risk shall be deemed to exist.

(b) *Proper use shall be made of radar equipment* if fitted and operational, including long range scanning to obtain early warning of risk of collision and *radar plotting* or equivalent systematic observation of detected objects.

(c) Assumptions shall not be made on the basis of scanty information, especially *scanty radar information*.

(d) In determining if risk of collision exists the following considerations shall be among those taken into account:
  (i)   such risk shall be deemed to exist if the compass bearing of an approaching vessel does not appreciably change;
  (ii)   such risk may sometimes exist even when an appreciable bearing change is evident, particularly when approaching a very large vessel or a tow or when approaching a vessel at close range.

Any discretion as to whether to make use of radar if fitted and operational, which may have existed under the previous rules, appears to have been removed by rule 7b. This section specifies that proper use shall be made of such equipment and the well established warning about 'scanty information' is now embodied in this rule.

7.12.5   Conduct of vessels in restricted visibility – rule 19

(a) This rule applies to vessels not in sight of one another when navigating in or near an area of restricted visibility.

(b) Every vessel shall proceed at a safe speed adapted to the prevailing circumstances and conditions of restricted visibility. A power-driven vessel shall have her engines ready for immediate manoeuvre.

(c) Every vessel shall have due regard to the prevailing circumstances and conditions of restricted visibility when complying with the rules of section I of this part.

(d) A vessel which *detects by radar alone* the presence of another vessel *shall determine* if a close-quarters situation is developing and/or *risk of collision exists*. If so, *she shall take avoiding action* in ample time, provided that when such action consists of an alteration of course, so far as possible *the following shall be avoided*:

   (i)   an alteration of course to port for a vessel forward of the beam, other than for a vessel being overtaken;

   (ii) an alteration of course towards a vessel abeam or abaft the beam.

(e) *Except where* it has been determined that a *risk of collision does not exist, every vessel* which hears apparently *forward of her beam the fog signal* of another vessel, or which cannot avoid a close-quarters situation with another vessel forward of her beam, *shall reduce her speed to the minimum* at which she can be kept on her course. She shall if necessary take all her way off and in any event navigate with extreme caution until danger of collision is over.

7.12.5.1   The development of a close-quarters situation

In cases where a target is detected by radar alone, rule 19d places a specific obligation on the observer to determine whether a close-quarters situation is developing. To comply with this requirement, the target should be plotted and its CPA and TCPA determined. With ARPA, this information can be made available in alphanumeric form if the target is designated. (The TCPA will assume particular importance if a close-quarters situation is developing.)

At this juncture, it is the duty of the officer of the watch to decide if the CPA constitutes a close-quarters situation; the CPA which would suggest that the encounter be deemed 'close quarters' will depend upon:

(a) The geographical position of the vessels.

(b) The handling capability of the ship.

(c) The density of the traffic.

7.12.5.2   Manoeuvres to avoid collision

If it is decided that a close-quarters situation is developing, the observer must take action to resolve the situation in ample time, subject to the recommendations laid down in rule 19d(i) and (ii). Any avoiding manoeuvre not based on a knowledge of the true motion of all relevant targets would be unseamanlike and could certainly attract criticism as an assumption based on scanty radar information.

When ARPA is being used, the true-motion data may be obtained in alpha-numeric form and cross-checked by interpretation of the graphical presentation but, since these are often generated from the same database, a good comparison should not be taken as an assumption of accuracy of the information. It is important to remember that the success of the action by own ship may be influenced by recent changes in the target's true motion. It is thus essential to check, by using the *history* presentation on the ARPA, whether such changes have occured.

7.12.6   Action to avoid collision – rule 8

(a) Any action taken to avoid collision shall, if the circumstances of the case admit, *be positive*, made *in ample time* and with due regard to the observance of *good seamanship*.

(b) Any alteration of course and/or speed to avoid collision shall, if the circumstances of the case admit, *be large enough* to be readily apparent to another vessel *observing* visually or *by radar*; a *succession of small alterations* of course and/or speed should be avoided.

(c) If there is sufficient sea room, alteration of course alone may be the most effective action to avoid a close-quarters situation provided that it is made in good time, is substantial and does not result in another close-quarters situation.

(d) Action taken to avoid collision with another vessel shall be such as to result in passing at a safe distance. *The effectiveness of the action shall be carefully checked* until the other vessel is finally past and clear.

(e) If necessary to avoid collision or *allow more time to assess* the situation, a vessel shall *slacken her speed* or take all way off by stopping or reversing her means of propulsion.

7.12.6.1   *The forecast*

Rule 8d requires that action taken to avoid collision with another vessel shall be such as to result in a safe passing distance. This rule applies to all states of visibility but, in restricted visibility, the safe passing distance may have to be greater than that which would be tolerated in clear weather.

When employing radar and ARPA, passing distances may and should be determined by the construction of a 'predicted OA line' on the plot or the use of the 'trial manoeuvre' facility which all ARPAs are required to have. Such a forecast will also enable the observer to check that the manoeuvre will not result in a close-quarters situation with other vessels (rule 8c) and can often indicate where targets may manoeuvre to avoid each other.

It is essential to remember that a further criterion for an acceptable manoeuvre is that it must be readily apparent to another vessel observing by radar (rule 8b). In making this judgement one must consider own ship's speed and the speeds of target vessels. Further, it must be appreciated that, even if the target vessel is equipped with radar, the plotting facilities may be very basic. Hence the rate at which the observer can extract data, and thus become aware of changes, may be slow and the ability to identify small changes may be particularly limited (for this reason, rule 8b gives a warning about a succession of small alterations).

Finally, the possibility that a target vessel may not be plotting, or may not even have an operational radar, must be continually kept in mind.

7.12.6.2   *The effectiveness of a manoeuvre*

Rule 8d requires that the effectiveness of the avoiding action be checked until the other vessel is finally past and clear. This requirement can be satisfied by monitoring:

(a) *The true motion* of all relevant targets (to ensure early detection and identification of target manoeuvres).

(b) *The relative motion* of all relevant targets to check for the fulfilment of the forecast nearest approach.

7.12.6.3   *Resumption*

When the target is finally past and clear, the decision must be made to resume course and/or speed.

As in the case of the avoiding manoeuvre, prior to resuming, the apparent motion of the target after resumption (see Section 7.5.7) or the trial manoeuvre on the ARPA should be employed to verify that a safe passing distance will be achieved with respect to all relevant targets. It should be remembered that the resumption will be most obvious to other observing vessels if it is performed as a single manoeuvre as opposed to a series of small alterations. The common practice of resuming course in steps by 'following the target round' will make it difficult for other observing ships to identify the manoeuvre positively and could be considered to be in contravention of the spirit, if not the letter, of rule 8b.

7.12.7   The cumulative turn

This set of related manoeuvres based on wrongly interpreted radar information (in restricted visibility) has probably done more than anything else to give radar a bad name and to indicate the need for a proper appreciation and use of the data displayed on the screen.

A number of elements have been identified which are common in the majority of the cases which have come before the courts and which are of interest when endeavouring to understand just how, in spite of repeated warnings, the same fatal scenario has been played out on so many occasions.

The common elements are:

(a) The encounter is end-on or nearly end-on.

(b) In most cases, only the two ships are involved, i.e. no constraints by other vessels or by the land etc.

(c) There was no proper assessment of the situation

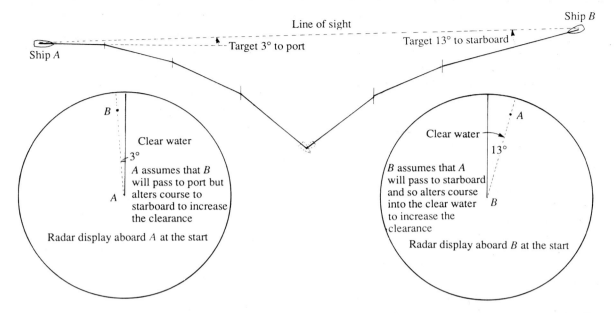

Figure 7.38 The cumulative turn

based on acceptable plotting techniques, but rather a subjective judgement based on casual observation of the display. Because of the small change in bearing, each assumes (on scanty information) that the other vessel is on a reciprocal course.

(d) With only one *other* ship on the screen, each considers that there is no need to go to the trouble of a formal plot.

(e) Speeds have invariably been excessive.

(f) Small alterations of course have been seen as adequate and usually the justification has been that it was done 'only to give the other vessel a wider berth'.

(g) Each vessel alters into the 'clear water', i.e. *A* alters to starboard while *B* alters to port (Figure 7.38).

(h) The misunderstanding of the true situation can be aggravated by the use of a ship's-head-up unstabilized relative-motion display where, after the completion of the manoeuvre, the impression obtained from the casual observation of the display is that the target will now pass farther off (Figure 7.39).

(i) In the agony of the final moments any manoeuvre might be ordered but, in general, the wheel will be put hard over and the engines put astern. The outcome or the intention of the manoeuvre is extremely difficult to predict and rarely has time to take effect.

With the aid of ARPA, the true situation can be more readily understood at an early stage in the encounter so that if early and substantial action is taken to avoid the collision followed by rigorous subsequent monitoring, the irretrievable situation should not be allowed to develop. Where there is no ARPA assistance, it is essential that both the letter and spirit of the collision avoidance rules are adhered to in terms of plotting, predicting ahead, monitoring target manoeuvres, while at the same time making an early and substantial avoiding manoeuvre. The importance of 'making time to plot' by reducing speed at an early stage in the encounter cannot be too strongly stressed.

Classical cases which have followed the above scenario with fatal consequences are: the *Stokholm – Andrea Doria*; *Crystal Jewel – British Aviator*; *Dalhanna – Staxton Wyke*, as well as the *Canopic – Hudson Firth* and many more which followed the same basic pattern but in which no lives were lost.

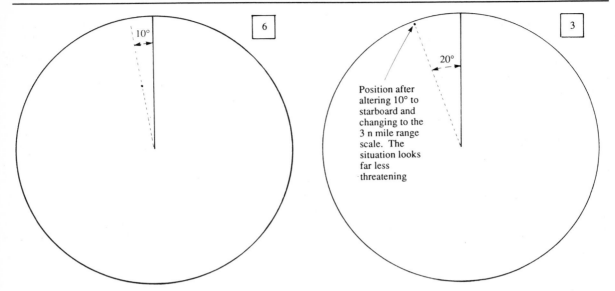

Figure 7.39 The effect of altering course and changing range scale on a ship's-head-up unstabilized radar presentation

Table 7.2 Summary of the Regulations for Preventing Collision at Sea as applied to radar and ARPA

1	Use ARPA and radar if they can be of the slightest assistance	(a) (b)	Clear weather with heavy traffic Proper lookout (especially at night)
2	Does risk of collision exist, and/or is a close-quarters situation developing?	(a)	Analyse displayed information ● Relative tracks, CPA and TCPA ● True tracks – course and speed ● History of past position
3	Determine best manoeuvre	(a) (b)	Trial facility ● Will targets pass safely? ● Will targets have to manoeuvre? Avoid A/C to port, or turning toward converging overtaking ships
4	Manoeuvre	(a) (b) (c) (d)	Bold – avoid succession of small A/C Large – obvious to others In good time – time to correct Good seamanship
5	Ensure its effectivenes	(a) (b)	Continuous check of relative motion and history Watch for changes in true motion of targets
6	Resume	(a) (b) (c)	Are targets clear? Trial – check other vessels for likely manoeuvres Make one manoeuvre

7.12.8   Conclusion

In any potential collision situation, particularly in restricted visibility, the interpretation of displayed radar information facilitates the determination and execution of action to avoid close-quarters situations. Traditionally this is achieved by a decision based on data extracted by manual plotting. ARPA should be seen as a device that extracts and presents such data. It thus reduces the workload on the observer by carrying out routine tasks and allows him more time to carry out decision making on the basis of the data supplied.

The ability of the ARPA equipment to carry out routine tracking and computation in no way relieves the observer of the need to understand fully the principles of radar plotting, or of being capable of applying such principles to a practical encounter, such as might be the case in the event of an equipment failure.

It is imperative that the observer is capable of interpreting and evaluating the data presented by the ARPA system. Equally essential is the ability to detect any circumstances in which the equipment is producing data which is inconsistent with the manner in which a situation is developing as observed, say, from the raw radar.

In general, it is vital that the observer understands the limitations of the system in use and hence is aware of the dangers of exclusive reliance on the data produced by an ARPA. In particular, the implicit reliance on the validity of the prediction of small non-zero passing distances should be avoided. The CPA errors tabulated in sections of the Performance Standards for ARPA (see Section 9.3) clearly indicate that predicted passing distances of less than one mile should be treated with the utmost caution.

8 Navigation techniques using radar and ARPA

8.1 Introduction

The availability of information from radar and ARPA forms the basis of a number of techniques which may assist in the safe navigation of vessels. Successful and safe use of these require an ability to relate the echoes displayed by the radar to the information shown on the chart and an understanding of the levels of performance and accuracy which can be achieved under given circumstances. Where radar information is used in making a landfall, the ship's position may be in considerable doubt and it may be difficult positively to identify specific echoes, particularly if the observer is unfamiliar with the locality. In routine coastal navigation there may be more general certainty as to the vessel's position, but effective use of these techniques will require organization, skill, practice and a thorough awareness of the capability of the radar system. They will also be found to be of assistance in certain pilotage situations but it has to be said that current civil marine radar equipment has a very limited ability to contribute to the docking of vessels.

This chapter discusses the difficulties of making comparison between the radar picture and charted features before passing on to describe the navigation techniques in terms of the underlying theory covered elsewhere in this text.

It is often stressed that radar is *only an aid* to navigation. This does not mean that radar information is necessarily of any less value than that obtained from other sources. What it does mean is that radar data

should not be used in isolation and to the exclusion of that available from other sources. The radar system should be seen as one element in a variety of data sources which must be taken into account in arriving at decisions related to directing the safe navigation of the vessel. The exercise of command decision-making based on an evaluation of navigation information derived from all sources is referred to as *navigation control* and is the subject of *The Navigation Control Manual*.

8.2 Identification of targets and chart comparison

It is sometimes suggested that the radar picture offers a *bird's-eye view* of the area surrounding the observing vessel. This analogy is imperfect on a number of counts but two are particularly evident in the use of radar for navigation. The radar aerial does not look down on the terrain from a great height and thus its *view* can be obstructed. Further, it does not offer the optical resolution (see Section 2.6.5) which the use of the word 'eye' may imply. As a consequence, the radar picture may be an incomplete and fairly coarse version of the chart's finely detailed plan view of the terrain. This may limit the observer's ability to identify positively elements of the terrain echoes and relate them to the charted representation.

Interpretation of the displayed picture involves consideration of a number of factors each of which will be discussed in turn.

8.2.1 Long range target identification

When making a landfall, the radar must be carefully observed in order to obtain an early indication of the presence of the terrain. In the absence of clutter (see Sections 3.6 and 3.7) the first echoes will have to be found against the background of receiver noise (see Section 2.5.2.3). If the observer knows the approximate bearing and range at which to expect the first echoes, early detection may be assisted by, from time to time, temporarily setting the gain control a little higher than the normal optimum level (see Section 6.2.4.1). A slight loss of contrast is traded for an increase in received signal strength and this may be beneficial when looking in a specific area as opposed to scanning the entire screen area. Where an echo stretch facility (see Section 6.11.1) is provided, it may be found similarly helpful. A knowledge of where to look for the expected echoes on the screen pre-supposes other sources of information concerning the vessel's likely position and the probable detection range of specific terrain features. Such information may stem from dead reckoning techniques, knowledge of leeway and tidal streams, other position-fixing systems, and an assessment of specific target detection ranges in the light of radar, target and environmental characteristics (see Chapter 3). This emphasises the complementary nature of the various data sources available for the safe navigation of the vessel.

Initially the presence of the land may be indicated by only a few responses and these will be considerably distorted by the angular width of the resolution cell (see Sections 2.6.5 and 8.2.2) which will be large at long range. Under these circumstances it will be extremely difficult, if not impossible, to identify positively specific terrain features from the few distorted echoes which are being observed. It must be appreciated that the use of the echo stretch technique is likely to exacerbate the problem by adding radial distortion and it should be switched off after it has fulfilled its role of assisting initial detection. Identification may be assisted if the observer knows which parts of the terrain are likely to show first and also the approximate range and bearing at which they should appear. As indicated in the previous paragraph this pre-supposes other sources of information related to probable position and target detection considerations.

To exploit fully the use of radar in making a landfall, adequate preparation should be made in terms of collating the information from other sources. An up to date and best available estimate of the ship's position should be maintained using information from all available sources. Prior to making the landfall, the chart and the Admiralty Sailing Directions should be consulted in order to assess the ranges at which the radar should detect specific terrain features which are likely to be easy to identify. This assessment should take into account the characteristics of the radar system, the characteristics of the target, the atmospheric conditions and any limits to detection which may be imposed by clutter or attenuation, all of which are dealt with in detail in Chapter 3. In particular it should be remembered that frequently coastlines are backed by higher terrain and at long ranges it must be borne in mind that the first land to show is not necessarily the *coastline* (see Section 3.8.1). Failure to appreciate this can be dangerously misleading because the measured range will suggest that the vessel is farther to seaward than is in fact the case. Also, as the land is closed, responses will be obtained from land which is lower and closer than that originally detected and as it comes above the horizon it may give an exaggerated impression of the speed at which the vessel is approaching the land. When a particular landfall has been made on more than one occasion, it may be possible to establish a list of good landfall targets which may supplement those tabulated in the Sailing Directions.

It has to be recognised that, while civil marine radar offers early warning of the presence of most land formations, long range target identification is not a function at which it excels. A coded racon (see Section 3.5.2.1) is probably the only sure source of early positive target identification and its range may well be limited by the height of its aerial. Positive identification of just one target is a major step forward because it may then be possible to identify other terrain echoes by virtue of their known range and bearing from the identified target. A *free EBL* (see Sections 6.9.6 and 8.4.6.1) is ideally suited to making the necessary measurements.

Care must be taken not to jump to conclusions when a radar echo appears in the general area in which a particular point of land is expected by DR. There appears to be a great temptation to ascribe immediately and unquestioningly the hoped-for identity to the target. This temptation must be resisted until cross-checks have established that any fix so obtained is consistent with all other available sources of information.

8.2.2 The effect of discrimination

In the previous section attention was drawn to the difficulty of identifying targets in the landfall situation because of the effect of the size of the resolution cell on the few echoes which may be detected at extreme ranges. Even at the more moderate ranges likely to be employed when using the radar for routine coastal navigation, the effect of resolution (see Section 2.6.5) may

still be to make it difficult to identify specific coastal features, despite the fact that there will be a larger aggregation of land responses forming some sort of *chart-like* coastline on the PPI.

The angular width of the resolution cell produces an angular distortion on both sides of all targets by an amount equal to half the horizontal beamwidth plus the spot size effect. Neglecting for the moment the spot size effect, it is evident that if two headlands forming the entrance to a bay are separated by less than the horizontal beamwidth, their echoes will overlap. Thus the effect of the limited bearing discrimination may be to mask coastal features such as bays, river entrances, sea lochs and other similar inlets. The echoes of an island close to the mainland may appear as a peninsula and small islands close together may appear as one large island. Thus a charted coastline having many indentations may translate to a featureless coastline on the PPI. It must be borne

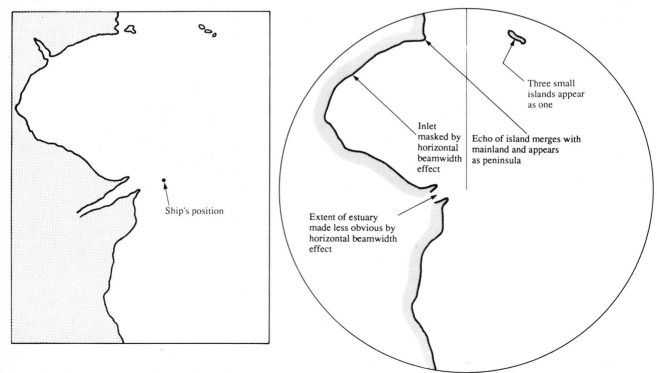

Figure 8.1 The radar display of charted features

in mind that, while the width of the beam is a fixed angle, the linear measurement of the arc it cuts off increases in direct proportion to the range at which it is considered. Thus features which are masked at a distance may become identifiable as their range decreases.

The pulse length/spot size dimension of the resolution cell will produce radial distortion of all responses. Except at very short ranges this will have an effect which is much less significant than that of the angular distortion. However, where two features lie one behind the other, for example an island or a buoy located close to the shore, they may appear as one feature due to the limited range discrimination.

The observer's ability to minimize the effects of the angular and radial distortion are fairly limited. In both cases the spot size effect will be reduced by using the shortest appropriate range scale. Where a dual or inter-switched system (see Section 2.7.8) is available, selection of the aerial having the narrower beamwidth will assist, as would a modern raster-scan display offering beam processing (see Section 3.9.5.1). A temporary reduction in the setting of the gain control may help to locate features which have been masked by angular distortion but this requires some practice and is not invariably successful. Use of differentiation (see Section 3.7.4.4) may improve the picture by combating the radial distortion. However, this technique must be used with care as if two echoes overlap and the farther is the weaker of the two, the effect of differentiation may be to remove the remote echo.

Thus, due to the inherent difficulty of relating the radar picture to the chart, care must be taken to ensure positive identification of any target before selecting it for use in position fixing (see also Section 8.3).

8.2.3 Shadow areas

Because the line of sight of the radar system is substantially horizontal, some features of the terrain may be shadowed by others. These shadows are a further factor which may make it difficult to relate the radar picture to that of the chart, the problem being compounded by the fact that the shadow pattern will vary with the position of the observing vessel.

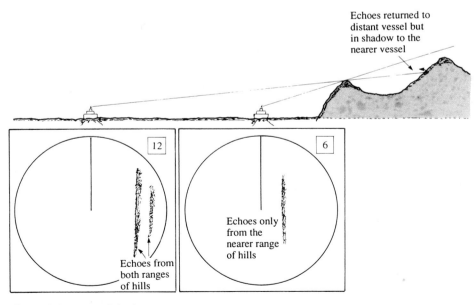

Figure 8.2 Vertical shadowing

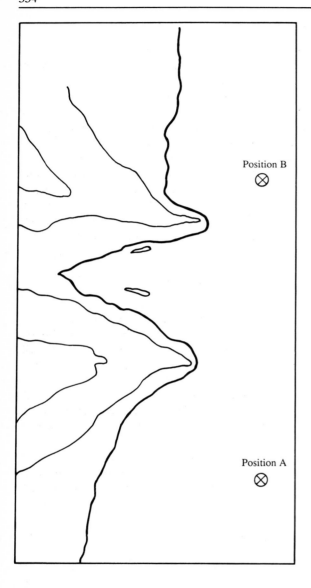

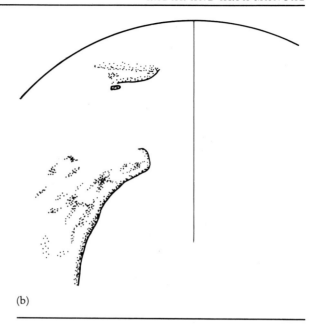

(b)

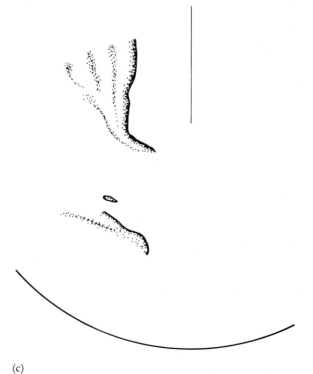

Figure 8.3 Horizontal shadowing
(a) The chart
(b) The radar picture from position A: shadowing takes effect particularly in the south, west and northwest areas of the bay
(c) The radar picture from position B: shadowing takes effect particularly in the north, west and southwest areas of the bay

(c)

8.2.3.1 Vertical shadowing

Figure 8.2 shows an example of vertical shadowing. To a vessel which is close inshore, the lower range of coastal hills may shadow higher mountains lying inland, whereas from another vessel farther offshore, the radar may be able to 'see' the mountains over the top of the coastal range.

Bearing in mind that, as described in Section 8.2.1, a vessel making landfall on such a coastline may well detect the higher inland mountains first, it is evident that if a ship closes the coastline from seaward the character of the radar picture will change through three distinct phases. Initially the vessel will observe the higher mountains only, then both coastal and inland mountains and finally only the coastal range. If there are gaps in the coastal range, horizontal shadowing (see Section 8.2.3.2) will also take place, further complicating the pattern.

8.2.3.2 Horizontal shadowing

Figure 8.3 shows an example of horizontal shadowing from which it is clear that the radar picture obtained by a vessel at location A looks quite different from that which would be obtained at location B. It follows that a ship whose course takes it from A to B will notice a progressive change in the character of the radar picture.

8.2.3.3 Composite shadowing

In many cases both vertical and horizontal shadowing occur and the interaction between the two as a ship steams past the terrain may produce a complex and changing pattern of responses. In the early days of radar some experimental attempts were made to produce radar *maps* by producing a collage of radar photographs. Such attempts proved to be of little practical value, because the character of the radar picture portrayed by each element in the collage was heavily dependent on the location at which the photograph was taken and the characteristics of the radar installation used.

If a ship is uncertain of its position, the complex shadow pattern may make it difficult to recognise the particular stretch of coastline or to identify specific targets on the terrain.

8.2.4   Rise and fall of tide

The radar picture may appear quite different at various states of the tide. The changes will depend very much on the character of the area. For example, at low water an area with off-lying, drying sandbanks may produce large areas of no response (where the smooth sloping surfaces reflect the radar energy away from the aerial) surrounded by fringes of clutter (where the water breaks) which depend on the strength and direction of the wind. By contrast, at high water, in calm conditions there may be no response at all whereas in strong winds there may be extensive clutter in the shallow water over the banks. The ability to understand and recognise such effects may be of value to the radar observer in identifying specific targets.

8.2.5   Radar-conspicuous targets

A radar-conspicuous target is one which produces a good response that can be positively identified. While the ability of radar waves to penetrate fog is of great assistance to vessels navigating in restricted visibility, all targets obscured visually by the fog are not necessarily conspicuous when viewed by the radar.

A particularly important example is a lighthouse, which traditionally represents a key navigational mark whose charted position is known. It is visually conspicuous and can be identified beyond doubt. Unless other adequate sources of position lines are available, it is a serious loss to the navigator if the lighthouse is obscured by poor visibility and that loss may not be made good by the radar. In general, the shape of a lighthouse makes it an inherently poor target (see Section 3.3.4) and, unless it is situated on an isolated rock, whatever response there is tends to be lost in the land echoes from the terrain surrounding it. Thus, unless the lighthouse is fitted with a radar beacon (see Section 3.5), in many cases it may be difficult or impossible to identify on the radar. Buoys represent another example of navigation marks which, because of their inherently poor reflecting characteristics, may be difficult to detect and hence identify unless fitted with a reflector or a racon (see Sections 3.4 and 3.5). This may be particularly so in cases where vessels anchor in the vicinity of a floating navigation mark such as a fairway buoy.

However, some man-made features are particularly conspicuous when observed on radar. Tank farms and small built-up areas are particularly good examples. Their response is among the strongest likely to be encountered and, if isolated from other areas of response, they may be very conspicuous. Naturally occuring features such as small isolated islands offer a further example of radar-conspicuous and potentially identifiable targets.

Sloping sandy coastlines may be quite conspicuous to the eye even when fairly low-lying, but their radar response is likely to be poor because most of the energy is not reflected back toward the aerial. The response may be improved if waves are breaking on the beach, but this will only be experienced at fairly short range.

8.2.6   Pilotage situations

In most pilotage situations targets are so close that detection scarcely presents a problem. However, identification may be a problem, and an urgent one given the proximity of hazards and the speed with which manoeuvres must be effected.

In estuary and port approach situations, the need for continuous position monitoring may well be met by using parallel indexing techniques (see Section 8.4), provided that suitable preparation has been carried out beforehand and the necessary indexing targets can be easily and positively identified. Some high-definition radars are designed with very short range scales, low minimum range and good discrimination that suit them for use in pilotage. In the absence of such equipment the observer must attempt to make the best use of the available system. In an interswitched system, aerial siting, beamwidth, pulse length, and the setting of gain and clutter controls should receive attention. Where a single system is fitted, fine detail can be improved by use of the shortest pulse length and differentiation.

In the docking phase of pilotage, the presence at very close range of targets which produce strong and spurious responses (see Section 3.9) will conspire with the limited discrimination of the radar system (see Sections 2.6.5.5 and 2.6.5.6) to obscure the fine detail of the picture. On the short range scales in use under such circumstances, only relative-motion presentation will be

available and the consequent movement of the land echoes on the screen, together with the changes in shadow areas and indirectly reflected echoes, will greatly exacerbate this effect and make it very difficult to identify the extent of berths, lock entrances and other essential features.

While the problem can be to some extent reduced by judicious use of differentiation, it has to be said that the docking phase of pilotage is one for which current civil marine radar equipment is not particularly suited. In the past the docking of very large vessels has been assisted by the siting of doppler equipment ashore to measure the rate of approach of the vessels. There is considerable debate at the present time as to how the problem might be solved for the frequent and regular berthing of ferries in fog. The more traditional suggestion is to use radar having a wavelength of a few millimetres while more recent thinking suggests the use on the vessel of precision sensors which detect position and attitude. At present no suitable system is commercially available.

8.3   Position fixing

Essentially two types of position lines are available directly from the radar, namely radar range circles and radar bearings. These can of course be used in association with position lines from other sources. In making a decision as to which particular position lines should be used to obtain a fix in any given circumstances, consideration must be given to the accuracy that can be obtained. This will depend on the targets chosen and the type of position lines selected.

8.3.1   Selection of targets

In selecting targets for position fixing, attention must be given to the certainty with which they can be identified and the suitability of their angular disposition.

8.3.1.1   Target identification

The importance of positive target identification and the difficulties of achieving this have been discussed at length in the preceeding sections of this chapter. Mistaken identification can seriously mislead the observer as to the vessel's most probable position. Even where the feature has been correctly identified, unless it is small, it is essential to identify which part of the feature has reflected the radar energy; otherwise, accuracy may suffer. For example, when measuring a range from a sloping surface, the high level of ranging accuracy can be lost if the range is not laid off from the correct contour on the chart.

Similarly, if taking a bearing from the edge of the radar echo of a point, considerable thought must be given to the effect of any slope of the terrain and the beamwidth effect of the radar before deciding from which charted position to lay off the observed bearing. In general, if radar bearings are used it is better to attempt to avoid the effect of the half beamwidth distortion by using the centre of small isolated targets or, if it is necessary to use a point of land, to take a bearing which runs along the axis of the headland rather than one which is tangential to it.

8.3.1.2 Angle of cut

In selecting targets for position fixing, the considerations given to angles of cut are not particular to radar but are based on the general principles of position lines. Where two position lines are involved, the angle of cut should be as close to 90° as possible as this minimizes the displacement of the fix due to any errors in the position lines used. To provide cross-checking, good practice dictates that where possible at least three position lines should be used. Under these circumstances, angles of cut less than 30° or greater than 150° should be avoided as small errors in the position lines can produce relatively large errors in the fix.

8.3.2 Types of position line

The position lines available from radar and other sources can be used in a variety of combinations. The considerations of radar accuracy affecting these combinations are discussed in turn.

8.3.2.1 The use of radar range circles

The inherent accuracy of radar range circles is very high,

the IMO Performance Standards (see Section 10.2) requiring that the fixed range rings and the variable range marker should enable the range of a target to be measured with an error not exceeding 1.5 per cent of the range scale in use or 70 metres, whichever is greater. On the 12 mile range scale the error should not exceed 334 metres and this compares very favourably with most other position-fixing systems. Care must be taken in using the facilities provided for range measurement to ensure that the full potential accuracy is realized. The practical procedures for doing this are summarized in Section 6.9.8. Additionally, as indicated in Section 8.3.1.1, it is essential to establish with certainty the charted location of the reflecting surface. There is little point in measuring with a high degree of accuracy the range of a target which has been incorrectly identified. Assuming that the foregoing procedures are followed, radar range circles have the potential to produce a highly accurate fix.

8.3.2.2 The use of radar bearings

When compared with that of radar ranges, the inherent accuracy of radar bearings is very much lower. In Section 6.9 the various error sources set out in the IMO Performance Standard are discussed and it is shown that the inherent accuracy of radar bearings is such that a bearing measured from the display can be in error by as much as 2.5° without the system being in breach of the Standard. The arc subtended by an angle of 2.5° at 12 miles is approximately 870 metres, which does not compare favourably with the inherent accuracy offered by radar range circles. Suitable practical procedures must be followed to ensure that the potential accuracy is realized; these are summarized in Section 6.9.9. Additionally, care must be exercised to ensure that the target has been correctly identified (see Section 8.3.1.1).

In general, given the relative inherent accuracy levels, wherever possible radar ranges should be used in preference to radar bearings.

8.3.2.3 The combination of radar ranges and bearings

Inevitably, circumstances will arise in which a combination of ranges and bearings will have to be used. Where only one feature is available for fixing, a single range and bearing fix does have the virtue that the angle of cut is 90°. However, in such circumstances the respective accuracies of the two position lines must be borne in mind.

8.3.2.4 *The use of single position lines*

A single radar range or bearing can be used in the same way as any other single position line to exploit the various general navigation techniques, such as the running fix, which maximizes the use of such observations.

8.3.2.5 *The combination of radar position lines with those from other sources*

Radar ranges and bearings should be seen as one of several sources of position lines all of which may be combined to arrive at a decision as to the vessel's most probable position.

A particular example is the situation which arises in clear weather when only one feature can be positively identified. Under such conditions the accuracy of a visual bearing (which is higher than that of a radar bearing) can be combined with that of a radar range circle to produce a fix having a potentially high degree of accuracy. In conditions of poor visibility of course the lower accuracy of a radar bearing would have to be substituted for the visual.

In general, the radar should be seen as one source of position-fixing information which should be compared and combined with the others that are available. Any disparity between the information available from different sources such as is manifest by a 'cocked hat' should alert the observer to consider carefully why the disparity exists. Serious thought should precede any decision to discount a particular data source. In particular, a large 'cocked hat' should be a warning to check all position lines and not an excuse for discarding the one which is most embarrassing.

8.4 Parallel indexing

8.4.1 Introduction

While navigating from one port to another, it is inevit-

able that for part of the time the ship will be in confined waters, be it the approaches to the port and berth, or in a busy waterway such as the Dover Strait or Malacca Strait. Leaving aside for the moment any consideration of avoiding collision with other vessels, restrictions on the available sea room require the navigator to monitor the vessel's position, not just with an increased accuracy commensurate with the reduced safety margins and clearing distances imposed upon him, but also with an increased frequency to ensure that environmental and other forces that take the vessel off her desired track are recognised in sufficient time for corrective action to be taken and the vessel to be maintained on a safe track.

Traditionally the navigator would identify the vessel's proximity to the track or danger by putting a fix on the chart, the data for this fix having been obtained from one of a variety of navigation instruments. Depending upon which navigation system is being used, the time needed to establish the fix will probably be, at best, about two minutes. However, a single fix does not reveal the whole story, merely the ship's position some two minutes ago. Before the navigator can take corrective action, it is necessary to know the trend of the movement, i.e. a series of fixes is required – probably three or more, bearing in mind the inherent imprecision of most fixing systems. Consequently, there may be a time delay of the order of six to ten minutes between the vessel beginning to deviate from its desired track to the time when proper considered action is taken to return the vessel to safety.

If the reason for the deviation is a five knot cross-current and the shoal water is only a few cables away, a reaction time in excess of six minutes is too great.

One might expect that, under conditions such as these, where the shoal water is so close, there ought to be sufficient visual navigation marks nearby to enable the person conning the vessel, be it the master, pilot or officer of the watch, to react almost instantly to any deviation from the planned track. This will probably be the situation in a port approach with moderate to good visibility. In poor visibility, however, when all the visual marks disappear, conning becomes extremely difficult even with the radar giving the relative positions of some of these marks. Consider also the very large vessel fully laden. Its deep draft means that it may be in 'confined' waters well away from port approaches in an area where the navigation marks necessary for the visual conning are sparse.

The usefulness of parallel indexing in the above circumstances is indisputable. There have been numerous incidents of grounding which have resulted from the navigator using a position-monitoring method that had too long a reaction time for the conditions in which the vessel was operating (for instance, the *Metaxa*, and also the *Sundancer* casualties) or where the navigator failed to recognise that the data he was appraising was insufficient on which to base remedial action.

It is in situations like these that parallel indexing shows its true worth by enabling the navigator to monitor the vessel's progress moment by moment and by providing enough data to allow corrective manoeuvres to be made in a time scale which is very similar to that of visual conning, i.e. about two to three minutes.

8.4.2   Preparations and precautions

8.4.2.1   Pre-planning

Navigators who conduct their vessels in confined waters using blind pilotage techniques such as parallel indexing must never lose sight of the fact that safety margins are often minimal and on no account must operator errors be allowed to creep in to the parallel indexing data. By the time an error becomes apparent it can very likely be too late to recover the situation. Considerable care must be taken therefore in deriving the parallel indexing data from the navigation chart and transferring it onto the radar reflection plotter, to ensure that it is as accurate as possible. All data should be cross-checked and, indeed, the whole process of acquiring the parallel indexing data is best carried out when there is a minimum of pressure and distraction. It would be inviting trouble to attempt to derive and use parallel indexing data in quantity when the vessel is already proceeding through the confined area. Most 'off the cuff' work suffers from inadequate checking and hence is susceptible to error. On occasions, parallel indexing may be employed directly from the radar screen without any pre-planning (see Section 8.4.7) but generally the need for parallel indexing should be assessed during the passage planning stage and all the

necessary data to carry out the task, extracted from the chart and stored in suitable form (see Section 8.4.3.5), hours before it is intended to make use of the data. Only by doing this can one be sure of reliable data of sufficient quality to realize the full benefits of parallel indexing.

8.4.2.2   Preparing the on-board equipment

The radar set is an integral part of the parallel indexing process and must be in proper working order, able to display the *indexing* target, be operated correctly orientated and stabilized and with proper discrimination and accuracy. Particular care must be exercised with the tuning, gyro compass error and heading marker accuracy (see practical setting-up procedures in Chapter 6). Ancillary systems such as the reflection plotter must be properly adjusted to remove parallax and other errors.

Assuming that the mechanical cursor is to be used to lay off bearings, then it is essential to centre the start of the timebase on the PPI. Alternatively, if the electronic bearing line is to be used, the readout accuracy must be confirmed. Similarly, if the variable range marker is to be used, then any errors must be removed or known so that due allowance can be made. Distance measurement,

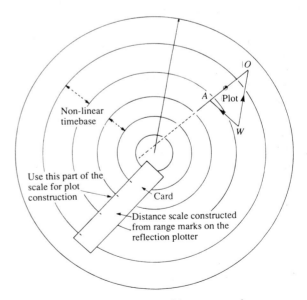

Figure 8.4   Constructing a working range scale

when working on the reflection plotter, has proved to be a prolific source of inaccuracy. The observer must derive his own distance scale from the PPI and (being unable to use dividers on the reflection plotter) using a piece of paper or plastic, attempt to transfer distances from the derived scale to his drawing on the face of the reflection plotter (see Figure 8.4). This process is difficult and considerable care must be taken to minimize inaccuracies in the distances laid off.

With some older radar sets, (and some which are not so old), the timebase is not perfectly linear, especially near the start of the timebase (see Section 6.9.1). Hence, a distance scale derived from this timebase will also be non-linear. With this in mind, it is advisable always to use that part of the range scale which is at a similar distance from the centre of the PPI to that where the plot is being constructed.

8.4.2.3   The radar presentation

In theory, parallel indexing can be employed either on a relative-motion north-up gyro-stabilized display or on a ground-stabilized true-motion display.

There are practical difficulties in achieving a reliable ground-stabilized display (see also Sections 6.8.3 and 8.4.5). For instance:

1 Obtaining the present tidal rate and set can be time-consuming and not necessarily very accurate. Even if good values are obtained, changing conditions may mean that the values need to be frequently re-assessed.
2 An accurate knowledge of our own ship's course and speed through the water is not always easily available, especially when using unreliable speed logs.
3 Given good information regarding the vessel's movement over the ground, it still remains for the radar equipment to track accurately in response to this information. On some radar sets, this cannot be taken for granted.

Bearing in mind that parallel indexing is intended to improve navigational safety, the operational difficulties mentioned above that could influence the reliability of this work means that true-motion parallel indexing must be considered second best to relative-motion parallel indexing.

A further disadvantage of reflection plotter work on a true-motion display is that all the constructions must be done as they are needed, since most true-motion presentations do not have the ability to determine precisely where the origin will be situated at any given instant. Because of this, the parallel indexing construction on the reflection plotter cannot be pre-worked.

Some modern radar equipments have the ability to draw electronic lines (see Sections 5.4 and 8.4.6.3) for navigational purposes on the PPI. Once drawn, these may be moved around at will on the screen using the tracker ball or joystick. This feature overcomes the disadvantage mentioned above as experienced with reflection plotters and at the same time introduces a distinct advantage in that the construction can be transferred between range scales with no effort on the part of the operator.

8.4.2.4   Selecting the indexing target and its effect on
             accuracy

The *indexing target* is a chosen radar target which appears on the PPI and whose movements relative to the observing vessel as it transits a particular confined area will be closely monitored. If everything goes according to plan, the ship will be manoeuvred to make this target track along the lines that have been drawn on the reflection plotter, or at least within certain limits from these index lines, and in so doing the navigator can ensure that the vessel follows the chosen track line.

For a target to be suitable, there are certain conditions which must apply to the indexing target:

1 It must be a good radar target, i.e. clearly visible on the PPI at the ranges at which it is intended to use it.
2 It must be identifiable among all the other land targets in the area and also there must be some recognisable feature on the target to which all the measurements can be related. This latter requirement can be difficult to resolve in the case of non-point targets, since most change their radar aspect and therefore their appearance as the relative position of the ship changes (see Section 8.2).

The navigator, in preparing for parallel indexing, must study the chart of the area with particular care to find the most suitable indexing targets, such as the end of a breakwater, the tip of a headland, small islands, isolated rocks, isolated lighthouses etc. Lighted navigation marks are of no consequence in this context of course and it is advisable never to rely on a floating navigation mark as an indexing target (except as provided in Section 8.4.7), not so much because of their slight variations in position but because of the possibility of their not being there at all when the vessel arrives. It is impossible to change all the pre-worked parallel indexing data to another target at short notice.

Note Whenever a vessel is operating in a confined area where parallel indexing can be useful, the navigator is advised to watch the radar picture carefully with a view to identifying suitable indexing targets for use on a future occasion. This method is far more certain than studying the chart. This information should be stored for future use, e.g. by marking the chart.

Another inportant consideration is the choice of the working range scale for the radar. Inevitably, the longer the range scale, the lower the accuracy with which one can monitor the position. The navigational requirements will determine the accuracy required and also the safety margins which will apply. The navigator must therefore be sure that the working range scale of the radar meets this accuracy requirement and that the selected indexing target will be 'in range'. This should not be taken to imply that a complete parallel index transit should be completed on one range scale. As accuracy requirements change, so should the working range scale. Similarly, as the vessel progresses through the confined area, so the indexing target will also need to be changed.

8.4.2.5   *Preparing the navigation data*

Parallel indexing is part of the navigation of the ship and therefore any guidance lines that appear on the reflection

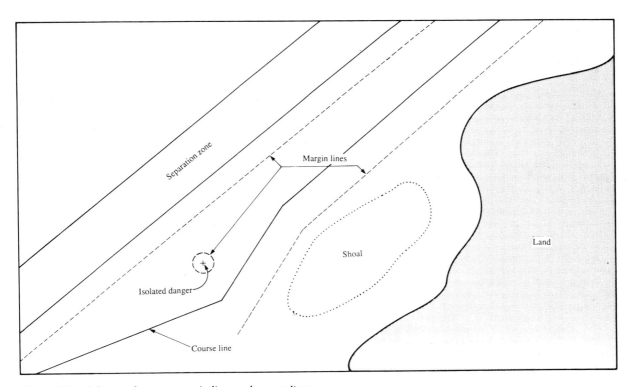

Figure 8.5   Adjacent dangers, margin lines and course lines

plotter should be directly related to actual data of navigational significance on the chart, e.g. the safety margins and course lines (Figure 8.5).

In planning a passage through a confined area, the adjacent dangers need to be assessed in detail. Adjacent dangers in addition to shoal water can include areas of strong tidal sets and the boundaries of traffic separation schemes (for a full treatment of passage planning techniques, refer to Chaper 15 of *The Navigation Control Manual*). The navigator should also assess the state of preparedness of the vessel for the passage, i.e. for the time of the intended transit, speed and engine readiness, method of steering and turning circles, preparedness for anchoring and manning levels etc. and, with these factors in mind, decide on a safe distance at which to clear the adjacent dangers.

This data is put onto the chart as a safety or 'margin' line spaced away from the danger by the estimated safe distance.

Common sense and experience must be relied upon here when estimating where to position the margin lines,

as it is impracticable to draw a 'contour' line around every adjacent danger. Furthermore, it is extremely difficult to reproduce curved lines from the chart on the plotter with any degree of accuracy. The purpose of this part of the passage planning process is to identify clearly all the clear water that can safely be used by the vessel during a transit of the area. Naturally the intention is to maintain the course line but unfortunately the seaways have to be shared with many other vessels and therefore one must be prepared to leave the course line should an anti-collision manoeuvre be required at any time.

The final stage of this navigation process is to draw in the course lines on the chart, taking care at all times to keep within the defined safe/clear water areas.

8.4.3 Parallel indexing, the technique

8.4.3.1 *The parallel indexing principle*

On a relative-motion compass-stabilized radar display, a land target will always move across the screen in a direction which is the reciprocal of the observing vessel's

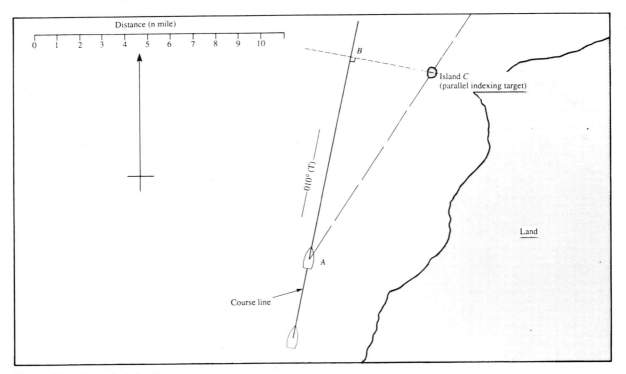

Figure 8.6   A simple index line
(a)   A charted plan

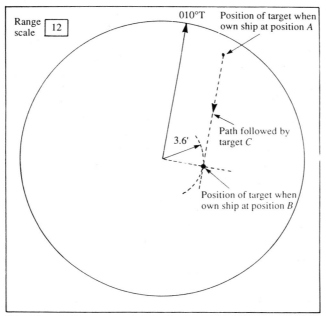

(b) The relative movement of a fixed target on the PPI

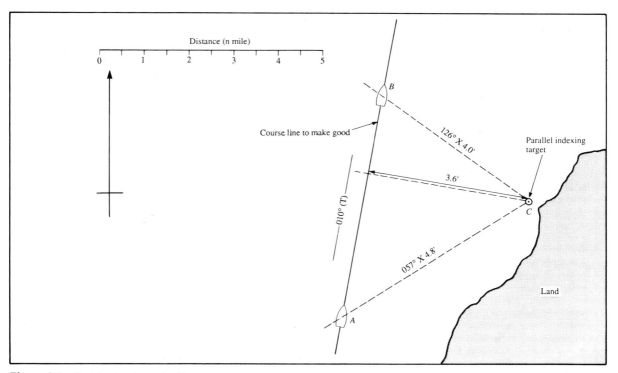

Figure 8.7 Positioning the index lines

(a) A charted plan navigation plan

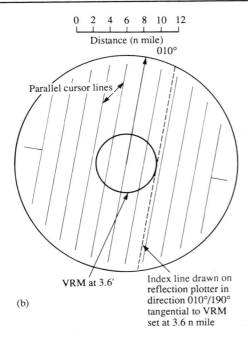

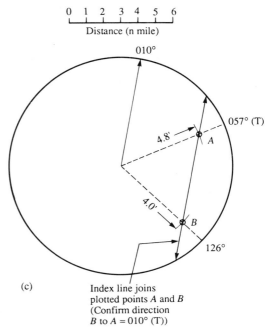

(b)   Positioning the index line by beam distance

(c)   Positioning the index line by ranges and bearings

course made good over the ground and at a rate directly related to the vessel's speed over the ground.

In the example shown in Figure 8.6(a), as the vessel steams from position A to position B (3.6 miles off island C), the radar echo of the island on the PPI will move from a position on the starboard bow until it is 3.6 miles off on the starboard side bearing 100°(T), having moved in a direction 190°(T), i.e. reciprocal to the ship's course made good over the ground.

With an understanding of this principle, it is possible for the navigator to predict the movements of an echo on the PPI, of a 'fixed' object while the ship follows a series of course lines near this object and to draw lines (index lines) on the reflection plotter to represent these movements prior to arriving in the area.

8.4.3.2   Positioning the index line on the reflection plotter

In the example illustrated in Figure 8.7(a) it is intended to make good a course of 010°(T) and to pass 3.6 miles off the island C (the indexing target). The index line can be positioned on the reflection plotter in one of two ways: either

(a)   Set 3.6 miles on the variable range marker and then turn the mechanical cursor to 010°/190°(T). Now, using a suitable straight edge, draw the index line at a tangent to the variable range marker and parallel to the cursor as shown in Figure 8.7(b); or

(b)   Measure the range and bearing of the indexing target from a chosen position on the course line (any position will do, but preferably a beam position, an alter-course position or another position where the highest accuracy is needed). Plot the range and bearing on the reflection plotter, turn the cursor to 010°/190°(T) and draw in the index line, parallel to the cursor and passing through the plotted position.

As a variation on method (b), if two points on the course line are fixed and plotted on the reflection plotter then they can be simply joined by a straight line. This method is useful in that it allows a simple cross-check, i.e. fix the start and end of a particular index line and then confirm from the chart, the actual direction and distance between the two (see Figure 8.7(c)).

Figure 8.8(a) shows a more complex series of intended

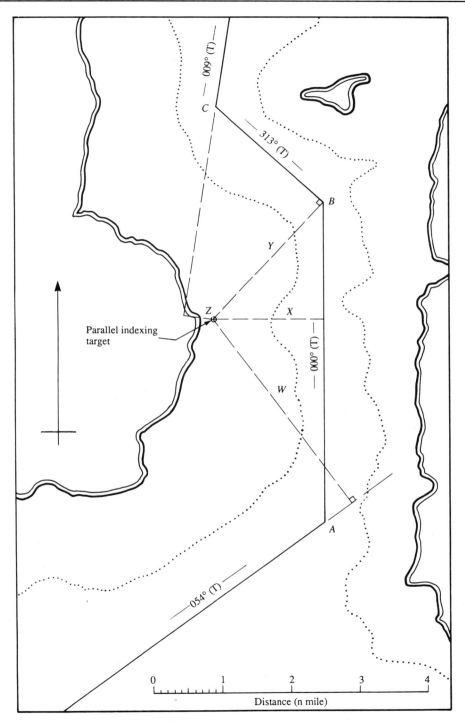

Figure 8.8   More complex indexing
(a)   A complex charted plan

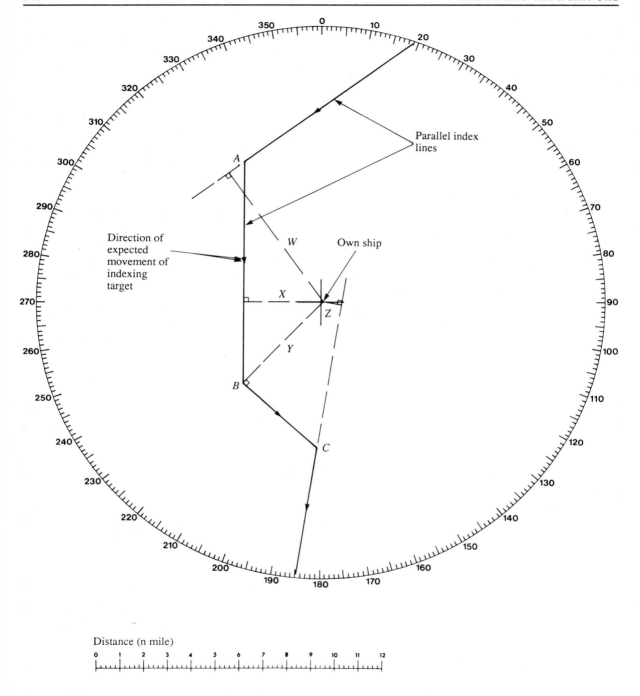

(b) A series of parallel index lines

tracks within a parallel indexing area and Figure 8.8(b) illustrates how this data translates onto the reflection plotter.

Example 8.1 Figure 8.8(a) has been drawn to scale. Extract the appropriate data and then, using either (a) the beam distance method or (b) the range and bearing method, construct the parallel indexing lines as they would be drawn out on the reflection plotter. The accuracy of the construction should be verified by measuring the directions and distances *A* to *B* and *B* to *C* or the distances *W*, *X*, *Y* and *Z*, as appropriate. The plot should appear as in Figure 8.8(b).

8.4.3.3 Transferring the margin lines to the reflection plotter

(a) *Normal lines.* Adding the margin line data to the parallel indexing plot is simply an extension of what has already been done, i.e. draw another series of lines on the plotter representing the acceptable limits for deviation of the indexing target. These

are usually drawn in such a way as to distinguish them from the normal cross-index lines. See Figures 8.9(a) and (b).

(b) *The danger circle.* Figures 8.9(a) and (b) also illustrate the special case of an isolated danger with a circular margin of safety or 'danger circle'. In this case, its position on the reflection plotter is determined by first measuring the position of the indexing target from the isolated danger and then transferring that to the reflection plotter. Then the margin of safety is drawn as a circle of appropriate radius centred on the plotted point *X*.

Note Although position *X* has been plotted on the reflection plotter, this should not be misinterpreted as the actual position of the isolated danger relative to the observing vessel. As the ship transits the area, the indexing target moves along the index line. When the index target reaches position *Z* (the alter-course position), the vessel is 2.8 n mile away from the danger, i.e. by the distance *XZ*.

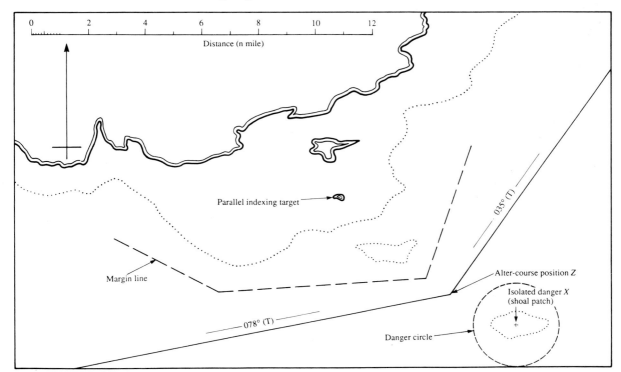

Figure 8.9 Margin lines and danger circles
(a) A navigation plan including margin lines and a danger circle

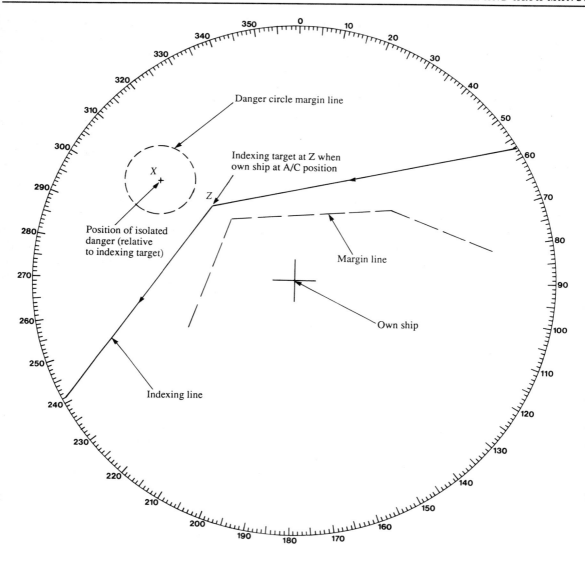

Danger circle margin line

Indexing target at Z when own ship at A/C position

X

Position of isolated danger (relative to indexing target)

Z

Margin line

Own ship

Indexing line

Distance (n mile)

(b)   A parallel indexing plot of margin lines and a danger circle

(c) *An alternative method of defining margin lines.* In confined waters where the margin lines are relatively close to the course line, it may be found more convenient to fix the margin lines on the plotter using the index lines as the datum rather than the indexing target. This technique is depicted in Figure 8.10(a) and (b).

Note that the distances being measured from the chart are the beam distances between the alter-course positions 1 and 2 and the adjacent margin line for both headings. The margin lines on the final 310° course are additionally referenced by the directions and distances.

As confirmation that the resultant margin lines on the plotter are in the correct position, check that their individual directions and lengths agree with those laid off on the chart. Provided that the distances *A*, *B*, *C* etc., are relatively small, it will not be found necessary to measure the beam angle but to lay off the direction by eye and measure the appropriate distance.

With this method, where a lot of distance measuring is being done, it is necessary to construct a distance scale, either on an unused area of the reflection plotter or on a separate straight edge (see Figure 8.4).

8.4.3.4 The 'wheel-over' position

When transiting a very confined channel and/or conning a large vessel, it is advisable to plan the wheel-over positions using a knowledge of the ship's turning characteristics including any interaction effects (see *The Navigation Control Manual*, Section 15.3.3). Use of this data should make it possible to keep on the track line required. This information will appear on the chart as a point on the course line spaced a calculated distance back from the alter-course position. This distance can be used on the reflection plotter to indicate the point on the index line where the ship should begin to turn. See Figures 8.11(a) and (b).

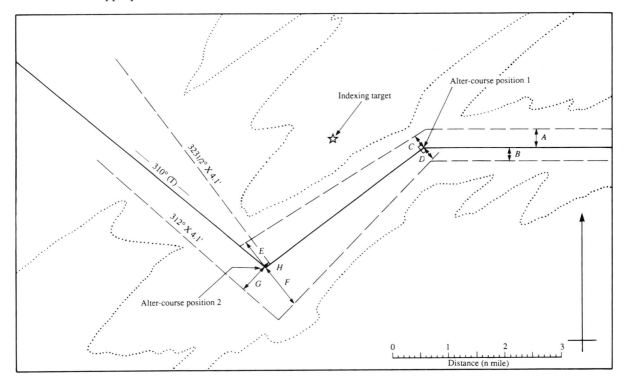

Figure 8.10 Narrow margins
(a) A navigation plan with narrow margins

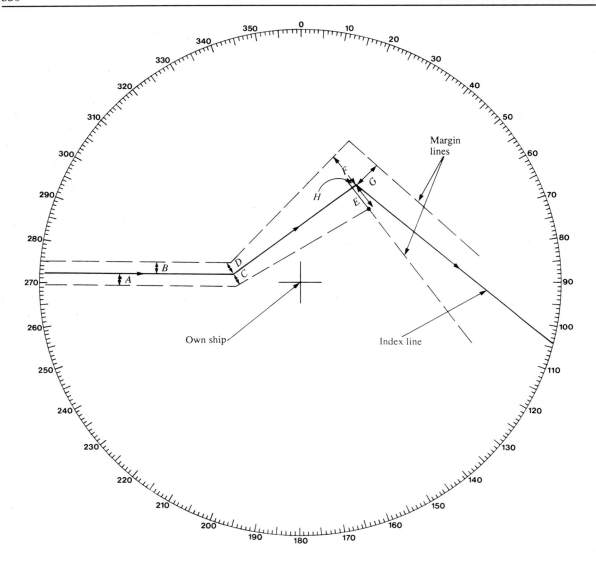

Distance (n mile)

(b)   A parallel indexing plot with margin lines fixed relative to index lines

Note It is advisable to make these turning predictions for a moderate value of helm (10° to 15°) on the understanding that, if the conditions are other than calm (and assuming deep water), the actual turn as executed may not correspond with the predictions. Consequently the person conning the ship should be prepared to increase or reduce the amount of helm applied in order to meet the precise requirements of the turn.

The track line may be regained using the wheel-over position. When the vessel is not exactly on the course line and is approaching an alteration point, provided circumstances allow, it is common practice to take the new course either early or late, as necessary, in order to recover the course line (see Figure 8.12(a)).

To identify the position at which to begin the alteration of course, a construction line is drawn through the wheel-over position and parallel to the new course line. On the parallel index plot (see Figure 8.12(b)). when the indexing target reaches the construction line through the wheel-over position, the turn begins.

8.4.3.5 *Recording the parallel indexing data*

Having spent the necessary time and effort in planning a coastal passage or port approach and having defined the areas where parallel indexing will be used, the data needed for the reflection plotter must be extracted and recorded in a suitable form, i.e. either in a notebook or in a diagrammatic form so that, when the time comes to use the data, it can be put on the reflection plotter and used with an absolute minimum of delay. It is essential to remember that no mistakes can be tolerated at this stage.

The diagrammatic method of data storage gives the operator the additional advantage of being able to cross-check by direct comparison of the indexing lines drawn on the reflection plotter with the previously prepared data.

An extension of the diagrammatic method involves drawing the parallel indexing data accurately on one or more acetate sheets which have been cut to fit the face of the reflection plotter. Apart from the normal parallel

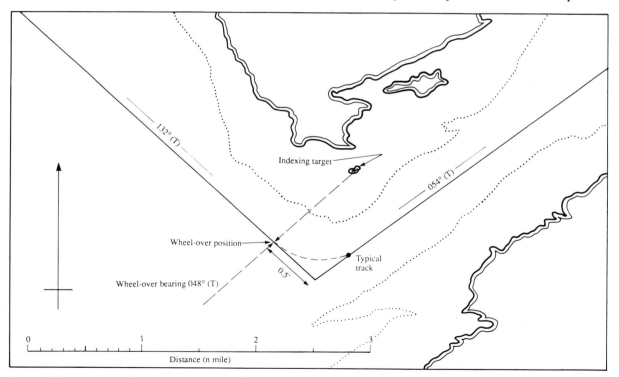

Figure 8.11   Incorporating the wheel-over position
(a)   A navigation plan with alter-course and wheel-over positions

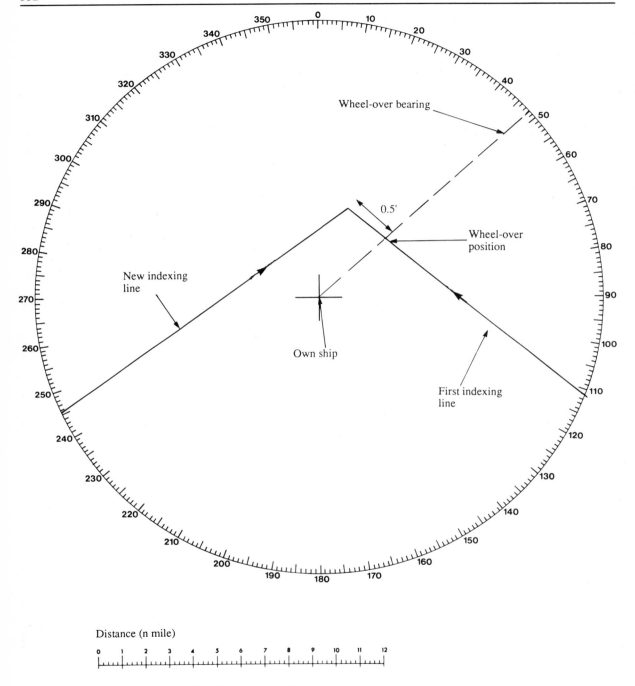

Distance (n mile)

(b)   A parallel indexing plot with the wheel-over position marked

indexing data, these sheets would need careful marking with reference points for centre and north.

The recording of this navigational data is part of the normal passage-planning process and the operator should not look on the data as permanent and able to be used repeatedly on future occasions without amendment. It should be remembered that, in deciding on the margin of safety lines, the tide and present vessel status, for example, are important factors. Hence the parallel indexing data contained on the acetate overlays should not be used subsequently without first checking that the data is still valid.

Included with the parallel-indexing lines will be the operational instructions, such as the point at which to begin using the data, the range scale to use, the appropriate point/time to change range scale or to change the indexing target.

8.4.4 Progress monitoring

As described in Section 8.4.2.4, the intention while navigating using parallel indexing is to keep the indexing target on the indexing line that has been drawn for it, or at least within the margin lines that may apply. To do this the navigator must continuously monitor the movement of the indexing target and take particular note of (a) the actual position of the indexing target relative to the index line and safety margin lines and (b) the present trend of movement relative to the desired direction of movement.

Simple observation of the echo and its afterglow can provide this information but it is advisable to plot the indexing target with grease pencil to make the data more obvious. The actual position of the indexing target relative to the margin lines confirms that the vessel is in

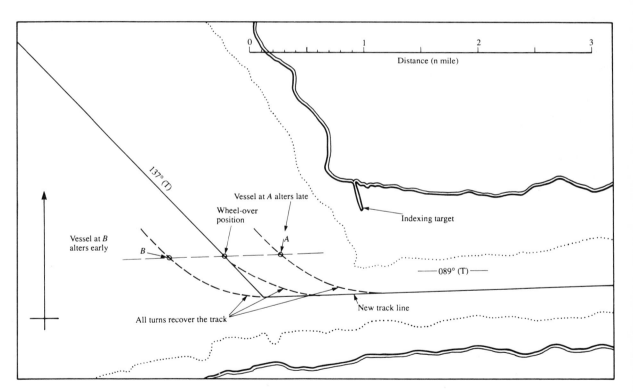

Figure 8.12 Recovering the track
(a) A navigation plan to recover the track line using the wheel-over line

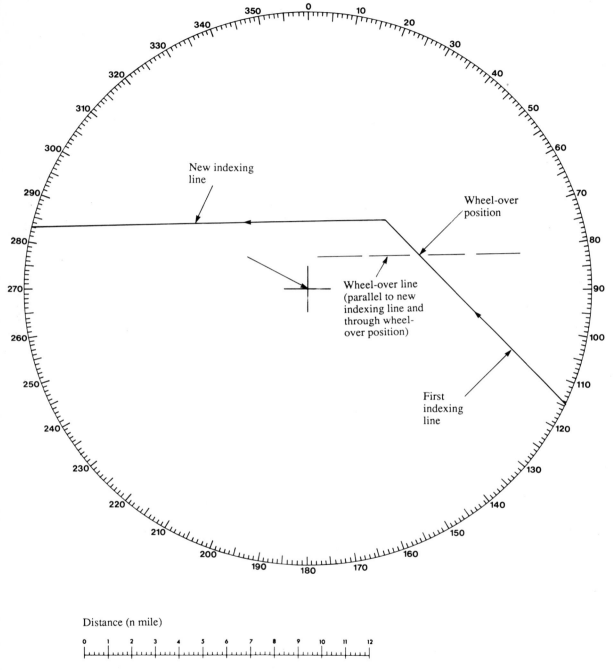

Distance (n mile)

(b)   A parallel indexing plot with wheel-over line to assist in the recovery of the track line

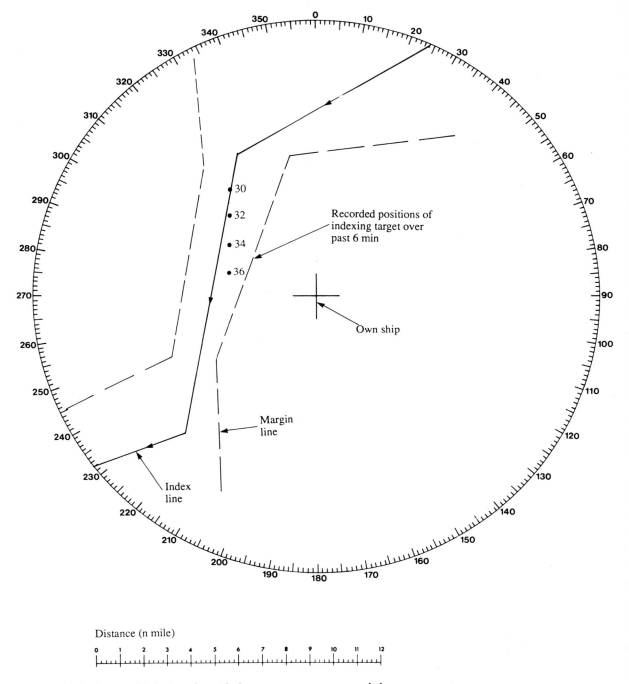

Figure 8.13 A parallel indexing plot with the target movement recorded

safe water and how much sea room is presently available. The trend of movement as provided by the plotting confirms whether or not the vessel is at that time making good the required track. The navigator can now decide, on the basis of these two pieces of information, whether corrective action is needed, either to regain the planned course line or to make good the required track direction.

For example, in Figure 8.13, monitoring the indexing target as the vessel transits the narrow channel shows that over the past few minutes the indexing target has left the indexing line and is approaching the margin line. This indicates that the ship is being set to the west and that the required corrective action is to turn to starboard by a few degrees so that the indexing target moves back onto the index line, or at least does not move any farther away from it.

Notice that no reference is made to the ship's head in this process because what in fact is relevant here is the course which is being made good rather than the direction in which the ship is pointing. The difference between the two can be large in a tideway when the ship's speed is low. When visibility is restricted, these differences can be very disorientating. It is not being suggested here that the ship's head should be totally disregarded; obviously there should be some logical relationship between the two directions provided by a knowledge of the tidal set and rate.

As the indexing target moves along the indexing line there is no need to keep the lines behind it and these may be progressively cleared from the plotter. While the vessel is being navigated using parallel indexing it is very important to fix the ship's position on the chart by normal methods at frequent intervals as confirmation that the ship *is* in fact in safe water and *is* in fact moving in agreement with the parallel indexing information.

8.4.5   Parallel indexing on a true-motion display

As explained in Section 8.4.2.3, the use of a true-motion radar presentation for parallel indexing requires an ability to ground-stabilize the display reliably. Assuming that this condition can be met, the PPI may be used as an extension of the chart. The navigational data additional to the radar targets already on the PPI, such as course lines and margin-of-safety lines, can be marked on the reflection plotter.

The data needed to be transferred to the plotter is identified during passage planning in exactly the same way as when working with relative motion, except that the lines will be located relative to any fixed recognisable target on the PPI rather than to a single indexing target. This implies that, if the data is to be maintained at a high level of accuracy, careful consideration must be given to the identification of these fixed targets. In addition, the overall accuracy of this process will be enhanced by using the shortest range scale which is capable of showing the required data and by using reference navigation marks that are the nearest available. Each individual line should also be crossed-checked by confirming from the chart the direction and length of each leg. Figure 8.14(a) shows the navigational situation with own ship approaching an alter-course position north of island Y, to be followed by the transit of a narrow passage. Suitable radar navigation marks are identified at point X, island Y and point Z. The alter-course position and margin lines are referenced relative to these points. As our vessel approaches the area (see Figure 8.14(b)), the radar echoes of the selected navigation marks are identified and the navigation lines are drawn on the reflection plotter using the previously recorded ranges and bearings. Each individual line should also be cross-checked by confirming, from the chart, its length and direction.

As the ship transits the area in question, the navigator must be prepared to reset the origin and/or change the range scale at the appropriate time. Where the navigation data is on the reflection plotter, this necessitates redrawing, therefore the point at which to do this needs to be pre-planned and the data stored in a form suitable for rapid application to the plotter. It has to be recognised that if ground-stabilization is not perfectly maintained, the fixed targets will drift away from their marks on the reflection plotter. The picture reset controls are normally fairly coarse and it may be difficult or even impossible to recover from this situation without redrawing the lines. Many users believe that this limitation of true-motion parallel indexing renders the technique unsuitable for practical use.

8.4.6 Modern radar navigation facilities

8.4.6.1 The electronic range and bearing line (ERBL)

This feature (see Section 6.9.6) is fitted to many modern radars and can make a considerable contribution to the speed and accuracy with which parallel indexing data can be applied to the reflection plotter, as it removes any requirement to rely on the mechanical parallel cursor lines and the 'homemade' distance scale (see Section 8.4.2.2). Using a joystick or similar control, the electronic bearing line can be moved to any part of the screen and orientated to any chosen direction. A separate control can then adjust the length of this line or put a marker on the line at any chosen distance from its origin. Digital read outs indicate the values of range and direction.

Using this device, the positions at which to draw the parallel indexing lines can quickly be established and checked. This is particularly valid when working with the true-motion presentation where being off-centred makes the use of the mechanical cursor more difficult.

8.4.6.2 Ground-stabilization using ARPA (see also Section 5.3)

The target-tracking capability of the ARPA can provide the navigator with an important and potentially very useful piece of data to help with the navigation problem, namely a continuously updated rate and set of the current being experienced. This is a significant improvement on the previous situation where relatively long periods of plotting or position fixing were needed to be able to deduce the rate and set experienced over that period. The navigator then had to assume that this data was constant and use it to plan future action, naturally with varying degrees of success as this data can be very time-variable.

There are two pre-requisites for the ARPA to provide the navigator with accurate tidal data:

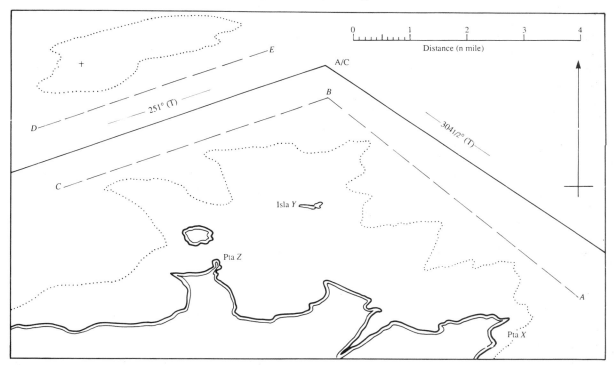

Figure 8.14 Parallel indexing on a true-motion ground-stabilized presentation
(a) A navigation plan to transit a narrow passage

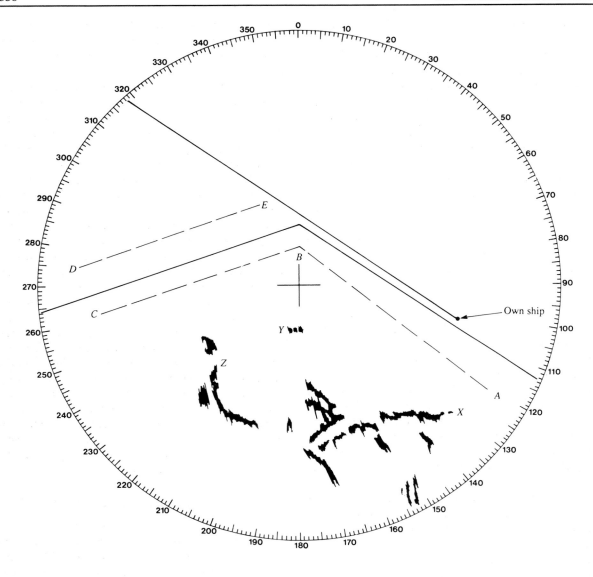

Distance (n mile)

(b)   A parallel indexing plot on a true-motion ground-stabilized presentation

1 The computer must be provided with accurate values of own ship's motion *through the water*, i.e. true heading and speed (see Sections 6.8.1.2 and 6.8.1.3)

2 There must be a radar echo from a known fixed target showing on the PPI and capable of being tracked by the ARPA. In most cases this means that it must be small and isolated, otherwise the point being tracked will tend to wander randomly within the echo area and so provide random spurious data. In some geographical areas, this type of fixed target can be hard to find. However, the rigorous selection requirements associated with parallel indexing targets (see Section 8.4.2.4) do not apply in this case and, provided that the target is small and isolated and does not move its geographical location during the period of time that it is being used for this purpose, it will suffice. Hence floating marks are acceptable with due caution in this regard.

The accuracy of the tidal data calculated is dependent not only on the accuracy with which the reference target is tracked (yielding the ground track) but also on the accuracy of the input of the observing vessel's water track since the tidal values are deduced from the vector difference of these two tracks. For practical purposes, the accuracy of the set and drift so obtained should be at least as good as would be obtained by using more traditional methods, i.e. better than ± 0.5 knot for rate and $\pm 20°$ for direction. The fact that it has been obtained very rapidly and with only token effort by the navigator makes it an ideal source of information with which to ground-stabilize the radar presentation. This may be done by setting in the relevant values on separate controls, or the radar manufacturer may provide a direct internal route such that, at the touch of the appropriate control, the tidal data is automatically applied to the tracking of own ship (see Section 5.3). Since the tidal data is continually updated, the result is an almost perfect degree of ground-stabilization where own ship and all target motions are now indicated with respect to the ground.

Note When the display is being automatically ground-stabilized, the accuracy of own ship's perceived movement through the water does not affect the indicated movements on the screen. If, however, a read-out is taken of tidal rate and set, then the computation involves own ship's input course and speed data and this factor must therefore be correct.

The reliability with which the ARPA continues as a ground-stabilized display depends on how well it continues to track the *reference* fixed target. Tracking can be lost under certain circumstances (see Section 5.3) and, remembering the purpose for which ground-stabilization is selected for the radar presentation, it is advisable to pay close attention to the performance of the ARPA in this respect. In particular, always try to keep the reference target visible on the PPI and under observation. Other fixed targets suitable for the purpose of ground-stabilizing should already be being tracked and available for use at short notice. Some ARPA manufacturers allow the simultaneous tracking of several fixed targets from which the mean value of tidal data is derived and applied. This makes the system less vulnerable to the loss of tracking of a single reference target.

Once the radar presentation has been stabilized, the additional navigational data can be applied to the reflection plotter as described in Section 8.4.5. Although the automatic ground-stabilizing function is not affected by changing range scales or by repositioning the display origin, the lines drawn on the plotter will be out of position and to the wrong scale and hence will have to be redrawn. Even if the navigator returns to the original range scale, it is not always possible to re-position the origin with the precision needed.

8.4.6.3 *Electronic navigation lines (see also Section 5.4)*

Most ARPAs obviate the need for the observer to draw the index lines on a reflection plotter by providing some form of optional navigation line package. This facility allows the navigator to use graphics to draw electronic lines directly on the screen. A major advantage of such a facility is that the observer has complete freedom to reset the origin of the picture and change range scale, because the lines are automatically scaled and referenced to suit the selected range scale and presentation.

In theory, the pattern of lines may be referenced to the observing vessel, or to the ground. There is considerable variety in the way manufacturers have approached the provision of this facility, and both modes are not necessarily available in any given package.

Where the lines can be referenced to the observing vessel they will maintain constant position on the screen when the relative-motion presentation (see Section 1.5.1) is selected, thus facilitating relative-motion parallel indexing as described previously.

The ready availability of automatic ground-stabilization in ARPA systems makes it simple to generate a line pattern which remains stationary on the screen when the ground-stabilized true-motion presentation (see Section 1.5.2.2) is selected. This facilitates true-motion parallel indexing as described previously in Section 8.4.5 and, additionally, allows the navigator to arrange the lines in such a way as to form simple maps giving a *chart-like* presentation. It is essential to appreciate that in the case of many systems this will be accompanied by ground-stabilization of the true vectors, as a result of which they will *not* represent the headings of other vessels. If the radar is also being used for collision avoidance, the observer may be dangerously misled. This important limitation of ground-stabilization is discussed in Sections 8.4.8.2 and 5.3. In some ARPA systems it is possible to display ground-referenced lines when the relative-motion presentation is selected. In such a situation the map or other pattern should maintain its registration with a ground-stationary target.

The format in which navigation line data is read into the computer is not standardized and many different systems exist while yet others are being developed. In general, the method will involve one of the following:

(a)   A series of ranges and bearings.
(b)   A cartesian co-ordinate system.
(c)   A series of latitudes and longitudes.

In each case the navigator must have some datum from which to measure so as to establish the relationship between the chart and the radar picture (e.g. if a navigation line is referenced on the chart relative to a prominent navigation feature such as the end of a breakwater, then, when the vessel arrives in the area in question and the breakwater echo appears on the radar screen, the navigation line can be positioned in the correct relationship to the radar echo of the breakwater and will thus take up its proper geographical location).

The navigator must be very aware of the accuracy with which the datum can be defined and, similarly, of the accuracy with which the lines can be positioned on the screen. It is also a condition that the datum used must be an identifiable radar target.

Many ARPA 'navigation' packages provide a storage facility such that the map can be drawn at some convenient time prior to use and put into the computer's memory. Depending on the sophistication of the particular package, several maps of varying sizes may be stored simultaneously and called up when required. When recalled to the PPI, the map needs precise positioning; to assist in this function, a *map align* control is usually provided. It is worth remembering that it may be impossible to turn the map in azimuth once drawn and therefore, before constructing any map, the navigator must check that the radar presentation is accurately north-referenced and stabilized.

A fundamental precaution that must be taken by all navigators designing maps which are to be used to assist with navigation in confined waters is the inclusion of check marks within the map such that, at any time while the maps are being used, it is possible for the navigator to confirm by simple inspection of the PPI screen that the lines drawn are in correct registration with geographical features. Happily, the lines drawn on the chart do not move without warning, but this may happen with electronic lines. For any ARPA there is likely to be one or more sets of circumstances that would allow the maps to shift their position. Usually the drift is very slow but therein lies the danger, for the gradual movement easily escapes detection unless there are obvious marks within the map to highlight the discrepancy. Generally, when the ARPA presentation has been ground-stabilized by *fixed target* reference, the map stabilization is reliable provided that the ground-stabilization is accurately maintained. The commonest form of check is to include points or lines in the map which correspond to recognisable fixed radar targets. Only when these markers lie on the appropriate radar echoes is the map known to be properly positioned. These markers, if they include floating reference marks, have the complementary function of attracting the attention of the navigator to buoys which are out of position or missing.

8.4.7 Unplanned parallel indexing

Occasionally, the navigator may realize a need for parallel indexing data while actually conning the vessel in an area where the passage planning appraisal had not foreseen the need. In such a case it is necessary to devise a strategy which, with the minimum of measurements, will allow a simple and rapid application of data to the reflection plotter or a rapid input of data to the facility which generates the navigation lines.

For example, suppose that the vessel is experiencing difficulty, due to tide or wind, in making an alter-course position off a buoy or other radar target:

(a) With a relative-motion radar presentation, set the variable range marker (VRM) at the required passing distance (CPA) from the radar target and draw a line on the plotter from the radar target at a tangent to the VRM. Thereafter, steer the vessel so that the echo remains on the index line.

(b) With a true-motion ground-stabilized radar presentation, set the VRM at the required passing distance from the radar target, then draw a line on the plotter through the radar echo at a tangent to the VRM. Thereafter, steer the vessel to maintain the tangent relationship between the VRM and the index line.

The advantage of these methods is their instant response to a particular need. Navigators should not, however, lose sight of the dangers inherent in failing to pre-plan thoroughly, such as the absence of cross-checking and the inability to detect the proximity of danger. The navigator also needs to be able to pick out, at short notice, a reliable indexing target.

8.4.8 Anti-collision manoeuvring while parallel indexing

Parallel indexing is purely a radar navigational technique which is unlikely to be employed unless navigational constraints are present and which requires the continuous attention of the navigator. However, non-navigational obstructions in the form of other vessels may appear at any time requiring anti-collision action. This action must not take the vessel into unsafe water

and it is in integrating this anti-collision action with the navigational constraints that the *margin-of-safety lines* included in the parallel indexing data show their true value.

8.4.8.1 Using a relative-motion presentation

Unless ARPA data is available, the relative-motion display with parallel indexing data on the plotter is most unsuitable as a source of anti-collision data, mainly due to the disruption it causes to the navigation process while the plotting is taking place. To determine the motion of a target, it is preferable to use one of the following techniques:

(a) Use a second radar set solely for anti-collision data acquisition. In a confined water situation, true-motion would probably be of assistance as it allows the tactical situation to be more apparent and, consequently, possible action by targets to be more predictable.

(b) Plot the target's position on the navigation chart. A period of such plotting puts the anti-collision problem into its proper context and the navigator can then plan his actions to avoid the traffic while still remaining in safe water.

When working on the relative-motion plot, it can be difficult to assess rapidly the importance of any particular moving target and much time and effort can be used in plotting each one as it appears. A 'rule of thumb' method to resolve this problem is to take an approximate range and bearing of the moving target from own ship, transfer the line defined by this vector to the indexing target (the end of the line which intersected the target to be placed on the indexing target). The other end of the line now indicates the position of the moving target relative to the fairway. If it is in or close to the fairway of margin lines then it should be given further consideration immediately. If, however, it falls completely away from the parallel indexing fairway then it can be discounted for the time being as it is not in or close to the intended route. Obviously it could subsequently enter the fairway so it cannot be ignored completely.

In Figure 8.15, while indexing on the present heading

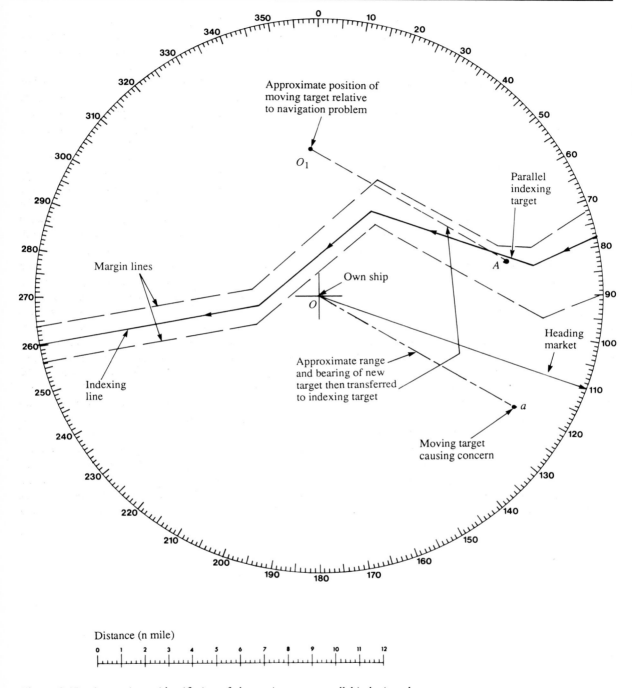

Figure 8.15   Approximate identifiction of obstructions on a parallel indexing plot

of 110°(T), target *a* has appeared on the starboard bow. By transferring line *Oa* so that *a* lies on the indexing target at *A*, it is established that the target is well outside the fairway at O_1 and the observing vessel expects to turn to 020°(T) before reaching the target.

Where ARPA facilities are provided, it should be possible to extract collision-avoidance data in the usual way.

8.4.8.2   *Using a true-motion ground-stabilized presentation*

(a) *Without ARPA.* Moving targets within the vicinity are soon recognised after a small amount of plotting on the reflection plotter. Their positions and approximate movements with respect to the navigation problem can be deduced. However, it is essential to bear in mind that all targets will exhibit their ground tracks.

With the non-ARPA display, this limitation is resolved by turning the tidal speed control to zero for long enough to assess the course and speed of the target through the water, i.e. two to three minutes, depending on the range scale. (*Note*   The parallel indexing lines on the plotter are now out of position and the origin will need to be reset to restore the parallel indexing plot.)

(b) *With ARPA.* Echoes of moving targets can be tracked in the normal manner and their true vectors displayed. The relative vectors or data will provide CPA and TCPA information as required.

However, the true vectors may well represent the movement of the targets *over the ground* and if the tidal component is significant there could be a large discrepancy between the ARPA ground tracks and the target's course and speed *through the water* (see Section 5.3). Since it is the *course through the water* which provides the aspect, the distortion of this piece of information can result in a complete misunderstanding of the situation which is facing the navigator. For example, in clear visibility at night, as a vessel approaches a port and is presented with an array of lights from moving targets against a backdrop of shore lights, unless there is a fairly close correlation between observed aspects and those illustrated on the PPI, the navigator may become disorientated or, alternatively, begin to lose faith in the equipment, all at a critical point in the passage. In reduced visibility, the fact that the data is distorted may go completely unnoticed and result in the navigator having a completely erroneous understanding of the traffic situation. This could lead to the wrong anti-collision action being taken.

The solution to this particular problem is that the navigator should not use a radar presentation that is primarily intended for navigation to deal with an anti-collision problem. The correct information on which to base collision-avoidance action comes from a sea-stabilized display and should always be made use of prior to making an anti-collision decision. With ARPA, remove the fixed target reference and return to the display of sea-stabilized data. Most of these changes of presentation are simple and quick with modern radars and there is no excuse for attempting to guess the effect that removing the tide would have. Having assessed the relevant information, the navigator can then return to his navigation problem by re-selecting the reference and re-aligning the navigation lines which will have drifted.

9 ARPA – accuracy and errors

9.1 Introduction

Errors present in the data displayed on the ARPA screen or by the alphanumeric read-out will affect decision making. The observer must therefore have a knowledge of the level of accuracy that can be expected and the errors which will affect it. It is not a simple matter to specify the accuracy because it depends on, among other things, the geometry of the plotting triangle. For this reason, the IMO Performance Standards specify accuracy in terms of what must be achieved by the ARPA in the case of four carefully chosen test scenarios. The scenarios are described and illustrated in Section 9.2 and the accuracy levels to be achieved are set out in Section 9.3.

9.2 The test scenarios

These test scenarios are generated by a simulator and fed to the ARPA which must give the results specified in Tables 9.1 and 9.2.

In the scenarios, the target's motion is specified in terms of its *relative* course and speed, neither of which is particularly helpful to the practical ARPA operator; in fact, the use of these terms on the bridge of a ship can give rise to dangerous confusion. While recognising that specification in this way is suited to a scientific test carried out in a laboratory, it is believed that, to be of

Table 9.1 ARPA accuracy values (95% probability) required after one minute

Scenario	Relative course (degrees)	Relative speed (knots)	CPA (nautical miles)
1	11	2.8	1.6
2	7	0.6	
3	14	2.2	1.8
4	15	1.5	2.0

Table 9.2 ARPA accuracy values (95% probability) required after three minutes

Scenario	Relative course (degrees)	Relative speed (knots)	CPA (nautical miles)	TCPA (min)	True course (degrees)	True speed (knots)
1	3.0	0.8	0.5	1.0	7.4	1.2
2	2.3	0.3			2.8	0.8
3	4.4	0.9	0.7	1.0	3.3	1.0
4	4.6	0.8	0.7	1.0	2.6	1.2

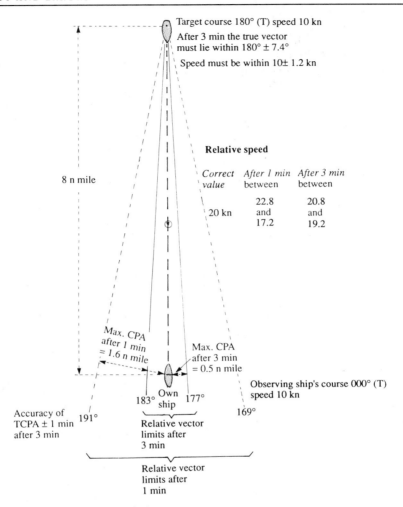

Target course 180° (T) speed 10 kn

After 3 min the true vector must lie within 180° ± 7.4°

Speed must be within 10± 1.2 kn

Relative speed

Correct value	*After 1 min between*	*After 3 min between*
20 kn	22.8 and 17.2	20.8 and 19.2

8 n mile

Max. CPA after 1 min = 1.6 n mile

Max. CPA after 3 min = 0.5 n mile

Observing ship's course 000° (T) speed 10 kn

Accuracy of TCPA ± 1 min after 3 min

191°   183°   Own ship   177°   169°

Relative vector limits after 3 min

Relative vector limits after 1 min

Figure 9.1   Test scenario 1

practical value to the user, it is more helpful if the target's true motion is known. To this end, the illustrations (which do not form part of the Performance Standard) show the scenarios in this way (Figures 9.1 – 9.4).

Test scenario 1 (Figure 9.1)

Own ship course 000°; own ship speed 10 kn; target range 8 n mile.
Target: bearing 000°; relative course 180°; relative speed 20 kn.

Test scenario 2 (Figure 9.2)

Own ship course 000°; own ship speed 10 kn; target range 1 n mile.
Target: bearing 000°; relative course 090°; relative speed 10 kn.

Test scenario 3 (Figure 9.3)

Own ship course 000°; own ship speed 5 kn; target range 8 n mile.

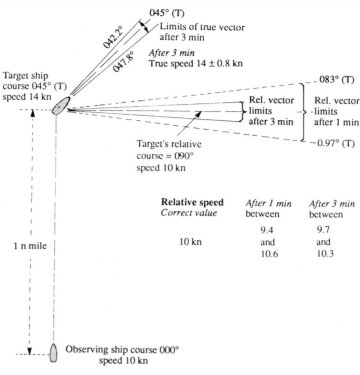

Figure 9.2 Test scenario 2

Target: bearing 045°; relative course 225°; relative speed 20 kn.

Test scenario 4 (Figure 9.4)

Own ship course 000°; own ship speed 25 kn; target range 8 n mile
Target: bearing 045°; relative course 225°; relative speed 20 kn.

9.3 The accuracy of displayed data required by the Performance Standard

The ARPA should provide accuracies not less than those given in Tables 9.1 and 9.2, for the four scenarios defined in Section 9.2, with the sensor errors specified in Section 9.5.6. The values given relate to the best possible manual plotting performance under environmental conditions of ± 10 degrees of roll.

An ARPA should present within one minute of steady state tracking, the relative motion trend of a target with the accuracy values shown in Table 9.1 (95% probability values).

An ARPA should present within 3 minutes of steady state tracking, the motion of a target with the accuracy values shown in Table 9.2 (95% probability values).

When a tracked target, or own ship, has completed a manoeuvre, the system should present in a period of not more than one minute, an indication of the target's motion trend, and display within three minutes the target's predicted motion, in accordance with Tables 9.1 and 9.2

The ARPA should be designed in such a manner that under the most favourable conditions of own ship motion, the error contribution from the ARPA should remain insignificant compared to the errors associated with the input sensors, for the scenarios depicted in Figures 9.1 – 9.4.

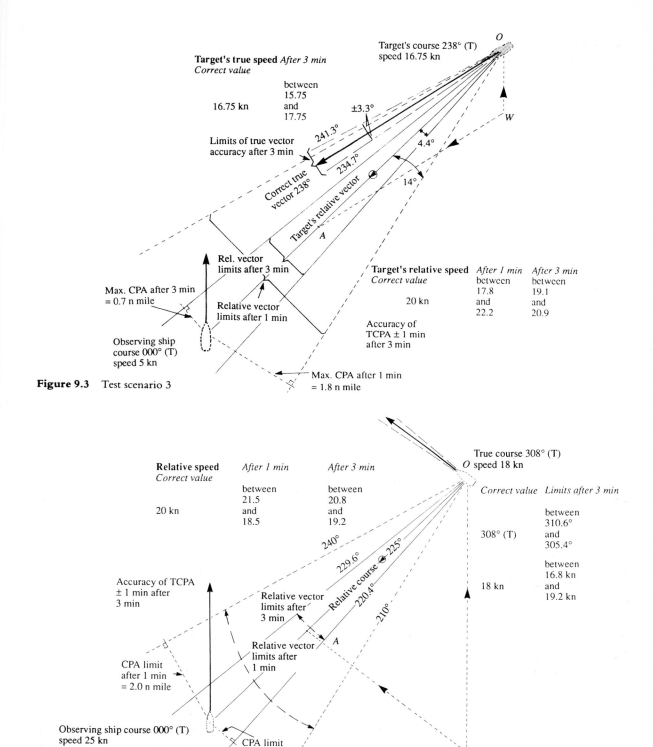

Figure 9.3 Test scenario 3

Figure 9.4 Test scenario 4

It should be noted that the tables give 95% probability values. This is necessary because any such error treatment is essentially statistical in its nature and means that the results must be within the tolerance values on 19 out of 20 occasions.

It is important to appreciate that even though the data is analysed by a computer, this does not mean that the results are perfect. Further, the errors considered in arriving at these tabulated values *do not* include 'blunders' or errors that result from the input of incorrect data.

Data obtained from the radar, log and gyro compass will be subject to random variations which all contribute to the uncertainty of the results as predicted by the computer. It should be appreciated that, because of the very short time period over which the computer plots (usually 1 minute or 3 minutes, see Section 4.3.6), and the consequent positional precision required, a whole new appreciation of radar errors is required. Errors which were not even considered with conventional radars in the past now become significant. In any case, the tables included in the specification should be taken as a guide as to what can be expected, especially with regard to CPA. It should be noted that this only considers up to 10° of roll. Where this is exceeded in practice, poorer results might be expected.

9.4   The classification of ARPA error sources

The accuracy levels discussed in the previous section are dependent on the chosen level of sensor errors but can also be affected by other errors. All errors which can affect the accuracy of displayed data can be conveniently arranged in three groups as follows:

1 Errors which are generated in the radar installation itself, the behaviour of the signals at the chosen frequency and the limitations of peripheral equipment such as logs, gyro compasses and dedicated trackers.
2 Errors which may be due to inaccuracies during processing of the radar data, inadequacies of the algorithms chosen and the limits of accuracy accepted.
3 Errors in interpretation of the displayed data.

9.5   Errors that are generated in the radar installation

Errors in the radar, gyro compass and log which feed data to the ARPA system will result in errors in the output data. Range and bearing errors which remain constant or nearly so during the encounter, e.g. a steady gyro compass error of a few degrees, will introduce an error into the predicted vectors of other ships, but are unlikely to cause danger since all data will be similarly affected, including own ship. The effect of errors on the predicted data depends on the kind of error, the situation and the duration of the plot for which the data is stored for processing and prediction. This time is typically in the range of 1 to 3 minutes and in this respect it must be appreciated that errors which in the past could be considered to be negligible may have a significant effect on derived ARPA data. In the following examples, the situation is assumed to be a near miss or a collision.

9.5.1   Glint

As a target ship rolls, pitches and yaws, the apparent centre of its radar echo moves over the full ship's length; this is termed glint. Its distance from amidships is random with a standard deviation of one-sixth length, i.e. for a 200 m ship it is probable that the error does not exceed ± 33 m. Since the beam of a ship is usually small by comparison with its length, transverse glint is negligible. If the target ship's aspect is beam-on, glint introduces random bearing errors.

9.5.2   Errors in bearing measurement

These cause false positions to be recorded on each side of the relative track of the other ship, leading to errors in the observed relative track and therefore in the predicted CPA and also in the displayed aspect of the other ship. Unfortunately, the greatest errors in displayed aspect occur in those cases where the real aspect is near end-on. Bearing errors may result from the following causes.

9.5.2.1 Backlash in gearing

Backlash can occur between the rotating antenna and its azimuth transmitter. Air resistance on the rotating antenna will tend to maintain geartooth contact, but bounce and reverse torque due to aerodynamic forces will break the contact and allow some backlash to occur. This problem has been to a large extent overcome by the use of more modern forms of bearing transmission (see Section 2.6.6.4).

9.5.2.2 Unstable platform or antenna tilt

Ship motion causes the axis of rotation of the radar antenna to tilt. When the ship is heeled to an angle of B radians, a bearing error of $-(\frac{1}{2}B^2 \sin \theta \cos \theta)$ radians is produced, where θ is the bearing of the target off own ship's bow. This error is quadrantal, i.e. zero ahead, astern and abeam, rising to alternate plus and minus maxima at 45° and 135° etc. It will not be reversed by the opposite roll since B is squared.

When the ship is rolling, the tilt has two components, a random variation between zero and a maximum, according to the value of B (i.e the actual roll angle which happens to be present when the aerial is directed on the bearing) and a rise and fall of the maximum over periods of about one or two minutes with wave height variation. For a relative bearing of 45° and a roll of 7.5° toward or away from the other ship, the error is $-0.25°$ maximum.

9.5.2.3 Parallax due to roll of own ship (Figure 9.5)

If the radar antenna is mounted at a height H above the roll axis of the ship and the ship rolls to an angle B, the antenna moves transversely by $H \sin B$. The measured bearing of a target at a bearing of θ from the ship's head and at a range R will be in error by an angle e which is given by

$$e = \frac{180 \, H \sin B \cos \theta}{\pi R} \text{ degrees}$$

(Note H and R must be in the same units.)

This error will vary sinusoidally with time and has a period equal to the roll period.

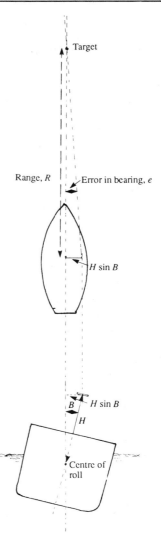

Figure 9.5 Parallax due to roll of own ship

$$\tan e = \frac{H \sin B}{R} \times \cos \theta$$

where θ is the relative bearing
The error is maximum when $\theta = 0°$ and 180°
minimum when $\theta = 090°$ and 270°
i.e. it varies with $\cos \theta$
Since e is small,

$$e = \frac{180 \, H \sin B \cos \theta}{\pi R} \text{ degrees}$$

9.5.2.4 *Asymmetrical antenna beam*

The ARPA should take the bearing of the target as that of the centre of the echo. If the antenna beam is asymmetrical, the apparent position of the echo may change with the echo strength. Errors due to this cause can become very large in some systems if the echo strength is sufficient for the close-in side-lobe pattern of the antenna to become apparent. At least one system employs special techniques to eliminate this problem.

9.5.2.5 *Azimuth quantization error (Figure 9.6)*

The antenna position must be converted to digital form before it can be used by the computer, for example, by using a shaft encoder (see Section 2.6.6.4). A 12-bit shaft encoder has a least significant bit (LSB) equivalent to 0.09° (360°/4096) so that the restriction to 12 bits introduces a quantization error of 0.045°. The same error will arise if the computer truncates the input azimuth information to 12 bits. Antenna azimuth is often taken to a resolution of either 12 or 13 bits.

Note Since many gyro compass repeater systems are step-by-step, with a step size of $\frac{1}{6}°$, there is no real point in making the antenna encoder bit size very much smaller.

9.5.3 Errors in range measurement

9.5.3.1 *Range change due to roll of own ship*

If the radar antenna is mounted at a height H above the roll axis of the ship and the ship rolls to an angle B, the antenna moves transversely by $H \sin B$. For a target bearing θ from the ship's head, the measured range will be in error by a distance d which is given by

$$d = H \sin B \sin \theta$$

Pitch error is much less significant, but if roll and pitch occur together the effects add non-linearly and must be worked out separately.

9.5.3.2 *Range quantization error (Figure 9.6)*

The range of a target must be converted into a digital

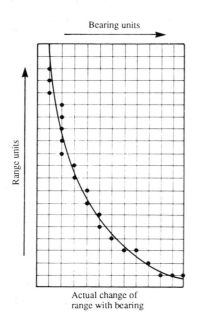

Actual change of
range with bearing

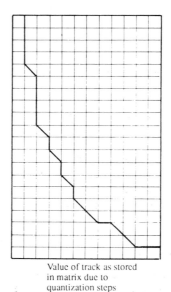

Value of track as stored
in matrix due to
quantization steps

Figure 9.6 Quantization errors

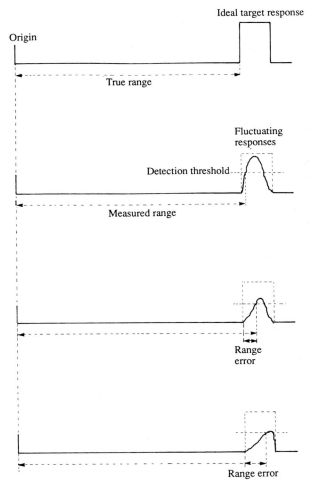

Figure 9.7   The error due to pulse amplitude variation

The equipment will typically measure the range of an echo at the point at which the echo strength rises above a pre-set threshold. Because of the finite bandwidth of the radar receiver, the echo pulse will have a sloping leading edge and the measured range will vary with the pulse amplitude (see Section 2.3.2.3). For the pulse length commonly used on anti-collision range scales, the receiver bandwidths are chosen for long range performance rather than for discrimination, so that it is likely that the leading edge slope will be nearly as long as the transmitted pulse.

The resulting apparent range variation will depend upon some assumptions about echo amplitude variations but is likely to be about 40 metres as a maximum.

9.5.4   The effect of random gyro compass errors

A gyro compass master unit, mounted at an arbitrary height above the roll axis of the ship, is subject to transverse acceleration at each extremity of the roll. This includes a false vertical as the pendulous unit tilts in its gimbals. This puts an error into the gyro compass output affecting all bearings; it has random and slowly varying components in just the same way as the radar tilt error. Observation at sea indicates that 0.25° is the error in many typical installations.

The gyro compass also has other errors. Long term errors (e.g. settling point ±0.75°) are unimportant if they remain sensibly constant, as they normally do, but short term random errors (e.g. settling point difference ±0.2°) are significant.

9.5.4.1   Gyro compass deck-plane (gimballing) errors

The true heading of a vessel is the angle between the vessel's fore-and-aft line and the meridian when measured in the horizontal plane. In several gyro compass designs, the sensitive element has sufficient degrees of freedom to assume a north-south, horizontal attitude. However, the compass card may be constrained to the deck plane. In this case there can be a discrepancy between the compass card reading and the ship's heading detected by the sensitive element.

number for the computer to use and it is likely that this will be done by measuring the range using counting techniques. A convenient clock rate is that corresponding to 0.01 n mile steps on the 12 mile range scale (see Section 2.6.6.3).

Typical step functions due to range and bearing quantizing are shown in Figure 9.6.

Note   During some periods, it will appear that the target is on a collision course, i.e. steady bearing, although this is never the case in fact.

9.5.4.2 *Yaw motion produced by the coupling of roll and pitch motions*

When a ship is rolling and pitching, these two motions interact to produce a resultant yawing motion. The motion can be resolved into horizontal and vertical components. The horizontal component is the yaw motion and is detected by the gyro compass sensing element.

9.5.5 The effect of random log errors

An error in own ship's log will produce a vector error in every tracked ship's true speed and course. This will also result in an error in the displayed aspect of other ships; however this aspect error is minimum in all cases where the real aspect is end-on. A further effect will be to produce non-zero speed indications on all stationary targets being tracked. This cause may also produce large errors in the aspects of very slow-moving targets. If this error is assumed not to exceed 0.4 knots, it will give rise to a positional error of some 15.5 metres in a plot time of 75 seconds.

Where true tracks are stored by the tracker (see Section 4.3.6.2), a fluctuating log error can also affect the relative vectors. However, the errors being considered here are the small random variations in the log output and not the large fluctuations which can occur if the log's performance becomes erratic due to technical malfunction or problems caused by outside influences such as fouling or aeration. Such larger flunctuations are more appropriately considered under errors in input data (see Section 9.6.3).

9.5.6 The magnitude of sensor errors specified in the Performance Standard

The accuracy figures quoted in Section 9.3 are based upon the following sensor errors and are appropriate to equipment complying with Performance Standards for shipborne navigational equipment. Note that σ denotes standard deviation.

Radar

Target glint (scintillation) (for 200 m length target)

Along length of target $\sigma = 30$ metres (normal distribution)
Across beam of target $\sigma = 1$ m (normal distribution)

Roll-pitch bearing The bearing error will peak in each of the four quadrants around own ship for targets on relative bearings of 045°, 135°, 225° and 315° and will be zero at relative bearings of 0°, 090°, 180° and 270°. This error has a sinusoidal variation at twice the roll frequency.

For a 10° roll the mean error is 0.22° with 0.22° peak sine wave superimposed.

Beam shape Assumed normal distribution giving bearing error with $\sigma = 0.05°$.

Pulse shape Assumed normal distribution giving range error with $\sigma = 20$ metres.

Antenna backlash Assumed rectangular distribution giving bearing error $\pm 0.5°$ maximum.

Quantization

Bearing Rectangular distribution $\pm 0.01°$ maximum.

Range Rectangular distribution ± 0.01 n mile maximum.

Bearing encoder assumed to be running from a remote synchro giving bearing errors with a normal distribution $\sigma = 0.03°$.

Gyro Compass

Calibration error 0.5°
Normal distribution about this with $\sigma = 0.12°$

Log

Calibration error 0.5 knots.
Normal distribution about this with $3\sigma = 0.2$ knots.

9.6 Errors in displayed data

9.6.1 Target swop

When two targets are close to each other, it is possible for the association of past and present echoes to be confused so that the processor is loaded with erroneous data.

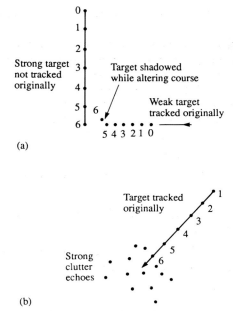

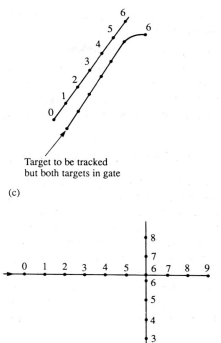

Figure 9.8 Target swop
(a) At position 6, tracker transfers to stronger target
(b) At position 6, and later, the profusion of echoes confounds tracker accuracy. The tracker may easily pick up random clutter instead of the target ship
(c) Targets travel close together for a period, then separate. The tracker may not follow the diverging target ship
Note It is often difficult to acquire a target that is close to others already being tracked

(d) Two tracked targets pass close to each other, so that both are in the tracking gate at one time
Note In this case, longer rate aiding may be an advantage

The result is that the historical data on one target may be transferred to another target and the indicated relative (and true) track of that ship will be composed of part of the tracks of two different target motions. Target swop can occur with any type of tracker but is least likely in those which use a diminishing gate size as confidence in the track increases and those which adopt rate aiding. It is most likely to occur when two targets are close together for a comparatively long time and one target echo is much stronger than the other, see Figure 9.8. It is particularly likely to occur if one target shadows the other (see also Section 4.3.5).

9.6.2 Track errors

The motion of a target is rarely completely steady and even steady motion will return positions which are randomly scattered about the actual track, due to basic radar limitations. Quantization errors in range and bearing which are introduced by the translation of the basic radar information to the processor database further exacerbate the effects of these system errors. The only way in which the tracker can deal with these is to use some form of smoothing over a period of time by applying more or less complicated filtering techniques (see also Section 4.3.6). The aim of the filtering is to give the best possible indication of the steady track and at the same time detect real changes quickly.

Given the need to satisfy these two conflicting requirements it is inevitable that the tracker will be limited in its ability to predict precisely the relative and true motion of a tracked target at any instant and thus track errors will result. The effect of these errors should of course fall within the limits set out in Section 9.3 but the prudent observer will use suitable clear weather opportunities to gain some evaluation of the practical performance of the tracker which is producing the ARPA data. Such performance can be usefully judged against two important criteria. These are the stability of the track shown on the display for a vessel which is observed to be standing-on and the rapidity with which the track responds to a target which has been observed to manoeuvre. It has to be recognised that alterations of course are easy to detect by visual observation whereas speed changes are not. However, in clear weather the former are very much more common than the latter, except in very confined waters.

Accuracy is most difficult to achieve with targets whose track movement is slow. In the case of relative track storage (see Section 4.3.6.2) this will affect a target whose course and speed are close to those of the observing vessel. The length of the relative track will be small and thus the system errors are a much more significant proportion of track length than would be the case with a target having a rapid relative motion. Thus the inherent accuracy of CPA data will be low. Conversely, in the case of true track storage (see Section 4.3.6.3) a near-stationary target will suffer the same low accuracy in the prediction of its true motion.

In general the tracker is likely to offer the best indication of both the relative-motion and the true-motion when both the target and the observing vessel maintain their course and speed for a full smoothing period. In the changing situation the track errors will depend on the nature of the changes and the form of track storage adopted (see Sections 4.3.6.2 and 4.3.6.3).

Where only the target manoeuvres there will be a finite response time in which the displayed vector will seek to follow the change and to stabilize on the new track. Under such circumstances, irrespective of whether the tracker smoothes relative or true tracks, there should in theory be no difference in the tracker performance when measured in terms of the accuracy with which it provides output of both relative and true vectors. In both cases the vectors may be erratic when the processor reverts to smoothing over the short period.

Where only the observing vessel manoeuvres, the method of storage is significant because the relative tracks of all targets will be curves for the duration of the manoeuvre. If the smoothing is applied to relative tracks, the tracker will be faced with the task of trying to produce a straight line from a curve and will hence obtain a mean track. Errors in the relative track will result and the relative vectors of all targets may be erratic in the short term. True-motion data derived from this will also be in error, just as where a manual plotter constructs an OAW triangle on the basis of an apparent motion which is not uniform (see Section 7.2). The effect may be exacerbated by the fact that, during the vessel's manoeuvre, the path traced out by the mass of the vessel, and hence the aerial, may differ significantly from that indicated by the gyro compass and log. Systems which smooth true tracks should derive a more accurate indication of the target's true track during the observing vessel's manoeuvre, as the true track is in theory rendered independent of changes in the observing vessel's course and speed. This independence will be reduced by any difference between the velocity of the ship's mass during the manoeuvre and the direction and speed fed in by the gyro and log. Again, all errors must fall within the limits of the Performance Standards but the prudent observer can assess the effect of manoeuvres on the performance of the tracker by observing a known stationary target during a manoeuvre. In this connection it must be remembered that, even in steady state conditions, a land-stationary target may display some component of motion due to the effect of tide, and water-stationary targets may have small non-zero vectors due to system errors.

Where both observing vessel and target manoeuvre at the same time, it is unlikely that any system will commence to provide a reliable indication of any target data until either the observing vessel or the target ceases to manoeuvre.

If targets are tracked down to very close ranges, the relative motion will give rise to very rapid bearing changes and this may make it impossible for the tracker to follow the target; thus the 'target lost' condition may arise, not because the echo is weak, but because the gate cannot be moved fast enough or opened up sufficiently to find it. It is also worth remembering that the use of true vectors as an indication of target heading is based on the assumption that the target is moving through the water in the direction in which it is heading. Leeway is the prime example of a case where this may not be correct. Unless one can see the target it is impossible even to begin to make an estimate of leeway. In poor visibility and high winds the observer must be alert to the possibility and use the displayed data with additional caution.

In summary, it must be remembered that whenever the steady state conditions are disrupted there will be a period in which the data will be particularly liable to the track errors described above, in the same way as is the case when a target is first acquired. When the steady state is regained, accuracy and stability will improve, first over the short smoothing period and then over the long period. Any track data extracted during periods of non-steady-state conditions must be viewed with suspicion.

9.6.3 The effect on vectors of incorrect course and speed input

From the theory of manual radar plotting (see Section 7.2) it is evident that it is possible to deduce the relative-motion of a target without using a knowledge of the true-motion of the observing vessel (other than to produce stabilized bearings). Deduction of the true-motion of the target requires a knowledge of the true-motion of the observing vessel to allow resolution of the *OAW* triangle and the accuracy of the result depends largely on the accuracy of the course and speed data used. Extrapolation of this reasoning suggests that the accuracy of relative vectors and the associated CPA data are independent of the accuracy of the course and speed input, whereas the accuracy of true vectors and the associated data are dependent on the accuracy of the input course and speed. In the case of systems which smooth relative tracks, this is invariably correct; in the case of systems which store true tracks, it is correct sub-

ject to the qualification that the input errors are constant. In the case of a fluctuating error input, the two storage approaches will produce different results. For this reason the effect of steady input errors on relative and true vectors is discussed in Sections 9.6.3.1 and 9.6.3.2 respectively, while the case of a fluctuating error is treated separately in Section 9.6.3.3.

Whatever approach the tracker uses, it is essential for the observer to ensure that the correct course and speed inputs are fed in when setting up (see Section 6.12.3) and that regular and frequent checks are made to ensure that the values remain correct. Failure to do this will in general result in the erroneous display of true data which may seriously mislead the navigator when choosing a suitable avoiding manoeuvre.

9.6.3.1 Relative vectors

The relative vectors and the associated CPA/TCPA data should be unaffected if the observer allows a fixed erroneous input of course and speed data to be applied. In the case of relative storage the information is not used in the calculation. In the case of true storage it is used twice and one could say that this illustrates a classic case of 'two wrongs making a right', as illustrated by Figure 4.9 in Section 4.3.6.3.

A fixed gyro compass error present at the point at which the bearings are digitized (see Section 2.6.6.4) would result in the picture being slewed but would not affect the CPA/TCPA data.

9.6.3.2 True vectors

The true vectors will be displayed incorrectly if the observer allows an erroneous input of course and speed data to be applied, irrespective of the storage format. This may give the observer a seriously misleading impression of the other vessel's heading and speed and may prompt an unsafe manoeuvre. Such a situation is illustrated by Figures 9.9 and 9.10.

Figure 9.9 shows a target which is moving at a similar speed to the observing vessel, is showing a red light and which will pass clear down the starboard side. Incorrect speed input could make this appear to be a slower vessel in a broad crossing situation or a faster ship passing green to green.

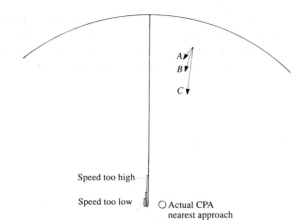

Figure 9.9 The effect of incorrect speed input on a true-vector presentation
Vector *B* is correct
Speed input 'too high' shows Vector *A*, a crossing slow ship
Speed input 'too low' shows vector *C*, a fast target on near parallel crossing

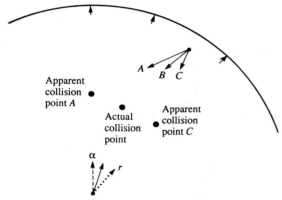

Figure 9.10 The effect of incorrect compass input on a true-vector presentation
Vector *B* is correct
Incorrect compass input to the left at alpha shows a target broad crossing to port and faster than own ship
Incorrect compass input to the right at *r* shows a target fine crossing to starboard and slower than own ship

The effect of an incorrect heading input will have a similar capacity to produce misleading results, as illustrated in Figure 9.10

9.6.3.3 *The effect of fluctuating input error*

The most probable source of a fluctuating input error is the log. There are a number of circumstances in which this might arise. An example is the case of some doppler logs which tend to give erratic output in bad weather when the transducer has to operate through an aerated layer. The fluctuating effect will affect the display of the true vectors whatever the form of storage but the behaviour of the relative vectors will depend on the mode of storage used. Where relative tracks are smoothed the fluctuating error will have no effect on the relative vectors and the associated CPA/TCPA data. Where true tracks are smoothed, the relative vector will tend to change erratically in sympathy with the input flunctuations, since the relative vector is derived from the smoothed true track and the instantaneous input course and speed data.

The difference in effect can be considered by an example shown in Figure 9.11. Consider the case where the observing vessel has been on a steady course and speed for a full smoothing period and the correct course and speed data has been consistently fed in. Both methods of smoothing will have settled to produce the correct relative and true vectors.

Suppose that the log develops an instantaneous fault and reads half the correct speed. The relative track system, shown in Figure 9.11(a), will show no change in the relative vector (because the relative track is smoothed) but the true vector will immediately go to the erroneous value because it is derived from the smoothed relative track and the instantaneous course and speed input.

The true track system will show no immediate change in the true vector, because it is insulated by the smoothing, whereas the relative vector will immediately go to an erroneous value since it is derived from the smoothed true track and the instantaneous course and speed input. If no further change takes place in the error and the vectors are observed over a full smoothing period, the true vector will gradually change to the erroneous value while the relative vector will gradually come back to the correct value as the previously smoothed track is progressively discarded. Thus, in this type of storage, if the speed input flunctuates the relative vector will also flunctuate. This disadvantage has to be set against the advantage gained in being able to maintain a stable relative vector when the observing vessel is manoeuvring (see Section 9.6.2).

An erratic course input would have a similarly dis-

ruptive effect. However, such a condition would also affect the digitization of bearings. This would tend to cause targets to jump and it would be fairly obvious to even a casual observer that something was wrong.

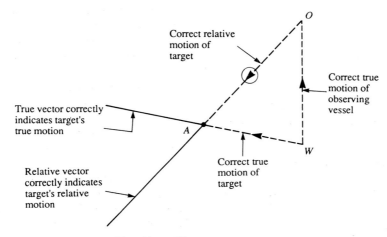

(i) **Course and speed input correct for a full smoothing period**

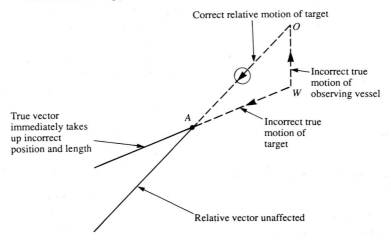

(ii) **Speed input instantaneously drops to half of correct value due to log error**

Figure 9.11   The effect of a step change in the error of speed input
(a)   Where relative track storage is used

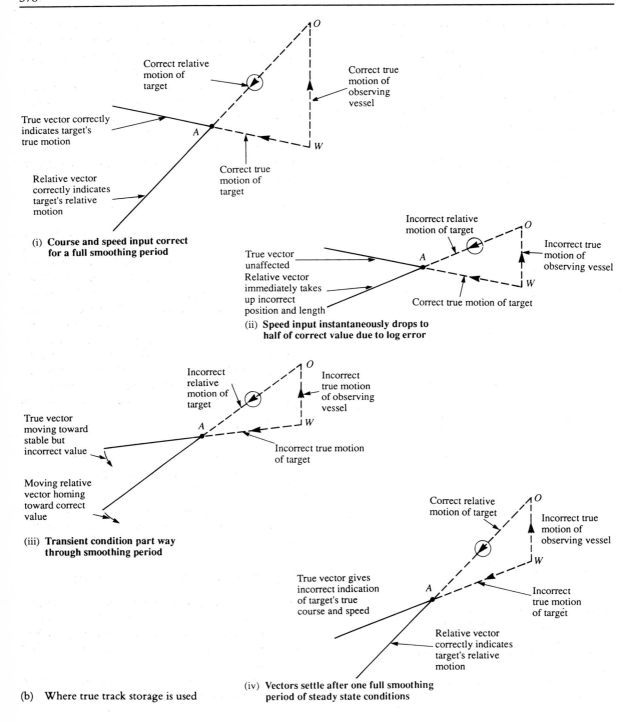

Correct relative motion of target

Correct true motion of observing vessel

True vector correctly indicates target's true motion

Correct true motion of target

Relative vector correctly indicates target's relative motion

(i) **Course and speed input correct for a full smoothing period**

Incorrect relative motion of target

Incorrect true motion of observing vessel

True vector unaffected

Relative vector immediately takes up incorrect position and length

Correct true motion of target

(ii) **Speed input instantaneously drops to half of correct value due to log error**

Incorrect relative motion of target

Incorrect true motion of observing vessel

True vector moving toward stable but incorrect value

Incorrect true motion of target

Moving relative vector homing toward correct value

(iii) **Transient condition part way through smoothing period**

Correct relative motion of target

Incorrect true motion of observing vessel

True vector gives incorrect indication of target's true course and speed

Incorrect true motion of target

Relative vector correctly indicates target's relative motion

(iv) **Vectors settle after one full smoothing period of steady state conditions**

(b) Where true track storage is used

9.6.3.4 Comparison of relative and true vectors

Given that one or other of the vectors can be affected by input errors in a way which may be dependent on the tracker philosophy, it is important to stress the need for the observer continuously to compare one data source with another to ensure that, in all cases, indications given from relative vectors and true vectors sensibly agree.

9.6.4 The effect on the PPC of incorrect data input

9.6.4.1 Errors in speed input

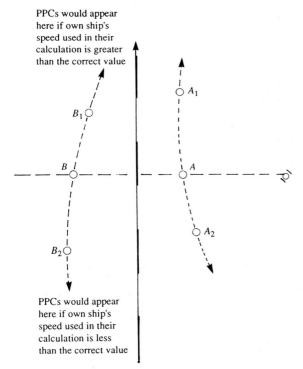

Figure 9.12 The effect on the PPC of a speed error
A, target passing astern, correct speed used
B, target passing ahead, correct speed used
A_1, B_1, PPC appears here if a speed greater than the correct value is used
A_2, B_2, PPC appears here if a speed less than the correct value is used

If incorrect speed is input to a collision situation, the collision point will still appear correctly on the heading marker, but at an incorrect range, and will move down the heading marker at an incorrect speed.

In the case where there is, in fact, a miss distance, the collision point will appear in the wrong position, which may give rise to a misjudgement of the danger or urgency of the situation. Figure 9.12 shows how the collision point may be displaced due to a speed error in the two cases where the target is crossing ahead and crossing astern.

9.6.4.2 Errors in course input

The behaviour of the collision point when an error in the course is input is too complex to allow definition of a pattern. If the error occurs only in the calculation and does not appear in the position of the heading marker, the collision point could appear on the heading marker in a miss situation. More dangerously, a collision point could appear off the heading marker in a collision situation. When the same error appears in both heading marker and calculation, as might occur due to a gyro compass error, the collision case will always show the collision point on the heading marker. Similarly, if a miss distance exists, the collision point will not be on the heading marker.

9.7 Errors of interpretation

These errors are not within the system but are those likely to be made by the operator through misunderstanding, inexperience or casual observation.

9.7.1 Errors with vector systems

In the case of vector systems, the most common mistakes arise because the observer, either from lack of concentration due to stress of the moment or through lack of knowledge, confuses relative and true vectors. Typical blunders are:
(a) measuring the CPA as the tangential distance at which the true vector passes the origin;

(b) mistaking the direction of the relative vector for the target's true heading.

A further source of error sometimes occurs where the observer runs out the true vector to see the dynamic development of the situation (which in itself is a useful ploy) to assist in determining collision avoidance strategy, but deduces the point of closest approach as being where the vectors cross. This is of course only correct in the collision case. Attempts to find the passing distance by trial and error using this technique also frequently mislead the observer and are not necessary when the CPA is so easily available from other sources.

Some equipments fit spring-loaded switches to ensure that the equipment always reverts to either true or relative vector mode in an attempt to reduce the chance of misinterpretation of the data.

Other common errors include the confusion of real and trial values of CPA and the omission to set in the correct trial speed where analogue controls are provided (see Section 4.4.3). Where the displayed vectors and history of a different type are simultaneously presented, the difference between the two may be mistaken for a manoeuvre by the target.

During the second and third minute of tracking, the vectors will be stabilizing and care must be taken not to be misled into assuming that this is an alteration by the target or that it is yawing.

9.7.2 Errors with PPC and PAD systems

In the case of PPCs and PADs, the commonest mistakes arise when attempting to interpolate or extrapolate data from the display. Typical errors arise because of failure to appreciate the following:

1 The line joining the target to the collision point is not a time-related vector and does not indicate speed (see Figure 9.13(a).
2 The collision point gives no indication of miss distance.
3 Changes in collision point positions do not necessarily indicate a change in the target's true course or speed.
4 The area of danger does not change symmetrically with a change in the selected miss distance (see Figure 9.13(c)).

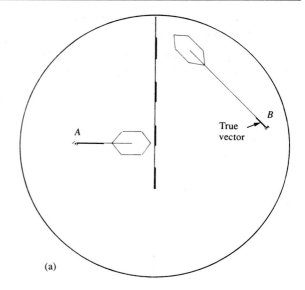

(a)

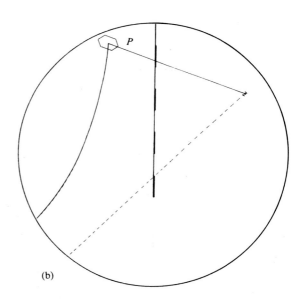

(b)

Figure 9.13 Errors of interpretation
(a) Target *A* is faster and target *B* is slower than own ship, despite appearances
     Note Vectors will show this
(b) The solid line shows the track of the PPC from *P*. The apparent track of the echo is shown by the broken line

5 The collision point is not necessarily at the centre of the danger area (see Figure 9.13(d).

It is always important to realize that the areas of danger generated on the screen apply only to own ship and the target, and that they do not always give warning of a mutual threat between two targets. If two areas of danger overlap, it is reasonable to suppose that the two targets involved will also pass each other within the stated miss distance (see Figure 9.13(f)), but separated

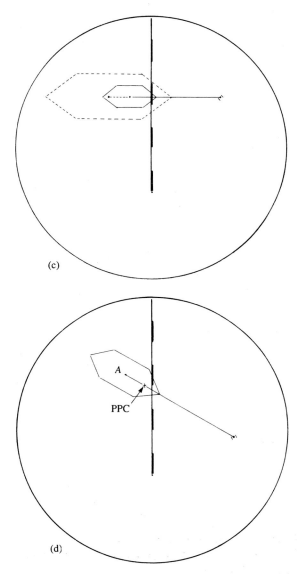

(c)

(d)

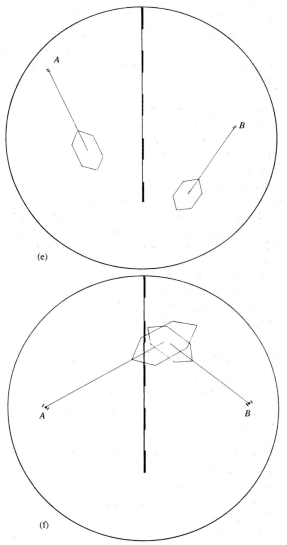

(e)

(f)

(c) The broken line shows the PAD for 2 miles The solid line shows the PAD for 1 mile

(d) The PPC is not at *A*, the centre of the hexagon

(e) Targets *A* and *B* will collide, although this is not apparent from the display

(f) Targets *A* and *B* will not collide, although they may pass within the miss distance

danger areas do not imply safe passing between the targets. Two targets may eventually have a close passing although their danger areas, as applied to own ship, appear to be well separated (see Figure 9.13(e)).

9.7.2.1   Resumption of course

Where a 'chained' bearing cursor is available and the chain divisions are an indication of time, care must be exercised in the measurement of time to resume course. As shown in Figure 9.14, the marker correctly indicates the time own ship will cross ahead and astern on the target track, but the time at which the required miss distance occurs cannot be determined.

9.7.3   The misleading effect of afterglow

Because the vector mode (i.e. relative or true) is not necessarily the same as the radar presentation which has been selected, vectors and afterglow trails may not match. When true vectors are selected on a relative-motion presentation, the vectors and the afterglow will not correlate. When relative vectors are selected while using a true-motion presentation, the true afterglow will not match the relative vector.

9.7.4   Accuracy of the presented data

Over-reliance on, and failure to appreciate inaccuracies in, presented data which has been derived from imperfect inputs should be avoided at all costs. It must always be borne in mind that a vector/PAD/alphanumeric read-out is not absolutely accurate, just because it has been produced by a computer, no matter how many micro-processors it may boast. An indication by the ARPA that a target will pass one cable clear of own ship should not be regarded as justification for standing-on into such a situation.

The errors given in Table 9.2 are quite typical and should always be allowed for.

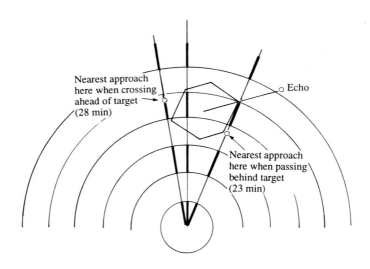

Figure 9.14   The misleading effect of using the bearing cursor to determine the time to resume course
Note   There are four intervals to the point of crossing ahead and five intervals to the point of crossing astern, but nearest approaches occur, as indicated, at 4.9 and 3.6 intervals, respectively

9.7.5 Missed targets

An automatic acquisition system may totally fail to detect and acquire a target of vital importance, for one of a number of reasons. Similarly, it may also drop or cancel a fading target. In the latter case, the target may subsequently be re-acquired and present a course and speed which may indicate that the target has manoeuvred when, in fact, the track is new and has not yet established its long term accuracy.

10 Extracts from official publications

10.1 Extract from Regulation 12, Chapter V of the IMO-SOLAS (1974) Convention as amended to 1983

Within the extracts the paragraph numbering of the original publications has been retained.

The requirement to carry Radar and ARPA

(g) Ships of 500 tons gross tonnage and upwards constructed on or after 1 September 1984 and ships of 1600 tons gross tonnage and upwards constructed before 1 September 1984 shall be fitted with a radar installation.

(h) Ships of 10 000 tons gross tonnage and upwards shall be fitted with two radar installations, each capable of being operated independently of the other.

(i) Facilities for plotting radar readings shall be provided on the navigating bridge of ships required by paragraph (g) or (h) to be fitted with a radar installation. In ships of 1600 tons gross tonnage and upwards constructed on or after 1 September 1984, the plotting facilities shall be at lest as effective as a reflection plotter.

(j) (i) An automatic radar plotting aid shall be fitted on:
      (1) Ships of 10 000 tons gross tonnage and upwards, constructed on or after 1 September 1984;
      (2) Tankers constructed before 1 September 1984 as follows:
        (aa) If of 40 000 tons gross tonnage and upwards, by 1 January 1985;
        (bb) If of 10 000 tons gross tonnage and upwards, but less than 40 000 tons gross tonnage, by 1 January 1986;
      (3) Ships constructed before 1 September 1984, that are not tankers, as follows:
        (aa) If of 40 000 tons gross tonnage and upwards, by 1 September 1986;
        (bb) If of 20 000 tons gross tonnage and upwards, but less than 40 000 tons gross tonnage, by 1 September 1987;
        (cc) If of 15 000 tons of gross tonnage and upwards, but less than 20 000 tons gross tonnage, by 1 September 1988.

  (ii) Automatic radar plotting aids fitted prior to 1 September 1984 which do not fully conform to the performance standards adopted by the organization may, at the discretion of the administration, be retained until 1 January 1991.

  (iii) The administration may exempt ships from the requirements of this paragraph, in cases where it considers it unreasonable or unnecessary for such equipment to be carried, or when the ships will be taken permanently out of service within two years of the appropriate implementation date.

10.2 Extracts from IMO Resolutions A222(VII), A278(VIII), A477(XII)

10.2.1 Performance Standards for Navigational Radar Equipment installed before 1 September 1984

1 Introduction

1 The radar equipment required by Regulation 12 of Chapter V should provide an indication in relation to the ship of the position of other surface craft and obstructions and of buoys, shorelines and navigational marks in a manner which will assist in avoiding collision and in navigation.

2 It should comply with the following minimum requirements:

(a) Range performance

The operational requirement under normal propagation conditions, when the radar aerial is mounted at a height of 15 metres above sea level, is that the equipment should give a clear indication of:

(i) Coastlines:
At 20 nautical miles when the ground rises to 60 metres
At 7 nautical miles when the ground rises to 6 metres.

(ii) Surface objects:
At 7 nautical miles a ship of 5000 tons gross tonnage, whatever her aspect
At 3 nautical miles a small ship of length 10 metres
At 2 nautical miles an object such as a navigational buoy having an effective echoing area of approximately 10 square metres.

(b) Minimum range

The surface objects specified in paragraph 2(a) (ii) should be clearly displayed from a mimimum range of 50 metres up to a range of 1 nautical mile, without adjustment of controls other than the range selector.

(c) Display

(i) The equipment should provide a relative plan display of not less than 180 mm effective diameter.

(ii) The equipment should be provided with at least five ranges, the smallest of which is not more than 1 nautical mile and the greatest of which is not less than 24 nautical miles. The scales should be preferably of 1:2 ratio. Additional ranges may be provided.

(iii) Positive indication should be given of the range of view displayed and the interval between range rings.

(d) Range measurement

(i) The primary means provided for range measurement should be fixed electronic range rings. There should be at least four range rings displayed on each of the ranges mentioned in paragraph 2(c) (ii), except that on ranges below 1 nautical mile range rings should be displayed at intervals of 0.25 nautical mile.

(ii) Fixed range rings should enable the range of an object, whose echo lies on a range ring, to be measured with an error not exceeding 1.5 per cent of the maximum range of the scale in use, or 70 metres, whichever is the greater.

(iii) Any additional means of measuring range should have an error not exceeding 2.5 per cent of the maximum range of the displayed scale in use, or 120 metres, whichever is the greater.

(e) Heading indicator

(i) The heading of the ship should be indicated by a line on the display with a maximum error not greater than $\pm 1°$. The thickness of the display heading line should not be greater than 0.5°.

(ii) Provision should be made to switch off the heading indicator by a device which cannot be left in the 'heading marker off' position.

(f) Bearing measurement

(i) Provision should be made to obtain quickly the bearing of any object whose echo appears on the display.
(ii) The means provided for obtaining bearings should enable the bearing of a target whose echo appears at the edge of the display to be measured with an accuracy of ±1° or better.

(g) Discrimination

(i) The equipment should display as separate indications, on the shortest range scale provided, two objects on the same azimuth separated by not more than 50 metres in range.
(ii) The equipment should display as separate indications two objects at the same range separated by not more than 2.5° in azimuth.
(iii) The equipment should be designed to avoid, as far as is practicable, the display of spurious echoes.

(h) Roll

The performance of the equipment should be such that when the ship is rolling ±10° the echoes of targets remain visible on the display.

(i) Scan

The scan should be continuous and automatic through 360° of azimuth. The target data rate should be at least 12 per minute. The equipment should operate satisfactorily in relative wind speeds of up to 100 knots.

(j) Azimuth stabilization

(i) Means should be provided to enable the display to be stabilized in azimuth by a transmitting compass. The accuracy of alignment with the compass transmission should be within 0.5° with a compass rotation rate of 2 r.p.m.

(ii) The equipment should operate satisfactorily for relative bearings when the compass control is inoperative or not fitted.

(k) Performance check

Means should be available, while the equipment is used

operationally, to determine readily a significant drop in performance relative to a calibration standard established at the time of installation.

(l) Anti-clutter devices

Means should be provided to minimize the display of unwanted responses from precipitation and the sea.

(m) Operation

(i) The equipment should be capable of being switched on and operated from the main display position.

(ii) Operational controls should be accessible and easy to identify and use.

(iii) After switching on from cold, the equipment should become fully operational within 4 minutes.

(iv) A standby condition should be provided from which the equipment can be brought to a fully operational condition within 1 minute.

(n) Interference

After installation and adjustment on board, the bearing accuracy should be maintained without further adjustment irrespective of the variation of external magnetic fields.

(o) Sea or ground stabilization

Sea or ground stabilization, if provided, should not degrade the accuracy of the display below the requirements of these performance standards, and the view ahead on the display should not be unduly restricted by the use of this facility.

3 Siting of the aerial

The aerial system should be installed in such a manner that the efficiency of the display is not impaired by the close proximity of the aerial to other objects. In particular, blind sectors in the forward direction should be avoided.

10.2.2 Performance Standards for Navigational Radar Equipment installed on or after 1 September 1984

1 Application

1.1 This Recommendation applies to all ships' radar equipment installed on or after 1 September 1984 in compliance with Regulation 12, Chapter V of the International Convention for the safety of Life at Sea, 1974, as amended.

1.2 Radar equipment installed before 1 September 1984 should comply at least with the performance standards recommended in resolution A.222(VII).

2 General

The radar equipment should provide an indication, in relation to the ship, of the position of other surface craft and obstructions and of buoys, shorelines and navigational marks in a manner which will assist in navigation and in avoiding collision.

3 All radar installations

All radar installations should comply with the following minimum requirements.

3.1 Range performance

The operational requirement under normal propagation conditions, when the radar antenna is mounted at a height of 15 metres above sea level, is that the equipment should in the absence of clutter give a clear indication of:

.1 Coastlines:
   At 20 nautical miles when the ground rises to 60 metres
   At 7 nautical miles when the ground rises to 6 metres.

.2 Surface objects:
   At 7 nautical miles a ship of 5000 tons gross tonnage, whatever her aspect
   At 3 nautical miles a small ship of 10 metres in length
   At 2 nautical miles an object such as a navigational buoy having an effective echoing area of approximately 10 square metres.

3.2 Minimum range

The surface objects specified in paragraph 3.1.2 should be clearly displayed from a minimum range of 50 metres up to a range of 1 nautical mile, without changing the setting of controls other than the range selector.

3.3 Display

3.3.1 The equipment should without external magnification provide a relative plan display in the head up unstabilized mode with an effective diameter of not less than:

.1 180 millimetres on ships of 500 tons gross tonnage and more but less 1600 tons gross tonnage;

.2 250 millimetres on ships of 1600 tons gross tonnage and more but less than 10 000 tons gross tonnage;

.3 340 millimetres in the case of one display and 250 millimetres in the case of the other on ships of 10 000 tons gross tonnage and upwards.

Note Display diameters of 180, 250 and 340 millimetres correspond respectively to 9, 12 and 16 inch cathode ray tubes.

3.3.2 The equipment should provide one of the two following sets of range scales of display:
.1 1.5, 3, 6, 12 and 24 nautical miles and one range scale of not less than 0.5 and not greater than 0.8 nautical miles; or
.2 1, 2, 4, 8, 16, and 32 nautical miles.

3.3.3 Additional range scales may be provided.

3.3.4 The range scale displayed and the distance between range rings should be clearly indicated at all times.

3.4 Range measurement

3.4.1 Fixed electronic range rings should be provided for range measurements as follows:

.1 Where range scales are provided in accordance with paragraph 3.3.2.1, on the range scale of between 0.5 and 0.8 nautical miles at least two range rings should be provided and on each of the other range scales six range rings should be provided; or

.2 Where range scales are provided in accordance with paragraph 3.3.2.2, four range rings should be provided on each of the range scales.

3.4.2 A variable electronic range marker should be provided with a numeric readout of range.

3.4.3 The fixed range rings and the variable range marker should enable the range of an object to be measured with an error not exceeding 1.5 per cent of the maximum range of the scale in use, or 70 metres, whichever is the greater.

3.4.4 It should be possible to vary the brilliance of the fixed range rings and the variable range marker and to remove them completely from the display.

3.5 Heading indicator

3.5.1 The heading of the ship should be indicated by a line on the display with a maximum error not greater than ± 1°. The thickness of the displayed heading line should not be greater than 0.5°.

3.5.2 Provision should be made to switch off the heading indicator by a device which cannot be left in the 'heading marker off' position.

3.6 Bearing measurement

3.6.1 Provision should be made to obtain quickly the bearing of any object whose echo appears on the display.

3.6.2 The means provided for obtaining bearing should enable the bearing of a target whose echo appears at the edge of the display to be measured with an accuracy of ± 1° or better.

3.7 Discrimination

3.7.1 The equipment should be capable of displaying as separate indications on a range scale of 2 nautical miles or less, two small similar targets at a range of between 50 per cent and 100 per cent of the range scale in use, and on the same azimuth, separated by not more than 50 metres in range.

3.7.2 The equipment should be capable of displaying as separate indications two small similar targets both situated at the same range between 50 per cent and 100 per cent of the 1.5 or 2 mile range scales, and separated by not more than 2.5° in azimuth.

3.8 Roll or pitch

The performance of the equipment should be such that when the ship is rolling or pitching up to ± 10° the range performance requirements of paragraphs 3.1 and 3.2 continue to be met.

3.9 Scan

The scan should be clockwise, continuous and automatic through 360° of azimuth. The scan rate should be not less than 12 r.p.m. The equipment should operate satisfactorily in relative wind speeds of up to 100 knots.

3.10 Azimuth stabilization

3.10.1 Means should be provided to enable the display to be stabilized in azimuth by a transmitting compass. The equipment should be provided with a compass input to enable it to be stabilized in azimuth. The accuracy of alignment with the compass transmission should be within 0.5° with a compass rotation rate of 2 r.p.m.

3.10.2 The equipment should operate satisfactorily in the unstabilized mode when the compass control is inoperative.

3.11 Performance check

Means should be available, while the equipment is used operationally, to determine readily a significant drop in performance relative to a calibration standard established at the time of installation, and that the equipment is correctly tuned in the absence of targets.

3.12 Anti-clutter devices

Suitable means should be provided for the suppression of unwanted echoes from sea clutter, rain and other forms of precipitation, clouds and sandstorms. It should be possible to adjust manually and continuously the anti-clutter controls. Anti-clutter controls should be inoperative in the fully anti-clockwise positions. In addition, automatic anti-clutter controls may be provided; however, they must be capable of being switched off.

3.13 Operation

3.13.1 The equipment should be capable of being switched on and operated from the display position.

3.13.2 Operational controls should be accessible and easy to identify and use. Where symbols are used they should comply with the recommendations of the organization on symbols for controls on marine navigational radar equipment .

3.13.3 After switching on from cold the equipment should become fully operational within 4 minutes.

3.13.4 A standby condition should be provided from which the equipment can be brought to an operational condition within 15 seconds.

3.14 Interference

After installation and adjustment on board, the bearing accuracy as prescribed in these performance standards should be maintained without further adjustment irrespective of the movement of the ship in the earth's magnetic field.

3.15 Sea or ground stabilization (true motion display)

3.15.1 Where sea or ground stabilization is provided the accuracy and discrimination of the display should be at least equivalent to that required by these performance standards.

3.15.2 The motion of the trace origin should not, except under manual override conditions, continue to a point beyond 75 per cent of the radius of the display. Automatic resetting may be provided.

3.16 Antenna system

The antenna system should be installed in such a manner that the design efficiency of the radar system is not substantially impaired.

3.17 Operation with radar beacons

3.17.1 All radars operating in the 3cm band should be capable of operating in a horizontally polarized mode.

3.17.2 It should be possible to switch off those signal processing facilities which might prevent a radar beacon from being shown on the radar display.

4 Multiple radar installations

4.1 Where two radars are required to be carried they should be so installed that each radar can be operated individually and both can be operated simultaneously without being dependent upon one another. When an emergency source of electrical power is provided in accordance with the appropriate requirements of Chapter II-1 of the 1974 SOLAS Convention, both radars should be capable of being operated from this source.

4.2 Where two radars are fitted, interswitching facilities may be provided to improve the flexibility and availability of the overall radar installation. They should be so installed that failure of either radar would not cause the supply of electrical energy to the other radar to be interrupted or adversely affected.

Symbols for controls on marine navigational radar equipment
1 List of controls to be identified by symbols
The following switches and variable controls are considered to be the minimum required to be marked by symbols:

Radar on – standby – off switch
Aerial rotation switch
Mode of presentation switch – north up or ship's head up
Heading marker alignment control or switch
Range selection switch
Pulse length selection switch – short or long pulse
Tuning control
Gain control
Anti-clutter rain control (differentiation)
Anti-clutter sea control
Scale illumination control or switch
Display brilliance control
Range rings brilliance control

Symbols for controls on marine navigational radar equipment

1	Off	To identify the 'off' position of the control or switch	
2	Radar on	To identify the 'radar on' position of the switch	
3	Radar stand-by	To identify the 'radar stand-by' position of the switch	
4	Aerial rotating	To identify the 'aerial rotating' position of the switch	
5	North up presentation	To identify the 'north up' position of the mode of presentation switch	
6	Ship's head up presenta-tion	To identify the 'ship's head up' position of the mode of presentation switch	
7	Heading marker alignment	To identify the 'heading marker alignment' control switch	
8	Range selector	To identify the range selection switch	
9	Short pulse	To identify the 'short pulse' position of the pulse length selection switch	
10	Long pulse	To identify the 'long pulse' position of the pulse length selection switch	
11	Tuning	To identify the 'tuning' control	
12	Gain	To identify the 'gain' control	

13		Anti-clutter rain minimum	To identify the minimum position of the 'anti-clutter rain' control or switch

14		Anti-clutter rain maximum	To identify the maximum position of the 'anti-clutter rain' control or switch

15		Anti-clutter sea minimum	To identify the minimum position of the 'anti-clutter sea' control

16		Anti-clutter sea maximum	To identify the maximum position of the 'anti-clutter sea' control

17		Scale illumination	To identify the maximum position of the 'scale illumination' control or switch

18		Display brilliance	To identify the maximum position of the 'display brilliance' control

19		Range rings brilliance	To identify the maximum position of the 'range rings brilliance' control

20		Variable range marker	To identify the 'variable range marker' control

21		Bearing marker	To identify the 'bearing marker' control

22		Transmitted power monitor	To identify the on position of the 'transmitted power monitor' switch

23		Transmit/ receive monitor	To identify the on position of the 'transmit/receive monitor' switch

Variable range marker control
Bearing marker control
Performance monitor switch – transmitted power
monior or transmit/receive monitor.

2 Code of practice

The following code of practice should be used when
marking radar sets with recommended symbols:

2.1 The maximum dimension of a symbol should not
be less than 9 mm.

2.2 The distance between the centres of two adjacent
symbols should not be less than 1.4 times the size of the
larger symbol.

2.3 Switch function symbols should not be linked by a
line. A linked line infers controlled action.

2.4 Variable control function symbols should be
linked by a line, preferably an arc. The direction of
increase of controlled function should be indicated.

2.5 Symbols should be presented with a high contrast
against their background.

2.6 The various elements of a symbol should have a
fixed ratio one to another.

2.7 Multiple functions of controls and switch positions
may be indicated by a combined symbol.

2.8 Where concentric controls or switches are fitted,
the outer of the symbols should refer to the larger diameter control.

3 Symbols

3.1 The symbols attached hereto should be used for
controls on marine navigational radar equipment.

3.2 The circles shown around the following symbols
are optional:
Symbol 4: aerial rotating
Symbol 9: short pulse
Symbol 10: long pulse
Symbol 17: scale illumination
Symbol 22: transmitted power monitor
Symbol 23: transmit/receive monitor.

10.3 Extract from IMO Resolution A422(XI)

10.3.1 Performance Standards for Automatic Radar Plotting Aids (ARPA)

1 Introduction

1.1 Automatic radar plotting aids (ARPA) should, in
order to improve the standard of collision avoidance at
sea:

.1 Reduce the workload of observers by enabling
them to automatically obtain information so that
they can perform as well with multiple targets as
they can by manually plotting a single target
.2 Provide continuous, accurate and rapid situation
evaluation.

1.2 In addition to the general requirements for electronic navigational aids (resolution A.281(VIII)), the
ARPA should comply with the following minimum
performance standards.

2 Definitions

2.1 Definitions of terms used in these performance
standards are given in annex 1 to this resolution.

3 Performance standards

3.1 Detection
3.1.1 Where a separate facility is provided for detection of targets, other than by the radar observer, it
should have a performance not inferior to that which
could be obtained by the use of the radar display.

3.2 Acquisition
3.2.1 Target acquisition may be manual or automatic.
However, there should always be a facility to provide
for manual acquisition and cancellation: ARPA with
automatic acquisition should have a facility to suppress
acquisition in certain areas. On any range scale where
acquisition is suppressed over a certain area, the area of
acquisition should be indicated on the display.

3.2.2 Automatic or manual acquisition should have a performance not inferior to that which could be obtained by the user of the radar display.

3.3 Tracking

3.3.1 The ARPA should be able to automatically track, process, simultaneously display and continuously update the information on at least:

.1 Twenty targets, if automatic acquisition is provided, whether automatically or manually acquired

.2 Ten targets, if only manual acquisition is provided.

3.3.2 If automatic acquisition is provided, a description of the criteria of selection of targets for tracking should be provided to the user. If the ARPA does not track all targets visible on the display, targets which are being tracked should be clearly indicated on the display. The reliability of tracking should not be less than that obtainable using manual recordings of successive target positions obtained from the radar display.

3.3.3 Provided the target is not subject to target swop, the ARPA should continue to track an acquired target which is clearly distinguishable on the display for five out of ten consecutive scans.

3.3.4 The possibility of tracking errors, including target swop, should be minimized by ARPA design. A qualitative description of the effects of error sources on the automatic tracking and corresponding errors should be provided to the user, including the effects of low signal-to-noise and low signal-to-clutter ratios caused by sea returns, rain, snow, low clouds and non-synchronous emissions.

3.3.5 The ARPA should be able to display on request at least four equally time-spaced past positions of any targets being tracked over a period of at least 8 minutes.

3.4 Display

3.4.1 The display may be a separate or integral part of the ship's radar. However, the ARPA display should include all the data required to be provided by a radar display in accordance with the performance standards for navigational radar equipment.

3.4.2 The design should be such that any malfunction of ARPA parts producing data additional to information to be produced by the radar as required by the performance standards for navigational equipment should not affect the integrity of the basic radar presentation.

3.4.3 The display on which ARPA information is presented should have an effective diameter of at least 340 mm.

3.4.4 The ARPA facilities should be available on at least the following range scales:

.1 12 or 16 miles
.2 3 or 4 miles.

3.4.5 There should be a positive indication of the range scale in use.

3.4.6 The ARPA should be capable of operating with a relative motion display with north up and either head up or course up azimuth stabilization. In addition, the ARPA may also provide for a true motion display. If true motion is provided, the operator should be able to select for his display either true or relative motion. There should be a positive indication of the display mode and orientation in use.

3.4.7 The course and speed information generated by the ARPA for acquired targets should be displayed in a vector or graphic form which clearly indicates the target's predicted motion. In this regard:

.1 An ARPA presenting predicted information in vector form only should have the option of both true and relative vectors.

.2 An ARPA which is capable of presenting target course and speed information in graphic form should also, on request, provide the target's true and/or relative vector.

.3 Vectors displayed should either be time adjustable or have a fixed time-scale.

.4 A positive indication of the time-scale of the vector in use should be given.

3.4.8 The ARPA information should not obscure radar information in such a manner as to degrade the process of detecting targets. The display of ARPA data should be under the control of the radar observer. It should be possible to cancel the display of unwanted ARPA data.

3.4.9   Means should be provided to adjust independently the brilliance of the ARPA data and radar data, including complete elimination of the ARPA data.

3.4.10   The method of presentation should ensure that the ARPA data is clearly visible in general to more than one observer in the conditions of light normally experienced on the bridge of a ship by day and by night. Screening may be provided to shade the display from sunlight but not to the extent that it will impair the observer's ability to maintain a proper look-out. Facilities to adjust the brightness should be provided.

3.4.11   Provisions should be made to obtain quickly the range and bearing of any object which appears on the ARPA display.

3.4.12   When a target appears on the radar display and, in the case of automatic acquisition, enters within the acquisition area chosen by the observer or, in the case of manual acquisition, has been acquired by the observer, the ARPA should present in a period of not more than 1 minute an indication of the target's motion trend, and display within 3 minutes the target's predicted motion in accordance with paragraphs 3.4.7, 3.6, 3.8.2 and 3.8.3.

3.4.13   After changing range scales on which the ARPA facilities are available or resetting the display, full plotting information should be displayed within a period not exceeding four scans.

3.5   Operational warnings

3.5.1   The ARPA should have the capability to warn the observer with a visual and/or audible signal of any distinguishable target which closes to a range or transits a zone chosen by the observer. The target causing the warning should be clearly indicated on the display.

3.5.2   The ARPA should have the capability to warn the observer with a visual and/or audible signal of any tracked target which is predicted to close to within a minimum range and time chosen by the observer. The

target causing the warning should be clearly indicated on the display.

3.5.3   The ARPA should clearly indicate if a tracked target is lost, other than out of range, and the target's last tracked position should be clearly indicated on the display.

3.5.4   It should be possible to activate or deactivate the operational warnings.

3.6   Data requirements

3.6.1   At the request of the observer the following information should be immediately available from the ARPA in alphanumeric form in regard to any tracked target:

.1   Present range to the target
.2   Present bearing of the target
.3   Predicted target range at the closest point of approach (CPA)
.4   Predicted time to CPA (TCPA)
.5   Calculated true course of target
.6   Calculated true speed of target.

3.7   Trial manoeuvre

3.7.1   The ARPA should be capable of simulating the effect on all tracked targets of an own ship manoeuvre without interrupting the updating of target information. The simulation should be initiated by the depression either of a spring-loaded switch, or a function key, with a positive identification on the display.

3.8   Accuracy

3.8.1   The ARPA should provide accuracies not less than those given in paragraphs 3.8.2 and 3.8.3 for the four scenarios defined in annex 2 to this resolution. With the sensor errors specified in annex 3, the values given relate to the best possible manual plotting performance under environmental conditions of $\pm 10°$ of roll.

3.8.2   An ARPA should present within 1 minute of steady state tracking the relative motion trend of a target with the following accuracy values (95 per cent probability values):

Scenario	Relative course (degrees)	Relative speed (knots)	CPA (nautical miles)
1	11	2.8	1.6
2	7	0.6	—
3	14	2.2	1.8
4	15	1.5	2.0

3.8.3 An ARPA should present within 3 minutes of steady state tracking the motion of a target with the following accuracy values (95 per cent probability values):

Scenario	Relative course (degrees)	Relative speed (knots)	CPA (nautical miles)	TCPA (min)	True course (degrees)	True speed (knots)
1	3.0	0.8	0.5	1.0	7.4	1.2
2	2.3	0.3	—	—	2.8	0.8
3	4.4	0.9	0.7	1.0	3.3	1.0
4	4.6	0.8	0.7	1.0	2.6	1.2

3.8.4 When a tracked target, or own ship, has completed a manoeuvre, the system should present in a period of not more than 1 minute an indication of the target's motion trend, and display within 3 minutes the target's predicted motion, in accordance with paragraphs 3.4.7, 3.6, 3.8.2 and 3.8.3.

3.8.5 The ARPA should be designed in such a manner that under the most favourable conditions of own ship motion the error contribution from the ARPA should remain insignificant compared with the errors associated with the input sensors, for the scenarios of annex 2.

3.9 Connections with other equipment

3.9.1 The ARPA should not degrade the performance of any equipment providing sensor inputs. The connection of the ARPA to any other equipment should not degrade the performance of that equipment.

3.10 Performance tests and warnings

3.10.1 The ARPA should provide suitable warnings of ARPA malfunction to enable the observer to monitor the proper operation of the system. Additionally, test programs should be available so that the overall performance of ARPA can be assessed periodically against a known solution.

3.11 Equipment used with ARPA

3.11.1 Log and speed indicators providing inputs to ARPA equipment should be capable of providing the ship's speed through the water.

Annex 1 Definitions of terms to be used only in connection with ARPA performance standards

Relative course	The direction of motion of a target related to own ship as deduced from a number of measurements of its range and bearing on the radar, expressed as an angular distance from north.
Relative speed	The speed of a target related to own ship, as deduced from a number of measurements of its range and bearing on the radar.
True course	The apparent heading of a target obtained by the vectorial combination of the target's relative motion and own ship's motion, expressed as an angular distance from north.
True speed	The speed of a target obtained by the vectorial combination of its relative motion and own ship's motion.

Note For the purpose of the definitions of true course and true speed there is no need to distinguish between sea and ground stabilization.

Bearing	The direction of one terrestrial point from another, expressed as an angular distance from north.
Relative motion display	The position of own ship on such a display remains fixed.
True motion display	The position of own ship on such a display moves in accordance with its own motion.
Azimuth stabilization	Own ship's compass information is fed to the display so that echoes of targets on the display will not be caused to smear by changes of own ship's heading.

North up	The line connecting the centre with the top of the display is north.
Head up	The line connecting the centre with the top of the display is own ship's heading.
Course up	An intended course can be set to the line connecting the centre with the top of the display.
Heading	The direction in which the bows of a ship are pointing, expressed as an angular distance from north.
Target's predicted motion	The indication on the display of a linear extrapolation into the future of a target's motion, based on measurements of the target's range and bearing on the radar in the recent past.
Target's motion trend	An early indication of the target's predicted motion.
Radar plotting	The whole process of target detection, tracking, calculation of parameters and display of information.
Detection	The recognition of the presence of a target.
Acquisition	The selection of those targets requiring a tracking procedure and the initiation of their tracking.
Tracking	The process of observing the sequential changes in the position of a target, to establish its motion.
Display	The plan position presentation of ARPA data with radar data.
Manual	Relating to an activity which a radar observer performs, possibly with assistance from a machine.
Automatic	Relating to an activity which is performed wholly by a machine.

Annex 2   Operational scenarios

For each of the following scenarios predictions are made at the target position defined after previously tracking for the appropriate time of one or three minutes:

Scenario 1

Own ship course	000°
Own ship speed	10 knots
Target range	8 nautical miles
Bearing of target	000°
Relative course of target	180°
Relative speed of target	20 knots

Scenario 2

Own ship course	000°
Own ship speed	10 knots
Target range	1 nautical mile
Bearing of target	000°
Relative course of target	090°
Relative speed of target	10 knots

Scenario 3

Own ship course	000°
Own ship speed	5 knots
Target range	8 nautical miles
Bearing of target	045°
Relative course of target	225°
Relative speed of target	20 knots

Scenario 4

Own ship course	000°
Own ship speed	25 knots
Target range	8 nautical miles
Bearing of target	045°
Relative course of target	225°
Relative speed of target	20 knots

Annex 3   Sensor errors

The accuracy figures quoted in paragraph 3.8 are based upon the following sensor errors and are appropriate to equipment complying with the performance standards for shipborne navigational equipment.

Note σ means standard deviation

Radar
Target glint (scintillation)(for 200 m length target)
Along length of target $\sigma = 30$ metres (normal distribution)
Across beam of target $\sigma = 1$ metre (normal distribution).

Roll-pitch bearing The bearing error will peak in each of the four quadrants around own ship for targets on relative bearings of 045°, 135°, 225° and 315° and will be zero at relative bearings of 0°, 90°, 180° and 270°. This error has a sinusoidal variation at twice the roll frequency.

For a 10° roll the mean error is 0.22° with a 0.22° peak sine wave superimposed.

Beam shape	Assumed normal distribution giving bearing error with $\sigma = 0.05°$
Pulse shape	Assumed normal distribution giving range error with $\sigma = 20$ metres
Antenna backlash	Assumed rectangular distribution giving bearing error $\pm 0.5°$ maximum.

Quantization

Bearing	Rectangular distribution $\pm 0.01°$ maximum
Range	Rectangular distribution ± 0.01 nautical miles maximum.

Bearing encoder assumed to be running from a remote synchro giving bearing errors with a normal distribution $\sigma = 0.03°$.

Gyro compass
Calibration error 0.5°.
Normal distribution about this with $\sigma = 0.12°$.

Log
Calibration error 0.5 knots
Normal distribution about this with $3\sigma = 0.2$ knots.

10.4 Extracts from IMO Resolutions A423 (XI) and A277 (VIII), Radar Beacons, Transponders and Reflectors

10.4.1 Marine uses of radar beacons and transponders

1 Introduction

1.1 The uncontrolled proliferation of radar beacons and transponders could cause significant degradation of a ship's navigational radar display, produce incompatibilities among devices developed for different uses, or necessitate a succession of modifications to shipborne radars to accommodate progressive developments of radar beacons and transponders.

1.2 To avoid these possibilities, the following recommendations are made concerning the appropriate applications for radar beacons and transponders, where an operational requirement for such a device exists, and measures for general administration of radar beacons and transponders.

1.3 The terms 'radar beacon' (racon) and 'transponder', as used in these performance standards, are understood to have the following meanings:

1.3.1 *Radar beacon (racon):* A receiver-transmitter device associated with a fixed navigational mark which, when triggered by a radar, automatically returns a distinctive signal which can appear on the display of the triggering radar, providing range, bearing and identification information. The terms 'radar beacon' and 'racon' should be reserved exclusively for this use and include devices mounted on fixed structures, or on floating aids anchored at fixed positions, for navigational purposes. Whether used alone, or mounted on another aid to navigation (such as a visible mark) the racon itself is considered a separate aid to navigation.

1.3.2 *Transponder:* A receiver-transmitter device in the maritime radionavigation service which transmits automatically when it receives the proper interrogation, or when a transmission is initiated by a local command. The transmission may include a coded identification signal and/or data. The response may be displayed on a radar PPI, or on a display separate from any radar, or both, depending upon the application and content of the signal.

2 General operational characteristics

2.1 *Swept frequency radar beacon:* A radar beacon in the maritime service which is capable of transmitting a warning signal, automatically, to any radar-equipped ship in its vicinity:

.1 the beacon will be triggered automatically by the transmissions of any radar operating in the appropriate radar band;

.2 the return signal is to be displayed on the PPI of the triggering radar.

2.2 *Fixed frequency radar beacon:* A radar beacon in the maritime radio-navigation service which is capable of responding automatically to any radar-equipped ship in its vicinity, and which returns a signal on a fixed frequency which can be displayed on the PPI of a suitably configured radar:

.1 the beacon will be triggered automatically by the transmission of any radar operating in the appropriate radar band;

.2 the signal may be displayed continuously, either separately or super-imposed on the radar picture, or may be switched off, at the option of the operator.

2.3 *Transponders:* A transponder is a device, which, when properly interrogated, can provide for:

.1 ship radar target identification and echo enhancement with the proviso that such enhancer should not significantly exceed that which could be achieved by passive means on the radar PPI of an interrogating ship or shore station;

.2 radar target correlation with voice or other radio transmission for identification on the radar PPI of an interrogating ship or shore station;

.3 operator selectable presentation of transponder responses either super-imposed on the normal PPI display, or free of clutter and other targets;

.4 transfer of information pertinent to avoidance of collision or other hazards, manoeuvre, manoeuvring characteristics, etc.

3   Operational uses

3.1   Swept frequency radar beacons should be used only for the following purposes; under no circumstances should they be used to enhance the detection of marine craft:

.1★ ranging on and identification of positions on inconspicuous coastlines;

.2★ identification of position on coastlines which permit good ranging but are featureless;

.3★ identification of selected navigational marks both seaborne and land-based;

.4★ landfall identification.

.5 as a warning device to identify temporary navigational hazards and to mark new and uncharted dangers.

3.2   Fixed frequency radar beacons★★ should be used only for the following purposes:

.1 ranging on and identification of positions on inconspicuous coastlines;

.2 identification of position on coastlines which permit good ranging but are featureless;

.3 identification of selected navigational marks both seaborne and landbased;

.4 landfall identification;

.5 identification of offshore structures.

3.3   Transponders should be used to meet the operational requirements for any of the following purposes:

.1 identification of certain classes of ships (ship-to-ship);

.2 identification of ships for the purpose of shore surveillance;

.3 search and rescue operations;

.4 identification of individual ships and data transfer;

.5 establishing positions for hydrographical purposes.

★   If a fixed frequency radar beacon system is internationally agreed and introduced, swept frequency systems may, subject to review by the Organization, continue to be provided for these purposes at the discretion of the navigation authority concerned.

★★   If studies show that the present development of fixed frequency radar beacons justifies their use for the identification of marks used for general navigational purposes, they should be introduced in the following stages:

.1 international operational standards are prepared;

.2 international technical specifications are prepared;

.3 details of a beacon facility requirement are incorporated in the IMO performance standards for navigational radar equipment;

.4 the requirement for a beacon facility is included in national specifications for navigational radar;

.5 the International Convention for the Safety of Life at Sea, 1974, is amended to provide that all new radars installed on board ships be equipped with a beacon facility;

.6 fixed frequency radar beacons to identify navigational marks are introduced in addition to swept frequency devices.

Note: Some of these stages may be introduced simultaneously.

4 General administration of radar beacons and transponders

4.1 The use of all radar beacons should be authorized by an Administration or by a competent navigation authority. Before authorizing or approving the use of a radar beacon, account should be taken of the density of such devices in the particular area and the need to prevent degradation of ships' navigational radar displays.

4.2 The use of all transponder systems designed to respond in a frequency band used by marine radars should be authorized by an Administration. Before authorizing such use, account should be taken of the effect such transmissions would have on ships' navigational radars.

Operational standards for swept frequency radar beacons

1 Introduction

1.1 Swept frequency radar beacons should conform to the following minimum operational standards.

1.2 Swept frequency radar beacons should be operationally compatible with navigational radar equipment which conforms to the standards recommended by the International Maritime Organization.

2 Operating frequencies

2.1 Radar beacons designed to operate on a wavelength of 3 cm should be capable of being interrogated by any navigational radar equipment operating on any frequency between 9320 MHz and 9500 MHz and respond within the frequency band 9320 MHz to 9500 MHz.

2.2 Radar beacons designed to operate on a wavelength of 10 cm should be capable of being interrogated by any navigational radar equipment operating on any frequency between 2920 MHz and 3100 MHz and respond within the frequency band 2920 MHz and 3100 MHz.

3 Transmitter tuning characteristics

3.1 The tuning characteristics of the transmitter should be such that the beacon response can appear on a radar display in a recognizable form at least once every two minutes.

4 Operating range

4.1 The operating range should be compatible with the navigational requirements for the radar beacon at its location and should not normally exceed 30 nautical miles.

5 Response characteristics

5.1 On receipt of an interrogating signal, the radar beacon should commence its response in such time that the gap on the radar display between the radar target and the beacon response does not normally exceed approximately 100 metres. In certain cases the operational use of beacons may allow this delay time to be increased. Under such circumstances the delay time should be as short as practicable and the details should be shown in appropriate navigational publications.

5.2 The duration of the response should be approximately 20 per cent of the maximum range requirement of the particular beacon, or should not exceed 5 miles, whichever is the lower value.

5.3 The leading edge of the response should be sufficiently sharp to permit satisfactory range determination. Where identification coding is used, the leading edges of any other dots and dashes in the response should be such that they may, if required, be substantially removed from a radar display with minimum degradation to the radar echoes.

6 Identification code

6.1 In some applications coded response formats may be required.

6.2   The form of identification coding when required should comprise the full length of the radar beacon response being divided into dashes and dots, with a ratio of 1 dash equal to 3 dots and 1 dot equal to 1 space.

6.3   The coding should normally commence with a dash and the design of beacons should permit the use of an additional three dots or dashes.

7   Construction

7.1   Radar beacons should be designed to operate continuously and with high reliability when permanently installed in a marine environment.

Note   Beacons which sweep the whole marine radar frequency band in less than 20 microseconds may not meet some of these operational requirements and some other requirements may not apply to them.

Operational standards for fixed frequency radar beacons

1   Introduction

1.1   Fixed frequency radar beacons should conform to the following minimum operational standards.

1.2   Fixed frequency radar beacons should be capable of being interrogated by a radar which conforms to the standards recommended by the International Maritime Organization.

2   Operating frequencies

2.1   Radar beacons designed to operate on a wavelength of 3 cm should be capable of being interrogated by any navigational radar equipment operating on any frequency between 9320 MHz and 9500 MHz and re: ond within the frequency band 9300 MHz and 9320 N Hz.

2.2   .adar beacons designed to operate on a wave ngth of 10 cm should be capable of being interrogated by any navigational radar equipment operating on any frequency between 2920 MHz and 3100 MHz and respond within the frequency band 2900 MHz to 2920 MHz.

3   Operating range

3.1   The operating range should be compatible with the navigational requirements for the radar beacon at its location and should not normally exceed 30 nautical miles.

4   Response characteristics

4.1   On receipt of an interrogating signal, the radar beacon should commence its response in such time that the gap on the radar display between the radar target and the beacon response does not normally exceed approximately 100 metres.

4.2   The duration of the response should be approximately 20 per cent of the maximum range requirement of the particular beacon, or should not exceed 5 miles, whichever is the lower value.

4.3   The leading edge of the response should be sufficiently sharp to permit satisfactory range determination.

4.4   When a beacon is required to respond to several interrogators, interruptions in responding to each particular interrogator should be kept to a minimum.

5   Identification coding

5.1   The form of identification coding when required should comprise the full length of the radar beacon response being divided into dashes and dots, with a ratio of 1 dash equal to 3 dots and 1 dot equal to 1 space.

5.2   The coding should normally commence with a dash and the design of beacons should permit the use of an additional three dots or dashes.

6   Construction

6.1   Radar beacons should be designed to operate continuously and with high reliability when permanently installed in a marine environment.

Transponders

1   The design of transponder systems should ensure that there is no significant degradation of fixed frequency radar beacons, and the response of a transponder should not be capable of being interpreted as being from a radar beacon of any type.

2 Where a transponder is to be used with a marine navigational radar any modifications necessary to the radar should not degrade its performance, be kept to a minimum, be simple and be compatible with a fixed frequency radar beacon facility.

3 In-band transponders should not be used to enhance the detection of marine craft, except when specially authorized by Administrations for use in survival craft.

10.4.2 Performance standards for radar reflectors

1 Introduction

1.1 Small craft referred to in paragraph 2 should be fitted with radar reflectors to improve the range and probability of their radar detection.

1.2 Radar reflectors should comply with the minimum performance requirements.

1.3 In the following paragraphs the echoing areas specified are those for the frequency of 9.3 GHz (corresponding to a wavelength of 3.2 cm).

2 Application

2.1 All ships of less than 100 tons gross tonnage operating in international waters and adjacent coastal areas should, if practicable, be fitted with a radar reflector.

2.2 The radar reflector should be of an approved type with an adequate polar diagram in azimuth, and an echoing area:

.1 preferably, of at least $10 \, m^2$, mounted at a minimum height of 4 m above water level; or
.2 if this is not practicable, of at least $40 \, m^2$, mounted at a minimum height of 2 m above water level.

3 Performance

3.1 Reflectors should be capable of performance

around 360° in azimuth using a typical marine navigational radar.

3.2 The echoing areas referred to in paragraph 2 correspond to the maximum values of the main lobes of the polar diagram.

3.3 The azimuthal polar diagram should be such that the response over a total angle of 240° is not less than −6 dB with reference to the maxima of the main lobes and that the response should not remain below −6 dB over any single angle of more than 10°.

4 Construction

The reflector should be capable of maintaining its reflection performance under the conditions of sea states, vibration, humidity and change of temperature likely to be experienced in the marine environment.

5 Installation

5.1 Fixing arrangements should be provided so that the reflector can be fitted either on a rigid mount or suspended in the rigging.

5.2 If there is a preferred orientation of mounting this should be clearly marked on the reflector. In the case of an octahedral reflector, the correct method of mounting is one corner cavity at the top and one at the bottom. Any other method might reduce its performance below that in paragraph 3.3.

10.5 Extract from United Kingdom Merchant Shipping Notice M1158 The use of radar including ARPA

General

3.1 Collisions have been caused far too frequently by failure to make proper use of radar; by altering course on insufficient information; and by maintaining too high a speed, particularly when a close-quarters situation is developing or is likely to develop. It cannot be emphasised too strongly that navigation in restricted visibility is difficult and great care is needed even though all the information which can be obtained from radar observation is available. Where continuous radar watchkeeping and plotting cannot be maintained, even greater caution must be exercised.

Interpretation

3.2 It is essential for the observer to be aware of the current quality of performance of the radar set (which can be most easily ascertained by a performance monitor) and to take account of the possibility that small vessels, small icebergs and similar floating objects may escape detection.

3.3 Echoes may be obscured by sea or rain clutter. Adjustment of controls to suit the circumstances will help, but will not completely remove this possibility.

3.4 Masts and other obstructions may cause shadow sectors on the display.

Plotting

3.5 To estimate the degree of risk of collision with another vessel it is necessary to forecast her closest point of approach. Choice of appropriate avoiding action is facilitated by knowledge of the other vessel's course and speed, and one of the simplest methods of estimating these factors is by plotting. This involves knowledge of own ship's course and distance run during the plotting interval.

Choice of range scale

3.6 Although the choice of range scales for observation and plotting is dependent upon several factors such as traffic density, speed of the observing ship and the frequency of observation, it is not generally advisable to commence plotting on short range scales. In any case advance warning of the aproach of other vessels, or changes in traffic density, should be obtained by occasional use of the longer range scales. This advice applies particularly when approaching areas of expected high traffic density when information obtained from the use of the longer range scales may be an important factor in deciding on a safe speed.

Appreciation

3.7 A single observation of the range and bearing of an echo can give no indication of the course and speed of a vessel in relation to one's own. To estimate this a succession of observations at known time intervals must be made.

3.8 Estimation of the other ship's course and speed is only valid up to the time of the last observation and the situation must be kept constantly under review, for the other vessel, which may or may not be on radar watch, may alter her course or speed. Such alteration in course or speed will take time to become apparent to the radar observer.

3.9 It should not be assumed that because the relative bearing is changing there is no risk of collision. Alteration of course by one's own ship will alter the relative bearing. A changing compass bearing is more to be relied upon. However, this has to be judged in relation to range, and even with a changing compass bearing a close-quarters situation with a risk of collision may develop.

3.10 Radar should be used to complement visual observation in clear weather to assist in the assessment of whether risk collision exists or is likely to develop. It also provides accurate determination of range to enable action taken to avoid collision to be successful, bearing in mind the manoeuvring capabilities of own ship.

Clear weather practice

3.11 It is important that shipmasters and others using radar should gain and maintain experience in radar observation and appreciation by practice at sea in clear weather. In these conditions radar observations can be checked visually and misinterpretation of the radar display or false appreciation of the situation should not be potentially dangerous. Only by making and keeping themselves familiar with the process of systematic radar observation, and with the relationship between the radar information and the actual situation, will officers be able to deal rapidly and competently with the problems which will confront them in restricted visibility.

Operation

3.12 If weather conditions by day or night are such that visibility may deteriorate, the radar should be running, or on standby. (The latter permits operation in less than 1 minute, whilst it normally takes up to 4 minutes to operate from switching on.) At night, in areas where fogbanks or small craft or unlighted obstructions such as icebergs are likely to be encountered, the radar set should be left permanently running. This is particularly important when there is any danger of occasional fogbanks, so that other vessels can be detected before entering the fogbank.

3.13 The life of components, and hence the reliability of the radar set, will be far less affected by continuous running than by frequent switching on and off, so that in periods of uncertain visibility it is better to leave the radar either in full operation or on standby.

Radar watchkeeping

3.14 In restricted visibility the radar set should be permanently running and the display observed, the frequency of observation depending upon the prevailing circumstances, such as the speed of one's own ship and the type of craft or other floating object likely to be encountered.

The use of parallel index techniques as an aid to navigation by radar

3.15 General Investigations of casualties involving the grounding of ships, when radar was being used as an aid to navigation, have indicated that a factor contributing to the grounding was the lack of adequate monitoring of the ship's position during the period leading up to the casualty. Valuable assistance to position monitoring in relation to a predetermined navigation plan could have been given in such cases if the bridge personnel had used the techniques of parallel index plotting on the radar display. Such techniques should be practised in clear weather during straightforward passages, so that bridge personnel become thoroughly familiar with this technique before attempting it in confined difficult passages, or at night, or in restricted visibility.

3.16 The basic principle of parallel index plotting can be applied to either a stabilized relative motion display or a *ground* stabilized true motion display.

3.17 On a stabilized relative motion display the echo of a fixed object will move accross the display in a direction which is the exact reciprocal of the *course made good* by own ship at a speed commensurate to that of own ship over the ground. A line drawn from the echo of the fixed object tangential to the variable range marker circle set to the desired passing distance will indicate the forecast track of the echo as own ship proceeds. If the bearing cursor is set parallel to this track it will indicate the course to make good for own ship. Any displacement of the echo from the forecast track will indicate a departure of own ship from the desired course over the ground.

3.18 On a ground stabilized true motion display, the echo of a fixed object will remain stationary on the display and the origin of the display (own ship) will move along the course made good by own ship at a speed commensurate to that of own ship over the ground. A line should be drawn from the echo of the fixed object tangential to the variable range marker circle set to the desired passing distance. If the electronic bearing marker is set parallel to this line it will indicate the course to be made good by own ship at a speed commensurate to that of own ship over the ground. Any departure of own ship from this course will be indicated by the drawn line not being tangential to the variable range marker circle. (The variable range marker circle should move along the line like a ball rolling along a straight edge.)

3.19 The engraved parallel lines on the face of the bearing cursor can be used as an aid to drawing the index lines on, say, a reflection plotter and to supplement the bearing cursor.

3.20 It should be borne in mind that parallel indexing is an aid to safe navigation and does not supersede the requirement for position fixing at regular intervals using all methods available to the navigator.

When using radar for position fixing and monitoring, check:

(a) The radar's overall performance
(b) The identity of the fixed object(s)

(c) Gyro error and accuracy of the heading marker alignment

(d) Accuracy of the variable range marker, bearing cursor and fixed range rings

(e) On true motion, that the display is correctly ground stabilized.

3.21 It must be remembered that parallel index lines drawn on the reflection plotter are applicable to one range scale only. In addition to all other precautions necessary for the safe use of the information presented by radar, particular care must therefore be taken when changing range scales.

3.22 Some ARPA equipments provide a facility to generate synthetic lines which may be used as aids to parallel indexing techniques. These can be particularly useful where changes of range scale make the use of reflection plotters inappropriate.

Regular operational checks

3.23 Users of radar are reminded that frequent checks of the radar performance should be made to ensure that it has not deteriorated.

3.24 The performance of the radar equipment should be checked before sailing and at least once every four hours whilst a radar watch is being maintained. This should be done by using the performance monitor where fitted.

3.25 It is recommended that checks of the heading alignment should be made periodically to ensure that correct alignment is maintained. The following procedures are recommended:

(a) *Centring the trace* Each time the radar is switched on, and at the commencement of each watch when the radar is used continuously and whenever bearings are to be measured, the observer should check that the trace is rotating about the centre of the display and should, if necessary, adjust it (the centre of the display is the centre of rotation of the bearing scale cursor).

(b) *Aligning the heading marker and radar antenna* Visually aligning the radar antenna along what appears to be the ship's fore-and-after line is not a sufficiently

accurate method of alignment. The following procedure is recommended for accurate alignment:

(i) Adjust accurately the centre of rotation of the trace. Switch off azimuth stabilization. Rotate PPI until the heading marker lies 0° on the bearing scale.

(ii) Select an object which is conspicuous but small visually and whose echo is small and distinct and lies as nearly as possible at the maximum range scale in use. Measure simultaneously the relative visual bearing of this object and the bearing on the PPI relative to the bearing scale. It is important that the visual bearing is taken from a position near the radar antenna in plan. Repeat these measurements twice at least and calculate the mean difference between bearings obtained visually and by radar.

(iii) If an error exists, rotate the PPI picture until the radar bearing is the same as the visual bearing.

(iv) If necessary adjust the heading marker contacts in the antenna unit to return the heading marker to 0° on the bearing scale.

(v) Take simultaneous visual and radar bearings as in (iii) above to check the accuracy of the alignment.

3.26 Alignment of the heading marker or correcting the alignment on a ship berthed in a dock or harbour, or using bearings of a target that has not been identified with certainty both by radar and visually, can introduce serious bearing errors. The procedure for alignment of heading marker should be carried out on clearly identified targets clear of a confusion of target echoes. The alignment should be checked at the earliest opportunity.

Automatic plotting aids (ARPA)

3.27 In addition to the advice given above, and the instructions given in the appropriate operating manual, users of ARPA should ensure that:

(a) The test programs (where fitted) are used to check the validity of the ARPA data.

(b) The performance of the radar associated with the ARPA is at its optimum.

(c) The heading and speed inputs to the ARPA are satisfactory. Correct speed input, where provided by manual setting of the appropriate ARPA control(s) or by an external input, e.g. Doppler log, is vital for correct processing of ARPA data. Serious errors of output data can arise if heading and speed inputs to the ARPA are incorrect. In this context users should be aware of the possible hazards of using a ground stabilized mode of ARPA display when information on the movement of other ships is being used to assess a potential collision risk, particularly in areas where significant currents and/or tidal streams exist. On some ships, should the master gyro fail, the transmitting magnetic compass can operate the gyro repeaters and provide heading information to other equipment, including ARPAs and true motion radars. Users should bear in mind that in this mode the errors involved are magnetic and should be ascertained and applied accordingly.

(d) The use of audible operational warning signals to denote that a target has closed on a range, or transits a zone chosen by the observer, does not relieve the user from the duty to maintain a proper look-out by all available means. Such warning devices, when the ARPA is operating in an automatic acquisition mode, should be used with caution especially in the vicinity of small radar inconspicuous targets.

Users should familiarize themselves with the effects of error sources on the automatic tracking of targets by reference to the ARPA operating manual.

10.6 Extracts from United Kingdom Statutory Instrument 1984, No 1203

Part III   Radar installation

Radar performance standards and interswitching facilities

18(1)   Every radar installation required to be provided shall comply with the performance standards adopted by the organization and shall, in addition, comply with the relevant performance specifications issued by the Department of Transport.

(2)   Interswitching facilities:

(a) Where such a radar installation includes additional radar units and facilities for interswitching, at least one arrangement of units when used together shall comply with all the requirements of this part of these regulations.

(b) Where two radar installations are required to be provided on a ship, they shall be so installed that each radar installation can be operated individually and both can be operated simultaneously without being dependent upon one another.

Provision of plotting facilities

19   Facilities for plotting radar readings shall be provided on the navigating bridge of every ship required to be fitted with a radar installation. In ships of 1600 tons gross tonnage and upwards constructed on or after 1 September 1984 the plotting facilities shall be at least as effective as a reflection plotter.

Radar watch

20(1)   While a ship which is required to be fitted with a radar installation is at sea and a radar watch is being kept, the radar installation shall be under the control of a qualified radar observer, who may be assisted by unqualified personnel.

(2)   In every such ship a record shall be kept in the deck log book of the times at which radar watch is commenced and discontinued.

Serviceability and maintenance of radar installations

21(1)   The performance of the radar installation shall be checked before the ship proceeds to sea and at least once every four hours whilst the ship is at sea and radar watch is being maintained.

(2)   Every ship of 1600 tons or over required to be fitted with a radar installation which is going between the United Kingdom and locations in the unlimited trading area or between locations in the unlimited trad-

ing area shall be provided with at least one officer or member of the crew adequately qualified to carry out radar maintenance: provided that:

(a) If on an occasion on which a ship goes to sea, the officer or member of the crew adequately qualified to carry out radar maintenance is not carried because of illness, incapacity, or other unforeseen circumstance, but all reasonable steps were taken to secure the carriage on that occasion of a duly qualified officer or crew member, the provisions of this regulation which require such a ship on such a voyage to carry an officer or crew member adequately qualified to carry out radar maintenance shall not, subject to compliance with the conditions in subparagraph(b) below, apply to the ship during a period beginning with the day on which the ship goes to sea and ending either 28 days later or with the day on which the ship sails from its next port of call, whichever is the later.

(b) The conditions are that one such period shall not be followed immediately by any further period at sea during which the ship does not carry an officer or crew member adequately qualified to carry out radar maintenance and that the master, when going to sea on such an occasion shall:
    (i) Notify a proper officer of his intention not to carry a suitably qualified officer or crew member; and
    (ii) Make an entry of that notification in the ship's official log.

Qualifications of radar observers and radar maintenance personnel
22(1)   For the purposes of these regulations, a person shall be deemed a 'qualified radar observer' if he holds:

(a) A valid Radar Observer's Certificate granted by the Secretary of State; or
(b) A valid certificate of attendance granted at the conclusion of a radar simulator course which has been approved by the Secretary of State; or
(c) A valid Electronic Navigation Systems Certificate granted by the Secretary of State; or
(d) A valid Navigation Control Certificate granted by the Secretary of State; or

(e) A certificate recognized by the Secretary of State as being equivalent to any of the certificates mentioned in (a), (b), (c) or (d).

(2)   For the purpose of these regulations, an officer or crew member shall be deemed qualified to carry out radar maintenance if he holds:

(a) A Radar Maintenance Certificate granted by the Secretary of State; or
(b) An Electronic Navigational Equipment Maintenance Certificate granted by the Secretary of State; or
(c) A certificate recognized by the Secretary of State as being equivalent to either of the certificates mentioned in (a) or (b); or
(d) A certificate of proficiency to carry out maintenance on specified types of radar installations granted at the conclusion of a radar manufacturer's course which has been approved by the Secretary of State; or
(e) A special certificate to carry out maintenance on specified types of radar installations issued by the Secretary of State upon satisfactory written evidence that the applicant's employment, over a period of not less than 10 years between 25 May 1960 and 24 May 1980 has included the maintenance of marine radar installations.

Siting of radar installation
23(1)   The antenna unit of the radar installation shall be sited so that satisfactory overall performance is achieved in relation to:

(a) The avoidance of shadow sectors;
(b) The avoidance of false echoes caused by reflections from the ship's structure; and
(c) The effect of antenna height on the amplitude and extent of sea clutter.

(2)   The radar display shall be sited on the bridge from which the ship is normally navigated. The siting of one of the displays shall be such that:

(a) An observer, when viewing the display, faces forward and is readily able to maintain visual lookout;

(b) There is sufficient space for two observers to view the display simultaneously.

(3) The radar installation shall, where practicable, be mounted so as to prevent the performance and reliability of the installation being adversely affected by vibration and so that the installation will not, whilst in service, normally be subject to greater vibration than that specified in the General Requirements for Marine Navigational Equipment, 1982, issued by the Department of Transport.

Alignment of heading marker

24 The radar heading marker (and stern marker if fitted) shall be aligned to within 1° of the ship's fore-and-aft line as soon as practicable after the radar installation has been installed in the ship. Where interswitching facilities are provided, the heading marker shall be aligned with all arrangements of units. The marker shall be realigned as soon as practicable whenever it is found to be substantially inaccurate.

Measurement of shadow sectors

25 The angular width and bearing of any shadow sectors displayed by the radar installation shall be determined and recorded. The record shall be shown on a diagram adjacent to the radar display and be kept up to date following any change likely to affect shadow sectors.

Display sizes

26 A radar installation required to be provided which is installed on board a ship on or after 1 September 1984 shall provide a relative plan display having an effective diameter, without external magnification of not less than:

(a) 180 millimetres on ships of 500 tons or over but less than 1600 tons;

(b) 250 millimetres on ships of 1600 tons or over but less than 10 000 tons;

(c) 340 millimetres in the case of one radar installation and 250 millimetres in the case of the other on ships of 10 000 tons or over.

Part VIII   Automatic radar plotting aid installation

Automatic radar plotting aid performance standards

39 Every automatic radar plotting aid installation required to be provided shall comply with the performance standards adopted by the organization and shall, in addition, comply with the relevant performance specifications issued by the Department of Transport.

Siting and other requirements of automatic radar plotting aid installations

40(1)   Where the automatic radar plotting aid installation is provided as an additional unit to a radar installation it shall be sited as close as is practicable to the display of the radar with which it is associated.

(2)   Where the automatic radar plotting aid installation forms an integral part of a complete radar system, that radar system shall be regarded as one of the radar installations required by regulation 3(4)(b) and accordingly shall comply with the relevant requirements of part III of these regulations.

(3)   The automatic radar plotting aid installation shall be interconnected with such other installations as is necessary to provide heading and speed information to the automatic radar plotting aid.

Use of an automatic radar plotting aid to assist in the radar watch

41   When at any time on or after 1 September 1985 a ship required to be fitted with an automatic radar plotting aid is at sea and a radar watch is being kept on the automatic radar plotting aid, the installation shall be under the control of a person qualified in the operational use of automatic radar plotting aids, who may be assisted by unqualified personnel.

Qualifications of observers using an automatic radar plotting aid to assist in keeping a radar watch

42   For the purpose of Regulation 41 of these regulations, a person shall be deemed to be qualified in the operational use of automatic radar plotting aids if he holds:

(a) A valid Electronic Navigation Systems Certificate granted by the Secretary of State; or

(b) A valid Navigation Control Certificate granted by the Secretary of State; or

(c) A valid Automatic Radar Plotting Aids Certificate granted by the Secretary of State; or

(d) A certificate recognized by the Secretary of State as being equivalent to any of the certificates mentioned in (a), (b) or (c).

Glossary of acronyms and abbreviations

AEB	area exclusion boundary	LSB	least significant bit
AFC	automatic frequency control	LSR	least sampling rate
ARB	area rejection boundary	MHz	megahertz
ARPA	automatic radar plotting aid	ms	millisecond
BCR	bow crossing range	MSB	most significant bit
BCT	bow crossing time	n mile	nautical mile(s)
CFAR	constant false alarm rate	OAW	plotting triangle symbols
CPA	closest point of approach	PAD	predicted area of danger
CRT	cathode ray tube	PFN	pulse-forming network
CSR	controlled silicon rectifier	PPC	possible/potential point of collision
dB	decibel	PPI	plan position indicator
DSC	digital scan converter (conversion)	PRF	pulse repetition frequency
EBI	electronic bearing indicator	PRP	pulse repetition period
EBL	electronic bearing line	PRR	pulse repetition rate
EBM	electronic bearing marker	Radar	Radio detection and ranging
EHT	very high voltages	RDF	radio direction-finder
ERBL	electronic range and bearing line	RF	radio frequency
FTC	fast time constant (rain clutter control)	RH	relative humidity
FTE	false target elimination	SCR	silicon controlled rectifier
GHz	gigahertz	SI	Statutory Instrument
GRP	glass reinforced plastic (Fibreglass)	SOD	sector of danger
HBW	horizontal beamwidth	SOLAS	Safety of Life at Sea
HM	heading marker	SOP	sector of preference
Hz	hertz	STC	sensitivity time control
IF	intermediate frequency	TCPA	time to closest point of approach
IKBS	intelligent knowledge-based system	VHF	very high frequency
IMO	International Maritime Organization	VRM	variable range marker
kHz	kilohertz	VBW	vertical beamwidth
kn	knot(s)	UHF	ultra-high frequency
kW	kilowatt	μs	microsecond

Index

Acquisition of targets, 196 *et seq.*, 269, 396
  automatic, 393
  performance standard, 392
  selection criteria, 393
  suppression areas, *see* Area rejection boundaries
Adaptive gain, 163, 266, 267
Aerial, *see* Antenna
Afterglow:
  misleading effect of, 382
  real, 9, 72, 108
  synthetic, 113, 116
Alarms, *see* Warnings, ARPA
Amplifier, *see also* Receiver
  intermediate frequency, 59
  linear, 63
  logarithmic, 64
  noise, *see* Thermal noise
  radio frequency, 56
  saturation, 59
  video, 66
Antenna:
  beamwidth, horizontal, 8, 42, 43
  beamwidth, vertical (roll), 28, 48, 386, 388
  characteristics, 40 *et seq.*, 127
  function, 28
  gain, 42
  performance standard, 389
  polarization, 42
  principles, 40 *et seq.*
  rotation rate, 50, 386, 388
  siting, 117, 386
  squint, angle of, 47
  synchronization with trace, 9, 52
Appraisal aids, *see* Threat assessment markers
Area rejection boundaries (ARBs), 196, 198

ARPA:
  accuracy and errors, 364 *et seq.*, 382, 394, *see also*
    Errors associated with ARPA
  alarms and warnings, *see* Warnings, ARPA
  connection to other equipment, 217, 395
  data brilliance control, 213, 394
  data presented on, 213, 394
  definition of terms, 395
  display modes, 213
  display sizes, 393
  integral/stand alone, 194
  malfunction of, 212, 393, 395
  requirement to carry, 384
  observer qualification, 195, 407
  over-reliance on, 382
  performance standards – IMO, 195, 392 *et seq.*
  setting-up, 268 *et seq.*
  siting, 407
  test programmes, 217, 404
  test scenarios, 364, 395, 396
Aspect:
  plotting term, *see* Plotting, radar
  target characteristic, 129
Assessment aids, *see* Threat assessment markers
Atmospheric conditions, 173 *et seq.*
  ducting, 179
  standard, 173
  sub-refraction, 177
  super-refraction, 178
Attentuation due to precipitation, 168, 172
Auto drift, *see* Stabilization, ground

Bandwidth, 61
Beamwidth, *see* Antenna

Bearing:
   accuracy, 264
   discrimination, 43, 89
   facilities for measurement of, 214, 256 *et seq.*
   performance standard, 385, 387
   principle of measurement of, 8 *et seq.*
   storage of, 97
Bearing errors, 259, 262, 264, 370
Blind sectors, 117
Buoy patterns, 143

Cathode ray tube (CRT):
   colour television, 114
   monochrome television, 106
   principles of, 69 *et seq.*
Close-quarters situation, 325 *et seq.*
Clutter, precipitation, 166 *et seq.*, 267 *et seq.*
   attenuation in precipitation, 168
   combating the attenuation caused by precipitation, 172
   detection of targets beyond, 172, 267
   detection of targets in, 166 *et seq.*, 267
   effect of precipitation type, 168
   exploiting ability to detect, 173
   nature of, 167
   performance standard, 386, 388
   rain clutter circuit, 169
   rain clutter control, 267
   suppression of (practice), 267
   suppression of (theory), 169
Clutter, sea, 154 *et seq.*, 265 *et seq.*
   control, 159, 265, *see also* Adaptive gain;
      Rotation-to-rotation correlation
   detection of targets in, 154 *et seq.*, 265
   nature of, 155
   performance standard, 386, 388
   suppression of (practice), 265
   suppression of (theory), 159
Collision:
   action to avoid, 324
   points, *see* Possible points of collision
Collision avoidance regulations, *see* Regulations for
   preventing collisions at sea
Colour, use of in raster-scan picture generation, 115
Compass:
   safe distances, 123

   stabilization, *see* Stabilization
Controls, *see* Setting-up of operational radar controls
CPA, 24, 25, 204, 210, 214
   accuracy of, 207
   determination of, 274 *et seq.*
   safe limits, 216, 394
Cumulative turn, 326

Data (ARPA):
   accuracy of displayed, 366, 382
   alphanumeric display of, 214, 394
   analysis, 201
   storage of, 204 *et seq.*, 378, 379
Deflection system, 73
Detection of targets, *see* Target, detection
Detector, 66
Differentiator, *see* rain clutter circuit *under* Clutter,
   precipitation
Digital scan conversion, 109, 202, 204
Digital storage, *see* Storage
Discrimination, 332
   bearing, 89
   performance standard, 386, 388
   range, 88
Display:
   A-scan, 3
   ARPA, performance standard, 393
   alphanumeric data, 214, 394
   function, 29
   history, *see* History, ARPA tracking
   non-linearity, 257, 319
   preparing the, 232, 241
   principles, 69 *et seq.*
   radar performance standard, 385
   radial-scan, *see* Radial-scan display
   raster-scan, *see* Raster-scan display
   real-time, 75
   relative-motion, *see* Relative-motion display
   setting-up procedure, 230, 236, 240, 268
   siting, 122
   size, 213, 385, 387, 407
   synthetic, 6, 100
   true motion, *see* True-motion displays
   vector, *see* Vectors

'E' plot, 322
Echo paint, 84
    effect of beamwidth, 86
    effect of pulse length, 86
    effect of spot size, 85
Echo principle, 1
Echo reference, *see* Stabilization, ground
Echo stretch, 268, 331
Echoes, unwanted, *see* False echoes
Electron gun, 70
Equivalent flat plate area, 134
Errors associated with ARPA:
    due to incorrect data input, 375 *et seq.*
    displayed data in, 375 *et seq.*
    interpretation in, 379 *et seq.*
    quantization, 96, 203, 370, 373
    sensor, for test scenarios 372, 396
    sources of, 364 *et seq.*
    target swop, 372
    tracking errors, 373
Errors associated with manual plotting, 313 *et seq.*
Errors associated with the true-motion presentation, 317 *et seq.*
Exclusion areas, *see* Area rejection boundaries

False echoes, 179 *et seq.*
    due to power cables, 193
    indirect, 120, 180
    multiple, 184
    radar to radar interference, *see* Interference
    reflected, *see* False echoes, indirect
    second-trace, 187, 268
    side, 184
False target elimination, (FTE), 268
Focus, 71, 232, 243
Frequency:
    intermediate, 59
    pulse repetition, 31
    transmitter, 37
FTC, *see* rain clutter circuit *under* Clutter, precipitation

Gain:
    control, *see* Setting-up of operational radar controls
        overall, 59

stage, 59
Gate, tracking, *see* Tracking
Glint, 368, 396
Graphic presentation, *see* Predicted areas of danger
Grey-level, 105, 239
Ground lock, *see* Stabilization, ground
Guard rings and zones, 197 *et seq.*, 215, 394

Hazards;
    high voltage, 123
    radiation, 121, 122
Heading marker:
    alignment of, 404, 407
    performance standard, 385, 387
    production of, 10, 54
    setting-up, 233, 243
History, ARPA tracking, 207, 393
Hit matrix, 202

IMO:
    ARPA carriage requirements, 384
    ARPA performance standards, 392
    radar carriage requirements, 384
    radar performance standards, 385 *et seq.*
Intelligent knowledge-based systems (IKBS), 322
Interference:
    radar to radar, 185, 386, 389
    suppression of, 186, 267
Inter-switching, 123, 389, 405
Isotropic source, 42

Joystick, 196, 262

Limiting, *see* Saturation
Log errors, 364 *et seq.*
Lookout, proper, 198, 213, 215, 323, 405
Lunenburg lens, 141

'M' notice No. 1158 extract, 401
Magnetron, 389
Manoeuvre;
    avoidance, 325
    characteristics, 287 *et seq.*
    forecasting effect of, 283, 326, *see also* Trial
        manoeuvre

resumption, 326
target, effect of a, 281
trial, *see* Trial manoeuvre
Map presentation, 221, 360
Material, reflecting properties, 130
Mixer principle, 56
Modulator unit, 35
Multiple installations, *see* Inter-switching

Navigation lines, 221, 359
Noise, *see* Thermal noise

Operational controls, 230 *et seq.*
Operational warnings, *see* Warnings, ARPA
Orientation of picture, 11 *et seq.*, 231 *et seq.*, 243, 259
  et seq., see also Stabilization, azimuth
  choice of, 17
  course-up, 14, 233, 260
  ship's-head-up, 11, 233, 259
  true-north-up, 14, 233, 260

Parabolic reflector, 43
Parallel indexing, 338 *et seq.*
  clear weather practice, 403
  collision avoidance while, 361
  cursor, 261, 310, 339
  margin lines, 347
  technique, 342, 403
  true-motion display, on, 340, 351
  unplanned, 361
  wheel-over position, 349
Past positions, *see* History, ARPA tracking
Performance monitoring, 404
  equipment, 243 *et seq.*
  performance standard, 386, 388
  procedure, 243, 248
Performance standards – IMO:
  ARPA, 392
  radar beacons and transponders, 397 *et seq.*
  radar installed before 1 September 1984, 385
  radar installed after 1 September 1984, 387
  reflectors, 401
Performance tests, ARPA 366

Perspex cursor, 232, 258, 310
Picture, *see also* Display
  build up of, 9
  optimum, 234, 237, 243
  storage of, 6, 91 *et seq.*
  synthetic, 6, 100
Pilotage situations, 336
Plotting, radar, 271 *et seq.*, 396, 402
  accuracy and errors, 313 *et seq.*
  aids, 320 *et seq.*
  avoiding action, 325
  facilities for, 405
  need for, 323
  PADs 227, 302
  PPCs, 222, 297
  practicalities of, 277
  relative, 271
  SODs, 302
  SOPs, 305
  stopping distances, 287, 293
  tide, in, 305
  true, 279
  turning circles, 292
  when own ship only manoeuvres, 283
  when own ship only resumes, 295
  when target only manoeuvres, 281
Point radiating source, 40
Polarization, 42, 159, 172
Position fixing, 336 *et seq.*
Possible points of collision (PPCs), 222 *et seq.*
  error due to incorrect sensor input plotting of, 297
Power density, 42
Precipitation, *see* Clutter, precipitation
Predicted areas of danger (PADs), 227 *et seq.*
  errors of interpretation, 380 *et seq.*
  plotting and construction of, 302
Presentation of picture:
  choice of, 24
  ground-stabilization, *see* Stabilization
  relative motion, 18 *et seq.*
  sea-stabilization, *see* Stabilization
  true-motion, 21 *et seq.*
Prime register, 202
Prioritization, 197
Processor, 194, 195, 202 *et seq.*

Progress monitoring, 249, 353
Pulse-forming network, 31, 35
Pulse repetition frequency, 31, 39
Pulse, transmitted:
    frequency, 37
    length, 32, 39
    power, 33
    shape, 35

Qualifications:
    ARPA observer, 407
    maintenance personnel, 406
    radar observer, 406

Radaflare, 151
Radar beacons and transponders, 143 *et seq.*
    chart symbols, 153
    operation of radar with, 389
    performance standards for, 397 *et seq.*
    racon, 143 *et seq.*
    ramark, 150
    sources of information, 151
    survival craft, for, 154
Radar cross-section of target, 134
Radar horizon, 173 *et seq.*
Radar log, 405
Radar maintenance, 405
Radar range equation, 126
Radar reflectors, 137 *et seq.*
    arrays of, 139
    corner, 137
    performance standards, 401
Radar systems;
    block diagram, 27
    characteristics, 127 *et seq.*
    obligation to use, 324
    operational principles, 26 *et seq.*
    performance standards, 385 *et seq.*
    siting of, 406 *et seq.*
    requirement to carry, 384
    use in clear weather, 402
Radar watchkeeping, 403, 405, 407
Radial-scan display:
    build up of picture, 9
    generation of, 75 *et seq.*

principle of, 4
    setting of controls, analogue, 230 *et seq.*
    setting of controls, synthetic, 236 *et seq.*
Radiation:
    hazards, 121, 122
    intensity, 41
Radio waves, velocity of, 2
Rain, *see* Clutter, precipitation
Ramark, *see* Radar beacons and transponders
Range:
    accuracy, 262
    as a function of time, 2
    discrimination, 32, 68, 88, 97
    facilities for measurement of, 214, 256 *et seq.*
    maximum detection, 126, 173
    minimum detection, 128, 385, 387
    performance standard, 385, 387
    principles of measurement, 1 *et seq.*
    storage of, 6, 94, 97
Range scales:
    changing, 214
    choice of, 402
    relationship with pulse repetition frequency and pulse
        length, 39
Raster-scan display:
    future of, 116
    PPI, 110
    principle, 6, 106
    setting-up of controls, 240
Rate aiding, 199
Rayleigh roughness criterion, 136
Real-time picture generation, *see* Display
Receiver, *see also* Amplifier
    characteristics, 127
    function, 28
    noise, *see* Thermal noise
    principles, 55 *et seq.*
Reflection plotters, 309 *et seq.*, 344, 405
    on raster-scan displays, 312
Reflectors, *see* Atmospheric conditions
Refraction, *see* Atmospheric conditions
Regulations for preventing collisions at sea:
    application of, 323 *et seq.*
    summary, 328
Relative-motion display, 18 *et seq.*

Resolution cell, 87, 132, 332
Restricted visibility, 324
Rotation-to-rotation correlation, 165, 266

'S' band characteristics, 38, 158, 167
Safe speed, 324
Sailing directions, 331
Saturation, receiver, 59
Scanner, *see* Antenna
Scanty radar information, 324
Scenarios, operation, ARPA, 364, 396
Screen:
    characteristics, 72
    marker, 196, 262
Sea clutter, *see* Clutter, sea
Sea stabilization, *see* Stabilization
Search and rescue transponder (SART), 154
Sensor errors, 372, 396
Setting-up of operational radar controls:
    brilliance of tube, 232, 241
    centring, 232, 243, 404
    changing range scale/pulse length, 249
    clutter, rain, 267
    clutter, sea, 265
    contrast, 237, 242
    focus, 232, 243
    gain, 234, 237
    heading marker, 233, 243, 404
    tuning, 235, 239
Setting-up procedure for:
    ARPA displays, 268 *et seq.*
    radial-scan analogue displays, 230
    radial-scan synthetic displays, 236
    raster-scan synthetic displays, 240
    true-motion, 250 *et seq.*
Shadow areas, 333
    sectors, 117, 407
Shaft encoding, 98
Side lobes, 43
Signal processing, 103, 113
Siting of units, 116 *et seq.*, 406
Sloping surface, effect on target response, 132 *et seq.*
Slotted waveguide, 46
Spot size, 71, 85
Stabilization:

azimuth, 14, 78, 386, 388, 393
ground, 23 *et seq.*, 219 *et seq.*, 251, 254, 255, 357, 360, 363, 386, 389, 403, 405
sea, 21 *et seq.*, 251, 255, 386, 389, 395
Stand-by control, 250, 386, 389, 403
Statutory instrument No. 1203 of 1984, extract, 405
Storage:
    bearing, of, 97
    digital, 6, 91, 93
    range, of, 94
Surface texture (of target), 129
Switching-off, 270
Switching-on, 231, 236, 240, 386, 389
Symbols for radar controls, 389 *et seq.*
Synthetic picture, *see* Display
Systematic observation of detected echoes, 19, 324, *see also* Plotting, radar

Target:
    aspect, 129
    characteristics, 129
    detection in clutter, 154 *et seq.*
    detection of, 126 *et seq.*, 385, 387, 392, 396
    detection, minimum range, 128
    enhancement, active, 143 *et seq.*
    enhancement, passive, 137 *et seq.*
    equivalent flat plate area, 134 *et seq.*
    identification of, 330 *et seq.*
    loss of, 200, 216, 393
    material, 130
    radar conspicuous, 335
    radar cross-section, 134
    responses from specific, 136
    shape, 130
    size, 131
    sloping surface, 132
    strikes per point, 51
    surface texture, 129
    swop, 200, 393
TCPA, *see* CPA
Thermal noise, 60, 234
Threat assessment markers, 321, *see also* aids *under* Plotting, radar
Threshold:
    detection, 93
    video, 102, 103, 238

Tidal controls, 254, *see also* Stabilization, ground
Timebase:
  calibration of, 4
  constant speed, 7
  non–linear, 319
  storage, 6, 94
Trace:
  as a line on CRT, 3 *et seq.*
  generation of, 73
  synchronization with scanner, 9, 52
Track file, 202
Tracker:
  ball, *see* Joystick
  'Full' warning, 219
  philosophy, 201
Tracking, 198 *et seq.*, 396
  errors, 373
  gate, 196, 199
  number of targets, 200
  performance standards, 198, 393
Transmitter:
  characteristics, 127
  choice of frequency, 38, 124
  function, 26
  principles, 29
  siting, 121
Transponder, *see* Radar beacons and transponders
Trend of targets motion, 201, 203, 394, 396
Trial manoeuvre, 211 *et seq.*
  alarm, 219
  performance standard, 394
True-motion display;
  presentation, 21 *et seq.*
  provision of facilities, 80 *et seq.*
  sea and ground-stabilization, *see* Stabilization
  setting up procedure, 250 *et seq.*
Tuning:
  automatic, 58

control, *see* Setting-up of operational radar controls
  manual, 58

Vectors, 209 *et seq.*, 393
  mode, 269
  relative, 210
  time control, 269
  trial, 211
  true, 210
Video:
  amplifier, 66
  correlated, 165, 185, 266
  levels, 102, 103, 238
  quantized,106

Warnings, ARPA:
  anchor watch, 219
  CPA/TCPA, 216, 219
  guard rings/zones, 215
  loss of sensor input, 218
  malfunction, 217, 395
  operational, 394, 405
  performance standards, 394
  safe limits, 269, 394
  target lost, 216, 394
  time to manoeuvre, 219
  track change, 218
  tracks full, 219
  wrong request, 219
Waveguide:
  linking transceiver and antenna, 26
  slotted, 46

'X' band characteristics, 38, 158, 167

Yaw, effect of, 13

Zero-speed control, 253